The Cuisine of
PAUL
BOCUSE

The Cuisine of
PAUL BOCUSE

Translated by Colette Rossant and Lorraine Davis

GRANADA
London Toronto Sydney New York

Granada Publishing Limited
8 Grafton Street, London W1X 3LA

First published in Great Britain by Granada Publishing as *The New Cuisine* 1978
Reprinted 1979
Reissued under the title *The Cuisine of Paul Bocuse* 1982
Reprinted (in paper covers) 1985

Copyright © Flammarion 1976
This translation Copyright © 1977 by Random House, Inc.

British Library Cataloguing in Publication Data

Bocuse, Paul
The cuisine of Paul Bocuse
1. Cookery, French
I. Title   II. La cuisine du marché. *English*
641.5944   TX719

ISBN 0-246-12754-6

Printed in Great Britain by R J Acford, Chichester, West Sussex.

To my father
and
in tribute to
Alfred Guérot and Fernand Point,
who inspired *La Nouvelle Cuisine Française*

CONTENTS

FOREWORD

Paul Bocuse, who may well be the world's greatest chef, is a man of Lyonnais charm and a captivating Napoleonic air. In discussing his recipes, he talks about his book with the assurance of one who holds the title of Meilleur Ouvrier de France Cuisinier (best chef-craftsman in France), awarded him by the President of the French Republic, along with the Légion d'Honneur.

Bocuse sees his book first as a novel, to be read for enjoyment. Reading this volume, he says, should whet your appetite; then, without any specific recipe in mind, go to the market to see what is available. Only then should you choose a recipe. The recipes, he adds, although precise, should be considered only guidelines. Bocuse believes that cooking is an art like painting or music. Both imagination and common sense must be employed. Quality is the most important criterion in the choice of ingredients. As he explains in his introduction, in Lyons, Bocuse himself goes to the market every morning, to choose his menu for the day. Whatever he finds fresh and in season is what will appear on his table for lunch or dinner.

In following one of Bocuse's recipes, consider first what is available. If the ingredients are of first quality, the dish will be a success regardless of whether or not you have every one of the seasonings.

Every meal should be a pleasure to make, Bocuse insists. And since eating a Bocuse dish is a feast in itself, Bocuse recommends that only one recipe in a menu should be taken from his book. If the home cook, therefore, concentrates on one chosen recipe, the rest of the meal should be simplicity *par excellence*. If you make a beautiful leg of lamb, seasoning it and cooking it to perfection, serve it with a simple salad of slices of tomato. Or if you devote your efforts to the first course – a soufflé or a soup – the rest of the meal may be unadorned, easy to prepare and very light.

Here are a few points to remember in using the recipes in this book:

French cream – *crème fraîche* – is slightly fermented and has a slightly sharp flavour. In the recipes double cream (which has the same butterfat content) has been substituted for *crème fraîche*, but you can make a closer equivalent in the following way: Stir 1 tablespoon of sour cream or buttermilk into $2\frac{1}{2}$–4 dl ($\frac{1}{2}$–$\frac{3}{4}$ pt) of double cream. Heat until lukewarm (about 75–85°F, 24–29°C). Pour into a bowl or jar, cover and leave to thicken in a warm place (for example an airing cupboard) at about 75°F (24°C). This will take between 8 and 24 hours, depending on the temperature. When whipping *crème fraîche* you will need to thin it with 1 part cold milk, water or crushed ice to 3 parts cream.

Fresh pork fat can be replaced by salt pork or unsmoked bacon; you may blanch these briefly to remove some of the salt.

In all the recipes unsalted butter should be used; salted butter contains more moisture.

If crayfish are not available, they can be replaced by a small lobster or large prawns. Substitutes for Mediterranean fish and other ingredients are listed in the recipes.

Fresh truffles are difficult to find and very expensive. You can replace them with tinned truffles, using the liquid in which the truffles came as flavouring in the sauce or the dish itself.

In numerous recipes Bocuse uses a mortar and pestle. You can blend the same ingredients easily with an electric blender, but you must experiment with the timing, and the ingredients should be rubbed through a sieve afterwards.

The dough and pastry recipes specify rather large quantities. When making any dish that requires a smaller amount, you can either cut down the amounts of the ingredients or follow the recipe as given, use the amount of dough needed, and freeze the remaining dough for future use.

Baking temperatures are indicated, but each cook knows his or her own oven best. Experiment to discover how to set yours for comparable results. Wherever oven cooking is specified, the oven should be properly preheated.

The roasting times are for very rare meat and you may need to allow longer to suit English tastes.

Above all enjoy what you are doing; follow the recipes, but don't let them stifle your own imagination.

– Colette Rossant

Paul Bocuse was born on 11 February 1926 in Collonges-au-Mont-d'Or; his restaurant is in that same house today. In the intervening years Bocuse has been around the world countless times, teaching and practising the fine art of cooking. But the Bocuse family has lived in this part of France since 1634, as millers and restaurant proprietors, and Bocuse always returns to his beloved market in nearby Lyons.

Bocuse's father, also a chef, made a grand tour as well, serving as an apprentice in many of the most celebrated restaurants in France, before settling in Collonges and taking over the restaurant from his grandfather.

In 1941 his son, young Paul, was apprenticed to one of his father's friends, Claude Maret, in Lyons. But Paul was soon caught up in the Second World War and wounded. When the war ended, he quickly won a place at a three-star restaurant, the renowned establishment of La Mère Brazier, outside Lyons. From there he moved to another three-star restaurant, the Pyramide, run by another of his father's friends, Fernand Point, and then to still another three-star post, at the Restaurant Lucas Carton, where he completed his education.

Finally, in 1959, he succeeded his father at Collonges, and in only two years he won his first star, and at the same time the accolade of Meilleur Ouvrier de France Cuisinier. A second star followed in 1962 and a third in 1965. In February of 1975 Bocuse was made a member of the Légion d'Honneur by President Valéry Giscard d'Estaing in recognition of his services as an ambassador of French cuisine. On that occasion Bocuse prepared the official dinner at the Elysée Palace.

Bocuse has won numerous other awards for his restaurant, and he is a culinary consultant to Air France. He has also taught in Japan, and in his restaurant in Tokyo introduced his own contribution to the ancient art of cooking – *la nouvelle cuisine*, the new style of French cooking, which combines traditional French culinary knowledge with the innovativeness that has won France its unique position in world cooking and Bocuse his unrivalled place at its head.

INTRODUCTION

Every morning I go to the market and wander about among the stalls. This is a Lyonnais tradition which I find hard to abandon. I do my own shopping because I know that one stallholder will have the best artichokes, another particularly good spinach and that a third brings his own delicious goat cheese fresh to the market every morning. Quite often I have not decided what dishes to prepare for lunch: the market makes up my mind for me. This I believe is the basis of good cooking.

In planning menus I also take account of the season. When hare is available, we have hare; in spring, young lamb and new spring vegetables. The calendar too plays its part in the drawing up of a menu.

In presenting this volume to the public, I must explain the philosophy behind it. All the recipes in it – simple or elaborate – will only succeed if the cook carefully selects the finest quality ingredients needed for the dish in the local market or shops. Even if your first attempts at an elaborate and prestigious dish are not a complete success I feel sure that you will not produce a total failure so long as you are working with really good ingredients. This may seem obvious but it is often forgotten. In successful cooking, method and experience are certainly important, but careful shopping and the choice of ingredients seem to me just as vital.

It is often said that the quality of market produce has declined, that fine raw ingredients are no longer to be found. As early as 1908 the author of a cookery book was complaining that good produce was not available, and in 1860 the Goncourts felt that meat had lost its flavour. I could easily go back to the eighteenth century to complete this catalogue of culinary complaint.

Surprisingly enough I personally believe that nowadays the finest produce is available everywhere, thanks, among other things, to modern transport methods. All you have to do is take your time and look around. The trouble is that people today are gradually ceasing to be aware of the seasons, losing the sense of ritual and ceremony as each season brings its own particular foods. They want to eat asparagus at Christmas, strawberries on New Year's Day, game at Easter and they have to be reminded that tomatoes are at their best in August, cherries in June – that the calendar has its part to play in preparing a menu.

I advise you not to look through my book and decide on a particular dish. Instead go to the market. There you will see what is available and then you can choose a suitable recipe. If you are determined to buy sole and do not change your mind even when you see beautiful, glistening, bright-eyed whiting or bream, you will probably end up with inferior sole and your meal may be spoiled.

'LA NOUVELLE CUISINE FRANÇAISE'

Sometimes I am criticized because I do not go to my famous market everyday, because I am in Japan, the United States or somewhere else. Certainly I do travel, but my trips are always very short – three days here, forty-eight hours there, rarely more. I think it is very important to visit other countries, to realize what scope for improvement there is at home. The more I travel the more I realize that other people are making advances too and that their experience can benefit others. This is why I feel I must go and see them. After all, the cook's trade makes him part of a brotherhood. A French chef must go all over France – perhaps several times – and nowadays he must travel round the world if he really wishes to develop his skills. Every time I visit another country I return with plenty of ideas. In Hong Kong for example I discovered that they cooked vegetables excellently, in just a few moments. Thus while my book reflects the current interest in France in returning to the roots of traditional French cooking, it also shows how much we can learn if we are open to new ideas from other countries, near or far. In short it combines both the old and the new.

Journalists interview me, my customers question me – they all want to know what exactly is meant by '*La nouvelle cuisine française*' – new French cuisine. Basically it is the truest form of cooking. More specifically it depends, as I have said, on the careful choice of good ingredients. Never cut corners, but look for the very finest meat, vegetables and so on. This is as true if you are cooking at home as for the most famous restaurant: whether you are buying whiting or salmon, make sure you only use the best.

One of the tenets of *la nouvelle cuisine* is that the food must keep its own taste, making the most of the original flavour. Previously in French cooking there was a concern with ostentatious effect which had little to do with cooking. In *la nouvelle cuisine* everything must be done for a purpose. Let us take one of my specialities, *Loup en croûte*, sea bass in pastry stuffed with lobster mousse. The fish is cooked in a pastry case, but you do not have to eat the pastry if you do not want to; it is there to keep in the juices of the fish. Nor do you have to eat the stuffing, which is intended to keep the fish moist as it tends to dry up otherwise. The disciples of *la nouvelle cuisine* obey other rules which I have mentioned in passing: do not decide your menu in advance but go to the market in the morning and plan according to what is available. This automatically involves simpler, lighter menus. There is no longer any need for rich stocks and sauces, lengthy marinading and preparations. Before the last war Fernard Point, whom I regard as my master, had already dispensed with all the sauces, complicated rich dishes and elaborate garnishes which were the rule during the nineteenth century. These simplified preparations also affect cooking times. Fish, for example, is always overcooked, and should still be pink around the bone, surprising though this may sound. French beans should be slightly crunchy. Pasta should be firm.

I never forget another of Fernand Point's maxims: you can only cook well, he used to say, if you cook with love, creating friendship and fraternity round your table. I believe that this is essential. The home cook as well as the great chef must only cook dishes he or she enjoys preparing. When you prepare a meal – for example when you are roasting a succulent chicken – you must do it with love. I think it is very much easier to cook well for people you love or like. Another important point: whenever you are cooking you should always allow for improvisation. A great conductor used to say that he always left room for imagination and improvisation when performing a long-rehearsed work in public. Similarly when cooking at home you must not feel that you have to obey recipes to the letter; at the last moment you can substitute one ingredient for another depending on what is to hand. For example if you have decided to make *coq au vin* and find you have no small onions or pork, don't worry. So long as the chicken is good and you have used good wine, so long as the seasoning is exactly right, you can use shallots or leeks instead of onions. You must not be a slave to the book: you must take initiatives – and even risks. Even if you do not believe you have any special gifts, the fact that you are attempting a particular recipe shows you care. You can allow yourself room for manoeuvre and fantasy, within the bounds of common sense.

These, I believe, are the main characteristics of *la nouvelle cuisine française*. I am proud to be one of those who has made the new tradition more widely known on board the planes of Air France and also in Japan. In Osaka I had the honour of teaching French cooking in the largest hotel school there – Shizuotsuji – to 1,500 pupils from a 14-year-old apprentice to an 82-year-old chef on a refresher course. But again, I think I learned as much there as I taught.

MEALS

I find that meals are always too large. I think one should leave the table still feeling slightly hungry. One hot dish in a meal seems to me enough, even on an important occasion.

At home if you cook a single hot dish and cook it well, it is sure to satisfy your guests. Meals with hot hors-d'oeuvre, hot fish, hot meat and a hot dessert are lethal. Especially since they demand an enormous amount of work, and there is nothing sadder for guests than to see the host or hostess exhausted after a day spent in the kitchen, not able to join them, but obliged to stay at the stove. You must know your limitations and not compete with professional chefs. If you want to go to a restaurant, go to a restaurant. But if you stay at home choose the simplest recipes and do not arrive at table smelling of cooking oil. Serve a cheese soufflé you know how to make well, followed by some delicious cold dish. As a general rule choose dishes that can be cooked in advance; then you can relax when you sit down to dinner. One more piece of advice: concentrate on dishes you know how to cook. Perfect two or three dishes and keep in practice. Perhaps you can make a cheese soufflé superbly or an unforgettable gratin of potatoes. If you also know how to make chicken with a cream sauce or cook a leg of lamb, the battle is won.

QUANTITIES

In his cookery book Fernand Point does not give any proportions or quantities. I think he went a little too far. In my book the quantities are approximate. If I write '12 onions', this does not mean that the dish will not come out right if you use 9 or 14. The same is true for the flour for flaky pastry. '2 oz flour' does not mean much. It depends on the quality of the flour. In my town of Collonges we have had the same miller for the last twenty years. We know that a pound of his flour is the amount needed for flaky pastry – but if, for one reason or another, we ever had to use another miller, we should have to revise all our recipes that include flour. Every time one stands in front of a stove, one has to start from scratch. So do not take what is written here absolutely literally. I shall outline a certain kind of cuisine and you, with your own taste, imagination and inspiration will do the cooking.

I use many of Guérot's recipes, which I think are marvellous. Alfred Guérot is one of the greatest and most accomplished chefs of the first half of this century. He has managed to combine, with deep understanding and great skill as a writer, all the trends in our profession. His recipes are the most perfect in existence, and in this book I draw on them extensively. In cooking one does not invent. The basic ingredients are always the same – poultry, meat, vegetables and so on. And then there is tradition, although there is also the margin for innovation that I have been talking about. I have adapted Guérot's recipes and transformed them – and you should do the same with my advice.

COOKING TIMES

Perhaps the only thing one can take directly from a cookery book is timing. And even then you may have an oven that when set to heat to 400° really only heats to 350°F (200° or 180°C). The only instruction which leaves no room for doubt is 'boil for 15 minutes'. But with an oven one is never sure of the temperature. If there is 1 chicken in the oven, it does not cook in the same way as when there are 3. As a general point, you must make sure that your oven is heating up properly.

WINE

I think one can well serve champagne throughout the meal. It is simple and delicious. Choosing wines to suit each dish is a much more delicate task. Here again I think that you should not be afraid to innovate. You can perfectly well drink a red wine with oysters; I see no objection to that. With game you can serve an Alsatian Riesling, with a fruity and very distinctive flavour. But take care, and if you are not sure of yourself, it is better to follow the traditional rules. What is most important is the quality of the wine and for that you must know where and from whom to buy. When buying French wine look on the label for the name of the property on which the wine was grown; this is a sign of quality, but there are of course other good wines as well. I personally serve wine very cool. Beaujolais in particular. Burgundies are served at 50–54°F (10–12°C); white wines at 46–50°F (8–10°C); Bordeaux at 59–61°F (15–16°C). Many people believe that to *chambrer* a wine – to serve it 'at room temperature' – means standing it near the fireplace or radiator. On the contrary, it means putting it in an unheated room. The wine will have all the time it needs to warm up in the glass when you pour it.

PRESENTATION

I often surprise people by saying that presentation is not very important. It is certainly true that today we have moved far away from the culinary art of the beginning of the century, when each dish had to be prepared by someone who had all the talents of a painter and an architect besides knowing how to cook. Fish, meat, vegetables and desserts had to look like pyramids, Chinese pavilions or cathedrals.

Today you can serve a dish without turning it into a caterer's display. For example if you are serving a lobster, you need only cut it in half and serve it with its court-bouillon. Provided the lobster has been cooked at the last moment and cut while still warm, your guests will have a fine meal. *Grande cuisine* does not mean complicated cooking. *Grande cuisine* can be boiled turkey, freshly cooked lobster, a salad picked from the garden and dressed at the last minute.

I hope that in these few pages of introduction I have given the essential rules of the art of *la nouvelle cuisine française*. You will find in this book all the detailed information necessary to the success of a simple or complicated meal.

I would like to add that this book owes a great deal to Louis Perrier and I must thank him for all the help he has given me.

I wish my readers good luck. Do not be discouraged if you cannot create culinary masterpieces immediately. I often wonder whether knowing how to cook is a gift one is born with. Sometimes it seems predestined. For more than seven generations there have always been cooks in my family. In 1634, my ancestors were millers at Collonges; and, in 1765, part of the mill was transformed into a restaurant. I started in 1942 in a small restaurant in Lyons, run by Claude Maret. It was during the Second World

War and there was nothing to eat, one had to pick one's way through the labyrinths of the black market and make do with scarce supplies. This background was a great help to me and I mastered the art of coping pretty well. Since then, times have changed, but I continue to cook. One day, soon I hope, I shall buy a house in the country. I shall build a kitchen according to my own specification. I shall install my stove and a beautiful wooden table, and if I still have health and will I shall serve Bocuse cooking to four or five people every day. You will be allowed to drink water (if you must), but you will not be allowed to smoke. I shall continue my work for pleasure and for friendship. A French moralist once said that the table is an altar that should be raised to celebrate the cult of friendship. The cook should never lose sight of this maxim; if you cook with pleasure and with love, you are certain to succeed with one of the delectable dishes described in this book.

Paul Bocuse

COOKING TECHNIQUES

Cooking procedures, simple or complex, are all based on principles that must be carefully observed if one wishes to succeed in the various steps involved in cooking a perfect dish.

These rules concern the preparation of ingredients, the preliminary steps, cooking processes, carving and presentation.

PRELIMINARY STEPS

The preliminary steps consist of:

Boning, trimming, cutting and interlarding meat or prepared joints;

Gutting, cleaning, trussing, barding and stuffing poultry and game;

Peeling, washing and blanching vegetables;

Gutting and scaling fish, rinsing the fillets.

These are the steps that are carried out before you start cooking:

Trimming: giving a piece of meat a neat appearance, getting rid of gristle and removing excess fat.

Interlarding: inserting small sticks of fat (*lardons* or lardoons) here and there in a piece of meat. This is done with a larding needle, inserting the fat in close, neat rows in the surface of the meat. The aim is to lubricate the meat as the fat melts during cooking. This is how one interlards a fillet of beef, calf's sweetbreads, lean veal, a saddle of rabbit or hare, etc.

Larding: This is similar to interlarding and is used for bigger pieces of meat that are to be braised. The difference is that the lardoons are cut to the length of the piece of meat being prepared. The lardoons are first seasoned and marinated for 2 hours and stuck, with a larding needle, through the thickness of the meat, from end to end following the direction of the grain.

Barding: Protecting the fleshy parts – for example the breast of poultry or game – with pieces of fresh pork fat about 3–6 mm ($\frac{1}{8}$–$\frac{1}{4}$ inch) thick. This prevents the heat of the oven from drying out the meat and the white meat cooks more slowly than it would otherwise; the rest of the dark meat, which is less tender, has longer to cook.

Blanching: This means scalding. Blanching starts off the cooking process. It hardens the skin of certain cuts of meat, takes away the bitterness or the strong taste of certain vegetables or softens them. Very often, after blanching, ingredients are cooled quickly in cold water, then drained. Ingredients are blanched either by plunging them into boiling water or by bringing them to the boil in cold water.

COOKING METHODS

There are five cooking methods: braising, poaching, pot-roasting, roasting and grilling. It is these different methods and the different results they produce which bring to French cooking its infinite variety.

Braising is used mainly for large cuts of meat which are nearly always marinated for 5–6 hours and are often interlarded. The piece of meat is drained, dried and browned in butter or any other fat on top of the stove; then it is moistened with some of the marinade and some veal stock or bouillon is added. The pot is hermetically sealed, and cooking continues very slowly at a simmer.

Poaching is a barely perceptible simmering in a lesser or greater amount of liquid.

Pot-roasting – or casserole-roasting – must be done over a very low flame. The only liquid is the butter used at the beginning of the cooking and the juices which run out of the meat. After the meat is browned, the pot is kept well covered. Baste frequently. At the end of the cooking time the concentrated juices will be full of goodness.

Roasting can be done in two ways – in the oven or on a spit. The second method is certainly superior to the first. In both cases fierce heat drives the juices towards the centre of the joint and creates a brown exterior crust that seals in the juices. These juices flow outwards again and impregnate all the tissues when the roast is no longer exposed to this strong heat. During roasting frequent basting with the fat but not the juice of the roast is recommended.

Grilling follows the same principles as roasting – quick searing and browning of the meat by direct heat, which seals in and concentrates the juices. The art is in knowing how to co-ordinate the heat of the grill and the speed at which the meat is seared with the size and thickness of the meat. A piece of grilled meat is turned only once, with a spatula – never with a fork or pointed utensil which would let the juices escape.

Stewing, sautéing and frying derive from these basic processes. These theories will be explained in the relevant chapters.

PRESENTATION

This is the last step before eating.

Food should be presented in an attractive but simple way – especially hot dishes – so that the quality and flavour of the dish is not affected. Never sacrifice substance to form.

If silver, gold plate or glass serving dishes are used they must always be sparkling and bright and just the right size; the rim of the dish should never be covered with food.

The ideal arrangement is one that makes serving easy. Avoid over-elaborate, cumbersome presentations which interfere with carving or serving.

CARVING

It is very difficult to carve well without any knowledge of anatomy. Learn by observation. If you are carving a joint of meat, note the direction of the grain and always cut across it. A slice of meat carved like this is easier to chew. If meat is cut with the grain even tender meat will seem tough.

SEASONING, HERBS AND SPICES, CONDIMENTS

Seasoning with the correct amount of salt is a simple but very important operation, requiring a subtle sense of taste, care and discretion.

Herbs and spices. The herbs and spices used in cooking must, except in a very few cases, blend into the general flavour of a dish, heightening the taste in a more or less pronounced way. Herbs and spices come from aromatic plants. The following are the main ones, most widely used:

Dill, betel, cinnamon, cloves, coriander, bay, mace, mustard, nutmeg, pepper, thyme, aniseed, star aniseed, basil, cumin, fennel, juniper, ginger, horseradish, rosemary, sage, paprika, saffron, curry, chervil, tarragon, parsley, vanilla, tea, chocolate, coffee and zest of lemons, oranges and tangerines.

You can instead use a ready prepared herb and spice mixture

(*épices composées*). This is more convenient but has the disadvantage of giving a standardized flavour.

Here is one of the best combinations. Mix together about 10 g ($\frac{1}{4}$ oz) dried bay, dried thyme, mace, nutmeg, white pepper, dried red pimento (seeds removed), rosemary, basil;
  15 g ($\frac{1}{2}$ oz) cloves;
  20 g ($\frac{3}{4}$ oz) cinnamon.

These are pounded in a mortar and put through a fine sieve to make a very fine powder; the fragments left in the sieve are then pounded again and put through the sieve until nothing is left. The mixture can be stored indefinitely in tightly sealed jars in a dry place. [*Editor's note:* You can also make this mixture in a blender, sieving it carefully before storing it.]

To make spiced salt mix 3$\frac{1}{2}$ tablespoons salt and 1$\frac{1}{4}$ tablespoons pepper with 4 teaspoons of this spice mixture.

Condiments can be divided into six categories.

Acid condiments: vinegar, verjuice (sour apple or grape juice), lemon juice;

Pungent condiments: garlic, shallots, spring onions, onions, chives, leeks, horseradish, radish;

Sugars or sweetening condiments: cane or beet sugar, honey;

Fat condiments: oil, butter, fat;

Pickled condiments; mustard and all its derivatives, piccalilli, gherkins, onions, tiny melons, capers, green nasturtium seeds, small green tomatoes, cauliflower, etc., all pickled in vinegar.

HORS-D'OEUVRE

Hors-d'oeuvre form the start to a lunch menu, as an addition to the main courses. Intended as a contrast to the main dish, they should whet the appetite, not satisfy it, and so should be light, varied and delicate.

Hot hors-d'oeuvre are mainly served at dinner.

The list of hors-d'oeuvre is endless. The range of possible combinations depends on the fertility of the cook's imagination, so this chapter will give practical examples rather than classic definitions.

Cold Hors-d'oeuvre
This group is divided into several categories:

Charcuterie
Salads
Shellfish
Fish
Mushrooms and other vegetables
Eggs
Canapés, etc.

Hot Hors-d'oeuvre
This group includes:

Shellfish
Mushrooms
Mixtures based on vegetables
Soufflés
Hors-d'oeuvre served on toast
Croquettes
Fritots and *beignets* (fritters of various kinds)
Croustades (pastry or toasted bread shells with various fillings)
Petites bouchées (little puff pastries with various fillings)
Pâtés and pies
Ramequins (cheese tartlets) and *paillettes* (puff pastry cut into very thin strips)
Hot *charcuterie* and sausage dishes

The section ends with several compound butters which are a great help in the preparation of a variety of hors-d'oeuvre.

Dressings for simple or mixed salads

First method (vinaigrette sauce)

Combine in a salad bowl salt, pepper, *fines herbes* (parsley, chives, tarragon, chervil) or other condiments as specified. Pour in 1 tablespoon of vinegar, then add 3 tablespoons of oil.

Second method

Instead of oil and vinegar, use the juice of 1 lemon and 3 tablespoons of cream.

Third method

Rub 2 hard-boiled egg yolks through a sieve. They should be firm but not overcooked; if they are too hard they will be very dry instead of creamy. Mash the yolks in a salad bowl with salt, pepper and a teaspoon of mustard. Mix well with a wire whisk and meanwhile slowly add 1 tablespoon of vinegar and 3 tablespoons of oil. The sauce should be thick and light. Finish by adding the egg whites cut into very thin strips.

Fourth method

Cube a strip of fat bacon. Sauté the bacon until brown in a frying pan, and pour the bacon and fat over a salad seasoned with pepper and very lightly salted. Add vinegar that has been warmed quickly in the same frying pan while still hot. This method does not include oil – the bacon fat replaces it.

Fifth method

The salad ingredients are lightly seasoned with salt, pepper and *fines herbes*, and then bound together with a very light mayonnaise (page 128) containing mustard.

Some mixed salads may be regarded as hors-d'oeuvre or as accompaniments to other cold dishes. Others are really main dishes in their own right.

Mixed salads are usually served in a glass or china salad bowl. They should be simply and tastefully decorated with ingredients used in the salad itself.

Cold Hors-d'oeuvre

FRENCH BEAN SALAD
Salade de haricots verts
For 6 people

1 kg (2 lb) young French beans, washed

4 tomatoes, peeled and quartered

50 g (2 oz) fresh truffles

225 g (8 oz) white mushrooms

Vinaigrette:

5 cl (1¾ fl oz) walnut oil

2 cl (1¾ fl oz) wine vinegar

2 shallots, finely chopped

Salt and freshly ground pepper

Snap off the ends of the beans and string them; cook quickly in a large quantity of rapidly boiling water. Make sure the beans remain crunchy.

When the beans are cooked, cool them under cold water and drain at once. Pat dry.

Place the beans in a salad bowl. Top them with the tomatoes, the truffles and the mushrooms cut into juliennes (matchsticks).

Season at the table with vinaigrette sauce to which finely chopped shallots are added.

Salade niçoise

One part boiled potatoes

One part ripe tomatoes

One part cooked French beans

One part lettuce hearts

Dressing:
Oil
Vinegar
Salt
Pepper
1 onion
Chervil

Peel and thinly slice the potatoes. Remove the stalks of the tomatoes; peel, seed and cut them into quarters. Trim the ends and strings of the beans and cook in salted water. Separate the leaves of the lettuce.

Mix all the ingredients in a salad bowl. Dress with the oil, vinegar, salt and pepper and add a finely chopped onion and plenty of fresh chervil.

Salade Café de Paris

Inner leaves of a
  lettuce
Salt
Pepper
Oil
Vinegar
Cooked chicken
  breast or
  drumsticks
Mayonnaise (page
  128)
Lettuce heart
Anchovy fillets
Green olives, stoned
Hard-boiled eggs,
  quartered
1 tablespoon
  vinaigrette sauce

Separate the lettuce leaves. Wash and dry them. Season with salt, pepper, oil and vinegar; pile into a mound in a salad bowl. Cover the top with slin slices of cooked breast of chicken arranged in a fan shape – the drumsticks can also be used – and cover with a light layer of mayonnaise. Dip a lettuce heart in vinaigrette sauce and place on top of the mound. Arrange anchovy fillets, cut into two long strips, green olives and hard-boiled eggs around the lettuce heart.

Salade demi-deuil

One part potatoes
One part truffles

Mustard Sauce:
1 heaped teaspoon
  mustard
1 teaspoon vinaigrette
  sauce
Salt and pepper
1 tablespoon cream

Boil some potatoes; peel and cut them into large dice. Add an equal part of truffles, cooked or raw, cut into large julienne. Season with mustard sauce. Mix in a salad bowl.

LOBSTER OR CRAWFISH SALAD
Salade de homard ou de langouste

Prepare a salad with hearts of lettuce. Season with vinaigrette sauce to which is added the sieved yolk of a boiled egg, just set. Arrange in a china or glass bowl, and on top, in the shape of a crown, set the cooked lobster or crawfish tail meat cut into thin slices. Cover the lobster with light mayonnaise (page 128) and decorate the slices with anchovy fillets cut into diamond shapes, capers and quartered hard-boiled eggs.

BEET SALAD
Salade de betteraves

First method

Cook very red beetroots, preferably by baking in a 375°F (190°C, gas mark 5) oven for 45 minutes, or in boiling water. Peel the beetroot and cut them into thick strips or thin slices. Season with salt, pepper, vinegar, oil and chopped chervil or parsley.

Second method

Prepare as above but add for each medium beetroot 1 medium-sized onion that has been baked for 15 minutes in a 325°F (170°C, gas mark 3) oven, cooled, and cut in slices.

Third method

Prepare as above. Peel, and cut into thick strips, dice or thin slices. Season with salt, pepper, lemon juice, cream and strong mustard.

Proportions for the seasonings: juice of half a lemon, 2 tablespoons of cream, 1 teaspoon of mustard.

Arrange the beetroot in a shallow dish or a salad bowl. Just before serving, sprinkle a little chopped chervil on top.

POTATO SALAD
Salade de pommes de terre

1 kg (2 lb) yellow potatoes
6 tablespoons dry white wine
Salt
Pepper
Vinegar
Oil
Chopped parsley
Chopped chervil
1 chopped onion or shallot (optional)

Cook the potatoes in salt water. Dry them in a 275°F (140°C, gas mark 1) oven. Peel the potatoes while still hot, cut into slices immediately and marinate, still hot, in dry white wine; then season with salt, pepper, vinegar, oil and chopped parsley and chervil. A finely chopped onion or shallot may be added.

TOMATO SALAD
Salade de tomates

First method

Choose well-ripened tomatoes; remove the core and the stem. Plunge the tomatoes into boiling water for 6 seconds; drain, cool them under cold water and peel them. Remove the juice and seeds, and cut into slices about 6 mm ($\frac{1}{4}$ inch) thick. Place the slices in a shallow dish. Pour vinaigrette sauce over them, and sprinkle with chopped tarragon. Leave to stand for a few minutes before serving.

Second method

Peel the tomatoes as above; squeeze them gently to remove the juice and the seeds and cut into quarters instead of slices. Season in a salad bowl with vinaigrette sauce, chervil, chopped tarragon and chopped onion; leave to stand for 1 hour. Transfer to a glass bowl and decorate with thin onion rings overlapping one another in a crown; add a pinch of chopped chervil in the centre. At table, before serving, mix one last time, so that the different ingredients will be well seasoned.

CUCUMBER SALAD
Salade de concombre

Peel a cucumber and slice in two lengthwise; remove the seeds and cut into very thin slices. Spread slices on a plate and sprinkle them with salt; mix well and transfer to a bowl. Let stand for 1 hour, so that the cucumber will release its water. Drain well; season with pepper, oil, vinegar and chopped chervil. Serve in a shallow dish.

CAULIFLOWER SALAD
Salade de chou-fleur

Divide a white firm cauliflower into small florets and peel each stem. Wash in water to which vinegar has been added to get rid of any tiny slugs. Boil the cauliflower for 5 minutes, drain, then place again in boiling salted water (10 g ($\frac{1}{4}$ oz) of salt per litre ($1\frac{3}{4}$ pts) of water). Simmer slowly in order to avoid breaking the florets. Drain again and arrange in shallow dishes or small bowls. Pour over vinaigrette sauce to which mustard and chopped chervil have been added.

Mix carefully at table and serve.

CELERY SALAD OR RÉMOULADE
Salade de céleri ou rémoulade

Use the white heart of a celery. Divide each stalk into 8- or 10-cm (3- or 4-inch) pieces. Cut the pieces lengthwise in thin strips, without completely cutting them apart at one end. Soak in cold water for 40 minutes and drain carefully.

Season with a strong vinaigrette sauce made with mustard; or use a dressing made with salt, pepper, mustard, lemon juice and sour cream or double cream; or rémoulade sauce (page 130).

CELERIAC SALAD OR RÉMOULADE
Salade de céleri-rave ou rémoulade

First method

1 large or 2 small celeriac
Salt

Sauce:
1 teaspoon mustard
Pinch salt
Pinch freshly ground pepper
$\frac{1}{2}$ teaspoon vinegar
$1\frac{1}{2}$ dl ($\frac{1}{4}$ pt) oil

Cut the celeriac into fine julienne; sprinkle lightly with salt; mix well in a bowl and let stand for 1 hour. Drain and dry the strips. For the sauce, put all the ingredients except the oil in a bowl and beat vigorously. Drop by drop, while beating, add the oil. Season the celeriac with the sauce. The pieces must be thoroughly coated when the mixing is finished. Serve in a shallow dish or salad bowl.

Second method

Scald the strips of celeriac for 5 seconds; drain and let cool. Then season as above.

Third method

Let the strips of celeriac stand for 30 minutes in lemon juice. Then season with a strong mustard mayonnaise or a rémoulade sauce (page 128 or 130).

RED CABBAGE OR SAVOY CABBAGE SALAD
Salade de chou rouge ou chou de Milan

First method:
1 small red or Savoy
    cabbage
Salt
Garlic cloves
Freshly ground
    pepper
Bay leaves
Boiled vinegar,
    cooled
Oil (optional)
Cooking apples
    (optional)

First method

Take the centre part of a small red or Savoy cabbage. Separate the leaves and cut off the rib stalks. Wash the leaves and drain them. Pile the leaves together and slice in thin shreds.

Parboil the shredded cabbage in boiling water for 6 minutes; drain thoroughly. Put into a bowl in layers, sprinkling each layer with a little salt. On top of each layer except the last, place a clove of garlic, a little freshly ground pepper and a tiny piece of bay leaf. Pour cooled boiled vinegar over all, so that the cabbage is entirely covered. Marinate for 2 days, checking to make sure that the vinegar is covering the cabbage. Cover the bowl, and set in a cool place. The cabbage can be used in the following ways:

1. Served as it is
2. Drained and seasoned with 2 tablespoons of oil to each 125 g (5 oz) of cabbage
3. Mixed, after seasoning, with an equal amount of cooking apples cut into thin slices

Second method:
1½ dl (¼ pt) vinegar
1 red or Savoy
  cabbage, shredded
Salt
Pepper
Oil

Second method

Boil vinegar in a saucepan. Add the cabbage, boil for an instant, then cool. Drain slightly and just before serving season with salt, pepper and oil.

Both these methods make the cabbage more tender and digestible.

BEEF AND POTATO SALAD
Salade de boeuf Parmentier

Mix leftover cooked beef (*pot-au-feu*), diced, with an equal amount of boiled potatoes, sliced thinly. Season while hot with salt, pepper, oil, vinegar, chopped onion and *fines herbes* to taste.

12 small red mullets
Salt and freshly
  ground pepper
4 tablespoons olive
  oil
1 dl (4 fl oz) dry
  white wine
4 tomatoes, peeled,
  seeded and cut into
  quarters
sprig thyme
½ bay leaf
1 garlic clove,
  crushed
1 pinch saffron
Lemon slices, peeled

RED MULLETS WITH TOMATOES, GARLIC AND SAFFRON
Petits rougets à l'orientale

Remove the mullet gills, but do not clean the fish. Dry them and place them side by side in a lightly oiled, ovenproof earthenware dish. Season with salt and freshly ground pepper. Mix the oil, white wine, tomato pulp and seasonings and pour over the mullets. Bake in a 425°F (220°C, gas mark 7) oven 8–10 minutes. Leave in the dish to cool. Serve cold with a slice of peeled lemon on each mullet.

There is a second recipe for this dish in the fish chapter, on page 176.

MARINATED MACKEREL
Maquereaux marinés

Marinade:
2 parts dry white
  wine
1 part vinegar
1 medium-sized
  carrot
1 large onion, thinly
  sliced
Thyme
$\frac{1}{2}$ bay leaf

12 small mackerel,
  gutted and cleaned
Salt and Freshly
  ground pepper
12 peeled lemon
  slices

Make a marinade of dry white wine, vinegar, the carrot, the onion, thyme and bay leaf. Cook for 20 minutes. Arrange the mackerel in an overproof earthenware dish; season with salt and freshly ground pepper. Cover the fish with the marinade and bake in a 425° F (220°C, gas mark 7) oven for 8–10 minutes; cool.
Serve very cold with a slice of lemon on each mackerel.

MARINATED HERRING
Harengs marinés

Prepare like the mackerel.

Note: It is advisable to prepare the fish at least two days before serving and keep them in the marinade, well chilled.

SAFFRON MUSSELS
Moules au safran

2 kg (4 lb) mussels,
  well cleaned
Sprig parsley
Sprig thyme
$\frac{1}{2}$ bay leaf
Pinch freshly ground
  pepper
Pinch saffron
2 dl (8 fl oz) dry
  white wine
1 large onion,
  chopped finely
4 tablespoons oil

In a pan combine the mussels, seasonings, herbs, wine and onion; heat rapidly and stir mussels frequently so that they all open. Remove from the heat. Drain the liquid into another pan, and reduce it by two-thirds. While it is boiling, add enough oil to make a light emulsion; let it cool. Remove half the shell of each mussel, and set the mussels on a plate or a shallow serving dish; pour the juice and oil mixture over them.
Serve very cold.

PASTRY STRAWS WITH ANCHOVY BUTTER
Paillettes d'anchois

Make some flaky pastry (page 531 or 533). Roll out a thin band about 6 cm (2½ inches) wide; prick well with a fork, and bake in a 425°F (220°C, gas mark 7) oven until golden brown.

After the pastry has cooled, spread a thick layer of anchovy butter (page 27) on it, and cut very thin strips. Serve as tit bits.

12 small artichokes
12 small white onions
½ l (1 pt) water
2 teaspoons salt
Juice of 3 lemons
10 peppercorns
Sprig thyme
½ bay leaf
1 celery stalk
Pinch dried fennel or
    fennel stalk
15 coriander seeds
2 dl (8 fl oz) oil

ARTICHOKES A LA GRECQUE
(cooked in oil)
Artichauts à la grecque

Cut off the stems of the artichokes and trim 2 cm (¾ inch) from the leaves with scissors; cut the artichokes into quarters and place them, with the onions, in a marinade prepared in the following way:

In a saucepan, combine the water, the salt and the lemon juice. Tie the peppercorns, thyme, bay leaf, celery, fennel and coriander in cheesecloth and add. Bring to the boil over high heat, and boil 5 minutes; add the oil, the artichokes and the onions. Simmer for about 20 minutes. Check whether the artichokes are cooked by pulling off one leaf: if it separates easily, they are done.

Put into a bowl and serve cold.

CAULIFLOWER A LA GRECQUE
Chou-fleur à la grecque

Divide a firm white cauliflower into small florets. Peel the stem of each floret, wash and put into salted boiling water (10 g (¼ oz) of salt per litre (1¾ pts) of water) for 5 minutes. Drain, rinse in cold water, drain again. Then follow the recipe for artichokes (above), adding 3 tomatoes, peeled, seeded and cut into quarters.

LEEKS A LA GRECQUE
Poireaux à la grecque

Cut the white parts of leeks into pieces 8–10 cm (3–4 inches) long and cook 10 minutes in boiling salted water. Drain, rinse in cold water and prepare like the artichokes above.

Pinch dried fennel or fennel stalk
Pinch powdered coriander or 10 seeds
Small sprig thyme
½ bay leaf
10 peppercorns
Small celery stalk
3 dl (½ pt) water
Juice of 2 lemons
1 teaspoon sugar
1 teaspoon salt
225 g (½ lb) very small mushrooms, firm and white
3 tablespoons oil
3 tablespoons dry white wine

MUSHROOMS A LA GRECQUE
Champignons à la grecque

Tie the herbs and spices in a piece of cheesecloth. Combine water, lemon juice, sugar, salt and spice bag in a saucepan and boil for 5 minutes. Clean and quickly wash the mushrooms and add. Boil rapidly for 5 minutes. At full boil, add the oil and wine. A light emulsion will form naturally.

Pour into a bowl, and serve very cold.

225 g (½ lb) medium mushrooms, firm and white
Salt and freshly ground pepper
Pinch powdered sugar
1 tablespoon lemon juice
3 tablespoons cream or oil
Fresh herbs and garlic

MUSHROOM SALAD
Salade de champignons

Carefully wash the mushrooms and wipe dry. Slice them thinly and put into a salad bowl; season with salt, pepper, sugar, lemon juice, cream (or oil); also add fresh tarragon, chervil; chopped fennel, or thyme, crushed garlic, spices, etc., depending on what is on hand and what you like.

500 g (1 lb) small
  onions
Dry white wine and
oil, in equal parts
3 large ripe tomatoes,
  peeled, seeded and
  mashed
Pinch salt
Freshly ground
  pepper
Garlic clove, grated
Coriander seeds
Pinch saffron

ONIONS WITH TOMATOES, GARLIC AND SAFFRON
Petits oignons à l'orientale

Choose very small onions of equal size. Peel them and put them into a frying pan big enough to hold them easily. Cover the onions with half dry white wine and half oil, then add the tomatoes. Season with salt, pepper, garlic, coriander and saffron. The saffron should be the dominant seasoning.

Cover, bring to the boil and simmer until the onions are completely cooked.

Pour into a bowl with the cooking juice and keep in a cool place until serving time.

STUFFED EGGS WITH PAPRIKA
Oeufs farcis au paprika

Cook eggs until they are just set. Shell them and cut in two lengthwise.

Place the yolks in a bowl and mash with a fork; mix with an equal quantity of unsalted butter or thick cream. Season this creamy paste with a pinch of salt and paprika to taste. Put the yolk mixture back into the egg-white halves and smooth into dome shapes.

Serve on a shallow dish.

HUNGARIAN CHEESE
Fromage hongrois
For 6 people

6 sweet green or red
  peppers
2 tablespoons finely
  chopped mild onion
50 g (2 oz) unsalted
  butter
500 g (1 lb) petit-
  Suisse or cream
  cheese
1½ tablespoons
  chopped chives
20 g (¾ oz) fine
  Hungarian paprika
1½ teaspoons cumin
  seeds
Salt and white pepper

Wash, dry and seed the peppers. Cook the chopped onion in the butter, covered. Cool and mix well with the cheese.

Mix in the chives, paprika and cumin, and season lightly with salt and pepper.

Stuff the peppers with this rich preparation.

Serve on a cheese tray.

Hot Hors-d'oeuvre

OYSTERS WITH SPINACH
Huîtres à la florentine
For 1 person

6 oysters
1 handful spinach
25 g (1 oz) unsalted
  butter
Salt
Dash grated nutmeg
Pinch sugar
  (optional)
Grated Parmesan or
  Gruyère cheese
Breadcrumbs

Shell the oysters and leave them in their juice; clean the shells carefully. At the same time prepare the spinach – a good handful for every 6 oysters. Remove the stems, blanch the leaves rapidly for 10 minutes in boiling water. Drain and rinse with cold water; drain again and squeeze to remove all the water.

In a frying pan rapidly heat about half the butter. As soon as it bubbles, add the spinach, seasoning it with salt and a dash of grated nutmeg. Add a pinch of sugar, if it is late in the season for spinach and it is bitter. Stir over high heat for 2 minutes. Remove from the flame, and add the rest of the butter.

Arrange the spinach in the centre of a heatproof dish. Surround it with the oyster shells, which have been lightly heated. Drain the oysters, remove their beards and place each on a shell. Sprinkle the oysters and the spinach with grated Parmesan or Gruyère cheese, mixed with a few breadcrumbs to form a crusty *gratin*. Sprinkle with melted butter, and place the dish under a very hot grill, very close to the flame, for 1 or 2 minutes, just long enough to brown the top.

Place the hot dish on a napkin and serve.

½ recipe pastry dough
(*pâte à foncer*, see
page 537)
50 g (2 oz) smoked
bacon cut into very
thin slices
50 g (2 oz) Gruyère
cheese, cut into
very thin slices
1 tiny onion, chopped
3 eggs
3 dl (½ pt) cream or
milk
A knob of butter

Quiche lorraine
For 4 people

Roll out the dough, and line a 20-cm (8-inch) flan tin. [*Editor's note:* This quantity of dough is ample for this size quiche. But since this dough freezes very well, you may want to make the full amount of the pastry recipe and freeze what is not needed here.]

Blanch the bacon in boiling water for 2 minutes and then cook slightly in a little butter. In the bottom of the crust lay alternate slices of bacon and Gruyère cheese.

Cook the onion, without browning, in the remaining butter. Beat the eggs with the cream or milk and mix in the onion.

Fill the crust with the mixture, which should be only lightly salted and peppered, as the bacon and the Gruyère are usually rather salty.

Bake 35 minutes in the oven at 425°F (220°C, gas mark 7).

Note: If you like you can partially bake the pastry case beforehand. To stop the bottom puffing up, line the case with foil or brown paper and weight it with a handful of cherry stones or dried beans kept for the purpose.

1 medium onion
50 g (2 oz) unsalted
butter
125 g (5 oz) rice
½ l (1 pt) white stock
6 chicken livers
6 large mushrooms
1 shallot, chopped
1 tablespoon veal
gravy, thickened

CHICKEN LIVERS WITH RICE
Risotto aux foies de volailles
For 4 people

Finely chop the onion and sauté in a third of the butter until transparent. Add the rice and heat in the butter. Add the stock, cover and cook on a low flame for 18 minutes. Then remove the rice from the fire, and carefully add about half the remaining butter, tasting to judge the amount. Pour the rice into a bowl.

Cut each liver in two, seasoning with salt and pepper, and sauté over a high flame in the remaining butter. Cook the livers until they are pink; add the mushrooms, quartered, and the shallot. Cook rapidly; then away from the flame finish with the veal gravy.

Note: Although the rice is well cooked, the grains should remain whole and separate and not be gummy.

4 small aubergines
4 medium-sized
  tomatoes, peeled,
  seeded and crushed
1 tablespoon oil
1 garlic clove,
  crushed
Salt and pepper
Breadcrumbs
Unsalted butter,
  melted
Tomato sauce
  (optional, page 111)

AUBERGINES WITH TOMATOES AND GARLIC
Aubergines provençales

Cut the aubergines lengthwise. Fry cut side down for 5 minutes; then remove the pulp and chop it coarsely. Retain the shells.

Sauté the tomatoes in the oil. Add the garlic and the aubergine pulp; season with salt and pepper to taste. Place the aubergine shells in a buttered ovenproof dish. Fill with the aubergine and tomato mixture. Sprinkle with breadcrumbs, and pour some melted butter over the tops. Bake until brown in the oven.

Serve the aubergines surrounded by a ring of tomato sauce, or pour over 2 tablespoons of foamy butter, melted in a frying pan at the last moment.

4 dl (¾ pt) milk
75 g (3 oz) flour
Salt, pepper, nutmeg
60 g (2 oz) Gruyère
  or Parmesan
  cheese, grated
25 g (1 oz) unsalted
  butter
4 eggs, separated
2 teaspoons milk

PARMESAN SOUFFLÉS
Soufflés au parmesan
For 4 people

Bring the milk to the boil. When it has cooled slightly, add to the flour in small quantities, stirring all the time to obtain a completely smooth mixture without any lumps. Add salt and a pinch of pepper and nutmeg. Bring to the boil again, stirring constantly. Remove from the heat and to this creamy sauce immediately add the cheese, the butter and egg yolks mixed with 2 teaspoons of milk.

Beat the egg whites until stiff; delicately fold them into the sauce, taking care that the whites fall as little as possible.

Pour the mixture into 4 well-buttered 8-cm (3-inch) porcelain soufflé dishes, and bake in a 325°F (170°C, gas mark 3) oven for 10 minutes.

Serve immediately.

HAM SOUFFLÉ
Soufflé au jambon
For 6 people

225 g (8 oz) lean cooked ham
25 g (1 oz) unsalted butter
Pinch paprika
½ l (¾ pt) béchamel sauce (page 110)
3 eggs, separated

Pound the ham in a mortar with the butter; rub it through a very fine strainer. Stir the ham purée and the paprika into very hot béchamel sauce. Add the egg yolks, then the whites, beaten stiff, being careful that they do not fall. Spoon the mixture into a buttered 1-litre (1-quart) timbale mould or into 6 buttered 8-cm (3-inch) porcelain soufflé dishes. Bake at 300°F (150°C, gas mark 2) until set. The mixture will double its volume above the mould. It must be served immediately.

[*Editor's note:* You can mince the ham fine in a mincer or chop it in a blender or food processor.]

SOFT ROE OF CARP ON TOAST WITH MUSTARD SAUCE
Laitance de carpe sur toast sauce moutarde

1 soft carp roe or 12 soft roe of herring
White wine
Lemon juice or vinegar
Thin slices of toast
1 tablespoon Dijon mustard

Rinse the soft roe in cold water, strip off the little black vessels that run along the sides, wash and dry.

Put the soft roe of a carp (or 12 soft roe of herring) into a sauté pan. Pour over a little court-bouillon made with white wine and water in equal parts and a few drops of lemon juice or vinegar; poach the roe lightly without boiling. As soon as it is cooked, drain and place on thin slices of toasted bread. Reduce cooking liquid and add the mustard. Continue cooking until the mustard sauce has thickened and cover the roe with it.

SOFT ROE AND ANCHOVY FRITTERS
Beignets de laitances et beignets d'anchois

12 soft roe or anchovy fillets
Dry white wine
Salt and pepper
6 tablespoons oil
Juice of ½ lemon
Frying batter (page 601)
Parsley

Slowly poach 12 soft roe in a court-bouillon made with equal parts of dry white wine and water, with salt and pepper; cool in the court-bouillon, drain and dry. Marinate the roe for an hour in oil and lemon juice.

Just before serving dip the roe one at a time into a frying batter, and plunge them immediately into hot deep oil to fry. Serve the roe on a napkin, garnished with a bouquet of fried parsley.

After the anchovy fillets have been marinated in oil, dry them, dip in frying batter and fry like the roe.

WELSH RAREBIT
Rôties galloises

Thin slices white bread, toasted and buttered
¼ l (½ pt) beer
½ teaspoon mustard (preferably English)
100 g (4 oz) Gloucester or Cheshire cheese
Dash cayenne pepper
25 g (1 oz) unsalted butter

Toast and butter thin slices of white bread; place in an ovenproof porcelain dish.

Reduce slightly by boiling the beer mixed with the mustard; add Gloucester or Cheshire cheese, cut into small cubes, and cayenne pepper. When the cheese is melted, remove from the flame and add butter. Pour the mixture over the warm toast, covering it completely.

Set in a 475°F (240°C, gas mark 9) oven to glaze quickly until the top is a beautiful golden colour. Serve immediately.

[*Editor's note:* Cheddar cheese may be substituted.]

FRITTERS
Fritots

Fritters are another way of using leftover fish, shellfish, chicken, meat, giblets, vegetables. They all can be cut into pieces, dipped in a frying batter (page 601), then deep fried, one at a time, in hot oil.

Serve with sauce or compound butter (pages 26–30) separately.

SHELLFISH CROQUETTES
Croquettes de coquillages

1 l (1 qt) mussels
225 g (½ lb) mushrooms
50 g (2 oz) unsalted butter
1 dl (¼ pt) thick béchamel sauce (page 110)
2 egg yolks

Open 1 litre (1 quart) of mussels (or other molluscs) that have been well washed and discard those that still contain mud. Remove the shells, cut off the beards and dice the meat.

Prepare the mushrooms. Wash rapidly, drain and dry; then dice. Melt the butter in a frying pan and cook the mushrooms rapidly over a high flame. Add the diced shellfish and béchamel sauce. Remove from the flame; thicken with the egg yolks, as explained in the recipe for chicken croquettes (below). Finish the dish in the same manner.

CHICKEN CROQUETTES
Croquettes de volaille

250 g (½ lb) leftover cooked chicken
100 g (¼ lb) cooked lean ham or tongue
50 g (2 oz) raw truffles (preferably in season)
100 g (¼ lb) mushrooms
50 g (2 oz) unsalted butter
4 dl (¾ pt) velouté sauce (page 109) made with chicken stock
50 g (2 oz) crumbs from stale bread
50 g (2 oz) flour
Oil
Tomato sauce (page 111)
4 eggs

Dice the chicken, the ham or tongue and the truffles and mushrooms. In a large frying pan melt the butter rapidly; add the mushrooms and a few seconds later the truffles, and then the chicken velouté. By boiling reduce rapidly by half, and add the chicken. Return to the boil, and immediately, away from heat, add 3 egg yolks. Mix well, and do not allow to boil again. Pour this mixture into a buttered dish, dab the surface with butter, and let cool.

While the meat mixture is cooling, prepare the breadcrumbs. Crush the bread, with a pinch of flour, in a cloth; then rub through a medium sieve or a strainer. This gives you freshly made, untoasted breadcrumbs.

Beat 1 egg in a bowl.

When the meat mixture is cool, divide into 50 g (2 oz) portions. Form each into the shape of a cork by rolling lightly in flour, then in beaten egg and then in breadcrumbs. (You can replace the fresh breadcrumbs with dry breadcrumbs, but this is not recommended.)

Fry the croquettes in very hot oil just before serving; they should be crisp on the outside and creamy inside, with a beautiful golden colour.

Serve on a napkin with tomato sauce separately.

BRAIN FRITTERS
Beignets de cervelle

1 calf's brain or 3
lambs' brains
½ tablespoon vinegar
Pinch salt
3 tablespoons olive
oil
Juice of ¼ lemon
Pinch chervil
Salt and pepper
Frying batter (page
601)
Oil
Parsley

Use 1 calf's brain or 3 lambs' brains; soak in cold water to remove the blood. Remove the surrounding membranes. Make a court-bouillon with ¼ l (½ pt) of water, ½ tablespoon of vinegar and a large pinch of salt. Start the brains in the cold court-bouillon and slowly bring to the boil; lower the heat and let it barely simmer for 10 minutes.

Drain; cut the brains into 2·5-cm (1-inch) cubes. Soak for about 20 minutes in a marinade made with olive oil and lemon juice, chervil, salt and pepper.

Meanwhile, prepare a frying batter; dip the cubes into the batter, and fry one at a time in very hot oil until golden brown.

Serve on a napkin, garnished with a bouquet of fried parsley.

CROUSTADE FILLED WITH CHICKEN, TRUFFLES AND MUSHROOMS
Croustade bressane

½ recipe pastry dough
(*pâte à foncer*,
page 537)

Filling
1 part chicken breast,
cooked
1 part truffles
1 part mushrooms,
diced coarsely
50 g (2 oz) unsalted
butter, plus extra
butter
Madeira or port
Cream or béchamel
sauce (page 110)

Roll the pastry dough quite thin. Cut with a round or oval pastry cutter to fit the size of the mould chosen (this recipe is suitable for a large flan tin or several smaller moulds). Line the mould or moulds with the dough; prick the dough with a fork. Line with wax paper or foil; fill with dried lentils or beans, or cherry stones kept for this purpose. Bake until lightly browned in a 350°F (180°C, gas mark 4) oven. Then remove the beans or other weights and the paper; keep the pastry warm.

Fill the *croustade* just before serving with a mixture of chicken, truffles and mushrooms, made as follows:

Cook the mushrooms first in butter, then add the truffles and, depending upon the quantity, 1 or more tablespoons of Madeira or port, then the chicken, and finally a few tablespoons of cream (or béchamel sauce, if you do not have any cream).

Boil rapidly to reduce by half, then thicken away from heat with 50 g (2 oz) of unsalted butter. The mixture should be very creamy. Correct the seasoning, garnish and serve.

The garnish for the bouchées (page 199) can be used for a *croustade*.

SAUSAGE PASTRIES
Petits pâtes à la bourgeoise

Make half recipe flaky pastry (page 531) and roll out 6 mm ($\frac{1}{4}$ inch) thick. Cut the dough with a pastry cutter into circles 6 cm ($2\frac{1}{2}$ inches) in diameter or into 5-cm (2-inch) squares. Place half the circles or squares on a pastry sheet, moisten the edges with a brush or cloth dipped in water.

In the centre of each piece of pastry, place 1 tablespoon of sausage meat. Cover each with a second piece of pastry.

Press lightly all around the edges with your thumb or with a pastry wheel in order to seal the pastry.

Brush tops with beaten egg and score dough with the point of a knife. Bake in 425°F (220°C, gas mark 7) oven for 15 minutes.

---

125 g (4 oz) flour
60 g (2 oz) unsalted butter
4 eggs
$\frac{1}{4}$ l (8 fl oz) milk
Pinch salt
Pinch grated or ground nutmeg
Grated Gruyère cheese

CHEESE PASTRIES
Ramequins au fromage

Prepare a chou pastry (page 550) with the flour, butter, eggs (save about $\frac{1}{2}$ egg for glaze), milk, salt, nutmeg. Do not add any sugar.

Fill a tablespoon with dough and push the dough on to a baking sheet with the blade of a knife, leaving about 8 cm (3 inches) between the puffs. Frequently dip the blade in warm water so that the dough does not stick to it.

Brush the puffs with the reserved $\frac{1}{2}$ beaten egg. Sprinkle with grated Gruyère cheese, and then press cheese into the puffs lightly with a knife.

Bake in a 425°F (220°C, gas mark 7) oven for about 15 minutes.

½ recipe flaky pastry
(page 531)
200 g (8 oz) grated
Parmesan or
Gruyère cheese
Paprika or cayenne
pepper (optional)

CHEESE STRAWS
Paillettes au parmesan

Make half recipe flaky pastry. Sprinkle grated Parmesan or Gruyère cheese on to the pastry board before the last two turns so that the grated cheese will be distributed evenly into the dough.

Roll out the dough and divide into strips 10 cm (4 inches) wide and 3 mm (⅛ inch) thick. Cut the strips crosswise into strips 6 mm (¼ inch) wide. Place them on a baking sheet and bake in a 450°F (230°C, gas mark 8) oven until golden brown.

The *paillettes* can be served as a garnish for various clear soups. They can also be seasoned with a pinch of paprika or cayenne pepper.

ANCHOVY STRAWS
Paillettes aux anchois

Follow the directions above for pastry straws, but do not add cheese. Roll the dough and cut into strips 10 cm (4 inches) wide and 6 mm (¼ inch) thick. Moisten the surface with a brush or cloth dipped into beaten egg. Cut crosswise in 1-inch strips.

Cover the tops of the pastry strips with anchovy fillets rinsed, dried and cut into small rectagles about 2 cm (¾ inch) long. Place them on a baking sheet and bake for 12 minutes in a 425°F (220°C, gas mark 7) oven.

POTATOES WITH CRAYFISH
Pommes de terre Nantua

Bake some fairly small potatoes of a firm-fleshed variety. Cut off the tops and scoop out the pulp. Replace it with a ragoût of crayfish tails bound with a Nantua sauce (page 121).

Place a folded napkin on a serving plate and serve the potatoes on it.

SAUSAGES IN WHITE WINE
Saucisses au vin blanc

6 chipolata sausages
Unsalted butter
Croûtons, fried in butter
1 tablespoon dry white wine
1 tablespoon veal stock
1 teaspoon tomato sauce or ½ teaspoon fresh tomato pulp

Cook the sausages in butter in a small frying pan, and place them on rectangular croûtons (bread squares that have been sautéed in the same butter as the sausages). Arrange on a hot serving dish. Add dry white wine to the frying pan; boil until reduced by two-thirds, then add veal stock and tomato sauce or tomato pulp. If you are using pulp, let it cook for a few minutes. When this sauce has reduced and is very hot, add 2 pats of butter, stirring vigorously away from the flame until the sauce is perfectly blended. Keep the sausages very hot, and pour the sauce over them.

POACHED SAUSAGE WITH POTATOES
Saucisson chaud à la lyonnaise
For 4 people

An 800-g (1½-lb) pure pork sausage
[*Editor's note*: Italian *cotechino* may be used.]
1 kg (2 lb) yellow, waxy potatoes, all about the same size

Put the sausage in a saucepan or an earthenware pot. Cover with 2–3½ litres (2 or 3 quarts) of cold water.

Heat on top of stove just to boiling point; maintain a constant heat without boiling for 25–30 minutes.

Remove the pan from the heat for a quarter hour to complete the poaching. Peel and steam the potatoes or cook them in salted water and serve with the hot sausage and unsalted butter.

This very simple dish, typical of Lyons, is eaten at the beginning of a meal. The sausage must be of excellent quality, not the usual English mixture with a high percentage of cereal.

‰‹⟨⟩‹⟨⟩‹⟨⟩‹⟨⟩‹⟨⟩‹⟨⟩‹⟨⟩‹⟨⟩‹⟨⟩‹⟨⟩‹⟨⟩‰

SAUSAGE IN DOUGH
Saucisson en brioche
For 5–6 people

A 1-kg (2-lb) pure pork sausage, about 30 cm (12 inches long)

[*Editor's note:* Italian *cotechino* may be used.]

¼ l (½ pt) Beaujolais wine

1 recipe ordinary brioche dough (page 524)

1 egg yolk, beaten

Flour

Périgueux sauce (optional, page 116)

Cover the sausage with cold water and cook for 30 minutes, simmering without boiling on a low flame. Leave the sausage to cool in its water away from the heat. Then remove it from the water and strip off the skin. Place in a 475°F (240°C, gas mark 9) oven for a few minutes to melt more of the fat. Drain off the accumulated fat; deglaze the pan with wine, scraping up the concentrated juices, and boil to reduce the wine.

Roll the brioche dough so that it is about 8 cm (3 inches) longer at each end than the sausage and about 15 cm (6 inches) wide.

Brush the sausage with the egg yolk, then roll in flour. Wrap the sausage in the brioche dough, making sure that the dough sticks to the sausage. If necessary, moisten the dough lightly.

Brush the entire surface of the dough with the beaten egg; decorate with some of the reserved dough or simply with designs made with the point of a knife.

Set the sausage in dough on a cooking sheet, and let the dough rise until it doubles. Bake in a 425°F (220°C, gas mark 7) oven for about 30 minutes.

The sausage in dough is served sliced, sometimes accompanied by an excellent Périgueux sauce.

Compound Butters

Compound butters are prepared by mixing unsalted butter with substances such as cooked meats, fish, seafood, vegetables, herbs or spices, crushed in a mortar then put through a very fine sieve or cheesecloth.

These butters are used in the preparation of some hors-d'oeuvre or to finish a sauce.

In many cases the compound butters are cooked or melted with the other ingredients.

This is how shrimp butter, crayfish butter, lobster butter, etc., are prepared.

[*Editor's note:* You can experiment with an electric blender in making these butters.]

ANCHOVY BUTTER
Beurre d'anchois

15 anchovy fillets
200 g (8 oz) unsalted
butter

Rinse the anchovy fillets in water to rid them of salt. Dry them and pound in a mortar with butter. Rub through a fine sieve.

GARLIC BUTTER
Beurre d'ail

8 cloves of garlic
1 teaspoon salt
300 g (12 oz) unsalted
butter

Prepare in the same way with garlic cloves and salt.

GREEN OR WATERCRESS BUTTER
Beurre vert pré ou de cresson

Chervil
Tarragon
Burnet (if available)
Parsley
Chives
Finely chopped
watercress
Unsalted butter

Put into boiling water equal parts of chervil, tarragon, burnet, parsley and chives; boil 1 minute, then rinse under cold water and press well to squeeze the water out. Weigh the herbs, chop fine, and pound in a mortar with an equal weight of unsalted butter. Season and pass through a very fine sieve. Add to the butter a handful of finely chopped watercress, which should dominate the flavour.

GOOSE LIVER BUTTER
Beurre de foie gras

150 g (6 oz) cooked
foie gras
150 g (6 oz) unsalted
butter
Dash cayenne pepper

First method

In a mortar mash together the *foie gras* and butter. Season, and put through a fine sieve. Add a dash of cayenne pepper.

100 g (4 oz) cooked
  foie gras
100 g (4 oz) unsalted
  butter
1 tablespoon port
Pinch salt
Dash cayenne pepper

Second method

Put lightly cooked *foie gras* through a fine sieve. Melt the butter and beat in the sieved *foie gras* and port.

Season with a pinch of salt and a dash of cayenne pepper.

ROQUEFORT BUTTER
Beurre de Roquefort

Mix 200 g (8 oz) of Roquefort cheese with 200 g (8 oz) of unsalted butter.

SNAIL BUTTER
Beurre d'escargots

100 g (4 oz) good
  quality unsalted
  butter, slightly
  softened
Coarse salt
Ground pepper
Dash grated nutmeg
3 or 4 cloves crushed
  garlic
1 tablespoon chopped
  shallots
1 tablespoon sweet
  almonds
2 tablespoons finely
  chopped parsley

Mix in a mortar the salt, pepper, nutmeg, garlic, shallots and almonds. With the pestle pound these ingredients into a smooth paste. Then add the parsley and the slightly softened butter. Again with the pestle, pound all the ingredients until they are smooth.

You can store the snail butter in an earthenware jar in the refrigerator.

ALMOND BUTTER
Beurre d'amandes

Drop 100 g (4 oz) of almonds into boiling water; drain almost immediately and remove the skins. Do this by holding each almond between the thumb and the forefinger and pressing slightly. Pound the almonds in a mortar, adding a few drops cold water as the almonds are blended into a paste, to avoid their becoming oily. Add about 125 g (5 oz) of unsalted butter and mix until smooth.

½ **glass dry white wine**
½ **tablespoon chopped shallots**
100 g (4 oz) unsalted butter
225 g (8 oz) beef marrow
1 teaspoon chopped parsley
Juice of ½ lemon
Pinch salt
Freshly ground pepper

BERCY BUTTER
Beurre Bercy

Boil dry white wine with shallots until reduced by half. Let the liquid cool, then add the butter, mixing with a whisk or a wooden spoon. Dice and poach beef marrow in salted water for 3 to 4 minutes, then drain. Add along with chopped parsley, lemon juice, salt and freshly ground pepper.

This butter is served warm, with grilled meat or fish.

SHRIMP BUTTER
Beurre de crevettes

Pound in the mortar equal weights of cooked shrimps and unsalted butter. Rub through a fine sieve. To obtain a fine mixture, put the butter through a sieve along with the sauce or the soup for which the butter is intended.

CRAYFISH BUTTER
Beurre d'écrevisses

Sauté crayfish in butter. Pound together an equal weight of unsalted butter and the shells and trimmings of the crayfish following the directions for shrimp butter. For 12 crayfish, add 1 teaspoon of *mirepoix* (half carrots and half onions, diced very small and slowly cooked until very soft in seasoned butter). Let the creamy parts of the crayfish stick to the shells.

[*Editor's note:* Crayfish may be replaced by a small lobster or unshelled large prawns.]

LOBSTER BUTTER
Beurre de homard ou de langouste

Follow the same proportions and directions as above.

MUSTARD BUTTER
Beurre de moutarde

Mix 100 g (4 oz) of unsalted butter with 1 rounded teaspoon of Dijon mustard.

NUT BUTTER
Beurre de noix

Follow the directions and quantities for almond butter above.

PAPRIKA BUTTER
Beurre de paprika

Mix 100 g (4 oz) of unsalted butter with a little paprika.

HORSERADISH BUTTER
Beurre de raifort

In a mortar pound 50 g (2 oz) of grated fresh horseradish. Add 100 g (4 oz) of unsalted butter. Rub the mixture through a fine sieve.

PÂTÉS, TERRINES, TIMBALES AND PIES

FILLINGS FOR PÂTÉS AND TERRINES

350 g (¾ lb) veal fillet
350 g (¾ lb) lean pork
500 g (1 lb) fresh pork fat
2 tablespoons spiced salt (page xxiv)
3 eggs
½ glass cognac

[When the filling is to be used for a game pâté or terrine, replace the veal with game meat.]

Remove the gristle and membranes carefully from the meat and remove the skin from the pork fat. Dice the meat, then chop or mince it fine. Add the salt, then the eggs, one at a time, and then the cognac.

Check the seasoning by poaching a spoonful of filling in a little boiling water.

VEAL TERRINE
Terrine de veau

1 recipe filling for pâtés and terrines (above)
350 g (¾ lb) veal fillet
350 g (¾ lb) lean pork
500 g (1 lb) fresh pork fat
300 g (10 oz) cooked lean ham
1 tablespoon cognac
Thin slices pork fat to line the terrine and cover the pâté
Salt, pepper and spice and herb mixture (page xxiv)

Carefully remove all the gristle and membranes and cut meat and pork fat into 2·5-cm (1-inch) dice or 1-cm (½-inch) thick strips. Season with salt, freshly ground pepper and spice and herb mixture and mix in a bowl with cognac; marinate for 2 hours.

Line the terrine with the thin slices of pork fat. Combine the filling with the marinated meat and fill the terrine with this mixture.

Or, after lining the terrine, fill with a layer of filling, then a layer of the lardons (veal, pork, pork fat and ham by turns), then another layer of stuffing and so on, until you have used all the ingredients.

Cover the meat with a thin slice of pork fat. Make a hole in the centre, and on either side of the hole place a small piece of thyme and a bay leaf. Cover and set the terrine in a *bain-marie* (a roasting pan half filled with hot water). Bake in 350°F (180°C, gas mark 4) oven for at least 1½ hours.

The cooking time depends on the shape of the terrine and the kind of meat used. The terrine is cooked when it is surrounded by clear juice. By that time, the meat juices will have become a good meat glaze.

Remove the terrine from the oven. Take off the cover and on top of the pâté put a piece of wood cut to fit the terrine, and on top of this set a weight – a heavy object weighing at least 225 g ($\frac{1}{2}$ lb), such as a tin of food, or a brick.

The pressure of the weight during cooling improves the texture of the pâté and prevents it crumbling when sliced.

On the other hand, if you use too heavy a weight, the fat will rise and the pâté will not be so well flavoured.

To serve, carefully wash the outside of the terrine and set it on a plate on top of a folded napkin.

Terrine du cordon bleu

Meat as for veal terrine (page 33)
Salt and pepper
Pinch thyme
Ground bay leaf
Dash nutmeg
2 tablespoons cognac
25 g (1 oz) unsalted butter
Thin slices pork fat to line the terrine
1$\frac{1}{2}$ dl ($\frac{1}{4}$ pt) meat jelly

This terrine can be made with veal, poultry or game.

The ingredients are the same as for the veal terrine, but the preparation is different.

Carefully remove the gristle and membrane from all the meat and cut into strips about 1 cm ($\frac{1}{2}$ inch) wide and 8 cm (3 inches) long.

Season the meat with salt, pepper, thyme, bay leaf and nutmeg, and stir carefully in a large bowl until well mixed. Pour over 1 tablespoon of cognac and marinate for 3 hours.

Then drain the meat very well. Reserve the marinade in a bowl.

Heat the butter in a frying pan; when bubbling, add the meat and cook over high heat, stirring with a spatula or wooden spoon until firm.

Remove the meat from the butter with a slotted spoon and place in a bowl.

Pour the reserved marinade into the frying pan; add a second tablespoon of cognac and let boil for a minute or two to deglaze the coagulated juices of the meat. Then pour this mixture over the meat in the bowl and let it cool.

Line the terrine with fat as explained in the recipe for the veal terrine (page 33). Fill with layers of meat and stuffing alternately, and pour over some of the marinade left in the bottom of the meat bowl. Cook in the same way as the veal terrine in a *bain-marie* in a 350°F (180°C, gas mark 4) oven for 1$\frac{1}{2}$ hours.

After cooking, let the terrine cool without removing the cover. When it is nearly cold, lift the cover and pour in 1$\frac{1}{2}$ dl ($\frac{1}{4}$ pt) of good meat jelly made with veal, game or poultry bones and pork rind and calf's foot which contain natural gelatine.

The jelly will penetrate the meat and set when cold. Slice like an ordinary terrine.

✄━━━━━━━━━━━━━━━━━━━━━━━━━━✄

CHICKEN TERRINE
Terrine de volaille Paul Mercier

Filling:
4 chicken livers
25 g (1 oz) unsalted butter
½ glass Madeira
225 g (½ lb) lean pork
225 g (½ lb) veal
500 g (1 lb) fresh pork fat
¼ teaspoon coarse salt
4 freshly ground peppercorns
1 teaspoon spice and herb mixture (page xxiv)
½ glass cognac
1 egg

1 tender chicken, about 1·8 kg (4 lb)
Salt, pepper, spice and herb mixture
½ raw *foie gras*, marinated in Madeira and seasoned
2 good-sized truffles, cut into quarters
6 slices fresh pork fat
½ glass cognac
1 bay leaf
Thyme

Filling.　Sear chicken livers in butter in a small frying pan; away from the heat, pour over half the Madeira and let cool. Put the mixture in a bowl. Cut the pork, the veal and the pork fat into thick cubes. Add to the liver and mix together. Mince everything or pound fine in a mortar; then rub through a fine sieve. Put the purée in a bowl and add the salt, pepper, herb and spice mixture, the rest of the Madeira, the cognac and the egg. Mix well with a wooden spoon. Test the seasoning by poaching a small piece of the stuffing in water.

Chicken.　Bone the chicken by making an incision in the skin of the back from the tail to the neck. Cut off the thighs and wings, and carefully cut the flesh from the carcass. Spread the flesh on the table and remove any remaining bones. Season with salt, pepper, spice and herb mixture. Spread on top of it a layer of filling about 1 cm (½ inch) thick. Place the *foie gras* in the middle and surround with the truffles. Cover with another layer of filling and re-form the chicken body over it.

Terrine.　Line an oval terrine with thin slices of pork fat. Cover the fat with a layer of the filling about 1 cm (½ inch) thick. Place the stuffed chicken in the terrine and pour over ½ glass of cognac. Cover with a layer of filling, a slice of pork fat, a bay leaf, a little piece of thyme. Chop up the carcass quite fine and sprinkle on top, with the bones. Cover.

Cooking.　Place the terrine in a *bain-marie* (a roasting pan two-thirds full of hot water). Bake in a 350°F (180°C, gas mark 4) oven for 2½ hours. When the cooking is done, remove from the oven, uncover, and take out the pieces of carcass, the thyme and the bay. Place a piece of wood on the meat and on the wood an object weighing about 225 g (½ lb). During the cooling, this weight will produce a smoooth pâté. If it is too heavy, it will squeeze out the fat and spoil the texture of the terrine.

When cold, remove the weight and the wood. Cover the meat with a layer of lard about 1 cm (½ inch) thick and refrigerate. This terrine can be kept for 2–3 months in the refrigerator or a cool place.

COLD CHICKEN MOUSSE
Mousse de volaille froide en terrine

Carefully roast a fine 1·3 kg (2½ lb) chicken, following the directions in the chapter on chicken. Cool, but do not put in the refrigerator.

Then remove the skin and take the flesh off the breastbone and the thighs, which should give you about 350 g (12 oz) of meat.

Pound the chicken flesh in the mortar and rub this purée through a fine sieve; follow the directions for the cold ham mousse (page 302).

EEL PÂTÉ
Pâté d'anguilles

1·5 kg (3 lb) eels
Salt, pepper and
　nutmeg
Oil
1 glass white wine
2 tablespoons cognac
100 g (4 oz) unsalted
　butter
3 shallots, chopped
1 tablespoon chopped
　parsley
4 hard-boiled eggs,
　sliced
Semi-flaky dough
　(page 533) about 6
　mm (¼ inch) thick
　and the size of the
　baking dish
1 egg, beaten
1½ dl (¼ pt) demi-glace
　sauce made with
　fish essence (see
　page 108)
1 tablespoon reduced
　fish fumet

Skin, wash and gut the eels. Make an incision along both sides of the bone, and cut them in half lengthwise. Remove the bone. Cut the fillets crosswise into pieces about 8 cm (3 inches) long. Plunge them into boiling salted water. When the water comes back to the boil, remove the eel pieces immediately, rinse them in cold water and drain. Dry them, and season with 1 tablespoon of salt, ¼ teaspoon of pepper and a dash of nutmeg; add a tablespoon or so of oil, ½ glass of dry white wine and the cognac. Marinate the eel pieces for 2 hours. Drain the eel, reserving the marinade.

Melt 50 g (2 oz) of butter in a large sauté pan and cook the shallots briefly; add the eel and cook for 10 minutes; sprinkle with chopped parsley.

In a deep round ovenproof earthenware or porcelain dish put layers of the sliced eel, alternating with layers of sliced, hard-boiled eggs seasoned with salt, pepper and nutmeg.

Pour over the remaining ½ glass of white wine and the reserved marinade to cover the eel and eggs. Add more wine if needed. Cut the remaining butter in small pieces and spread on top. Cover the whole with the dough rolled to fit the dish.

Brush the dough with beaten egg. With the point of a knife make a design – flowers or leaves – on the dough, and a hole in the centre of the dough to let the steam escape. Bake at 350°F (180°C, gas mark 4) for 1½ hours.

About 5 minutes before the baking has been completed, finish the demi-glace sauce with a little butter and the fish fumet. When ready to serve, pour the demi-glace sauce into the pâté through the centre hole.

***

1 plump duckling
100 g (¼ lb) firm white
**   mushrooms**
1 kg (2 lb) filling
**   (recipe below)**
1 recipe pastry dough
**   (page 536)**
1½ dl (¼ pt) Madeira
**   sauce (page 113)**
Truffles (optional)
Thyme and bay leaf
1 egg, beaten

HOT OR COLD DUCKLING PÂTÉ
Pâté chaud ou froid de caneton Gaston Richard

Roast the duckling in a 425°F (220°C, gas mark 7) oven for 15 minutes; it should be very rare. Remove the two wings from the breast, remove the breast skin and slice the meat thinly. Cut the mushrooms into thin slices and rapidly cook in the same pan used to roast the duckling; they will absorb the seasoning and cooking juices.

Next, butter a straight-sided, 1-litre (2-pt) charlotte mould and line it with the pastry dough. Cover the dough with a layer of stuffing about 1 cm (½ inch) thick.

For the bottom layer make a bed of sliced duckling and follow with a layer of mushrooms. Slices of raw truffles can also be added. Spread another layer of stuffing, and continue until you have used all the ingredients, finishing with a layer of stuffing.

On the last layer, sprinkle pinches of powdered thyme and bay leaf. Cover the pâté with a sheet of pastry dough, sealing the edges by moistening with water. Brush the pastry with beaten egg, and make some light incisions; then make a hole in the centre to allow the steam to escape.

Bake in a 325°F (170°C, gas mark 3) oven for 1 hour.

To serve, unmould the pâté onto a round plate. Carefully cut away the bottom crust of the pâté 1 cm (½ inch) from the edge to preserve the shape and remove carefully. Divide this pastry into wedges, one per guest, and set them around the pâté.

Pour 1 tablespoon of Madeira sauce over the uncovered stuffing and serve the rest of the sauce in a sauceboat.

Just before serving, you can decorate the top of the pâté if you like. Place a large mushroom cap, cut in the shape of a rose, or fluted, and cooked in butter in the centre. Around this arrange slices of truffle and cover with Madeira sauce.

The pâté can be served cold without the sauce.

225 g (8 oz) fresh
 pork fat
125 g (5 oz) unsalted
 butter
225 g (8 oz) veal fillet
225 g (8 oz) calf's or
 pig's liver
4 shallots
50 g (2 oz)
 mushrooms
125 g (5 oz) raw
 truffles
Bay leaf, crushed
Pinch thyme
2 teaspoons salt
Large pinch freshly
 ground pepper
6 tablespoons demi-
 glace sauce (page
 108)
Madeira to moisten
6 egg yolks

Filling. Remove the rind from the pork fat. Dice fat, and brown in 50 g (2 oz) of butter in a sauté pan.

Drain the pork fat with a slotted spoon and reserve on a plate. In the same butter, brown the veal, cut into large dice. Drain and add to the pork. In the same pan rapidly sear the pork or veal liver, cut into large dice and add the duckling liver. Add the chopped shallots, mushrooms, truffles, bay leaf, thyme, salt and pepper. Return the pork fat and veal to the pan. Mix and cook everything for 2 minutes. Remove from heat, and baste with the Madeira. Then pour the mixture into a mortar, add the thigh meat of the duckling, cut in cubes, and reduce the mixture to a fine paste by pounding vigorously. Finish the pounding by adding the remaining butter and the egg yolks, one at a time.

Rub the mixture through a fine sieve. Test the seasoning by tasting a small piece of stuffing poached in salted water. Pour into a terrine and smooth with a wooden spoon.

At this point, the stuffing is ready to use.

In the days of the great chef and *pâtissier* Antonin Carême the timbale was a complicated dish made of partially cooked or uncooked ingredients, combined in a charlotte mould, poached and turned out for serving.

The classic *Timbale à la milanaise* is a typical example of the timbale which may be made in individual portions or in a large mould for 6–12 people.

MACARONI TIMBALE
Timbale à la milanaise
For 6 people

Fine unsweetened pastry dough (page 536)
225 g (8 oz) macaroni or spaghetti
$\frac{3}{4}$ tablespoon salt
125 g (5 oz) grated cheese, half Gruyère, half Parmesan
100 g (4 oz) unsalted butter
5 tablespoons thick tomato purée
100 g (4 oz) cooked lean ham
Freshly ground white pepper
***Financière* sauce**
1 egg, beaten

Roll fine unsweetened pastry dough 3 mm ($\frac{1}{8}$ inch) thick and line a 2-litre (4-pt) charlotte mould, following the method on page 37. Prick the dough with a fork. Reserve remaining dough.

Cook 225 g (8 oz) of good quality macaroni or spaghetti in the following way: plunge the pasta whole in a large pot of boiling water with 10 g ($\frac{1}{4}$ oz) of salt for each litre (quart). Bring back to boiling point, stirring the pasta with a wooden spoon to prevent the pieces from sticking together. Reduce the heat and simmer steadily, covered, for about 20–25 minutes. Make sure that the pasta remains firm.

Drain thoroughly and put back into the saucepan; heat for a few minutes to dry the pasta. Sprinkle with grated cheese, half Gruyère and half Parmesan if possible. On top scatter 100 g (4 oz) of butter cut into small pieces. Add the tomato purée and the ham, cut into thin julienne.

Sprinkle 3 or 4 grinds of white pepper on top. Take the saucepan off the heat and shake it several times until the cheese melts. This prevents the pasta breaking.

While the pasta is cooking, prepare a garnish of *financière* sauce, using a thick demi-glace sauce well flavoured with tomato (page 108).

There are two ways to finish the timbale:

1. In the charlotte mould lined with pastry make alternate layers of macaroni and *financière* sauce. When the mould is nearly full, roll out an additional pastry round using the reserved dough. Cover the mould with the round of pastry and seal carefully by moistening the edge of the crust. Decorate the

crust and brush with beaten egg; bake in 325°F (170°C, gas mark 3) oven for about 40 minutes.

Unmould carefully and serve.

2. Cover the pastry in the charlotte mould with paper or foil and fill with fruit stones or dried beans; bake in a 425°F (220°C, gas mark 7) oven until golden brown.

Remove the pastry from the oven, empty the timbale and turn out. Brush inside and out with beaten egg. Set the shell in the oven again for a few seconds to dry it and to give it a beautiful golden colour.

In the prepared crust make alternate layers of the macaroni and *financière* sauce, which should have been kept warm meanwhile.

Using reserved dough, make a dome-shaped lid of the same diameter as the timbale, shaping it round a wad of paper. Decorate the lid with leaves made of pastry dough. Bake at 425°F (220°C, gas mark 7) until golden brown and place on top of the filled crust.

Serve on a folded napkin.

Note: The second method is more convenient for household cookery.

❦━━━━━━━━━━━━━━━━━━━━━━━❦

SWEETBREAD PIE
Tourte des gastronomes
For 6 people

Semi-flaky pastry (page 533)
3 prepared calf's sweetbreads (page 325)
Madeira
100 g (¼ lb) white mushrooms, thinly sliced
Salt
Pepper
50 g (2 oz) unsalted butter, melted
1 egg, beaten

Prepare two rounds of semi-flaky pastry, about 35·5 cm (14 inches) in diameter and 6 mm (¼ inch) thick. Use one of the rounds to line a tart tin and prick it with the point of a knife in seven or eight places.

Prepare the sweetbreads according to the recipe on p. 328 for sweetbreads braised *à blanc*. Reserve the cooking liquid. Cut the sweetbreads in half. Arrange them on the pastry round, keeping them about an inch in from the edge. Sauté the mushrooms lightly in 25 g (1 oz) of butter and season with salt and pepper. Scatter over the sweetbreads and moisten with 25 g (1 oz) of melted butter.

Moisten the edges of the pastry base and cover with the second round. Press round with your thumb and seal by rolling the lower edge over the upper. Brush the top with beaten egg and decorate by making incisions in the dough with a knife or by making designs cut out of another piece of dough. Make a hole in the centre with the point of the knife to allow the steam to escape.

Bake for 25–30 minutes in a 425°F (220°C, gas mark 7) oven.

Serve the dish immediately. With it serve a sauce made with the cooking liquid from the sweetbreads, flavoured with a little Madeira. Put about ½ tablespoon of sauce on each plate beside each helping of pie.

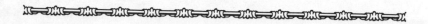

EGGS

Eggs, plain or garnished, make a good light entrée. You should generally allow two eggs per person.

For flavour – and safety – eggs should always be eaten very fresh. You can judge freshness by weight or by holding the egg up to a bright light like a candle. A standard-sized, day-old egg weighs about 60 g (2 oz). At this stage the air space at the round end of the shell is imperceptible, but it gradually increases in size each day. A very fresh egg will make no noise if you shake it next to your ear, but if it is not so fresh you will hear a faint muffled sound. A fresh egg will sink to the bottom if placed in water; a ten-day-old egg will float.

Poaching is the fundamental method on which the methods used for hard and soft-boiled eggs, *oeufs mollets*, shirred eggs, fried eggs and eggs cooked in a mould or cocotte are based. The methods for omelets and scrambled eggs are quite different.

SHIRRED EGGS
Oeufs sur le plat

Although apparently simple, there is a knack to this method of cooking eggs. The eggs are perfectly cooked when the white takes on a milky look and the soft-cooked yolk is covered with a light, mirror-like film. Take care that the eggs do not stick to the bottom of the dish.

Method. For 2 eggs, use about 15 g ($\frac{1}{2}$ oz) of unsalted butter. Put half the butter into a shallow, fire proof dish (for 1 serving) and heat. When the butter begins to bubble, break the eggs one at a time onto a plate so that you can check their freshness. Slide the 2 eggs into the butter. Pour the rest of the melted butter on top. Season the egg whites with a pinch of fine salt. Bake in a 350°F (180°C, gas mark 4) oven for about 4–5 minutes.

Wait for the egg whites to set and the yolks to film over for the perfect result described above.

Instead of using the oven, you can cook the eggs on top of the stove, continually basting the tops, while they are cooking with butter spooned up from the side of the dish.

Presentation.   If the shirred eggs are to be served with a garnish, the garnish should be put in the bottom of the dish before cooking the eggs or added on top of the eggs afterwards.

EGGS WITH BACON
Oeufs au bacon

Take two rashers of bacon and remove the rind. Cook them in boiling water for 3 minutes, drain and brown lightly in a shallow pan with a small knob of unsalted butter. Break 2 eggs on top. and cook them according to the method above.

SHIRRED EGGS WITH HAM
Oeufs sur le plat au jambon

Put a very thin slice of raw ham in $\frac{1}{2}$ l (1 pt) of cold water. Heat slowly to boiling point. Drain, then heat in an egg dish with a small knob of unsalted butter; turn once and, 2 seconds later, break in 2 eggs. Cook by the method above.

SHIRRED EGGS WITH SPINACH
Oeufs sur le plat à la florentine
For 6 people

350 g ($\frac{3}{4}$ lb) spinach
75 g (3 oz) unsalted
 butter
Salt
Pepper
Pinch of grated
 nutmeg
75 g (3 oz) lean
 cooked ham
6 eggs

Remove the stems from the spinach and cook in boiling, salted water. Drain, rinse, squeeze firmly to get rid of the water. Rub spinach through a sieve. Put this purée in a sauté pan with 25 g (1 oz) of very hot butter. Season with salt, pepper and a pinch of grated nutmeg. Heat rapidly; then mix in away from the flame 25 g (1 oz) of butter and 50 g (2 oz) of lean cooked ham, diced very small.

   Butter 6 individual baking dishes. In the bottom of each put a thin slice of ham and a layer of hot spinach purée. Then break

1 egg into each dish; baste each egg with a few drops of melted butter, add a pinch of salt and cook in the oven by the method above.

SHIRRED EGGS WITH TOMATOES
Oeufs sur le plat aux tomates

First method

Peel and seed tomatoes (1 per egg) and simmer in butter. Season with salt and a pinch of sugar. Spread them on the bottom of a buttered dish, then break the eggs on top and cook them as described above.

Second method

Cook eggs by the method above and garnish them after cooking with a purée of chopped tomato made in the same way as the spinach purée in the previous recipe.

SHIRRED EGGS WITH BLACK BUTTER
Oeufs sur le plat au beurre noir

Cook the eggs by the basic method above, basting with a drop of vinegar and unsalted butter which have been cooked together until the butter turns light brown.

Butter cooked this way has a delicious taste but is rather indigestible. Do not use too much of it.

POACHED EGGS
Oeufs pochés

Poached eggs must be absolutely fresh. In poaching, the white sets immediately on contact with boiling water, enveloping the yolk and forming an evenly shaped oblong. If the eggs are not very fresh, the white spreads as it sets and the yolk remains uncovered, giving a flat, irregular shape.

Method.   Use a shallow saucepan or sauté pan. Fill it two-thirds full with water, adding 1 tablespoon of vinegar for each quart. Bring the water to the boil. Break the egg, smell for freshness and drop it into the liquid exactly where the water is bubbling, so that the yolk remains intact. Continue this operation, breaking up to 8 eggs, one at a time.

Keep the sauté pan on the edge of the flame so that the water simmers very gently.

The poaching takes $3\frac{1}{2}$ minutes.

Remove the eggs carefully, one by one, with a slotted spoon. Check if they are done by pressing lightly with your finger – they should be very soft. Drain them and plunge them one at a time into a bowl of cold water to stop the cooking. Remove the loose ends of egg white and return eggs to water – tepid and slightly salted if they are to be served warm, cold if they are to be served cold.

Poached eggs are very versatile and can be served in a great variety of ways.

They can be served on rice prepared in various ways, covered with a sauce, for example curry or tomato.

They can be served on top of a purée of mushrooms, poultry, asparagus, etc., or on top of chopped fish, shellfish, meat, poultry or game, surrounded by duchesse potatoes (page 497), and covered with a suprème, Mornay, béchamel, cream or hollandaise sauce (see Index).

They are delicious with a good consommé.

Cold poached eggs can be served in aspic flavoured with port or Madeira. They can also be served on toast or slices of bread spread with a compound butter (see pages 26–30).

They can be served cold decorated with tarragon leaves (blanched in boiling water for a minute) or ham, tongue, truffles or sweet peppers cut into short, narrow strips, placed over the eggs and covered with a few spoonfuls of aspic.

You also can serve poached eggs with simple or mixed salads, with asparagus tips, Russian salad, etc. In these cases, the eggs are served with a light mayonnaise, perhaps with some cream added.

Finally, they can be served with vegetables, such as sorrel purée (page 484) or spinach with butter, cream or velouté sauce (page 109).

In general, all garnishes used for poached eggs can be used for *oeufs mollets* and vice versa.

Bouchées (page 541)
Sliced bone marrow
Poached eggs

Bordelaise sauce:
2 lumps sugar
3 glasses red
   Bordeaux wine
1 tablespoon chopped
   shallots
Bouquet garni
Pinch salt
Pinch pepper
15 g ($\frac{1}{2}$ oz) *beurre
   manié* (2 teaspoons
   unsalted butter and
   1 teaspoon flour)
Half clove garlic
1 teaspoon chopped
   parsley
25 g (1 oz) unsalted
   butter
Veal or beef gravy
   (optional)

POACHED EGGS WITH BORDELAISE SAUCE
Oeufs pochés à la bordelaise

First prepare small *bouchées* – little flaky puff-pastry patties (page 541), baked unfilled. Allow 2 per person and the same number of slices of bone marrow about 3 mm ($\frac{1}{8}$ inch) thick.

Next poach eggs following the basic method above and drain them carefully.

Into each hot *bouchée* put the following:

$\frac{1}{2}$ tablespoon of Bordelaise sauce (recipe below)
1 hot poached egg
1 slice of bone marrow (first poach marrow by placing it in a bowl of boiling salted water for 3–5 minutes; then drain). Cover the marrow with 1 tablespoon sauce.

Bordelaise Sauce

Dissolve the sugar in a pan and boil until it turns to a light brown caramel; add the wine, the shallots, the bouquet garni a big pinch of salt and a pinch of freshly ground pepper. Cook until the liquid has reduced by one-third. With a fork blend the *beurre manié* in a bowl. Add in little pieces to the boiling wine; it will thicken almost immediately. Beat lightly with a whisk, remove from the flame, and take out the bouquet garni. Finish the sauce with half a garlic clove chopped finely and the parsley; heat again to boiling point and then strain the sauce through a very fine sieve or through cheesecloth. Then add about 25 g (1 oz) of butter, and correct the seasoning.

The flavour of the sauce is improved by a little veal or beef gravy, or a little meat glaze. If these are salted, do not salt before reducing the sauce.

Serve this rich, smooth sauce with the eggs.

POACHED EGGS WITH SPINACH
Oeufs pochés à la florentine

500 g (1 lb) spinach
Salt
50 g (2 oz) unsalted butter
Pepper
Grated nutmeg
Pinch sugar (optional)
8 poached eggs
Mornay sauce (page 120)
Fresh breadcrumbs
Grated Gruyère or Parmesan cheese

Remove the stems from the spinach, wash well and cook in boiling water, salted with $\frac{3}{4}$ tablespoon of salt per quart. It must cook rapidly so that the spinach remains green. Drain the spinach and rinse under cold water; drain again, and press firmly to remove the water.

Heat 25 g (1 oz) of butter in a sauté pan. Add the spinach, season with salt and pepper and a dash of grated nutmeg – plus a pinch of sugar if the spinach is at the end of its season and rather bitter. Stir in 25 g (1 oz) of butter off the flame.

Spread the spinach in a shallow ovenproof porcelain dish; place on top 8 hot poached eggs, well-drained, and spread lightly with Mornay sauce. On each egg sprinkle a mixture of equal amounts fresh breadcrumbs and grated Gruyère or Parmesan cheese; baste with a few drops of melted butter, and brown in a 425°F (220°C, gas mark 7) oven.

The eggs can also be placed in individual dishes, cocottes or ramekins, allowing 2 eggs per person.

POACHED EGGS WITH ARTICHOKES
Oeufs pochés Henri IV

8 artichokes
Court-bouillon (page 106)
Unsalted butter
Salt
Pepper
8 poached eggs
Béarnaise sauce (page 127)
Stewed tomato
3 tablespoons veal gravy
Mushroom or tomato purée (optional)

Remove the outer leaves from the artichokes, dip them in boiling water, remove the chokes, and then cook the hearts in a court-bouillon.

Heat 25 g (1 oz) of butter in a sauté pan. Add the artichoke hearts and season with salt and pepper. Cook slowly, covered, for 15 minutes, turning them once. Put a small pat of butter in each heart.

Then place the hearts on a very hot platter. On top of each one put a hot poached egg, well drained. Spread 1 tablespoon of béarnaise sauce on each egg and on top of the sauce a spoonful of tomato stewed in butter.

In the pan in which the artichoke hearts were cooked bring the lightly salted veal gravy to the boil; reduce by half and away from the flame incorporate 15 g ($\frac{1}{2}$ oz) of butter. Pour this gravy round the artichokes.

To make this dish richer, the artichoke hearts can be garnished with a mushroom purée or a thick, buttery tomato purée to which a pinch of chopped tarragon has been added.

POACHED EGGS WITH SORREL
Oeufs pochés à l'oseille

Serve poached eggs on a purée of sorrel; baste each one with $\frac{1}{2}$ tablespoon of good veal gravy.

EGGS IN A MOULD
Oeufs moulés

Generously butter small moulds (such as castle pudding moulds), allowing 2 per person. Carefully break a very fresh egg into each, adding a pinch of salt and a tiny pinch of white pepper. Place the moulds in a pan big enough to hold them easily. Fill the pan with boiling water two-thirds of the way up the moulds. Cover and poach for about 10 minutes.

When using a *bain-marie* in this way the water must not boil; add 2–3 tablespoons of cold water to the pan whenever you notice that the water is about to boil.

When the eggs are done the white will have set and should feel about as firm as a soft-boiled egg when you press it.

EGGS IN A MOULD WITH *FOIE GRAS* AND OYSTERS
Oeufs moulés Antonin Carême

Cook eggs in moulds by the method above; then place each one on a medallion of *foie gras* that has been quickly seared in butter. Top each egg with a poached oyster, trimmed neatly, and covered with a little cream sauce.

BOILED EGGS
Oeufs à la coque

To be really perfect, boiled eggs must be extremely fresh – ideally laid the same day.

Make sure that the shells have no cracks. Carefully put the eggs into a strainer and plunge it into boiling water so that the eggs are totally submerged.

From the instant the water starts boiling again count three minutes; then drain. Immediately put the eggs into a bowl of very hot water, and serve them at once.

A perfect boiled egg should have a milky white. If it is not cooked enough, the inside is cold and the white is watery; if overcooked, the white is leathery and the yolk is partly hard.

EGGS BAKED IN RAMEKINS
Oeufs en cocotte

This method derives from the boiled egg. The results are excellent. Lightly butter the insides of ovenproof ramekins and place them in a pan with hot water two-thirds of the way up their sides. In each one put a few grains of salt; then break a very fresh egg into each. Bake 8 minutes at 375°F (190°C, gas mark 5).

Remove the ramekins from the pan, wipe them well, sprinkle a dash of salt on each and set on a napkin to serve.

BAKED EGGS WITH CREAM
Oeufs en cocotte à la crème

Place 6 cocottes in a pan and pour boiling water about two-thirds of the way up their sides. Boil 6 tablespoons of cream with a small pinch of salt, and pour 1 tablespoon of cream into each cocotte. Break an egg into each one, and add 2 small knobs of un-salted butter.

Cover and bake 8–10 minutes at 375°F (190°C, gas mark 5).

Remove the pan from the oven, and take the ramekins out of the hot water; wipe them, and place each one on a plate on top of a folded napkin.

BAKED EGGS WITH TOMATOES
Oeufs en cocotte aux tomates

Remove the stems and the core of 2 ripe tomatoes. Plunge for 10 seconds into boiling water and peel. Cut in half and press out the juice and seeds.

Dice the tomatoes, and cook in a sauté pan with 15 g ($\frac{1}{2}$ oz) of butter; season with salt and pepper. Cook until the tomatoes have the consistency of jam.

Butter 6 ramekins and cover the bottoms with the tomato purée. Break an egg into each one and cook in a *bain-marie* in the oven as in the basic recipe above. Remove the eggs from the oven, and put $\frac{1}{2}$ teaspoon of tomato purée and a little chopped parsley on top of each one.

You can add 1 tablespoon of finely chopped onion to the tomatoes. In that case, cook the onion in butter without browning in the pan before cooking the tomatoes.

BAKED EGGS WITH MUSHROOMS
Oeufs en cocotte aux champignons

Prepare a mushroom purée with 100 g (4 oz) of clean firm white mushrooms. Wash and slice thinly. Put 25 g (1 oz) of unsalted butter in a sauté pan. When it is bubbling, add mushrooms and sauté for 3 minutes, then mash through a fine sieve into a bowl. Add 1 tablespoon of cream. Season with a dash of salt.

Butter 6 cocottes, and pour this purée into them; break an egg in each. Cook in the oven in a *bain-marie*, as in the basic recipe above. When you remove them from the oven, pour 1 teaspoon of cream over each egg.

HARD-BOILED EGGS
Oeufs durs

Boil water in a suitable-sized pan. Put the eggs into a strainer and lower into the boiling water. The instant the water starts boiling again, count 9 minutes for eggs of average size, and 10 minutes for large ones.

Remove the strainer of eggs and plunge immediately into cold water; this will make peeling easier.

Do not cook longer than indicated, or the white will become tough and the yolk very dry.

HARD-BOILED EGGS WITH ONIONS
Oeufs durs aux oignons dits à la tripe

3 medium-sized
  onions
25 g (1 oz) unsalted
  butter
25 g (1 oz) flour
Pinch salt
Pinch freshly ground
  white pepper
Dash grated nutmeg
½ l (1 pt) boiling milk
25 g (1 oz) unsalted
  butter or 1
  tablespoon cream
6 hard-boiled eggs

Cut the onions into julienne; if they are not young onions, soak them in boiling water for 5 minutes, drain and dry. Put the onions in a small pan in which 25 g (1 oz) of butter has been melted; half-cook, covered, very slowly without browning.

Then add 25 g (1 oz) of flour, a pinch of salt, a pinch of freshly ground white pepper, a dash of grated nutmeg. Cook this white *roux* slowly for 10 minutes; remove from the heat and let cool. Then with a whisk, mix in ½ l (1 pt) of boiling milk, a little at a time. Bring the mixture to the boil, stirring to avoid lumps. Cook over low heat for 2 minutes. Away from the heat add 25 g (1 oz) of butter or 1 tablespoon of cream.

At the same time, hard-boil 6 eggs, and remove the shells. Just before serving, add the hot eggs, cut into quarters or thick slices, to the sauce.

The sauce may be rubbed through a fine sieve first, mashing the onions to a purée in order to incorporate them in the sauce, which them becomes a kind of thin onion purée.

Note: The flour, butter and milk may be replaced by a béchamel sauce (page 110).

HARD-BOILED EGGS WITH CREAM OF SORREL
Oeufs durs à la crème d'oseille

500 g (1 lb) sorrel
50 g (2 oz) unsalted
  butter
15 g (½ oz) flour
4 dl (¾ pt) milk
Salt
Pepper
50 g (2 oz) unsalted
  butter or 2
  tablespoons cream
6 hard-boiled eggs

Cut 500 g (1 lb) of young sorrel with the stems carefully removed into thin strips.

Put the sorrel in a pan with 50 g (2 oz) of unsalted butter; heat slowly and cook until the juices have completely evaporated. Add 15 g (½ oz) of flour; cook over a low flame 5 minutes, and let cool. Stirring with a wooden spoon all the while, gradually add 4 dl (¾ pt) of boiling milk seasoned with salt and pepper. Bring to the boil, and then simmer for 15 minutes.

Strain the sauce through a very fine sieve, rubbing with a wooden spoon. Bring the sauce back to boiling point and test the seasoning. As soon as it comes to the boil, off the flame add 50 g (2 oz) of unsalted butter or 2 tablespoons of cream. Peel 6 hot hard-boiled eggs, put in a deep dish and cover with the sauce.

HARD-BOILED EGGS WITH VEGETABLE PURÉES
Oeufs durs sur purées divers

Hard-boiled eggs, like poached eggs, can be served with most vegetable purées. Purées of asparagus, watercress, chicory, celery, mushrooms, carrots, lettuce, spinach and chestnuts would be the most suitable.

SOFT-BOILED EGGS
Oeufs mollets

Soft-boiled eggs are prepared in the same way as hard-boiled ones. Place them in a strainer with large holes and plunge into boiling water. The instant the water starts boiling again, count 6 minutes for eggs of average size. Remove the strainer and plunge it immediately into cold water. Shell the eggs carefully, and keep them in hot salted water if they are to be served hot.

Soft-boiled eggs can be served in the same way as poached or hard-boiled eggs (though not stuffed of course) and vice versa.

Here are some recipes besides those given for poached and hard-boiled eggs.

SOFT-BOILED EGGS WITH ONIONS
Oeufs mollets soubise

4 large onions
50 g (2 oz) unsalted butter
8 tablespoons thickened béchamel sauce (see page 110)
2 tablespoons cream or 50 g (2 oz) butter
8 large mushroom caps
8 soft-boiled eggs, kept warm in salted water

Dice the onions; cook them in boiling water for 5 minutes, then drain. Put the onions in a small saucepan with 25 g (1 oz) of butter and a pinch of salt, and cook on a low flame, covered. The onions must remain white. After cooking, rub the onions through a very fine strainer into a sauté pan. Add the reduced béchamel sauce; bring to the boil and remove from the heat immediately. Add cream or butter; taste. Grill the mushrooms or cook gently in 25 g (1 oz) of butter with a few drops of lemon juice. Afterwards the butter may be carefully poured into the onion purée.

To serve place the mushroom caps upside down on a hot round plate. On top of each one, place a soft-boiled egg and cover with the rich, smooth purée of onion and cream.

SOFT-BOILED EGGS WITH BÉARNAISE SAUCE
Oeufs mollets béarnaise

25 g (1 oz) unsalted butter
8 artichoke hearts cooked in a white court-bouillon (see page 106)
8 soft-boiled eggs
4 dl (¾ pt) béarnaise sauce (page 127)

Melt butter in a sauté pan. Add the artichoke hearts and season with a pinch of salt and one grind of the pepper mill. Cook for 15 minutes on a low flame, turning once; place on a hot serving platter. Pour the butter used to cook the artichoke hearts over them and place a soft-boiled egg on top of each one; cover with the béarnaise sauce. Serve the remaining sauce in a sauceboat.

PAN-COOKED EGGS
Oeufs poêlés

Pan-cooked eggs are a variant of shirred eggs.

For 2 eggs, heat 25 g (1 oz) of unsalted butter in a frying pan until it reaches a light brown or hazelnut colour. Browning the butter first gives the eggs a particularly delicious flavour.

Continue by following the recipe for shirred eggs (see page 45).

Pan-cooked eggs may be served with ham, bacon or vegetables.

PAN-COOKED EGGS WITH TOMATOES
Oeufs poêlés aux tomates

Peel a large, ripe tomato; cut it in half, and squeeze out the seeds and juice. In a frying pan heat 1 tablespoon of olive oil until it smokes. Place the tomato, cut side down in the pan, season with salt and pepper and cook over a high flame. Turn the tomato halves over carefully with a spatula, and break an egg into each. Season with a dash of salt on the egg whites. Cook rapidly in a 350°F (180°C, gas mark 4) oven until the tops of the eggs have filmed over and slide them on to a hot plate. Cook 15 g ($\frac{1}{2}$ oz) of butter in a small pan until it becomes dark brown (this is *beurre noir*, or black butter). Baste the eggs with this hot butter.

FRIED EGGS
Oeufs frits

Break a fresh egg into a bowl. Heat about 1$\frac{1}{2}$ dl ($\frac{1}{4}$ pt) of oil in a frying pan. When it starts to smoke, tilt the pan slightly so that the oil runs to one side. Slide the egg into the oil. The white will set immediately, forming large bubbles. Quickly fold the white round the yolk, with a spoon dipped in oil, and roll the egg over so that the white completely surrounds the yolk, which should remain soft. Cook the egg for 1 minute until golden. Drain on a cloth or kitchen paper and season with a pinch of salt.

Cook the egg just before serving.

Fried eggs can be served on slices of raw ham sautéed in a little butter or rashers of grilled or sautéed bacon. They can be accompanied by a garnish of mushrooms sautéed in butter with *fines herbes*, or leaf spinach cooked in butter.

They may also be served with grilled kidneys, chipolata sausages or grilled or sautéed lamb chops. They form part of the classic garnish for chicken Marengo and calf's head *à la tortue*. Tomato, Périgueux, Italian or other sauces are often served with the eggs.

FRIED EGGS WITH MACARONI
Oeufs frits à la milanaise

175 g (6 oz) spaghetti
  or macaroni
Salt
Pepper
2 tablespoons tomato
  sauce (page 111) or
  2 tomatoes
25 g (1 oz) grated
  Parmesan or
  Gruyère cheese
50 g (2 oz) unsalted
  butter
6 fried eggs
6 grilled tomato
  halves

Boil 1 litre (1 quart) of water with 1 teaspoon of salt; add 175 g (6 oz) of spaghetti or macaroni, and cook covered without boiling for 20 minutes. Drain thoroughly. Pour the pasta into a bowl, season with salt and pepper. Add 2 tablespoons of tomato sauce or 2 tomatoes, peeled, with the juice and seeds squeezed out, seasoned with salt and pepper, and cooked in a little butter in a small frying pan. Add grated Parmesan or Gruyère cheese and 50 g (2 oz) of butter.

Mix well without breaking the pasta.

Pour into a well-buttered timbale mould and shake down well. Place the mould in a *bain-marie* half filled with hot water and bake at 350°F (180°C, gas mark 4) for 18–20 minutes. Let stand 5 minutes, then unmould on a hot round plate. Around the timbale, arrange 6 fried eggs and 6 grilled tomato halves alternately. Serve with tomato sauce.

FRIED EGGS WITH HAM AND TOMATOES
Oeufs frits à l'Américaine

Serve the fried eggs on a slice of cooked ham, surrounded by grilled tomatoes.

Omelettes

Omelettes may be folded or flat according to taste and depending on the garnish. Successful omelette-making is a skill which only comes with experience – practice is more important than advice.

If the omelette has a filling or garnish, use 3 eggs for 2 people. Otherwise allow 2 eggs per person.

If you are using more than 8 eggs it is advisable to make several omelettes.

Beat the eggs lightly with a fork, to mix the whites and yolks, but so that the white is still viscous. Excessive beating makes the eggs too liquid. They will not rise when cooked in hot butter and the result is a heavy omelette with a poor flavour.

Method. Break the eggs, add salt and beat lightly at the last minute to prevent them turning brown. Melt the butter (15 g ($\frac{1}{2}$ oz) for every two eggs) in an omelette pan over high heat. When it sizzles and starts to turn a very light brown colour pour in the eggs.

On contact with the hot butter the eggs will set first round the edge of the pan. With a fork quickly draw the edges to the centre so that the omelette cooks evenly. When it reaches the desired consistency (well-cooked but still creamy in the centre) leave the pan on the heat for a second longer. Then, with your left hand, tilt the pan towards the burner. Holding the fork in your right hand fold the omelette towards the far lip. With your right hand give your left hand a light tap to shake the pan. This loosens the omelette so that it folds over correctly. Quickly put a little piece of butter into the pan to brown the omelette very lightly. Then slide it out on to a long hot serving dish. If necessary push it into shape and rub the top with a little piece of butter on the point of a knife to make it shiny.

This delicious, golden, neatly folded omelette should be served immediately.

Omelettes usually have a filling or garnish or some form of seasoning.

GARNISHED AND FILLED OMELETTES
Omelettes garnies et fourrées

The garnish or filling for omelettes must be prepared beforehand.
The recipes for omelettes number hundreds; here are some of the
most common and the easiest for a home cook. The quantities
are for a 6-egg omelette.

MUSHROOM OMELETTE
Omelette aux champignons

Put 50 g (2 oz) of mushroom caps, washed rapidly and sliced thin,
in an omelette pan; sauté in 25 g (1 oz) of unsalted butter until
lightly browned. Pour in the eggs and cook as directed above.

HAM OMELETTE
Omelette au jambon

Mix 50 g (2 oz) of diced cooked lean ham with the beaten eggs.
Cook as directed above.

CHEESE OMELETTE
Omelette au fromage

Mix 50 g (2 oz) of grated Gruyère cheese with the beaten eggs.
Cook as directed above.

BACON OMELETTE
Omelette au lard

Cut 50 g (2 oz) of lean bacon, with the rind removed, into small cubes. Blanch for 6 minutes, drain and wipe dry with a cloth. Brown in a pan with 25 g (1 oz) of unsalted butter.

Pour in the beaten eggs and cook as directed above.

SORREL OMELETTE
Omelette à l'oseille

A dozen leaves of young sorrel, well washed, dried and cut in thick strips, cooked gently in 15 g ($\frac{1}{2}$ oz) of unsalted butter in an omelette pan. Add $\frac{1}{2}$ teaspoon of chopped chervil leaves to the beaten eggs and pour into the pan with the sorrel. Cook as directed above.

HERB OMELETTE
Omelette aux fines herbes

Add to the beaten eggs 1 teaspoon of chopped fresh parsley and 1 teaspoon of chopped chives. Cook as directed above.

ONION OMELETTE
Omelette lyonnaise

Cut 1 medium onion into fine strips; cook with 25 g (1 oz) of unsalted butter in an omelette pan. When the onion is golden brown, pour in the beaten eggs. Cook as directed above.

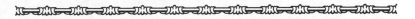

CREAM OMELETTE
Omelette à la crème

Beat 3 tablespoons of double cream; as soon as the cream is light and thick (be careful not to turn it into butter by beating it too long), fold in the beaten egg and pour the mixture into the pan. Cook as directed above.

TRUFFLE OMELETTE
Omelette aux truffes

Slice 2 medium-sized raw truffles into not too thin slices or dice. Heat them quickly in 25 g (1 oz) of unsalted butter in an omelette pan, and pour in the beaten eggs. Cook as directed above.

TOMATO OMELETTE
Omelette aux tomates

Remove the stem and the core from a large ripe tomato. Squeeze out the juice and the seeds, and cut the tomato in large dice. Season with salt and pepper and a pinch of sugar, and cook in a pan with $\frac{1}{2}$ tablespoon of oil or with 15 g ($\frac{1}{2}$ oz) of unsalted butter. When the tomato is reduced, pour it into the beaten eggs, add a pinch of chopped parsley and cook as directed above.

CHICKEN LIVER OMELETTE
Omelette aux foies de volaille

Cut 2 chicken livers into medium dice, season lightly with salt and freshly ground pepper; cook rapidly in 15 g ($\frac{1}{2}$ oz) of very hot unsalted butter in a small pan until firm, but still pink. Remove the chicken livers from the pan and keep warm on a plate. Add

1 tablespoon of Madeira or port to the pan; reduce by half; add 2 tablespoons of strong veal stock. Again reduce the mixture by half. Away from the heat add a knob of butter. Then add the livers and coat them in this rich sauce.

Make the omelette, following the method on page 60. Before folding the omelette, garnish the centre with two-thirds of the chicken livers without sauce. Fold the omelette; then turn on to a long heated plate. Make a shallow cut lengthwise on top; push open the cut and coat the inside with $\frac{1}{2}$ tablespoon of the sauce. Finish the omelette by filling the cut with the remaining $\frac{1}{3}$ of the chicken livers. Then pour the rest of the sauce around the omelette.

OMELETTE WITH CHICKEN LIVERS AND MUSHROOMS
Omelette chasseur

Prepare the ingredients as in the recipe for the chicken liver omelette; add 1 small chopped shallot and 4 medium mushrooms, diced, cooked over a high flame in the butter used to sauté the livers.

Finish as you would for the chicken liver omelette.

KIDNEY OMELETTE
Omelette aux rognons

This omelette is prepared exactly as in the recipe for the chicken liver omelette. Choose lamb kidneys preferably, about 1 per person; remove the thin outer skin and the inside tubes before dicing coarsely.

OMELETTE WITH ASPARAGUS TIPS
Omelette aux pointes d'asperges

Remove the tips from a bunch of green asparagus and cut them to the size of small peas. Barely cook in salted water; drain, and while still hot put in a pan with 25 g (1 oz) of unsalted butter; mix them off the heat. Reserve one-third of the asparagus tips to garnish the omelette, and place the other two-thirds inside the omelette before it is folded.

FLAT OMELETTES
Omelettes plates

These omelettes are generally garnished. They are not folded, but are flat and round, and are turned in the same way as a pancake.

WALNUT OMELETTE
Omelette aux noix

Use 8 eggs and about 20 walnuts. If the walnuts are fresh, remove the thick skin that covers the nut. Chop coarsely and place in the pan as the butter starts to foam. Immediately pour in the beaten eggs and season. As soon as the omelette is the desired consistency, let it brown for a second. Turn the omelette as you would a pancake and cook the other side lightly. Slide the omelette on to a round heated platter.

Note: Use a pan of the right size, so that the omelette, which will have the same diameter as the bottom of the pan, will be about $2\frac{1}{2}$–3 cm (1–$1\frac{1}{2}$ inches) thick.

2 medium-sized
potatoes, peeled
and boiled
75 g (3 oz) unsalted
butter
8 eggs
Salt
Pepper
50 g (2 oz) grated or
thinly sliced
Gruyère or
Parmesan cheese
1 teaspoon chopped
chervil

CHEESE AND POTATO OMELETTE
Omelette à la savoyarde

Slice the potatoes. Put half the butter into an omelette pan and cook the potatoes. When they are golden, add the rest of the butter and heat. Pour in the 8 beaten eggs, season with salt and pepper, and add the grated or thinly sliced Gruyère or Parmesan cheese, and chopped chervil.

When the omelette is golden on one side, flip it over as you would a thick pancake and brown the other side. Slide the omelette on to a round heated platter.

POTATO OMELETTE
Omelette Parmentier

Peel 2 medium-sized potatoes, cut evenly into thin slices; wash in cold water, drain and wipe dry.

In an omelette pan heat 25 g (1 oz) of unsalted butter. When the butter is bubbling, add the potatoes, being careful to separate the slices. Cook the potatoes, turning them frequently, so that they are golden brown and crisp. When the potatoes are cooked, add 50 g (2 oz) of butter and heat. Pour in 8 beaten eggs, season with salt and pepper and 1 teaspoon of fresh chopped parsley; finish by following the recipe above.

COURGETTE OMELETTE
Omelette aux courgettes

Peel a medium-sized courgette, and slice very thinly. Season with salt and pepper. Sauté in 15 g ($\frac{1}{2}$ oz) of unsalted butter in an omelette pan. When the courgette starts to brown, add 50 g (2 oz) of butter and heat. Pour in the 8 beaten eggs, seasoned, and add 1 teaspoon of chopped parsley.

Finish the omelette as above.

GOOSE LIVER OMELETTE
Omelette au foie gras

Cook diced *foie gras* in unsalted butter in an omelette pan; pour in the beaten eggs, and cook as for the basic flat omelette.

SCRAMBLED EGGS
Oeufs brouillés

In making scrambled eggs properly it is essential to mix the egg whites and yolks smoothly so that they are creamy, with no lumps. This can be done in the following way:

Break the eggs into a bowl, season with salt and pepper, and beat lightly as you would for an omelette.

Melt 15 g ($\frac{1}{2}$ oz) of unsalted butter per egg in a fairly small saucepan. Add the eggs and cook slowly, stirring continuously with a wooden spoon. It is best to do this in a *bain-marie* (double boiler). When the eggs are cooked, they should have a creamy consistency; remove from the heat and stir in 15 g ($\frac{1}{2}$ oz) of butter for every 2 eggs.

Scrambled eggs are served in a covered dish, in small *croustades* (shells of bread or flaky pastry), in small individual dishes, or on a large serving dish surrounded by a garnish. Most of the garnishes used for omelettes can be used for scrambled eggs, and vice versa.

SCRAMBLED EGGS WITH BACON
Oeufs brouillés au bacon

Dice 100 g (4 oz) of bacon, first removing the rind. Blanch the bacon in boiling water for 5 minutes and drain; brown lightly in 15 g ($\frac{1}{2}$ oz) of unsalted butter in the pan to be used to scramble the eggs. Set the bacon aside on a plate and keep warm. Cook the scrambled eggs, following the method above; then add the bacon, mix and serve.

SCRAMBLED EGGS WITH MUSHROOM PURÉE
Oeufs brouillés à la purée de champignons

Use 125 g (5 oz) of firm white mushrooms. Clean the mushrooms and wash them quickly; drain, and wipe dry. Slice very thin. Add the mushrooms immediately to a pan in which 25 g (1 oz) of unsalted butter has been heated. Sauté for 3 minutes over a high flame. Season with a pinch of salt and a few drops of lemon juice. Turn the mushrooms into a very fine sieve over a bowl and pound them through with a pestle.

In the pan used to cook the mushrooms, cook the eggs by the method above and finish the cooking by adding the mushroom purée.

SCRAMBLED EGGS WITH ASPARAGUS TIPS
Oeufs brouillés aux points d'asperges

Simmer green asparagus tips in water and finish in unsalted butter. Carefully mix them into the scrambled eggs just before serving. Place a bunch of asparagus tips on top of the eggs.

SOUPS

I have divided soups into two main groups: clear soups and thick soups.

There are many varieties of each.

In the first group you will find bouillons and consommés, with and without garnishes.

The second group includes soups thickened by dissolving or mashing the basic ingredient of the soup (as in purée soups) and soups to which one or more thickening ingredients are added (for example, a roux, cooked rice, bread boiled to a pulp, egg yolks or cream).

Soup should always be served piping hot in well-heated plates.

Le pot-au-feu

The *pot-au-feu* is one of the fundamentals of French cooking. It is the stock pot which provides the broth used as the main liquid in many soups and a supply of stock used in making a great many sauces and other dishes.

If the stock is to be kept it must be carefully strained (vegetables, especially carrots, left in it will quickly turn it sour) and then boiled up again. It should be left to stand uncovered, in a glazed earthenware or enamelled receptacle, in an airy place so that it cools as quickly as possible.

A *pot-au-feu* for 12 people should be made with enough meat for at least two meals.

Beef:

1·5 kg (3 lb) shin

500 g (1 lb)
   forequarter flank

500 g (1 lb) bladebone

500 g (1 lb) rump

500 g (1 lb) oxtail

200 g ($\frac{1}{2}$ lb) rib bones

5 beef marrow bones
   cut into 3-cm.
   (1$\frac{1}{2}$-inch) lengths

Other meat:

500 g (1 lb) knuckle
   of veal

500 g (1 lb) neck of
   lamb

1·5 kg (3 lb) chicken

Vegetables:

350 g ($\frac{3}{4}$ lb) leeks

350 g ($\frac{3}{4}$ lb) carrots

3 large tomatoes

2 celery hearts

350 g ($\frac{3}{4}$ lb) turnips

350 g ($\frac{3}{4}$ lb) onions

1 fennel bulb

1 parsnip

1 head garlic

Cloves

Bouquet garni

Salt

Black peppercorns

Truffles (optional)

Method. Lay the rib bones on the bottom of the stock pot so that the meat itself does not touch the bottom and stick. Lay the beef shin, flank, bladebone and oxtail on top of the bones. On top of them place the knuckle of veal and neck of lamb. Fill the pot with cold water to cover the meat completely. Do not add salt at this stage – wait until after skimming. Cook uncovered over high heat, otherwise the stock will become cloudy.

Meanwhile peel the vegetables. Wash the leeks and celery well to get rid of any earth or sand. Prepare a bouquet garni, wrapping $\frac{1}{2}$ bay leaf, parsley, chervil and thyme in the green leaves of the leeks. Tie a slice of carrot at either end of the pieces of bone marrow to seal in the marrow.

Skim the stock when it has been cooking for about 20 minutes. Use a ladle, not a skimmer, and gently remove the scum and grease. Move the pot to the side of the heat so that the scum rises to one side. Lower the heat and leave to simmer for another 20 minutes. Skim again. Season with coarse salt (allowing about 10 g ($\frac{1}{4}$ oz) to every 1 l (2 pts) of liquid) and a few black peppercorns wrapped in a piece of muslin. Now add the trussed chicken (having first, if you like, inserted a few slices of truffle under the skin). Add the bouquet garni, the onions, each studded with four cloves (one of the onions should previously have been cut in half and browned in a hot oven for half an hour or so; this will give the stock a good colour), the garlic and all the vegetables except the tomatoes. Tie the leeks together. Skim again and simmer gently for 40 minutes, skimming from time to time. Remove the parsnip after 15 minutes.

As soon as the vegetables are cooked (check with a skewer to see if they are done) carefully lift them out with a slotted spoon. Put them in a covered dish, moisten with a couple of ladles of stock and keep warm on the side of the stove. Take out the chicken and keep it hot in another dish.

Let the meat cook for another 30 minutes, skimming from time to time, then remove the veal knuckle and neck of lamb. Leave the rest of the meat to simmer gently for another hour. Then add the rump steak, attached to the handle of the pan with a piece of string. Add the pieces of marrow bone and the tomatoes and skim again. Cook for a further 12–15 minutes, depending on how thick the piece of rump is. Take out the meat and the marrow bones (when you remove the slices of carrot the marrow will be intact inside) and put the chicken and vegetables back in the liquid to reheat for a moment.

Place the shin of beef in the middle of a large serving dish and arrange the rest of the meat, the chicken and the vegetables around it. Moisten with broth. More broth is served separately in a soup tureen.

The *pot-au-feu* provides three separate courses, all served in soup dishes.

1. The broth, served with toasted bread, grated cheese, freshly ground black pepper, coarse salt and red wine if you like.
2. The chicken, carved into pieces, surrounded by the knuckle of veal and the oxtail and served with broth or a sauce made of 1 tablespoon wine vinegar, 4 tablespoons walnut oil, salt, pepper and chopped chervil.
3. The shin of beef served with a little of the lamb, bladebone, vegetables and broth.

Note: If you are cooking for a large number of people, you can add further ingredients to this dish – for example, a turkey, pheasant or partridge, a piece of pork collar or knuckle (fresh or salt), a leg of lamb (cooked in the same way as the rump steak) and some cabbage or cauliflower (cooked separately in salted water).

Petite marmite

For 6 people

1 kg (2 lb) shin of beef
1 small chicken
2 l (4 pts) stock
225 g ($\frac{1}{2}$ lb) carrots (core removed)
225 g ($\frac{1}{2}$ lb) turnips
175 g (6 oz) leeks, white part only
2 sticks celery, sliced
Small marrowbones
Slices toasted bread
Grated Gruyère cheese

Cube beef shin, blanch and drain.

Place in a large stock pot. Brown a small chicken in a 450°F (230°C, gas mark 8) oven for 15 minutes. Put the chicken into the pot.

Cover with stock and $\frac{1}{2}$ litre (1 pint) of cold water. Slowly bring to the boil, and remove the scum as it rises to the surface.

Add the carrots, the turnips cut down to the size of large olives, the leeks cut into pieces 6 cm (2$\frac{1}{2}$ inches) long and the celery. Cook steadily at a simmer for 4$\frac{1}{2}$ hours.

Serve in the pot, with small marrowbones poached in a little of the soup, thin slices of toasted bread and grated Gruyère cheese.

Note: With slow, careful simmering you should only lose about $\frac{1}{2}$ litre (1 pint) of liquid through evaporation. No extra salt will be needed.

'WOODEN LEG SOUP'
Soupe à la jambe de bois

Here is the recipe for the so-called *soupe à la 'jambe de bouâ'* or 'wooden leg soup', given me by Henry Clos-Jouve. This is how it has been made in Lyons for a very long time. [*Editor's note:* This recipe is delightful reading, but not one to be attempted lightly!]

'Take an earthenware soup pot or a copper one. Clean well. Place in it a beautiful leg of beef and cover with cold water, adding salt, onions, cloves and anything else that will give it flavour. Let simmer very slowly on a low flame. Skim the soup well. Once the soup is very clear, add leeks, turnips, celery. Add 2 or 3 veal knuckles, a shoulder of pork, turkey, partridge, a juicy leg of lamb and a juicy beef rump. Half an hour before serving, add a couple of large chickens and, moments later, a pork sausage larded with truffles and pistachio nuts. When all are cooked set one shin bone right across the stew pot so that everyone will recognize the "Wooden Leg Soup". Serve a Beaujolais wine, and don't be skimpy with it. *Bon appétit!*'

Consommés

For 2 l (4 pts) consommé:
700 g ($1\frac{1}{2}$ lb) topside of beef, the fat completely removed
Chicken giblets
$\frac{1}{2}$ carrot
3 leeks, white part only
1 egg white
$2\frac{1}{2}$ l (5 pts) meat stock

A consommé is a meat stock, lightly salted, its flavour enhanced with meat juices, seasoning and flavouring.

Chop the meat and giblets very fine. Cut the carrot and the leeks into tiny cubes. In a stock pot combine the chopped meat, vegetables and egg white; mix well. Add the meat stock, cold or warm, stirring with a wooden spoon.

Bring slowly to the boil, continuing to stir constantly. As soon as the soup starts to boil, reduce the heat and keep the soup at a simmer, partially covered, for $1\frac{1}{2}$ hours.

The bouillon is enriched by the juices from the meat and the flavour of the vegetables. With this added body it has now become consommé. Strain it through cheesecloth soaked in warm water and wrung out.

The consommé should now be absolutely clear because of the albumin from the meat and the egg white.

CHICKEN CONSOMMÉ
Consommé de volaille

This consommé has a clear and characteristic flavour of chicken, obtained by adding a small roasting chicken, 2 lots of giblets, and the carcass of another chicken, finely chopped, to the ingredients for an ordinary consommé.

Proceed exactly as for the consommé above.

The small chicken can be used later to make delicious hot or cold dishes such as chicken croquettes or chicken salad.

CONSOMMÉ WITH SPRING VEGETABLES
Consommé printanier

To the basic consommé add cooked carrots and turnips from the *pot-au-feu*. Cut into matchsticks about 2·5 cm (1 inch) long and 3 mm ($\frac{1}{8}$ inch) thick, or shape into tiny rounds or fluted ovals. Add an equal part of tiny peas and string beans cut into small diamond shapes and cooked in a little soup. Complete the soup with a few chervil leaves.

Consommé Colbert

This is a *consommé printanier* (recipe above) with a small poached egg added for each guest.

Consommé Célestine

This consommé is slightly thickened with tapioca and garnished with a pancake, made without sugar, cut into very fine strips.

Consommé à la royale

The consommé is thickened lightly with tapioca and garnished with a *royale* or moulded custard (recipe below), made without sugar and cut with a pastry cutter into decorative shapes, such as diamonds.

Royale for soups

4 eggs
¼ l (½ pt) milk
½ l (1 pt) bouillon, with all fat removed
Salt
Pinch grated nutmeg

Beat the eggs and strain them through a very fine strainer. Add the milk, the hot soup (not boiling), the salt and nutmeg. Pour into a cake tin or flat biscuit pan, and bake in a 325°F (170°C, gas mark 3) oven in a *bain-marie* like a baked custard. Do not let the water in the *bain-marie* boil as this causes tiny holes in the custard.

Cool, unmould and cut into even strips, and then cut each strip into small decorative shapes – squares, stars or diamonds. When putting the pieces of custard into very hot consommé be careful not to break them.

Consommé aux profiteroles

Garnish the soup with tiny *profiteroles* (little pastries the size of hazelnuts) of chou pastry made with the addition of Gruyère or Parmesan cheese and baked in a very hot oven.

CONSOMMÉ WITH DICED VEGETABLES
Consommé brunoise

225 g (½ lb) carrots (core removed)
225 g (½ lb) turnips
2 leeks, white part only
Small stick of celery
2 tablespoons stock
Chervil (optional)

Dice carrots, turnips, leeks and celery finely. Mix everything together, blanch and drain.

Cook over a very low flame, in a small pan with 2 tablespoons stock. Use 2 teaspoons of the vegetables to garnish each portion of consommé. A few chervil leaves may be added at the end.

Croûte-au-pot

Garnish the consommé with carrots, turnips and leeks from a *pot-au-feu*. Cut the vegetables into the shape of an olive and simmer in a little stock. With the soup serve a separate dish of grated Gruyère cheese and crusts of French bread, with the soft part removed, baked slowly in the oven and arranged on a plate covered with a folded napkin.

You could add $\frac{1}{4}$ small cabbage, cooked in a couple of tablespoons of stock.

COLD CONSOMMÉ
Consommé froid

Cold consommé is generally served in a cup, very cold but not iced. It should be the consistency of a very soft jelly, not set solid.

To achieve this, the consommé must be very rich in meat juices. As an economy measure, you can add a thickening ingredient, such as tapioca or cornflour, but I do not recommend cornflour which blunts the flavour of the consommé. A small amount of tapioca does not have this drawback. You can also make up for a lack of natural jelling by the discreet use of gelatine. However, tapioca is preferable as it is more natural and has a better flavour.

Since raw tomatoes are 90 per cent water, adding them to a consommé dilutes its flavour. To avoid this, use tomatoes that have been cooked beforehand and reduced to a thick purée.

CHICKEN CONSOMMÉ
Consommé de volaille

Sprinkle 4 tablespoons of tapioca into 1 l (2 pts) of boiling chicken consommé made from the basic recipe for consommé. Stir and cook very slowly for 15 minutes.

Put through a fine strainer, cool and serve in a cup.

CELERY-FLAVOURED CONSOMMÉ
Consommé au fumet de céleri

Proceed as for the chicken consommé. After stirring the tapioca into the consommé, add ½ heart of celery. Cook slowly for 25 minutes. Finish as above.

TARRAGON-FLAVOURED CONSOMMÉ
Consommé au fumet d'estragon

Follow the same procedure as for the celery-flavoured consommé, replacing the celery with a sprig of tarragon. Cook for only 15 minutes.

TOMATO-FLAVOURED CONSOMMÉ
Consommé madrilène

First method

First method:
6 ripe tomatoes
1 l (2 pts) consommé
Tarragon
Garlic clove
4 tablespoons tapioca

Choose large ripe tomatoes; cut them in half and squeeze to remove the juice. Force through a very fine sieve. Add this purée to the consommé; put in a small sprig of tarragon and garlic. Thicken with tapioca, and cook slowly for 40 minutes. Strain through a napkin and let cool.

Second method

Second method:
1 l (2 pts) chicken
   consommé
6 ripe tomatoes,
   cooked to a purée
4 tablespoons tapioca

Proceed as directed above for the chicken consommé and add a purée made from the ripe tomatoes. Thicken with tapioca, and cook slowly for 25 minutes. Strain through a napkin and let cool.

Whether you use the first or the second method, the consommé must be absolutely clear.

Note: You need not add tapioca for thickening if the consommé is sufficiently rich in meat juices and natural gelatinous ingredients.

CONSOMMÉ WITH POACHED EGGS
Consommé aux oeufs pochés

Serve 1 poached egg for each guest in ordinary consommé or chicken consommé.

1 l (2 pts) consommé
1 carrot (core removed)
1 turnip
1 leek, white part only
Celery
1 tablespoon fresh peas

CONSOMMÉ WITH VEGETABLE JULIENNE
Consommé julienne

Cook the outer part of 1 carrot, 1 whole turnip, the white of 1 leek, and a little celery, all cut into julienne, in stock. Towards the end of the cooking, add 1 tablespoon of fresh peas.

To serve add 1 tablespoon of these vegetables for each guest to a very good consommé.

CONSOMMÉ WITH CHICKEN QUENELLES
Consommé aux quenelles de volaille

Poach tiny quenelles (page 381), the size of small olives, made with chicken and cream, in chicken consommé.

TRUFFLE CONSOMMÉ
Consommé aux truffes

Cook finely diced raw truffles for two minutes in chicken consommé. Add a little port just before serving.

Hearty Soups

A French *soupe* (as distinct from a *potage*) has as its base one or more vegetables mashed to a purée, cut into julienne strips or cut into quarters and then sliced very thinly.

If carrots are used they should be scraped or peeled thinly, cut in half lengthwise and the tough, strong-tasting centre part removed. Slice the rest finely, blanch and rinse in cold water. These steps are not necessary with very young carrots. Turnips should be fairly thickly peeled, as you will see if you examine a turnip cut in half. In general allow just over 600 g ($1\frac{1}{4}$ lb) of vegetables for $1\frac{1}{2}$ l (3 pts) of liquid.

When the vegetables are ready, start cooking them as follows.

Choose a saucepan just the right size for the quantity of soup you plan to make. Put it on the heat with some butter and when hot add the vegetables. Sweat gently on a very low heat so that the juices run and the butter absorbs the flavour of the vegetables.

Then add salted water or stock, bring to the boil and simmer slowly for just the right amount of time. Overcooking spoils the flavour, so time the soup carefully to be ready at the right moment.

CLEAR OXTAIL SOUP
Oxtail clair

1·5 kg (3 lb) oxtail
3 onions
3 medium-sized carrots
100 g (4 oz) unsalted butter
Bouquet garni
Celery stick
$\frac{1}{2}$ glass Madeira
2 tablespoons cognac
3 l (6 pts) consommé
Carrots, turnips and celery heart (for garnish)

Brown the oxtail cut into pieces, the onions and the carrots cut into quarters with the butter in the oven.

Then transfer the meat and vegetables to a large saucepan. Add a bouquet garni, a stick of celery, the Madeira and cognac. Reduce slowly, covered, on low heat. Then pour in the consommé and $\frac{1}{2}$ l (1 pt) of water. Cook very slowly for 4 hours; the soup should barely simmer.

Strain soup through cheesecloth, reserving some of the best pieces of oxtail, 1 per guest. Serve with a garnish of carrots and turnips, cut into the shape of small olives, and a celery heart, cooked separately in a little consommé. Allow a tablespoon of vegetables per helping.

Serve very hot.

GARLIC SOUP
Soupe à l'ail

2 cloves
Sprig sage
1 tablespoon salt
Pinch pepper
20 garlic cloves
20 slices French bread
Grated Gruyère or
    Parmesan cheese
Few drops olive oil

In a saucepan, combine 2 l (4 pts) of water with the cloves, sage, salt, pepper and garlic.

Bring to the boil and cook slowly for 15 minutes.

Slice the French bread; put slices on a baking sheet and cover each with a little grated Gruyère or Parmesan cheese; sprinkle with a few drops of olive oil and brown in a 475°F (240°C, gas mark 9) oven.

Place the bread in a soup tureen; taste the soup and correct the seasoning if necessary. Then pour the very hot soup through a fine strainer on to the bread.

Serve immediately.

TRUFFLE SOUP
Soupe aux truffes Élysée
For 1 person

2 tablespoons
    matignon (equal
    parts carrots,
    onions, celery,
    mushrooms;
    unsalted butter)
50 g (2 oz) fresh raw
    truffles
20 g (1 oz) *foie gras*
¼ l (½ pt) strong
    chicken consommé
60 g (2½ oz) flaky
    pastry (page 531)
1 egg yolk, beaten

Use individual ovenproof soup bowls.

Remove the woody centre from the carrots and chop all the vegetables into tiny dice. Stew gently in butter until soft to make a *matignon*. Put 2 tablespoons of this *matignon* into each soup bowl with the roughly sliced truffles and *foie gras* and the consommé.

Take a thin layer of flaky pastry, brush with egg yolk and cover the soup bowl with it, sealing the edges tightly.

Put the bowl into a 425°F (220°C, gas mark 7) oven, to cook very quickly. The pastry will puff up and turn a beautiful golden colour when cooked.

To eat the soup, break the pastry with your spoon so that it falls in flakes into the bowl.

I created this truffle soup for M. and Mme Valéry Giscard d'Estaing. The occasion was the magnificent luncheon which gathered together all the finest cooks in France on Tuesday 25 February 1975, when the French president presented me with the cross of the Légion d'Honneur, as an ambassador of French cooking.

2 medium potatoes
6 endives (Belgian
  chicory)
2 leeks, white part
  only
125 g (5 oz) unsalted
  butter
1 l (2 pts) water
½ l (1 pt) milk
½ loaf French bread
Salt

POTATO AND ENDIVE SOUP
Soupe ardennaise

Clean the vegetables, peel the potatoes. Cut the endives and the whites of the leeks into julienne, and the potatoes into very thin slices. Heat 50 g (2 oz) of butter in a saucepan. Add the vegetables, and stew slowly, covered, for 15 minutes. The vegetables must be softened but not browned. Add the water, and salt. Simmer 45 minutes. Add the milk at the end of the cooking time.

Cut the French bread into thin slices; brown lightly in a 425°F (220°C, gas mark 7) oven and place in a soup tureen with the rest of the butter.

Correct the seasoning of the soup. Pour the boiling soup over the bread just before serving.

2 carrots
4 leeks, white part
  only
¼ cabbage
2 medium turnips
2 medium potatoes
125 g (5 oz) unsalted
  butter
2 l (4 pts) stock or
  water
Salt
½ loaf French bread or
  the equivalent
  quantity of white
  bread

VEGETABLE SOUP
Soupe fermière

Wash, peel and remove the woody centres from the carrots: use only the outer portion.

Shred the leeks and the cabbage finely; peel the other vegetables and cut them into very thin slices. Heat 50 g (2 oz) of butter in a saucepan; add all vegetables except the potatoes, and stew slowly for 15 minutes.

When the vegetables are softened, add the stock or water. Simmer just at boiling point for 25 minutes; then add the potatoes and cook for another 20 minutes.

Cut the bread into very thin slices, brown in a 425°F (220°C, gas mark 7) oven, and place in the soup tureen with the remaining butter. Just before serving, correct the seasoning of the soup and pour it over the bread. Cover the bread completely, so that it will soften.

SALT PORK AND VEGETABLE SOUP

Soupe auvergnate

3 carrots
2 medium turnips
1 small cabbage
4 leeks
100 g (4 oz) lentils
1 kg (2 lb) salt pork
Slices bread

Wash and peel the vegetables; remove the woody centres from the carrots; soak the lentils for 2 hours in cold water and drain.

In a saucepan cover the salt pork and vegetables with 4 l (8 pts) of water, and cook on a low flame for 3 hours.

To serve, remove pork and vegetables and arrange on a platter. Pour the soup over slices of bread in a tureen.

PUMPKIN SOUP

Soupe de courge

For 6–8 people

1 3–4 kg (6–8 lb) pumpkin
225 g (8 oz) toasted croûtons (see page 91)
100 g (4 oz) grated Gruyère cheese
Salt and pepper
3 l (6 pts) single cream

Cut the top off the pumpkin to give it the shape of a soup tureen. Set the top aside.

Remove all the pumpkin seeds. Inside make alternate layers of toasted croûtons and grated Gruyère. Add salt and pepper and fill with the cream. Close the 'soup tureen' with its pumpkin top as tightly as possible.

Place the prepared pumpkin in a 425°F (220°C, gas mark 7) oven. It will take about 2 hours to cook.

To serve, place the pumpkin tureen on the table. Remove the lid. With a spoon, scoop out the pumpkin flesh. Mix it into the soup with a ladle to make the soup rich and smooth. If necessary, correct the seasoning.

500 g (1 lb) onions
125 g (5 oz) unsalted
  butter
15 g ($\frac{1}{2}$ oz) flour
Salt and freshly
  ground pepper
1 small bouquet garni
  (see page 259)
$\frac{1}{2}$ loaf French bread
225 g (8 oz) grated
  Gruyère cheese
4 egg yolks
1 tablespoon Madeira

ONION SOUP GRATINÉE
Gratinée lyonnaise
For 4–6 people

Chop the onions finely. Sauté them in the butter in a heavy frying pan until brown, without burning them.

Then sprinkle on the flour and stir to form a roux. Put it in a large saucepan with $2\frac{1}{2}$ l (5 pts) of water.

Add salt, pepper and the bouquet garni. Cook over a low flame for about 40 minutes.

Discard the bouquet garni. Rub the onions and the stock through a sieve or a food mill.

In an ovenproof soup tureen, put the bread cut into very thin slices and lightly dried in the oven. Over each layer of bread sprinkle grated Gruyère, using about half of it. After correcting the seasoning, pour the stock over the bread. Cover the surface with the remaining grated Gruyère.

Set the soup tureen in a 425°F (220°C, gas mark 7) oven. The Gruyère will melt and the surface of the *gratinée* will take on a beautiful golden colour.

Put the 4 eggs yolks into a bowl and add the Madeira.

Pour the mixture into the soup tureen. Stir immediately with a ladle to thicken the soup and mix in the eggs thoroughly.

Note: In Lyons this soup is very popular for a family supper or after a show.

50 g (2 oz) unsalted
  pork fat
4 leeks
1 onion
1 celery stick
2 medium potatoes
Salt
$\frac{1}{2}$ l (1 pt) milk
1 l (2 pts) water
$\frac{1}{4}$ loaf bread
Grated Gruyère or
  Parmesan cheese

Soupe savoyarde

Remove the skin from the pork fat, dice fat and melt in a heavy saucepan. Add the leeks, onions and celery cut into julienne. Slice the potatoes thinly and add. Cook gently for 15 minutes, stirring from time to time. Pour in 1 l (2 pts) of water, salt lightly and cook 35 minutes; add the milk, and return to the boil for a second.

Cut the bread into thin slices and place them on a baking sheet or roasting pan; sprinkle them with grated Gruyère or Parmesan cheese and brown in a 425°F (220°C, gas mark 7) oven.

Put the bread into the soup tureen, and just before serving pour in the boiling soup.

Soupe Nîmoise

50 g (2 oz) unsalted
butter
3 leeks, white part
only
350 g ($\frac{3}{4}$ lb) cabbage
1 celery heart
100 g (4 oz) pearl
barley or rice
Pinch crushed basil
$\frac{1}{2}$ tablespoon salt
2 l (4 pts) water
Grated Gruyère
cheese

Heat the butter in a heavy saucepan. Add the vegetables, cut into thin strips, and stew slowly, letting them soften; stir from time to time. Add the barley, the basil, the salt and 2 l (4 pts) of water. Cook 45 minutes.

If using rice, first cook the soup for 15 minutes; then add the rice and continue cooking for 30 minutes.

Serve with a dish of grated Gruyère cheese.

Soupe ménagère

3 carrots
2 turnips
4 medium leeks
3 potatoes
225 g ($\frac{1}{2}$ lb) cabbage
175 g (6 oz) celery
225 g ($\frac{1}{2}$ lb) bacon (in
the piece)
$2\frac{1}{2}$ l (5 pts) water
$\frac{1}{4}$ loaf bread

Wash and peel the vegetables; remove the woody centres from the carrots and cut the vegetables into large pieces. Put into a large saucepan with the water and the bacon. Cook $1\frac{1}{2}$ hours.

Remove the bacon, and cut it into tiny pieces. Put the bacon into a soup tureen together with the bread cut into thin slices; correct the seasoning, and pour the soup over the bread.

Soupe à la normande

Proportions:
$\frac{1}{3}$ carrots (cores
removed)
$\frac{1}{3}$ potatoes
$\frac{1}{3}$ leeks, white part
only
Rice
Toasted bread

Cut the carrots and the potatoes into very thin slices and the leeks into thin strips. Stew the carrots and the leeks in stock or water and salt to taste. Cook for an hour, then add the potatoes and a small amount of rice. Continue the cooking for 30 minutes. Put the soup through a food mill off the flame, and pour into a soup tureen with slices of toasted bread. Serve with unsalted butter.

Soupe paysanne

Leeks, white part
only
Unsalted butter
Cabbage heart
Stock or water
Salt
2 large floury
potatoes
Slices toasted bread

Cut the leeks into julienne and sauté in butter as you would an onion for soup. When it is lightly browned, add the firm heart of a cabbage, cut into thick julienne and blanched. Cook gently. Add the stock or water; salt to taste. Cook for an hour. Then add the potatoes, and continue the cooking for 30 minutes. Mash the potatoes coarsely and pour the soup into a tureen lined with slices of toasted bread. Serve with fresh butter.

SORREL SOUP
Soupe à l'oseille

Proceed as for the leek and potato soup (page 99), replacing the leeks with sorrel. Sorrel takes only a few minutes to cook.

Potée bourguignonne

To the ingredients for *petite marmite* (page 73) add:
A piece of lightly salted pork
A raw garlic sausage
The heart of 1 cabbage
Potatoes, quartered
White bread

This is the same as the recipe for *petite marmite* (see page 73) with the addition of the ingredients listed here. The potatoes should be added just a half hour before serving.

Put the meat and vegetables on a platter. Pour the stock over white bread and serve separately but at the same time.

MINESTRONE
Soupe minestra

100 g (4 oz) fresh pork fat or bacon
1 medium-sized onion, chopped
2 leeks, white part only, diced
1 carrot (core removed), diced
1 medium-sized turnip, diced
1 celery stick, diced
Heart of 1 small cabbage, diced
Salt, pepper, pinch sugar
1½ l (3 pts) stock or water
2 tomatoes
1 cup fresh peas
Handful French beans
1 large potato, diced
100 g (4 oz) broken-up spaghetti or small pasta
Garlic clove, basil, chervil

In a heavy saucepan melt half the pork fat or bacon cut into tiny dice. Add an onion, chopped, and the white of 2 leeks cut into tiny dice. Sauté until golden. Add the carrot, turnip, celery stalk and cabbage all cut into tiny dice. Season with salt, pepper and sugar. Mix well, cover and stew for 15 minutes. Pour in lightly salted stock or water.

Bring to the boil and simmer for 30 minutes.

At this point, add the tomatoes, skinned, seeded and diced, the peas, the beans cut into 2.5-cm (1-inch) lengths, the potato and the pasta.

Let the soup simmer for an hour.

Just before serving, bring to the boil; add remaining pork fat, chopped very fine and mashed with a garlic clove, basil and chervil.

GARBURES

There are many versions of this delicious soup, which is typical of Béarnais district. Although they have different names, they are all variations of this basic recipe.

Turnips
Carrots
Cabbage
French beans
White haricot beans
Piece of smoked
  bacon
Piece of *confit d'oie*
Salt
Slices toasted bread
Grated Gruyère
  cheese
Freshly ground
  pepper

Garbure béarnaise

In a fireproof earthenware pot place any fresh vegetables in season – turnips, carrots, cabbage, French beans, white beans – and the bacon and *confit d'oie* (goose meat cooked in goose fat or lard and preserved, see page 378). Cover the vegetables and the meat completely with water. Bring to the boil, and simmer for 3 hours.

Halfway through the cooking time, taste and correct seasoning, adding salt if necessary. When the 3 hours are up, pour off the soup and set aside.

In an ovenproof dish arrange layers of vegetables, bacon and the *confit d'oie* cut into pieces. On top place slices of toasted bread; sprinkle them with grated Gruyère cheese and freshly ground pepper. Moisten with a couple of tablespoons of soup and set in a 325°F (170°C, gas mark 3) oven to simmer and brown for 15 minutes. Serve the broth in a soup tureen or in its earthenware cooking pot, along with the dish of vegetables and *confit d'oie*.

Note: There are many variations on this recipe – for example *garbure Crécy* (made with carrots), *limousine* (with chestnuts), *fermière* (a thicker version of *soupe paysanne*), *fréneuse* (with turnips) and *dauphinoise* (with potatoes and marrow). All derive from the recipe above and are generally served with slices of bread fried in butter covered with a thick coat of vegetable purée made from the soup, then sprinkled with cheese and browned under the grill. These slices are placed in the serving tureen before the soup is poured in.

ONION GARBURE
Garbure à l'oignon

This onion soup is thickened with a large potato, mashed and spread on slices of toasted bread. They are copiously sprinkled with grated cheese and pieces of butter, then baked in the oven until a golden crust is formed.

Soupe cultivateur

Use all the vegetables in season, cut into coarse dice. Cook gently with diced bacon. Cover with white stock or with water, salted to taste, and cook 1 hour.

Halfway through the cooking time, add potatoes, fresh peas, and French beans cut into pieces.

Pour into a soup tureen over slices of bread dotted with butter.

RUSSIAN BORSCHT
Bortsch à la russe

225 g ($\frac{1}{2}$ lb) beets
1 medium-sized leek, white part only
1 onion
225 g ($\frac{1}{2}$ lb) cabbage heart
1 celery stick
1 fennel stalk
Unsalted butter
1$\frac{1}{2}$ l (3 pts) stock or water
$\frac{3}{4}$ kg (1$\frac{1}{2}$ lb) forequarter flank of beef
1 small duckling or giblets of 2 ducks
6 tablespoons beetroot juice
6 tablespoons sour cream

Thinly slice all the vegetables except the fennel. Mix the rest together and season with a pinch of salt; cook gently in butter in a fireproof earthenware pot large enough to hold the soup.

Pour in 1$\frac{1}{2}$ l (3 pts) of stock or water; add salt or more water as needed. Bring to the boil. Scald the beef in boiling water and add to the soup. Skim the soup, and cook very slowly for 2$\frac{1}{2}$ hours. Then add the duck browned in butter or, for economy, the giblets of 2 ducks. Add the fennel, and continue cooking for 40 minutes.

Drain the beef and duck (or giblets).

Cut the beef into large dice and remove the bones and membranes; slice the breast of the duck; and return both to the boiling soup. Off the flame pour in the beetroot juice and sour cream mixed.

PANADE

Panades are made with coarsely diced bread, sometimes fried in butter, and cooked in milk, which may be diluted with water.

The soup is then thickened with egg yolks mixed with cream or milk. To this soup one may add shredded sorrel, lettuce, spinach or watercress.

The soup has the consistency of a cream soup or velouté.

Generally stale bread is used.

1½ kg (3 lb) white fish
4 medium onions, chopped
3 cloves garlic, crushed
2 cloves
1 bay leaf
15 fennel seeds or 1 fresh fennel stalk
2 ripe tomatoes, peeled, de-seeded and chopped
25 g (1 oz) salt
Pinch pepper
½ glass dry white wine
3 l (6 pts) water
¼ l (½ pt) oil
8 slices bread
Garlic clove
1 tablespoon chopped fresh parsley

Panade au céleri

This is a variation of the *panade*, flavoured with celery or celeriac.

Fish Soups

This is a basic recipe for 8 servings. For flavour use several varieties of fish.

Cut the fish into pieces and put them into a heavy saucepan that will sit firmly on the burner. Add vegetables, seasoning, herbs, white wine and 3 l (6 pts) of water. Bring to a rapid boil; add the oil. Boil rapidly for 15 minutes.

While this is cooking, slice the bread and place it on a baking sheet; coat the slices lightly with oil, and toast them in the oven. If you like, rub the bread with a clove of garlic. Put the bread into a soup tureen. Strain the soup if you wish. Pour into the tureen just before serving, and finish with a tablespoon of fresh chopped parsley.

If the soup has been strained, the pieces of fish may be served on the side.

Here are some suggestions for suitable types of fish: scorpion-fish, monk or angler-fish, conger eel; John Dory; weever; gurnard.

4 l (8 pints) mussels
1 bottle Pouilly-
    Fuissé
3 shallots, chopped
3 tablespoons chopped
    parsley
100 g (4 oz) unsalted
    butter
$\frac{1}{4}$ l ($\frac{1}{2}$ pt) olive oil
300 g (10 oz) onions
    finely chopped
300 g (10 oz) leeks,
    cut into strips
4 l (8 pts) water
4 kg (8 lb) fish
$1\frac{1}{2}$ kg (3 lb) tomatoes,
    seeded and cut into
    pieces
2 fennel stalks,
    chopped
2 cloves garlic,
    chopped
$\frac{1}{2}$ bay leaf
1 sprig thyme
Saffron
Salt and pepper
$\frac{1}{4}$ l ($\frac{1}{2}$ pt) cream
Croûtons
Grated cheese

MUSSEL SOUP
Soupe de moules
For 10 people

Cook the mussels with $\frac{1}{4}$ of the white wine, the shallots, parsley and butter until they open. Heat the olive oil in a large saucepan. Add the onions and the leeks, and cook over a low flame for 5 minutes. Then pour in 4 l (8 pts) of water, the remaining wine and the liquid the mussels cooked in; add the fish, the tomatoes, the herbs and seasonings, and cook for 40 minutes.

Then put the stock through a very fine strainer, rubbing all the ingredients to extract the juice and the flesh of the fish. Pour the stock into a smaller saucepan and bring to boiling point. At the last moment, add the mussels and the cream. Cook for 2 minutes.

Serve in a soup tureen, with croûtons (see page 91) of toasted bread and grated cheese served separately.

175 g (6 oz) rice
1 l (2 pt) white stock
175 g (6 oz) unsalted
　butter
2 tablespoons diced
　carrot, core
　removed
2 tablespoons diced
　onions
1 sprig parsley
1 sprig thyme
1 bay leaf fragment
20 crayfish, about 50 g
　(2 oz) each
Cognac
White wine
Salt and pepper
Stock or double
　cream (see recipe)
Pinch cayenne

CRAYFISH SOUP
Soupe d'écrevisses

Carefully wash the rice and cook rapidly in two-thirds of the stock. While the rice is cooking, put the carrots and the onions into a frying pan with a pat of butter, and cook slowly without letting them brown. Add parsley, thyme and bay leaf; raise heat; add the crayfish and salt and pepper. Sautée quickly on high heat; the crayfish will turn red at once. Moisten with the cognac, *flambé* and put out the flame immediately by pouring in the white wine. Cook for 8 minutes. Remove 10 crayfish, take out the flesh and reserve in a small amount of stock. Put these shells, along with everything else, into a mortar; rinse the frying pan out with a few tablespoons of reserved stock and add to mortar.

Pound the mixture to a fine paste; mix in the very hot rice, and pound again, working on the texture until it has the consistency of cream.

Strain into a fine sieve rubbing through until nothing is left but the crushed shells. Put into a saucepan and bring to the boil adding some stock or double cream to give the consistency of a thick soup. Then off the fire add the remaining butter. Correct the seasoning and add a pinch of cayenne.

Serve the soup with the reserved crayfish tails cut in pieces. The colour of the soup should be a pinkish red, the same as the crayfish after they have been cooked.

Thick Soups

This general heading covers purées, veloutés, cream soups and shellfish bisques in which the thickening or liaison is achieved in different ways.

Purées are usually made from a single vegetable or combination of vegetables. Some vegetables, turnips, carrots, cauliflower and pumpkin for example, need an extra farinaceous ingredient, like beans or lentils, or a thickening agent, such as potatoes, rice or *beurre manié*. Purées made from poultry are thickened with rice, those made from game with lentils, those made from shellfish with rice or fried croûtons. Croûtons, fried in butter or toasted, and then simmered gently in the soup, provide a particularly smooth liaison.

A really good soup should have a velvety texture. Often farinaceous or starch ingredients have to be held in suspension in the liquid by adding a small amount of a thickening ingredient such as *beurre manié* (equal amounts of flour and unsalted butter mashed together) or a *mitonnade* (bread simmered in the soup). With a soup made from a purée of, for example, lentils, dried or fresh peas, or beans, this prevents the purée and the liquid separating once the soup is served.

Fresh vegetables should be sliced very thin and then cooked gently in butter, allowing 100 g (4 oz) of butter to every 700 g (1½ lb) of vegetables. Dried vegetables should be soaked for up to two hours before cooking. Some vegetables are blanched and rinsed in cold water. Each recipe gives precise instructions.

The liquid used is stock, milk or water. The proportions are one-third purée to two-thirds liquid.

Remember that the flavour of a soup is fresher and clearer the less time it has to wait once cooked and finished. Work out how long it will take to cook and start preparing it so that it is just ready at the time it is to be eaten.

Finish the soup at the last minute with unsalted butter or cream, allowing 75 g (3 oz) to every 1 l (2 pts) of soup. Add away from the heat, so that the soup is hot but not boiling. Never boil a soup after butter has been added; the flavour will be spoilt and some of the nutritional value lost.

Velouté Soups

Veloutés are made from butter, flour and a liquid ingredient. A purée of poultry, game, fish, shellfish or vegetables and a liaison of egg yolks and cream are added to finish the soup.

The method of preparation is always the same.

Melt the butter in a heavy saucepan. Add an equal weight of flour, mix and cook gently for 15 minutes, stirring frequently with a wooden spoon. Do not let this mixture brown or turn golden – it must stay white. Let it cool to prevent lumps forming and then pour in the boiling liquid, a little at a time, stirring vigorously all the while. The liquid used is white stock made from meat, poultry, game or fish, or milk. Bring to the boil, stirring continuously, and leave on a very low heat to simmer gently for 35 minutes.

While cooking a skin will form on the surface of the velouté and this should be removed from time to time with any impurities from the flour and cooked butter which rise to the top. After 35 minutes strain the velouté and bring it back to the boil. Now add the purée called for in the particular recipe. Away from the heat add the liaison of egg yolks and cream, first diluted with a little velouté to prevent the egg yolks setting hard. Heat the soup to about 185°F (85°C), whisking all the time. Do not let it boil.

The soup should be creamy and the consistency of a very light sauce.

Note: To thicken the soup, take it off the heat so that it is no longer boiling. Separate the yolks from the whites and place the yolks (allowing 3 for every 1 l (2 pts) of soup) in a bowl with 6 tablespoons of double cream. Take care to remove any little bits of egg white. Mix well together with a small whisk and little by little add $\frac{1}{4}$ l ($\frac{1}{2}$ pt) of soup, whisking all the time. Whisk the soup and pour in the liaison. Replace on the heat to start cooking the yolks, but remove from heat before it comes to the boil. Finish by adding 100 g (4 oz) of butter in small pieces to every 1 l (2 pts) of soup. Taste, correct the seasoning if necessary and serve.

Cream Soups

Cream soups are prepared in the same way as veloutés. However, the liquid used is always lightly salted milk, sometimes with a proportion of white stock. For the liaison double cream is used, without egg yolks.

―――

CREAM OF ASPARAGUS
Crème d'Argenteuil ou d'asperges

$\frac{3}{4}$ kg (1$\frac{1}{2}$ lb) thick white asparagus
1 l (2 pts) cream soup
1$\frac{1}{2}$ dl ($\frac{1}{4}$ pt) double cream
Seasoning

Peel and cut up the asparagus. Boil in salted water for 8 minutes. Drain and add to 1 l (2 pts) of cream soup. Continue cooking.

When the asparagus is tender, pour the soup into a fine sieve, rubbing through the pieces of asparagus to incorporate them into the soup.

Set the soup on the stove, bring to the boil and keep warm in a *bain-marie* (double boiler) until you are ready to serve it. Add the cream just before serving. If the soup is too thick, thin it with boiling milk. Correct the seasoning, and pour into a hot tureen.

175 g (6 oz) rice flour
or cornflour
½ l (1 pt) cold milk
1½ l (3 pts) stock
1 celery heart
6 tablespoons double
cream

CREAM OF CELERY
Crème de céleri

Mix the flour with cold milk. Heat the stock to boiling point
and pour in the mixture, whisking vigorously. Parboil the
celery heart and add. Cook slowly for 2 hours. Put in a sieve and
rub the celery through. Finish the soup with the cream.

225 g (8 oz) sorrel
75 g (3 oz) unsalted
butter
1 l (2 pts) good meat
stock
10 egg yolks
1½ dl (¼ pt) double
cream
Chervil
Croûtons, fried in
butter
Pinch cayenne pepper
(optional)

CREAM OF SORREL
Crème Germiny
For 4–6 people

This soup is one of the most delicate of all cream soups. It is very
simple to make, but it needs the same care as a *crème anglaise* (or
light custard sauce) which is made by the same principle.

Remove the stems of the sorrel, and chop. Soften the sorrel in
25 g (1 oz) of butter in a saucepan; then add the stock.

Bring to the boil.

While the soup is boiling, combine the egg yolks and the
cream in a bowl. Mix well, stirring with a spatula, and very slowly
pour into the sorrel soup, off the flame. Return to a low heat; if
you are not very experienced use a *bain-marie* (double-boiler).
Cook as you would a custard sauce, stirring the soup continuously
until it becomes creamy, without letting it boil. As soon as it
has reached the proper consistency, remove from the flame and add
50 g (2 oz) of butter and some chopped chervil or chervil leaves.
Pour immediately into a soup tureen in which there are some
tiny croûtons fried in butter.

This soup should be completed just before serving; it should not
be allowed to stand. Correct the seasoning, and add a pinch of
cayenne pepper, if you wish.

20 crayfish, 40 g (1½
oz) each
125 g (5 oz) rice
1 l (2 pts) white
stock
50 g (2 oz) diced
carrots, core
removed
50 g (2 oz) diced
onion
125 g (5 oz) unsalted
butter
1 sprig thyme
1 bay leaf fragment
1 parsley stalk
½ glass cognac
1 glass dry white
wine
1½ dl (¼ pt) double
cream

CRAYFISH BISQUE
Bisque d'écrivisses

Wash the rice carefully and cook it quickly in two-thirds of the stock. Meanwhile cut the carrot and the onion into tiny dice (*mirepoix*) and cook slowly, without letting them brown, in a pat of butter in a frying pan.

Add the thyme, bay leaf and parsley. Raise the flame and add the crayfish to the *mirepoix*. Add salt and pepper. Sauté rapidly; the crayfish will turn red immediately. Moisten with the cognac, ignite and extinguish immediately by pouring in the white wine; cook for 8 minutes.

Shell the crayfish. Set aside the tails for the garnish and pound the shells in a mortar. Add the pounded shells to the rice and the cooking liquid from the crayfish and rub this mixture through a sieve.

Put this purée in a saucepan and add the rest of the stock. Bring to the boil and keep hot in a *bain-marie*.

At the last minute finish with the rest of the butter, cut into small pieces, and the cream. Correct the seasoning and serve, garnished with the diced crayfish tails.

CREAM OF WATERCRESS AND SORREL
Crème de cresson et d'oseille

Follow the directions for a velouté soup (page 92), add the watercress (half a bunch per 1 l (2 pts) of soup) to the hot cream soup. Cook for 5 minutes and rub through a sieve. The sorrel is added to the soup just before serving, about 1 teaspoon per serving, finely shredded and wilted in unsalted butter. Finish the soup with a pinch of chervil and small croûtons fried in butter.

CREAM OF LOBSTER
Crème de homard

Prepare a 600–700-g (1–1½-lb) lobster as for lobster *à l'américaine* (page 203). Crush the lobster in a mortar and rub it through a very fine sieve; then put it through cheesecloth.

Add the lobster to ¾ l (1½ pts) of cream soup. Correct the consistency by adding double cream.

CHICKEN VELOUTÉ WITH ASPARAGUS TIPS
Velouté princesse

2 l (4 pts) velouté soup, made with chicken stock
Chicken breasts
6 tablespoons double cream
100 g (4 oz) unsalted butter
6 egg yolks
Asparagus tips

Prepare the velouté soup, using stock made with a tender chicken.

Remove the meat from the chicken breast and skin it; pound in a mortar with the cream and butter. Rub through a very fine strainer and reserve in a bowl.

Thicken the soup with the egg yolks, following the velouté recipe.

Just before serving, correct the seasoning and finish the soup with the purée of chicken and cream. Garnish with tips of green asparagus, cooked in salted water.

Purée Soups

PEA SOUP
Purée de pois

350 g (12 oz) split
   peas
$1\frac{1}{2}$ l (3 pts) water
$2\frac{1}{2}$ teaspoons salt
$2\frac{1}{2}$ teaspoons sugar
50 g (2 oz) pork fat
   or bacon
2 tablespoons diced
   carrot
1 onion
Parsley
Small leek
Sprig thyme
$\frac{1}{2}$ bay leaf
Stock or milk (to
   finish)
Pat *beurre manié*
75 g (3 oz) unsalted
   butter
Croûtons fried in
   butter
Chervil

Wash the split peas, pick them over, wash in several changes of water until it becomes absolutely clear; soak for 2 or 3 hours in cold water.

In a saucepan combine the drained peas with the water, salt and sugar. Bring to the boil, and skim carefully. Add a *mirepoix* made with the bacon or pork fat diced, scalded and sautéed with the diced carrot and onion. Add a bouquet made of a few sprigs of parsley, a small leek, a sprig of thyme and $\frac{1}{2}$ bay leaf. Cook for 2 hours, then sieve. Return to the saucepan and thin to the proper consistency by adding stock or milk. Bring to the boil and add a pat of *beurre manié*. Finish with the unsalted butter added away from the flame.

Serve with small croûtons fried in butter and a few chervil leaves.

Note: The thickening with the *beurre manié* prevents the pea purée separating from the liquid and sinking to the bottom of the bowl after the soup is served. The same result can be obtained with some croûtons fried in butter and simmered with the peas.

POTATO SOUP
Potage Parmentier

2 leeks, white part
   only
75 g (3 oz) unsalted
   butter
1 pound floury
   potatoes, peeled and
   cut into quarters
1 l (2 pts) stock or
   water
Milk
15 g ($\frac{1}{2}$ oz) *beurre
   manié*
2 tablespoons double
   cream
Croûtons, fried in
   butter
Chervil

Wash and slice the leeks, and cook slowly in 25 g (1 oz) of butter. Add the potatoes. Pour over the stock or water; if water is used, salt to taste. Cook 25 minutes. Sieve, mashing the leeks through. Return the purée to the saucepan, and add enough milk to thin the soup to the desired consistency. Bring to the boil, adding the *beurre manié* in small pieces. Finish the soup away from the flame with the cream and 50 g (2 oz) of butter.

Serve with small croûtons fried in butter and a few chervil leaves.

WATERCRESS SOUP
Potage cressonière

First method

Follow the recipe for *potage Parmentier* (above), using a handful of watercress instead of leeks. Garnish with a few leaves of blanched watercress.

Second method

Wash a bunch of watercress carefully. Cut it coarsely and cook gently in 25 g (1 oz) of unsalted butter for a few minutes. As soon as the cress is wilted, add 225 g ($\frac{1}{2}$ lb) of floury potatoes, sliced, and pour over 1 l (2 pts) of stock or water. If using water, add salt to taste.

Cook for 20 minutes. Put through a sieve and return to the saucepan. Bring to the boil, and correct the consistency of the soup with boiling milk.

Add butter or cream off the flame.

CAULIFLOWER SOUP
Potage Dubarry ou crème de chou-fleur

500 g (lb) cauliflower
175 g (6 oz) unsalted butter
350 g ($\frac{3}{4}$ lb) new potatoes, peeled and quartered
1 l (2 pts) milk
$\frac{1}{4}$ l ($\frac{1}{2}$ pt) stock or water
Salt
Milk or double cream
Chervil
Croûtons, fried in butter

Clean and blanch the cauliflower. Rinse and drain. Put in a saucepan with 100 g (4 oz) of melted butter; stew for 20 minutes. Add the potatoes, milk, stock or water and salt. Cook slowly for 20 minutes.

Put through a sieve, mashing all the vegetables through. Put the purée into a saucepan, bring to the boil, and off the flame add boiling milk or cream to give it the proper consistency.

Add the rest of the butter to the soup just before serving. Add a few chervil leaves and croûtons diced small and fried in butter.

LEEK AND POTATO SOUP
Potage poireaux et pommes de terre

5–6 medium-sized leeks, white part only

100 g (4 oz) unsalted butter

1 l (2 pts) stock or water

Salt

500 g (1 lb) floury potatoes

Slices bread

Wash and cut the leeks into strips; stew in 50 g (2 oz) of butter. Pour over the stock or water. Check the seasoning, and add salt if necessary. Simmer slowly for 1 hour, then add the potatoes, peeled and cut into very thin, even slices. Continue cooking for another 20 minutes.

Pour into a soup tureen containing slices of bread dried in the oven and spread with butter.

STOCKS AND SAUCES

Sauces, with all their variety and subtlety, are the glory of French cooking, and this chapter is therefore a key one. However, I will confine it to sauces which are within the scope of the home cook, leaving out complicated recipes which demand years of professional experience and extensive preparations impractical in the average kitchen.

Sauces are divided into two main categories, white and brown.

Some are made with a roux (white, pale or brown) moistened with milk or specially prepared stock; others with egg yolks combined with butter, cream or oil; others are *coulis* or liquid purées, sometimes based on meat stock.

The white sauces, béchamel and velouté, and brown espagnole sauce are the basic sauces which have given rise to a host of other sauces, some of which are listed in this chapter.

Béchamel is made with a white roux and milk, velouté with a pale roux and white stock, espagnole with a brown roux and brown stock. In household cookery ordinary broth may be used instead of these specially prepared stocks, but the sauce will not have such a good flavour.

Stocks

In the soup chapter I have included the recipe for the classic *pot-au-feu* which provides an ordinary white or brown broth.

BROWN STOCK
Jus ou fond brun
For 2 l (4 pts)

1 kg (2 lb) veal meat
225 g ($\frac{1}{2}$ lb) bones
1 medium carrot
2 medium onions
100 g (4 oz) pork rind
3 l (6 pts) water
Bouquet garni
Salt

To prepare this use veal meat and bones: knuckle, loin, neck, shoulder or breast.

In a buttered or greased roasting pan, spread the meat, cut into cubes, and the bones, broken into small pieces; brown in 375°F (190°C, gas mark 5) oven. Stir frequently until the meat is well browned.

Meanwhile peel and slice the vegetables and put them into a large saucepan. Cover them with the pork rind; then put the browned meat and bones on top. Let the pot stand for 10 minutes at the side of the stove or over a very low flame to allow the vegetables to sweat their juices. Pour 1 cup of boiling water into the roasting pan and stir to dissolve the substances that have stuck to it; then pour this water into the saucepan, bring to the boil and reduce by half. Do this last step again, adding another cup of water. Be careful to turn off the heat when the liquid has thickened and it is reduced to 1 tablespoon. This procedure is called *faire tomber à glace* (reducing to a glaze).

Then add the rest of the water, the bouquet garni and a good pinch of salt. Slowly bring to boiling point. Skim, and place the pot on a low flame and cook very slowly, partially covered, for about 5 hours.

Then strain the stock through a very fine sieve into a bowl. Let it stand 15 minutes; then carefully remove the fat, which can be used for other dishes. When the stock is cool, strain it through cheesecloth into another bowl. Discard the sediment at the bottom of the bowl.

The stock made in this way will be clear, well-flavoured and a beautiful amber colour.

In traditional French cooking, this stock was called *blond de veau*.

WHITE STOCK
Jus ou fond blanc

White stock is prepared exactly like brown stock except that the meat is not browned.

The clarity characteristic of a white stock is obtained by boiling the stock slowly and watching it very carefully.

BROWN OR WHITE CHICKEN STOCK
Fond de volaille brun ou blanc

To the respective recipes above add 1 boiling fowl or the giblets of 4 chickens. For a white stock do not brown the ingredients.

GAME STOCK
Fond de gibier

Use the cheaper cuts of large game, venison for example, or use a hare or rabbit, allowing about 2 kg (4 lb) weight, plus a partridge, an old pheasant or several carcases.

Add a medium-sized carrot, a medium-sized onion, a sprig of sage, a few juniper berries, and a bouquet garni. Follow the recipe for brown stock (page 103) to brown the meat and bones and to cook the vegetables.

After browning the game in the oven add 1 glass of dry white wine and 2½ l (5 pts) of water. Cook very slowly for 4 hours.

FISH STOCK
Fond de poisson dit 'fumet de poisson'

For 1 l (2 pts) water:
1 kg (2 lb) fish or sole bones
2 large onions, sliced thinly
Parsley or parsley root
2 tablespoons mushroom peel or stalks
Juice of ¼ lemon
Salt

For this recipe use any readily available white fish such as hake, whiting, cod or haddock. However, none of these can compare with sole bones which alone can produce an authentic fish stock.

The procedure is very simple.

In a deep pot, put the fish or sole bones with the cold water. After the water starts to boil, skim, add the onions, a few sprigs of parsley or a parsley root, the mushroom peel or stalks, lemon juice and a pinch of salt. Fish stock is almost always intended to be reduced for use in sauces or combined with butter or cream without a roux or egg yolks. That is why no salt or very little is added to a fish stock.

Reduce the heat, and boil slowly for 30 minutes. Strain through a cloth into a glazed bowl and keep cool.

Courts-bouillons

COURT-BOUILLON FOR VARIOUS DISHES
Blanc pour cuissons diverses
For 1 l (2 pts)

For 1 l (2 pts) water:
8 g (¼ oz) salt
1 tablespoon flour
2 teaspoons vinegar
    or juice of ½ lemon

Optional ingredients:
1 onion stuck with 1
    clove
1 medium-sized
    carrot, quartered
Bouquet garni
2 tablespoons
    chopped suet

The expression *blanc* describes a court-bouillon made from water, salt, flour and vinegar or, in certain cases, lemon juice.

Mix the flour and the water before placing them on the heat. Then slowly bring to the boil.

Add a garnish of vegetables, such as onions, carrots and a bouquet garni.

When the court-bouillon is to be used to cook offal, add some raw chopped suet which will melt during cooking to form a protective layer to keep out the air, which would darken the ingredients.

Cook the stock for 30 minutes; strain it through a fine sieve, and let it cool. Use it when required for a recipe.

This court-bouillon is used for cooking offal, for such delicacies as cocks' combs or kidneys, and for certain vegetables such as artichoke hearts, cardoons (a vegetable in the artichoke family) or salsify. The suet is omitted for vegetables.

COURT-BOUILLON FOR MUSHROOMS
Cuisson ou blanc pour champignons

1½ dl (¼ pt) water
Salt
50 g (2 oz) unsalted
    butter
Juice of ½ lemon
300 g (10 oz)
    mushrooms,
    cleaned and quickly
    washed

Bring the water to the boil; add a pinch of salt, the butter and lemon juice. Return to a fast boil and add the mushrooms. Boil rapidly for 5 minutes, then pour into a glazed earthenware pot and cover with a piece of buttered paper to prevent any contact with air.

Roux

The roux is the thickening element of the sauce, except for such emulsified sauces as hollandaise or béarnaise, in which the roux is replaced by egg yolks. The roux must be cooked with care and attention.

A roux may be brown, pale or white. In all three cases, the proportions are identical: 50 g (2 oz) of butter to 60 g (2½ oz) of flour.

Method.   Melt the butter and cook it until it is clarified, that is, when the moisture in the butter has evaporated. Add the flour, and blend it into the butter with a spatula or wooden spoon.

Heat the mixture slowly and cook very gently to allow the active element of the flour – the starch – to turn into dextrin, a soluble substance that has the property of thickening a liquid.

Stir frequently, and if you want a brown roux, continue cooking until it reaches the desired colour. Cook the roux less for a pale roux, and even less for a white one.

Any roux must be cooked for at least 15 minutes.

The roux can be prepared in advance and kept in a cool place in an earthenware pot.

A roux is always used cold. To avoid lumps when mixing it with a boiling liquid, follow these directions:

Put the roux into the saucepan in which the sauce or soup will be cooked. Dilute the roux by adding a small amount of boiling liquid (stock, bouillon or milk) and mixing with a whisk; the result should resemble a paste. When the mixture is very smooth, repeat the operation, adding liquid and at the same time heating slowly to boiling point until the flour absorbs the entire quantity of liquid specified.

Note: In making brown sauce, I recommend the method called *torréfaction* (roasting) of the dry flour. This thickener is less perishable and very simple to make. Spread the flour on a baking sheet, and brown it in a 325°F (170°C, gas mark 3) oven. Store the browned flour in a tightly sealed jar, so that it is ready for use at any time. Dilute it with the cold liquid and then bring to the boil.

Basic Sauces

A brown roux combined with brown stock as described above, produces espagnole sauce; if the roux is pale-coloured and the liquid ingredient is a white stock, the sauce is called a velouté; if the liquid ingredient is milk, the sauce is a béchamel.

⚜━━━━━━━━━━━━━━━━━━━━━━━━━━━━━━━━━⚜

ESPAGNOLE SAUCE
Sauce espagnole
For 1 l (2 pts)

50 g (2 oz) diced
   bacon or fat pork
1 medium carrot,
   finely diced
1 medium onion,
   finely diced
1 sprig thyme
Piece of bay leaf
175 g (6 oz) cooked
   brown roux
2 l (4 pts) veal stock
   or brown bouillon,
   lightly salted
½ glass dry white
   wine
1½ dl (¼ pt) thick
   tomato purée

Melt the pork fat or bacon in the pot in which you are going to cook the espagnole sauce. Add the diced vegetables and seasonings and cook slowly until lightly browned.

Drain off the melted fat or lard, add the roux, the stock or other liquid (following the instructions above), and then add the white wine.

Cook on a low flame and simmer 2 hours, skimming frequently to remove the impurities and the fat that rises to the top.

If the roux has not been prepared in advance, it should be cooked first, in the same pot. Then brown the diced vegetables in a small frying pan, and add. Deglaze the frying pan by pouring in the white wine and stirring up the brown bits on the bottom; add the flavoured wine to the sauce, and continue cooking for 2 hours as above.

At this point, strain the sauce through a fine sieve, then return it to the stove and add the thick tomato purée (page 507).

Cook very slowly for another hour, skimming frequently.

If the sauce is not to be used for a while, strain it through a fine sieve into a glazed earthenware bowl and stir it very frequently with a wooden spoon until it is completely cool; this prevents the formation of a thick skin and lumps.

⚜━━━━━━━━━━━━━━━━━━━━━━━━━━━━━━━━━⚜

RICH BROWN SAUCE
Demi-glace

The demi-glace sauce is a derivative of espagnole sauce. The sauce has been reduced to two-thirds of its volume and then brought to the desired consistency by adding a rich, well-flavoured veal stock. This explains why the basic sauces and the stocks with which they are made should always be salted very lightly.

Finish the demi-glace sauce away from the heat with some Madeira.

VELOUTÉ OR WHITE SAUCE
Sauce velouté ou sauce blanche

This sauce is made by mixing a pale roux with white stock or bouillon, about 125 g (5 oz) of roux to 1 l (2 pts) of liquid.

Proceed following the recipe given for the roux; cook slowly for an hour and a half and skim as directed for espagnole sauce.

The French word velouté means velvety and the sauce should fit this description.

THICK VELOUTÉ SAUCE
Sauce allemande appelée aussi sauce parisienne

1 l (2 pts) velouté sauce
5 egg yolks
Pinch coarse-ground pepper
Pinch grated nutmeg
4 tablespoons cooking juice from mushrooms
½ teaspoon lemon juice
125 g (5 oz) unsalted butter

Just as demi-glace sauce is a derivative of espagnole, this sauce is a derivative of velouté.

It is a velouté sauce thickened with egg yolks. To thicken *allemande* sauce properly, proceed in the following manner:

Method.   Bring the velouté sauce to the boil; reduce until it reaches the consistency of light cream, stirring constantly with a wooden spoon. The sauce should become shiny and should coat the wooden spoon evenly. Put the egg yolks, a pinch of coarse-ground black pepper, a pinch of grated nutmeg, the cooking juice from mushrooms, lemon juice and 25 g (1 oz) of unsalted butter in a bowl.

With a whisk, beat the egg-yolk mixture, pouring some of the velouté sauce into it, a tablespoon at a time. Then, off the flame, slowly pour the thickening ingredients into the sauce with your left hand while you beat the velouté vigorously with your right. Put the sauce back on the stove and heat it slowly to boiling point, whisking continuously.

Remove from the flame immediately, and strain the sauce through a fine sieve into an earthenware pot. Continue stirring until the sauce is completely cool.

Just before using the sauce, correct the seasoning, and away from the flame mix in the remaining butter. After this sauce has been thickened, it should not be boiled except to preserve it.

Sauce suprême

1 l (2 pts) velouté
sauce
1 l (2 pts) chicken
stock, reduced to
$\frac{1}{4}$ l ($\frac{1}{2}$ pt)
3 dl ($\frac{1}{2}$ pt) double
cream
100 g (4 oz) unsalted
butter

This very fine sauce is derived from velouté sauce, with rich chicken stock and double cream added.

Method. In a small, heavy saucepan combine the velouté and reduced chicken stock. Bring this to boiling point on a high flame, stirring continuously with a wooden spoon. Little by little, as the sauce is reduced, add two-thirds of the cream. Continue this reduction until the mass of the velouté, the stock and the cream have reduced to one-third their original volume. At that point, strain the sauce through a fine sieve, correct the seasoning, and finish by stirring to prevent a skin from forming and adding the rest of the cream and the butter.

This sauce should be light, glossy and full of flavour.

BÉCHAMEL SAUCE
Sauce béchamel

For 125 g (5 oz) roux:
1 l (2 pts) milk
50 g (2 oz) veal
25 g (1 oz) unsalted
butter
1 onion, finely
chopped
Sprig thyme
Pinch crushed pepper
Pinch grated nutmeg
Pinch salt

Prepare a white roux and, for each 125 g (5 oz) of roux, add 1 l (2 pts) of milk. Bring to the boil, stirring continuously to obtain a perfectly smooth sauce. Then add 50 g (2 oz) of lean white veal, diced and cooked gently in butter with the onion, thyme, pepper, nutmeg and salt.

Cook slowly for an hour. Pour the sauce through a sieve taking care not to dislodge the particles that stick to the sides of the saucepan, which generally get somewhat browned during cooking. Strain the sauce into a glazed earthenware bowl.

Film the surface of the sauce with butter to avoid skin and lumps forming.

To save time or money the veal can be omitted entirely. Obviously, the flavour of the sauce will not be so rich.

This sauce can also be prepared without meat; replace the veal with white fish.

BUTTER SAUCE
Sauce au beurre

125 g (5 oz) unsalted
  butter
50 g (2 oz) flour
3 dl ($\frac{1}{2}$ pt) very hot
  water
Pinch salt
Few drops lemon
  juice (optional)
2 egg yolks

Make a pale roux with 50 g (2 oz) of flour and just over 50 g (2 oz) of butter. Cook the roux for 15 minutes, let it cool; then add the very hot water, whisking the mixture vigorously to obtain a smooth paste. Add a pinch of salt and, if the recipe calls for it, a few drops of lemon juice. Bring to the boil, remove from the flame and add 50 g (2 oz) or more of unsalted butter. This sauce should be creamy, and can be finished with a little more lemon juice. Finally, thicken the sauce with 2 egg yolks, as in the recipe for *allemande* sauce but do not bring to the boil.

Note: The butter and the flour can be mixed without cooking a roux: stir the flour into softened butter and moisten with water that is nearly boiling. Bring to the boil, then remove from the flame to add the final butter. The result is just as good.

TOMATO SAUCE
Sauce tomate
For 1 l (2 pts)

50 g (2 oz) fat pork
  or bacon
1 medium-sized
  carrot, diced finely
1 medium-sized
  onion, diced finely
Sprig thyme
$\frac{1}{2}$ bay leaf
25 g (1 oz) unsalted
  butter
15 g ($\frac{1}{2}$ oz) flour
1·5 kg (3 lb) very ripe
  tomatoes, juice and
  seeds removed
4 garlic cloves
Pinch salt
Pepper
3 dl ($\frac{1}{2}$ pt) white
  stock
2 cubes sugar
1 scant tablespoon
  wine vinegar

Prepare a *mirepoix* with the pork or bacon, a carrot, an onion, thyme, a bay leaf and butter. Mix everything together and sauté until lightly browned in the pan in which the sauce will be made. Sprinkle with the flour. Mix and cook gently like a pale roux. Add the tomatoes, garlic, salt, a little pepper, white stock and 2 cubes sugar, melted until they are beginning to take on a light caramel colour. Deglaze with wine vinegar.

Bring to the boil while stirring. Then cook gently, covered, in a 275°F (140°C, gas mark 1) oven for at least 1$\frac{1}{2}$ hours.

Strain, then bring to the boil again and remove any sediment; pour into a glazed bowl and store until ready to use. Dab the surface with unsalted butter to prevent a skin forming.

Compound Brown Sauces

THICKENED STOCK
Jus lié

1 l (2 pts) brown veal stock
1 teaspoon arrowroot or cornflour or, preferably, 1 teaspoon tapioca

Bring the veal stock to the boil and cook until reduced by three-quarters. Then thicken with 1 teaspoon arrowroot or cornflower mixed with a little cold veal stock. Boil 2–3 minutes; keep warm.

The sauce should be clear and smooth, the consistency of the juices left in a casserole after a piece of veal has been braised in it.

The use of cornflower or arrowroot as a thickening agent is a culinary trick that gives an appetizing appearance but it rather spoils the flavour. It is better to use tapioca instead in the quantity specified. The tapioca must be cooked at least 15 minutes, barely bubbling, so that the gravy remains clear.

RED WINE SAUCE WITH BEEF MARROW
Sauce bordelaise

25 g (1 oz) unsalted butter
1 teaspoon chopped shallot
1 glass red Bordeaux wine
Pinch crushed pepper
Small piece bay leaf
Sprig thyme
1½ dl (¼ pt) demi-glace sauce (preferably) or espagnole sauce
50 g (2 oz) beef marrow, very fresh

In a saucepan, heat 15 g (½ oz) of butter. When the butter is very hot, add the shallots; brown lightly. Add the wine and seasoning, bring the sauce to the boil, and reduce rapidly until 2 tablespoons remain. Add the demi-glace sauce and boil for 15 minutes. Strain the sauce through a very fine sieve; bring to the boil again, correct the seasoning and set aside until ready to serve. Poach the marrow in a bowl of lightly salted hot water for 3–5 minutes. Drain and set aside. When ready to serve, warm the sauce slightly. Off the flame, add the rest of the butter to the sauce, stirring continuously with a wooden spoon while adding the marrow.

MADEIRA SAUCE WITH MUSHROOMS
Sauce madère et champignons

225 g (8 oz) mushrooms, small and very white
50 g (2 oz) unsalted butter
½ l (1 pt) demi-glace sauce (preferably) or espagnole sauce
½ glass Madeira

Clean mushrooms and wash rapidly; do not let mushrooms stand in water or they will turn brown.

Heat about 15 g (½ oz) of butter in a sauté pan. When the butter is very hot and starting to turn brown add the mushrooms, drained, and sauté rapidly over a high flame; then add the demi-glace sauce. Boil the Madeira to reduce it slightly; then away from the flame add it, slightly cooled, to the sauce. Add the rest of the butter while stirring.

Correct the seasoning before serving.

MADEIRA SAUCE
Sauce madère

This sauce is the same as the one above but made with mushroom trimmings or stems, which are then strained through a fine sieve before the sauce is finished with the Madeira and the butter.

WHITE WINE SAUCE WITH ONION AND GHERKINS
Sauce charcutière

1 medium sized onion, chopped finely
75 g (3 oz) butter
1 glass dry white wine
3 dl (½ pt) demi-glace or espagnole sauce
50 g (2 oz) small gherkins, chopped or sliced

In a small sauté pan melt 15 g (½ oz) of butter; when the butter is very hot, add the onion. Brown slowly, then pour in the white wine. Reduce the mixture until 2 tablespoons remain; add the demi-glace or espagnole sauce. Cook slowly for 15 minutes; then, just before serving, away from the flame add the rest of the butter and the gherkins, stirring continuously.

~~~~~~

PIQUANT SAUCE WITH ONION, SHALLOTS AND GHERKINS
Sauce piquante

1 medium-sized onion, chopped finely

2 large shallots, chopped finely

75 g (3 oz) butter

3 tablespoons red wine vinegar, reduced to 2 teaspoons

3 dl ($\frac{1}{2}$ pt) demi-glace or espagnole sauce

2 medium-sized gherkins, chopped

Freshly ground pepper

Finely chop 1 medium onion and 2 shallots. Heat 15 g ($\frac{1}{2}$ oz) of butter in a sauté pan, add the onion and shallots, and cook slowly until they begin to soften; when lightly browned, add the reduced wine vinegar and demi-glace or espagnole sauce.

Cook slowly for 15 minutes, and away from the flame add the rest of the butter. Finish the sauce by adding the gherkins and a few turns of the pepper mill.

Sauce Robert

This is a *sauce piquante* (recipe above) to which 2 teaspoons of mustard and a pinch of caster sugar are added just before the butter.

Never let the mustard boil.

~~~~~~

TARRAGON SAUCE
Sauce à l'estragon

1 glass dry white wine reduced by half

Sprig tarragon

3 dl ($\frac{1}{2}$ pt) demi-glace or espagnole sauce or thickened stock

50 g (2 oz) unsalted butter

1 teaspoon chopped tarragon leaves

Reduce the wine, add the tarragon sprig, and let stand for 10 minutes. Then add the demi-glace or espagnole sauce, or thickened stock. Reduce the sauce by one-third, strain through a very fine sieve, then away from the flame add the butter.

Season with 1 teaspoon of chopped tarragon leaves.

MUSHROOM SAUCE
Sauce gratin

225 g (8 oz)
  mushrooms
50 g (2 oz) unsalted
  butter
6 shallots, chopped
1 glass dry white
  wine
½ l (1 pt) demi-glace
  or espagnole sauce
Sprigs parsley
Juice ¼ lemon

Clean and wash the mushrooms quickly and drain immediately. In a sauté pan, heat 15 g (½ oz) of butter until light brown; add the shallots and cook slowly. Then add the mushrooms, finely chopped at the last moment to keep them from turning brown. Cook the mushrooms on a very high flame. Stirring constantly let the juices reduce. Add the white wine and reduce it almost completely. Then add the demi-glace or espagnole sauce.

Simmer over a low flame for 10 minutes. Finish the sauce off the flame by adding the remaining butter and, at the last minute, 1 teaspoon of chopped parsley and the juice of ¼ lemon. This sauce should be quite thick.

MUSHROOM SAUCE WITH TOMATOES
Sauce chasseur

50 g (2 oz) unsalted
  butter
2 tablespoons oil
100 g (4 oz)
  mushrooms, white
  and firm
1 teaspoon chopped
  shallots
3 ripe tomatoes
  (preferably) or 3
  tablespoons tomato
  purée
½ glass dry white
  wine
2 dl (¼ pt) demi-glace
  or espagnole sauce
Chopped chervil and
  tarragon

In a sauté pan heat the butter and the oil, add the mushrooms, sliced finely or chopped; brown on a high flame. At that point add the shallots and heat for a few seconds. If you are using fresh tomatoes remove the stems and the skin, the seeds and the juice; chop coarsely and add to the sauce after the shallots. If you are using tomato purée, first add the white wine and reduce by one-half. Finally add the demi-glace or espagnole sauce and tomato purée.

Off the flame, just before serving, finish the sauce by adding the rest of the butter and a sprinkling of chopped chervil and tarragon.

PEPPERY SAUCE
Sauce diable

Follow the recipe for *sauce charcutière* (page 113), but omit the gherkins and replace the onions with 3 shallots. Strain the sauce through a fine sieve and spice it heavily with freshly ground black pepper or a pinch of cayenne pepper. However I do not really recommend cayenne – it is not so much a flavour as a fire that burns the palate.

BROWN SAUCE WITH HAM AND MUSHROOMS
Sauce italienne

50 g (2 oz) unsalted butter
100 g (4 oz) very white mushrooms, chopped
1 teaspoon chopped shallots
½ glass dry white wine
1 tablespoon thick tomato purée or 3 ripe tomatoes
2 dl (¼ pt) demi-glace or espagnole sauce
50 g (2 oz) finely diced lean ham
¼ lemon
Chopped parsley

In a frying pan heat 15 g (½ oz) of butter; add chopped mushrooms and brown lightly; add shallots and white wine. Reduce the mixture to 2 tablespoons; add tomato purée or the ripe tomatoes, peeled, seeded and chopped. Reduce the mixture again, and add the demi-glace or espagnole sauce and the ham.

Boil slowly for 10 minutes; off the flame add the butter and lemon juice. Correct the seasoning, and finish the sauce with a pinch of chopped parsley.

This sauce is also very good with a pinch of chopped tarragon, depending on how it is to be used.

MADEIRA SAUCE WITH TRUFFLES (1)
Sauce Périgueux

Prepare a Madeira sauce (page 113); finish by adding, for ½ l (1 pt) of sauce, 100 g (4 oz) of chopped truffles. If you are using canned truffles, add the juice in which they come. If they are fresh, chop them raw, then sauté quickly in hot butter for a few seconds and pour the truffles and butter into the Madeira sauce.

MADEIRA SAUCE WITH TRUFFLES (2)
Sauce périgourdine

This sauce is the same as the one above, but the truffles here are sliced extremely thin instead of being chopped.

PORT SAUCE
Sauce au vin de Porto

Follow the recipe for Madeira sauce (page 113), replacing the Madeira wine with port. Finish this sauce by adding the juice of a very ripe and very sweet orange and the juice of $\frac{1}{2}$ lemon.

RED WINE SAUCE
Sauce au vin rouge

1 large onion, diced
1 medium-sized carrot (core removed), diced
50 g (2 oz) unsalted butter
2 garlic cloves, crushed
$\frac{1}{2}$ l (1 pt) red wine
Pinch salt
Pinch sugar
$\frac{1}{2}$ l (1 pt) demi-glace or espagnole sauce

Cook the onion and carrot gently in 15 g ($\frac{1}{2}$ oz) of butter for 20 minutes, stirring often; do not let the mixture brown. When this *mirepoix* is well cooked, add the garlic. Heat the mixture for a minute and pour in the red wine. Season with a pinch of salt and a pinch of sugar. Reduce the sauce to two-thirds, then add the demi-glace or espagnole sauce, cook slowly for 20 minutes. Strain through a fine sieve, pushing the vegetables through. Bring the sauce back to the boil; finish away from the flame by adding the rest of the butter.

BORDELAISE SAUCE WITH DUCK LIVERS
Sauce rouennaise

½ l (1 pt) bordelaise sauce prepared without marrowbones (page 112)
3 raw duck livers
1 tablespoon cognac
50 g (2 oz) unsalted butter or purée of *foie gras*
Freshly ground pepper

Prepare bordelaise sauce without any marrowbones. Rub the duck livers through a very fine sieve into a bowl and dilute with a little bordelaise sauce. Heat the sauce. When it is hot but not boiling, add the duck livers, stirring continuously until it reaches the boiling point.

Remove from the heat and strain through a fine sieve – the livers should then be completely incorporated into the sauce, giving it a creamy appearance. Finish by adding the cognac and butter or *foie gras*.

Correct the seasonings. Spice with a couple of turns of the pepper mill.

PEPPER SAUCE
Sauce poivrade
For game

1 medium-sized carrot (core removed), diced very finely
2 medium-sized onions, diced finely
1 celery stalk, diced finely
25 g (1 oz) unsalted butter
½ l (1 pt) game marinade
¾ l (1½ pt) demi-glace or espagnole sauce
Game trimmings or carcasses
Freshly ground pepper
1 teaspoon redcurrant jelly (optional)
1 teaspoon Dijon mustard (optional)

Cook the carrot, onions and celery in the butter until they are lightly browned.

Pour over a pint of liquid drained from the marinade in which the game has steeped. Reduce by two-thirds and add the demi-glace or espagnole sauce, and the carcases or trimmings from the game.

Cook covered, on a low flame, for 3 hours.

Strain through a fine sieve, pressing the vegetables and the game trimmings well.

Deglaze the meat juices in the pan in which the game has roasted and add to the sauce. Away from the flame add, if liked, 1 teaspoon of redcurrant jelly and 1 teaspoon of Dijon mustard. Do not let the sauce boil again.

Season with freshly ground pepper.

TOMATO SAUCE WITH GARLIC
Sauce portugaise

1 large onion
2 tablespoons oil
700 g (1½ lb) ripe
  tomatoes
3 garlic cloves,
  crushed
Salt
Pepper
Sugar
Bouquet garni
50 g (2 oz) unsalted
  butter

Finely chop the onion; brown lightly in the oil. Add the large, ripe tomatoes, peeled, seeded, drained and chopped coarsely, the garlic, a pinch each of salt, pepper and sugar, and the bouquet garni.

Cook slowly for 30 minutes.

Correct the seasonings. If the sauce is not to be used to deglaze the pan juices of the dish it will accompany, before serving it, add the butter off the heat.

MUSHROOM SAUCE
Sauce duxelles

1 teaspoon chopped
  shallots
100 g (4 oz) unsalted
  butter
100 g (4 oz) white
  mushrooms
½ glass dry white
  wine
3 dl (½ pt) demi-glace
  or espagnole sauce,
  or veal stock and 2
  tablespoons tomato
  sauce
1 teaspoon chopped
  parsley

In a frying pan lightly brown the shallots in 50 g (2 oz) of butter. Add the mushrooms, cleaned, washed quickly and chopped finely.

Cook until dry on a high flame, then add the wine and cook until it evaporates. Add the demi-glace or espagnole sauce or a good veal stock; if you use veal stock, finish the sauce with 2 tablespoons of very thick and concentrated tomato sauce.

Cook for a few minutes, reducing the sauce by one-third.

Away from the flame add the rest of the butter and chopped parsley; correct the seasonings.

Note: For certain dishes, the duxelles is used without any liquid ingredients. Follow the instructions in the recipe.

MARROWBONE SAUCE
Sauce à la moelle
For vegetables

This sauce is prepared in the same way as bordelaise sauce (page 112), but the red wine is replaced by white wine and the quantity of marrowbone is doubled. Half the marrow should be diced and added to the sauce, while the other half should be sliced and added to the vegetables.

This sauce can also be served with poached eggs or *oeufs mollets*, or with grilled fish.

Compound White Sauces

½ l (1 pt) béchamel
  sauce
50 g (2 oz) grated
  Gruyère cheese
2 egg yolks
4 tablespoons cream
50 g (2 oz) unsalted
  butter

CHEESE SAUCE
Sauce Mornay

Bring the béchamel sauce to the boil. Add the grated Gruyère cheese. Boil, stirring until the cheese is completely melted. Take the pan off the flame so that it stops boiling, and thicken the sauce with the egg yolks mixed in a bowl with 1 tablespoon of cream (or milk). Heat gently, stirring quickly with a whisk, until it reaches boiling point.

Finish the sauce off the flame with 2 or 3 tablespoons of cream and the butter.

This sauce should be thick enough to cover the food with which it is served completely; although it looks thick, it must be creamy and well-flavoured.

When the sauce is to accompany fish, add some of the cooking juice, reduced.

½ l (1 pt) béchamel
   sauce (page 110)
1½ dl (¼ pt) double
   cream
50 g (2 oz) crayfish
   butter (page 29)

CRAYFISH SAUCE
Sauce Nantua

Prepare the béchamel sauce, add the cream. Reduce rapidly, stirring with a spatula, until it reaches the proper consistency – slightly thickened. Off the flame finish the sauce with the crayfish butter. Beat the sauce well and correct the seasoning.

LOBSTER SAUCE
Sauce cardinal

Follow the recipe above and finish the sauce with lobster butter (page 30) replacing the crayfish butter. This sauce is better if it is stronger than the Nantua sauce. To do this add 1½ dl (¼ pt) of strong fish stock (page 105) reduced to about 1 tablespoon. You can also add one tablespoon of truffle juice, when truffles are used to garnish the dish.

CAPER SAUCE
Sauce aux câpres commune

Mix a butter sauce (page 111) with capers, about 3 tablespoons for ½ l (1 pt) of sauce. Do not let sauce boil after adding the capers.

1 l (2 pts) béchamel
   sauce
3 dl (½ pt) double
   cream
50 g (2 oz) unsalted
   butter
Few drops lemon
   juice

CREAM SAUCE
Sauce crème

In a saucepan, mix the béchamel sauce and two-thirds of the cream. Bring to the boil, and then reduce the sauce on a high flame, stirring constantly with a spatula, until ¾ l (1½ pts) of sauce remain.

Strain through a fine sieve, bring back to the boil. Away from the flame add the rest of the cream, butter and lemon juice. Keep it hot in a *bain-marie* (double boiler). See that it does not boil again.

½ l (1 pt) velouté
sauce with fish
stock (page 105)
6 tablespoons fish
stock
½ glass dry white
wine reduced to 1
tablespoon
2 egg yolks
2 tablespoons double
cream
2 tablespoons cooking
juice from
mushrooms
100 g (4 oz) unsalted
butter

WHITE WINE SAUCE
Sauce au vin blanc
For fish

Prepare a velouté sauce made with concentrated fish stock, mixing in the fish stock and dry white wine reduced to 1 tablespoon; thicken with 2 egg yolks mixed with 2 tablespoons of cream and 2 tablespoons of cooking juice from mushrooms. Strain the sauce through a fine sieve; pour into a saucepan and, stirring constantly, heat to boiling point; add the butter away from the flame.

SHRIMP SAUCE
Sauce crevette

Use ½ l (1 pt) of white wine sauce and add 100 g (4 oz) of shrimp butter (page 29). This sauce should be a pale pink colour, which can be obtained by adding a little coloured butter – crayfish or lobster butter – or a little reduced tomato purée.

SHRIMP AND CRAYFISH SAUCE
Sauce Joinville

Prepare white wine sauce as above, and enrich it with the addition of as much butter as possible, consisting of half shrimp butter (page 29) and half crayfish butter (page 29). Finish the sauce with 1 tablespoon of truffles, cut into julienne, for each 3 dl (½ pt) of sauce.

BUTTER SAUCE WITH WHIPPED CREAM
Sauce Chantilly ou sauce mousseline commune

Prepare ½ l (1 pt) of butter sauce (page 111), and add, to finish it, 4 tablespoons of double cream, whipped until stiff with 1 tablespoon of milk. Be careful not to beat too long, or the cream may turn into butter.

EASY HOLLANDAISE SAUCE
Sauce hollandaise commune

Use ½ l (1 pt) of either butter sauce (page 111) or béchamel sauce (page 110) thickened with 3 egg yolks and mixed with 2 tablespoons of the liquid in which mushrooms have been cooked or with 1 tablespoon of water and a couple of drops of lemon juice. Then off the flame add unsalted butter. The more butter you add, the finer this sauce is. It should be thick but creamy.

FISH SAUCE
Sauce normande

Use ½ l (1 pt) of velouté sauce made with strong fish stock (page 105); add ¼ l (½ pt) of broth in which mushrooms have cooked and 1½ dl (¼ pt) of liquid in which oysters have poached. Reduce the sauce by one-third, then thicken with 4 egg yolks mixed with 3 tablespoons of double cream. Strain through a fine sieve and place over the flame; heat to boiling point, stirring continuously. Off the flame, immediately incorporate 100 g (4 oz) of unsalted butter by beating vigorously.

ONION SAUCE
Sauce soubise

225 g (½ lb) onions, chopped finely
75 g (3 oz) unsalted butter
½ l (1 pt) béchamel sauce (page 110)
2 tablespoons double cream

Cook the onions for 1 minute in boiling water; drain, rinse, drain well, and then stew slowly for 20 minutes in a frying pan with ⅓ of the butter. The onions must not brown. Add the béchamel sauce. Cook slowly, covered, for 20 minutes; then strain through a fine sieve, pushing through the onions to make a purée. Bring to the boil again and finish the sauce with the cream and the rest of the butter, stirred in away from the flame.

ONION SAUCE WITH TOMATO
Sauce soubise tomatée

Prepare a soubise sauce (as above) and mix with thickened tomato purée, 2 parts sauce for 1 part tomato purée (page 507).

HERB SAUCE
Sauce aux herbes

Use ½ l (1 pt) of butter sauce (page 111); season just before serving with 2 tablespoons of parsley, chervil and tarragon, all chopped, blanched, rinsed and pounded.

CREAM SAUCE WITH ONION
Sauce Smitane

1 large onion, finely chopped
50 g (2 oz) unsalted butter
1 glass dry white wine
½ l (1 pt) double cream
Pinch salt
Lemon juice

Blanch the onion for 1 minute, drain, rinse, drain well, and then cook slowly 20 minutes in a frying pan with 15 g (½ oz) of butter. Stir frequently and do not let brown. Add the wine, and boil until wine has evaporated. Add the cream and salt. Bring to the boil, reduce rapidly by one-third. Strain the sauce through a fine sieve. Bring back to the boil; then off the flame add the rest of the butter cut into tiny pieces; stir the sauce, and flavour with lemon juice so that it has a slightly tart taste.

WHITE WINE AND SHALLOT SAUCE

Sauce Bercy

For fish

2 teaspoons chopped shallots
1 glass dry white wine
1½ dl (¼ pt) strong fish stock (page 105)
¾ l (1½ pts) velouté sauce
100 g (4 oz) unsalted butter
Freshly ground pepper
Pinch chopped parsley

Cook the shallots in a little butter for 15 minutes without browning; add the wine and fish stock. Reduce by one-third. Add the velouté sauce made with strong fish stock.

Bring to the boil, and boil 10 minutes; finish the sauce away from the flame by adding the rest of the butter. Season the sauce with freshly ground pepper. Just before serving, add a large pinch of freshly chopped parsley.

CURRY SAUCE

Sauce au cari

1 medium-sized onion
25 g (1 oz) unsalted butter
Sprig thyme
½ bay leaf
Pinch mace
50 g (2 oz) flour
2 teaspoons curry powder
¾ l (1½ pts) white stock or strong fish stock
4 tablespoons double cream or coconut milk

Finely chop the onion; cook slowly, covered, in butter. Add thyme, bay leaf, a pinch of mace. Sprinkle with flour and curry powder. Cook for 10 minutes, stirring frequently.

Add the white stock or fish stock, if the sauce is for fish. Simmer for 30 minutes; strain the sauce through a fine sieve, squeezing all the ingredients well, and bring to the boil. Finish the sauce with cream, or coconut milk if available.

Note: Curry sauce can be made by a much simpler method. Add some good veal gravy to some strong chicken stock. Cook a chopped onion gently in butter, sprinkle in the curry powder, add the liquid and simmer for 35 minutes. Strain through a fine sieve and thicken with arrowroot.

Emulsified Rich Sauces

Sauce hollandaise

1 tablespoon white
wine vinegar
3 tablespoons water
Pinch crushed white
peppercorns
3 egg yolks
225 g (8 oz) best
unsalted butter

In a small saucepan combine the vinegar, 1 tablespoon of water and pepper; reduce this mixture to 1 teaspoon.

Cool the mixture; then add the egg yolks and 2 tablespoons of cold water. Mix together with a whisk and heat slowly, beating continuously and being careful to scrape up the sauce on the bottom of the pan so that all the egg yolks are incorporated.

For an inexperienced cook it is advisable to place the saucepan in a double boiler over very hot but not boiling water. The egg yolks will take longer to cook, but the success of the sauce is more certain. At this stage you are making a smooth liaison for the butter and if you use too much heat or cook the yolks too fast they will become granular, rather than thick and smooth.

This first step, the trickiest, consists of emulsifying the yolks over gradual heat to make them thick, smooth and creamy.

When the egg-yolk emulsion reaches the consistency of very thick cream, incorporate the butter, melted or cut into tiny pieces, bit by bit, whisking vigorously. Add a pinch of salt.

If you notice that the sauce is getting too thick and solid, from time to time, while whisking add a few drops of warm water. This method is preferable to suddenly adding extra liquid to lighten the sauce when it is finished.

This makes a well-flavoured, thick yet light hollandaise sauce. Correct the seasonings and keep warm in a double boiler over very low heat.

Too much heat will cause the yolks to separate from the butter, so that the sauce curdles.

If this happens, heat 1 tablespoon of water in a saucepan, then beating continuously add small quantities of the sauce that has separated.

You may omit the vinegar mixture, if wished.

If the vinegar is not used, the sauce is seasoned with a few drops of lemon juice.

These techniques and the use of best butter are sure guarantees of a successful and really delicious sauce.

As an economy measure, you can add a certain proportion of butter sauce (page 111) to this sauce. This makes the sauce cheaper and less likely to curdle, but the result is not as delicious.

HOLLANDAISE SAUCE WITH WHIPPED CREAM
Sauce mousseline

This is a hollandaise sauce, made as above, to which about one-third part of whipped double cream is added.

Sauce Béarnaise
For 6 people

225 g (8 oz) unsalted butter
3 medium shallots
3 tablespoons white wine vinegar
2 sprigs tarragon
$\frac{1}{4}$ teaspoon chopped chervil
Pinch salt
Pinch crushed peppercorns
4 egg yolks

In a small saucepan melt 15 g ($\frac{1}{2}$ oz) of butter. Add the shallots, finely chopped. Cook slowly 10 minutes; add vinegar, 1 sprig of tarragon, pinch of chervil and the salt and pepper. Reduce the mixture to about 2 teaspoons. Then proceed exactly as for hollandaise sauce heating the yolks until they have thickened.

Strain the finished sauce through a fine sieve. Add a pinch of finely chopped tarragon and chervil, and keep warm in a double boiler. This sauce should be much thicker than a hollandaise; that is why more egg yolks are required. The sauce should have the consistency of mustard.

Just as with the hollandaise sauce, this sauce can be adapted by adding butter sauce, but it loses much of its fine flavour.

TOMATO-FLAVOURED BÉARNAISE SAUCE
Sauce Choron

Make a béarnaise sauce, and add some very concentrated tomato purée equal to one-fourth the total amount of the béarnaise.

ORANGE-FLAVOURED HOLLANDAISE
Sauce maltaise

Make hollandaise sauce and add some blood orange juice and a few drops of curaçao liqueur.

Cold Sauces

Sauce mayonnaise

As the basic sauce for a number of cold sauces, mayonnaise deserves a detailed technical explanation.

The concept is simple and very old. There are clear references to it in the works of Apicius, and there may be even more ancient sources. Mayonnaise is easy to make under certain conditions.

It originated in the south and is sensitive to cold. Since it is made with a fluid ingredient that is quite inert, it requires strong beating to be light and well-flavoured.

The cook, therefore, should make sure that both the container in which the mayonnaise will be made and the oil are at room temperature, and should follow the instructions closely.

6 egg yolks, at room temperature
1 teaspoon salt
Large pinch freshly ground white pepper
1½ tablespoons wine vinegar or lemon juice
1 l (2 pts) oil, at room temperature

Method. Remove the stringy white from the egg yolks and put them in a bowl with salt, pepper and vinegar or lemon juice. Mix with a whisk to give more body to the yolks. Then add the oil, drop by drop in the beginning, continuously beating the mixture. If the mixture thickens too much, dilute with 1 teaspoon vinegar (or water if the sauce is tart enough). Continue adding oil at a faster speed as the volume of the sauce increases.

All the time you are making the sauce it should have a thick creamy consistency, so that it becomes smooth and light as you beat the air into it.

As with hollandaise sauce the fatty, liquid ingredient, the oil, adheres to the egg yolks, which serve as a thickening agent. This takes place slowly and requires vigorous beating to raise the temperature of the sauce and the surrounding air.

I recommend using a wooden spoon or spatula instead of a whisk when making mayonnaise at home. It takes longer but the results and the flavour are better.

Finally, when the mayonnaise is finished, it will be less liable to separate if you add one or two teaspoonfuls of boiling wine vinegar.

Mayonnaise that separates can be saved easily by reversing the errors made in preparing it – either the oil was too cold or it was poured in too fast. The remedy is to put 1 tablespoon of warm water in a bowl; then beat vigorously while adding, little by little, the mayonnaise that has curdled.

Pinch salt
Pinch freshly ground
  pepper
2 tablespoons capers
1 teaspoon chopped
  parsley
1 teaspoon chopped
  tarragon
1 teaspoon mustard
1 onion, finely
  chopped
2 tablespoons vinegar
5 tablespoons oil

VINAIGRETTE WITH CAPERS, HERBS AND ONION
Sauce ravigote

In a bowl combine salt, a pinch of freshly ground pepper, slightly crushed capers, chopped parsley, chopped tarragon, mustard and the onion. Beat vigorously with a whisk and gradually pour in the vinegar and oil.

8 garlic cloves
2 egg yolks
Pinch salt
3 dl (½ pt) oil
Juice of ½ lemon

GARLIC SAUCE
Sauce aïoli

Crush the garlic in a mortar; mix the egg yolks into the garlic paste, then add the salt. Add the oil, drop by drop, mixing continuously with the pestle. Keep the consistency creamy by adding a few drops of lemon juice from time to time (the lemon juice forms the acid element in the sauce) and warm water.

TOMATO-FLAVOURED MAYONNAISE WITH GREEN PEPPERS
Sauce andalouse

Add to some mayonnaise one-fifth its volume of very thick tomato purée and 2 sweet green peppers cut into very thin strips.

GREEN MAYONNAISE
Sauce verte

Prepare some mayonnaise. Then pound in a mortar or chop a large handful of spinach, washed clean and trimmed, mixed with a sprig of tarragon and a good pinch of chervil. Put the pounded herbs in cheesecloth, squeeze the juice into a small double boiler and heat.

The action of the heat will make the herb juices separate into solid and clear parts.

When the green substances are sufficiently solidified, strain everything through cheesecloth. This green paste is then mixed with the mayonnaise to turn it green. Finish the sauce with finely chopped chervil, parsley, chives and tarragon.

1 l (2 pts) mayonnaise
2 tablespoons capers
6 gherkins
Fines herbes (parsley, chervil, tarragon, chives)
1 teaspoon anchovy paste (optional)

ANCHOVY-FLAVOURED MAYONNAISE WITH HERBS, CAPERS AND GHERKINS
Sauce rémoulade

Mix mayonnaise with 2 tablespoons of capers and 6 gherkins, finely chopped, plus the *fines herbes* (parsley, chervil, tarragon, chives), and if liked 1 teaspoon of anchovy paste.

MUSTARD-FLAVOURED MAYONNAISE WITH HERBS, CAPERS AND GHERKINS
Sauce tartare

This has the same ingredients as rémoulade sauce above, but instead of anchovy paste, use 2 tablespoons of Dijon mustard.

GREEN MAYONNAISE WITH HARD-BOILED EGG YOLKS
Sauce Vincent

To $\frac{1}{2}$ l (1 pt) of green mayonnaise, add 12 leaves of young sorrel, finely chopped, and 3 hard-boiled egg yolks, rubbed through a fine sieve. Finish the sauce with 1 teaspoon of chopped chervil and tarragon.

HARD-YOLK MAYONNAISE WITH HERBS, CAPERS AND GHERKINS
Sauce gribiche

5 hard-boiled eggs
Salt
Pepper
1 teaspoon mustard
2 tablespoons vinegar
4 dl ($\frac{3}{4}$ pt) oil
1 teaspoon chopped chervil
1 teaspoon chopped tarragon
1 teaspoon capers
3 chopped gherkins

Put the egg yolks into a bowl with the salt, pepper and mustard. Mash them well; then add to this paste the vinegar and then the oil, drop by drop, as in making mayonnaise. Keep the sauce creamy all the time by adding small amounts of vinegar or warm water, if necessary. Finish the sauce by adding the chopped herbs, the capers, the gherkins and the white of 1 egg, diced very finely. Correct the seasoning.

This sauce is a mayonnaise in which the egg yolks are cooked instead of raw.

CREAM MAYONNAISE
Sauce mayonnaise à la crème

To mayonnaise made with lemon juice instead of vinegar, add $\frac{1}{4}$ part of whipped double cream.

Correct the seasoning.

1 teaspoon mustard
2 tablespoons vinegar
50 g (2 oz) finely
grated fresh
horseradish
Pinch of salt
50 g (2 oz) sugar
500 g (1 lb) white
bread
$\frac{1}{2}$ l (1 pt) double
cream

HORSERADISH SAUCE
Sauce raifort

Remove crusts from the bread, soak it in milk, and squeeze dry in a bowl. Dilute the mustard with the vinegar; mix in the horse-radish, salt, sugar and bread. Thin this paste with the cream.

1 large onion, finely
chopped
2 shallots, finely
chopped
$1\frac{1}{2}$ dl ($\frac{1}{4}$ pt) olive oil
1 glass dry white
wine
500 g (1 lb) tomatoes
Salt
Freshly ground
pepper
Juice of $\frac{1}{2}$ lemon

COLD TOMATO SAUCE
Sauce portugaise froide

Cook the onion and shallots slowly in a sauté pan with 3 table-spoons of olive oil. When they are transparent, pour over the wine and boil to reduce almost completely.

Add the tomatoes, peeled, seeded and chopped – do not squeeze out the juice. Season with salt and freshly ground pepper; cook and reduce until mixture has reached the consistency of a fairly thin purée. Away from the flame thicken the sauce by beating in the remaining olive oil; add the lemon juice. Correct the season-ing.

COLD BORDELAISE SAUCE WITH DUCK LIVERS
Sauce rouennaise froide

dl (¾ pt) bordelaise
  sauce (page 112)
duck's liver or 2
  chicken livers
Pinch salt
Freshly ground
  pepper
tablespoon cognac
tablespoons
  gelatinous veal
  stock
2 tablespoons sherry

Prepare the bordelaise sauce.

Meanwhile, sauté the liver of a small duck or 2 chicken livers and rub through a fine sieve. Season with a pinch of salt and a little freshly ground pepper. Then dilute the liver purée with good cognac.

Add the veal stock to the bordelaise sauce and reduce the mixture, over high heat, to about 3 dl (½ pt); correct the seasoning.

Away from the heat thicken the sauce with the liver purée, first adding a couple of tablespoons of the reduced sauce to the purée and then pouring the liver mixture into the sauce. Mix well with a whisk while pouring in the liver mixture. Strain through a cheesecloth, forcing the liver through.

When the sauce is warm, season with 2 tablespoons of sherry.

WHITE CHAUD-FROID SAUCE
Sauce chaud-froid blanche
For ½ l (1 pt)

75 g (3 oz) pale roux
¾ l (1½ pts) strong
  white chicken stock
  (or ½ l (1 pt) velouté
  sauce)
100 g (4 oz)
  mushroom peel or
  stalks
3 dl (½ pt) double
  cream
3 dl (½ pt) jellied
  stock (page 136)

Prepare the roux with the butter and flour in equal parts, thin with the chicken bouillon; bring to the boil, add the mushrooms and cook slowly for 1 hour. Skim carefully from time to time.

As an alternative replace the ingredients above with an equal quantity of a good velouté sauce.

In a saucepan combine two-thirds of the cream and the cooked sauce.

On a high flame reduce the sauce, stirring constantly with a spatula. Add the jelly.

When the sauce is again reduced to ½ l (1 pt) remove it from the heat and add the remaining cream. Strain through a fine sieve into a glazed earthenware bowl. Let it cool, stirring frequently to prevent the formation of a skin and lumps. Before the sauce jells, use it to coat the dish for which it is intended.

BROWN CHAUD-FROID SAUCE
Sauce chaud-froid brune

Reduce 4 dl ($\frac{3}{4}$ pt) of demi-glace sauce (page 108) seasoned with Madeira. Gradually add the same amount of good, lightly salted, jellied stock (p. 136).

When the mixture is reduced by half, strain it through a fine sieve into an earthenware bowl and let it cool, following the directions for the white chaud-froid sauce above. Use it before it has jelled.

This sauce can be flavoured with port, sherry, Marsala, etc.

Marinades

Marinades are used to preserve meats, to soften the fibres and to impregnate the meat with the flavour of the aromatic ingredients with which the marinades are made.

UNCOOKED MARINADE
Marinade crue
For meat or game

**1 medium-sized
  carrot
2 onions
4 shallots
1 celery stick
2 garlic cloves
Few sprigs parsley
Small sprig thyme
1 bay leaf
Pinch crushed pepper
2 cloves
1 l (2 pts) white wine
4 dl ($\frac{3}{4}$ pt) vinegar
1$\frac{1}{2}$ dl ($\frac{1}{4}$ pt) oil**

Slice the carrots, onions, shallots and celery very thinly. Place half these vegetables in the bottom of a bowl large enough to hold the pieces of meat to be marinated so that the marinade will cover the pieces entirely. Add the meat, then the rest of the vegetables and the spices and herbs. Add the white wine, vinegar and oil, which will remain on the surface and prevent the air touching the ingredients in the marinade; this will prevent spoilage.

Keep in a cool place, turning the pieces of meat frequently in the marinade. The time taken depends upon the quantity of the meat and surrounding temperature. The process is more rapid in summer than in winter. Very large pieces of meat may be left as long as 5–6 days in winter, 24–48 hours in summer.

COOKED MARINADE
Marinade cuite

The ingredients are the same as for the uncooked marinade.

Heat the oil in a saucepan and brown the vegetables slightly. Add the white wine, vinegar, herbs and spices, and cook slowly for $\frac{1}{2}$ hour.

Let cool completely before pouring over the meat that is to be marinated.

Storing Marinades. To keep the marinade from going off, especially in the summer, add 1 g of boric acid to every 1 l (2 pts) of marinade.

It is also necessary to bring the marinade to the boil every 3–4 days. In this case, add an extra glass of wine, since the boiling will reduce the amount of alcohol in the mixture.

Note: Red wine can be substituted for white wine for some dishes.

Brine

Brine is a solution of sea salt, sugar, saltpetre and water used to preserve foods by salting.

PRESERVING WITH SALT
Saumure au sel

In salting meat use 40 g (1½ oz) of saltpetre for 1 kg (2 lb) of sea salt. Put the meats coated with the saltpetre and the salt in a wooden bowl or tub. Do not leave any air spaces. Add 1 sprig of thyme and 1 bay leaf for each 1 kg (2 lb) of salt. Tightly seal the tub.

Meat put down in salt must be extremely fresh. The best time to salt meat at home is the months of December, January and February. Salt the meat 24 hours after slaughtering if possible.

5 l (10 pts) water
2¼ kg (5 lb) sea salt
150 g (6 oz) saltpetre
300 g (10 oz) sugar
12 peppercorns
12 juniper berries
Sprig thyme
1 bay leaf

PRESERVING IN BRINE
Saumure liquide

Place all these ingredients in a saucepan and bring to the boil. Then check the strength of the salt solution by dropping a peeled potato into the brine. If the potato floats, add more water until the potato starts to sink. If the potato sinks to the bottom of the pot immediately, add some salt or reduce the liquid until the strength of the saline solution keeps the potato nearly at the surface.

Let the brine cool, then pour into the bowl in which the meat will be marinated.

When the pieces of meat are placed in the brine, they should be completely submerged.

For 1 l (2 pts) meat
  jelly:
225 g (½ lb) veal
  knuckle
225 g (½ lb) veal
  bones, cut into
  small pieces
225 g (½ lb) beef shin
1 calf's foot, boned
  and blanched
50 g (2 oz) fresh pork
  rind
3 tablespoons diced
  carrot
3 tablespoons diced
  onion
1 leek, white only
1 celery stalk
Sprig thyme
½ bay leaf
1¼ l (2½ pts) water
1 teaspoon salt

Aspics

Meat jelly or aspic is obtained from the natural gelatine found in certain meats: veal knuckles, calf's or ox feet, pig's trotters and pork rind.

It can also be made by adding powdered or sheet gelatine to cooking stock (veal or chicken stock, bouillon, etc.). The second method is not recommended, but it can sometimes be used in summer to help the jelly set.

Method. Proceed exactly as for veal stock (page 103), lightly browning the ingredients if you are making a light-coloured jelly, and omitting this stage if the jelly is to be white. The total cooking time will be 6 hours.

Add poultry, or poultry bones, for poultry jelly. The addition of poultry greatly enriches any jellied stock.

Check the consistency of the jelly before clarifying it. Pour ½ tablespoon of stock into a bowl, and put it in a cool place. After it has cooled for a few minutes, the consistency can easily be tested and you can tell if it is necessary to add powdered gelatine.

To clarify jellies, combine ½ pound of lean beef, a pinch of tarragon and a pinch of chervil all roughly chopped, in a flat-bottomed saucepan.

Add 1 egg white, beaten with a whisk, and a little at a time pour in the jellied stock, just warm with all fat carefully removed. Degreasing is essential for a clear jelly.

Bring to the boil slowly, stirring constantly.

As soon as the stock starts to boil, reduce the heat very low and simmer 35 minutes. Then strain through a damp linen napkin, well wrung out.

Meat jellies are usually flavoured with wine or fortified wine such as Frontignan, port, Madeira, sherry or Marsala, added to the jelly while warm.

To every 1 l (2 pts) of jelly allow ½ glass of fortified wine or 1 glass of ordinary table wine (champagne, Alsace, Sauternes, etc.).

When making the jelly allow for the fact that adding wine will alter the proportions of gelatine.

FISH

FISH

Fish offers about the same food value as land animals. It is easily digestible, especially lean fish (sole, whiting, etc.), rich in phosphorus and an excellent nutritional source.

But it must meet one important condition: it must be absolutely fresh. Fish decays quickly and if it is not fresh, it can easily cause digestive upsets and food poisoning. You must therefore learn to recognize whether or not fish is fresh.

Fresh fish flesh is firm and smells clean. The eyes should not be sunk in the socket, but should be very bright. The scales should be shiny and brilliant. The gills should be bright red. If the fish has been caught and killed very recently, its body will be curved in a semicircle, the head turned towards the tail.

Cooked fresh fish tastes good, and the flesh is slightly resistant. If it is not fresh, it tastes insipid and flabby and has a dubious smell.

Preliminary preparation

Before beginning any recipe, you must gut the fish and scale it. Remove the dorsal, belly and caudal fins. Avoid pricking yourself while preparing the fish, as this is painful and sometimes dangerous. When scaling is difficult, soak the fish first for a few seconds in boiling water and the task will be easier.

This is the procedure. First remove the gills. Then scale the fish, using a knife with a strong blade, scraping against the direction in which the scales grow. Then make a short incision in the fish's belly to enable you to remove the entrails. Remove the line of blood that coagulates along the backbone. Finally, cut off the fins and trim the tail with strong scissors. Wash the fish inside and out in running water, wipe dry with a cloth and keep in a cool place.

Methods of cooking fish

1. Cooking in a court-bouillon, with or without seasoning
2. Braising (cooking very slowly with a small amount of liquid on a bed of aromatic vegetables and flavourings)
3. Poaching (cooking in liquid such as white or red wine, the broth mushrooms have cooked in or a strong fish stock)

4. Grilling
5. Frying
6. *A la meunière* (lightly floured and fried in butter)
7. *Au gratin* (with a sauce and a sprinkling of breadcrumbs or cheese, browned in the oven or under a grill)
8. *Au bleu* (plunged absolutely fresh into a court-bouillon with vinegar or wine)

Fish may be served hot or cold, whole or in pieces.

Cooking in court-bouillon

After the fish has been gutted, scaled and washed, inside and out, place it in a pot large enough to hold it comfortably. Lay large, whole fish on the rack of a fish kettle, if you have one, and pour in one of the cold court-bouillons (page 144) to reach 5 cm (2 inches) above the fish. Bring rapidly to the boil, then immediately reduce the flame. The fish should poach at a gentle simmer. If it boils vigorously, it will lose its shape and break into pieces.

When fish is cut into slices, they should never be less than 4 cm (1½ inches) thick; I suggest dropping them into the court-bouillon after it has started boiling, to seal in the juices and flavour the fish.

Braising

Braising is usually used for whole fish or large pieces, often larded with small pieces of pork fat, truffles, gherkins, carrots, etc., cut into small sticks about 6 mm (¼ inch) wide.

The pot should always be the same size as the fish. The bottom should be buttered thickly and covered with the usual seasonings – carrots, onions, shallots and mushrooms, all sliced very thin. Then season the fish on both sides and place it on top of the vegetables. Cover to three-fourths of its depth with 1 part white or red wine and 1 part strong fish stock. Bring it to the boil on a high flame and continue cooking in a 350°F (180°C, gas mark 4) oven, covered but with the lid slightly raised so that the liquid can evaporate very slowly, reducing the stock. The fish should be basted very often.

As the stock reduces, it becomes more flavourful; the frequent basting gives the fish a shiny, golden-brown coating or glaze and a fine flavour.

When the fish is cooked, drain it carefully and place on a serving platter, cover and keep warm.

The cooking liquid is then strained carefully, degreased, reduced if necessary and finished according to the recipe chosen.

Poaching

This method is one of the simplest and most satisfactory. Thickly butter a fireproof dish the same size as the fish to be cooked.

On the bottom sprinkle the ingredients specified in the recipe you have chosen, season lightly, then place the fish on top. Cover the fish with wine or concentrated fish stock, in the proportions given in the recipe. Cut a piece of butter into small knobs and spread them on the fish. Bring to the boil, then cook in a 350°F (180°C, gas mark 4) oven, basting often.

When the fish is cooked, it is usually drained and the cooking juices are used as the main ingredient in making the sauce to accompany the fish. Follow the chosen recipe to finish the dish.

Grilling

For grilling fish should be small or medium sized. Grilling a big fish presents technical difficulties for the amateur cook.

If the fish is medium sized, slash diagonally on either side to help the heat penetrate the flesh and make cooking easier.

The heat of the grill (charcoal, gas or electricity) should be adjusted according to the thickness of the fish.

If the heat is too fierce to start with the fish will not cook inside. It will form a protective coating which burns but prevents the heat penetrating properly.

A whole fish tapering towards the tail must be placed so that it cooks evenly. This is the secret of successful grilling.

Frying

The ideal oil for frying is one that can be heated to 575°F (300°C) without burning. There should be enough oil for the fish to be totally immersed.

The temperature of the oil can be judged by the smoke it releases as it is heated. The right temperature depends on the thickness of the fish.

Fried fish must be sealed, particularly if it is small. However if a medium fish is sealed too quickly, it will stop cooking. As with grilled fish, a protective coating forms that keeps the heat from penetrating.

When you plunge the fish into the smoking oil the temperature will drop. Make sure you restore the temperature quickly, raising the heat if necessary.

After each use strain the oil through a cloth to remove any sediment left made by the flour, breadcrumbs, etc., used to coat the fish.

Poissons à la meunière

See recipes for trout *à la meunière* (page 155) and sole *à la meunière* (page 184).

Court-bouillons

The court-bouillon is the cooking liquid in which the fish is completely immersed. These are the different types of court-bouillon.

White court-bouillon

3 l (6 pts) water
1½ dl (¼ pt) milk
40 g (1½ oz) salt
4 slices lemon, peeled and seeded

Mix the ingredients together and pour this cold court-bouillon over the fish, which should be barely covered. This court-bouillon is used for such fish as turbot, brill or halibut.

Court-bouillon with vinegar

3 l (6 pts) water
1½ dl (¼ pt) vinegar
40 g (1½ oz) salt
2 medium-sized carrots
2 large onions sliced thin
Sprigs parsley
Sprig thyme
½ bay leaf
Peppercorns

Bring to the boil, simmer for 40 minutes, adding the peppercorns 10 minutes before the end. Strain through a fine sieve. Cool before pouring over the fish to be cooked.

Court-bouillon with white wine

As for the court-bouillon with vinegar, but omit the vinegar and replace half the water with dry white wine. Cook as above.

Court-bouillon with red wine

The same ingredients as court-bouillon with vinegar, but omit the vinegar and use red wine instead of water. Simmer 40 minutes on a low flame.

Freshwater fish

EEL
Anguille

Eel must be kept alive to the last possible moment and skinned as soon as it is killed. If you have a live eel you can kill it with one blow on the back of the head. Holding it with a cloth to stop your hand slipping, make 2 or 3 incisions round the neck. Ease the skin away a little with a butcher's hook, and turn it back all round the neck. With your hand still wrapped in a cloth, tear off the skin in one go. Slit open the belly and gut the eel, making sure you remove the coagulated blood from the backbone. Remove the fins and wash in running water.

700–800 g (1½–1¾ lb
  eel
50 g (2 oz) onions,
  sliced
50 g (2 oz) carrots,
  sliced
Garlic clove
Bouquet garni
Salt
Freshly ground
  pepper
Red wine

20 small onions
Pinch sugar
20 small mushrooms
Beurre manié
100 g (4 oz) unsalted
  butter
15 g (½ oz) anchovy
  butter
Crayfish *à la nage*
  (page 202)
Croûtons fried in
  butter

EEL STEW (1)
Matelote d'anguille à la bourguignonne dite 'meurette'

[*Editor's note:* A *matelote* is a fish stew cooked in red or white wine. It is also called a *pochouse* or *meurette* according to which district the recipe comes from.]

Skin the eel, gut it, wash and cut it into pieces 8–9 cm (3–3½ inches) long.

Thickly butter a sauté pan and cover the bottom with a layer of thinly sliced onions and carrots; cook slowly, covered, 15–20 minutes.

Add a crushed garlic clove and a bouquet garni. Season with salt and freshly ground pepper. Add the pieces of eel and cover with red wine.

Bring rapidly to the boil and cook slowly, covered, for 20 minutes.

Remove the pieces of eel and put them into a bowl; over them pour the cooking liquid, strained through a very fine sieve.

Eel cooked in this way can be kept in a cool place, in its cooking liquid, which will jell when cold; or the fish can be used later for various recipes.

If the eel is served in a *matelote*, it should be garnished in the following manner:

Peel about 20 small onions, blanch and drain, and cook them in butter, covered, in a frying pan. Season with salt and a pinch of sugar.

The onions should colour slowly as they cook; when they are finished, they should be perfectly golden and glazed with the onion juice, which becomes slightly caramelized when the sugar melts.

When the onions are cooked, add about 20 small, firm, white mushrooms; sauté everything for a few seconds. Then pour just enough cooking liquid from the eel into the pan to cover the pieces. Bring to the boil, then add the pieces of eel. Bring to the boil again for 3–4 minutes.

Thicken with *beurre manié*. (Mix the *beurre manié* in the proportions 3 parts butter, to 2 parts flour and allow about 50 g (2 oz) *beurre manié* to each pint of cooking liquid (60 g per ½ l).) Add to the pan a teaspoonful at a time, swirling it round in the hot liquid. As it melts the sauce will thicken and coat the pieces of eel and their garnish.

Correct the seasoning and finish the sauce away from the heat by adding 100 g (4 oz) of butter.

You may add, at the same time, 15 g ($\frac{1}{2}$ oz) of anchovy butter, made with desalted anchovies pounded with an equal amount of butter and squeezed through a very fine sieve.

Place the eel on a hot serving dish, garnish with crayfish cooked *à la nage* and croûtons cut into diamond shapes and fried in butter.

EEL STEW (2)
Anguille en pochouse

The eel is prepared as for the *matelote à la bourguignonne*, with the addition of fat pork or bacon. Allow 125 g (5 oz) for an eel of 700–800 g ($1\frac{1}{2}$–$1\frac{3}{4}$ lb). Cut the fat into dice and soften them in the pan in which the onions and mushrooms will be cooked. Follow above recipe.

EEL IN CREAM WITH CRAYFISH
Anguille à la creme

700–800 g ($1\frac{1}{2}$–$1\frac{3}{4}$ lb) eel
Salt
12 crayfish (or giant prawns)
50 g (2 oz) unsalted butter
2 dozen mushrooms
Freshly ground pepper
1 tablespoon cognac
2 tablespoons dry white wine
$1\frac{1}{2}$ dl ($\frac{1}{4}$ pt) double cream
Beurre manié
Croûtons, fried in butter
Pastry shell as for *vol-au-vent* (page 539) (optional)

Skin, gut and wash the eel; cut it into large pieces. Sprinkle the pieces with salt and leave for $\frac{1}{4}$ hour; then cook as for a *matelote* with white wine.

Sauté the crayfish in butter on a high flame; add 2 dozen firm, white mushrooms; season with salt and freshly ground pepper. Cook 2 or 3 minutes; then add the cognac and wine. Boil 5 minutes; remove the crayfish and the mushrooms separately. Reserve the cooking liquid.

Remove the crayfish tails and add them to the mushrooms, along with the pieces of eel. Put them all in a sauté pan. Crush the heads and the shells of the crayfish in a mortar and put this mixture into a pan with the cooking liquid from the crayfish. Add the cooking liquid from the eel. Bring to the boil and reduce by one-third; then add two-thirds of the cream and bring to the boil. Strain through a fine sieve into the pan containing the eel, crayfish tails and mushrooms. Bring to the boil, and thicken with *beurre manié*, following the recipe for the *matelote bourguignonne* (page 146). The sauce should be thicker than for the *matelote*, however.

Correct the seasoning, and finish the sauce away from the heat with the rest of the cream to thin the sauce.

Place on a very hot serving platter and garnish with heart-shaped croûtons fried in butter.

This dish can also be served in a *vol-au-vent* shell (page 539).

700–800 g (1½–1¾ lb) eel
50 g (2 oz) unsalted butter
2 medium-sized onions, finely diced
Celery stalk, white part only
Dry white wine
Salt
Freshly ground pepper
125 g (5 oz) sorrel leaves
125 g (5 oz) watercress
1 teaspoon chopped parsley
1 teaspoon chopped chervil
Pinch sage
Pinch savory
Pinch fresh mint
4 egg yolks
2 tablespoons double cream

EEL WITH GREEN HERBS
Anguille à la flamande dite 'au vert'

Cut the eel into 6-cm (2½-inch) pieces. Brown the pieces in butter in a sauté pan. Then add the onions and celery.

When these ingredients are lightly browned, immediately add dry white wine to cover the pieces of eel. Season with salt and freshly ground pepper. Tie in a piece of cheesecloth the sorrel leaves, cut into strips, watercress, chopped parsley, chopped chervil, sage, savoury and fresh mint. Put in the pan.

Bring to the boil and boil rapidly for 15 minutes.

In a bowl beat 4 egg yolks with the cream. Remove the herbs and pieces of eel, being careful not to break them, and keep warm and covered.

Thicken the cooking liquid with the egg yolks and cream, as in making sauces and soups (see pages 92–93).

Place the pieces of eel in the sauce and coat them well by shaking the pan. Correct the seasoning, and serve hot or cold.

PIKE WITH WHITE BUTTER SAUCE
Brochet à la nantaise

Pike cooked in vinegar court-bouillon

3 shallots, finely chopped

2 tablespoons vinegar or ½ glass Muscadet

Pinch salt

Pinch freshly ground pepper

250 g (9 oz) unsalted butter

Cook a pike in a vinegar court-bouillon. As soon as it starts to boil, skim the court-bouillon and place the pan over the lowest possible flame. Poach the fish 20–25 minutes.

While it is poaching, very slowly cook the shallots in 25 g (1 oz) of butter in a frying pan. Add 1 tablespoon of water, 2 tablespoons of vinegar or ½ glass of Muscadet, a pinch of salt and a pinch of freshly ground pepper. Reduce by two-thirds.

Keep the sauce simmering, without boiling, and add piece by piece, 225 g (8 oz) of butter cut into small bits. With a whisk beat the mixture vigorously, without stopping. The butter, whipped like cream, will become very foamy and white – this is why the sauce is called *beurre blanc* (white butter).

Drain the pike and place on a napkin; serve the white butter separately as soon as it is ready. It must not wait.

Note: There are different regional methods which can be used to make an excellent white butter sauce. One of these methods is recommended for its simplicity. To the reduced sauce described above add 1½ dl (¼ pt) of pike court-bouillon. Reduce it by two-thirds on a high flame; then while it is at full boil, add the butter cut into pieces. As it melts the butter blends with the boiling liquid and forms an emulsion. Beat the sauce while this change is taking place and remove from the flame when the sauce is thickened.

2 kg (4 lb) pike
Salt
Pepper
225 g (8 oz)
mushrooms
1 glass sherry
1½ dl (¼ pt) white veal
stock (page 104)
225 g (8 oz) unsalted
butter
1½ dl (¼ pt) double
cream
1 tablespoon brandy

BRAISED PIKE WITH MUSHROOMS
Brochet braisé aux champignons

Gut and clean the pike. Wash it very carefully, season with salt and pepper on all sides, and place in a pan large enough to hold the fish, on a bed of very tiny white mushrooms.

Pour in the sherry and an equal quantity of white veal stock; on top, scatter 100 g (4 oz) of butter cut into small pieces.

Cook in a 375°F (190°C, gas mark 5) oven for 30 minutes. Do not cover the fish and baste frequently. At the end of the cooking time the pike should be perfectly golden.

Remove the fish to a serving platter, surround it with the mushrooms, well drained, and keep hot. Reduce the fish liquid by half in a pan, add the cream, reduce again slightly. Then off the flame add 100 g (4 oz) of butter and the brandy. Correct the seasoning, and pour the sauce, which should be a light ivory colour, over the pike.

Note: If more convenient, the veal stock may be replaced by an equal quantity of strong stock made from sole bones.

Pike cooked in a court-bouillon may be accompanied by various sauces – for example hollandaise (page 126), butter sauce (page 111) or ravigote sauce (page 129).

FISH QUENELLES OR FORCEMEAT
Quenelles de poisson ou farces

Fish quenelles or forcemeat are generally made with the flesh of whiting or pike, and nearly always with white fish of some kind. As with veal, chicken or game quenelles, there are two kinds: *mousseline* quenelles and ordinary quenelles.

The former are made in the same way as the chicken *mousseline* quenelles described on page 381. Both are composed of cream, egg whites and fish or meat. The proportions are exactly the same.

However, it is impossible to specify the proportions with mathematical precision. The forcemeat is held together by the albumin in the fish. As the amount of albumin varies with the size, age and species of fish, egg whites are added as necessary to bind the cream and fish. One therefore has to experiment to find the right proportions for the finest possible texture.

Ordinary quenelles are a mixture of fish, *panade* (or paste) and eggs, enhanced by adding cream or butter.

---

500 g (1 lb) pike fillets
500 g (1 lb) unsalted
   butter
12 eggs
3 egg whites
½ l (1 pt) milk
600 g (1¼ lb) flour,
   sifted
4 teaspoons salt
Fresh ground pepper
Grated nutmeg

PIKE QUENELLES
Quenelles de brochet à la Lyonnaise
For 20 quenelles weighing about 100 g (4 oz) each

There are three important steps in preparing quenelles – making the *panade*, mixing the forcemeat and poaching.

Making the panade. In a saucepan with a thick bottom bring the milk to the boil, add 100 g (4 oz) of butter and the sifted flour, and beat vigorously. As soon as the mixture is well thickened, turn the heat very low and stir constantly with a wooden spoon to dry the *panade*. After this step has been completed (about 20 minutes), set the *panade* in a cool place.

Combining the mixture. With a pestle pound the pike in a mortar, together with the salt, pepper and nutmeg. When it becomes a paste, push it through a fine sieve. Return to the mortar, work in the egg whites, and then the cooled *panade*.

When these are well mixed, add the whole eggs. When they have been incorporated smoothly, finish by adding the softened butter.

Before poaching, cool the quenelle mixture to make it firmer.

Poaching the quenelles. Bring to the boil 5 l (10 pts) of salted water. With a spoon shape the quenelles, which should be ovals weighing about 100 g (4 oz) each. Poach them in the hot, but not boiling, water, for about 15 minutes.

If they are not to be used immediately, plunge them into a bowl of fresh water until they are completely cool. Drain and set aside in the refrigerator. Quenelles can be prepared later as required with cream, *à la Nantua* (page 121), or *au gratin*.

Panade:
125 g (5 oz) sifted
flour
4 egg yolks
50 g (2 oz) unsalted
butter, melted
2 dl (8 fl oz) hot
milk, seasoned with
salt and nutmeg

Pike forcemeat:
225 g (8 oz) beef suet
(or 100 g (4 oz)
each suet and beef
marrow)
225 g (8 oz) pike
fillets, bones and
skin removed
1 teaspoon salt
Pepper
Nutmeg
3 egg whites
Mornay sauce (page
120)
Grated Gruyère
cheese

PIKE QUENELLES (OLD METHOD)
Quenelles de brochet

First make the *panade*. Put the flour and melted butter into a heavy saucepan with a flat bottom. Add the egg yolks and mix thoroughly. Gradually add the seasoned hot milk and bring to the boil, stirring all the time with a wooden spoon.

If you are using kidney suet in the pike forcemeat, remove the skin, fibres and sinews. Chop the suet and marrow fine. Pound the pike meat in a mortar until it becomes a smooth paste. Mix in the chopped fat and the seasonings. Pound again until the ingredients are completely mixed. Add the eggs one by one until you have the right consistency. Incorporate the cooled *panade* and push the mixture through a fine sieve. Spread it 2 cm ($\frac{3}{4}$ inch) thick in a dish, and place in the refrigerator until the next day.

Make the quenelles by hand on a table sprinkled with flour. With the tips of your fingers, roll the mixture into pieces the size of a walnut, or roll the entire mixture into a long sausage, as thick as a finger, and cut in 8-cm (3-inch) lengths.

Poach in boiling salted water, keeping the water at a low boil for 7 or 8 minutes. The quenelles are done when they resist slightly when pressed. Drain the quenelles well; arrange them in an ovenproof earthenware dish coated with a light Mornay sauce (page 120), and cover them with more of the sauce. Sprinkle with grated Gruyère cheese and fine breadcrumbs. Moisten with a little melted butter and place in a 425°F (220°C, gas mark 7) oven for 8–10 minutes.

Serve immediately, piping hot. This delicious dish is the great speciality of restaurants and chefs in Lyons.

Note: The beef suet can be partially or totally replaced by unsalted butter, which is preferable.

2 kg (4 lb) carp
2 large onions
3 shallots
4 dl ($\frac{3}{4}$ pt) oil
15 g ($\frac{1}{2}$ oz) flour
3 garlic cloves, crushed
Bouquet garni
White wine
Strong fish stock or white veal stock
Salt
Freshly ground pepper
Chopped parsley

SWEET-SOUR CARP
Carpe à la juive

Gut the carp and clean carefully. If it has a soft roe, reserve it. Cut the carp into 2·5-cm (1-inch) thick slices.

Chop finely the onions and shallots; cook them in $1\frac{1}{2}$ dl ($\frac{1}{4}$ pt) of oil heated slowly in a heavy pan big enough to hold all the pieces of carp flat. Place the fish slices on the onion and sauté for a few minutes in the hot oil, then turn them. Sprinkle with flour, mix carefully and cook for 5 minutes without browning. Add the garlic and the bouquet garni. Pour in liquid consisting of half white wine and half fish stock, veal stock or water, just to cover the fish. Add 4 tablespoons of oil. Season with salt and freshly ground pepper, and cook slowly, covered, for 20 minutes.

Drain the pieces of carp and set them, side by side in the shape of the original fish, on a long platter. Boil the cooking juice to reduce by two-thirds. Remove the bouquet garni, and away from the flame incorporate the rest of the oil into the reduced sauce, as in making mayonnaise. Correct the seasoning, pour the thickened sauce over the carp and let cool. The sauce will then jell.

Serve with chopped parsley sprinkled on at the last moment.

SOFT ROE OF CARP
Laitance de carpe

The soft roe of carp is very delicate and can be prepared poached or *à la meunière* or as a garnish for eggs, fish, etc. For family use, we advise *meunière* method (page 155), which is suitable for most fresh-water or sea fish.

PERCH
Perche

The small perch is an excellent frying fish. Cook it in the following way.

Choose small fish. Gut them with the point of a knife, wash, wipe and soak in a little milk. Drain and roll in flour, one at a time. When they are all ready, put into a frying basket and plunge into very hot oil. Cook 3 to 4 minutes. Drain on a cloth and sprinkle with salt.

Arrange the fish on a serving platter, accompanied by bouquets of fried parsley and lemon quarters. Serve immediately, very hot and crisp.

Any other small river fish can be cooked in the same way.

Larger perch, weighing 1–2 kg (2–4 lb) are treated like river trout as the flavour is similar.

HOT TROUT MOUSSE WITH CRAYFISH SAUCE
Mousse chaude de truite de rivière au coulis d'écrevisses

Mousse:
600 g (1¼ lb) trout, boned and skinned
¾ tablespoon salt
15 turns of the pepper mill
4 egg whites
1 l (2 pts) double cream

Sauce:
1 kg (2 lb) crayfish
6 tablespoons cognac
1 l (2 pts) fish fumet made with the trout bones
6 tablespoons cream
100 g (4 oz) unsalted butter
1 tablespoon flour

Pound the trout flesh in a mortar with the salt and pepper. Add the egg whites. When the mixture is smooth stand the bowl on ice and add the double cream.

Butter a large ring mould. Fill with the mousse and cook for ¾ hour in a *bain-marie* in a 375°F (190°C, gas mark 5) oven.

To make the *coulis*, scald the crayfish quickly in boiling water. Separate the tails, shell them and set aside. Pound the shells in a mortar and cook them in butter in a small pan to bring out the pink colour.

Add the cognac. Reduce by half and moisten with the well-seasoned trout fumet. Cook a few minutes over very low heat. Thicken slightly with *beurre manié* (flour and butter creamed together) and adjust the seasoning. Add the cream and pass this *coulis* through a fine sieve.

Turn the hot trout mousse out on to a large round china or

silver dish. In the middle place the crayfish tails, cooked gently in butter, seasoned and bound with a little of the very hot sauce.

Serve a sauceboat of the *coulis* and a bowl of pilaf rice separately.

Variation.   You can use small individual ring moulds. To make the dish richer, add a few slices of truffle on top and arrange *fleurons* – decorative motifs made of flaky pastry – round the edge of the dish.

BLUE TROUT
Truites au bleu

This simple way of preparing trout is one of the best but you really need live trout.

A few minutes before serving the trout fish them out of the tank, kill them by hitting their heads against a hard surface and remove the gills and intestines with the point of a knife. Without washing or wiping them so that you do not remove the slime which covers them, plunge them immediately into a fast-boiling court-bouillon well flavoured with vinegar.

Allow 7–8 minutes for fish weighing about 150 g (6 oz).

Drain the trout, which will have acquired a bluish tinge. Arrange them on a folded napkin and serve with steamed potatoes and a sauceboat of melted butter flavoured with a little lemon juice.

Truites au bleu may be served cold with ravigote sauce or a very light mayonnaise (see pages 128 and 129).

TROUT FRIED IN BUTTER
Truites de rivière 'à la meunière'

Remove the gills and intestines from the trout. Wash and dry them, coat them with salt and pepper mixed with a teaspoon of oil and roll them in flour. Shake them well and place in a frying pan in which a good lump of butter and a very small amount of oil is sizzling.

The fish will be seared as it touches the hot butter. Take care at this stage. The fish should be seared fairly quickly so that it does not stick to the pan, but not too much or the crust formed by the coating of oil and flour will become a barrier which prevents the trout cooking normally.

Cook the fish fairly quickly as it should fry gently, not boil in the fat.

When the trout is cooked on one side turn it over with a spatula and cook the other side in the same way.

When it is golden and crisp, the trout is placed on a well-heated plate. Squeeze a few drops of lemon juice over it and sprinkle with a good pinch of parsley, roughly chopped, blanched and drained at the very last minute. Then pour over the cooking butter and a little more butter cooked to a light brown colour. The piping hot butter and the moisture from the parsley make a delicious foam which is still on the fish when it is served to the guests, as soon as possible.

Fish from the Sea

BRILL
Barbue

Brill belongs to the same family as sole and turbot and is one of the finest sea fish. All sole and turbot recipes are suitable for it. When choosing brill, pick medium-sized fish.

GRILLED BRILL FILLETS
Filets de barbue grillés Saint-Germain

Gut and skin a medium-sized brill, and remove the fillet in the following way:

Make an incision in the flesh of the brill through to the bone, following the dorsal fin from the head to the tail. Make an incision round the fillets, starting at the small bones at the end of the backbone. Then, with the point of a flexible knife, starting with the dorsal fin, slide the blade, flat, under each fillet. Draw the knife towards you, detaching the fillets.

The bones and the head can be used to make a fish *fumet* or a soup.

Check the fillets to see that no bone or gristle remains. Dry them and season with salt and pepper mixed with a drop of olive oil. On one side of each fillet, sprinkle a few very fine breadcrumbs and press them down with the flat blade of a knife. Set the fillets on a glowing charcoal grill, with the breaded sides to the flame.

Adjust the distance from the coals according to the thickness of the fillets. For example, since the end of the fillet towards the tail is thinner, the coals at that end should be lower and that part of the fish farther away from the heat. If gas or electricity is used, put the thinner part of the fish farther away from the heat. It will cook evenly, and the thinner part will not dry out.

During the first part of cooking, sprinkle breadcrumbs on the uncoated tops of the fillets, pressing lightly with the blade of a knife. Moisten the breadcrumbs with a few drops of melted butter. When the fillets are cooked on one side, turn them over carefully with a spatula.

When the second side has cooked, arrange the fillets on a long, hot serving platter, sprinkle with the juice of $\frac{1}{2}$ lemon, then surround with a garnish of small tomatoes, seasoned and grilled. A tablespoon of rice – cooked *à la créole* or as a pilaf (page 514), or in salted water and then finished with unsalted butter – can be added to the tomatoes.

Serve with a sauce boat of béarnaise sauce (page 127).

A simpler way of cooking of the fillets is in a frying pan, with butter, *à la meunière* (page 155).

A whole brill can be grilled. In this case, remove only the black skin and carefully scrape the scales from the white skin. Cooking it this way requires more care, but the dish will be even more delicious because the bones contain juices that will enrich the flesh during cooking.

Bouillabaisse

For 6 people

1·5 kg (3 lb) freshly caught fish, including scorpion fish, whiting, red mullet, weever, John Dory, conger eel, lobster

Slices bread rubbed with garlic

Flavourings:
4 tablespoons finely chopped onion
1 medium-sized leek, white part only, finely chopped
2 tomatoes, peeled, seeded, and chopped (do not remove the juice)
1 tablespoon grated garlic
Large pinch coarsely chopped parsley
6 tablespoons olive oil
Sprig each thyme, laurel, savory
1 fennel stalk
Pinch saffron and aniseed
50 g (2 oz) unsalted butter
Salt and pepper

This typical Provençal dish, from Marseilles, is a fish stew first invented by fishermen who cook a kind of meatless *pot-au-feu* on their boats.

Southern tastes and the refinements contributed by professional cooks have combined to make this a divine dish.

Some people add shellfish such as mussels or cockles. I do not advise this. The taste of mussels is too strong, and the shells often leave sand at the bottom.

Method. Clean, scale, gut and trim the fish. Make an unsalted fumet (page 105) with the heads of the fish used or, if available, the bones of sole and brill and a turbot head.

Place the onion and leek in a saucepan with 2 tablespoons of oil. Heat slowly, stirring frequently, until they are both cooked but not brown. Then add the fish (except the lobster). Add all the flavourings and sprinkle with a teaspoon of salt and a pinch of freshly ground pepper. The aniseed and the saffron are the essentials; the saffron must dominate the soup.

Pour in the fumet to cover. Sprinkle over the butter cut into pieces, and the rest of the oil.

Start cooking over a high flame. As soon as the liquid boils, add the lobster cut into pieces. Cook on a high flame for 15 minutes. Meanwhile take the slices of bread that have been rubbed with garlic, sprinkle them with a few drops of oil and brown in the oven.

As it boils, the fish stock enhanced by the juices of the fish, the oil and the butter will mix and thicken to the consistency of a creamy soup.

It is essential to serve this fine and succulent dish, as soon as it's cooked. If it is forced to wait, the natural thickening that forms the charm of this dish will rapidly disappear.

Drain the fish carefully, and arrange the pieces on a serving platter. Pour the boiling soup into a soup tureen over the slices of bread.

Last and very important: before pouring the soup over the bread, correct the seasoning which is the key to the character of the bouillabaisse.

Saffron, with its flavour and its golden colour, must be the dominating note, but the fennel and aniseed are also vital. The proportions depend on the cook's palate and skill – he or she must have a precise notion of the fine flavour characteristic of this dish.

COD WITH POTATOES AND ONIONS
Cabillaud à la ménagère

Use a piece of cod about 30 cm (12 inches) long cut from the centre of the fish. Thickly butter an ovenproof earthenware dish big enough to contain the fish and its garnish. Put in the fish, well seasoned with salt and pepper on both sides, and surround it with small new potatoes and small new white onions. If you cannot get young vegetables, first, blanch, drain and season them with salt. Moisten the fish with melted butter and cook in a 425°F (220°C, gas mark 7) oven, basting frequently with additional melted butter, and a tablespoon of olive oil if liked.

The onions should constitute one-quarter of the total vegetable garnish. The vegetables should be placed around the fish, on the bottom of the dish, so that they brown evenly in the cooking butter.

Just before serving in the cooking platter, sprinkle the fish with fresh chopped parsley. Provide separately a lemon cut into quarters, to be squeezed over the fish when it has been served on hot plates.

Cod also can be poached or grilled in 2·5-cm (1-inch) thick steaks and served with a suitable sauce.

HAKE
Colin

The hake is a useful fish in family cooking. When available it is comparatively cheap. It has little waste and few bones and the flesh is white and delicate. It can be cooked by any method: served hot or cold, whole, in pieces, or in slices, poached, fried, grilled or *à la meunière* (page 155). Seasoned properly, it is always delicious.

It is nourishing and easily digestible, and as suitable for people who do heavy work as for sedentary workers and invalids.

350 g (12 oz) raw rice
1 kg (2 lb) very ripe
  tomatoes
1 large onion
1·5 kg (3 lb) hake
Salt
Freshly ground
  pepper
100 g (4 oz) unsalted
  butter
6 tablespoons olive
  oil
2 garlic cloves
1 glass dry white
  wine
Fresh chopped
  parsley

HAKE WITH TOMATOES AND RICE
Colin à la portugaise
For 6 people

Cook the rice in salted water for three-quarters of its cooking time. Remove tops, skins and seeds from the very ripe tomatoes – do not remove juice – and chop coarsely. Chop the onion and soften in butter and oil in a frying pan.

Cut the hake into 6 slices weighing about 225 g (8 oz) each. Season generously on both sides with salt and freshly ground pepper. Place the fish in a frying pan with 50 g (2 oz) of butter and 6 tablespoons of olive oil. Add the other ingredients – the onion, the garlic cloves, crushed, the tomatoes, the rice and the white wine.

Cover the frying pan, raise the heat and cook for 10 minutes; remove the cover and continue cooking for 8–10 minutes, to reduce part of the tomato juices and the white wine. Take off the flame, and remove the fish slices to an oval or round dish. Cut 50 g (2 oz) of unsalted butter into pieces and add to the frying pan and shake the pan to mix; the butter will blend into the rice and tomatoes. Correct the seasoning, and pour the mixture over the slices of hake.

Sprinkle fresh chopped parsley on top.

The rice and tomatoes and the cooking juices should be slightly thickened but not dry.

SEA BREAM
Daurade

The sea bream is protected by a thick layer of scales that must be removed completely in cleaning. When you gut the fish, if you find roe or soft roe, leave it in place. If the fish is to be served whole, leave the head on.

There are many species of sea bream. The true *daurade* or gilt-head bream, which lives in the Mediterranean, has a pearly transparent bulge between the eyes. It should not be confused with the sea bream that is native to the China Seas.

Small *daurades* can be cooked in the same way as red mullet – grilled, fried, *à la meunière* (page 155), etc. Medium or large, they can be cooked in a frying pan, poached, stuffed as for shad, *au gratin* like a sole, with white wine or red wine, *à la Bercy*, *à la dieppoise*, *à la portugaise*, etc.

SEA BREAM WITH WHITE WINE AND SHALLOTS
Daurade Bercy

Choose a *daurade* for 5 or 6 people: clean it, gut it, scrape it and wash it; gash lightly crosswise every 2 cm ($\frac{3}{4}$ inch) on the back and both sides. Season with salt and pepper and place in a gratin dish with the bottom thickly buttered and sprinkled with 2 chopped shallots and chopped parsley. Add dry white wine to one-third of the height of the fish and baste with 75 g (3 oz) of melted unsalted butter. Cook in a 350°F (180°C, gas mark 4) oven 25–30 minutes, basting frequently with the cooking liquid. Place the *daurade* on a long serving platter and keep warm and covered so that the fish does not dry out or cool.

If there is too much cooking liquid, reduce it to the quantity needed to serve with the fish. Stir in, off the heat, 100 g (4 oz) of unsalted butter cut into small pieces.

This thickened cooking liquid provides the sauce. Correct the seasoning, and pour it over the fish. Place for a few minutes in a 425°F (220°C, gas mark 7) oven or under a heated electric or gas grill, and the sauce will take on a pretty golden colour. Serve immediately.

If you do not have a sufficiently hot oven or grill, you may omit the last step.

This recipe can be made more economically by replacing the 100 g (4 oz) of butter with 50 g (2 oz) of butter mixed with 1 teaspoon of flour. Sprinkle this *beurre manié* little by little into the cooking liquid (reduced or unreduced) while it is boiling, stir for a few seconds and pour over the *daurade*; the sauce thickens immediately by the simple melting and cooking of the *beurre manié*.

STUFFED SEA BREAM
Daurade farcie
For 6 people

1·5 kg (3 lb) *daurade*
225 g (8 oz) unsalted
  butter
4 shallots, chopped
225 g (8 oz)
  mushrooms
Salt
Pepper
Pinch rosemary
2 glasses dry white
  wine
1 large tomato
100 g (4 oz) stale
  breadcrumbs
1 egg, beaten

Prepare the *daurade*. Very slowly melt 100 g (4 oz) of butter in a frying pan, and add the shallots, chopped; do not let brown. It will take 15–20 minutes until the shallots are cooked. Then raise the heat under the pan and add the mushrooms, carefully washed and chopped. Cook rapidly until dry, season with salt, pepper and rosemary; pour over 1 glass of dry white wine; add the tomato, peeled and seeded. Reduce quickly over a high flame. Finish away from the heat with the stale breadcrumbs and the beaten egg; mix in thoroughly and correct the seasoning.

If the *daurade* contains soft roe or roe, add it to the mixture; then stuff the mixture inside the fish through the gills. Place the fish on a thickly buttered ovenproof dish; season with salt and pepper; pour over 1 glass of dry white wine, and sprinkle on 1 tablespoon of fine breadcrumbs and 100 g (4 oz) of butter cut into small pieces.

Bake in a 375°F (190°C, gas mark 5) oven, basting frequently, for 40 minutes.

SMELTS
Éperlans

Always buy small smelts and fry them on a skewer or deep fry and serve arranged in a clump.

Large smelts can be prepared like whiting; they are very similar, except that they have an excessive number of bones for their size. This makes them difficult to eat.

STURGEON
Esturgeon

This is a migratory fish that, like the salmon, lives by turns in fresh or salt water. Sturgeon are found mainly in the large rivers of Russia and in limited quantities in the Gironde region of France. They can reach a very large size.

Sturgeon eggs, after special treatment, become caviare; the fish's flesh is firm and oily, but not of the finest quality.

Sturgeon is rarely available, but the receipes for it are the same as for braised veal.

BRAISED STURGEON
Fricandeau d'esturgeon

Cut a piece of sturgeon, with its skin removed, into slices about 4 cm (1½ inch) thick, larding with pork fat as for a cut of lean veal. Cover the bottom of a well-buttered sauté pan with sliced carrots and onions; place the slices of sturgeon on top and braise them for around 1 hour.

Serve the fish with the braised vegetables and a garnish of small onions, olives or vegetables – spinach, sorrel, courgettes, mashed potatoes *au gratin* or sautéed mushrooms.

SMOKED HADDOCK
Haddock ou aiglefin fumé

Whole or in fillets, smoked haddock is generally poached in water with some milk added. Cooking time, starting from boiling point, is 8–10 minutes for each 1 kg (2 lb).

Serve drained, on a napkin, accompanied by a sauceboat of melted butter and steamed potatoes.

HERRING
Hareng

This is a very popular fish because it is cheap and plentiful.

Eaten very fresh, herring is excellent but rather difficult to digest. It is best served as a lunch dish.

It can be prepared by grilling, frying or *à la meunière* (page 155), accompanied by a spicy sauce, such as mustard sauce, or it can be cooked in a marinade and served cold.

The soft roe of herring is a delicacy used for garnishes or for special dishes, for example, soft roe *à la Villeroy* (breaded and fried, and covered with a very reduced *allemande* sauce, page 109).

Kippers, or smoked herring, are grilled or marinated in fillets and served as an hors-d'oeuvre.

It is very simple to prepare herring. Gut the fish through the gills, without removing the soft roe or the roe, rub it vigorously to dry it and remove the scales. On each side of the back make small slashes to allow the heat to penetrate easily, which will make it cook more quickly. Season with salt and pepper mixed with a few drops of oil and cook on a grill, or roll the fish in flour and cook in a frying pan in very hot butter.

FRESH MARINATED HERRINGS
Harengs frais marinés

Clean and gut the herrings, rub with salt (a small handful of salt for a dozen herrings) and leave to stand for 6 hours.

Drain the fish, wipe and place in an oval earthenware dish, lined with thinly sliced onions and carrots, a couple of sprigs of parsley, sprig of thyme, 1 bay leaf, 3 crushed peppercorns and 2 cloves.

Moisten just to the top of the herrings with a mixture of half dry white wine and half vinegar; cover the fish with a second layer of onions and carrots, chopped, and cover with a sheet of waxed paper or foil.

Bring slowly to the boil, cover the dish and cook for 15 minutes. Cool, and keep fish in cooking liquid until serving time.

DAB AND LEMON SOLE
Limande — Limande-sole

These are flat fish that, if necessary, can be substituted for sole without, however, quite equalling its taste or its fineness.

Their flesh tends to be flaky and stringy, and not so delicate as sole.

All the recipes for sole and brill can be used for this fish.

MONKFISH OR ANGLER
Lotte de mer ou baudroie

Monkfish must be skinned before it can be eaten.

Its flesh, white and firm, is usually added to bouillabaisse or other fish soups.

It is generally prepared in the same way as fresh codfish or hake.

SAUTÉED SCALLOPS OF MONKFISH
Escalopes de lotte sautées

Fillet of monkfish
Salt
Freshly ground pepper
1 egg beaten
1 tablespoon oil
Pinch salt
Fine breadcrumbs
100 g (4 oz) unsalted butter
1 tablespoon olive oil
½ lemon
1 teaspoon chopped parsley
Tomato sauce (optional, page 111)

From the thick part of a monkfish fillet, cut 6 scallops, 2 cm ($\frac{3}{4}$ inch) thick. Flatten them slightly, season with salt and freshly ground pepper, dip in an egg beaten with 1 tablespoon oil and a pinch of salt, and roll in very fine breadcrumbs.

To make the breadcrumbs adhere to the fish, press lightly with the flat of a knife blade.

Heat the butter and olive oil in a sauté pan and place the scallops in it side by side. When they are half cooked and golden, turn them and cook the other side.

Arrange fish on a serving platter; squeeze ½ lemon over the tops and sprinkle with chopped parsley, blanched. Moisten with the cooking butter. If there is not enough butter, add another piece cooked in the pan until light brown.

A sauceboat of tomato sauce (page 111) can be served on the side.

FRIED FILLETS OF MONKFISH
Filets de lotte frits

The scallops are prepared as for the sautéed monkfish. Then soak them in milk, flour well and plunge into very hot oil.

Drain the scallops and place on a napkin, garnish with fried parsley and lemon quarters.

3 kg (6 lb) sea bass
Chopped chervil
Chopped tarragon
Salt
Pepper
Flaky pastry dough
  (recipe below)
Egg yolk
Melted butter

Lobster mousse:
225 g (8 oz) raw
  lobster meat
Coral
2 teaspoons salt
Freshly ground
  pepper
Dash grated nutmeg
1½ dl (¼ pt) double
  cream
100 g (4 oz) pistachios
  and truffles

Flaky pastry dough:
500 g (1 lb) sifted
  plain flour
1½ teaspoons salt
¼ l (½ pt) water
375 g (12 oz) unsalted
  butter

SEA BASS IN PASTRY
Loup de la Méditerranée en croûte
For 6–8 people

The Mediterranean sea bass has very fine, white flesh and an exquisite taste and aroma. It can be cooked many different ways – poached, braised, served whole cold, but it is probably at its best grilled with fennel or prepared in pastry.

Buy a fine, very fresh sea bass; gut and skin it carefully; leave the head and the tail intact.

Cut the fish along the back to the backbone. In this long slit, place freshly picked, chopped chervil and tarragon, salt and pepper, and close the fish. Do the same along the belly.

Next, roll out 2 thin sheets of flaky pastry dough (page 168), the length of the sea bass. Place the fish on top of one of the sheets of pastry, cover it with the other sheet of pastry. Seal the dough by pressing all around the fish to enclose it completely and follow its original shape.

With a very sharp knife, cut off the excess dough, leaving enough to make imitation fins. Make a few lines lengthwise on the fins and tail. Make gills and an eye with the remaining dough.

Glaze the dough with an egg yolk. To make it look more like a fish, reproduce the scales by pressing the dough with a little half-moon shape cutter. This careful work demands much patience and skill.

Place the sea bass thus prepared on a baking sheet, in a 425°F (220°C, gas mark 7) oven. When the dough is firm, reduce the heat to 350°F (180°C, gas mark 4) so that it cooks evenly, inside as well as outside, without burning the dough.

It will take about 1½ hours to cook.

To serve place the sea bass on a long platter and carve in front of the guests. Accompany it simply by melted butter.

Variation. Before it is wrapped in dough, the sea bass can be stuffed with this excellent lobster mousse:

Lobster mousse

In a mortar pound the lobster meat. Add the coral seasoned with salt, a turn of the pepper mill and finely grated nutmeg.

Rub the lobster meat through a very fine sieve into a bowl.

Set the bowl on ice, and beat into the lobster the cream and then the pistachios and truffles.

Flaky pastry dough

Place the flour on a pastry board, making a well in the middle for the salt and water. Mix and knead the flour with water until the dough is smooth and elastic. Roll into a ball and let stand for 20 minutes. Roll the dough out evenly into a sheet about 20 cm (8 inches) square. On top place the butter, which has been kneaded in the same way and has reached the same consistency as the dough.

Fold the ends of the dough over the butter so as to enclose it completely.

Let it stand again for 10 minutes; then give the dough two turns. Each turn consists of rolling the dough, on a marble slab with a rolling pin, into a rectangle 61 cm (24 inches) by 20 cm (8 inches) and 1 cm ($\frac{1}{2}$ inch) thick. Fold the pastry in three, forming a square again. The second turn consists of rolling the dough in the opposite direction and folding in three.

The purpose of turning and rolling is to distribute the butter evenly in the pastry, to ensure that it expands evenly during the cooking.

Give the dough two more pairs of turns, letting it stand 10 minutes between each pair of turns. The flaky dough is ready to be used and cut after 6 turns, which means 3 pairs of 2 turns.

1·5–1·8 kg (3–3½ lb) sea bass
1 glass dry white wine
2 handfuls fresh seaweed
Salt
Pepper

Sauce:
1 tomato
1 sweet pepper
2 tablespoons chopped *fines herbes*
Salt
Pepper
Juice of 2 lemons
6 tablespoons olive oil

SEA BASS WITH SEAWEED
Loup au varech à la façon de Michel Guérard

In a long, shallow ovenproof dish, place one-third of the seaweed. Gut, clean and season the sea bass; place it on top and cover completely with the remaining seaweed. Pour white wine over it.

Cover the dish with a piece of aluminium foil. Place it in an oven preheated to 400°F (200°C, gas mark 6). It will take about 30 minutes to cook.

Serve the sea bass accompanied by the following sauce, served separately.

In a bowl combine 1 tomato, seeded and finely chopped, 1 sweet pepper, cut into small dice, 2 tablespoons of chopped *fines herbes*, consisting of parsley, chervil, tarragon, basil and chives.

Mix, season with salt and pepper, and thin with the lemon juice and olive oil.

The chives can be replaced with a little chopped onion or shallot.

The sea bass can also be cooked in this way in a covered pan, over a low flame.

MACKEREL
Maquereau

Like herring, mackerel is very abundant in the spring, and it is an economical food, but rather difficult to digest. It is also simple to prepare: gut the fish through the gills and rub it vigorously to dry it. Cut off the fins and make a couple of slashes in the back.

GRILLED MACKEREL
Maquereaux grillés

Choose medium-sized mackerels. Prepare the fish and season with salt and pepper mixed with 1 tablespoon of melted butter or oil. Place on a very hot grill. Regulate the intensity of the flame according to the thickness of the fish, which taper towards the end, in order to cook them evenly. When the fish are half cooked, turn them over and complete cooking. Place the fish on a long platter and serve with a sauceboat of *maître d'hôtel* butter – a mixture of butter with *fines herbes*, vinegar or lemon juice, salt and pepper.

If the mackerels are very large, they can be cooked more easily by slitting them down the back without separating the two halves. Pour on some seasoned melted butter and place the opened fish on the grill, searing the inside first; then turn and cooking the skin side. Close the fish to serve.

Note: The thin end of the fish can be protected by sliding a slice of potato or any other vegetable between the tail and the flame. Do this after the mackerel has been seared.

MACKEREL IN BROWN BUTTER
Maquereaux au beurre noir

Prepare a court-bouillon with 1 l (2 pts) of water, 2 teaspoons of salt, 6 tablespoons of vinegar and a few crushed peppercorns. Place the mackerel in this cold court-bouillon and slowly bring to the boil; turn the heat as low as possible and poach for 10–15 minutes, depending upon the thickness of the fishes, which should be about the same size.

Drain the fish and place them on an ovenproof plate; dry for a few seconds in the oven. Sprinkle with chopped parsley and a few drops of vinegar or lemon juice and some unsalted butter cooked in a frying pan until brown. This last step is done just before serving.

6 large mackerel
Salt
Pepper
Strong fish stock
   (page 105)
Dry white wine
Unsalted butter
1·5 kg (3 lb) spinach
Cream
$\frac{1}{4}$ l ($\frac{1}{2}$ pt) Mornay
   sauce (page 120)
Grated cheese
Breadcrumbs

MACKEREL FILLETS WITH SPINACH
Filets de maquereaux à la florentine
For 6 people

Clean and fillet the mackerel.

This is done by dividing the fillet from the head end while the fish is lying flat. Then detach the fillet, starting from the tail, with the blade of the knife placed flat, resting slightly on the backbone. Do this on each side.

Place the fillets on an ovenproof serving platter. Season with salt and pepper and moisten with a mixture of half strong fish stock and half dry white wine, covering the fish halfway up. Sprinkle a few pieces of butter on top. Cook covered in a 375°F (190°C, gas mark 5) oven for 8–10 minutes.

Meanwhile, prepare the spinach in butter or cream, either puréed or in leaf. Make the fairly thick Mornay sauce.

Just before serving, spread the very hot spinach on a long platter and place the carefully drained mackerel fillets on top. Pour the remaining cooking juice from the fillets into the Mornay sauce without spoiling the consistency of the sauce. Coat the fillets and the spinach with the Mornay sauce and sprinkle with grated cheese mixed with breadcrumbs. Pour some melted butter over and brown under the grill.

WHITING
Merlan

The flesh of the whiting is very delicate, easy to digest and particularly good for invalids.

Because its flesh is very fragile, it is better to cook whiting whole. Gut it through the gills. Since there are few scales, it is enough to scrape it lightly and dry vigorously.

The best recipes for whiting are fried, *à la meunière* (page 155), *au plat* (page 172) and *au gratin* – although most of the recipes for white fish are applicable (see the recipes for sole).

FRIED WHITING
Merlan frit

Clean and gut 1 medium-sized whiting, make 5 or 6 slashes on each side and dip in milk and then in flour.

Just before serving, plunge into very hot oil.

Follow the advice given on frying (page 143).

If fish is seared too quickly it does not cook inside. On the other hand, if the oil is not hot enough, the fish boils instead of frying. This requires attention and the size of the fish must also be taken into account.

Drain the fish in a cloth. Sprinkle lightly with salt, and serve immediately so that it has a golden crusty coating.

Whiting is generally accompanied by fried parsley and lemon quarters.

WHITING AU PLAT
Merlan au plat

Split the whiting down the back, open it flat and season with salt and pepper. Set on an ovenproof dish, thickly buttered, and moisten with 2 tablespoons of white wine; on top sprinkle a few pieces of butter and the juice of $\frac{1}{4}$ lemon. Start cooking on top of the stove and continue in a 375°F (190°C, gas mark 5) oven, basting very often.

It will take 10–15 minutes to cook. At the end the white wine and the butter should be almost totally absorbed by the fish, which is glazed by the syrupy liquid.

SALT COD
Morue

Choose cod that is very dark on the back and silver on the belly, thick, with white flesh and short fibres.

Avoid flat, dry, yellow fish.

Before cooking, soak the cod under cold running water,

brushing the fish on both sides: cut the fish into pieces of about 100 g ($\frac{1}{4}$ lb) each and soak in cold water for at least 24 hours to desalt it before cooking. The water should be changed several times.

The cooking is very simple.

Drain the pieces after desalting. Roll each one up, with the skin on the outside, and tie with a thread.

Place the pieces of fish in a sauce pan and cover with cold water. As soon as the water starts to boil, reduce to the lowest possible heat. Skim off the foam. Cover, and poach 15–18 minutes, depending upon the thickness of the cod.

The cooked cod is ready for various dishes especially the most succulent of all described in the following recipe.

SALT COD WITH TRUFFLES
Brandade de morue aux truffes

Into the brandade, prepared as described below, mix truffles cut into large dice and heated in unsalted butter. Pile in a dome shape and arrange some slices of truffle in the centre and a ring of fried croûtons around the edge.

CREAM OF SALT COD
Brandade de morue à la ménagère
For 6–8 people

500 g (1 lb) very white salt cod
2–3 dl ($\frac{1}{4}$–$\frac{1}{2}$ pt) olive oil
1 crushed garlic clove
6 tablespoons cream or milk
100 g (4 oz) cooked potato
Pinch white pepper, very finely ground
Juice 1 lemon

Desalt the cod in fresh water 24 hours. Change the water several times.

Poach the desalted cod in water, placing the fish, cut into several pieces, in a saucepan with 3 l (6 pts) water. Bring to the boil. As soon as the water boils, turn the heat as low as possible and poach the fish 10–12 minutes.

Drain the pieces of cod. Remove the black and white skin and the bones. Break the flesh into fine flakes.

In a heavy-bottomed saucepan heat 6 tablespoons oil. Add the cod and the crushed garlic clove.

Work the mixture quickly with a spatula or a wooden spoon

until the fish is reduced to a fine paste. Then, lower the heat. Continue to beat the paste without stopping, adding the rest of the oil and the cream or milk.

Then, add the hot potato pulp and mix well (the potatoes should be boiled in the skin or steamed). Season with white pepper and, if necessary, salt. Then mix the lemon juice in well. When finished, the brandade should be a smooth paste, light and very white.

Serve the hot brandade in a mound on a serving dish. Surround with tiny bread croûtons, cooked golden in oil or butter.

SALT COD WITH ONIONS AND POTATOES
Morue à la lyonnaise

3 medium-sized onions
25 g (1 oz) unsalted butter
2 tablespoons oil
3 medium-sized potatoes
500 g (1 lb) salt cod
Pinch freshly ground pepper
Pinch chopped parsley
½ tablespoon vinegar

In a frying pan slowly cook the onions, cut into julienne, with 25 g (1 oz) of butter and 2 tablespoons of oil. Cook 3 potatoes in salted water, peel and cut into slices. When the onions are cooked but not brown, add the potatoes and sauté the mixture to brown lightly.

Poach the cod; remove the skin and bones, flake and dry over a low flame just long enough to evaporate the cooking water. Add to the mixture in the frying pan and sauté for a few minutes on a high flame. Correct the seasonings and add a pinch of freshly ground pepper.

Just before serving, stir freshly chopped parsley into the mixture. Pile on to a serving platter and add vinegar to the cooking pan; bring rapidly to the boil, and pour over the cod.

SKATE
Raie

Wash the skate under running water and scrub with a brush to remove the slimy matter that covers it. Then remove the wings, cut them into pieces of about 225 g (8 oz) each and place them in a heavy saucepan with the central part of the tail and the two sides of the head, where there are two fleshy knobs.

Cover with water, salt to taste and add 3 tablespoons of vinegar to each pint of water. Bring slowly to the boil, skim and, as soon as the water boils, lower the heat and poach for 15 minutes.

Drain the skate carefully. Remove the skin on both sides, arrange on a serving platter and serve as in the following recipe.

SKATE WITH BROWN BUTTER
Raie au beurre noir

Prepare the skate as directed above. While it is still very hot, season it with salt and freshly ground pepper. Sprinkle crushed capers and a pinch of chopped parsley on top. Baste it with hot browned butter and a splash of vinegar poured into the hot frying pan used for browning the butter for just a second. Serve steamed or boiled potatoes separately.

RED MULLETS
Rougets (rougets-barbets)

The red mullet has two barbels on its lower jaw; the back is red, the sides and belly a silver pink, and the tail scalloped. The flesh is white, fine and very delicate. This delicious fish lives at the bottom of the Mediterranean, where it feeds on small marine plants that grow on the rocks. It is also called the sea woodcock. It is at its finest grilled, while still very fresh.

Preparation is very simple: wipe, remove the gills, but do not gut the fish.

When the red mullets are cooked following the method for grilled fish on page 143, place them on a very hot serving platter and serve a sauceboat of *maître d'hôtel* butter (page 226), separately.

When the fish are served at table detach and remove the heads. Open the mullets down the back. Carefully scoop out the insides and mix with the *maître d'hôtel* butter. Remove the bones and spread the *maître d'hôtel* butter on the flesh of the fish. Season the fish with a few drops of lemon juice and one turn of a pepper mill; then serve this exquisite dish.

Small red mullets
Salt
Pepper
Flour
Oil

Tomato fondue:
1 kg (2 lb) ripe
   tomatoes
2 tablespoons oil
Salt
Pepper
Garlic clove
Pinch sugar
Pinch saffron
Fennel stalk
Sprig thyme
½ bay leaf
Few grains coriander
Pinch chopped
   parsley
Slices of peeled
   lemon
Chervil leaves

RED MULLET WITH TOMATOES, GARLIC AND SAFFRON
Rouget à l'orientale

Red mullet are also delicious eaten cold. Mullet *à l'orientale* makes an excellent hors-d'oeuvre or cold main dish (see page 11 for another version of this dish).

Use small red mullets. Season with salt and pepper. Roll them in flour and brown them rapidly in a frying pan in a little oil, as for *à la meunière*.

Place the fish in an oiled ovenproof dish and cover them with a fondue of tomatoes, prepared in the following manner.

Skin and seed ripe tomatoes, retaining the juice. Chop coarsely and put into a frying pan in which a little oil is heating. Season with salt and pepper and add a crushed garlic clove and sugar; cook slowly until the liquid is reduced by three-quarters.

The tomato fondue used for red mullet is seasoned with saffron, a fennel stalk, thyme and powdered bay leaf, coriander and chopped parsley.

Continue cooking the mullet covered with the fondue. Bring to the boil on top of the stove; then place, covered, in a 325°F (170°C, gas mark 3) oven for 8–10 minutes.

Cool and garnish to taste with thin slices of peeled lemon. Place a chervil leaf in the centre of each lemon slice; serve mullet at room temperature or slightly chilled.

RED MULLET WITH TOMATOES AND OLIVES
Rouget à la provençale

6 small red mullets
sautéed as above

1 onion, coarsely
chopped

6 tomatoes

1 garlic clove

Pinch chopped
parsley

100 g (4 oz) pitted
black olives

Pinch salt

Freshly ground
pepper

Few drops lemon
juice

Mullet *à la provençale* is a hot version of mullet *à l'orientale*.

Proceed as above with the mullets which are browned and placed in the ovenproof platter in which they will be served. Then add the onion to the oil in the frying pan and cook it slowly until it is just light brown. Add the tomatoes (peeled and seeded and drained), the garlic clove coarsely chopped, chopped parsley, black olives, salt and pepper. Simmer for 10 minutes and pour over the mullets. Finish the cooking in a 325°F (170°C, gas mark 3) oven for 10 minutes. Serve hot, with a few drops of lemon juice. This dish can also be served cold.

8 small red mullets,
   about 100 g (4 oz)
   each

Court-bouillon:
$\frac{1}{2}$ l (1 pt) white wine
$\frac{1}{4}$ l ($\frac{1}{2}$ pt) water
   (preferably bottled
   Evian water)
50 g (2 oz) chopped
   carrots
50 g (2 oz) chopped
   onions
50 g (2 oz) coarse salt
1 tablespoon each
   parsley, sliced
   celery, chopped leek
$\frac{1}{2}$ bay leaf
Small sprig thyme
2 teaspoons
   peppercorns
2 cloves
2 coriander seeds
4 slices orange
4 slices lemon

Pistou sauce:
1$\frac{1}{2}$ dl ($\frac{1}{4}$ pt) olive oil
2 tablespoons
   chopped basil
1 tablespoon chopped
   parsley
Chopped tarragon,
   chervil, chives
1 garlic clove,
   crushed
Juice of 1 lemon
2 teaspoons salt
3 turns of a pepper
   mill

RED MULLETS WITH PISTOU SAUCE

Rougets de la Méditerranée – Sauce au pistou

For 4 people

For this delicious dish you will need very fresh red mullets, which can be recognized by their bright eyes and beautiful red colour.

Prepare a court-bouillon with the listed ingredients. (Evian water is recommended as it does not have the taste of chlorine.) Bring the mixture to the boil, and boil for 15 minutes. Add the mullet; return to the boil. Lower the flame immediately and poach for fifteen minutes.

To make the sauce, mix all the ingredients. Keep in a cool place. In the summer these mullets can be eaten cold.

Sardines

Fresh sardines are rarely found in the average fishmonger's shop.

Around the Mediterranean sea, where the sardines are especially fine, they are eaten as soon as they have been caught, usually grilled and served with butter.

〰〰〰〰〰〰〰〰〰〰〰〰

SARDINES WITH TOMATO SAUCE
Sardines antiboises

500 g (1 lb) large, fresh sardines
2 tablespoons olive oil
2 large onions
½ glass dry white wine
6 tomatoes
Salt
Pepper
Anchovy butter (optional, page 27)

Scale, gut and wipe large fresh sardines.

Heat olive oil in a frying pan. When it smokes, add the sardines and brown them rapidly on both sides. Set aside on a plate.

Then slowly cook the onions cut into julienne in the oil used for the sardines; do not let them brown. Moisten with wine. Reduce by two-thirds, then add the tomatoes, peeled, seeded, drained and chopped coarsely: season with salt and pepper and simmer to reduce by half.

Pour the sauce in a gratin dish. Place the sardines on top and put in a 425°F (220°C, gas mark 7) oven for 5 minutes. Serve with a sauceboat of anchovy butter if liked.

〰〰〰〰〰〰〰〰〰〰〰〰

SALMON
Saumon

The salmon first lives in large rivers, then swims to the sea, and returns the rivers to reproduce. It often reaches a very large size – 1½–2 m (5–6 feet).

Choose a medium-sized fish, which means that the fish is adult but not old.

Salmon is cooked whole or cut into slices about 2.5 cm (1 inch) thick. I advise you to cook the fish whole unless you are grilling it or cooking it *à la meunière* (page 155).

The whole salmon is generally cooked in a court-bouillon (page 144) and served hot, with a hollandaise, mousseline, cream, shrimp or other sauce, or cold with mayonnaise, green, ravigote or other sauce (see index).

Salmon can also be poached, grilled or braised, following recipes suitable for large fish.

One can also make an excellent fish pastry or pie called *coulibiac*.

HOT SALMON IN PASTRY
Coulibiac de saumon

1 recipe firm unsweetened brioche dough (page 527)
350 g (12 oz) salmon
50 g (2 oz) mushrooms
1 medium-sized onion
100 g (4 oz) coarse semolina cooked in white stock
1 hard-boiled egg, coarsely chopped
225 g (8 oz) fresh *vésiga* or 50 g (2 oz) dried (if available)
Melted unsalted butter

Vésiga is the spinal cord of sturgeon. If available it should be soaked for 5 hours, cooked in water or white stock for 3 hours and then chopped.

Remove the backbone from the salmon, cut into slices 6 mm ($\frac{1}{4}$ inch) thick, season and sauté in butter until firm. Chop the onion and mushrooms, cook until soft in the salmon butter, cool and then sprinkle on the salmon.

As explained in the recipe for pâté Pantin on page 272, roll the brioche dough into a rectangle. On top place layers of the ingredients listed, leaving a good margin. Fold over the edges of the dough so that it encloses the fish and other ingredients, moistening the edges so that the pastry sticks together. Turn upside down on to a baking sheet and let stand at room temperature for 20 minutes, covered with a cloth. Brush the dough with melted butter. Mark it with a pattern of incisions and in the centre make a small hole to allow the steam to escape.

Bake in a 400°F (200°C, gas mark 6) oven for about 35 minutes. Before serving pour a couple of tablespoons of melted butter though the hole.

Note: The grains of the cooked, seasoned semolina should remain separate like rice, while becoming very soft.

¼ dl (½ pt) dry white
wine
¼ l (½ pt) dry white
vermouth
¼ l (½ pt) strong fish
fumet
6 tablespoons
chopped shallots
½ l (1 pt) cream
100 g (4 oz) sorrel
cooked in salted
water and drained
Salt
Pepper
1·5 kg (3 lb) fresh
salmon cut into
very thin scallops
6 tablespoons oil

SALMON SCALLOPS WITH SORREL

Escalope de saumon à l'oseille des frères Troisgros

For 8–10 people

In a saucepan, reduce the white wine, vermouth and fumet with the chopped shallots.

When the liquid becomes syrupy, strain it through a fine sieve. Add the cream, and reduce again to thicken. Season. Then add the well-drained sorrel.

Salt and pepper the salmon scallops. Place them in a frying pan with the hot oil. Do not let them dry out; a few seconds is enough to cook each side.

To serve, place the salmon scallops on warm plates; cover with the sorrel sauce or serve it separately.

As a garnish make a fish-shaped ornament of flaky pastry.

RAW SALMON

Saumon cru Renga-Ya

Japanese cooking was my inspiration for this recipe. Just before serving cut the salmon into scallops of about 125 g (5 oz) each.

Place the salmon scallops on very cold plates; salt them, and give them a turn of a pepper mill. Pour on each a tablespoon of olive oil, the juice of a quarter lemon and a pinch of chives.

Serve with thin slices of hot toast.

You can also add a tablespoon of caviare in the middle.

Sole

The sole is the finest of all the flat fish. Its flesh is white, firm, delicate and easy to digest.

To clean the sole remove its two skins, black and white. The latter is simply scraped when the sole is served whole, though this rule has some exceptions.

Cut the head off on the bias where the fillets begin. Trim the end of the tail. At the tail end ease away the black skin by scraping with the point of a knife. Grasp this end of the skin with the corner of a dish towel and pull sharply. The skin usually will detach itself in one pull. If the sole is not being filleted scrape the scales off the white skin. Otherwise remove the white skin in the same way as the black one.

Using strong scissors, cut off the lateral fins. Make a small incision above the intestines and remove them. Wash the sole under running water and dry it with a cloth.

Just before cooking the fish make a slash on the skinned side on the right and left of the backbone, which will guide the point of the knife. This helps the fish to cook better.

When the sole is to be filleted, and the two skins have been removed, with the point of a knife cut around the edges of each fillet. Detach the fillet by sliding the blade of a thin, flexible knife between the bones and the fillet, starting from the backbone and cutting close to the bones so as not to leave any flesh.

Then flatten the fillet lightly with a damp mallet or the side of a cleaver to tenderize the flesh.

Finally, if the sole is to be served whole, covered with a sauce, just before cooking cut the short bones from the edges of the fillets. This need not be done when the sole is fried or grilled, but it means that these many small bones do not get mixed into the sauce or the garnish as one serves the sole. Certainly the fillets lose some of their attractiveness, but it is easier to eat the fish, the sauce and the garnish since they are free of bones.

The bones and head are used to make a strong sole stock, to baste the fish while it is cooking.

Before cleaning, a sole for 2 people should weigh about 350–400 g (12–14 oz). The 4 fillets should average about 225 g (8 oz) net weight. Use 2 fillets per person.

FRIED SOLE
Sole frite

Clean the sole, remove the black skin and scrape the white one.

Soak the fish in milk, roll in flour, shake off the excesss, and plunge into a large pan of hot oil. Follow the basic instructions for frying (page 143); the cooking time for a sole of about 225 g (8 oz) will be 8–10 minutes. The fish will be crusty and golden when served.

When the sole is drained from the oil, pat it quickly with a cloth, sprinkle with salt and place on a plate with quarters of lemon and a bouquet of parsley plunged in very hot oil for a second and salted to taste. Serve without delay.

GRILLED SOLE
Sole grillée

Prepare the sole as above. In addition, with the point of a knife make a few diamond-shaped slashes in the white skin. Season with salt and pepper and dip into unsalted melted butter or a little oil. Place on a very hot grill, with the white skin side down. Adjust the heat of the flame according to the thickness of the sole. Place the thin tail end farther from the heat so that it does not cook more rapidly and dry out.

Cook for 3 minutes. Then slide a spatula between the grill and the sole, lift and shift it round about 2 cm ($\frac{3}{4}$ inch), skin side down still. Cook for another 3 minutes (for a 225 g (8 oz) fish). Slide the spatula a second time under the sole and turn the fish over with a rapid movement. The white skin will be golden and ornamented with an attractive diamond pattern left by the bars of the grill.

Moisten lightly with a few drops of melted butter while cooking the second side of the sole, and sprinkle with a little salt which will season the flesh as it melts.

Serve the sole with the diamond pattern up, accompanied by grilled tomatoes, grilled mushrooms and melted butter in a sauceboat, or *maître d'hôtel* butter, anchovy butter or a béarnaise or choron sauce (see Index).

Sole meunière

Sole
Salt
Pepper
Oil
Flour
75 g (3 oz) unsalted butter
1 tablespoon olive oil
Lemon slices and juice
1 teaspoon chopped parsley

Prepare the sole as directed above, leaving the well-scraped white skin on.

Season with salt and pepper mixed with a few drops of oil; then roll in flour.

Cook, white skin side down, in 25 g (1 oz) of very hot butter and 1 tablespoon of olive oil. Use a frying pan, preferably an oval one, to avoid using excess butter which often burns – the pan will be almost the same size as the fish.

Cook very quickly; when the sole touches the very hot butter, it will be seared so that it will not stick to the pan. The cooking butter should not bubble.

After 5 or 6 minutes, turn the sole with a spatula and continue cooking until it is done.

Place the fish on a very hot serving platter. Garnish the edges with a row of thin lemon slices, halved, with the peel cut into points.

Squeeze a few drops of lemon juice on to the sole; sprinkle with chopped parsley, blanched at the last moment and still damp. Add 50 g (2 oz) of butter to the cooking butter in the pan and heat until it turns brown. Pour over the sole.

When the hot butter touches the damp parsley, it produces a rich foam to cover the sole which is served immediately.

SOLE WITH CHAMPAGNE
Sole au champagne

Sole
Strong sole fumet
Champagne
Unsalted butter
Salt

Sauce 1
Unsalted butter
Flour

Sauce 2
Cooking juice from sole
3 tablespoons fish velouté or béchamel sauce (page 110)
1 egg yolk
1 tablespoon cold strong fish stock, milk or cooking juice from mushrooms
Unsalted butter

Sauce 3
1 egg yolk
1 tablespoon cold strong sole stock, milk or cooking juice from mushrooms
Unsalted butter

Prepare the sole by cutting away the short bones from the edges of the fillet. With the bones and the head make a strong sole fumet or stock using champagne instead of the usual wine.

Thickly butter a long fireproof dish the size of the fish; sprinkle with a pinch of salt, and place on it one or more soles, skinned side down.

Moisten, just to the top of the sole, with equal parts of dry champagne and strong sole stock. Sprinkle a few pieces of unsalted butter on top, and cover with a piece of buttered wax paper. Bring to the boil on top of the stove, then place in the oven to poach the fish slowly. The fish is cooked when the fillets can be detached easily from the backbone. This takes about 12–15 minutes.

Drain the fish with a spatula, and place it on a very hot serving platter; cover with another dish to keep it moist while the sauce is being prepared. The sauce can be thickened in various ways, but I am assuming that the home kitchen does not possess all the stocks that are available in a restaurant kitchen.

First method

Place the dish used for cooking the sole on the stove, and boil to reduce the stock until you have just enough to sauce 1 or 2 sole. Then add to the boiling sauce a mixture of 3 parts butter to 2 parts flour (by weight). The butter will melt immediately and thicken the sauce. Off the flame finish the sauce by adding 50 g (2 oz) of butter. Correct the seasoning. Add the juices from the serving platter that have drained from the sole. Pour the sauce over the fish.

Second method

Pour the cooking juice from the sole into a small saucepan. Boil to reduce the stock two-thirds, then add (for 1 sole) 3 tablespoons fish velouté or béchamel sauce. Stir the mixture. Bring to the boil, and thicken with 1 egg yolk beaten with cold strong sole stock, milk or mushroom juice. Be careful not to overcook the yolk; it should not boil but should thicken the sauce to the consistency of cream. Finish by adding butter away from the flame, as in the method above. Serve the same way.

Third method

Reduce the cooking liquid by two-thirds. Remove from the flame and thicken with 1 egg yolk mixed with cold strong sole stock, milk or mushroom juice. Cook without boiling on a low flame or in a double boiler, stirring with a whisk as for hollandaise sauce. Correct the seasoning. Away from the flame finish with 100 g (4 oz) of butter. Serve as in the two methods above.

This sauce should have the consistency of light cream.

1 shallot
Unsalted butter
Sole
Salt
Pepper
Dry white wine
Cooking juice from
   mushrooms or sole
   fumet
1 teaspoon chopped
   parsley
Few drops lemon
   juice

SOLE WITH WHITE WINE AND SHALLOTS
Sole Bercy

For 2 people

Thickly butter an ovenproof earthenware dish; on the bottom sprinkle a chopped shallot. Heat the dish slowly on the stove; cook the shallot without browning for about 10 minutes.

Season the sole on both sides with salt and pepper. Place on top of the shallot, the white skin side up, and moisten with dry white wine and the liquid mushrooms have cooked in and/or strong sole stock in equal parts. The liquid should just reach the top of the fish. Sprinkle pieces of butter over it. Bring to the boil on the stove, and continue to poach in a 325°F (170°C, gas mark 3) oven for about 10 minutes. Baste frequently.

Place the sole on a serving platter; cover with another platter to keep warm while you finish the sauce.

Pour the liquid from the sole into a small saucepan. Boil to reduce rapidly, until only 4 tablespoons of very syrupy liquid are left. Away from the flame shake the saucepan around to blend in 50 g (2 oz) of butter, cut into small pieces, which will thicken the sauce. Add 1 teaspoon of freshly chopped parsley, and squeeze in a few drops of lemon juice. Correct the seasoning; then cover the well-drained sole entirely with the sauce.

If you have a very hot oven, or a gas or electric grill, put the sole to brown for a few seconds. The sauce will get a beautiful golden colour. This last step must be done very quickly without letting the sauce boil, or the two main ingredients – the cooking liquid and the butter – will separate immediately.

This procedure, which is the simplest and the most delicious of all, can be utilized in many fish recipes. Only the seasonings and the garnishes will change.

Success depends on understanding the process rather than on skill. Remember that the liaison of the cooking liquid and the butter is only possible if the liquid is strong enough – if it contains enough concentrated fish juices – to hold the butter in suspension. If you reduce fish fumet to its furthest point you will see that a grey liquid gradually forms, syrupy at first, and finally becoming solid. This extract, called fish glaze, is the thickening element which gives the sauce its flavour.

For economy or convenience you can make the sauce for this classic dish by one of the methods described in the preceding recipe, for sole with champagne. In each case the cooking liquid is added to the prepared sauce or used to make it.

SOLE WITH MUSHROOMS
Sole aux champignons ou sole bonne femme

This recipe is identical to the preceding one.

The only change is the addition of 4 or 5 white mushrooms (for 2 people), finely chopped and spread on the chopped shallot after it is cooked.

Proceed as for sole Bercy.

SOLE WITH TOMATOES
Sole aux tomates ou à la portugaise

Use the same method of preparation as for sole Bercy and replace the mushrooms with 2 large ripe tomatoes, skinned, seeded, coarsely chopped and stewed in 15 g ($\frac{1}{2}$ oz) of butter.

1 pint mussels
1 tablespoon dry
white wine
15 g (½ oz) unsalted
butter
Sole, prepared as for
sole with
champagne

SOLE WITH MUSSELS
Sole aux moules dite marinière
For 2 people

Clean the mussels. Scrape them to be sure that no sand is left.
Boil with dry white wine and butter until they open.

Drain the cooking liquid and strain it through cheesecloth into
a bowl. Remove the mussels from their shells and clean them.
Add to the liquid.

Meanwhile, prepare a sole as for the sole with champagne,
above, moisten with the cooking liquid from the mussels, and
poach as in the recipe. Finish the sauce in the same way, adding
the mussels, which have been heated in a little of their cooking
juice and drained well.

Place the sole on a serving platter and cover with the sauce.

The hot mussels, well drained, can also be placed around the
sole on the serving platter and covered with sauce at the same
time as the fish.

I advise you not to reduce the mussel stock too much. If this
stock is concentrated excessively, it has too strong a flavour.

12 small onions
Unsalted butter
12 small mushrooms
Sole prepared as for
sole Bercy
6 tablespoons red
wine with pinch
sugar
4 tablespoons sole
fumet
Croûtons, fried in
butter

SOLE WITH RED WINE,
MUSHROOMS AND ONIONS
Sole à la bourguignonne
For 2 people

In a small saucepan cook the onions slowly in butter until brown.
When the onions are nearly cooked, add the mushrooms.

Prepare a sole as for sole Bercy. Place the onions and the mushrooms around the sole in the cooking dish. In a pan bring the
red wine (sweetened with a pinch of sugar) to the boil, and
reduce the liquid to 1 tablespoon. Then add 4 tablespoons of
strong sole stock. Moisten the sole with the reduced fish stock,
and continue the recipe as for the sole Bercy. Arrange the sole
on a platter and pour the sauce over, without putting it under
the grill. On top place some diamond-shaped croûtons fried in
butter.

2 ripe tomatoes
1 tablespoon unsalted
  butter
Pinch salt
Pinch sugar
Small garlic clove
Sole prepared as for *à
la meunière* (page
184)

SOLE MEUNIÈRE WITH TOMATOES AND GARLIC
Sole meunière à la niçoise

Remove the stems, cores and skins of the tomatoes and squeeze them to remove the seeds and the juice. Cut into quarters and sauté in a pan with the butter, salt, sugar and a piece of crushed garlic the size of a pea.

Reduce the mixture slightly, taste it. Place a sole prepared *à la meunière* on a serving platter and arrange the tomato mixture at either end.

Note: Courgettes, aubergines and cucumbers mix deliciously with tomatoes cooked as a garnish. If two vegetables are used, arrange separate spoonfuls of each alternating at either end of the serving platter.

Sole
Unsalted butter
Pinch salt
Sole fumet
1 tablespoon dry
　white wine
1 tablespoon cooking
　juice from
　mushrooms
Sauce normande
　(page 123)
Poached mussels
Shrimps
Poached oysters
Mushrooms stewed in
　butter with lemon
　juice
Truffles
Gudgeons rolled in
　breadcrumbs and
　fried
Crayfish cooked in a
　court-bouillon
　(page 144)
Flaky pastry
　ornaments

SOLE WITH SHELLFISH AND MUSHROOMS
Sole normande

Place the sole in a thickly buttered ovenproof dish, season with salt. Mix sole stock with 1 tablespoon of dry white wine and 1 tablespoon of mushroom juice. Pour over to reach the top of the fish. Dot with 1 tablespoon of butter cut into small pieces; cover with buttered wax paper, and poach slowly in a 325°F (170°C, gas mark 3) oven without boiling.

Drain the cooking liquid; reduce to 2 tablespoons, and incorporate into a sauce normande.

Put the sole on a long hot platter big enough to hold it and the garnish. For the classic garnish surround it with poached mussels (beards removed), shrimps, poached oysters, and mushrooms stewed in butter with a few drops of lemon juice. Coat the dish with the sauce normande. Place a row of sliced truffles on top and at either end of the platter a handful of gudgeons, rolled in breadcrumbs and fried. Add 1 crayfish, cleaned and cooked in a court-bouillon, per guest. Around the edge, arrange a row of *fleurons* or decorative motifs made of flaky pastry.

**1 slice fresh tuna,
about 1·2 kg (2½ lb)**

**0 g (2 oz) chopped
onion**

**3 tablespoons olive
oil**

Salt

Pepper

**300 g (10 oz) tomato
pulp**

1 glass white wine

**Small bouquet garni
(bay leaf, thyme,
rosemary and
parsley)**

BRAISED TUNA
Thon braisé à la ménagère

For 6 servings

Soak the tuna in cold water for about 1 hour to remove the blood.

In a saucepan with a heavy bottom sauté the chopped onion in the olive oil without letting it brown. Salt and pepper the slice of tuna, and place it on the onions and continue cooking. Turn after 5 minutes.

Add the tomato, the white wine and the bouquet garni. Season.

Cover the saucepan and simmer on a low flame for about 30 minutes. When the tuna is cooked, set it on a serving dish. Just before serving, cover the fish with the sauce, which should be very thick.

Serve the dish with a rice *à la créole* (page 514).

GRILLED TUNA
Thon grillé

Cut a piece of tuna into 2-cm (¾-inch) slices, season with salt and pepper, and marinate for about 1 hour with 1 onion, finely chopped, a couple of sprigs of parsley, a sprig of thyme, 1 bay leaf, 1 tablespoon oil, 1 tablespoon white wine and the juice of ½ lemon.

Just before grilling, drain and wipe the fish, moisten with a few drops of oil, and place slices on a very hot grill. Follow the instructions for grilling a fish (page 143).

Serve accompanied by a rémoulade sauce (page 130), sauce tartare (page 131) or mayonnaise (page 128).

TURBOT AND CHICKEN
TURBOT
Turbot et turbotin

The turbot is one of the best flat sea fish, with white flesh and a
fine flavour. The best turbot comes from the Straits of Dover
and the North Sea.

A 1–3 kg (2–6 lb) turbot is called a *turbotin* or chicken turbot.
For chicken turbot use the recipes for brill and sole. For large
turbot follow the more complicated recipes of the French *grande
cuisine* or simply poach them.

POACHED TURBOT
Turbot ou turbotin poché

Cook the turbot in a fish kettle, an indispensable utensil that has
a rack so that you can drain the fish without breaking it.

First gut and scrape the turbot, remove the fins and wash it.
Then make an incision along its back (brown side) the length of
the backbone and place the fish (white side up) on the rack of the
fish kettle. Cover with cold water, adding 3 dl ($\frac{1}{2}$ pt) of milk
and 1 tablespoon of salt for each 2 l (4 pts) of water; place on the
fire. As soon as the liquid starts to boil, skim, lower the heat and
simmer very gently. It will take about $\frac{1}{4}$ hour for each 1 kg (2 lb)
of fish, depending on its thickness.

It is not difficult to serve the fish, despite its shape and size.
Drain by lifting the rack out of the liquid and slide the fish on to
a serving platter or a clean piece of wood covered with a napkin.
Serve the turbot with potatoes boiled in their skins and a sauce –
melted butter, hollandaise, mousseline, caper, béarnaise, *maître
d'hôtel* butter, white wine, shrimp, etc. (see Index).

The meat of the turbot is extremely gelatinous, and does not
lend itself to being served cold.

Turbot leftovers can be served in scallop shells or used in other
recipes.

SHELLFISH AND CRUSTACEA

SCALLOPS
Coquilles Saint-Jacques

Scrub the outside of the scallop shells with a brush and place the scallops in a very hot oven until they open. Slide the blade of a knife between the flat shell and the muscle, and open them. Discard the flat shells.

With the blade of a flexible knife separate the white part from the concave shell.

Remove the membranes and the fringes that surround the white part and then the red part, called the coral. Wash the white part and the coral carefully under running water.

Scrub the insides of the concave shells with a brush and set them aside for further use, either to serve the scallops or to fill with other fish.

SCALLOPS WITH MUSHROOMS
Coquilles Saint-Jacques à la ménagère
For 6 people

12 scallops in shells
$\frac{1}{4}$ l ($\frac{1}{2}$ pt) water
$\frac{1}{2}$ glass dry white wine
Sprig thyme
$\frac{1}{2}$ bay leaf
1 medium-sized onion, 50 g (2 oz)
Pinch salt
Pinch pepper
225 g (8 oz) white mushrooms
300 g (10 oz) unsalted butter
1 tablespoon flour
2 egg yolks
Fine breadcrumbs

Prepare scallops in their shells as indicated above. Poach the cleaned scallops for 4 minutes in a court-bouillon made with the water, wine, thyme, $\frac{1}{2}$ bay leaf, medium-sized onion, finely chopped, a pinch of salt and pepper.

Drain the scallops and slice them about 6 mm ($\frac{1}{4}$ inch) thick. Melt 50 g (2 oz) of butter in a frying pan, and add the white mushrooms, cleaned and sliced very thin. Cook rapidly. Then add the scallop slices, mix well, and keep hot, covered.

In a sauté pan melt 100 g (4 oz) of butter, add 1 rounded tablespoon of flour and cook slowly like a roux for 10 minutes. Cool the roux. Strain the court-bouillon through cheesecloth, and add the hot liquid in small quantities to the cooled roux, stirring until the sauce is smooth. Bring to the boil, stirring with a whisk and cook for 1 minute.

Thicken the sauce, away from the heat, with 2 egg yolks diluted with 2 teaspoons of court-bouillon. Continue to beat while heating; remove from the heat when the mixture approaches boiling point.

Do not let the sauce boil or the yolk will cook and form small lumps. Add 100 g (4 oz) of unsalted butter and correct the seasoning.

Plunge 6 of the concave scallop shells into boiling water, drain and wipe them, and put 1 tablespoon of the sauce on the bottom of each shell. On top add the meat of about 2 scallops with the mushrooms and, finally, 2 pieces of coral. Cover with the sauce, and sprinkle over some fine breadcrumbs, moistened with a few drops of melted butter. Brown in a very hot oven.

Serve on a platter on top of a folded napkin.

SCALLOPS WITH FRESH TRUFFLES

Ragoût de coquilles Saint-Jacques aux truffes fraîches

For 1 person

3–5 scallops in their shells
3 tablespoons good demi-glace sauce (page 108)
50 g (2 oz) fresh truffles, chopped
50 g (2 oz) steamed spinach leaves
Unsalted butter
Salt and pepper

Open the scallop shells. Discard the parts that are not edible. Poach the meat in simmering demi-glace sauce with the truffles; 5–8 minutes is sufficient to cook them.

Drain the cooked spinach leaves. While hot, season with butter, salt and pepper.

To serve, place the spinach on a hot plate and cover with the ragoût of scallops with truffles.

Note: If the scallop shells are large, they can be used instead of plates.

OYSTERS

Huîtres

The section on hot hors-d'oeuvre includes a recipe for *Huîtres à la florentine* (with spinach). Here are two more useful recipes for cooked oysters.

However, for those who like them, good quality oysters eaten raw make a dish incomparable in its natural simplicity.

FRIED OYSTERS ON SKEWERS
Huîtres frites en brochettes

Remove the oysters from their shells, stiffen them by heating for
2 minutes in their juice together with the juice of 1 lemon. Drain
on a cloth and roll in beaten egg, then in fine breadcrumbs; place
6 oysters on each skewer, leaving a little space between them.
Plunge into very hot oil for 2 minutes. Serve with fried parsley
and a lemon quarter per skewer.

OYSTERS AU GRATIN
Huîtres au gratin

Detach each oyster from its shallow shell, leaving it in the concave
one. Sprinkle on top some chopped herbs, the juice of a lemon
and a pinch of fine breadcrumbs; moisten with melted butter.
Bake in a 425°F (220°C, gas mark 7) oven for 3–4 minutes.
    Serve in the shell.

MUSSELS
Moules

Mussels must always be carefully scraped, one by one, with a
knife, to remove all the filaments which hold them to the rocks
(or cork, when they are cultivated mussels). Test them by a light
pressure of the thumb and the forefinger, to close the two shells;
they always stay separate when they are filled with mud. Discard
the muddy ones; then wash the rest several times under running
water, turning them vigorously, and drain.
    The mussels are then ready to cook.

MUSSELS WITH WINE, ONION AND PARSLEY
Moules à la marinière

2 l (2 qt) mussels
1 medium-sized
 onion
100 g (4 oz) unsalted
 butter
½ glass dry white
 wine
3 sprigs parsley
Pinch freshly ground
 pepper

Prepare the mussels as explained above. Chop the onion very fine. In a saucepan big enough to hold the mussels in their shells, cook the onion very slowly in 50 g (2 oz) of butter without letting it brown.

When the onion is transparent, which should take 15–20 minutes, moisten with dry white wine, add the mussels, then 3 sprigs of parsley, chopped, and a pinch of freshly ground pepper. Cover the saucepan tightly, place over high heat, and let the mussels boil rapidly for a few minutes, until they open.

Remove the mussels with a slotted spoon and keep them warm in a covered soup tureen. Pour the liquid into another saucepan; be sure not to pour out the broth at the bottom of the pot, which will contain sand, despite careful cleaning. Boil to reduce the liquid by half, if you like it strong: less, if you prefer a more delicate flavour. Add the remaining butter, then pour the liquid over the mussels, sprinkle a pinch of chopped parsley on top, and serve.

Note: Mussels *à la marinière* must be cooked at the last moment, and the guests must wait for them. Mussels prepared in advance and kept warm get dark and dry and lose their flavour.

COURT-BOUILLON FOR SHELLFISH
Court-bouillon pour crustacés

3 l (6 pts) water
1 l (2 pts) white wine
¼ l (½ pt) vinegar
2 tablespoons salt
15 crushed
 peppercorns
1 bay leaf
2 sprigs thyme
1 celery stalk
Several sprigs parsley
1 onion, sliced

For 4 l (8 pts) of court-bouillon, place the ingredients in a saucepan and cook for 20 minutes before using.

CRABS
Crabes ou tourteaux

Cook the crabs in a court-bouillon prepared as above for 30 minutes; after letting them cook in the court-bouillon, remove the crab meat and the coral. This step must be done very carefully so that no bits of shell are left in the meat

    With this meat, you can prepare some delicious dishes, like those below.

CRAB IN PASTRY SHELLS
Bouchées de crabe

Fill small shells made of flaky pastry (page 541) with the cooked crab meat (recipe above) mixed with some of the sauce that will accompany the crabs – for example a sauce *américaine* (see recipe for lobster *à l'américaine*) a well-spiced tomato sauce, a cream, Mornay or curry sauce (see Index). Extra sauce should be served in a sauceboat.

CRAB WITH RICE
Crabe en pilaf

Line the bottom and the sides of a buttered shallow mould with a thick layer of hot cooked rice; fill with the cooked crab meat mixed with some of the sauce that will accompany the dish, and then cover with another layer of rice. Pack down and keep warm.

    Just before serving unmould and accompany with a sauceboat of curry sauce, sauce *américaine*, etc.

Crabe à la parisienne

Fill the shell of a crab with a salad made with one part cooked crab meat and one part cooked vegetables, all diced very small – carrots, turnips, potatoes, string beans. Bind the vegetables and crab with a well-seasoned mayonnaise, and sprinkle a pinch of chopped parsley and chopped hard-boiled egg on top.

SHRIMPS
Crevettes

Shrimps must be cooked alive, preferably in sea water; if that is not available, the water should be heavily salted, with 2 table-spoons of sea salt, a sprig of thyme, a bay leaf and 10 crushed peppercorns for each quart of water.

Plunge the shrimps into the boiling water for 3 minutes. Drain them and cool.

Unshelled shrimps are used as garnishes for fish and their sauces.

CRAYFISH AU GRATIN
Gratin de queues d'écrevisses Fernand Point
For 4–6 people

2 kg (4 lb) live
  crayfish

75 g (3 oz) unsalted
  butter

50 g (2 oz) chopped
  onions

50 g (2 oz) chopped
  carrots

$\frac{1}{4}$ glass cognac

$\frac{1}{2}$ l (1 pt) dry white
  wine

1 teaspoon tomato
  purée

Small bouquet garni,
  with several sprigs
  tarragon

Salt, pepper, cayenne

25 g (1 oz) flour

$\frac{1}{4}$ l ($\frac{1}{2}$ pt) cream

50 g (2 oz) truffles,
  cut into julienne

6 tablespoons
  hollandaise sauce
  (page 126)

Plunge the crayfish into boiling water for 5 minutes. Drain immediately, remove the tails and the claws, and shell. Pound the shells in a mortar.

In a saucepan, sauté in a little butter the pounded shells; add the onions and carrots, chopped fine.

Flame half the cognac and pour it over the mixture. Pour in the white wine and a little water to moisten. Add the tomato purée and the bouquet garni. Season with salt, pepper and a dash of cayenne.

Cook on a very low flame for about 20 minutes. Then rub the mixture through a very fine sieve and thicken with *beurre manié* to make a sauce.

Cook the tails and claws gently in 25 g (1 oz) of butter. Deglaze the pan with the remaining cognac. Add the cream and the crayfish sauce. After adding the truffles, bring to boiling point for a few minutes; then away from the heat mix in the hollandaise sauce.

Correct the seasoning, and combine the crayfish and the sauce in individual ovenproof porcelain gratin dishes.

Place under the grill to brown lightly.

This excellent dish must be served immediately.

1 carrot
2 medium-sized
  onions
2 shallots
½ l (1 pt) water
½ l (1 pt) dry white
  wine
2 teaspoons salt
Pinch pepper
Bouquet garni (1 bay
  leaf, 2 sprigs
  thyme, 1 celery
  stalk, 2 sprigs
  parsley)
Crayfish (at least 6
  per person)

CRAYFISH IN COURT-BOUILLON
Écrevisses à la nage
For 12 people

Thinly slice the carrot, onions and shallots; place the vegetables in a saucepan with the water, wine, salt, pepper and the bouquet garni. Simmer until the vegetables are completely cooked.

Wash the crayfish and remove the intestines. Bring the court-bouillon to the boil and plunge the crayfish into it; cook for 8–10 minutes.

Heap the crayfish in a glass bowl; reduce the cooking liquid by half and pour over the crayfish. Serve warm or cold.

24 crayfish
1 medium-sized
  carrot, core
  removed
1 onion
2 shallots
175 g (6 oz) unsalted
  butter
Pinch salt
Sprig thyme
Bay leaf
½ glass cognac
3 dl (½ pt) white wine
3 tablespoons tomato
  purée
Pinch chervil
Pinch tarragon

CRAYFISH WITH DICED VEGETABLES
Écrevisses à la bordelaise

Cut the carrot, onion and shallots into tiny dice. Cook slowly in 25 g (1 oz) of butter; add 50 g (2 oz) more butter, the cleaned and washed crayfish, salt, sprig of thyme and bay leaf. Sauté on a high flame until the crayfish are bright red. Pour over the cognac, wine and tomato purée. Cook covered for 8–10 minutes.

Spoon the crayfish into a bowl, and keep warm.

Boil to reduce the sauce by half; and finish by adding away from the heat the rest of the butter, a pinch of chopped chervil and a pinch of chopped tarragon.

Pour the sauce over the crayfish.

LOBSTER WITH WINE, TOMATO, GARLIC AND HERBS
Homard a l'américaine
For 3–4 people

800–900 g ($1\frac{3}{4}$–2 lb)
  live lobster
4 tablespoons oil
Salt
Freshly ground
  pepper
1 medium-sized
  onion, chopped
2 shallots, finely
  chopped
$\frac{1}{4}$ garlic clove,
  crushed
1 glass dry white
  wine
2 tablespoons fish
  fumet or water
$2\frac{1}{2}$ tablespoons cognac
2 medium-sized
  tomatoes, peeled,
  seeded, and
  chopped, or 6
  tablespoons tomato
  purée
3 sprigs tarragon
Dash cayenne pepper
100 g (4 oz) unsalted
  butter
Pinch chervil
Pinch tarragon
Chopped parsley

For this dish it is necessary to have a live lobster.

Cut up the lobster in the following way.

Hold the lobster with your left hand, the tail and the claws stretched out. Cut the claws off close to the body and crack the shells; cut the tail into 5 or 6 pieces. Slit the head in half lengthwise and remove the little sac close to the head, which contains sand, and the intestinal tract. In a bowl set aside the creamy part (the tomally) and the coral. This must be done rapidly.

In a sauté pan, heat the oil very quickly. Place the pieces of lobster in the very hot oil, season with salt and freshly ground pepper. Sauté until the shells become red. Remove the pieces of lobster, set aside and keep warm. Add the onion to the oil and cook, stirring constantly, without letting it brown. When the onion is nearly done, add the shallots, finely chopped, and the garlic. Cook briefly and drain off the oil. Pour in the white wine, the fumet (or water) and 2 tablespoons of cognac; add the tomatoes (or tomato purée), a bouquet of tarragon and a dash of cayenne pepper. Place the pieces of lobster on top and cook, covered, for 20 minutes.

Remove the pieces of lobster, place them in a bowl and keep warm. Remove the tarragon from the cooking liquid; boil to reduce by half, and thicken with the reserved creamy parts of the lobster, mixed with 50 g (2 oz) of unsalted butter, a pinch of chervil and a pinch of tarragon. As soon as the liquid boils, remove from the heat; add the remaining butter and cognac.

Pour the sauce over the lobster and sprinkle with chopped parsley.

Rice pilaf (page 514) may be served with the lobster and sauce.

Note: The lobster meat is often removed from the shells before serving. This procedure is recommended since it makes serving easier and eating less messy.

Live lobster
Salt
Pepper
Few drops oil
Melted unsalted
   butter

Sauce:
75 g (3 oz) unsalted
   butter
2 tablespoons flour
$\frac{1}{4}$ l ($\frac{1}{2}$ pt) milk, salted
1 egg yolk
2 tablespoons cream
1 teaspoon strong
   mustard
Mornay or
   hollandaise sauce
   (optional, pages 120
   and 126)

LOBSTER GRATINÉED IN ITS SHELL
Homard thermidor

Cut a live lobster in half lengthwise. Remove the sac and intestinal tract. Crack the claws and season the flesh with salt, pepper and a few drops of oil.

Place the 2 halves of lobster, shells down, in a roasting pan, and bake in a 425°F (220°C, gas mark 7) oven for 15 minutes. Baste from time to time with a little melted butter.

Prepare a sauce in the following manner: make a roux with 50 g (2 oz) of butter and 2 tablespoons of flour. Cook without letting it brown for 15 minutes; pour in the milk, bring to the boil and boil for 1 minute. Thicken away from the heat with 1 egg yolk diluted with two tablespoons of cream. Add the mustard.

Remove the lobster meat from the shells and slice it; mix with some of the sauce, then replace in the shells. Cover with the remaining sauce or, even better, with Mornay or hollandaise sauce. Brown in the oven.

---

1 lobster, cooked in
   court-bouillon
75 g (3 oz) unsalted
   butter
$\frac{1}{2}$ glass port
$1\frac{1}{2}$ dl ($\frac{1}{4}$ pt) cream
Salt
1 egg yolk
Dash cayenne pepper

LOBSTER WITH PORT
Homard au porto

Cut up a lobster that has been cooked in a court-bouillon. Heat the pieces slowly in 50 g (2 oz) of unsalted butter in a pan. Moisten with the port; let wine evaporate for a few minutes, then add the cream, salt lightly and boil 4–5 minutes. Remove the pieces of lobster, take the meat from the shell, and place the meat in a dish. Thicken the sauce, without boiling, with 1 egg yolk and the remaining butter; add a dash of cayenne pepper. Pour the sauce over the lobster.

1 lobster
100 g (4 oz) unsalted
  butter
1 tablespoon cognac
½ glass white wine
3 dl (½ pt) cream
Salt
Dash cayenne pepper
20 small truffle slices

LOBSTER WITH CREAM
Homard à la crème

Cut up a lobster as for lobster *à l'américaine* (above). Sauté pieces
rapidly in 50 g (2 oz) of butter. Moisten with cognac and white
wine; boil to reduce the wine. Then add the cream and season
with salt and cayenne pepper.

Cook, covered, for 15 minutes.

Remove the lobster and take the meat from the shells; mix it
with truffle slices.

Boil the sauce to reduce by one-third, and away from the
flame add the remaining butter. Place the lobster and the truffles
in a dish and pour the sauce on top.

LOBSTER SALAD
Mayonnaise de homard

Cook the lobster in a court-bouillon, let it cool, remove the meat
from the shell and cut it into small slices. Season with salt and
pepper and sprinkle with a few drops of oil and vinegar.

Cover the bottom of a salad bowl with chopped lettuce. Lay
the slices of lobster on top. Cover with mayonnaise (page 128)
and decorate with anchovy fillets, quartered hard-boiled eggs and
capers and place a small lettuce heart at the centre.

Mix the salad well at the table so the lettuce is well-coated
with mayonnaise.

CRAWFISH AND DUBLIN BAY
PRAWNS (OR SCAMPI)
Langoustes et langoustines

These are prepared in exactly the same way as lobster.

Note: Shellfish cooked in a court-bouillon which are to be
eaten cold should always be left to cool in the liquid. Do not
drain until they are completely cold. When you remove them

from the court-bouillon cut a small slit in the shell, at the top of the head. Stand the shellfish on its head so that any liquid inside drains out.

━━━━━━━━━━━━━━━━━━━━━━━━━━━━━━━━━━

GRILLED CRAWFISH WITH TWO SAUCES
La langouste grillée aux deux sauces
For 2 people

One 800 g (1½ lb) or two 400 g (¾ lb) live crawfish
50 g (2 oz) melted unsalted butter
Salt and freshly ground pepper
Sprigs parsley
Choron sauce (page 127)
Sauce *américaine* (page 203)

Plunge the crawfish into a large pan of boiling salted water for 2 or 3 minutes to kill it and stiffen the meat.

Remove the crawfish; split in half. Salt and pepper the meat, and brush with melted butter.

Cook the crawfish (meat up) under a moderately hot grill. Cooking time, about 15 minutes (do not let meat dry out).

To serve, place on a napkin or pleated paper. Decorate the plate with sprigs of parsley.

Serve with a timbale of creole rice (page 514).

Choron sauce and sauce *américaine* are served separately in sauceboats.

━━━━━━━━━━━━━━━━━━━━━━━━━━━━━━━━━━

SNAILS
Escargots

In France vine snails (*Helix pomatia*) and *petit-gris* (*Helix aspersa*) are the two species that are eaten.

Snails that are already sealed into their shells to hibernate for the winter are preferable; if not, you must starve the snails for a few days.

Wash the snails several times under running water, until the slime is completely gone. Blanch them by plunging into boiling water for about 5 minutes.

Drain, rinse, pull the snails from their shells and remove the black ends.

Place the snails in a saucepan; cover them with half white wine, half water; season each quart of cooking liquid with 1 medium-sized carrot, 1 onion, 2 shallots sliced thin, a bouquet garni made with a dozen parsley sprigs, a twig of thyme, a bay leaf, a pinch of crushed pepper, 1 teaspoon of salt. Bring to the boil and skim, then simmer for 3 hours. Pour in a bowl and let the snails cool in their liquid.

Meanwhile, wash the empty snail shells and boil them in a saucepan of water for $\frac{1}{2}$ hour. Drain, rinse and dry.

Note: It is important not to put salt in the water in which the snails are being purged. The quality and flavour of the snails will suffer.

SNAILS WITH PARSLEY AND GARLIC BUTTER
Escargots à la bourguignonne

Snail butter:
$\frac{3}{4}$ **tablespoon garlic**
2 tablespoons very finely chopped shallots
$1\frac{1}{2}$ **tablespoons finely chopped parsley**
2 teaspoons salt
Pinch freshly ground pepper
225 g (8 oz) unsalted butter

To prepare the snail butter crush the garlic, add the shallots, parsley, salt, pepper and butter. Mix well.

In each shell place a scant teaspoon of the special butter; then add a cold, drained snail. The snail will push the butter to the bottom of the shell. Seal the shell by adding more butter.

Arrange the snails on an ovenproof dish moistened with water. Sprinkle each snail with fine white breadcrumbs; bake in a 425°F (220°C, gas mark 7) oven for 8 minutes.

SNAILS WITH CHABLIS
Escargots à la mode de Chablis

The snails are prepared in the same way as snails *à la bourguignonne* (above). However, instead of putting the teaspoon of butter in the shell use $\frac{1}{2}$ teaspoon of white wine reduced with chopped shallots, then replace each snail in the shell and continue as in the recipe above.

SNAILS WITH MEAT STOCK
Escargots à l'alsacienne

Follow the same method as for the snails *à la bourguignonne* (above), with this slight difference:

Although the snails must be covered, they should be cooked in less liquid. Add a couple of fresh pork rinds and a small piece of veal knuckle to the liquid before putting the snails in it, to produce a well-flavoured, gelatinous stock.

After the snails have cooled in their cooking liquid, replace them in their shells, coated with some of the jellied stock which will blend with the special butter. Finish, as above, by sprinkling a pinch of fine white breadcrumbs on each snail, just before placing them in the oven.

FRIED FROGS' LEGS
Grenouilles frites

24 frogs' legs
Juice ½ lemon
Oil
1 teaspoon chopped parsley
1 garlic clove, crushed
Pinch salt
Pinch freshly ground pepper
Frying batter (page 601)
Bouquet fried parsley

[*Editor's note:* Frogs' legs are virtually unobtainable in England, though a great delicacy in France, where they are cooked in a variety of ways. Fried frogs' legs is the simplest method.]

Marinate 24 frogs' legs for 1 hour in lemon juice, a little oil, chopped parsley, garlic, salt and pepper.

Dip the legs, one at a time, in frying batter and plunge them one at a time into the very hot oil.

Drain the legs when they are golden, and serve on a napkin with a bouquet of fried parsley.

MEAT

Knowing how to recognize good quality meat and choosing the right cut for roasting, boiling, braising, grilling or stewing is the key to success in cooking a dish.

These are the chief characteristics of good quality meat:

1. The colour is red; the texture firm, smooth and slightly elastic to the touch.
2. It is plentifully streaked or marbled with fine fat veining.
3. It is covered with a thick layer of white or creamy fat.

Beef from a cow has a finer grain than that from a bull or bullock. Meat from an old bull is a dark brown-red. All lean meat which is limp, pale or very dark red is of inferior quality.

[*Editor's note:* French cuts of meat are different from English cuts and it is usually impossible to buy exactly the same cuts as in France. The recipes give English equivalents and alternatives to French cuts.]

PRIME CUTS

Prime cuts of beef come from the back of the animal, between the first ribs and the top of the haunch, the part known in French as the *aloyau*.

In France the *aloyau* is divided into four cuts: *filet* (fillet, the undercut); *faux-filet* or *contre-filet* (uppercut of the loin, separated from the fillet by the chine); *rumsteak* (rumpsteak) and *côtes couvertes* (sirloin).

The *aloyau* can be roasted whole or in large pieces, but the four cuts are usually treated separately.

The fillet is regarded as the finest and most tender cut. It is also the most expensive. Whole or in large pieces, trimmed and larded or barded, it makes a magnificent roast. For rare meat, allow 12–15 minutes per pound in the oven; 15–18 minutes per pound on a spit.

It may also be divided into five different cuts for steaks:

Filets grillés: 4-cm (1½-inch) steaks cut across the grain of the meat from the thick end of the fillet;

Châteaubriants: 4–5-cm (1½–2-inch) steaks cut across the grain of the meat from the first part of the centre of the fillet;

Coeurs de filet: (2½–4-cm (1–1½-inch) steaks cut across the grain of the meat from the second part of the centre of the fillet;

Tournedos: 4-cm (1½-inch) steaks cut across the grain of the meat from the third part of the centre of the fillet;

Filets. mignons: Steaks cut with the grain of the meat from the rib end of the fillet.

Boned *faux-filet* may be roasted whole or in large pieces in the same way as the fillet. It is also cut up into steaks for grilling. The *rumsteak* is treated in the same way.

The *train de côtes couvert* comes from between the eighth and last vertebrae. It may be roasted whole or in large pieces, preferably on the bone for flavour. For rare meat allow 15–18 minutes per pound in the oven; 20–22 minutes per pound on a spit. Or it may be cut against the grain of the meat into rib steaks for grilling (côtes or entrecôtes).

ROASTING

In roasting, grilling or sautéing a piece of meat, poultry or game, the cooking is done by concentrating the heat, which gradually penetrates the centre of the joint. This drives the juices inward, and creates a brown coating which seals them in.

When the heat has penetrated the meat, the meat should be removed from the direct action of the naked flame (if it is cooked on a spit) or radiant heat (if it is in an oven) and allowed to 'rest' at a lower heat. This allows the sealed-in juices to move slowly towards the surface, up to the brown coating. As the juices penetrate the tissues and cooking finishes, the meat acquires a nice pink colour.

The brown coating now becomes slightly softer and thinner until it is just a brown outline round the meat which exudes drops of succulent juices, pink or golden depending on whether the meat is red or white.

Methods of roasting

Roasts can be cooked in the oven or on a spit. The spit, though too seldom used nowadays, is far superior to the oven, because the open air causes moisture to evaporate. The meat browns more delicately and the flavour is better if you use certain woods, for example vine shoots, which transfer their aroma to the meat.

The oven is an enclosed environment which means that roasting is carried out in an humid atmosphere and this to some extent reduces the effectiveness of the browning process.

The heat must be intense enough to sear the meat, taking into account the size of the joint. When the browning has taken place, the heat is reduced. If roasting over an open fire add less wood, move the meat away from the heat or protect it with some kind of screen.

The joint should always rest on a rack to prevent it sitting in fat or cooking juices. It should be basted frequently with this fat, but not with the juice. When cooking on a spit, use a drip pan to collect the fat and juice.

With experience you can tell whether a roast (except poultry) is cooked by touching it. If you do not have this experience, consult a table of recommended cooking times, or the instructions in individual recipes. Then insert a needle or skewer into the meat so that a few drops of juice escape. If the meat is red (beef and mutton), it is cooked when the juice is pale pink. Fully cooked white meats (veal, lamb, pork) lose a few drops of colourless juice. Game is usually cooked to medium rare; when it is done its juice should be pale pink, as for red meats.

To test whether poultry is cooked, tilt it over a plate; when the juices inside run out completely clear and colourless, it is done.

Roasting juices

Except when otherwise indicated in a recipe, a roast should always be served with its cooking juices.

If you have carefully followed the cooking method for roasting, the juice gathered in the drip pan or roasting pan should be sufficient.

When roasting in an oven, carefully regulate the heat. If it is too high, it will reduce the juices and cause an overbrowning, which makes them bitter. The cooking butter will burn too.

This can be avoided by sliding something under the roasting pan or by pouring one or two tablespoons of water or white bouillon into the roasting pan.

The roasting juice can be degreased partially, but do not forget that much of the flavour is retained by the fat.

Serving and carving roasts

Generally, a roast is served simply on a long, heated dish and lightly sprinkled with one or two tablespoons of the roasting juice. The remaining juice is served in a sauceboat.

The vegetables accompanying the roast as a garnish are either served in a vegetable dish or placed attractively around the roast or at either end of the serving dish. Use a large enough dish so that the garnish fits on to it and is not balanced round the edge.

On ceremonial occasions a large roast may be decorated with silver or silver-plated *hâtelets*, ornamental skewers bearing crayfish, mushrooms, truffles, cockscombs, etc. from the accompanying garnish.

Carving consists of cutting thin slices across the grain of the meat. The reason for this is obvious. A piece of meat cut against the grain is easy to chew. If the slice has been cut along the grain it will be fibrous and more difficult to chew; tender meat will seem tough.

Preparing the meat for roasting

Before roasting there are particular ways of preparing the different cuts of beef, veal and lamb, poultry and game, etc.

Fillet of beef must have its fat and gristle removed; then it is larded or barded.

Faux-filet (upper fillet) has the gristle removed. This is done after lifting the fat that covers the gristle. It is put back into place afterwards.

Boned and rolled joints of beef are tied with string, to hold the meat together. Never tie the piece of meat too tightly. During cooking, the tissue swells and needs space. The string should be cut two-thirds of the way through the cooking.

A boneless veal roast should be larded.

The bone end of a leg of lamb is removed to facilitate carving. If the meat is larded with garlic, the cloves should be inserted between the membranes; always avoid cutting the meat to slide in a garlic clove.

Poultry and game birds are trussed and often barded.

Larding and barding

The purpose of larding meat – inserting tiny sticks of fresh pork fat into a piece of meat – is to keep the meat moist as the fat melts during cooking.

To bard a piece of meat is to cover it with a layer of fat. This protects it from the heat of an open grill or an oven. At the same time the melting fat keeps it moist.

GRILLING AND SAUTÉING

Grilling or sautéing a small cut of meat means cooking it over an open fire, under a grill or in a sauté pan or frying pan.

Grilling requires intense direct heat. The source may be charcoal, coke, gas, or electricity. How intense it should be depends on the size, especially the thickness, of the meat to be cooked.

All the rules for roasting discussed above should be observed.

The grill should be preheated. Brush the meat with melted butter and place it on the hot grill. After a few minutes, rotate the meat with a spatula, a quarter turn from its original position, so that the bars of the grill sear the meat, forming a checkerboard pattern. When the meat is done on one side, turn it over with a spatula and season with salt. This will dissolve in the meat juices that appear on the top of the meat and penetrate slowly into the meat's tissues. Give the second side a quarter turn, and when it is cooked, place it on a serving platter, with the side that was cooked last on top. This side is then seasoned.

For best results red meats (beef or mutton) should be cooked rare and left to stand a few minutes before serving. During this time, the sealed-in juices spread to the outer parts of the meat. Like roasted meat, grilled meat should be perfectly cooked and pink all the way to the brown surface. If the meat is not allowed to rest, it will be soft, much too raw in the centre, with a thin black crust on both sides.

Sautéed meats are cooked by the same method but in a sauté pan (ideally) or frying pan. The pan is deglazed to dissolve the coagulated juices which are served with the cooked meat.

BRAISING

A piece of braised meat requires a lot of attention to the minutest details. Braising meat is one of the most difficult operations to carry out successfully.

The best meat to braise is 3–6-year-old beef and 1–2-year-old mutton.

Younger animals are not suitable for braising (though they are for roasting). Older animals are stringy and dry; the long cooking period in braising accentuates this fault.

Beef for braising should always be larded when the pieces come from the leg or the chuck. When it is from the sirloin, larding is not necessary. If the animal is of good quality, this part is sufficiently marbled with its own fat.

All the cooking phenomena explained in the section on roasts also occur in braising. After reading and following all the advice given concerning roasts, the reader will have no difficulty in proceeding with the recipes for braising.

In the old school of French cookery the recipes for braising were different from those we use today. Reasons of economy and lack of time have obliged cooks to abandon that extremely rich and tasty method. Formerly a piece of braised meat was cooked so long that it was impossible to slice it with a knife. The meat was cooked to a compote which absorbed all the juices and the liquid used for braising; it became so tender and melting that it had to be served with a spoon.

Gourmets who are able to should follow this old method of braising, for nothing equals it in flavour.

POT-ROASTING

Pot-roasting a piece of meat or poultry is a very simple method, suitable for home cooking, and one of the best.

It consists of cooking a piece of meat in butter in a casserole of just the right size, and finishing it slowly, preferably in the oven, covered. Almost no evaporation takes place, and the meat produces delicious, rich juices.

DEEP-FRYING

For frying use a heavy, deep, round or oval pan. It should be fairly large and filled only halfway with fat or oil.

The ideal frying medium is absolutely tasteless groundnut oil. You can use animal fat, which can reach a high temperature without burning although it burns at a lower temperature than vegetable oil.

Beef suet is one of the best of all animal fats, but it cannot be heated very hot. Mutton fat is not recommended. Pork fat can be used, but it is better to keep it for recipes in which it is used for flavouring.

Butter burns at 265°F (130°C); it cannot be used for deep frying.

Animal fats start to smoke at 355°F (180°C).

Lard can go up to 480°F (250°C) before burning.

Vegetable oils start to burn at 575°F (300°C).

You can test the proper heat for frying in the following ways:

1. Medium hot: a parsley leaf thrown in starts to fry;

2. Hot: the fat sizzles and splutters if the parsley is slightly damp;
3. Very hot: the fat smokes and starts to smell.

After each use, strain the frying oil through cheesecloth, to remove the impurities left by the food that has fried in it. If these bits remain in the oil, they will burn and make the fat spoil more quickly. They also affect the taste of the food fried.

Store the frying fat in an earthenware or stone jar.

ROAST BEEF

A fine joint of roast beef – fillet, sirloin or rib – makes a welcome addition to any menu. The recipes are suitable for any cut, but the method of presentation varies.

In the general section on roasts I have described the method of preparation and cooking, with a rough indication of cooking times.

Any of the vegetable garnishes can accompany any of the cuts. Here I shall only give a few classic recipes.

FILLET OF BEEF RICHELIEU
Filet de boeuf Richelieu

Beef fillet
Lardoons of fresh pork fat
1 medium-sized carrot
1 large onion
Salt
Unsalted butter
1½ dl (¼ pt) veal stock, white stock or water

Garnish:
Braised lettuce
Mushroom purée
Stuffed mushrooms
Stuffed tomatoes
Potatoes
Chopped parsley
1 glass Madeira

Remove the fat and gristle from a piece of beef fillet, trimming the sinewy fibres along the sides of the fillet.

Lard the fillet with lardoons of fresh pork fat, matchstick strips about 4 cm (1½ inches) long.

To do this, put the fillet of beef on a dish placed upside down on a table, with the edges of the meat hanging down slightly around the dish. Hold the meat with the left hand. With the right hand insert the larding needle, piercing the meat in the direction of the grain just below the surface of the fillet. Leave the lardoon in the meat, with its two ends sticking out.

The lardoons are inserted in rows, about an inch apart. The rows are parallel, with the lardoons spaced to give a staggered arrangement.

The purpose of the larding fat is to keep the fillet moist and to provide it with the benefit of constant basting during cooking.

To hold the fillet together, tie the meat rather loosely every 6 cm (2½ inches) with string.

At the bottom of a roasting pan place 1 medium-sized carrot and 1 large onion, thinly sliced. Place the fillet of beef on top;

season with salt on all sides, and moisten with melted butter. Place in a 425°F (220°C, gas mark 7) oven. Cook following the general directions given for roasts.

Baste frequently, and be careful not to let the vegetables at the bottom of the roasting pan or the juices from the fillet brown too much.

If you have a suitable dish the joint can well be pot-roasted, still keeping the meat rare. In both cases the cooking time is 12–15 minutes per pound (not including 'resting' time).

When the meat has finished cooking (check whether it is done with a needle or skewer if you cannot tell by touching), place the fillet in a roasting pan and keep it hot while resting, the second stage of cooking.

Into the roasting or braising pan pour about $1\frac{1}{2}$ dl ($\frac{1}{4}$ pt) of good veal stock, white stock or water; simmer for 5 minutes, then strain through a fine sieve and keep warm.

Garnish.   This consists of braised lettuce stuffed with mushroom purée, stuffed mushrooms, stuffed tomatoes and potatoes cooked in butter (see the chapter on vegetables), allowing enough for the guests to have some of each.

Presentation.   Place the fillet of beef on a large platter, then surround it alternately, with one portion of lettuce, one mushroom, one tomato and potatoes. Finish the dish by sprinkling chopped parsley on the potatoes. Away from the flame add 1 glass Madeira to the juices that have run out of the meat during the resting time and a little of the cooking juice. Moisten the meat lightly with it. Serve with the remaining juice in a sauceboat.

Place very hot plates on the table while the meat is being carved. Serve one slice of fillet, one of each vegetable, a teaspoon of meat juice, poured on to the plate but not on to the meat, which should keep its beautiful light-pink colour. Finally, sprinkle on each slice a dash of powdered sea salt.

The fillet of beef Richelieu can be simplified. Without changing the cooking method, limit the garnish to one, two or three of the vegetables. It is still a fine dish, but the name is changed by substituting the name of the garnish – for example, beef with braised lettuce.

FILLET OF BEEF WITH VEGETABLE GARNISH
Filet de boeuf bouquetière

Lard the fillet; roast or pot roast following the method given for fillet of beef Richelieu.

To garnish surround the beef with small clumps of different vegetables: carrots, glazed turnips, string beans and peas with butter, potatoes cut in the shape of olives and browned.

FILLET OF BEEF WITH MADEIRA SAUCE AND MUSHROOMS
Filet de boeuf sauce madère et champignons à la ménagère

For 8 people

1·5 kg (3 lb) beef fillet (cut from the centre)
125 g (5 oz) fresh pork fat
50 g (2 oz) butter

Madeira sauce:
1 small carrot, diced
1 medium-sized onion, diced
100 g (4 oz) unsalted butter
50 g (2 oz) flour
1 glass dry white wine
1 l (2 pts) veal stock or juice, lightly salted
2 tablespoons thick tomato purée
Sprigs parsley
Sprigs thyme
½ bay leaf
225 g (8 oz) mushrooms
½ glass Madeira

This recipe is very suitable for home cooking. It can frequently be used as a basis for other recipes when the concentrated stocks generally required in *grande cuisine* are not available.

Prepare the fillet – trim it, remove the gristle, lard it, tie it and roast or pot roast it following the recipe for fillet of beef Richelieu.

To serve place the meat on a long platter; remove the strings, and surround it with fine mushroom caps taken from the vegetable garnish.

Sauce. The sauce will take 1½ hours to prepare and cook. Cook the carrot and the onion slowly in a saucepan big enough to hold the sauce, with 50 g (2 oz) of butter. When the vegetables are light brown, add the flour. Mix well, and cook this roux slowly, stirring constantly, until it turns dark brown; cool. Dilute the roux by slowly pouring in the white wine; then add the veal stock or juice, reserving about half a cup. Add the tomato purée, parsley, thyme and the bay leaf.

Bring to the boil, stirring with a whisk to avoid lumps, and simmer for 45 minutes.

Add the trimmings from the fillet, lightly browned, along with 4 or 5 mushroom stems, cleaned and chopped.

While it is simmering, from time to time skim off the fat and the skin that forms. This is necessary to remove the impurities from the flour and the fat, and leave a clear, light sauce at the end.

After 45 minutes of simmering, strain the sauce through a fine sieve into another saucepan, pressing the vegetables vigorously. Bring the sauce slowly to the boil and continue to clarify it by skimming. As needed, add 1–2 tablespoons of the remaining stock.

This second step will take 30 minutes.

Meanwhile prepare the mushrooms. They must be firm and very white. Cut off the ends and wash the mushrooms rapidly twice, without letting them soak. Drain immediately, and wipe dry.

Reserve a few whole mushroom caps to garnish the fillet; cut the rest into quarters.

Heat the remaining butter in a heavy saucepan big enough to hold the sauce as well as the mushrooms. When the butter is quite hot and a hazelnut colour, toss the mushrooms in; stir over a high flame until lightly browned.

Remove the mushrooms from the fire. Strain the sauce through a cloth and add to the mushrooms. Bring to the boil and simmer 5 minutes; remove again from the heat, correct the seasoning and keep warm without boiling until ready to serve.

Just before serving, add the Madeira and the cooking juices from the meat to the sauce. Do not let this sauce boil, as this would make the aroma of the Madeira evaporate with its alcohol and the meat juices would coagulate.

The Madeira sauce by now should be reduced to 5 dl (1 pt) – to about half of the liquid ingredients used – because of the clarifying and evaporation process.

Obviously if you have some demi-glace sauce (the recipe can be found on page 108), it will make a better-flavoured sauce. In that case, the recipe for the mushrooms remains the same, but they are moistened with 5 dl (1 pt) of demi-glace sauce instead of the sauce described above.

To finish the sauce with the Madeira, follow the instructions above.

FILLET OF BEEF WITH FINANCIÈRE GARNISH
Filet de boeuf à la financière

Lard a beef fillet and roast or pot roast it. At the same time prepare a Madeira sauce made preferably with demi-glace sauce (page 108), or with a sauce made by the recipe above. Add the following garnish.

Small mushrooms sautéed in butter; sliced truffles; cockscombs and kidneys (cooked in a court-bouillon made with white stock (page 106) with $\frac{1}{2}$ a tablespoon of flour and the juice of half a lemon or 1 tablespoon of vinegar per pint); veal quenelles (page 273) or braised sweetbreads, cut into slices 6 mm ($\frac{1}{4}$ inch) thick.

Ingredients

Beef fillet tenderloin
Béarnaise sauce (page 127) or *Valois* sauce

Garnish:
Pea purée:
1 kg (2 lb) peas
Spinach
100 g (4 oz) unsalted butter
2 tablespoons double cream
Pinch sugar
5 whole eggs
6 egg yolks

Glazed carrots:
Bunch of carrots
Pinch salt
Pinch sugar
75 g (3 oz) unsalted butter

Potatoes:
1 kg (2 lb) small new potatoes
50 g (2 oz) unsalted butter
Pinch salt
Chopped parsley

FILLET OF BEEF WITH PEA PURÉE
Filet de boeuf Saint-Germain
For 15 people

Lard the fillet and roast it or pot roast it.

Place the fillet on a platter and garnish it with 15 timbales filled with a purée of fresh peas, glazed carrots and potatoes cooked in butter.

Serve accompanied by the cooking juices and a sauceboat of béarnaise sauce or *Valois* sauce (béarnaise with added meat glaze).

Pea purée. Bring 3 l (6 pts) of salted water to the boil in a large saucepan and add the shelled fresh peas; cook rapidly on a high flame. Before peas are completely cooked, add a handful of spinach (the spinach is used to give the purée a strong green colour); boil for 5 minutes, remove from the heat and drain. Rub the peas and spinach through a fine sieve. Place the purée in a bowl, whip it vigorously with a wooden spoon to make it very smooth, and add the unsalted butter and cream. If the peas are not sweet enough, add a pinch of sugar. Beat together 5 whole eggs and 6 yolks without stirring too much. Add the eggs to the purée.

Generously butter 15 small cylindrical moulds; fill to about 6 mm ($\frac{1}{4}$ inch) from the top with the prepared purée. Bake in a *bain-marie* (a roasting pan half full of hot water). It should not be permitted to boil; watch it constantly and add 1–2 tablespoons of cold water if you see any sign of boiling.

Test as for a *crème renversée* (page 574); the purée should be a little firmer to the touch.

Keep warm in the *bain-marie* while waiting to unmould; unmoulding will be easier if you let the puréee rest for a few minutes after it is cooked.

Glazed carrots. Choose a bunch of new carrots, peel as thinly as possible. If carrots are small, leave them whole; if not, cut into halves or quarters and trim the ends slightly to give the pieces the shape of large garlic cloves.

Wash the carrot pieces and place in a heavy pan big enough to hold them in one layer; pour in water halfway up the carrots;

add a pinch of salt, a pinch of sugar and 50 g (2 oz) of butter. Bring to the boil and cook slowly without a cover so that the liquid will have evaporated almost completely when the carrots are cooked. Then the juices of the vegetables, the butter, the sugar and the moisture form a syrupy mixture.

Off the fire add 25 g (1 oz) of butter and stir gently; the carrots will be coated with a shiny glaze and very tender.

Potatoes cooked in butter. Use new potatoes no bigger than walnuts; peel and cook in 50 g (2 oz) of butter, with a pinch of salt, in a covered pan. They should be lightly browned and very tender.

Serving. Place the fillet of beef on a large platter; remove the string and baste with a little of the cooking juices. At either end of the platter, in a semicircle, arrange the timbales of puréed peas. Along either side of the beef alternate the carrots and the potatoes, piled in pyramids.

Top each pile of potatoes with a little chopped parsley.

2 kg (4 lb) fillet of
  beef, trimmed and
  tied
225 g (8 oz) carrots,
  cut into sticks
225 g (8 oz) turnips,
  cut into sticks
6 leeks, white part
  only
2 celery hearts
3 tomatoes, peeled,
  seeded and
  quartered
1 onion stuck with 3
  cloves
1 sprig each parsley,
  chervil and
  tarragon
1 tablespoon coarse
  salt
1 teaspoon
  peppercorns
Croûtons
Grated parmesan
  cheese

BOILED BEEF
Boeuf à la ficelle
For 6 people

Heat 3 l (6 pts) of water in a large soup pot, adding the vegetables
and seasonings.

After 5 minutes of boiling, plunge in the beef, tied by a string
to the handle of the pan – this will help in removing the meat.

After skimming well, continue to cook at a gentle boil. Allow
about 10–15 minutes for each pound; as for roast beef, the meat
should remain rosy red inside.

Serve the meat surrounded by the vegetables and accompanied
by tomato sauce (page 111) seasoned with tarragon and chives.
You also can serve the meat simply with coarse salt, gherkins and
small pickled onions. It can also be eaten with a rémoulade sauce
(page 130).

After lightly buttering the broth, serve it with small croûtons
and grated parmesan cheese.

Note: The top part of the rump, ribs of beef or a leg of lamb
can be prepared in the same way.

Steak tartare

Take 225 g (8 oz) of beef fillet from the thick end. Remove the
sinews and fat. Mince or chop fine, and season with salt and
freshly ground pepper. Shape the meat into a disc about 3 cm ($1\frac{1}{4}$
inches) thick; place on a serving plate, and make a hollow in the
centre with the back of a teaspoon dipped in cold water. Place
the yolk of a raw egg in the hollow.

Serve with a bowl of very hot consommé and surround with
three small dishes, one with capers, one with very finely chopped
onions, and one with chopped parsley.

STEAK WITH SHIRRED EGGS
Steak aux oeufs au miroir

Prepare minced steak, as described in the recipe for steak tartare (above). Cook in unsalted butter in a sauté pan until pink; place on a serving platter and cover with 2 eggs, cooked in the frying pan or the oven until the yolks are filmed over (see shirred eggs, page 45). The film can also be obtained by spooning some of the very hot cooking butter over the yolks.

Pour 2 tablespoons veal stock into the frying pan used for cooking, reduce by half, and surround the steak with the juice.

HAMBURGER
Hamburger ou steak haché

1 medium-sized onion
50 g (2 oz) unsalted butter
225 g (8 oz) beef fillet
Salt
Freshly ground pepper
1 tablespoon veal stock
Poached egg (optional)

Chop the onion fine; cook it slowly in a sauté pan with a knob of butter, but do not let brown.

Prepare minced steak as in the recipe for steak tartare (above), season with salt and freshly ground pepper, and mix in the cooked onion.

Shape the steak into a hamburger, cook it on both sides in butter in the same frying pan used for the onion (be sure that all the bits of onion have been removed, or they will burn). The hamburger is done when a drop of blood forms on the cooked upper surface.

Place the meat on a serving platter; put the rest of the butter in the frying pan with 1 tablespoon veal stock; bring to the boil, and boil 2 minutes. Pour over the steak.

If you wish, you may slide a poached egg on top of the steak.

BONED PORTERHOUSE STEAK
Châteaubriant

For this, use a piece of meat cut from the thickest part of the beef fillet, the fat and gristle removed.

A *châteaubriant* (also spelled *châteaubriand*) should not weigh more than 350–500 g ($\frac{3}{4}$–1 lb), so it can be evenly grilled.

Grill following the methods in the section on grilling (page 215), and serve accompanied by *maître d'hôtel* butter (below) or another compound butter and with soufflé potatoes (page 494), arranged at one end of the platter, and, at the other end, a bunch of watercress. Or serve with Pont-Neuf, matchstick or sautéed potatoes (see pages 492–3 or 501), or any other vegetable.

However, the classic garnish for a *châteaubriant* is soufflé potatoes accompanied by *maître d'hôtel* butter or béarnaise sauce (page 127).

100 g (4 oz) unsalted butter
1 teaspoon chopped fresh parsley
Large pinch salt
Couple of turns of the pepper mill
Juice of $\frac{1}{2}$ lemon

Beurre maître d'hôtel. Mix ingredients together until creamy. Serve separately or on the *châteaubriant* – the heat will melt the butter.

To serve the *châteaubriant* cut it on the serving platter, on the bias. Each slice is served on a heated plate, with some potatoes (or other garnish) and a few sprigs of watercress. A teaspoon of *maître d'hôtel* butter and some of the meat juice, which runs out as it is sliced, are put on the plate but not on the meat. The guests may season the meat with freshly ground sea salt and pepper.

SAUTÉED OR GRILLED FILLET STEAKS

Coeur de filet sauté ou grille

These are slices of fillet of beef, of about 175–225 g (6–8 oz), cut from the centre part of the fillet, with the gristle and the fat removed.

Sauté them like the *tournedos* (below) or grill them like the *châteaubriant*.

The garnish and the sauces for the other two steaks can be used.

Filet mignons

This cut uses the rib end of the fillet, which is too thin to be cut for *tournedos*.

The end piece is trimmed then sliced into thinner steaks following the grain of the meat.

Preparation of *filets mignons* is simple. Flatten them lightly with a mallet or the flat side of a cleaver or big kitchen knife; season with salt and freshly ground pepper and press in lightly with the flat part of a knife blade. Dip the steaks in melted butter and immediately into fine breadcrumbs, pressing the breadcrumb coating on with the blade of a knife. With the back of the blade, make a grid pattern on both sides of the meat; place the meat on a hot grill, pouring on some melted butter. Cook it rare.

Serve with vegetables and *maître d'hôtel* butter or a béarnaise, choron, Valois or other sauce.

Never pour a liquid sauce on to the *filets mignons* (for example, meat juice, Périgueux or Madeira sauce) as this would immediately make the breadcrumbs soggy. If you wish to use one of these sauces, serve separately in a sauceboat and pour $\frac{1}{2}$ tablespoon on to the plate next to the grilled meat, not on top.

TOURNEDOS AND MÉDAILLONS OF BEEF
Tournedos et médaillons

The *médaillon* is a sort of *tournedos*. They are both grilled or sautéed, and garnished the same way. All the recipes for *tournedos* are applicable to *médaillons*.

The steaks are cut from the centre of the fillet just before the rib end (the thinnest part of the fillet).

This part of the fillet must be trimmed, and the gristle, fat and sinews removed. The *tournedos* are cut about 5–6 cm (2–2½ inches) thick and each steak is wrapped in a strip of fresh pork fat (or bacon) of the same depth, tied firmly in place with a piece of string, giving the *tournedos* the appearance of a thick disc.

If the *tournedos* is grilled, follow the recipe given for the *châteaubriant* and serve with one of the garnishes listed there.

I prefer, however, to sauté *tournedos*; this method allows the deglazing of the pan and produces juices or sauces with a better flavour.

2 tablespoons oil
125 g (5 oz) unsalted
   butter
6 *tournedos*, 100 g
   ($\frac{1}{4}$ lb) each, wrapped
   in fresh pork fat
   and tied
Salt and pepper
6 tomatoes of equal
   size
2 medium-sized
   aubergines
1 tablespoon flour
   mixed with pinch
   salt
Oil for frying
2 large onions
1$\frac{1}{2}$ dl ($\frac{1}{4}$ pt) milk
Chopped parsley
1$\frac{1}{2}$ dl ($\frac{1}{4}$ pt) veal stock
$\frac{1}{2}$ glass Madeira

TOURNEDOS WITH AUBERGINES, TOMATOES AND ONIONS
Tournedos à l'arlésienne

In a sauté pan, heat 2 tablespoons of oil and 25 g (1 oz) of butter; when the butter sizzles, place the *tournedos* in the pan. The oil and the butter must be very hot (smoking) to sear the meat. Cook, covered, for 4 minutes. Turn the steaks with a spatula, so as not to prick them; season with salt and freshly ground pepper on the turned side and cook the other side for the same length of time.

One minute before the meat is finished, remove the strings and the pork fat; turn the *tournedos* on their sides and roll them in the cooking butter to seal the sides that were protected by the fat.

Place the steaks on a plate, turning them flat; season the second sides and keep warm. While waiting, the *tournedos* will finish cooking.

Garnish.   While cooking the *tournedos*, prepare the garnish of tomatoes, aubergines and onions.

Cut off the tops of the tomatoes and press to remove the seeds and the juice; season the insides with salt and pepper; and cook in 50 g (2 oz) of butter, covered, in a sauté pan.

Peel the aubergines. Slice very thin; sprinkle with a pinch of salt and 1 tablespoon of flour, well mixed; shake off excess flour, and fry slices in very hot oil. When slices are a nice golden colour, drain on a cloth and salt lightly; they should be very crisp.

Slice the onions and separate into rings; dip in a bit of milk, then sprinkle with flour, shake well, and plunge for 3 minutes into the hot oil, after cooking the aubergine. As soon as the rings are golden, drain on a cloth and salt lightly.

Presentation.   Arrange the tomatoes in a circle on a hot round platter; on top of each tomato, place a *tournedos* and, on top of the meat, some fried onion rings. Place the fried aubergine in a dome in the centre, and sprinkle with a pinch of chopped parsley. Pour 1 tablespoon of the following sauce into the bottom of the platter.

In the sauté pan, combine the cooking juices from the tomatoes and the veal stock. Boil to reduce rapidly to three-quarters; and away from the heat add the Madeira, the juice that has gathered in the plate from the *tournedos*, and the remaining butter. Shake to mix, and serve in a sauceboat.

TOURNEDOS WITH BÉARNAISE SAUCE
Tournedos à la béarnaise

Prepare and sauté 6 *tournedos* as in the recipe above. In butter fry slices of bread (croûtons) the same size as the steaks, about 2 cm ($\frac{3}{4}$ inch) thick Arrange in a circle on a hot round platter, and top each with a *tournedos*.

In the centre put a garnish of small new potatoes, cooked in butter and lightly browned, or château potatoes or potato balls (page 502), sprinkled with a pinch of chopped parsley.

Surround each *tournedos* with a border of béarnaise sauce (page 127) and, in the centre, pour $\frac{1}{2}$ teaspoon of the cooking juice, deglazed with good veal stock and buttered lightly away from the heat.

Serve the remaining béarnaise sauce in a sauceboat.

6 sautéed *tournedos*
Croûtons, fried in
  butter
½ glass dry white
  wine
6 tablespoons veal
  stock
25 g (1 oz) unsalted
  butter

Beurre Bercy:
3 shallots
½ glass dry white
  wine
125 g (5 oz) unsalted
  butter
225 g (8 oz) bone
  marrow
½ tablespoon chopped
  parsley
Pinch salt
Pinch pepper
Juice of ¼ lemon

TOURNEDOS WITH BEURRE BERCY
Tournedos Bercy

Place the *tournedos* on small round croûtons, 2 cm (¾ inch) thick
and 6–8 cm (2½–3 inches) in diameter, fried in butter. Pour the
white wine into the pan used to cook the meat, and reduce by
three-quarters. Add an equal amount of veal stock, and reduce
to two-thirds. Finish the sauce away from the heat with a knob
of butter, mixing it into the sauce by shaking the pan.

Pour the sauce over the *tournedos*, and on top of each steak
place 1 teaspoon of *beurre Bercy*.

Beurre Bercy.   Chop the shallots fine; cook them slowly with
25 g (1 oz) of butter, without browning. When the shallots are
very soft, add the white wine and boil to reduce to 3 tablespoons.
Away from the heat add to the pan used to cook the shallots:
100 g (4 oz) of butter, the diced marrow (poached for a few
minutes in nearly boiling salted water and then well drained),
chopped parsley, salt, pepper and lemon juice. Mix well to produce a thick creamed butter.

This butter can be served separately.

TOURNEDOS WITH RED WINE SAUCE AND BEEF MARROW
Tournedos sautés à la bordelaise

Arrange 6 sautéed *tournedos* on a hot round platter; on top of
each steak, place a substantial slice of marrow, poached in nearly
boiling salted water. Deglaze the pan with 8 tablespoons of
bordelaise sauce (page 112); finish the sauce away from the heat
with 50 g (2 oz) of butter. Pour some sauce on the meat. Sprinkle
the marrow with pinches of chopped parsley; serve very hot.

TOURNEDOS WITH MUSHROOMS (1)
Tournedos sautés aux champignons

Sauté 6 *tournedos*; arrange in a circle on a round heated platter. In the centre, place a garnish of small mushrooms with a large fluted mushroom cap on each steak.

Mushroom garnish. From 225 g ($\frac{1}{2}$ lb) of small very white mushrooms, cleaned and washed, choose 6 nice caps and flute them – use a vegetable knife to make cuts in the skin to form a rosette. If the other mushrooms are not tiny, cut each one into 2 or more pieces. In the pan in which the *tournedos* were cooked gently heat 100 g (4 oz) of butter. Make sure the meat juices left in the pan do not burn. Add the mushrooms, cook on a high flame for 5 minutes and add the dry white wine. Reduce by two-thirds; then add $1\frac{1}{2}$ dl ($\frac{1}{4}$ pt) of demi-glace sauce, or 3 dl ($\frac{1}{2}$ pt) of a good veal stock. If using veal stock, reduce by half; add the rest of the butter away from the heat. Correct the seasoning, then place the fluted mushrooms on the *tournedos* and the other mushrooms in the centre.

Coat the *tournedos* with the sauce, and finish the dish with chopped parsley on the fluted mushrooms.

TOURNEDOS WITH MUSHROOMS (2)
Tournedos chasseur

Follow the previous recipe for *tournedos* with mushrooms, cutting the mushrooms into slices. Just before adding the butter to the sauce also add $\frac{1}{2}$ teaspoon each of chopped tarragon and chopped parsley.

Do not boil the sauce after adding the herbs.

6 slices stale bread

75 g (3 oz) unsalted
   butter

6 *tournedos*, 100 g
   ($\frac{1}{4}$ lb) each

2 tablespoons oil

3 dl ($\frac{1}{2}$ pt) Choron
   sauce (page 127; 3
   parts béarnaise to 1
   part tomato purée)

6 artichoke hearts
   cooked in white
   court-bouillon

2 bunches green
   asparagus tips

1 kg (2 lb) large
   potatoes

6 tablespoons veal
   stock

TOURNEDOS WITH ARTICHOKES, ASPARAGUS AND POTATOES
Tournedos Choron
For 6 people

With the 6 slices of stale bread, prepare croûtons and fry them in 50 g (2 oz) of butter; place on a round platter and keep warm.

Cook the *tournedos* in the oil and 25 g (1 oz) of butter, following the general instructions for sautéing.

Place the steaks on the croûtons, arranged in a circle, and pour on each a border of Choron sauce.

Between the *tournedos*, place the 6 artichoke hearts, seasoned with salt and pepper and cooked on both sides in butter for 15–20 minutes. Garnish the artichokes with small bunches of asparagus tips cooked *à l'anglaise* (boiled in salted water, then drained and coated lightly, away from the heat, with unsalted butter). Correct the seasoning.

Fill the centre of the dish with the potatoes, cooked according to the recipe for Parisian potatoes (page 502).

Deglaze the pan with 6 tablespoons of veal stock, reduce by half, and pour a few drops on each *tournedos* in the centre of the circle of Choron sauce.

TOURNEDOS WITH PEAS
Tournedos Clamart

6 *tournedos*, 100 g
  ($\frac{1}{4}$ lb) each
3 large potatoes,
  baked
Salt and pepper
75 g (3 oz) unsalted
  butter
2 tablespoons oil
6 small tarts made
  with very short
  pastry, baked blind
500 g (1 lb) shelled
  green peas cooked *à
  la française* (page
  488)
$\frac{1}{2}$ glass sherry
1$\frac{1}{2}$ dl ($\frac{1}{4}$ pt) veal stock

Cut the baked potatoes in half; remove the pulp, place in a bowl, season with salt and pepper, and mix with a fork, adding 50 g (2 oz) of butter. With this paste, make 6 patties the shape and the size of the *tournedos* and brown them in a pan in butter. Turn them carefully with a spatula.

Arrange in a circle on a round platter and keep warm.

Cook the *tournedos* in 2 tablespoons of oil and 25 g (1 oz) of butter and place them on the potato patties.

Around the steaks put the small tart shells (baked at 400°F (200°C, gas mark 6) between two moulds so that they keep their shape, or lined with wax paper and filled with dried beans). Fill each tart with the green peas coated with butter.

Deglaze the pan with the sherry and the veal stock, reduce by two-thirds. Add butter away from the heat, and serve in a sauceboat. Do not pour the sauce on to the serving platter; it would spoil the crispness of the potatoes.

TOURNEDOS WITH WOODLAND MUSHROOMS
Tournedos forestière

6 slices stale bread
225 g (8 oz) unsalted
  butter
600 g (1$\frac{1}{4}$ lb)
  mushrooms
  (morels, ceps,
  girolles, etc.)
4 tablespoons oil
6 *tournedos*, 100 g
  ($\frac{1}{4}$ lb) each
Chopped parsley
6 tablespoons veal
  stock

Prepare 6 croûtons in 50 g (2 oz) of butter.

Clean and wash the mushrooms carefully; do not let them stand in water. Drain well and wipe dry. If they are medium-sized or a little large, slice them.

Heat the oil in a pan; as soon as it smokes, add the mushrooms, season with salt and cook over a high flame for 5 minutes, stirring frequently. Drain and place 50 g (2 oz) of butter in the pan. Heat until sizzling; add mushrooms and brown lightly. Correct the seasoning with salt, if needed, and add a couple of turns of the pepper mill.

Cook the *tournedos*; place them on the croûtons, arranged in a circle, and in the centre put the mushrooms. Sprinkle with chopped parsley.

Over the *tournedos*, pour sauce made by deglazing the pan with the veal stock, with the remaining butter added.

Serve very hot.

Note: If you like, you can add 1 teaspoon of chopped shallots to the mushrooms at the last minute.

TOURNEDOS WITH ARTICHOKE HEARTS AND BÉARNAISE SAUCE
Tournedos Henri IV
For 6 people

6 slices stale bread
2 tablespoons oil
6 *tournedos*, 100 g (¼ lb) each
700 g (1½ lb) large potatoes
100 g (4 oz) unsalted butter
6 artichoke hearts, cooked in a white court-bouillon
3 dl (½ pt) béarnaise sauce (page 127)
Chopped chervil and tarragon

Prepare the croûtons. Brush the steaks with the oil and grill them. Peel the potatoes and cut into ovals the size of a hazelnut; sauté in butter.

Slice the artichoke hearts, and place them in a pan in 50 g (2 oz) of sizzling butter. Brown lightly.

Place the *tournedos* on the croûtons and pour a circle of béarnaise sauce on each. Arrange the potatoes and artichokes round them alternately. Correct the seasoning of the vegetables. Finish the dish with chopped chervil and tarragon on the potatoes.

Serve the remaining béarnaise sauce separately.

TOURNEDOS WITH BEEF MARROW
Tournedos à la moëlle
For 6 people

6 *tournedos*, 100 g (¼ lb) each
6 slices beef marrow
6 tablespoons bordelaise sauce (page 112)

Grill the *tournedos*.

Poach marrow 5 minutes in a pan of nearly boiling salted water.

Place the *tournedos* on a round platter and put a slice of marrow on each piece. Coat with the bordelaise sauce, lightly reduced and buttered away from the heat.

ENTRECÔTE WITH BEEF MARROW
Entrecôte à la bordelaise

Grill the *entrecôte*. After it has been turned, when the second side is half cooked, completely cover the steak with slices of beef marrow about 3 mm ($\frac{1}{8}$ inch) thick, which have poached for 5 minutes in nearly boiling salted water.

As soon as the meat is cooked, carefully remove the *entrecôte* with a spatula and place on a long, hot serving platter. Sprinkle the marrow with a pinch of Bonnefoy sauce (a bordelaise sauce, page 112, made with white wine).

RIB OF BEEF WITH MARROW AND WINE
Côte de boeuf à la moëlle au vin de Brouilly
For 2 people

1 kg (2 lb) beef rib
Salt and freshly ground pepper
100 g (4 oz) unsalted butter
$\frac{1}{2}$ tablespoon chopped shallots
1 bottle Brouilly (or other Beaujolais)
1 tablespoon *beurre manié* (page 92)
100 g (4 oz) marrow

Salt and pepper the rib of beef. In a heavy-bottomed, fireproof casserole, cook the meat in melted butter, browning it on both sides. For very rare meat the cooking time is 5 minutes a side.

Remove the meat to a serving platter and keep warm.

Sauté the shallots without browning them in the cooking butter. To deglaze the pan and make the sauce, add the wine to the pan and let it boil until reduced by half.

Thicken the sauce with the *beurre manié*, and after correcting the seasoning, add the remaining butter to make the sauce more velvety.

Serve the rib of beef covered with slices of marrow, poached for 5 minutes in lightly salted water. It can be served coated with the sauce or the sauce can be served in a sauceboat.

Always cream the butter and add it at the last moment to any sauce made with wine; it will eliminate the acidity and improve the flavour.

BRAISED BEEF
Boeuf à la Mode

For 6 people, 2 meals – one cold and one hot

225 g (8 oz) fresh
  pork fat
Salt, pepper and herb
  and spice mixture
  (page xxiv)
½ glass cognac
1·8 kg (3½ lb)
  rumpsteak or
  silverside
Chopped parsley
Chopped thyme
Crushed bay leaf
4 dl (¾ pt) white wine
2 calf's feet
50 g (2 oz) fresh pork
  rind
50 g (2 oz) unsalted
  butter or pork,
  chicken or veal fat
1 medium-sized
  carrot, quartered
1 large onion,
  quartered
Bouquet garni (10
  parsley sprigs, bay
  leaf, sprig thyme)
5 garlic cloves
1 l (2 pts) lightly
  salted veal stock

Garnish:
500 g (1 lb) carrots
20 small onions
25 g (1 oz) unsalted
  butter

This dish must marinate for at least 5 hours before it is cooked, and it must cook for 5 hours. Cut the pork fat into pieces the width and length of a pencil; place them in a shallow dish, season with salt, pepper, herbs and spices. Add 2 tablespoons of cognac, mix and let macerate for 20 minutes, turning them from time to time.

Just before using the fat, sprinkle it with chopped parsley. With a larding needle introduce the pieces of fat into the meat by pushing the larding needle through in the direction of the grain of the meat. The pieces of fat should form a checkerboard pattern in each slice of meat when it is carved. Season the meat with salt and pepper and a pinch of thyme and crushed bay leaf. Place it in a bowl just big enough to hold it, so that when the remaining cognac and the white wine are added, the meat will be completely covered; let it marinate in the wine and cognac in a cool place for 5 hours, turning it from time to time to let the flavours penetrate the meat.

Have the butcher bone the calf's feet; retain the bones. Blanch the feet (place them in cold water and boil for 10 minutes), rinse and tie them in cheesecloth. Break the bones into tiny pieces.

Plunge the pork rind into boiling water, rinse, and tie in a bundle.

Drain the meat from the marinade, wipe carefully and tie it with string – not too tightly, just enough to hold the meat together. Put the butter or the fat in an ovenproof casserole big enough to hold the meat; heat well, and brown the meat on all sides. Add the carrot and the onion and brown lightly. Add the calf's feet, the bones, the pork rind, the bouquet garni and the garlic. Pour over the marinade and enough stock so that the meat is covered. Bring just to the boil, cover and continue cooking, preferably in the oven (325°F (170°C, gas mark 3)), slowly and evenly without interruption. Too-rapid boiling clouds the stock, makes it insipid and gives an unpleasant taste. This dish should simmer, not boil. The stock will then blend with the meat juices and the gelatinous ingredients of the pork rind and calf's feet. It will become rich and full of flavour. Cook for 4 hours.

Garnish. While this is cooking, prepare the carrots and the onions for the garnish. Cut the carrots into pieces the size of a walnut, rounding the edges. If they are old carrots, remove the cores, which are always hard and have a very strong taste. Plunge the cored carrots into boiling water for 15 minutes. If they are new carrots, omit the last two steps.

Peel the small onions and brown with 25 g (1 oz) of butter in a frying pan.

At the end of 4 hours remove the meat, the calf's feet, the pork rind and the large carrot and onion from the saucepan; strain the stock through a fine sieve, let it stand for 5 minutes, and then remove the fat from the surface.

Cut the calf's feet and the pork rind into pieces 1 cm ($\frac{1}{2}$ inch) square.

Place the meat back in a saucepan just big enough to hold the meat and the garnish and add the calf's feet, the pork rind, the carrot pieces, the small onions and the stock. Bring to the boil, cover and cook for 1 hour, as slowly as before. A larding needle should now penetrate the meat easily.

To serve, lift the meat carefully and place on a serving platter. Remove the string; surround the meat with the carrots, the onions, the calf's feet and the pork rind. Pour over just enough stock to moisten them.

At the end of the cooking time, if the recipe has been carefully followed, the stock should be syrupy and reduced to about 4 dl ($\frac{3}{4}$ pt).

To serve this cold, see recipe, page 248.

1 beef leg weighing about 40–50 kg (80–100 lb)

500 g (1 lb) crushed garlic cloves

Fine salt and finely ground pepper

Relish (for 10 people):

1 kg (2 lb) white onions

3 dl (½ pt) olive oil

1 kg (2 lb) fresh tomatoes, seeded and chopped

500 g (1 lb) green or red peppers, diced small

1 head garlic, crushed

Salt, pepper, paprika, cayenne

Bouquet garni

LEG OF BEEF ROASTED ON THE SPIT OVER CHARCOAL

Cuisse de boeuf rôtie au feu de bois

For 80 to 100 guests

Choose a leg of beef which has been carefully aged. The day before cooking trim it as you would a leg of veal (saw the knuckle and remove the end).

Pierce the flesh deeply with a larding needle every 10 cm (4 inches). In each hole, place a pinch of salt and finely ground pepper mixed with crushed garlic. Salt and pepper the surface of the meat rubbing it in with your hand so that the seasoning penetrates.

In a big fireplace with a spit prepare a wood fire, preferably of aromatic wood. When the logs are partly burned and the heat is strong, place the beef leg on the spit about 10 cm (4 inches) above the coals. Set the turn spit going. The cooking time for a leg of this size is 8 hours of steady cooking.

During this long time the fire will need more wood. The leg should be basted frequently with the juice and the fat that collect in the drip pan. To prevent the leg drying out it can also be basted with melted butter during the cooking.

Before serving it let the leg stand for 1 hour in a warm oven at a low temperature.

After this magnificent roast has been shown to your guests, carve it in front of them. When sliced, the flesh should be pink and juicy.

Serve with potatoes in their skins, cooked in the embers, along with this relish.

Chop the onions fine; sauté in the olive oil in a large pan, without letting them brown.

Add the tomatoes, the peppers and the garlic.

Season with salt and pepper, cayenne, paprika and add the bouquet garni. Cook slowly for ¾ hour, covered; remove the bouquet.

In Mexico this relish is very popular served with a leg of beef.

BEEF IN RED WINE, WITH BACON, ONIONS AND MUSHROOMS
Boeuf à la bourguignonne
For 6 people

1·5 kg (3 lb) rumpsteak or silverside

125 g (5 oz) fresh pork fat, with rind removed and reserved

½ glass cognac

1½ dl (¼ pt) Burgundy or red wine

1 calf's foot

100 g (4 oz) unsalted butter

2 tablespoons flour

1 l (2 pts) stock

Bouquet garni (sprigs parsley, sprigs thyme, 1 bay leaf)

500 g (1 lb) mushrooms

225 g (8 oz) lean bacon, cut in ¼-inch slices

2 dozen small onions, peeled

This dish will take 5 hours to cook. Lard the meat with the pork fat, and place it in a marinade of the cognac and wine for 3 hours.

Have the butcher bone the calf's foot; retain the bones. Plunge it into boiling water for 10 minutes, rinse, and tie it in cheesecloth; break the bones into tiny pieces. Plunge the pork rind into boiling water and rinse.

Drain the meat, wipe dry and brown in 50 g (2 oz) of butter as for the *boeuf à la mode*. When the meat is well browned, remove and set aside on a plate; add the flour to the butter and brown the mixture slowly, stirring constantly.

Dilute with the marinade and the stock. Bring to the boil, stirring with a whisk, and place the meat in the sauce, which should just cover the meat. Add the bouquet garni, the calf's foot, the bones, the pork rind and the stems of the mushrooms, well cleaned. Cover, and cook very slowly in a 325°F (170°C, gas mark 3) oven for 4 hours.

Plunge the bacon slices into boiling water for 5 minutes, drain and wipe dry. Brown in a frying pan with the remaining butter; remove to a plate. In the same pan brown the onions in the butter.

After 4 hours, remove the beef and the calf's foot; then strain the sauce through a fine sieve. Dice the calf's foot roughly and return to the pan with the beef. Add the bacon, the onions, the mushroom caps, quartered, and the strained sauce. Bring to the boil, and continue cooking in the oven, covered, very slowly for 1 hour.

At the end of this time the sauce should be reduced to 6 dl (1 pt). If more remains, boil the sauce until it is reduced to this point.

To serve, place the meat on a round, deep platter, surround with the garnishes, and pour the sauce over.

225 g (8 oz) fresh
  pork fat
Salt, pepper, herb
  and spice mixture
Pinch thyme and bay
  leaf
1 teaspoon chopped
  parsley
1·8 kg (3½ lb) of beef
  flank, topside and
  chuck, in equal
  parts
½ glass cognac
½ bottle red
  Burgundy
2 shallots, chopped
Sprigs parsley
100 g (4 oz) fresh
  pork rind
1 calf's foot
225 g (8 oz) lean
  bacon
Bouquet garni
4 large onions
4 garlic cloves
4 medium-sized
  carrots
50 g (2 oz) butter or
  fat
½ l (1 pt) lightly
  salted stock
Flour and water
  dough to cover

BRAISED BEEF WITH RED WINE AND VEGETABLES
Daube du maître Philéas Gilbert
For 6 people

This dish must marinate for at least 3 hours before it is cooked, and it must cook for 5½ hours.

Cut the fresh pork fat into lardoons (strips) as thick as a finger and 6 cm (2½ inches) long; season with salt, pepper, herbs and spices, or a pinch of thyme and a bay leaf; sprinkle with 1 teaspoon of chopped fresh parsley and marinate for 1 hour.

Cut the meat into 75-g (3-oz) cubes, and lard them with 4 lardoons, using a larding needle and piercing the meat in the direction of the grain. Season the meat with a pinch of salt, pepper, herbs and spices, mixed well; place the meat in a bowl, add the cognac, the red wine, the shallots and a couple of parsley sprigs cut into pieces. Marinate for 2 hours.

Place the pork rind and the boned calf's foot in cold water; blanch for 5 minutes, rinse and cut into small cubes. Break the calf's foot bones into tiny pieces. Cut the bacon into large dice and blanch. Coarsely chop the onions, mince the garlic with the point of a knife, mix well, and put between two plates to prevent the onion from browning when the air touches it; slice the carrots.

Drain and wipe the pieces of meat.

Heat the butter or the fat in a heavy pan. When it sizzles, add the meat, 5 or 6 pieces at a time, so that each piece browns on all sides.

Use an ovenproof earthenware terrine large enough to hold the meat. At the bottom of the terrine, place the calf's foot bones. On this bed of bones, put one-third of the meat; then half the carrots (with their cores removed, if they are not new carrots) cut into pieces; half the onions; the calf's foot; pork rind and one-third of the remaining lardoons. Sprinkle with a good pinch of salt, add another layer of meat. Then add the other half of the condiments – carrots, onions, calf's foot, pork rind, and another third of the lardoons; then a pinch of salt, a bouquet garni, and a third layer of meat. Finish by pouring in the marinade and the stock, which should reach 1 cm (½ inch) above the last layer of meat. Cover this with the remaining lardoons.

Place a cover on the terrine and seal it with dough made from flour and water, to prevent too-rapid evaporation during the cooking.

Place on the lowest possible heat. When it starts to boil continue cooking for 5½ hours in a 300°F (150°C, gas mark 2) oven so that it simmers slowly and evenly.

The ideal heat is a baker's oven, after bread has been baked in it – don't pass up the chance of cooking the meat that way, if you can.

After taking the dish out of the oven, let it stand for a few minutes so that the grease can be removed. Remove the bouquet garni, correct the seasoning and serve.

CASSEROLE OF BEEF
Estouffade de boeuf
For 6 people

225 g (8 oz) fresh pork fat
50 g (2 oz) unsalted butter
800 g (1½ lb) beef chuck
3 medium-sized onions, quartered
½ tablespoon salt
Pinch of ground pepper
2 tablespoons flour
2 garlic cloves, crushed
½ l (1 pt) good red wine
1 l (2 pts) veal stock or lightly salted bouillon
Bouquet garni
225 g (8 oz) mushrooms

Cut the pork fat into large cubes, blanch, drain and brown with 25 g (1 oz) of butter in a fireproof casserole just big enough to hold the meat and the stock.

Remove the pork fat, and in the same butter, half brown the meat cut into 75–100-g (3–4-oz) pieces. Add the onions and continue cooking until everything is browned.

Sprinkle with salt, pepper and flour. Mix well, and brown lightly, stirring constantly. Be careful that the onions do not brown too much or they will give the sauce a bitter taste.

Add the garlic, stir again for a few seconds, just long enough for the heat to bring out the perfume of the garlic; then add the red wine. Boil to reduce the wine by two-thirds, then pour in just enough veal stock or bouillon to cover the pieces of meat; bring to the boil, stirring, and finish by adding the sautéed pork fat and the bouquet garni. Cover the casserole and cook slowly in a 325°F (170°C, gas mark 3) oven for 3 hours. The dish should barely simmer.

Clean the mushrooms, wash rapidly and cut into quarters; sauté with remaining butter for 5 minutes over a high flame in a pan as big as the one previously used. Remove from the heat as soon as the mushrooms start to brown.

Remove the meat from the oven, and place the meat and pork fat on top of the mushrooms. Let the sauce stand in the original meat pan for 5 minutes, remove the fat and correct the consistency of the sauce by adding liquid or boiling to reduce it. By this time it should be lightly thickened and reduced so it will half cover the meat and the garnishes. Correct the seasoning, and strain the sauce through a very fine sieve on to the *estouffade*, rubbing it through with a wooden spoon.

Bring to the boil, and simmer on a very low flame for another 15–20 minutes.

Place in a deep serving platter and serve with a bowl of potatoes cooked in their skins.

Note: The garnish may be completed by adding to the mushrooms, 500 g (1 lb) of tomatoes, peeled, seeded, drained and cut into pieces. Be careful – raw tomatoes make the sauce more liquid because of the water in the pulp. When finishing the sauce, that important detail must be taken into account.

The *estouffade*, a delicious, traditional dish can also be made with white wine.

---

800 g (1½ lb) beef, chuck or boned rib
Salt and pepper
3 tablespoons fat
50 g (2 oz) unsalted butter
3 large onions
2 tablespoons flour
4 dl (¾ pt) beer
6 dl (1 pt) bouillon
1 teaspoon sugar
1 tablespoon vinegar
Bouquet garni

BEEF AND ONIONS BRAISED IN BEER
Carbonnade à la flamande
For 6 people

Cut the meat into small 50-g (2-oz) pieces, and season with salt and pepper.

Heat the fat and the butter in a heavy pan. As soon as it is smoking, brown the meat on all sides, remove and put aside on a plate.

Meanwhile, chop the onions fine and brown them lightly in the fat used to brown the meat.

Remove the onions and stir in the flour over a low flame until the roux has a dark-gold colour. Pour in the beer and the bouillon; add a pinch of salt, a pinch of pepper, the sugar and the vinegar.

Bring to the boil, stirring, and simmer on a very low flame for 15 minutes.

In an earthenware casserole or terrine large enough to hold all the meat, place the meat and the onions in layers. Put the bouquet garni in the centre.

Strain the sauce through a very fine sieve on to the meat; cover and seal tightly with a ribbon of dough made from flour and water; cook in a 325°F (170°C, gas mark 3) oven for 3 hours, until the meat is cooked and the sauce reduced and slightly thickened.

Take out of the oven; remove the cover and the bouquet garni. Let stand for 6 minutes, and skim off the fat. Correct the seasoning of the sauce, and serve in the cooking pot.

The carbonnade can also be served in a deep platter. In that case, strain the sauce through a very fine sieve, rubbing through the onions to make a purée.

Mix well, then heat and pour over the meat, which should be kept hot and covered so that it does not dry out during the last step.

BRISKET AND FOREQUARTER FLANK

Brisket and forequarter flank are usually reserved for a *pot-au-feu*. They are served with the traditional vegetable garnish and condiments of the *pot-au-feu* – coarse salt ground at the table with a salt mill, gherkins, horseradish with cream and mustard.

Other vegetable garnishes can be served – sauerkraut, braised cabbage, Brussels sprouts, red cabbage, stuffed cabbage, rice cooked in stock, purées of fresh or dried beans.

Very often, especially with leftovers, the dish is accompanied by a strongly spiced, sharp or peppery sauce such as *piquante*, *chasseur* or *Robert* (pages 114–115).

These cuts can also be pickled and salted and served with pasta – noodles, macaroni or spaghetti.

SALT BEEF
Accompagnement du plat de côtes salé
For 6 people

2 kg (4 lb) beef
  forequarter flank or
  brisket
2 handfuls sea salt
1 tablespoon saltpetre,
  crushed
Sprig thyme
1 bay leaf
Pinch pepper
2 medium-sized
  carrots, quartered
2 large onions,
  quartered and stuck
  with 2 cloves
Bouquet garni
350 g (¾ lb) pasta
Pepper, nutmeg, salt
100 g (4 oz) grated
  Gruyère or
  Cheshire cheese
50 g (2 oz) unsalted
  butter

The meat should be thick, well marbled and have a heavy coating of white or pale-yellow fat. Have the butcher saw the bones so that the meat can be carved easily and each guest can have a piece of meat with a bone.

In a bowl mix the sea salt with the saltpetre.

With a larding needle, pierce the meat; rub it all over with the salt and saltpetre. Sprinkle some of the salt on the bottom of an enamel baking dish big enough to contain the meat, put in the meat and pour the rest of the salt mixture on top. Break up the thyme and the bay leaf and place on the salt with the pepper.

Place the meat in a cool place for 10–12 days in the winter, 6–8 days in the summer or if the weather is humid. Every two days, turn the meat.

To cook, drain the meat and rinse it in cold water. Place in a saucepan, cover with cold water and add the carrots, onions and the bouquet garni. Bring to the boil and cook very slowly, as you would a *pot-au-feu* (page 71), for 3 hours. It need only simmer very slightly as long as it continues to cook steadily; a sudden stop might spoil the flavour.

Cook the pasta according to the instructions on the packet.

While the pasta is very hot, put it into a heated pan, give a couple of turns of the pepper mill, a dash of grated nutmeg, a pinch of salt (if needed – taste the noodles, taking into account the saltiness of the cheese) the grated cheese and the butter cut into pieces. Mix well with a fork until the cheese has coated the noodles.

Remove the meat from the saucepan and put on a long heated platter; place the pasta at either end or serve separately in a bowl, in which case, pour a ladle of the cooking bouillon over the meat.

800 g (1½ lb) boiled
  beef
6 large onions
50 g (2 oz) unsalted
  butter or chopped
  fresh pork fat
1 heaped tablespoon
  flour
2 tablespoons vinegar
½ l (1 pt) bouillon or
  veal stock
1 teaspoon thick
  tomato paste or 3
  tomatoes, peeled,
  seeded, drained and
  cut into pieces
2 garlic cloves,
  crushed
Pepper
1 teaspoon chopped
  parsley
1 tablespoon
  breadcrumbs
Melted butter

BOILED BEEF WITH ONIONS AND TOMATO SAUCE
Boeuf en miroton
For 6 people

Cut the onions into thin strips, boil for 5 minutes to remove the bitterness, drain and wipe dry.

In a saucepan or an earthenware pot heat the butter, add the onions and cook on a low flame, stirring often with a wooden spoon.

When the onions are golden, add the flour and continue to brown slowly. When the roux is browned, add the vinegar and let it cool. Gradually pour in the hot bouillon or stock, nearly boiling, whisking it into the flour in the same way as for a sauce, to prevent lumps from forming. Complete by adding the tomato and the crushed garlic; give the sauce a couple of turns of the pepper mill. Bring to the boil, then simmer for 20 minutes.

Fifteen minutes before serving cut the beef into slices 6 mm (¼ inch) thick; arrange on a fireproof earthenware dish; correct the seasoning of the sauce, then pour it over the beef, covering it completely. Heat on the stove to boiling point; then sprinkle with the chopped parsley and breadcrumbs, pour on a few drops of melted butter, and place in the oven to brown.

One teaspoon of mustard or grated horseradish or some sliced gherkins can be added to the sauce. In that case, do not let it boil after adding one of these ingredients. Dilute the condiments with vinegar and add to the sauce away from the heat; then add the beef to the sauce, cover the pot, and keep it warm without letting it boil.

The *miroton* is served in a heated dish and sprinkled with the chopped parsley. The edges of the dish can be decorated with sliced gherkins.

The *miroton* can be served with various garnishes:

1. Surround the meat with quartered, hot, hard-boiled eggs.
2. Serve the meat with a platter of sliced aubergine and onions, fried very crisp in oil.
3. Surround the meat, before the final browning, with a circle of boiled potatoes, cut up and moistened with the sauce.

COLD BEEF

Roast sirloin, rib or fillet of beef should all be pink inside when cooked.

The presentation is simple: trim the meat, removing the gristle, skin, fat or burned parts. Coat the meat with a thin layer of jelly spooned on when half set. The meat is either served on a large dish surrounded by the garnish; or on a rather smaller dish surrounded by chopped jelly or with a series of decorative motifs cut from jelly arranged around the edge.

The garnish is nearly always a mixed or plain vegetable salad. The vegetables are cooked and cooled, well drained, seasoned and bound with one of the following sauces: vinaigrette (page 129), rémoulade (page 130), or light mayonnaise (page 128). If the salad is to be moulded or placed in mounds around the meat, the mayonnaise should be made with 1 part half-set jelly for each 4 parts sauce.

It is not necessary to add jelly when the salad is served in a bowl.

COLD FILLET OF BEEF
Filet ou contre-filet froid ménagère

This recipe requires a piece of pot-roasted meat cooled naturally and not refrigerated. Trim it and slice evenly in 6 mm ($\frac{1}{4}$ inch) slices.

Moisten with the juices from the bottom of the pan, well degreased, strained through cheesecloth and half set; spoon a little on each slice.

Reshape the meat as a roast, and place on a serving platter surrounded with chopped jelly or watercress.

Serve with a vegetable salad.

COLD BRAISED BEEF
Daube froide

The leftovers of *daube* Philéas Gilbert (page 241), cooled in the cooking pan, make an excellent cold dish for a summer lunch.

The natural gelatine in the calf's feet, the pork rind and the meat are sufficient to jell the meat, which can be cut into slices like a pâté in a terrine.

COLD BOEUF A LA MODE
Boeuf à la mode froid

This dish, which is very pleasant in the summer, is a delicious way to serve leftovers of *boeuf à la mode* made according to the recipe on page 237 and intended for two meals.

Remove the garnish and the braising juices from the meat, and boil them for 2 or 3 minutes. Pour through a strainer and reserve the carrots, onions and calf's feet on a plate. Discard the pieces of pork rind, which lose their tenderness when cold.

If necessary, add some veal stock or some bouillon to the braising juices if there is not enough sauce to cover the beef and the garnish when they are placed in a mould. Add 2 or 3 sheets of gelatine, presoaked in cold water and brought to the boil to dissolve.

To test whether the jelly is strong enough, put 2 teaspoons of it on a plate and cool. The jelly should be firm enough to cut with a knife, without being rubbery. A jelly that is too stiff is rather unpleasant. Correct the seasoning, taking into account that, when it is cooled, the salt is less strong; and that a properly salted hot dish seems tasteless when eaten cold.

Use a charlotte mould of the size needed, or any straight-sided container, and pour in a little of the sauce prepared as directed above. Let it jell, then artistically arrange in it some of the carrots and the onions, then the beef, which must not touch the sides of the mould. Around the beef place the remaining carrots, onions and the calf's feet; then pour in the rest of the sauce.

The jelly must not overwhelm the garnish; be careful not to add too much veal stock or bouillon. Refrigerate the mould, which should not be served until the next day.

To serve dip the mould in hot water for a second, wipe and turn upside down on a cold platter; remove the mould. Decorate the edges of the jellied meat with gherkins.

This dish can be simplified in the following way.

Cut the meat into even slices, place them in a shallow dish, overlapping the slices. Around them place carrots, onions and calf's feet; cover with the braising sauce, with or without gelatine, and cool until the sauce has set.

Since this dish will not be unmoulded, the braising juices will probably be stiff enough without the addition of extra gelatine (test it first as explained above). The dish will taste better since gelatine diminishes its flavour.

Note: This preparation can be braised until tender enough to serve with a spoon. This procedure is not economical, but it reaches the heights of perfection.

Veal

Good quality veal is white or rather a very pale pink. The fat is very white, thick on the loin and breast. The meat and fat are very firm.

These superior qualities are found exclusively in animals two or three months old fed on their mothers' milk and grain and never allowed to graze.

Inferior quality meat is red, soft and often lean. If the meat is flabby and gelatinous, the animal was only a few weeks old and killed prematurely.

CUTS

In France a side of veal is divided into 3 main parts – the *cuisseau* (leg), *épaule* (shoulder) and, between them, the *longe* (loin) and *carré* (cutlets, neck). The entire back of the animal is known as the *selle* (saddle).

In France there are 4 leg cuts which do not correspond exactly to English cuts. They are *noix* (topside), *sous-noix* (silverside), *noix patissière* (thick flank) and *jarret* (knuckle). The first three are the prime cuts for roasting, braising or cutting up into escalopes, *grenadins* and paupiettes.

A *rouelle* is a joint cut across the thick part of the leg, corresponding more or less to the English fillet. However, this cut is not very common in France nowadays.

The end of the leg towards the tail is known as the *quasi* (chump end of loin).

The shoulder is used for stews or roasts.

The loin and neck are roasted or braised. They are also cut up into chops or cutlets.

Next to the shoulder are the *tendron* and *poitrine* (breast) and the *collet* (scrag end). Scrag end is used for stews. Breast is excellent stewed or sautéed and may also be braised whole or in pieces.

Veal offal consists of the head, the liver, the fat, the lungs, the heart, the sweetbreads, the brains, the tongue and the feet.

POT ROASTED CHUMP END OF VEAL

Quasi de veau bourgeoise

For 12–15 people

2–2·5-kg (4–5-lb) piece veal chump
1 calf's foot
225 g (8 oz) fresh pork rind
500 g (1 lb) veal bones
175 g (6 oz) unsalted butter
Salt and pepper
1 medium-sized carrot, sliced
2 large onions, sliced
Bouquet garni
2 tomatoes

Have the butcher bone the calf's foot; retain the bones. Plunge it with the pork rind in boiling water for 10 minutes. Break the extra veal bones and the bones of the calf's foot into tiny pieces, brown them in the oven with the carrot and onions.

Generously butter the bottom of a casserole or oven dish with a close-fitting cover. In it place the meat seasoned with salt and freshly ground pepper. Spread the rest of the butter over the meat. Place the pan in a 325°F (170°C, gas mark 3) oven, un-covered. Brown the meat slowly on all sides. Be careful that the butter does not burn.

When the meat has browned, remove it from the pan. Add to the pan the bones and the browned vegetables, the pork rind, the calf's foot, the bouquet garni and the crushed tomatoes. Return the meat, and cover tightly. Continue cooking for 2½ hours in a 325°F (170°C, gas mark 3) oven, basting frequently with the meat juices. If the cooking is done slowly, the liquid from the meat is turned into steam by the oven's heat. This steam, imprisoned under the tight cover, condenses and falls in drops on the meat, moistening and basting it before running down into the butter and the rich juices from the bones, the calf's foot, the pork rind and the vegetables, making enough light-coloured gravy, fragrant and syrupy, to sauce the veal.

If by any chance it cooks too rapidly the juice will reduce and may caramelize at the bottom of the pan. It could burn and give the dish a bitter taste, so moisten the bones with 1 cup of veal stock, bouillon or water.

When the cooking is over, remove the cover; place the meat, round side up, under the grill for a few minutes, basting it several times. The juice, which is now very rich, will give the meat a shiny glaze when it is ready to be served.

Strain the juice and serve it in a sauceboat without removing the fat; it should be rich, light in colour, and slightly syrupy.

Generally the veal is served with a vegetable garnish. The best ones are indicated below:

Bouquetière: Glazed carrots and turnips (trimmed very small), peas and green beans, cauliflower (divided into florets), served with butter or hollandaise sauce (page 126);

Bourgeoise: Glazed carrots and onions;

Jardinière: Glazed carrots and turnips, peas, French beans and kidney beans. Other possible accompaniments are spinach, chicory, endive, sorrel, tiny peas, celery, carrots; different types of noodles; lettuce, aubergine, courgettes, small onions; purée of mushroom, potatoes, celery, sorrel, etc.

Presentation.   At the table the veal is carved in very thin slices, cut crosswise against the grain. You will know if the meat is correctly cooked as soon as you start to carve – it will look very white and moist, and pearls of slightly pink, very clear juice will appear. If the meat is overdone, it will look dry and be tasteless.

Although the bones at the bottom of the pan will have cooked for 3 hours and be nearly dry, they will not yet have yielded up all the tasty ingredients they contain. Place them in a small saucepan with a carrot and an onion, sliced, then moisten with $1\frac{1}{2}$ l (3 pts) of water with a large pinch of salt. Bring to the boil and simmer for 3 hours; this will make a stock that can be used later in other dishes.

If the calf's foot has not been used with a vegetable garnish, it can be served as a hot hors-d'oeuvre with a vinaigrette sauce (page 129).

The pork rind, cut into strips, is an excellent addition to beans and carrots prepared *à la bourgeoise*.

TOPSIDE OF VEAL
Fricandeau

The *fricandeau* is a cut of meat from the upper part of the leg, cut parallel to the meat grain and about 6–8 cm (2½–3 inches) thick.

Pound the slice of meat to tenderize and lard with unsalted pork fat as you would a fillet of beef.

The *fricandeau* is cooked in the same way as the chump end. Only the cooking time is different, depending on its thickness.

This joint, moistened by the pork fat, can also be braised until it is so tender that it is served with a spoon. This dish, though expensive, is extremely succulent, hot or cold.

The garnishes described above can be used for the *fricandeau*.

VEAL FILLET
Rouelle de veau

This cut of veal, a cut 6–8 cm (2½–3 inches) thick, comes from the centre of the leg.

It need not be larded. It is cooked in the same way as a *fricandeau* – pot roasted or braised.

It is served with a purée of sorrel, spinach or endive or with a *fondue* of tomatoes.

SADDLE OF VEAL
Selle de veau

The saddle combines in one splendid joint the two halves of the veal loin. It is cut from the part of the animal between the rump and the bottom ribs.

The kidneys are removed, but most of the fat is left; the rib tips are cracked and folded so as to cover and protect the end of the fillet.

Slices of fresh unsalted pork fat are wrapped around the meat and held in place with string.

The saddle is cooked in the same way as topside (*noix*). It must be basted often. When the meat is nearly cooked, the pork fat is removed so that the surface of the meat can be well basted with the juice and take on a nice golden colour. It takes about 3 hours to cook in a 325°F (170°C, gas mark 3) oven.

The meat is carved in very thin slices, the knife placed flat on the fillet and turned towards the bone.

All the garnishes for the *fricandeau* and *rouelle* can accompany a saddle of veal. A saddle of veal is usually served for grand dinners. It is an impressive and succulent main course, and skilfully prepared as for a dish like saddle of veal Prince Orloff, one of the most celebrated recipes of the *grande cuisine*.

Saddle of veal
1 kg (2 lb) onions
225 g (8 oz) unsalted
  butter
Pinch salt
Large pinch sugar
1½ l (3 pts) béchamel
  sauce (page 110)
6 tablespoons double
  cream
Dash grated nutmeg
Foie gras, poached in
  port
Truffles
Grated Parmesan or
  Gruyère cheese
Artichoke hearts
  cooked in white
  stock
Green asparagus tips
  or peas

SADDLE OF VEAL WITH ONIONS, TRUFFLES AND FOIE GRAS
Selle de veau prince Orloff

Trim the saddle as explained above, and pot roast according to the principles outlined above.

Peel the onions, slice and boil for 5 minutes; drain, wipe dry and cook slowly with 100 g (4 oz) of butter, salt and sugar.

Prepare the béchamel sauce and reduce it until thick. Mix half the sauce with the onions, and use the other half for a Mornay sauce. Continue cooking the onions until they are completely softened and well mixed into the béchamel. Strain the onion sauce through a fine sieve into a saucepan, boil for 2 minutes and finish, away from the heat, with about 100 g (¼ lb) of butter and the cream, using enough of each to give this purée *soubise* a creamy consistency. Correct the seasoning. A dash of grated nutmeg will add an agreeable touch.

Remove the saddle of veal, perfectly cooked and golden, from the braising pot. Place it with the bone tips underneath on an ovenproof platter. Strain the juice through a very fine sieve and keep it warm.

Carve the saddle in the following way.

With the point of a knife run two deep incisions along 6 mm (¼ inch) from the outside edges of the two fillets. Do the same on each side of the backbone, keeping close to the bone. Then carefully detach the fillets from the bones.

Cutting slightly on the bias, carve slices 3 mm (⅛ inch) thick.

With the purée *soubise* cover the two cavities made in the saddle and replace the sliced fillets, each slice separated by 2 tablespoons of purée, a slice of *foie gras* poached in port, and a slice of truffle heated or cooked 2 minutes in the meat juice that was set aside.

Finish by mixing the remaing purée *soubise* into the Mornay sauce, which must be very creamy, and cover the surface of the saddle. Sprinkle with grated Parmesan or Gruyère cheese, moisten with melted butter and place under a hot grill or in a very hot oven to brown very quickly.

Place the saddle carefully on a long serving platter. All around put a garnish of small artichoke hearts cooked in white stock, stewed in butter, seasoned and then lightly browned in butter. On each artichoke place a small mound of green asparagus tips, boiled and coated with butter or cream in the pan in which the artichokes were cooked. Tiny peas can be substituted for the asparagus. On each mound place a slice of truffle heated with the artichokes for a few seconds beforehand. This truffle-flavoured butter will be absorbed by the asparagus.

Serve the roasting juice in a sauceboat; $\frac{1}{2}$ tablespoon poured on each slice is sufficient for each guest.

Prepared and served in this way a saddle of veal Prince Orloff is a magnificent dish.

BEST END OF VEAL
Carré de veau

The best end of neck is made up of ribs with the tips trimmed. I also advise removing the chine to make carving easier.

Remove the gristle and membranes, surround the veal with fresh pork fat, and lard it with additional pork fat on the top side, as you would a fillet of beef. Pot roast whole.

It can be served with any vegetable garnish.

VEAL CHOPS
Côtes de veau

The best end is usually cut up into veal chops. It is preferable to sauté the veal chops rather than grill them, because it makes them more juicy.

A veal chop weighing 225 g ($\frac{1}{2}$ lb) is enough for 2 people; if cut any thinner, the meat will dry out while cooking. Remove the end of the rib bone and the back bone that often comes with the chop.

Whatever garnish is chosen to accompany the chop, follow this method (for 6 servings):

In a sauté pan heat 25 g (1 oz) of unsalted butter and slowly brown 3 veal chops placed flat. When they are cooked on one side, turn them and season the browned surface with salt and freshly ground pepper.

Continue cooking for a total cooking time of 15–18 minutes.

Place the veal chops on a round heated platter, the seasoned surface underneath; sprinkle the top side with salt and pepper and cover to keep them warm while making the sauce or the garnish.

VEAL CHOPS WITH ONIONS AND POTATOES
Côtes de veau à la ménagère

Prepare veal chops and sauté in a small pan; when they are half cooked, surround them with small onions and small new potatoes (or potatoes cut like large olives) three-quarters cooked in butter, seasoned and well browned. Cover tightly until completely cooked. At the last moment for each chop add 1 tablespoon of veal stock, bouillon or water.

Deglaze the meat juices for 1 minute, sprinkle with a pinch of chopped parsley. Place the pan on a round platter to serve.

⫻━⫻━⫻━⫻━⫻━⫻━⫻━⫻━⫻━⫻

VEAL CHOPS WITH MUSHROOMS
Côtes de veau aux champignons
For 2 people

1 veal chop, sautéed in butter

50 g (2 oz) small whole mushrooms or medium-sized mushrooms, quartered

Pinch salt

1 tablespoon dry white wine

1 tablespoon veal stock, bouillon or water

25 g (1 oz) unsalted butter

Chopped parsley

Sauté the veal chop following the recipe above and place on a platter.

Add the mushrooms to the cooking butter. Brown lightly, season with a pinch of salt and add dry white wine. Reduce by half. Add veal stock, bouillon or water; bring quickly to the boil and finish the sauce away from the heat with the butter.

Pour the juice that has run out of the chop into the mushrooms, mix, and pour over the chops.

Sprinkle with chopped parsley.

⫻━⫻━⫻━⫻━⫻━⫻━⫻━⫻━⫻━⫻

VEAL ESCALOPES
Escalopes de veau

Escalopes are slices of veal about 1 cm ($\frac{1}{2}$ inch) thick cut from the fillet, the rib or the leg; they are always cut against the grain. Their average weight is 120–150 g (5–6 oz).

Since they are thin, escalopes must be sautéed on a high flame. They are often breaded, but this is not essential. If the meat is breaded, it is better not to moisten them with meat juice or sauce when serving; this would make the breadcrumbs soggy, and breaded escalopes should be crisp.

BREADED VEAL ESCALOPES WITH BROWN BUTTER

Escalopes panées au beurre noisette

For 6 people

6 veal escalopes, 125 g (5 oz) each
Salt, paprika (or pepper)
1 raw egg
3 tablespoons oil
125 g (5 oz) stale bread grated into fine crumbs
100 g (4 oz) unsalted butter
Juice ½ lemon

Flatten the escalopes with a mallet or the flat side of a cleaver. This breaks the fibres of the meat and spreads out the escalopes, which should then be 3 mm (⅛ inch) thick; season with salt and paprika (or pepper) on both sides. Beat 1 egg in a dish with a pinch of salt and 1 tablespoon of oil. Dip the escalopes in the egg mixture, then coat them with breadcrumbs on both sides; press the breadcrumbs down with the blade of a knife to make them stick.

Combine 50 g (2 oz) of unsalted butter and 2 tablespoons of oil in a pan big enough to hold the escalopes without over-lapping. Heat the oil–butter mixture and arrange the escalopes so as to sear them well; brown until the breadcrumbs are golden brown on both sides and finish cooking for a few minutes on the lowest possible heat. The total cooking time will be 8 minutes.

Place the veal escalopes on a heated platter. Pour the oil out of the pan and put in 50 g (2 oz) of butter; brown it lightly. Squeeze the juice of ½ lemon on the escalopes and pour the butter over. The breaded excalopes must be crisp. The guests should wait for them, not the escalopes for the guests. This remark applies to all the following recipes based on this one.

The best vegetable to serve with this dish is potatoes, boiled and then sautécd, or, better, sautéed raw. Or you could serve artichoke hearts, sliced and sautéed raw.

6 veal escalopes

Garnish:
1 large lemon
6 pitted olives
12 anchovy fillets
marinated in oil
2 teaspoons capers
1 hot hard-boiled egg
50 g (2 oz) unsalted
butter
2 teaspoons chopped
parsley

VEAL ESCALOPES WITH OLIVES, ANCHOVIES AND CAPERS
Escalopes de veau à la viennoise
For 6 people

Prepare 6 veal escalopes as explained in the previous recipe and garnish them the following way.

Place the escalopes on a serving platter. On top of each put 2 slices of peeled lemon with the seeds removed; on top of the lemon slices, place a pitted olive.

Around the lemon slices place the anchovy fillets, and around the plate small portions of capers and the chopped white of the egg.

Pour the lightly browned butter over the escalopes.

Serve the escalopes on hot plates. Mix the capers, the yolk of egg and the butter, and pour 1 tablespoon on to each escalope. Sprinkle with chopped parsley.

Serve with sautéed potatoes (parboiled beforehand if wished) well browned.

VEAL ESCALOPES WITH MACARONI
Escalopes de veau à la milanaise

Prepare in the same way as the breaded veal escalopes with brown butter but add to the breadcrumbs 25 g (1 oz) of grated Parmesan or Gruyère cheese.

Place the veal escalopes around a plate of macaroni *à la milanaise* (page 512). Serve with a buttery light tomato sauce.

Grenadins

For 6 people

800 g (1½ lb) veal
  fillet or boned best
  end
100 g (4 oz) fresh
  pork fat
Salt and pepper
100 g (4 oz) unsalted
  butter
1 medium-sized
  carrot, sliced very
  thinly
1 large onion, sliced
  very thinly
4 fresh pork rinds,
  blanched and
  drained
½ glass dry white
  wine
½ l (1 pt) veal stock
  or lightly salted
  bouillon, if the
  meat is to be
  braised
Bouquet garni (few
  sprigs parsley, sprig
  thyme, ½ bay leaf)

A *grenadin* is a smaller, thicker escalope, larded with tiny sticks of fresh pork fat, and pot roasted or braised like a miniature *fricandeau*.

Cut the *grenadins* 3 cm (1¼ inches) thick; lard them with the pork fat cut into small short sticks, and season with salt and pepper.

Heat the butter in a pan, and brown the *grenadins* slowly on both sides; remove and reserve on a plate. In the same pan soften and brown the carrot and the onion. Do this over very low heat. Do not raise the flame; this would burn the butter and caramelize the meat juices.

Add the pork rinds, then the *grenadins* placed side by side on top of the other ingredients.

Cover, and cook gently in a 325°F (170°C, gas mark 3) oven for 15 minutes. If the *grenadins* are pot-roasted on top instead of being put in the oven, continue cooking uncovered for 10 minutes, basting frequently with the meat juices. Be careful not to let the juice reduce too much. Add a couple of tablespoons of lightly salted veal stock or water if it begins to reduce.

If you are cooking them in the oven, braise them after 15 minutes, when they have sweated their juices. Moisten them with white wine, reduce the liquid by two-thirds, then add the veal stock to cover and the bouquet garni. Cook in a 375°F (190°C, gas mark 5) oven for 40 minutes to reduce the sauce by two-thirds. Towards the end of the cooking time, remove the cover, and baste very often in order to glaze the surface of the *grenadins* and brown the pork fat. By glazing, the tops of the *grenadins* get a shiny coat of reduced sauce, and the flavour is enhanced.

Set the *grenadins* in a circle around the garnish chosen. Correct the seasoning of the sauce, strain it through a very fine sieve and pour it over the meat.

Médaillons ou noisettes de veau

These small round pieces of veal, taken from the fillet, weigh about 100 g ($\frac{1}{4}$ lb) each. They are served one per guest.

The *médaillons* or *noisettes* correspond to the beef *tournedos*. They are cooked like veal chops and then served like a *tournedos*. All the sauces or garnishes for either can be used for *médaillons*.

VEAL MEDALLIONS WITH STEWED ONIONS
Médaillons de veau à la compote d'oignons

8 slices veal fillet, 100 g ($\frac{1}{4}$ lb) each, cut into medallions $\frac{1}{2}$ inch thick
Salt, pepper, flour
175 g (6 oz) unsalted butter
3 tablespoons Madeira
$\frac{1}{2}$ glass dry white wine
6 dl (1 pt) double cream
2 tablespoons fresh Périgord truffles cut into julienne

Stewed onions:
1·5 kg (3 lb) onions
Salt and pepper
75 g (3 oz) unsalted butter
2 tablespoons wine vinegar
6 tablespoons cream

Salt and pepper the veal medallions and flour them lightly. In a shallow saucepan with a heavy bottom sauté the veal pieces in 100 g (4 oz) of butter; keep them tender.

When they have cooked and lightly browned, arrange on a serving platter; cover with buttered waxed paper and keep the platter warm.

Deglaze the saucepan with the Madeira and the white wine, let reduce by three-quarters. Add the cream, correct the seasoning, reduce again over heat to produce a smooth sauce.

Briefly cook the truffles in butter (especially if they are raw); add to the sauce.

To serve, place each medallion on a portion of stewed onions and coat the whole dish with the delicious sauce.

The medallions can also be served individually, one on each plate; this way the food is hotter.

Onions. Chop the onions fine, season lightly with salt and pepper, and stew in butter in a covered saucepan. Halfway through the cooking add the vinegar and continue cooking for a couple of minutes. Then add the cream, stirring. Cook covered until tender.

6 veal medallions,
100 g ($\frac{1}{4}$ lb) each,
cut from the *filet
mignon* or loin

50 g (2 oz) unsalted
butter

3 tablespoons olive
oil

Salt and pepper

$\frac{1}{2}$ glass dry white
wine

3 dl ($\frac{1}{2}$ pt) good veal
stock

1 tablespoon chopped
fresh tarragon

Fresh tarragon leaves

VEAL MEDALLIONS WITH TARRAGON
Médaillons de veau à l'estragon
For 6 people

This will take 15–18 minutes to prepare and cook.

In a large pan combine half the butter and all the oil. When the fat is smoking, sear the medallions moderately on both sides, seasoning with salt and pepper as for veal chops and escalopes. Cook slowly 10–12 minutes.

Remove the medallions and keep warm between two plates. Pour out the butter–oil mixture and replace with the white wine; reduce by two-thirds, then add the veal stock. Reduce to the quantity needed for sauce and remove from the heat immediately.

Return the medallions to the pan and sprinkle with 1 tablespoon of chopped tarragon. Cover and let stand for 5 minutes, without boiling, on the side of the stove (boiling would toughen the meat and destroy the flavour of the tarragon).

Place the veal medallions on a round hot platter; decorate the top of each with 4 or 5 tarragon leaves, blanched in boiling water. Add the rest of the butter to the juice; correct the seasoning and pour over the medallions.

VEAL MEDALLIONS WITH TOMATO AND MUSHROOMS
Médaillons de veau sautés chasseur
For 6 people

100 g (4 oz) very white mushrooms

6 veal medallions, preferably cut from the fillet

Salt and pepper

3 tablespoons olive oil

50 g (2 oz) unsalted butter

2 shallots, finely chopped

½ glass white wine

1 tablespoon tomato purée or 2 fresh tomatoes, peeled, seeded, drained and cut into pieces

1½ dl (¼ pt) espagnole sauce (page 108) or demi-glace sauce (page 108) or a good veal stock

Large pinch each of chopped chervil, parsley and tarragon

Cornflour or *beurre manié* (page 92)

This will take 25 minutes to cook.

Clean and rapidly wash the mushrooms twice, drain and wipe dry. Cut into very thin slices.

Lightly flatten the veal medallions, season with salt and pepper. In a pan heat the oil and one-third of the butter. Add the veal and brown on one side; turn over, continue cooking until done, then remove and keep warm. This step requires 10–12 minutes.

In the butter in which the meat was cooked, cook the shallots until golden. Add the mushrooms and sauté them on a high flame, then add the white wine, reduce almost to nothing. Add the tomatoes and the sauce or the stock; boil to reduce for 5 minutes. If veal stock is used, thicken with a dash of cornflour diluted with cold water or with ½ tablespoon of *beurre manié*.

To finish the sauce, away from the heat add the chopped herbs and the remaining butter; taste to correct the seasoning, and add the juice that has escaped from the veal medallions while standing. Place the medallions in a circle on a heated round platter. Cover with the mushrooms and the sauce. Sprinkle a pinch of chopped herbs on top.

**6 veal escalopes,
    100 g (4 oz) each**
**6 slices fresh pork fat,
    cut very thin**
**50 g (2 oz) unsalted
    butter**
**1 small carrot, sliced
    thinly**
1 onion, sliced thinly
Few pork rinds
Bouquet garni
**1 glass dry white
    wine**
**1½ dl (¼ pt) veal stock
    or lightly salted
    bouillon**

Stuffing:
100 g (4 oz) veal
Salt, pepper, nutmeg
**1 medium-sized
    potato, boiled**
Milk
**50 g (2 oz) unsalted
    butter**
1 egg
**2 tablespoons double
    cream or béchamel
    sauce (page 110)**
**100 g (4 oz)
    mushrooms**
2 shallots, chopped
**1 teaspoon chopped
    parsley**

STUFFED ESCALOPES OF VEAL
Paupiettes de veau

Paupiettes are veal escalopes cut very thin from the *noix* or *sous-noix*. They are seasoned with salt, pepper and nutmeg; filled with a stuffing, the type determining the name of the dish; rolled like a pancake; wrapped in a layer of very thin pork fat held in place by a string; then braised.

This dish requires 2 hours for preparation and cooking.

Stuffing.   Remove the skin and gristle from 100 g (4 oz) of veal and pound in a mortar with a pinch of salt, a pinch of freshly ground pepper and a dash of nutmeg. Place in a bowl.

Slice the boiled potato thinly; place in a small saucepan, half cover with hot milk, and boil for 10–15 minutes to reduce the milk until you reach the consistency of a firm paste. Pour into the mortar, and while the potato is still hot, pound to a paste. Add the veal and 25 g (1 oz) of butter, mix well and then add 1 egg. Add a little cream or béchamel sauce to produce the proper consistency for a stuffing.

Rub the stuffing through a sieve into a bowl, and smooth the mixture with a spatula. Wash and clean the mushrooms, wipe dry and chop fine. Put 25 g (1 oz) of butter in a pan; brown lightly, add the mushrooms and shallots, and cook over a high flame for about 5 minutes. Add to the mixture in the bowl. Finish the stuffing with 1 teaspoon of chopped parsley, and season to taste.

Assembling the paupiettes.   Beat out the escalopes to 6-mm (¼-inch) thickness, sprinkle with a dash of salt, then spread a sixth of the stuffing on each one. Roll the meat like a pancake, wrap each with a slice of pork fat and tie with a string.

Use a fairly small, deep flameproof baking dish. First butter the dish generously; heat it, add the carrot and the onion and brown. Place the pork rinds on top of the carrot and onion, then the paupiettes, side by side, and place the bouquet garni in between.

Cover and bake for 15 minutes in a 325°F (170°C, gas mark 3) oven to sweat the meat – condense and evaporate the juices.

Add the white wine and boil to reduce it completely over a high flame; then add stock or bouillon to cover the meat. Bring to the boil, cover with buttered wax paper and then with a lid, and simmer in the oven for 1¼ hours.

During the cooking, baste more and more frequently, as the juices reduce.

To serve carefully remove the paupiettes; cut off the strings, take off the pork fat and place the veal rolls in a circle on a heated round plate. In the middle, place the garnish. Strain the juice through a fine sieve and pour over the paupiettes. If the juice is not thick enough, boil to reduce it to the right consistency before straining.

Some of the best garnishes to accompany the paupiettes are: mushrooms in cream (page 451) or with béchamel sauce (page 110), cucumbers sautéed in butter, tomato fondue (page 507), noodles or macaroni *à la milanaise* (page 512), small potatoes *dauphine* (page 288; served separately so that the meat juice does not soak into them), boiled asparagus tips or peas coated with butter, artichoke hearts sliced and sautéed in butter, a purée of mushrooms.

STUFFED AND BRAISED VEAL BREAST
Poitrine de veau farcie et braisée
For 6 people

Stuffing:
15 g ($\frac{1}{2}$ oz) unsalted butter
$\frac{1}{2}$ onion, chopped finely
125 g (5 oz) mushrooms
125 g (5 oz) lean pork
150 g (6 oz) fresh pork fat
Pinch spiced salt (page xxiv)
1 egg
Chopped parsley and tarragon
1 tablespoon brandy

This dish requires $3\frac{1}{2}$ hours for preparation and cooking.

Stuffing. Heat a knob of the butter in a pan and very slowly cook half the onion, finely chopped.

Clean, quickly wash and drain the mushrooms. Chop and add to the onions; dry over a high flame for 3–4 minutes; remove to a bowl.

Dice the pork and the pork fat, chop them separately and pound them together with the spiced salt in a mortar so that the ingredients are well mixed into a fine stuffing.

This mixture can be made in a bowl with a wooden spoon if you do not have a pestle and mortar, but the lean meat and the fat will never be completely mixed.

Mix together the pork stuffing and the chopped cooked onion and mushroom; then add the egg, the parsley, the tarragon and the brandy. Work the mixture with a wooden spoon to blend well.

Test the seasoning by poaching a little ball of the stuffing. Taste, and correct the seasoning, if necessary.

1 veal breast
Pinch spiced salt
1 medium-sized
carrot, sliced
½ onion, sliced
100 g (4 oz) unsalted
butter
1 pork rind
100 g (4 oz) veal
knuckle
Bouquet garni
½ glass dry white
wine
½ l (1 pt) lightly salted
bouillon, veal stock
or water

Preparing the breast.   Bone the breast; slit it horizontally through the centre without cutting the ends or the third side so that the cut forms a pocket. Season the inside with a pinch of spiced salt, and fill with the stuffing, making an even layer. Sew the opening with thick thread.

Using an ovenproof casserole, lightly brown the sliced carrot and onion and the bones cut into tiny pieces in 25 g (1 oz) of butter. On top place the pork rind cut into little pieces, the veal knuckle, the bouquet garni and then the veal breast; spread with the remaining butter. Place in a 325°F (170°C, gas mark 3) oven for 15 minutes.

Moisten with the white wine, boil to reduce nearly to nothing, then add the lightly salted bouillon, stock or water so that it barely covers the meat. Bring to the boil, cover the veal breast with buttered waxed paper; put on the lid, and simmer for at least 2 hours.

At the end of 2 hours, remove the cover, the paper and the bones. The braising juice should be reduced by two-thirds; if it is not, raise the heat until it has reduced, and during the next 20 minutes baste the veal breast frequently. This last step will give the surface of the meat a shiny coating with a beautiful golden colour.

Place the veal breast on a long platter, remove the sewing threads and pour over the meat juice strained through a fine sieve.

Serve the chosen garnish in a separate vegetable dish: celery braised and simmered with the veal breast during the final cooking; braised sauerkraut, cooked the same way with a couple of slices of *foie gras*; braised lettuce, spinach, endive or sorrel; small glazed carrots; any fresh or dry bean purée.

Tendron de veau

Tendron is the extreme end of the breast, the part where the ribs meet. The bones look more like cartilage; they are very gelatinous and give the cut its name – *tendron* means 'gristle'. It is indispensable in a *blanquette de veau*.

The simplest and most delicious way to prepare this meat is by braising; it is served with a vegetable garnish.

BRAISED END OF BREAST
Tendron de veau braisé

Cut a piece of end of breast in pieces of about 100 g ($\frac{1}{4}$ lb) each, they should be thicker than they are wide. Heat some butter in a pan large enough to hold all the pieces side by side; brown on both sides on a low flame.

Remove the meat and put aside. In the same pan, brown a few slices of carrots and onions. Season the veal with salt and pepper and place on top of the vegetables. Cover, and stew slowly in the butter in a 325°F (170°C, gas mark 3) oven for 1 hour.

Then moisten with dry white wine. Boil to reduce the wine nearly completely. Add a good veal stock lightly salted, covering the veal halfway. Continue cooking, uncovered, in the oven for 1 hour, basting very often. Add more stock if necessary.

At the end of the cooking time, strain the juice through a fine sieve; it should be thick and golden and the veal should be extremely soft and tender.

Cooled in the cooking juices, which will jell, this cut makes an excellent cold dish to serve with a vegetable salad.

1·5 kg (3 lb) milk-fed
  veal knuckle
Salt and pepper
75 g (3 oz) unsalted
  butter
1 large onion, diced
100 g (4 oz) new
  carrots, sliced
2 ripe tomatoes,
  seeded and crushed
6 tablespoons dry
  white wine
1½ dl (¼ pt) veal stock
Small bouquet garni

VEAL KNUCKLE WITH ONION, CARROTS AND TOMATOES

Jarret de veau à la ménagère

For 4 people

Season the veal knuckle with the salt and pepper. In a saucepan, preferably oval, brown the meat on all sides in butter. Then add the diced onion, the sliced carrots and, after these are browned, the tomatoes.

Moisten with the dry white wine and the veal stock. Add the bouquet garni, and cook covered in a 325°F (170°C, gas mark 3) oven or simmer on top of the stove for about 45 minutes.

Serve the veal in a shallow dish surrounded by the vegetables and coated with their juice; only the bouquet garni is removed.

This dish can also be served with fresh noodles with butter.

1 veal knuckle, sliced
 6 cm (2½ inches)
 thick
Salt
50 g (2 oz) unsalted
 butter
½ glass dry white
 wine
Bouillon, barely
 salted, or water
500 g (1 lb) shelled
 peas
2 lettuce hearts, cut
 into shreds
12 small white onions
½ cube sugar
Small bouquet garni
 or sprig of savory

VEAL KNUCKLE WITH PEAS
Jarret de veau aux petits pois printaniers

Have the butcher cut a veal knuckle into slices 6 cm (2½ inches) thick. Season with salt and brown in butter in a pan. Moisten with dry white wine and boil to reduce nearly completely. Then add a little barely salted bouillon or water, half covering the slices, and cook slowly, covered, for 2 hours.

In a saucepan mix together the peas, the lettuce hearts and the onions; add a pinch of salt, ½ cube of sugar; mix well, add 2 tablespoons of water and a small bouquet garni or a sprig of savoury.

Bring to the boil on a high flame; lower heat and simmer, covered, for 5 minutes. Then add to the veal knuckle slices, without the bouquet garni. Continue cooking for ½ hour, basting frequently; watch the sauce carefully, it should be thick while still covering the peas.

Correct the seasoning, and place the slices of veal knuckle in a shallow dish, surrounding them with the peas coated with the syrupy juice of the veal.

FRICASSEE OF VEAL
Fricassée de veau a l'ancienne
For 6 people

100 g (4 oz) unsalted butter

1 kg (2 lb) milk-fed veal (breast, best end and shoulder), cut into large cubes

Salt and pepper

1 medium-sized carrot, quartered

1 onion quartered and stuck with a clove

2 tablespoons flour

White bouillon or water

Bouquet garni (5 sprigs parsley, sprig thyme, 1 bay leaf

12 small onions

100 g (4 oz) mushrooms

¼ lemon

2 egg yolks

1½ dl (¼ pt) single or double cream, or milk

Nutmeg

Small croutons of white bread or fleurons of flaky pastry

In a pan heat 50 g (2 oz) of butter; add the veal, seasoned with salt and pepper, and the carrot and onion. Stew slowly for 15–20 minutes, stirring from time to time.

Sprinkle with the flour, mix well and cook over a low flame for 10 minutes, like a roux, but without letting it brown.

Moisten with barely salted white bouillon just covering the meat; if using water, salt lightly. Bring to the boil, stirring to thicken the sauce smoothly, and simmer in the oven or over a low flame on top of the stove for 2 hours with the bouquet garni.

Blanch the small onions, drain and stew in about 25 g (1 oz) of butter until they are cooked. They must remain white; watch them carefully.

Clean the mushrooms and wash them rapidly in water, drain and wipe dry. Cut off the stems and put them to simmer with the meat; quarter the caps, sauté them in a pan with 15 g (½ oz) of butter for 2 minutes on a high flame; season with a pinch of salt and squeeze in a few drops of lemon juice. When the onions are cooked, add the mushrooms to the onions. Cover the pan and set aside.

Place the egg yolks in a bowl with 3 tablespoons of white bouillon (or milk or cream), 15 g (½ oz) of butter in pieces, and a dash of grated nutmeg. Mix well.

When the meat is cooked, remove from the heat, and with a skimmer and a fork, take out the pieces of meat, reserving them separately. Scatter the mushrooms and the small onions over the veal, cover and keep warm.

To thicken the sauce, place the pan with the vegetable garnish over a high flame and reduce the liquid by half, stirring with a wooden spoon. As it reduces it will become very thick. Add just enough cream or milk to give the sauce the smooth consistency and subtle flavour characteristic of this delicious dish.

Remove the pan from the flame, and slowly mix a ladleful of the sauce into the egg-yolk mixture, stirring rapidly with a sauce whisk.

Squeeze the rest of the lemon juice into the egg yolks and sauce. Add the mixture in a stream to the sauce in the pan, whipping it with a whisk continuously. If this is done quickly, while the sauce is still very hot the egg yolks start to cook without losing their thickening and enriching qualities.

If for any reason the sauce cools off too much, preventing the yolks and the sauce blending, put the pan back on the flame. Stirring with a whisk, blend the yolks and start them cooking. Too much heat may scramble the eggs – success is a matter of experience.

To finish the perfectly thickened sauce add a tablespoon or so of butter cut in small pieces; beat into the sauce with a whisk. Correct the seasoning.

Strain the sauce through a fine sieve, pressing the quartered carrots and onions lightly; pour the sauce over the veal and garnish, which have been kept warm. Spread carefully with a spatula, so that the meat is well coated with the sauce; serve on very hot plates with creole rice (page 514) or boiled potatoes in their skins.

Around the fricassee arrange small heart-shaped croûtons, made of white bread and fried in butter; or *fleurons*, small semi-circular shapes cut with a fluted cutter from flaky dough or the trimmings of flaky dough, well browned in the oven.

Blanquette de veau

This uses the same ingredients as the fricassee of veal above.

Cook the veal in a seasoned court-bouillon, which is used to moisten the roux. The egg yolks and cream make a smooth velouté sauce. The total cooking time is $2\frac{1}{2}$ hours.

75 g (3 oz) unsalted
  butter
2 tablespoons olive
  oil
1 kg (2 lb) veal
  (breast, best end
  and shoulder), cut
  into large cubes
1 carrot, quartered
2 medium-sized
  onions, quartered
25 g (1 oz) flour
2 garlic cloves,
  crushed
½ glass dry white
  wine
500 g (1 lb) fresh
  tomatoes, peeled,
  seeded and
  quartered, or 1½ dl
  (¼ pt) tomato
  purée
Bouquet garni (sprig
  parsley and thyme,
  ½ bay leaf)
½ l (1 pt) veal stock,
  bouillon (barely
  salted) or water
12 small onions,
  peeled
100 g (4 oz)
  mushrooms
¼ lemon
6 croûtons cut into
  heart shape and
  fried in butter
1 teaspoon chopped
  fresh parsley

VEAL STEW WITH MUSHROOMS AND TOMATOES

Sauté de veau Marengo

For 6 people

This will take 2 hours to prepare and cook. In a pan, heat 50 g (2 oz) of butter and the oil; when the mixture is smoking, add the pieces of veal, the carrot and the onions. Season with salt and freshly ground pepper; cook on a high flame until browned.

Sprinkle the meat with the flour, mix well and brown the flour slightly; add the crushed garlic, heat for a second, then add the white wine; reduce by two-thirds. Then add the tomato purée or the fresh tomatoes, the bouquet garni and the veal stock, bouillon or water. If using water, salt lightly. Bring to the boil, stirring with a spatula; cover and simmer on a low flame, or in the oven, for 1 hour.

If you do not have new onions, scald them, drain and wipe dry; cooked until glazed in a pan with 15 g (½ oz) of butter.

Clean the mushrooms, wash carefully and quickly, and drain. Put the stems in the pan with the veal. Quarter the caps, if they are large; trim them if medium-sized. Add the peels to the veal. Do not cut the mushrooms if they are small. Prepare a second pan or a saucepan and heat 15 g (½ oz) of butter; add the mushrooms and stir over a high flame until they are browned; remove from the heat and add to the small onions.

When the veal is half cooked, remove the pieces of meat from the pan and place them in the second pan on top of the mushrooms and the glazed onions. Let the sauce stand for a few minutes until the fat comes to the surface and you can remove it easily. Degrease the sauce; strain through a fine sieve on to the meat, rubbing the vegetables through. Correct the seasoning and simmer until completely cooked, about 20 minutes.

To serve, squeeze lemon juice over the veal and put it into a dish or a deep serving platter. Place the croûtons around and sprinkle some chopped parsley on top.

VEAL AND PORK PIE
Pâté Pantin du maître Ferdinand Wernet
For 10 people

Dough:
500 g (1 lb) flour,
  sifted
½ tablespoon salt
150 g (5 oz) unsalted
  butter
1 egg
2 dl (¼ pt) water, or
  more, depending
  upon the quality of
  the flour

Forcemeat and filling:
500 g (1 lb) veal,
  rump or topside
800 g (1½ lb) fresh
  pork fat
225 g (8 oz) lean ham
175 g (6 oz) pork
  fillet
1 tablespoon spiced
  salt (page xxiv)
Pinch thyme
Pinch powdered bay
  leaf
½ glass brandy
2 eggs

Dough. Make the day before; after 12 hours it loses its elasticity. Keep it firm, give it four turns, as explained for flaky dough (page 531).

Filling. From the veal cut 8 pieces 15 cm (6 inches) long and 2 cm (¾ inch) thick.

Cut the fresh pork fat into 2 large bards, 20 cm (8 inches) wide and 30 cm (12 inches) long, or into 4 bards, 15 cm (6 inches) long, and 8 lardoons the same length as the pieces of meat.

Cut pieces of ham the same size. Combine the meat and the lardoons in a shallow dish; season with the spiced salt, thyme and powdered bay leaf; mix well, so that the meats will be permeated by the spices, and pour the cognac over. Marinate until ready to be used, stirring from time to time.

Forcemeat. Cut the pork fillet, the remaining veal, pork fat and ham into large cubes; season with spiced salt, thyme and powdered bay leaf, then mince finely or chop by hand. Pound the meats in a mortar and mix vigorously, adding the beaten eggs, and any cognac not absorbed by the meat while marinating.

If you do not have a mincer or mortar, after chopping by hand mash the meat together in a bowl with a wooden spatula.

To be sure the seasoning is correct, poach a ball of forcemeat in boiling water and taste it.

Method. Roll out three-quarters of the dough after the last two turns, making a rectangle 36 cm (14 inches) long and 6 mm (¼ inch) thick; place it on a pastry sheet.

In the centre of the dough, place a bard of pork fat and spread a layer of the forcemeat on top, then a layer of veal, then pork fat, then ham, then a second layer of forcemeat. Continue the same way until you have used up all the meats, arranging them symmetrically. Finish with a layer of forcemeat and cover it with the final bard of pork fat.

Moisten lightly with a wet cloth or pastry brush all around the edges of the dough. Lift the two long sides of the rectangle of dough up over the top of the pork fat, so that the two edges of dough meet. With a rolling pin, roll out the two ends of the dough and lift them up so that their moistened edges meet the top dough and stick, pressing lightly with your fingers.

Brush the whole surface of the pie with a wet brush or cloth and place on top a rectangle of dough of the same size (first cut into the dough all around with a knife, so that it will puff up while cooking).

Pinch the edges together with a pastry wheel or with your thumb and forefinger. Brush the surface with 1 tablespoon of beaten egg; decorate the top surface with designs lightly incised in the dough. Finally, with the point of a knife make two 6-mm ($\frac{1}{4}$-inch) openings in the centre of the decorated dough and insert in each a little funnel of buttered paper to allow the steam to escape from the liquid ingredients.

Place in a 350°F (180°C, gas mark 4) oven. When the dough is golden brown, protect the pastry by covering it with good quality white paper, lightly damped, which will not flavour the pie as it gets hot.

The pie takes about $1\frac{1}{4}$ hours to cook. After an hour in the oven some juice runs out round the paper funnels and little by little solidifies to form a meat glaze. This is a sure sign it is done.

The pie is ready to be served hot, warm or cold; if served hot, it is harder to cut.

Note: This recipe can be enriched with truffles, *foie gras*, poultry or game. It is a superb combination of ingredients.

VEAL QUENELLES WITH BUTTER
Quenelles de veau au beurre
For 1 pound of forcemeat

Panade:
2 dl (8 fl oz) water
Pinch salt
50 g (2 oz) butter
100 g (4 oz) sifted flour

Forcemeat:
225 g (8 oz) veal rump or topside
125 g (5 oz) unsalted butter
$\frac{1}{2}$ tablespoon salt
Pinch pepper
Dash grated nutmeg
2 eggs, beaten

Panade. Combine in a saucepan the water, a pinch of salt and 50 g (2 oz) of butter. Bring to the boil. Add the flour away from the flame, and mix until smooth. Put back on a high flame, stirring constantly to evaporate part of the water. The dough will pull away from the sides of the pan in one ball when it is dry enough. Let it cool on a plate.

Forcemeat. Dice the veal and chop fine in a mincer or with a hand chopper. Place the chopped meat in a mortar and pound vigorously, adding the cold *panade*; pound until the two are blended. Add the butter, and continue to work the mixture with the pestle until all the ingredients are completely mixed. Add the salt, pepper and nutmeg; then little by little work in the beaten eggs.

With the pestle rub the meat through a fine sieve over a bowl. Mash the sieved meat for a few moments with a wooden spatula, place it in a cool place or refrigerate, covering the surface with a round of white paper to protect it from the air until ready to use.

Method. With a tablespoon pack the stuffing into a pastry bag fitted with a simple tube 6 mm ($\frac{1}{4}$ inch) in diameter. Close the bag and press to push the stuffing through the tube on to a shallow baking dish. Squeeze out little sticks about 8 cm (3 inches) long; leave them about 5 cm (2 inches) apart.

Fifteen minutes before serving, cover the quenelles with lightly salted water and place the baking tin on the heat so that the water barely simmers. The quenelles are done when they float in the water and are resistant when pressed lightly with a finger.

These quenelles are used in certain recipes for *vol-au-vent*, *bouchées à la reine*, etc., or are served alone for entrées accompanied by a sauce such as a light Mornay (page 120).

Note: This recipe can be refined by adding some double cream, which makes the quenelles more delicate. In that case, use less *panade* or none and increase the number of egg whites. To be sure of the right consistency, test the mixture by poaching a little ball of it before shaping the quenelles.

COLD VEAL
La veau froid

Any cut of roasted, braised or pot-roasted veal can be served cold like roast beef.

If veal is to be served cold, it is best pot roasted. The stock, well degreased and strained, makes a marvellous jelly to serve with the meat.

Serve with a garnish of cold vegetables, seasoned like a salad, for example a mixture of vegetables coated with mayonnaise.

Mutton and Lamb

Mutton comes from an adult animal over a year old and is bright red, firm, close-grained and fat. The leg is well covered with meat. The saddle is a good size with plenty of fat. The fat is well distributed, plentiful and very white and firm.

A young lamb of between 5 and 9 months is more succulent and tender than full-grown mutton and a lighter red. In France this type of lamb is known as *agneau de pré-salé*, after the salty grasses along the Channel and Atlantic coasts which are thought to produce the best lamb, particularly in the Coutances district of Normandy.

Milk-fed lamb 2–3 months old (*agneau de lait*) is lamb which has not yet been weaned and has never grazed. The meat is pale pink, almost white. In France *agneau de Pauillac* is regarded as the finest milk-fed lamb.

In summer, during shearing time, mutton is not at its best. It is strong-tasting and the flavour becomes stronger with cooking.

[*Editor's note:* As good, well-aged mutton is hard to come by in England, the recipes for lamb and mutton are interchangeable, though milk-fed lamb is best prepared by special recipes.]

CUTS

Lamb and mutton cuts are the same.

The prime cuts are leg, saddle and best end. Then come the shoulder, breast and scrag end, and finally the offal.

The two legs together are the hindquarters. The hindquarters and saddle together are known as a baron. These are joints for important occasions and are almost always roasted.

The saddle can be cut up into pieces 4–5 cm ($1\frac{1}{4}$–2 inches) thick to give chump chops and loin chops. Best end can be divided into cutlets.

These cuts can be roasted, pot-roasted, sautéed or grilled according to size and cut.

Shoulder is roasted or braised and is also the main ingredient for stews.

Scrag end and breast are also used in stews and breast makes a number of light entrées.

ROAST LEG OF MUTTON
Gigot de mouton rôti

To carve the leg more easily, I recommend boning the chump end.

It is an excellent idea to insert garlic cloves in the leg, according to taste; do not, however, pierce the muscles with the point of a knife but insert the garlic between the muscles and the bone or at the chump end.

Place the leg on a rack in a roasting pan; coat with butter, season with salt and place in a 375°F (190°C, gas mark 5) oven.

Cooking time: For medium-rare meat allow about 10 minutes per pound for a fairly large leg. Leave time for the meat to 'rest' after roasting.

Baste frequently. At end of the cooking, add 6 tablespoons hot water to deglaze the pan juices, without letting them boil. Let the roast stand in a warm place before serving.

Serve the juices in a sauceboat without degreasing them.

If the leg of mutton is very fat, it is preferable to remove some of the fat before cooking.

A leg of mutton should be cooked rare, although the heat should reach the bone.

ROAST LEG OF LAMB
Gigot de pré-salé rôti

This can be given the same preparation and cooked for the same length of time as the leg of mutton.

A leg of lamb or mutton can also be roasted on a spit. Increase the roasting time by 5 minutes for each pound. Serve the juices gathered in the drip pan separately.

The garnishes for a roast leg of lamb are: French beans or haricot beans, potato purée, new potatoes cooked and browned in butter, potatoes *à la sarladaise* (sliced boiled potatoes with thinly sliced truffles, page 504), etc., or any fresh or dried vegetables.

**Leg of mutton or
lamb
12 small carrots
4 turnips
4 onions quartered,
one stuck with 1
clove
Bouquet garni
4 large potatoes
1 celery stalk
100 g (4 oz) unsalted
butter
75 g (3 oz) flour
2–3 teaspoons capers**

BOILED LEG OF MUTTON OR LAMB
Gigot bouilli à l'anglaise

Trim the leg, shorten the shank bone, and remove the bone at the chump end. Place in a braising pan with sufficient boiling water to cover it completely.

Add to the cooking water: 1 scant tablespoon salt for each quart of water, the carrots, turnips, onions, bouquet garni, potatoes and celery. As soon as the water starts boiling again, lower the flame so that it barely simmers. From that point, calculate the cooking time at 15 minutes per pound.

To serve drain the leg of lamb and serve it alone on a serving platter. Remove the carrots and the onions from the braising pan carefully with a skimmer and serve in a separate bowl. In another bowl serve the turnips, mashed with a little butter, a pinch of salt and a pinch of freshly ground pepper. In a sauceboat serve the butter sauce prepared in this way:

Make a roux with 100 g (4 oz) of butter and 75 g (3 oz) of flour. Let it brown, then moisten with the cooking liquid from the leg of lamb to make a moderately thick sauce. Cook slowly for 10 minutes, strain and add 2–3 teaspoons of capers.

**500 g (1 lb) white
haricot beans
1 medium-sized
onion, chopped
finely
1 tablespoon unsalted
butter or fatty
lamb juice
½ glass dry white wine
½ dl (¼ pt) thick
tomato sauce or
500 g (1 lb) fresh
tomatoes, peeled,
seeded and chopped
2 garlic cloves, crushed
1 teaspoon chopped
parsley**

ROAST LEG OF LAMB OR MUTTON WITH HARICOT BEANS
Gigot rôti aux haricots à la bretonne

Roast the leg of lamb following the classic method above and serve with its own juice (do not degrease it even if it is quite fatty) and a dish of white haricot beans (*flageolets, soissons* or *suisses* are suitable varieties available in France) cooked *à la bretonne* as described below.

First, cook the beans, fresh or dried.

Then prepare 3 dl (½ pt) of Breton sauce. Cook the onion very slowly with a little butter or lamb juice. When the onion is golden, add the dry white wine (reduced by two-thirds) and the tomato sauce or fresh tomatoes. Simmer for 10 minutes, add the garlic and chopped parsley. Away from the flame add two or three turns of the pepper mill.

Drain the beans and mix them with the sauce to coat them lightly. If the lamb juice is very fatty, the excess fat can be added to improve the flavour of the beans.

Note: The beans should not be allowed to turn into a purée. The juice or sauce should be about as thick as the braising liquid from a joint of veal and the beans when served should be very moist and juicy – not dry or swimming in liquid.

How to carve a leg of lamb

Hold on tightly to the leg bone.

First method

Hold the bone with your left hand and lift it slightly, with the other end on the platter rump side down.

With your right hand, cut parallel to the bone, slicing from right to left. The slices should be thin. When you reach the bone, turn the leg of lamb over and slice the rump, with the blade at an angle towards the bone.

Second method

Hold the leg of lamb as above but keep the sharp edge of the blade at right angles to the bone. The carving is also done in two stages. In both cases, the bone will be completely clean.

Since the juice is very fatty, all plates must be very hot. Without this essential step, the fat congeals rapidly and this delicious dish loses much of its appeal.

HINDQUARTERS, BARON AND SADDLE
Double, baron et selle

The hindquarters, the baron and the saddle are prepared in the same way as the leg of lamb. The same vegetable garnishes can be used.

The cooking time for the saddle, for medium rare meat, is 10 minutes per pound. Allow time for the roast to 'rest' before serving.

It is easy to tell when the saddle is done. Plunge a larding needle into the marrow for 1 minute. Remove, and place it immediately against the back of your hand. If the needle is cold, the meat needs more cooking; if it is quite warm, the meat is done; if it is definitely hot, the saddle is overdone. Let the meat rest for 10 minutes in a warm oven.

How to carve a saddle of lamb

Before placing the meat in the oven, trim the thin hindquarter flank, fold it under the saddle and tie in place with a string.

When the saddle of lamb is removed from the oven, place it on a platter, the cut end facing the carver. Make a deep incision on either side of the back bone.

The carving knife should be held flat in a position that will enable the carver to cut from right to left, towards the back bone, cutting thin slices the length of the saddle. When one side is carved, turn the platter around to carve the other side the same way.

Then turn the saddle over and carve the meat underneath.

The cooking temperatures and times for the leg of lamb are the same for the baron and the saddle.

If the cooking juice is too lightly salted, sprinkle a dash of ground sea salt on each slice of meat; it gives a better flavour.

The juice must be served very hot. Never pour the juice over a rare slice of lamb; pour 1 tablespoon on the plate next to the meat which will keep its good colour and all its flavour.

SADDLE OF LAMB WITH TRUFFLES, CHESTNUTS AND MUSHROOM TARTS

Selle d'agneau de pré-salé des gastronomes

For 12 people

1 saddle of lamb,
 weighing 2.5 kg
 (5 lb)
Veal bones
Salt and pepper
75 g (3 oz) unsalted
 butter
¼ l (½ pt) good veal
 stock, barely salted

Garnish:
¼ l (½ pt) white
 bouillon
12 cock kidneys
12 truffles, all
 medium sized
½ glass cognac
24 chestnuts
Mushroom purée
 made with 500 g
 (1 lb) mushrooms
 (page 447)
12 small
 unsweetened tart
 crusts (page 536)
1 glass champagne
 brut
Cayenne pepper
12 tablespoons good
 veal stock, barely
 salted
½ tablespoon flour
½ teaspoon vinegar or
 juice ¼ lemon
1 teaspoon port or
 Madeira
1 celery stalk
75 g (2 oz) unsalted
 butter

Lamb. Trim the saddle, by removing the membrane over the fat covering the meat. Score the fat, forming a checkerboard pattern with the point of a knife to allow the heat to penetrate the meat. Remove the two balls of fat that surround the kidneys. Trim the two thin hindquarter flanks and fold over the tenderloin strips to protect them and to make the saddle sit firmly. Keep in place with five pieces of string, not too tight. If the saddle is tied too tightly. the muscles cannot expand; the meat must be allowed to swell.

Cook by pot roasting. At the bottom of a braising pan just big enough to hold the meat place either a rack or (preferably) veal bones broken into tiny pieces. Place the saddle on top with the fat side up; season with salt and pepper and moisten with 75 g (3 oz) of melted butter, good veal fat or fresh pork fat. Roast in a 425°F (220°C, gas mark 7) oven, turning three times and basting frequently. The fat will give the saddle a nice golden colour.

The cooking time is estimated at 10 minutes per pound for rare meat. When the meat should be done, probe the marrow by inserting a larding needle; if after 1 minute inside the marrow, the needle is just warm when placed against the back of your hand, the meat is done. Remove it from the hot oven, place on a platter, and let stand for 15 minutes in a very slow oven.

Pour the veal stock into the braising pan and boil for 5 minutes to dissolve the solidified juices on the bones and in the pan.

Strain the juices into a small deep saucepan; and after waiting a few minutes, remove the fat that floats to the top. Taste the gravy and correct the seasoning by adding salt or water, which-ever is needed.

Garnish

While the saddle is roasting in the braising pan, prepare the garn-ish. To reduce the amount of work before a big dinner so that you can give more care and attention to the final details, it is essential to make certain preparations the night before or several hours before serving time. Make a white bouillon for the cock kidneys. Scrub the truffles and steep in the cognac in a tightly sealed jar. Peel the chestnuts. Clean the mushrooms. Make the tart crusts. This means that during the braising of the saddle, only these steps will remain to be done:

Truffles.   In a small saucepan with a close-fitting lid place the whole uncooked truffles, the champagne, the cognac, a pinch of salt and a dash of cayenne pepper. Bring to the boil on a high flame for 5 minutes. Remove from the heat; drain the truffles, place in a bowl, cover and keep warm.

To the remaining champagne, add 4 tablespoons veal stock, and boil to reduce to 3 tablespoons. Return the truffles to the saucepan and coat them in the reduced juice until they have completely absorbed it.

Kidneys.   Prick the cock kidneys with a needle to prevent them bursting. Poach them in a white bouillon made with 3 dl ($\frac{1}{2}$ pt) of white stock or salted water, $\frac{1}{2}$ tablespoon of flour and $\frac{1}{2}$ teaspoon of vinegar or the juice of a quarter of lemon. Plunge the kidneys, well soaked in fresh water, into the white bouillon and remove the saucepan from the heat without letting it boil. Leave to stand for 5 minutes.

Reduce 6 tablespoons of veal stock almost completely. Drain the kidneys and coat with the reduced liquid, which can be flavoured, away from the heat, with 1 teaspoon of port or Madeira.

Chestnuts.   Place the chestnuts in a 425°F (220°C, gas mark 7) oven for 5–6 minutes or plunge into hot oil or boiling water for 2 minutes (see page 478). Peel. Boil in white stock to cover with the celery for 20 minutes very slowly, so that the chestnuts remain whole and slightly firm.

When they are done, drain and brown (as you would glaze small onions) in butter in a pan large enough for them to fit in one layer on the bottom.

Mushrooms.   Make a mushroom purée, using 50 g (2 oz) of butter.

Tarts.   Make the tarts beforehand with unsweetened dough (page 536) and place in small moulds; cook them between two moulds to keep their shape, and fill with the mushroom purée.

Serving.   Place the saddle on a long platter big enough to hold the garnish around the meat comfortably without covering the rim. Arrange the garnish around the meat, alternating 1 tart with the mushroom purée and 1 cock kidney, then a truffle and 2 chestnuts.

Pour 1–2 spoons of cooking juice over the saddle and serve the rest of the juice, very hot, in a sauceboat.

To reduce the carving time at the table and to make it easier, the saddle can be carved in the kitchen, the slices put back in their places, and the tenderloin strips reshaped carefully.

Do not forget to put very hot plates on the table just before serving.

BEST END OR FILLET OF LAMB
Carré d'agneau de pré-salé ou filet rôti

The *carré* is the best end of neck joint, consisting of the cutlets. The bones should be trimmed to the length of ordinary lamb chops and the ends cleaned. The chine bones must be removed to facilitate carving; the membrane covering the layer of fat must also be removed.

Cooking time: 12 minutes per pound at 425°F (220°C, gas mark 7). The meat must 'rest' once it is seared.

The fillet is made up of half the saddle, cut lengthwise along the spinal cord.

To roast remove the covering membrane. Trim the hind quarter and bone it completely; season the inside with salt and pepper and reshape. Hold in place with string.

Cooking time in a 425°F (220°C, gas mark 7) oven for the fillet, 10 minutes per pound for searing; then the meat must 'rest'.

To serve, remove most of the fat. Deglaze with a little bouillon, veal stock or water to dissolve the solidified juices sticking to the roasting pan; serve the juices in a sauceboat with the chosen garnish.

All the garnishes for leg of lamb, and lamb chops can be used with the best end and fillet.

Note: It is preferable to cook the loin with the bone in; the flavour will be better, but it is more difficult to carve.

FILLET OF LAMB WITH POTATOES
Filet d'agneau de pré-salé Parmentier

Trim and bone the loin, roast in butter in a large baking dish. As soon as the meat is golden, surround it with 2 large potatoes diced in 2-cm ($\frac{3}{4}$-inch) cubes, washed (to remove the starch and to prevent their sticking to each other), and carefully dried. Sprinkle with a pinch of salt. Continue cooking in a 425°F (220°C, gas mark 7) oven, stirring the potatoes from time to time. Baste the meat often. To serve, place the meat on a long heated platter, with the potatoes piled at each end. Sprinkle the potatoes with a pinch of chopped parsley.

Deglaze the roasting pan with 2 tablespoons of veal stock and pour over the meat.

CHOPS AND CUTLETS

The ribs and loin are cut into chops – chump chops, loin chops and cutlets.

The best way to cook lamb or mutton chops is to grill them. When the meat is nearly cooked, turn the fatty part of the chop towards the flame to grill it as well. Expose the inside of the chops to the flame to sear that as well.

Let the meat rest in a warm oven for a few minutes; serve with a bunch of watercress (trim the stems and gather together into a tight bunch so that the stems do not show) and an additional vegetable as garnish.

All vegetables can be served with mutton or lamb, grilled or sautéed. However, green vegetables coated with butter are usually best, such as French beans, peas, haricots, asparagus tips or artichoke hearts. Also potatoes, usually fried (soufflé, Pont-Neuf, matchstick, straw, chips, etc.) or puréed (pages 492–496).

LAMB CHOPS WITH TOMATOES AND MUSHROOMS
Côtelettes d'agneau à la parisienne

Grill the chops, place them on a platter and garnish with grilled tomatoes and mushrooms.

If the tomatoes are large, cut them in two round the middle; if they are medium-sized, cut off the top part and the stem. In both cases, squeeze them carefully to remove the juice and the seeds.

Season with salt and pepper inside, cover with oil or melted butter and place under a very hot grill. Turn them over halfway through the cooking.

The mushrooms should be large and regular in shape. Remove the stems; wash the caps, wipe and cover with oil or melted butter. Season and place under the grill, top side up first, under a medium flame.

Turn the caps over halfway through the cooking and in each stem cavity place a pat of butter, which will soak into the mushroom during the second part of the cooking.

Arrange the lamb chops in a semicircle, overlapping; in the centre place a bunch of watercress and on the outer edge alternate the mushrooms and the tomatoes.

Note: The mushroom stems can be used to make *duxelles*.

BREADED LAMB CHOPS, SAUTÉED OR GRILLED
Côtelettes d'agneau panées, sautées ou grillées

If sautéing the chops, dip them in seasoned, beaten egg, then in breadcrumbs. Press lightly to make the breadcrumbs adhere.

Heat some clarified butter in a pan and place the chops in it. Cook slowly so that the browning of the breadcrumbs and the cooking of the chops are completed at the same time. When the chops are turned the first time, sprinkle them with a pinch of salt; do this a second time on the other side after the chops are cooked.

To grill chops, brush them with oil or melted butter, season and sprinkle with very fine breadcrumbs, white or light brown.

Sprinkle again with a few drops of melted butter. Place on a very hot grill, and grill gently, reducing the heat at that point.

For sautéed chops, serve with a purée of potatoes or fresh peas. For grilled chops serve with fried potatoes.

SAUTÉED MUTTON CHOPS WITH CEPS
Côtelettes de mouton sautées aux cèpes

4 tablespoons olive oil
6 mutton chops
500 g (1 lb) ceps
50 g (2 oz) unsalted butter
Pinch chopped parsley
Finely chopped garlic
Pinch freshly ground pepper
2 tablespoons reduced white dry wine
2 tablespoons light tomato sauce

Heat 2 tablespoons of olive oil in a pan. When the oil is smoking, place 6 mutton chops, trimmed, lightly flattened and seasoned, in one layer in the pan.

Halfway through the cooking turn the chops over and finish cooking.

Place the chops in a circle on a heated round platter with paper frills on the bones. Garnish the centre with the ceps sautéed in 2 tablespoons of oil and 25 g (1 oz) of butter. Brown them well and at the last minute complete the seasoning with a pinch of chopped parsley, garlic and a pinch of freshly ground pepper.

Deglaze the pan with dry white wine (reduced) and the tomato sauce.

Away from the heat add 25 g (1 oz) of butter, and pour over the chops.

6 mutton chops from the best end

50 g (2 oz) unsalted butter

Salt and pepper

2 large onions, peeled and sliced thinly

$\frac{1}{2}$ l (1 pt) bouillon or white veal stock

Bouquet garni

6 medium-sized yellow potatoes, peeled, washed, dried and sliced thinly

2 garlic cloves, finely chopped

MUTTON CHOPS WITH POTATOES AND ONIONS

Côtelettes de mouton à la Champvallon

For 6 people

This will take $1\frac{1}{2}$ hours to prepare and cook. In a pan big enough to hold the chops in one layer, heat the butter. When it bubbles, add the chops; sprinkle each chop with a pinch of salt and a dash of pepper. Brown slowly to avoid burning the butter; then turn over, season a second time and brown again.

Remove the chops and place on an ovenproof earthenware platter that has been rubbed with garlic.

Put the onions in the pan. Brown them, stirring frequently. Add half the bouillon or veal stock, boil for 5 minutes and pour over the chops, spreading the onion on top. If the bouillon does not quite cover the lamb chops, add more as needed. Bring to the boil, insert the bouquet garni between the chops, cover and cook in a 400°F (200°C, gas mark 6) oven for 30 minutes.

Spread the potatoes over the chops; add the remaining bouillon, bring to the boil and continue cooking in the oven, covered, for 20 minutes more.

Then remove the cover, sprinkle the garlic on the potatoes and baste with the juice. Continue cooking uncovered in the oven for another 20 minutes, basting often with the juice, which will reduce and thicken slightly. When the cooking is finished, the cooking juice should be largely absorbed by the meat and the potatoes, which will be very soft; the top of the vegetables will be browned to a beautiful dark golden colour.

Sprinkle the dish with chopped parsley, and serve on the cooking platter.

MUTTON CHOPS WITH CROQUETTE POTATOES
Côtelettes de mouton Pompadour

Sauté the chops; place them in a circle on a round, heated platter, and place a paper frill at the end of each bone.

In the centre, form a pyramid of walnut-sized potato croquettes, fried just before serving (recipe below). In butter stew 1 artichoke heart per guest for 15 minutes. Arrange them around the chops in a circle.

Garnish with a purée of lentils or any other dry or fresh vegetable, buttered well. Deglaze the pan with a few table-spoons of veal stock, demi-glace (page 108) or Périgueux sauce (page 116). Flavour away from the heat with Madeira and serve in a sauceboat.

Potato croquettes

Potato croquettes:
500 g (1 lb) potatoes
100 g (4 oz) unsalted butter
4 egg yolks
Salt and nutmeg
1 whole egg
Breadcrumbs

Peel the potatoes, cook them in salted boiling water until soft; do not wait until the potatoes fall apart.

Drain the potatoes well and replace them in the saucepan; leave them for a few seconds on very low heat so that the moisture evaporates.

Turn the potatoes into a sieve and press them through to form a purée. Do not rub them through with a circular motion as this makes the pulp stringy.

Reheat the pulp in a saucepan and beat in the butter vigorously, using a wooden spatula. When well beaten, the potatoes will still be white. Still beating, incorporate the egg yolks and a little nutmeg. Add more salt if needed.

Turn the mixture out on a buttered plate, butter the top to prevent a crust forming and let stand until cool. Divide into pieces the size of a walnut. Roll them on a lightly floured table. Dip in beaten egg and roll in breadcrumbs, patting to make the crumbs adhere.

Plunge into very hot deep fat for a few minutes; drain. The outsides should be crisp. Arrange on the platter and serve.

NOISETTES OF SPRING LAMB WITH DAUPHINE POTATOES
Noisettes de pré-salé à la dauphine

Prepare the *noisettes*. These are round slices cut from a boned loin of lamb, 4 cm ($1\frac{1}{2}$ inches) thick. Trim the meat and flatten it slightly; sauté in butter in a pan. Season the meat on both sides while cooking. The centre should be pink.

Place the meat in a circle on a large round platter on top of croûtons fried in butter (the bread slices should be the same size as the meat and 6 mm ($\frac{1}{4}$ inch) thick).

Around the edge, like a string of big pearls, place croquettes of *dauphine* potatoes.

Deglaze the pan with 2 tablespoons of dry white wine, reduce nearly completely, then add 6 tablespoons of good veal stock. Reduce again by one-third, and add butter away from the heat; pour a little over the *noisettes*. Serve the remaining juice in a sauceboat.

Potatoes Dauphine

Mix together 2 parts potato croquette mixture (recipe above) with 1 part batter for unsweetened soufflé fritters (page 604).

Form into large sausages on a lightly floured table and cut into pieces as big as walnuts. Roll each piece in the shape of an egg and dip it in an egg beaten with salt and pepper and a few drops of oil, then in breadcrumbs. Roll each croquette between your palms so that the breadcrumbs stick.

Place the croquettes in a frying basket and plunge at once into very hot oil for 7–8 minutes. Shake the frying basket carefully so that the croquettes move in the oil or fat.

Drain on a paper towel, sprinkle with salt and serve.

ROAST SHOULDER OF LAMB
Epaule d'agneau de pré-salé rôtie

The meat of a shoulder is rather sinewy so only shoulder of lamb can be roasted. Mutton shoulder should be braised or stewed.

Shoulder of lamb can be roasted with or without the bone. In boning, the butcher lifts out the blade bone. The central bone is easily removed without slitting the shoulder. The leg bone is sawn off near the stump and left in.

Season the meat inside with salt and pepper and roll it like a sausage. Tie it with string.

For better flavour do not bone the joint. Naturally the carving is not so easy and cooking the meat in this way is only suitable for a family dinner or when the number of guests warrants cooking the whole shoulder.

Place the shoulder on the rack of a roasting pan; season, and baste with melted butter. Cook in a 425°F (220°C, gas mark 7) oven, basting frequently. Watch the bottom of the roasting pan so that the meat juices do not burn.

Cooking time will be about 15 minutes per pound to sear the meat. It should then be left to 'rest' in a low oven.

Deglaze the roasting pan with 3–4 tablespoons of bouillon or water. Serve this juice after correcting the seasoning, without degreasing it.

1 young lamb
  shoulder, boned or
  unboned
50 g (2 oz) unsalted
  butter
3 medium-sized
  onions
4 large baking
  potatoes

SHOULDER OF LAMB WITH POTATOES
Epaule de pré-salé boulangère
For a whole shoulder

Prepare the shoulder as you would for roasting. Brown it quickly in a 450°F (230°C, gas mark 8) oven in an ovenproof earthenware dish that holds the meat easily.

Peel the onions and the potatoes; dry them. Cut the onions into julienne and thinly slice the potatoes; sprinkle with salt.

Remove the shoulder from the dish and spread the onions, then the potatoes, in thin layers on the bottom of the dish. Place the shoulder on top, pour over some melted butter and continue cooking until done in a 375°F (190°C, gas mark 5) oven.

Serve in the cooking dish. Remove the string carefully, if the shoulder has been boned.

Note: The onions and the potatoes will brown slightly and will absorb the butter and the lamb juice. If the garnish sticks to the pan it does not matter; it can be loosened with a serving spoon at the table.

BRAISED SHOULDER OF MUTTON WITH TURNIPS
Épaule de mouton braisée aux navets

50 g (2 oz) unsalted butter
15 small onions, peeled
500 g (1 lb) turnips
Pinch sugar
1 lamb shoulder, boned, seasoned and tied
1 glass dry white wine
½ dl (1 pt) lightly salted bouillon
Bouquet garni
Garlic clove

Heat the butter in an oval saucepan or fireproof dish and brown the onions slowly; remove them.

Peel the turnips thickly, quarter them lengthwise, and trim to the shape and size of large walnuts. Place them in the same butter, sprinkle with a pinch of sugar and brown. Then set aside with the onions.

Place the lamb shoulder in the pot and brown it. Moisten with the white wine, reduce the wine almost completely, then add the bouillon, covering the shoulder. Add the bouquet garni and garlic, bring to the boil, and cook, covered, in a 400°F (200°C, gas mark 6) oven for 2 hours.

As the braising juices reduce, baste more and more frequently.

After the meat has cooked for 2 hours, add the onions and turnips. If the juices have reduced too much to cover the garnish, add a little bouillon or water to prevent the dish becoming too salty.

Simmer, covered, for 25–30 minutes. Baste often.

Serve the shoulder in a shallow dish, surrounded by its garnish, and moistened with the braising juices – there should be just enough to serve with the meat.

STUFFED SHOULDER OF MUTTON

Épaule de mouton farcie à la mode du Berry

1 lamb shoulder, boned

Stuffing:
1 medium onion, chopped
25 g (1 oz) unsalted butter
225 g (8 oz) good sausage meat
1 clove garlic, finely chopped
1 egg
1 teaspoon chopped parsley
2 slices white bread, soaked in bouillon and squeezed
Salt, pepper, herb and spice mixture (see page xxiv)

Garnish:
3 leeks, white part only
2 celery stalks
Bouquet garni
1 onion stuck with a clove
2 medium-sized carrots, peeled
500 g (1 lb) celeriac, peeled and quartered
3 large baking potatoes, peeled
100 g (4 oz) unsalted butter
Salt and pepper

To make the stuffing, cook the onion in butter. Combine in a bowl with the sausage meat, the garlic, the egg, the chopped parsley, the squeezed bread and the seasoning. Mix well, and spread the stuffing on the shoulder where the bones were. Roll the meat to enclose the stuffing and tie with string.

Place the shoulder in a braising pan; add water to reach halfway, add salt (2 teaspoons per 1 l (2 pts) of water, or to taste), pepper and seasoning.

Bring to the boil, and add the following from the garnish: the leeks, celery, bouquet garni, the onion stuck with the clove and the carrots.

Cook slowly for 1¼ hours; then surround the shoulder with the pieces of celeriac. Simmer for another 25 minutes, and add the potatoes.

When the potatoes are cooked (they should be firm), drain all the vegetables and rub them through a fine sieve into a pan. Dry this purée over a high flame, stirring constantly with a spatula. When the purée has thickened, add the butter, away from the heat. Add salt and grind in 3 or 4 peppercorns. Correct the consistency, if necessary, with a couple of tablespoons of the cooking juices.

To serve, place the meat on a long serving platter, remove the string, and pour over a little of the cooking juices. Serve the meat with a sauceboat of the cooking juice and the vegetable purée in a bowl.

LAMB BREAST AND CUTLETS
Poitrine ou épigrammes d'agneau
For 6 people

500 g (1 lb) breast of lamb
1 glass dry white wine
1 onion, sliced
1 carrot, sliced
Bouquet garni
1 egg
125 g (5 oz) white breadcrumbs
6 lamb cutlets
25 g (1 oz) unsalted butter, melted

Combine the lamb breast, the white wine, the vegetables and the bouquet garni in a heavy pan. Add enough water to cover the meat and the vegetables. Add salt and bring to the boil. Simmer, covered, for 40 minutes. Before the 40 minutes are up, check the meat; it has cooked enough when the bones can be removed from the meat easily.

Then drain the breast and place it flat on a plate; remove the bones. Lay the breast on half of a dish towel and cover it with the other half. Place on a baking sheet and put a weight of about 1 kg (2 lb) on top. Let the meat cool under the weight.

When the meat is completely cooled, cut into pieces the size of a lamb chop, 1 per guest. Dip each piece first in egg beaten with a little oil and a pinch of salt, then in breadcrumbs. Press the breadcrumbs on to the meat with a knife blade, so that they stick.

Lightly flatten and season the lamb chops and coat in the same way, or pour some melted butter over them and roll in breadcrumbs.

Pour some melted butter on the pieces cut from the breast and the chops and grill them under a low flame.

Place in a ring on a round platter, alternating the breast pieces and the chops.

In the centre place a vegetable garnish – mixed vegetables, green peas, asparagus tips, a vegetable purée, braised endive, etc. – arranged in the shape of a pyramid.

LAMB STEWS OR SAUTÉS
Ragoûts, sautés et navarin

The breast, the neck, the best end and the shoulder are the cuts of the lamb or mutton best suited for sautés, stews and navarins.

LAMB STEW — CLASSIC RECIPE
Navarin
For 6 people

1 kg (2 lb) lamb or mutton: breast, neck, best end and shoulder, in equal parts
Oil or unsalted butter
1 large onion, peeled and quartered
1 medium-sized carrot, peeled and quartered
Pinch sugar
2 tablespoons flour
2 garlic cloves, crushed
2 tablespoons tomato purée or 3 fresh tomatoes, peeled, seeded and chopped
Bouquet garni
400 g ($\frac{3}{4}$ lb) small potatoes, peeled
24 small onions
125 g (5 oz) lean bacon

Have the shoulder and best end boned and cut into pieces weighing about 50 g (2 oz). Have the breast and the neck cut the same way but not boned.

In a pan brown the meat in very hot oil or butter with the onion and the carrot, seasoned with salt and pepper.

When the meat is well browned, drain off some of the fat; sprinkle the meat with a pinch of sugar and stir over a high flame, so that the sugar just caramelizes – it will give the *navarin* a nice colour. Then add the flour, mix and brown for a few minutes.

Add the crushed garlic to the meat, and mix well for a few seconds to heat it; cover the meat with water. Add the tomato purée or the fresh tomatoes and the bouquet garni.

Bring to the boil and simmer in a 325°F (170°C, gas mark 3) oven, covered, for 1 hour.

After 1 hour, pour the meat into a strainer over a bowl. Take out the meat, removing the bones and skin, and separate from the vegetable garnish; place the meat in a clean pan. Scatter the potatoes on top – if they are too large, cut and trim them to the size of a small egg. Brown and glaze the onions. Cut the bacon into small pieces, blanch and brown. Add the onions and bacon to the meat.

Degrease the sauce which has been allowed to stand; taste and correct the seasoning. Pour the sauce over the meat and potatoes. If there is not enough sauce, add some water.

Bring to the boil again, cover, and simmer in the oven for 1 hour more.

Serve the stew in a round dish.

Garnish:
12 small onions,
 browned and glazed
20 pieces cored
 carrots, trimmed to
 the size and shape
 of large olives
20 small turnips
Unsalted butter
20 small new
 potatoes
100 g (4 oz) peas,
 shelled
Handful French
 beans, cut into $1\frac{1}{2}$
 inch pieces
Chopped parsley and
 chervil

LAMB STEW WITH SPRING VEGETABLES
Ragoût de mouton printanier

This stew is the same as the *navarin*; only the garnish is different.

Follow the preceding recipe until the meat has been cooking for an hour. Then add the onions, carrots and turnips, stewed in butter for 15 minutes, and the new potatoes.

Moisten with the sauce, bring to the boil and cook in the oven for 25 minutes; add the green peas and beans.

Continue cooking slowly in the oven for 30 minutes.

Serve in a bowl, sprinkled with chopped parsley and a little chervil.

1·5 kg (3 lb) lamb
 shoulder, breast,
 neck and best end,
 in equal parts
Salt and pepper
2 tablespoons curry
 powder
75 g (3 oz) unsalted
 butter
1 large onion,
 chopped
2 tablespoons flour
Bouquet garni
225 g (8 oz) eating
 apples
1 banana
1 dl (4 fl oz) double
 cream
150 g (6 oz) rice

LAMB CURRY WITH APPLES
Cari de mouton aux reinettes
For 6 people

Have the shoulder and best end boned and cut into 50-g (2-oz) pieces.

Season the meat with salt, pepper and curry and mix well so that all the pieces of meat are impregnated with the spices. In a pan heat 25 g (1 oz) of butter (or lard) and sear the meat in it.

When the lamb is half browned, sprinkle the chopped onion on top and continue browning, stirring often. As soon as the onion starts to brown, sprinkle the meat with the flour; stir again to coat the meat, and brown lightly.

Be careful not to burn the onion during this last step.

Cover the meat with water, add the bouquet garni and bring to the boil, stirring with a wooden spatula. Cook in a 325°F (170°C, gas mark 3) oven for $2\frac{1}{2}$ hours.

Peel the apples, cut them into quarters, remove the seeds and core.

Peel the banana and cut into 3 pieces.

Brown the apples and the banana in 50 g (2 oz) of butter in a pan big enough to hold the curry. Take the curry out of the oven, remove the pieces of meat and add them to the apples and the banana.

Cool the sauce, degrease it and reduce by one-third; pour in enough cream to bring it back to the original quantity and to thicken it. Correct the seasoning and strain the sauce over the meat through a fine sieve.

Shake the pan round to coat the meat and garnish with the sauce. There should be enough sauce to season the rice too.

Serve in a shallow dish with a bowl of rice cooked according to the recipe for Indian rice on page 514 served separately.

Note: The dish can be improved by replacing the water with coconut milk. This milk is obtained from the grated pulp of coconut, fresh or dry. The grated or pounded coconut is steeped for 1 hour in warm water.

Pour the water and the pulp into a cloth or fine sieve over a bowl and squeeze to extract the milk.

IRISH STEW
Ragôut de mouton à l'irlandaise
For 6 people

1·5 kg (3 lb) lamb shoulder, best end, breast and neck, in equal parts
3 large floury potatoes, peeled, quartered and thinly sliced
3 large onions, peeled and finely chopped
Salt and pepper
Bouquet garni
12 small new potatoes
12 small onions
2 celery stalks, the white only
Pinch crushed sage
Chopped parsley

This will take about 2½ hours to cook.

Bone the shoulder and the best end, cut them with the breast and neck into 50 g (2 oz) pieces.

Place the potatoes and onions on a plate with the bouquet garni.

In a heavy pan big enough to hold the stew, sprinkle one-third of the onion and one-third of the sliced potatoes. On this layer place half the pieces of meat. Season with salt and freshly ground pepper. Add the bouquet garni. Then add half the remaining onion and potatoes. Cover with the remaining meat; season with salt and pepper, and finish with a layer of the remaining onion and potatoes. Add more pepper; this stew should be highly seasoned.

Cover just to the top of the meat and vegetables with hot water. Bring to the boil, cover and cook slowly and evenly in a 300°F (150°C, gas mark 2) oven for 1½ hours.

Peel the new potatoes; if they are not small enough, cut them and trim them into little ovals. Leave them in cold water until adding them to the stew.

After 1½ hours remove the stew from the oven; the potatoes and the onions should be completely disintegrated. If some pieces remain, rub them through a strainer. Add the small onions, the celery cut into sticks and the raw potatoes; push them down into the stew and sprinkle with a pinch of sage. If the sauce is too thick add some hot water.

Bring to the boil, correct the seasoning. Over the stew, place a piece of buttered wax paper the size of the pan; cover, and continue cooking in the oven for 45 minutes.

Test the potatoes and, if they are cooked, serve in a very hot shallow platter; sprinkle some chopped parsley on top.

Note: If you want a smoother sauce, take out the pieces of meat and place them in a clean pan. Rub the sauce through a fine sieve, pressing the vegetables with a pestle. Reheat the stew quickly.

The stew should be served piping hot on well-heated plates.

BARON, LEG, LOIN OR QUARTER OF MILK-FED LAMB ROASTED WITH PARSLEY

Baron, gigot, carré ou quartier d'agneau de lait rôti et persillé

The meat of baby lamb has little taste, so flavour must be added to it during the cooking. I think that roasting with parsley is the best way.

Season the meat with salt and pepper; place it on a rack in a roasting pan. Baste generously with melted butter, and put it in a 350°F (180°C, gas mark 4) oven for about 20 minutes per pound. While the meat is roasting, it must be basted frequently with the cooking butter.

Meanwhile, prepare a mixture of 1 tablespoon of chopped parsley mixed with 2 tablespoons of fresh coarse breadcrumbs.

Five minutes before the end sprinkle the breadcrumb mixture on top of the meat; baste with melted butter, and raise the heat so that the breadcrumbs turn golden brown.

Serve very hot, basted with the cooking butter.

Serve a bowl of sautéed potatoes sprinkled with chopped parsley separately.

SAUTÉED MILK-FED LAMB WITH SPRING VEGETABLES
Sauté d'agneau de lait printanier

Cook the spring vegetables – carrots, turnips, small onions, peas and French beans – separately.

The carrots and the turnips should be trimmed to the shape of an olive or chopped; cook them following the recipe for glazed vegetables (page 429). Prepare the peas in the French (page 488) or English way (page 487). Cook the beans in water.

Meanwhile, cut a quarter of lamb into 100–125-g (4–5-oz) pieces and sauté in unsalted butter in a pan big enough to hold them flat.

Season with salt and pepper and cook slowly, covered; turn the pieces of meat when they are browned on one side. Season again.

When the meat is cooked, place on a round platter; turn the vegetables over in the cooking butter, add 2 or 3 tablespoons of good veal stock, bring to the boil, pour over the lamb and serve.

COLD LAMB AND MUTTON

Loin, leg, baron, saddle, shoulder or best end can all be served cold after they have been roasted, with jellied stock, a vegetable salad, a green salad or condiments (such as gherkins) and a cold sauce (see pages 128–134).

Pork

Pork meat is fat, firm and nearly white because all the blood is drained from the carcass after butchering. Pork is difficult to digest but combines easily with other ingredients. It is rather rich for young children.

In general when the meat is red, flabby and not very fat, the animal is old or of poor quality. Never buy such meat, especially if the pork is to be used for salting, which improves many cuts. In France the cuts of pork most often used fresh are the *échine* (spareribs and bladebone), the *filet* (hind loin), the *côtelettes* (fore loin) and the *jambon* (leg). The *plat de côtes* (hand), *poitrine* (belly) and *jambonneaux* (knuckles) are placed in a salting tub for 2–3 days to make salt pork.

[*Editor's note:* It is well worth knowing how to salt and cure your own meat as the results are most rewarding. Full details are given below.]

The blood, fat, intestines, stomach, feet, liver and skin of the pig are used in making black pudding, cooked or raw pork sausages, pigs' trotters rolled in breadcrumbs or with truffles, *andouilletes*, pâté, brawn, etc.

HAM

Preparation. The best period for salting a ham is the cold season (15 December to 15 January); this is also the time when pigs are usually fat, especially if they have been fed with corn, chestnuts, potatoes and grain mixed with milk products.

The ham is cut from the back leg, from the base of the spine to above the knee. To prepare it, remove the thigh bone.

The pork shoulder can be prepared in the same way.

The salting mixture. This must be prepared during dry weather. In a very clean bowl, mix 225 g (8 oz) of sea salt, finely crushed with a rolling pin or a wine bottle, 125 g (5 oz) of brown sugar and 50 g (2 oz) of saltpetre.

Salting or curing. *First step.* Place the ham, skin side down, on a very clean table. Hold the bone with your left hand; with your right hand rub the ham up and down with the salt mixture so that it penetrates the meat. Do the same for the skin side; then start again on the other side and cover all sides of the ham, until you have used up all the salt.

The nice pink colour of the ham depends upon this first step; it is therefore very important. The care and the time spent are always repaid in the end by success.

Second step. Place the ham, skin side down, in a scrupulously clean salting tub made of wood or stoneware. The salting tub should be close to the size of the ham to avoid wasting salt.

Cover the ham with 500 g (1 lb) of sea salt. Cover the salting tub with a cloth and then the lid. Let stand for 2 days; then turn the ham, handling it as little as possible. Cover again with 500 g (1 lb) of sea salt. Let stand again for 2 days.

Two days later remove the ham, set it on a platter in a cool place and cover with a dish towel. Empty the salting tub into a very clean saucepan and add 2 quarts of cold water, 125 g (5 oz) of sugar, 2 bay leaves, a large sprig of thyme, a sprig of rosemary, 4 sage leaves, 25 peppercorns, 25 coriander seeds, 6 cloves, 12 juniper berries, a clump of parsley with its root well washed, 1 tablespoon crushed cinnamon stick, a pinch each of marjoram, nutmeg, savoury, mace and cumin.

Boil for 3 minutes. Remove from the heat. Cover and let cool.

Replace the ham in the salting tub and pour in the brine, well cooled and strained through a cloth.

The quantity of brine specified above should be enough to immerse the ham completely, if the salting tub is the right size.

Turn the ham over every 2 days with a special fork. Never use your fingers. If the ham is not covered completely by the brine it will have to be turned every day.

It will take 20 days to cure a ham from a pig weighing 90–100 kg (180–200 lb).

If the ham is not going to be kept for several months, the time can be reduced by half, but the ham must be cooked and eaten as soon as it is taken out of the salting tub, without soaking to remove the salt.

Smoking. A salted ham can be preserved smoked. But whether or not it is smoked it must be dried, suspended in a dry airy place.

The smoking is done in a fireplace. The ham is hung fairly high. Underneath the leaves and stems of aromatic and resinous plants are burned: oak, bay, juniper, broom, vine shoots, etc.

After 6 months of drying, the ham can be sliced very thin and can be eaten raw.

After the ham has soaked for 20 days, it can be served cooked at any time after it is removed from the brine. However, it must be soaked in water for 6–12 hours, depending upon the length of the drying. The longer the ham is dried, the stronger and saltier the flavour becomes.

Cooking. Weigh the soaked ham to determine the cooking time. Scrub it well and wash it in cold water; place in a stew pan or a braising pan and immerse in cold water. Add a large handful of hay, tied in a bunch. Bring to the boil, and reduce the heat to a simmer. The ham should be poached gently, allowing 20 minutes per pound.

Let the ham cool completely in the cooking liquid, unless it is to be served hot, in which case drain it and prepare following the recipes below.

Presentation

First method

Remove the skin and trim the excess fat, which can be used in cooking cabbage or sauerkraut. Sprinkle the ham with icing sugar and place in very hot oven or under the grill. This step must be done quite quickly; the sugar melts, caramelizes and covers the layer of fat with a shiny, amber-coloured coating. The meat has a more appetizing appearance and a better flavour.

Second method

Glaze by braising the ham. Thirty minutes before the ham is cooked, take it from the pot and remove the skin. Trim off the excess fat, and place ham in a braising pan. Baste it with 2 glasses of Madeira, port, Frontignan, sherry or Marsala.

Place the braising pan, covered, in a 300°F (150°C, gas mark 2) oven for about an hour.

Baste often. Then sprinkle the ham with icing sugar and continue cooking as above.

Hams served hot are usually accompanied by a vegetable garnish and by Madeira (page 113) or demi-glace sauce (page 108) flavoured with the cooking liquid carefully degreased.

Among the best vegetables to serve with ham are: braised sauerkraut, spinach, chicory, braised celery, cucumbers with Mornay sauce, a *jardinière* garnish, noodles, green peas, braised lettuce.

HAM TURNOVER WITH TRUFFLES AND MUSHROOMS
Chausson Lucas-Carton

300 g (10 oz) braised ham from close to the knuckle (where the meat is more gelatinous and softer), with some fat left on

1 large fresh truffle

50 g (2 oz) unsalted butter

100 g (4 oz) fresh *foie gras*

100 g (4 oz) firm, white mushrooms, chopped

2 tablespoons port

1 recipe brioche dough (page 524)

Salt, freshly ground pepper, mace

1 egg, beaten

6 tablespoons demi-glace sauce (page 108)

Cut the ham into pieces. Slice the truffle thickly and heat in butter in a pan. Cut the *foie gras* into 2 or 3 slices and sear in the same butter. Remove and add the mushrooms. Sauté rapidly and moisten with 2 tablespoons of port, then reduce almost completely and away from the heat coat with a knob of butter. Roll the dough 6 mm ($\frac{1}{4}$ inch) thick into an oval shape; prick several times with a fork. On one half of the dough (the other half will be folded over as a cover), spread alternate layers of ham, truffle, *foie gras* and mushrooms.

The layers of truffle, *foie gras* and mushrooms should be seasoned with a pinch of salt, freshly ground pepper and just a dash of mace.

Fold the other half of the dough over the ham and the other ingredients, first moistening the edges with beaten egg. Seal well by pressing lightly with your fingers to fasten the bottom layer to the top one.

The turnover is now shaped like a semicircle. Place it on a baking sheet. Brush the top with beaten egg.

Cut small diamond-shaped designs out of dough. With the back of a knife blade draw leaf veins on them, and arrange them like leaves on the turnover. Brush them with beaten egg and bake in a 400°F (200°C, gas mark 6) oven until golden brown, at least 30 minutes.

Degrease the demi-glace sauce and reduce; flavour away from the heat with 1 tablespoon of port and 1 tablespoon of butter per guest. Add a dash of freshly ground white pepper.

The strong flavour of this sauce is enhanced by the rich bouquet of the port and the fresh taste of the butter, both added away from the heat.

Serve this dish as soon as it comes from the oven, accompanied by a sauceboat of demi-glace sauce.

Note: This delicious turnover can be made with flaky pastry (page 531).

The turnover should be served as it is, as a hot hors-d'oeuvre, or as a main dish accompanied by morels (or other mushrooms) sautéed in butter and covered with double cream flavoured with port.

HOT HAM WITH VEGETABLES
Jambon chaud garni de légumes divers

Cold ham is very often reheated and served with a vegetable garnish and the thickened pan juices or a brown sauce. However, it can be a disappointing dish unless you follow the method given below.

Prepare the chosen vegetable garnish and place it, piping hot, on a very hot platter. Cut slices of ham as thin as possible and serve several slices per guest rather than one thick slice of ham, which is less appetizing. Place the slices on top of the very hot vegetables, cover with a glass bell or a shallow dish, then serve. The heat from the vegetables under this improvised cover will be enough to heat the ham.

Be sure to give each guest a well-heated plate.

Ham served this way is always accompanied by a little demi-glace sauce (page 108) or some thickened veal stock (page 112) flavoured with Madeira, sherry, port or some other fortified wine.

COLD HAM MOUSSE
Mousse froide de jambon

500 g (1 lb) leftover cooked lean ham
1½ dl (¼ pt) velouté sauce (page 109)
4 dl (¾ pt) double cream
1½ dl (¼ pt) jelly made with pale Madeira (page 136)

Cut the ham into tiny cubes and pound thoroughly in a mortar till smooth. Add the very cold velouté sauce a little at a time.

Put this purée in a very fine sieve, and with a pestle rub it through into a bowl. Place the bowl on top of crushed ice, then work the purée vigorously with a wooden spatula, adding little by little two-thirds of the jelly, half melted. Correct the seasoning and add the cream, half whipped.

Pour the remaining half-melted jelly into a 1½-l (3-pt) mousse mould, and coat the mould by turning it on a bed of ice, to make the jelly set. Fill the mould with the mousse and refrigerate.

Unmould, ideally on a silver platter, by dipping the mould for a second in hot water. Dry the mould to avoid marking the platter. Place the platter upside down on top of the mould and, with a quick movement, turn platter and mould right side up. Lift off the mould. The mousse will look pink under the shiny transparent layer of jelly. Serve immediately.

3 kg (6 lb) smoked
ham, lightly cured
225 g (½ lb) hay,
fresh or dry
Sprig thyme
2 bay leaves
6 cloves
10 juniper berries

HAM COOKED WITH HAY
Jambon au foin

The night before using the ham, soak it in cold water to remove
the salt, after sawing the knuckle and removing the end of the
bone.

Place the ham in a large pan, cover it completely with cold
water, add the hay and the seasonings.

Put the pan on the stove and, without letting it come to the
boil, simmer gently, allowing about 20 minutes per pound.

Remove the skin when the ham is cooked.

Ham cooked with hay can be served hot or cold.

Andouillettes et andouilles, boudins blanc et noir, saucisses

Andouillettes and *andouilles* are tripe or chitterling sausages;
boudin blanc is white pudding made from white pork meat or
chicken; *boudin noir* is black or blood pudding. *Saucisses* are fresh
pork sausages with scarcely any cereal content compared with
the standard English sausage.

All these sausages are usually bought ready prepared at a
charcutier's shop in France. They require very little cooking and
are simply grilled or sautéed.

Accompaniments: puréed potatoes, puréed green or dried
peas, puréed lentils or white beans, other fresh or dried vegetables,
sautéed potatoes, rice prepared in various ways, cauliflower,
cabbage, Brussels sprouts, braised lettuce or celery, etc.

SAUTÉED ANDOUILLES WITH ONIONS
Andouilles sautées aux oignons

First, cut 1 medium-sized onion per guest into julienne and cook
slowly in butter in a pan.

Then cut a piece of *andouille* in slices 1 cm (½ inch) thick and
brown them in another pan. Then add the sausage to the onions;

raise the heat and cook rapidly for 2 minutes, adding a pinch of freshly ground pepper and a splash of vinegar. Away from the heat, finish the dish with a pinch of chopped fresh parsley. Serve very hot with sautéed or fried potatoes.

GRILLED WHITE PUDDING WITH POTATO PURÉE
Boudins blancs grillés purée mousseline

Plunge some white puddings made of pork or chicken into boiling water. Immediately move the pot from the heat to stop the boiling; lower the heat, and poach gently for 12 minutes.

Drain and cool.

Prick each sausage with a pin; wrap it in white buttered paper and place it on a grill. Grill under a low flame.

Serve with a purée of potatoes *mousseline* (page 500).

BLACK PUDDING WITH APPLES
Boudins noirs aux pommes reinettes

For each guest, allow a piece of black pudding and one good eating apple.

Peel the apple, remove the core, cut into quarters and cook in butter until brown and tender.

Spice the apples with a dash of salt and a small pinch of powdered cinnamon.

Make shallow slashes in the sausage skin to let the heat penetrate, and brown in a pan in butter. When the sausage is cooked, add the apples; simmer 4–5 minutes, so that the ingredients flavour one another.

Serve very hot.

2 fresh pork sausages
25 g (1 oz) unsalted butter
Slice of bread 6 mm ($\frac{1}{4}$ inch) thick
1 tablespoon white wine
1 tablespoon veal stock
$\frac{1}{2}$ teaspoon *beurre manié* made with equal parts of flour and butter

SAUSAGE WITH WHITE WINE
Saucisses au vin blanc
For 1 person

This will take 15 minutes to cook. Thickly butter a shallow baking dish and place the sausages in it; baste with melted butter and place in a 375°F (190°C, gas mark 5) oven to cook slowly.

Butter the slice of bread and brown in the oven.

Remove the sausages from the dish and keep them warm. Pour the white wine into the same dish, reduce nearly totally. Add the veal stock and thicken with *beurre manié*. Bring to the boil and turn off the heat.

Place the slice of bread on a hot plate and put the 2 sausages on it; pour over the sauce, adding a little extra butter away from the flame at the last minute.

PORK CHOPS
Côtes de porc

Pork chops must be at least $2\frac{1}{2}$ cm (1 inch) thick. If they are thinner, they will be dry when cooked. Pork chops are grilled or sautéed.

To grill, before placing on the grill, coat the chops with unsalted butter or melted lard, season with salt and pepper, and sprinkle with breadcrumbs.

To sauté, cook over a low flame. The chops should brown slowly and not dry out.

Deglaze the grill or sauté pan for the accompanying sauce, generally a spicy one – Robert (page 114) or *charcutière* (page 113), and serve with vegetables: a potato purée (page 496), potatoes *dauphine* (page 498), sautéed potatoes (page 501), apple sauce, etc.

SALT PORK WITH STUFFED CABBAGE
Échine de porc, petit salé d'échine aux choux farcis

During the cold season, lightly salt a piece of pork blade bone or spare rib. Rub it vigorously with crushed, spiced salt (page 135). Place it on a plate and cover it with sea salt. The next day remove the sea salt and again rub with spiced salt. Place in a clean earthenware pot with 1 sprig of thyme, 1 bay leaf, and 1 tablespoon of sugar; cover completely with salt. Cover the pot with a dish cloth, and put it in a cool place. Let stand for 8 days; if the salt does not cover the meat completely as it dissolves, turn the meat over with a fork every day. Do not touch the meat with your fingers.

After 8 days, drain the meat, wash and cook in cold water brought slowly to the boil. Add a carrot cut into quarters and an onion stuck with a clove. Cook the meat in the way described above for poaching a ham.

Serve on a round platter surrounded with stuffed cabbage leaves. Serve boiled potatoes and a sauceboat of the cooking liquid separately.

FRESH PORK LOIN AND FILLET
Carré et filet de porc frais

We will give two methods of cooking a pork loin or fillet.

First method

Do not bone the loin but saw through the backbone at $2\frac{1}{2}$–4-cm (1–$1\frac{1}{2}$-inch) intervals to make the carving easier. Two hours before roasting, season with salt and pepper.

Place the meat in a metal or earthenware roasting pan, baste with melted lard and roast in a 375°F (190°C, gas mark 5) oven. Baste and turn the meat often until completely cooked. Rare pork is indigestible and even dangerous. Cooking time: 25–30 minutes per pound, depending on the thickness of the meat.

Second method

Follow the preparation explained above, then place the loin in a casserole or braising pan with carrots, an onion studded with 3 cloves, a head of garlic, the white of 2 leeks, 1 celery stalk, as for a *pot-au-feu*. Pour over cold water to cover the meat.

Add 1 tablespoon of salt for each quart of water. Bring to the boil, skim, lower the heat and simmer, continuing to poach the meat without ever letting the water boil.

If the cooking liquid is not going to be used because of its strong taste, the joint can be placed directly in boiling liquid, rather than starting in cold water.

The cooking time is the same as in the first method.

When the meat is done, drain and place in a roasting pan with 2–3 tablespoons of smoking hot lard. Baste the meat with the hot lard and place it in a 425°F (220°C, gas mark 7) oven to brown quickly.

Serve with Robert (page 114) or piquante sauce (page 114) or with a tablespoon of veal stock and a little of the fat used to brown the pork.

SAUERKRAUT WITH PORK
Choucroute à la strasbourgeoise
For 6 people

2 kg (4 lb) sauerkraut
4 large slices fresh
    pork fat, cut very
    thin
1 large carrot, peeled
    and sliced
1 onion stuck with a
    clove
Bouquet garni
Juniper berries
225 g (8 oz) goose fat
    or lard
1 pork knuckle
500 g (1 lb) smoked
    bacon in the piece
1 slice cooked ham,
    per guest
1 kg (2 lb) smoked
    pork loin
1 large garlic sausage
2 glasses white
    Alsatian wine or
    dry white wine
1 l (2 pts) light
    bouillon
1 frankfurter per
    guest

Three hours before cooking the sauerkraut, soak, wash, drain and squeeze it by handfuls to remove all the water. Spread the handfuls of sauerkraut on a cloth; grind some peppercorns over them and mix well.

Blanch the pork fat by boiling briefly, drain and rinse; trim the edges.

Line the sides and the bottom of a deep saucepan or braising pan with the slices of pork fat. Over them place one-third of the sauerkraut and then add half the carrot, the onion, bouquet garni, juniper berries tied in cheesecloth, and one-third of the goose fat or lard. Add another third of the sauerkraut, the remaining carrot, the pork knuckle, and another third of the goose fat. Then add the bacon, the slices of ham, the pork loin, the sausage pricked with a pin, and finally the remaining sauerkraut. The remaining goose fat is spread on top.

Pour over enough white wine and bouillon to cover the sauerkraut.

Bring to the boil top with a greased white paper, then cover with the lid. Place in a 325°F (170°C, gas mark 3) oven. The cooking must proceed slowly and continue until the liquid has been almost totally absorbed.

After 35 minutes, remove the sausage carefully; after an hour. the bacon; after an hour and a half, the loin. Set them aside.

Twenty minutes before serving, place the frankfurters in boiling water and poach them for 10 minutes without letting the water boil.

Remove the sauerkraut from the oven and take off the paper. Top the sauerkraut with the bacon, the sausage and the frankfurters.

Cover and let stand for 10 minutes.

To serve remove all the meats that will accompany the sauerkraut, including the pork knuckle, and keep hot on a covered plate.

Remove the vegetables and stir the sauerkraut with a fork.

Pile the sauerkraut up on a long wide platter. Overlap the slices of ham in a straight line on top of the sauerkraut, alternating with slices of bacon, thick slices of sausage, and slices from the pork knuckle. Finally, surround the dish with the frankfurters placed round the edge.

Serve a bowl of very creamy potato purée or steamed potatoes separately.

This dish must be served very hot, on hot plates.

COLD ROAST PORK WITH GREEN OR RED CABBAGE SALAD
Porc rôti froid avec salade de chou vert ou rouge

Whether the meat comes from a leftover roast or is specially cooked for the purpose, cold pork should be carved in very thin slices just before serving.

Place the slices on a round platter, overlapping in a ring. Decorate with gherkins.

Serve with a green cabbage salad using the firm, white heart, or red cabbage cut into thin shreds and soaked in boiling vinegar. Just before serving, mix in some chopped eating apples.

Cold pork can also be served with a vegetable salad – potatoes, cauliflower, French beans, white beans or mixed vegetables with gherkins, capers, etc.

All cold sauces made with a mayonnaise base are excellent accompaniments.

POTTED PORK
Rillettes de porc

Remove the ribs, the gristle and the skin from a fresh pork belly. Rub vigorously all over with 100 g (4 oz) of sea salt, crushed very fine and flavoured with bay leaf, thyme, mace, cinnamon, sage, marjoram, basil, nutmeg, cloves and pepper. Wrap the meat in a dish towel, and leave for 2 hours.

Cut the meat into 2½-cm (1-inch) squares. Melt 75 g (3 oz) of pork fat in a heavy saucepan, add the pieces of meat and fry slowly, browning them on all sides but keeping the fat clear and white.

With a skimmer remove the pieces of fat which have turned golden; drain the melted fat into a container and set aside. Chop the pieces of fat, and return them, with 1 cup of water, to the pan. Cook very slowly for 7–8 hours, stirring often and maintaining the level of liquid by adding more water as the water in the pan evaporates.

At this point in the cooking the water should be almost totally reduced; remove from the heat, and season with 1 teaspoon of paprika. Add the drained fat to the purée of cooked meat and fat, and mix well until the meat is completely cold. It should be a fine smooth paste which melts in the mouth, as a result of the slow cooking.

Divide the *rillettes* among medium-sized earthenware pots of about $\frac{1}{2}$ l (1 pt) capacity. Pack down to avoid pockets of air, and cover with a 3-mm ($\frac{1}{8}$-inch) layer of melted lard. To preserve the *rillettes* for a long time, when you have filled the pots, heat them in a *bain-marie* for 25 minutes. While cooling, stir each pot often to keep the contents perfectly smooth.

Cover with fat and aluminium foil.

BRAWN
Fromage de tête de porc

1 small pig's head, about 3–4 kg (6–8 lb)
500 g (1 lb) fresh pork rind
Spiced sea salt (page 135)
Salt and pepper
2 large carrots
2 large onions each stuck with 1 clove
1 small head garlic, peeled
Large bouquet garni

Singe the head and scrape carefully; remove the brain and the tongue, then cut the head in two. Cut each half in two. Rub each piece and the tongue with crushed spiced sea salt.

Repeat the salting step 5 times. Place the pieces of head, tongue, and the pork rinds in a bowl. Sprinkle lightly with a layer of salt, cover with a cloth and leave for 4 days in a cool place.

Then remove the meat from the bowl and the salt; wipe each piece. Place the meat with the tongue, the rinds, the carrots, the onions, the garlic and the bouquet garni in a pan just big enough to hold everything. Cover with water.

Bring to the boil slowly; remove the scum as it rises to the surface. Reduce the heat and simmer, covered, for 3 hours. The water should barely quiver.

After the meat is cooked, drain the pieces of head, the tongue and the rinds. Let cool, then remove all the bones. Reserve the flat part of the ears. Cut the meat, the tongue, and the thick part of the ears into $2\frac{1}{2}$-cm (1-inch) cubes and place in a bowl.

Check the saltiness of the meat, and add more salt if necessary. Spice with a couple of turns of the pepper mill, and add $\frac{1}{2}$ cup of the cooking juice strained through a very fine sieve (taste beforehand for seasoning). Mix everything well.

Line a terrine with the pork rinds, or use a bowl which is

wider at the top and can be unmoulded easily. First pour in one-third of the mixture of meat and cooking liquid. On top, spread half the flat parts of the ears; then another third of the meat and the remaining ears. Finish with the remaining meat.

Cover the mould with a round piece of white paper or a piece of foil and top with a piece of wood the same size. On top of the wood, place a pound weight.

Let cool for 24 hours.

The brawn can be served unmoulded or in the terrine. It is best to leave it in the terrine if it is not going to be eaten at one meal. To keep the edges from drying up, protect the cut side with a piece of foil.

PORK LIVER PÂTÉ
Pâté de foie de porc

225 g (8 oz) ham fat or fresh pork fat
225 g (8 oz) lean pork or veal, all gristle removed
500 g (1 lb) pork liver
50 g (2 oz) salt
Pinch herb and spice mixture (page xxiv)
2 shallots, finely chopped
1 medium-sized onion, finely chopped
1 tablespoon cognac
225 g (8 oz) bread soaked in milk and squeezed
1 tablespoon chopped parsley
3 eggs
4 slices fresh pork fat
1 bay leaf
Sprig thyme
Flour-and-water dough

Cut the ham or pork fat, the lean pork or veal, and the liver into 2½-cm (1-inch) cubes. Place all these ingredients on a plate and season with the salt and seasonings.

In a pan partially melt the pork fat. Brown lightly, then add the liver; sauté. As soon as the liver is seared, sprinkle with the shallots and onion; sauté again for a few seconds. Then add the meat; sear quickly, remove from the heat and pour on the cognac. Mix to dissolve the juices that have stuck to the pan. Empty everything into a bowl and let cool.

Chop everything, with a chopper or a mincer, not too fine. Add the bread, the chopped parsley and the eggs. Work the mixture with a wooden spatula until it is blended.

Check the seasoning by poaching a small ball of pâté in boiling water or in the oven. Correct the seasoning, if necessary, with added salt and seasonings.

Line the bottom and sides of a pâté terrine or mould (just big enough to hold the mixture) with 3 slices of pork fat. Fill the terrine with the meat, cover with the fourth pork fat slice, and top with the bay leaf and thyme. Place the lid on the terrine and seal with a layer of dough made with flour and water.

Place the terrine in a roasting pan half filled with hot water; keep it at the same level by adding more boiling water during the cooking.

Place in a 300°F (150°C, gas mark 2) oven for about 1 hour.

The pâté is cooked:

1. When the fat that rises to the surface is clear not cloudy;
2. When the meat juices which collect round the edge of the terrine become meat glaze;
3. When a thin barding needle, inserted into the pâté and removed after 2 minutes, is hot against your hand.

Remove from the oven, and take off the cover. Cool for 15 minutes, then press down with a piece of wood the same size as the terrine, weighted with a one-pound weight. Let cool completely under the weight. The purpose of the weight is to press down the ingredients of the pâté while it is being cooled without squeezing out the fat before it sets. Adjust the weight and pressure as appropriate, using your common sense. If there has been no pressure, the pâté will crumble when cut; if there is too much pressure, the fat will be squeezed out and the pâté will become dry and lose all its flavour and smoothness.

Wipe the outside of the terrine and serve on a long platter on a napkin. Cut slices 6 mm ($\frac{1}{4}$ inch) thick at the table.

Offal

The term *triperie* or offal includes:

Ox liver, heart, lungs, tongue, kidneys, brain, spinal marrow (*amourette*), cheeks, trotters and tripe;
Calf's liver, heart, lights, kidneys, spinal marrow, sweetbreads, mesentery, head, trotters and brains;
Lamb's kidneys, liver, brains, tongue, sweetbreads and trotters;
Pig's liver, kidneys, brains, trotters, head, blood, stomach and intestines.

Most of the recipes for the liver, heart, kidneys, spinal marrow and brains of these four animals are interchangeable.

The recipes for some – sweetbreads and tongue for example – depend on their size. There are special recipes for trotters, depending on whether they come from an ox, calf, lamb or hog. The same applies to the belly, stomach, liver, lights and head.

Pig's blood and intestines are mainly used for pork sausages.

SPINAL MARROW OF BEEF OR VEAL
Amourette de boeuf ou de veau

Veal marrow is finer than beef marrow.

Soak the marrow in water for at least 12 hours, changing the water several times. Remove the membrane and the cords that surround it, being careful not to crush the central substance, which is rather like brains.

Poach the marrow for 5 minutes in a court-bouillon made with salted water, 1 tablespoon of vinegar per quart of water, 1 sprig of thyme and 1 bay leaf. Place the marrow in the cold court-bouillon then slowly bring to the boil, cool and leave in the cooking liquid. It is then prepared in the same way as brains.

LAMB'S, CALF'S OR PIG'S BRAINS
Cervelle de mouton, de veau, de porc
For 1 brain

1 lamb's, calf's or pig's brain
1 l (2 pts) water
½ tablespoon salt
1 tablespoon vinegar or juice of ½ lemon
½ bay leaf
Sprig thyme
1 medium-sized carrot
1 medium-sized onion (both chopped, cooked for 25 minutes, cooled and drained)

Soak the brains for 12 hours in cold water, changing the water often. Remove the membranes and the coagulated blood that surround the brain and soak again until the brain is very white.

Unless you are using a recipe calling for uncooked brains, poach the brains in a court-bouillon made with 1 l (2 pts) of water, flavoured with salt, vinegar or lemon juice, bay leaf, thyme, carrot and onion.

Place the brains in the cold court-bouillon, bring slowly to the boil, skim and poach without boiling on a very low flame for 10–15 minutes, depending on the weight.

If the brains are not going to be used immediately, keep in the court-bouillon.

BRAINS IN BROWN BUTTER
Cervelle au beurre noir

When the brains are poached and warm, cut into slices 1-cm (½-inch) thick, and place flat on a hot plate; season with a pinch of salt, a dash of freshly ground pepper, and a pinch of fresh chopped parsley. Moisten with *beurre noir* (brown butter) or with *beurre noisette* (hazelnut-coloured or light-brown butter) cooked in a frying pan just before serving.

Add a splash of vinegar to the very hot frying pan after the butter has been removed, and pour quickly over the brains.

BRAINS FRIED IN BUTTER WITH LEMON AND PARSLEY
Cervelle à la meunière

Use raw brains, soaked and with the membranes removed. Cut into slices about 1 cm (½ inch) thick, season with salt and pepper, then sprinkle with flour.

Meanwhile heat 25 g (1 oz) of unsalted butter in a heavy frying pan; sear the slices of brains, brown on both sides and cook slowly for 5 minutes.

Place the slices on a hot plate. Squeeze a quarter of a lemon over them, sprinkle with some chopped parsley and baste with the cooking butter and some extra butter if necessary.

BRAIN FRITTERS WITH TOMATO SAUCE
Beignets de cervelle sauce tomate ou Orly

Cook the brains in a court-bouillon, and cut into large dice or slices. Salt and pepper, dip in a light frying batter and plunge one at a time into very hot deep oil.

When the batter is crisp and golden, drain the fritters, pat dry, sprinkle with a pinch of salt and place in a pile on a round platter on top of a folded napkin.

On top place a bouquet of parsley, fried for a second in the hot oil; around the base place two lemon halves.

Serve a sauceboat of tomato sauce (page III) separately.

Sweetbreads can be prepared the same way.

SAUTÉED BRAINS WITH TOMATOES AND OLIVES
Cervelle sautée à la niçoise

1 large tomato per
serving, peeled,
seeded, drained, cut
into pieces
1 tablespoon olive oil
Salt, freshly ground
pepper
$\frac{1}{2}$ garlic clove,
crushed
Pinch parsley,
chopped, with a
tarragon leaf
6–8 small black cured
olives, pitted
15 g ($\frac{1}{2}$ oz) butter

Follow the recipe for brains *à la meunière*. Place the slices in a circle on a round hot plate and cover them with a thick tomato sauce *à la Provençale*.

In a pan heat the olive oil; when it is smoking, add the tomatoes. Season with salt and freshly ground pepper. Cook for 10 minutes. Then add the garlic, parsley, tarragon and olives. Heat for 2 or 3 seconds; then away from the heat add the butter. Correct the seasoning of the sauce, which should be rather thick; it should leave a clear taste of tomatoes and fresh butter on the palate.

LIVER
Le foie

Ox liver is often sinewy and of poor quality. Pig's liver is usually used in terrines and pâtés. Lamb's liver is often used with the heart and lungs. Calf's liver is certainly the finest.

20 large lardoons of
fresh pork fat

Salt and pepper, herb
and spice mixture
(page xxiv)

Chopped parsley

1·5 kg (3 lb) piece of
calf's liver cut
from the thickest
part

1 veal or pork caul

25 g (1 oz) unsalted
butter

Pork rind

100 g (4 oz) onions,
peeled and
quartered

225 g (8 oz) carrots,
core removed,
peeled and
quartered

Bouquet garni (10
sprigs parsley, sprig
thyme, ½ bay leaf)

2 garlic cloves

1 tablespoon cognac

BRAISED CALF'S LIVER
Foie de veau a l'étuvée
For 6 people

This is a Burgundian speciality.

Prepare the lardoons, cutting them into thin strips. Place them on a plate, season with salt and pepper, a pinch of chopped parsley and seasonings. Mix well and leave 15 minutes. Insert the lardoons in the liver with a larding needle as you would for *boeuf à la mode* (page 237).

Season the liver with salt and pepper and seasonings and wrap in the caul. Hold the caul in place with string.

In a saucepan, earthenware pot or terrine just big enough to hold the liver, heat the butter and brown the liver. It must be seared to seal in the juices. Turn it over with a skimmer, so as not to prick it, and brown on all sides.

When the caul is golden, place the pork rind under the liver. Around the liver add the onions, the carrots, the bouquet garni and the garlic – everything sprinkled with a pinch of salt and a dash of pepper. Cover tightly.

Heat slowly. When you hear a light frying sound from inside the pan, place in a 300°F (150°C, gas mark 2) oven.

This dish can also be cooked on top of the stove or over charcoal, using a pot with a deep lid in which hot coals are placed. This is the oldest and best method.

Cook for 3 hours. Halfway through add the cognac.

Since the pan is tightly closed, the steam cannot escape. It cooks very slowly and there is hardly any reduction of the juices from the meat and the vegetables. When the cooking is finished, the gravy should come halfway up the liver.

To serve place the liver on a plate and remove the strings and what is left of the caul. Remove the bouquet garni and rub the vegetables through a strainer. Put this purée in a small saucepan. Degrease the cooking juices. Mix the juices into the purée until it has the consistency of a light tomato sauce.

If properly cooked, the purée should absorb all the juice.

Pour the sauce over the liver and serve very hot.

Note: This dish is delicious served cold. Cool the liver in the sauce and remove it to carve.

CALF'S LIVER ON SKEWERS
Brochettes de foie de veau

225 g (8 oz) large firm
white mushrooms

2 shallots

25 g (1 oz) unsalted
butter

2 tablespoons dry
white wine

2 tablespoons tomato
purée

3 dl ($\frac{1}{2}$ pt) veal stock

Beurre manié

1 teaspoon chopped
parsley

225 g (8 oz) salt belly
of pork

500 g (1 lb) calf's
liver

4 tablespoons oil or
chicken fat

2 tablespoons fine
breadcrumbs

Tomato sauce (page
111) or *maître
d'hôtel* butter (page
226)

Preparation. Clean the mushrooms, wash them and remove the stems; peel the curved cap of each mushroom and the sides of the stem. Reserve the caps. Chop the stems and peel very fine and add to the shallots, which have been chopped and softened in butter in a pan. Dry quickly over a high flame.

Moisten with dry white wine, boil to reduce almost totally; add the tomato purée and veal stock. Reduce by one-third and thicken with *beurre manié* made with 25 g (1 oz) of butter and 1 teaspoon of flour well mixed with a fork.

As soon as the *beurre manié* has melted in the boiling sauce, remove from the heat, correct the seasoning and add the chopped parsley.

Remove the pork rind and cut the fat into 4-cm (1$\frac{1}{2}$-inch) squares, 6 mm ($\frac{1}{4}$ inch) thick. Place in cold water and bring to the boil. Blanch for 5 minutes and drain.

Cut the liver into 5-cm (2-inch) squares, 2$\frac{1}{2}$ cm (1 inch) thick.

Preliminary cooking. Heat the oil in a pan; as soon as it is smoking, add the mushroom caps cut into slices 6 mm ($\frac{1}{4}$ inch) thick. Sear them, season with a pinch of salt, then sauté on a high flame for 1 minute. With a slotted spoon remove to a plate.

Reheat the oil, and sear the liver squares; season with salt and pepper and sauté on a high flame just long enough to stiffen them; drain the liver and remove to a plate.

Do the same for the squares of pork fat, but let them brown slightly.

Threading the skewers. In a bowl, combine the liver, the pork fat, the sliced mushroom caps and the sauce prepared with the mushrooms stems (*duxelles*). Mix well, so that the meat is well coated with the sauce.

On metal skewers, string one piece of liver, one piece of pork fat and one slice of mushroom. Continue doing this until you end with a piece of liver.

Roll each skewer in fresh breadcrumbs and set aside on a plate.

Grilling. Fifteen minutes before serving, sprinkle the food on the skewers with unsalted melted butter and place under a medium-hot grill. Turn them all round until the breadcrumbs are golden brown. Serve on the skewers with a sauceboat of tomato sauce or *maître d'hôtel* butter.

GRILLED CALF'S LIVER WITH BEEF MARROW, SHALLOTS AND WHITE WINE
Foie de veau grillé Bercy
For 6 people

6 slices liver, 2 cm (¾ inch) thick (100 g (4 oz) each)
50 g (2 oz) unsalted butter
Salt, pepper and flour
100 g (4 oz) beef marrow, soaked
1 shallot, finely chopped
½ glass dry white wine
1½ dl (¼ pt) veal stock
***Beurre manié* made with 25 g (1 oz) flour and 100 g (4 oz) unsalted butter**
Chopped parsley
Juice of ¼ lemon

Brush the slices of liver with melted butter; sprinkle with salt, pepper and flour. Shake off the excess flour and sprinkle each slice with a few drops of melted butter; place under a very hot grill or over charcoal.

After two minutes give each slice a quarter turn; the bars of the grill will sear a square design into the liver. In another two minutes turn the liver over; after it has cooked for 2 minutes on this side give another quarter turn. Remove the liver slices from the grill and place them on a serving platter. Cover and keep warm.

Cut the marrow into very thin slices with a knife dipped in hot water. Place in a saucepan of boiling salted water and poach for 5 minutes without boiling.

Heat a knob of butter in a small pan. Add the shallot, and cook slowly without letting it brown. Moisten with white wine and boil to reduce to 2–3 tablespoons, then add the veal stock and reduce by half. Add the *beurre manié*; then the marrow, well drained, a pinch of salt, a pinch of pepper, chopped parsley and the lemon juice.

Heat slowly, shaking the saucepan so that the sauce thickens as the *beurre manié* melts.

Drain the liver juice from the platter; add it to the sauce, and pour the sauce over the liver slices. Sprinkle with chopped parsley and serve with a bowl of steamed potatoes.

50 g (2 oz) unsalted
   butter
6 slices liver
Salt and pepper
Flour
4 large onions
1 tablespoon vinegar
Chopped parsley

SAUTÉED CALF'S LIVER WITH ONIONS
Foie de veau sauté à la lyonnaise
For 6 people

Heat half the butter in a pan. Meanwhile, season the liver with salt and freshly ground pepper; flour the meat and shake off the excess. Sear in the butter when it has turned a light-brown colour. Cook on a high flame for 2 minutes; turn the slices and cook for another 2 minutes; remove to a serving platter. Cover and keep warm.

Heat the remaining butter in the same pan. When it is hot, add the onions cut into fine julienne or chopped fine; cook over moderate heat until brown, stirring constantly. When the onions are well softened, add the vinegar, without boiling, and the juice drained from the liver on the platter. Shake the pan until all the juices sticking to the bottom of it have dissolved. Pour the onions and the juice over the liver. Sprinkle with chopped parsley.

Pig's liver can be cooked the same way.

OX TRIPE
Gras-double de boeuf

Ox tripe or stomach is usually bought cooked. If not, soak it in water, scrub carefully, wash again and blanch in boiling water for 25 minutes.

Drain the tripe, rinse, scrape with a knife to remove any traces of scum or odour.

Cook the tripe for 6 hours in salted water, using $\frac{1}{2}$ tablespoon of salt per litre (2 pts) of water. The water should boil slowly. To the cooking liquid, add 2 carrots cut into pieces, 2 onions, each stuck with 1 clove, a bouquet garni made largely of thyme and bay, and 1 garlic head.

When the tripe is cooked, remove from the heat, let cool in the liquid, then drain. Roll up the tripe and refrigerate until ready to use.

4 large onions
4 tablespoons oil
25 g (1 oz) unsalted
   butter
700 g (1½ lb) cooked
   ox tripe (see above)
Salt and pepper
Chopped parsley
1 teaspoon vinegar

TRIPE AND ONIONS
Gras-double à la lyonnaise
For 6 people

Cut the onions into fine julienne; heat the oil in a pan big enough for the tripe to be placed flat. As soon as the oil is smoking, add the onions and cook them slowly, stirring often. Towards the end of the cooking, raise the heat to brown onions well.

Lift the onions on to a plate with a slotted spoon, leaving the oil in the pan; add the butter.

Cut the tripe into large strips, about 6 mm (¼ inch) thick. Heat the butter and the oil, and sear the tripe. Taste a piece to see if there is enough salt, and correct the seasoning. Add some freshly ground pepper. Sauté the tripe on a high flame to brown it slightly. When it is light brown, add the onions, sauté and mix well; finish by adding chopped parsley.

Place the tripe in a bowl, and pour the vinegar into the hot pan, then pour over the tripe. Add another pinch of chopped parsley and serve on very hot plates.

OX OR LAMB'S TONGUE
Langue de boeuf ou de mouton

Ox tongue is served fresh or salted. It should always be soaked in water for 2–3 hours. Remove all inedible parts and the skin – this is easy after it has been placed in a large pan of cold water and boiled for 20 minutes. Then drain and remove the skin.

Place the tongue in a bowl, and as soon as it is cold, cover it with a large handful of sea salt; let it stand for 24 hours before cooking it. Turn the meat from time to time when the salt starts to dissolve.

※━━━━━━━━━━━━━━━━━━━━━━━━━━━━━━━━━━※

BRAISED OX TONGUE
Langue de boeuf braisée à la bourgeoise

Follow the recipe for *boeuf à la mode* (page 237), but instead of larding the tongue, wrap it in one or more pieces of pork fat.

※━━━━━━━━━━━━━━━━━━━━━━━━━━━━━━━━━━※

LAMB'S TONGUES WITH LENTIL PURÉE
Langues de mouton à la purée de lentilles

For 6 people

6 lamb tongues
75 g (3 oz) pork rind, blanched
1 carrot, sliced thickly
1 medium-sized onion, sliced thickly
Bouquet garni
1 glass dry white wine
½ l (1 pt) bouillon or lightly salted veal stock

Lentil purée:
500 g (1 lb) dried lentils
1 onion stuck with 1 clove
1 small carrot, cut in half
½ head garlic
Small bouquet garni
125 g (5 oz) salt pork belly
25 g (1 oz) unsalted butter
Peppercorns

The dish will take 2½ hours to cook.

Soak the tongues in cold water for 2 hours, changing the water several times.

Pick over the lentils to remove small stones or grit. Wash and soak in warm water for 2 hours.

Place the tongues in a saucepan, cover with cold water and boil for 8 minutes. Remove with a slotted spoon and plunge into a bowl of cold water. When cold, drain, cut off the larynxes and remove the skins. Set aside on a plate.

Drain the soaked lentils and place in a saucepan, cover with water and boil for 5 minutes; drain again.

Choose a pan big enough to hold the tongues in one layer. Melt a few lardoons cut from the pork fat and brown the sliced carrot and onion in this fat. Take out the vegetables and set aside. Add the tongues and brown lightly. Set aside. Now make a layer of the carrots and tomatoes on the bottom of the pan, add the bouquet garni and cover with the blanched pork rind. Place the tongues on top.

Pour over the white wine, and boil to reduce by two-thirds; then cover with the bouillon.

Place a piece of buttered wax paper cut the same size as the pan over the tongues, cover and cook in a 300°F (150°C, gas mark 2) oven for 2 hours.

Lentil purée

Put just enough water in a saucepan to cover the lentils. Add a teaspoon of salt per litre (2 pts) of water, the onion stuck with a clove, the carrot, the garlic, the small bouquet garni and the pork fat without the skin (the skin is used for braising the tongues). Bring to the boil and add the lentils, skim and lower the heat; simmer over the lowest possible flame for $1\frac{3}{4}$–2 hours.

When the lentils are cooked, drain, remove the garnish and rub the lentils through a very fine sieve. (When starchy foods are cold, it is harder to put them through a sieve.) Pour the purée into a saucepan, and reduce over a high flame, stirring with a wooden spatula. When the purée has thickened, return it to the proper consistency by adding some braising juice from the tongues. Butter away from the flame and grind a few peppercorns over the top; do not boil.

Presentation. By now the juice in which the tongues are cooking has been reduced through evaporation in the course of the braising. At the last minute uncover the tongues, baste with their juice and raise the oven heat to its highest temperature. The juices will caramelize slightly and cover the tongues with a shiny coating. The result is an attractive and tasty glaze.

Pile the lentil purée in a shallow dish, then add the tongues, the tips up and the glazed side showing.

Baste each tongue with a tablespoon of the braising sauce, strained through a very fine sieve. Place 6 slices of salt pork fat round the bottom.

Serve the remaining sauce separately in a sauceboat after correcting the seasoning.

Note: This dish can be served cold with mayonnaise or a mayonnaise-based sauce such as tartare sauce (page 128–131).

CALF'S OR LAMB'S KIDNEYS
Rognons de veau ou de mouton

Lamb's, calf's and pig's kidneys should not boil while cooking. They should be grilled, sautéed or pot-roasted quickly at a high temperature just before serving. The principle of cooking kidneys is always the same.

When kidneys are grilled, place them, slit open, on a very hot grill over glowing coals or under a very hot grill.

When they are sautéed, place them in a large pan so that the pieces of kidney lie flat and are seared as soon as they come into contact with the hot butter.

Calf's kidneys are usually pot-roasted. Place them in a hot oven-proof dish with hot butter to sear them.

Never overcook kidneys as this makes them dry. Lamb's kidneys should be pink when cooked, calf's and pig's kidneys pale brown.

---

2 lamb's kidneys or ½ calf's kidney per serving
50 g (2 oz) unsalted butter
6 tablespoons Espagnole or demi-glace sauce or thickened veal stock (page 112 or page 108)
½ glass Madeira
Salt and pepper

SAUTÉED KIDNEYS WITH MADEIRA
Rognons sautés au madère

Cut the lamb's kidneys in two lengthwise, remove the membrane and cut each half in two diagonally. Calf's kidneys should be diced. Remove the tubes and the fat. On a plate, season with salt and freshly ground pepper.

Heat a knob of butter in a pan. As soon as it starts to bubble sear the kidneys; sauté rapidly over a high flame. During this step, do not let the kidneys stew in liquid – they will harden. Brown lightly and place on another plate.

In the pan boil the Madeira to reduce by half; add the Espagnole or demi-glace sauce. Bring to the boil for 2 minutes; away from the flame add the remaining butter to the sauce. Serve very hot in a bowl. Instead of the Espagnole or demi-glace sauce, you can use lightly salted veal stock; boil to reduce by half, and thicken with a little cornflour or 1 tablespoon of butter mixed with 1 tablespoon of flour.

SAUTÉED KIDNEYS WITH MUSHROOMS
Rognons sautés aux champignons

Sauté the kidneys as described above, replacing the Madeira with white wine. Then in the cooking butter used for the kidneys, for each serving, sauté 4 mushrooms, quartered, with a pinch of salt; add the mushrooms to the kidneys and finish the sauce as described above for the sautéed kidneys with Madeira.

12 lamb's kidneys
100 g (4 oz) *maître d'hôtel* butter (page 226)

GRILLED LAMB'S KIDNEYS
Rognons de mouton grillés
For 6 people

Split the kidneys lengthwise two-thirds of the way through; remove the thin membrane that covers them. Open the kidneys and put on skewers, 2 skewers for each kidney, forming a diagonal cross. Brush with melted butter, season with salt and pepper and place on a very hot grill. Grill at medium heat. Turn after 3 minutes; cook until slightly pink. Place on a long hot platter. In the centre of each kidney, put 1 teaspoon of *maître d'hôtel* butter and arrange the garnish at each end of the platter.

Usually fried potatoes are served – straw, Pont-Neuf, soufflé, matchstick, etc. (pages 492–494).

175 g (6 oz) unsalted butter
2 large onions, finely chopped
500 g (1 lb) long-grain, good quality rice
1 l (2 pts) bouillon or white stock
3 calf's kidneys or 6 lamb's kidneys
Chopped parsley
Madeira sauce

CALF'S OR LAMB'S KIDNEYS WITH RICE PILAF
Rognons de veau ou de mouton au riz pilaf
For 6 people

Heat 100 g (4 oz) of butter in a pan. When it starts to foam add the onions, and cook slowly without letting them brown. Wash the rice several times until the water is clear.

When the onions are soft, add the rice. Stir the rice over a low flame until it is completely coated with butter.

Add the hot bouillon or white stock.

Cook in a 325°F (170°C, gas mark 3) oven, covered without stirring for 18–20 minutes.

Remove from the oven; cut 25 g (1 oz) of butter in small pieces, scatter on the rice and mix in with a fork.

While the rice is cooking, remove the skins and tubes from the kidneys. Slice and sauté in butter, following the recipe for sautéed kidneys with Madeira.

Pack the rice in a ring mould and unmould on a round platter. In the centre place the kidneys and sprinkle with chopped parsley. Pour the Madeira sauce around the rice.

Note: Rice cooked this way can be varied by adding seasonings or garnishes as listed in the section on rice (pages 513–516).

CALF'S KIDNEYS WITH MUSTARD
Rognons de veau à la moutarde
For 6 people

3 calf's kidneys
Salt and pepper
1 shallot, finely
  chopped
100 g (4 oz) unsalted
  butter
1 tablespoon cognac
  or fine champagne
  brandy
4 tablespoons double
  cream
1 teaspoon Dijon
  mustard
Chopped parsley
Juice of ¼ lemon

Remove the membrane and fat from the kidneys and season with salt and freshly ground pepper.

Cook the shallot in a small pan with a knob of butter without browning.

Heat 50 g (2 oz) of butter in a fireproof earthenware casserole and brown the kidneys quickly on all sides. Place in a 425°F (220°C, gas mark 7) oven for 12 minutes; remove while the kidneys are still very pink.

Put the kidneys on a plate, cut into slices 6 mm (¼ inch) thick and replace in the casserole. Baste with two teaspoons of the cognac and flambé, stirring all the time.

Remove the kidney slices and add to the shallot in the pan. Cover and keep warm.

While the casserole in which the kidneys cooked is still very hot, add the cream and boil to reduce by half. Then away from the heat season with the mustard and a few turns of the pepper mill. The mustard should not boil.

Pour the kidneys, the shallots and the juice from the kidneys into the casserole. Add the remaining butter in small pieces and sprinkle with the chopped parsley, then the remaining cognac. Mix well, so that all the ingredients are coated with the thickened sauce.

Correct the salt, squeeze in the lemon juice and serve on very hot plates.

The kidneys should be cooked until half done if the cooking is to be finished by flaming in brandy, though this step is optional.

Sweetbreads

Sweetbreads are not a common dish in France because of their high price, but they are without question one of the great delicacies of *haute cuisine*.

The preliminary preparations are always the same. Sweetbreads must be soaked in water for 5–6 hours, changing the water several times.

Scald by placing in a saucepan of cold water and slowly heating to boiling point, stirring from time to time with a wooden spoon, until the outer tissues stiffen. Drain, and rinse under running water.

Trim the sweetbreads, which means separating the round lobes (heart) from the long lobes (throat) and removing the filaments of fat and any gristle or tubes.

From this point on, the preparation differs according to the recipe used.

---

6 sweetbreads from
  young calves
50 g (2 oz) chopped
  onions
50 g (2 oz) chopped
  carrots
100 g (4 oz) unsalted
  butter
½ glass vermouth
½ glass dry white
  wine
½ l (1 pt) white stock
Bouquet garni
½ l (1 pt) double
  cream
100 g (4 oz) fresh
  mushrooms,
  washed and sliced
400 g (14 oz) shelled
  crayfish
25 g (1 oz) truffles,
  cut into julienne
600 g (1 lb 4 oz) tiny
  green peas

SWEETBREADS WITH CRAYFISH AND PEAS

Ris de veau aux écrevisses et aux pois gourmands

For 6 people

Soak the sweetbreads in water for 24 hours. Blanch briefly, rinse and trim.

Stew the chopped onions and carrots in butter in a saucepan. Place the sweetbreads on top. Moisten with the vermouth, white wine and white stock. Season. Add the bouquet garni, cover and cook very slowly 20–30 minutes.

Remove the sweetbreads. Strain the sauce through a fine sieve. Boil to reduce nearly to a glaze.

Add the cream and mushrooms. Reduce again until the sauce thickens and becomes very smooth.

Correct the seasoning; then add the sweetbreads, the shelled crayfish and the truffles.

Cook the green peas in salted water, then sauté in the remaining butter and season; place in a shallow dish. Arrange the sweetbreads on top, covering them generously with the sauce along with the crayfish, the truffles and the mushrooms.

Serve immediately on hot plates.

The green peas can be replaced with spinach cooked in butter.

BRAISED SWEETBREADS
Ris de veau poêlé

6 sweetbreads
Fresh pork fat for larding
1 large onion, sliced
1 medium-sized carrot, sliced
Fresh pork rind cut into pieces
Small bouquet garni
Melted unsalted butter
2 croûtons, fried in butter

Soak, scald and trim the sweetbreads as described above. Wrap in a dishtowel and place on a plate; cover with a piece of wood with a 2-kg (4-lb) weight on top. Leave under the weight for at least an hour. Using a thin larding needle, lard the sweetbreads with several rows of thin strips of fresh pork fat as explained for the fillet of beef Richelieu (page 217).

Choose a fireproof dish just big enough to hold the sweetbreads. Butter the bottom well and put in it 1 large onion, sliced, and 1 medium-sized carrot, sliced.

Heat slowly over a low flame until the vegetables begin to brown.

Add the fresh pork rind, cut into pieces, and place the sweetbreads on top, the larded side up. Sprinkle with salt.

Finish by filling any empty spaces with the trimmings of the sweetbreads and adding a small bouquet garni.

Baste with melted butter and cook in a 300°F (150°C, gas mark 2) oven for 25–30 minutes, depending upon the size of the sweetbreads. Baste often with the cooking butter and the juice that escapes from the sweetbreads. If the sauce boils down too rapidly, add a few tablespoons of good veal stock and cover the dish.

As the cooking proceeds and the basting becomes more frequent, the sauce will become syrupy and caramelize, coating the sweetbreads with a tasty glaze of a beautiful shiny golden colour. To produce this glaze, finish the cooking uncovered.

The cooked sweetbreads should not fall apart; the meat should remain firm when sliced.

To serve, place the sweetbreads on 2 croûtons of bread fried in butter and arrange on a heated round platter; baste the sweetbreads with 1 tablespoon of the cooking juice, strained through a very fine sieve. Too much juice would soak the croûtons.

Serve the remaining juice in a sauceboat.

If the braising is properly done, the juice will be reduced but there will be enough to serve with the sweetbreads. This rich, golden and naturally thickened juice is delicious as it is.

Serve the dish with a vegetable: green peas *à la française* or cooked in butter; asparagus tips coated with cream; mushrooms of all kinds; spinach; French beans; braised vegetables; lettuce, chicory, celery; purées of various vegetables; truffles; rice pilaf; noodles; braised or sautéed tomatoes; or one of the classic garnishes like *financière*, *Nantua* or *périgourdine*.

ꝏꝏꝏꝏꝏꝏꝏꝏꝏꝏꝏꝏꝏ

WHITE BRAISED SWEETBREADS
Ris de veau braisé à blanc

A 'white' braising of sweetbreads uses the same recipe as above, but without browning the ingredients: the sweetbreads are cooked, covered, in a 275°F (140°C, gas mark 1) oven.

This recipe is used when the sweetbreads are accompanied by a garnish thickened with a white sauce, such as velouté, cream or béchamel sauce; or if the sweetbreads are going to be served in a vol-au-vent, a timbale or puff pastry cases with a white sauce.

ꝏꝏꝏꝏꝏꝏꝏꝏꝏꝏꝏꝏꝏ

GRILLED SWEETBREADS
Ris de veau grillé maréchal
For 6 people

800–900 g (1¾–2 lb) sweetbreads
12 small artichoke hearts
150 g (6 oz) unsalted butter
Salt and pepper
1 bunch green asparagus
6 medium-sized truffles
1 tablespoon cognac or fine champagne brandy
6 tablespoons mushroom purée (page 447)

Soak, scald, rinse and trim the sweetbreads as described above.

Cook the artichoke hearts in a clear stock, drain and cook gently in butter. Season with salt and pepper.

Cook the asparagus in a large saucepan of boiling water, the tips tied together and the tender part of the stalks cut into small dice. Drain and cook gently in butter. Remove the asparagus tips and place them on a plate; away from the heat add a knob of butter to the remaining asparagus. Season with salt and pepper.

Cut the truffles into thick slices and sauté rapidly in very hot butter. Season with salt and pepper. Moisten with the brandy and cook to reduce almost completely. Away from the heat, add another knob of butter.

Meanwhile split the sweetbreads in half, brush with melted butter, season with salt and grill under a low flame.

Place the sweetbreads on a hot round platter, arranging them in the shape of a cross. Between the arms of the cross, arrange 3 artichoke hearts. Garnish the centre ones with the truffle slices and the others with the diced asparagus, and on top the asparagus tips. Inside the cross, pile the mushroom purée. Baste the sweetbreads with 1 tablespoon of melted butter.

SAUTÉED SLICED SWEETBREADS
Escalopes de ris de veau sautées

Prepare the sweetbreads as described above. Slice each into 3 or 4 pieces, season with salt and pepper, dust with flour and sauté in very hot butter as you would veal escalopes. Place in a circle on a round platter with a vegetable garnish in the centre. With 2 tablespoons of veal stock dissolve the meat juices sticking to the bottom of the pan, and pour these juices, mixed with the cooking butter, over the sliced sweetbreads.

1 young calf's head, unboned
1 lemon
10 l (20 pts) water
50 g (2 oz) flour
1½ dl (¼ pt) white vinegar
2 carrots
2 medium onions, stuck with 4 cloves
1 head garlic
Bouquet garni
Salt and pepper

CALF'S HEAD
Tête de veau

For 12 people

Trim and clean the calf's head. Soak in water for 24 hours. Drain and rub with lemon all over – nose, cheeks, ears, etc.

Prepare a *blanc* (a white court-bouillon). Fill a big pot with 10 l (20 pts) of water; mix the flour with some of the liquid and add, with all the other ingredients.

Place the calf's head in this well-seasoned liquid. Bring to the boil. Cook about 2 hours on a low flame, skimming regularly.

The calf's head is served whole and carved at table. It is accompanied by a variety of sauces: vinaigrette, green, gribiche, tartare, rémoulade, etc.

SHEEP'S TROTTERS
Pieds de mouton

In France sheep's trotters are usually bought already blanched. First singe the feet and with the point of a knife detach the small woolly tufts between the two parts of the hoofs.

Sheep's trotters are cooked exactly the same way as calf's head and trotters, in a *blanc*, but with a little less flour. Place the feet in the stock when it starts to boil.

Let simmer for 2½–3 hours.

The trotters are cooked when the main bone (the shin) comes away from the skin easily without breaking it.

Let the trotters cool in the cooking liquid and drain in a sieve. Separate any from old animals and those that are not fully cooked. Cook them again.

Be sure to remove the shin bones while the trotters are still hot, without breaking them. Place the trotters in a bowl with the cooking stock, strained through a fine sieve. Keep refrigerated; the cooking liquid will jell and will preserve the trotters for several days.

4 or 5 sheep's or lamb's trotters
50 g (2 oz) firm, white mushrooms
Pinch chopped parsley
1 cup poulette sauce (recipe below)
4 tablespoons water
15 g ($\frac{1}{2}$ oz) unsalted butter
Juice of $\frac{1}{4}$ lemon
Pinch salt

Poulette sauce (for 1 l (2 pts):
175 g (6 oz) unsalted butter
60 g (2 oz) flour
1 l (2 pts) white bouillon
Mushroom stems, peel and cooking liquid from the caps
4 egg yolks
Dash nutmeg
Juice of $\frac{1}{4}$ lemon
Chopped parsley

SHEEP'S TROTTERS WITH POULETTE SAUCE
Pieds de mouton à la poulette
For 1 person

Cook the sheep's trotters following the recipe above; cool them in a little of their cooking liquid, drain on a plate and remove the small bones – without spoiling the shape of the feet if possible.

Place the trotters in the cooking liquid again, and heat to boiling point. They are then ready to be used.

Mushrooms. Clean the bottoms of the mushroom stems; wash in two different waters without letting them stand, quickly, so that the mushrooms do not turn brown.

Cut off the stems close to the caps and 'turn' the caps. This means peeling them neatly so that they look machine-turned at the end. Flute the caps by making small, regular grooves in the skin with a sharp vegetable knife. Holding the knife in your right hand and the mushroom in your left, start at the top of the cap and cut a groove round it, finishing at the edge, giving the mushroom a quarter turn against the blade of the knife with your left hand. The finished mushroom is a delicately fluted rosette.

Reserve the stems and peels to be used later.

As the mushroom caps are 'turned', place them in a hot bouillon made with water, butter, lemon juice and salt. When the mushrooms are all in the bouillon, cover the saucepan, raise the heat, and boil for 3 minutes; drain and place the mushrooms in a bowl, covered with a piece of buttered paper and cut so that it will rest flat on the mushrooms; reserve the cooking liquid.

Sauce. Melt 50 g (2 oz) of butter in a 2-l (4-pt) saucepan. When it bubbles, add the flour, mix and cook slowly without letting it brown for 10 minutes. Stir often with a wooden spoon.

Let the mixture cool; then slowly add the boiling bouillon and most of the mushroom cooking liquid to the roux. As you slowly pour in the liquid, mix with a whisk while the sauce thickens, to avoid lumps. As soon as the sauce comes to the boil, add the mushroom stems and peels; reduce the heat and simmer very slowly for 30 minutes. From time to time, remove the scum and the impurities that come to the surface at the edges of the saucepan.

Note: The same quantity of velouté sauce (page 109) could replace the sauce above.

Strain the sauce through a very fine sieve into a saucepan, and away from the heat thicken with the egg yolks as follows:

Place the yolks, with the white bits removed, in a bowl with a few tablespoons of the reserved mushroom cooking liquid, 50 g (2 oz) of butter in small pieces and a dash of grated nutmeg.

While mixing the egg yolks with a whisk, add a ladleful of the boiling sauce little by little to prevent the yolks cooking. When the mixture is smooth, pour it all back into the sauce, beating all the while. Heat the sauce slowly almost to boiling point.

Remove from the heat and enrich with additional butter.

Correct the seasoning.

Presentation. Drain off the cooking liquid from the trotters and wipe them dry with a cloth; place in a heavy saucepan. Reheat the mushroom caps and their stems in a little of their cooking liquid. Then drain, scatter them over the trotters and cover with sauce – about $1\frac{1}{2}$ dl ($\frac{1}{4}$ pt) of sauce to 5 trotters. Squeeze the lemon juice over the top.

Heat everything together to coat the trotters and the mushrooms with sauce; when everything is well mixed, pour into a warm bowl. Sprinkle with chopped parsley and serve on very hot plates.

SHEEP'S TROTTERS WITH RÉMOULADE SAUCE
Pieds de mouton sauce rémoulade

Cook the trotters in a *blanc*, then carefully drain, bone and coat with a rémoulade sauce made with a generous quantity of mustard and seasoned with finely chopped raw onion.

Place in a bowl and sprinkle with chopped chervil and parsley.

PIG'S TROTTERS
Pieds de porc

Pig's trotters can be prepared like calf's head (page 329) and braised like sheep's trotters. They are, however, usually prepared in a special way which makes a delicious dish.

PIG'S TROTTERS WITH RÉMOULADE SAUCE
Pieds de porc grillés sauce rémoulade

Use front trotters, which are better than hind ones. Singe or scald them and scrape.

Wrap each trotter in a strip of cloth tied firmly with string to prevent it losing its shape during cooking.

Place the trotters in a braising pan, cover with cold water and add vegetables and seasonings as for a *pot-au-feu* (page 71), adding also 1 l (2 pts) of dry white wine for each 10 l (20 pts) of water. Add salt.

Bring to the boil, skim, cover, simmer very slowly, either in the oven or on top of the stove, for 10 hours.

Let the trotters cool in the cooking liquid, drain and remove the strips of cloth. Dip in melted butter, then in fresh breadcrumbs.

To serve, sprinkle with melted butter and grill slowly.

Serve with a bowl of sautéed potatoes or potatoes *mousseline* (page 500) and a sauceboat of rémoulade sauce (page 130). Serve on very hot plates.

GRILLED PIG'S TROTTERS WITH BÉARNAISE SAUCE
Pieds de porc grillés sauce béarnaise

Use the same method and garnish as for the grilled trotters with rémoulade sauce. Instead of rémoulade sauce use a béarnaise sauce (page 127).

POULTRY

This chapter includes turkey, guinea fowl, duck, goose, pigeon and above all chicken. There are several categories of chicken, according to age. The French types and their English equivalents are: *poularde* (large roaster); *chapon* (capon); *poulet reine* (medium-sized roaster or spring chicken); *poulet de grain* (small roaster or spring chicken); and *poussin* (baby chicken).

The giblets consist of the pinions, neck and gizzard, used for certain light entrées, and the liver, combs and kidneys, used in certain garnishes.

Large roasters and capons may be roasted, poached or pot-roasted – a roast farmyard chicken is a most delicious dish. These are the prime birds, carefully reared and tended, weighing 1·8–3 kg (4–6½ lb) or sometimes more. Their characteristics are their size, white flesh and fine-grained skin. The neck and feet are large, the breast-bone should be flexible at the tip. These features are found in all young birds. Old birds have scraggy necks and long spurs.

Large roasters and capons are prepared in the same way whether they are to be roasted, poached or pot-roasted. They are drawn, cleaned and singed and any pinfeathers buried in the skin are removed. They are then trussed in one of two ways. If the chicken is to be roasted or poached, the legs are first singed or blanched and plucked, and the spurs are shortened. The legs are left sticking out from the drumsticks which are trussed against the body. If the chicken is to be pot-roasted the legs are prepared in the same way, then folded back on the drumsticks and the outer sinews severed; the legs are tucked into incisions made in the breast skin so that they are fastened close to the drumsticks on either side of the breast.

If the chicken is to be poached, rub the breast with a quarter of a lemon to keep it white and cover with a piece of fresh pork fat.

If the chicken is going to be studded with truffles, this operation is easier if you first firm the meat by dipping the breast and thighs in boiling bouillon or white stock for a few seconds.

Poussins or baby chickens are ready for eating at 7–10 weeks old. They are generally roasted in a casserole or grilled.

Poulet de grain (small roaster or spring chicken) is 4–5 months old. It is usually cooked in a casserole, grilled, roasted or sometimes sautéed.

A *poulet à la reine* (medium-sized roaster or spring chicken) comes between a *poulet de grain* and a *poularde*. It is used for *suprêmes* of chicken and is usually sautéed. It can also be roasted, cooked in a casserole or braised.

TRUFFLED ROAST CHICKEN
Poularde de Bresse truffée rôtie
For 6 people

1·8-kg (4-lb) roasting chicken (about 1·4 kg (3½ lb) drawn weight)
500 g (1 lb) truffles
2 tablespoons Madeira
1 tablespoon cognac
2 tablespoons oil
Sprig thyme
½ bay leaf
Salt
Pepper
Herb and spice mixture (page xxiv)
500 g (1 lb) fresh pork flair fat
100 g (4 oz) raw *foie gras* (if unavailable, add 4 oz extra pork fat)
2 slices fresh pork fat for barding
Melted butter or chicken fat

Before cooking the chicken, stuff it.

Scrub and wash the truffles carefully (they will lose about 100 g (4 oz) in this process); peel and retain the peels. From the largest truffles cut a dozen thick slices, place in a bowl and add 1 tablespoon of Madeira; the truffles should soak in it for a little while.

Cut the remaining truffles in quarters and marinate in the cognac, the remaining Madeira, oil, thyme, bay leaf, a pinch of salt, a few turns of the pepper mill and a dash of herbs and spices.

Skin the pork fat and cut into small pieces, removing any gristle. Pound in a mortar. When completely crushed, add the *foie gras* and work the mixture into a fine paste. Put the mixture in a terrine and leave in a warm place to soften the fat so that it will go through a fine sieve easily.

Strain into a bowl and add the quartered truffles, the truffle peels (finely chopped), and the remaining marinade and seasonings. Remove the thyme and the bay leaf, and mix well to obtain a smooth paste.

The chicken should be drawn entirely through the neck. Lift the breast skin and slide the slices of truffles set aside between the skin and the meat. Put the stuffing into the chicken, fold the neck skin over the hole and truss and bard the bird.

To roast the chicken, cover with buttered white paper to protect the breast. Place the bird in a roasting pan on a rack so that it does not sit in the melted fat. Brush with melted butter or chicken fat and place in a 350°F (180°C, gas mark 4) oven.

The cooking should be slow, at an even temperature. The chicken should not be basted, but it should be turned from time to time. It will take 1½ hours to cook (it is a longer roasting time because the stuffing was not previously cooked).

Ten minutes before the end of the cooking time, remove the paper and the barding and let the bird brown very lightly; during this time, baste it with the melted fat from the stuffing.

Test the chicken to see if it is done by pricking with a trussing needle at the thickest point of the thigh. If the juice runs clear and white, the chicken is cooked; if the juice runs pink, let the bird stand for a few minutes in a low oven, protecting the breast with the fat removed earlier.

Serve with the juice of the chicken, partly degreased.

The melted fat has a delicious flavour and can be used in many ways.

POT-ROASTED CHICKEN WITH CHESTNUTS
Poularde poêlée châtelaine
For 6–8 people

1·8-kg (4-lb) chicken (1·4 kg (3½ lb) drawn)
2 slices fresh pork fat for barding
50 g (2 oz) unsalted butter
50 chestnuts
4 dl (¾ pt) bouillon or veal stock
1 celery stalk

Clean the chicken, season it inside and out, truss and bard it. Place in a casserole with 25 g (1 oz) of melted butter.

Cover and cook for 40–50 minutes in a 325°F (170°C, gas mark 3) oven or simmer on top of the stove. Keep an eye on it, turning the chicken on its sides and its back, and as little as possible on its breast.

Since there is almost no evaporation, the juice that collects in the bottom of the pan will be rich, well-flavoured and golden.

Slowly grill the chestnuts or fry them; peel and poach in a little bouillon or clear veal stock. Flavour the stock with the celery and the remaining butter. The chestnuts should still be slightly firm when removed from the heat.

Fifteen minutes before the end of the cooking time remove the bard and the trussing, and place the poached chestnuts around the chicken.

Simmer, uncovered. Baste often taking care not to break the chestnuts. The breast will brown slightly.

Place the chicken on a long platter and arrange the chestnuts around it, like a necklace of large pearls. Baste with the chicken juice.

CHICKEN WITH COARSE SALT
Poularde au gros sel

1·6-kg (3½-lb) chicken
10 carrots, cut and trimmed in the shape of olives
10 small turnips, cut and trimmed in the shape of olives
10 small onions
6 leeks, white part only, cut into pieces 5 cm (2½ inches) long
Bouillon or white veal stock
Coarse salt

Draw, singe and truss the chicken. Place in a saucepan just big enough to hold it easily. Add the carrots, turnips, onions and leeks.

Cover with bouillon or veal stock. Bring to the boil, skim and poach, covered, on a very low flame.

Drain the chicken and place on a round platter; arrange the vegetables in small clusters as a garnish.

Serve the bouillon separately. If the saucepan used for poaching was of the correct size, it will be very well flavoured because of the limited quantity of liquid used.

Serve a dish of coarse rock or sea salt separately.

POACHED CHICKEN WITH TARRAGON AND RICE
Poularde pochée à l'estragon et au riz

Poach the chicken as in the recipe above, but use only one-third of the vegetables.

Place the chicken on a round platter and with it serve separately:

1. A sauceboat of the bouillon in which you have cooked a teaspoon of tapioca until completely dissolved. Let a few leaves of tarragon steep in this bouillon, lightly thickened by the tapioca. Strain through cheesecloth.
2. A dish of rice pilaf (page 514).

CHICKEN WITH RICE AND SUPRÊME SAUCE
Poularde de Bresse au riz sauce suprême

1·6-kg (3½-lb) chicken, prepared as for chicken with coarse salt (above)

1¼ l (2 pts) bouillon or white stock

1 medium-sized carrot

1 onion stuck with a clove

Bouquet garni

225 g (8 oz) rice

175 g (6 oz) unsalted butter

1 tablespoon flour

6 tablespoons double cream

½ teaspoon lemon juice

Dash grated nutmeg

Trim, prepare the chicken and poach following the recipe for chicken with coarse salt (above). The cooking liquid should be about 1¼ l (2 pts) with carrot, onion and bouquet garni added.

Wash the rice in cold water, changing the water several times until it is quite clear. Place the rice in a saucepan and add enough cold water to cover generously; boil 5 minutes, stirring from time to time. Drain, wash again in warm water to remove the starch, which would make the grains stick together. Moisten with 6 dl (1 pt) of cooking liquid from the chicken and 50 g (2 oz) of butter, bring to the boil, cover and cook in a 425°F (220°C, gas mark 7) oven for 15 minutes.

When the rice is cooked, separate the grains with a fork, adding 50 g (2 oz) of butter.

Sauce. In a saucepan, melt 25 g (1 oz) of butter; mix in the flour; cook 10 minutes without browning.

Let the mixture cool; then add, stirring, 3 dl (½ pt) of very hot stock from the chicken. Bring to the boil, stirring with a whisk until the sauce is at boiling point; simmer 10 minutes slowly.

Strain the sauce through a very fine sieve into a heavy saucepan. Raise the heat, and boil to reduce the sauce by half, stirring with a wooden spoon. The sauce will be too thick, so thin it with cream. Away from the heat season the sauce with lemon juice and grated nutmeg. Correct the salt, if necessary, and finish the sauce by adding the remaining butter. The sauce should be very white and creamy.

To serve

First method: Pile a bed of rice on a long platter. Remove the pork fat and the strings from the chicken, leaving the breast exposed, and place on top. Cover the breast with a coating of the finished sauce.

Serve the remaining sauce in a sauceboat.

Second method: Serve the chicken on its own on a serving platter, after removing the pork fat and the strings. Baste the bird with 1 tablespoon of the poaching stock.

Serve the rice separately and the suprême sauce in a sauceboat.

POACHED CHICKEN WITH ASPARAGUS, ARTICHOKES AND TRUFFLES
Poularde pochée princesse

Follow the above recipe but do not make the rice.

To the suprême sauce add pieces or slices of truffles, cooked gently in butter; add this butter to the sauce. If you use canned truffles, add the truffle juice to the sauce.

Serve as above; around the chicken, place artichoke hearts cooked in white stock and finished in butter. Top with steamed asparagus tips coated with butter or a spoonful of suprême sauce.

CHICKEN SUPRÊMES, FILLETS AND CUTLETS
Suprêmes de volaille, filets et côtelettes de volaille

These names are useful cooking terms but have little to do with the anatomy of the bird. They are synonyms for the same part of the chicken – the tender white breast meat. In France the term *suprême* generally refers to a *poularde* or large roaster, *filet* and *côtelette* to a *poulet à la reine* and *poulet de grain* (medium and small roaster) respectively.

The breast is removed from the bird in three stages. First remove the wing, then the skin covering the breast. Then make a deep incision right through to the carcass, cutting along on either side of the breastbone. Finally, insert your knife at the wing joint and slide it up close to the carcass, removing the breast meat in one piece. If properly done this operation leaves the bones clean of any flesh.

The breast of a large roaster is divided into 3 pieces – the *filet mignon*, which is easily separated, and the *filets*, which are divided into 2 or 3 strips cut on the bias, giving heart-shaped pieces which should be flattened lightly.

Breasts from small or medium roasters are left whole, without skin or bone.

Côtelettes keep part of the wing bone attached. The same term is used for chopped raw chicken or finely diced chicken bound with a sauce and reshaped to look like a cutlet.

The three basic cooking methods for this extremely delicate cut are essentially the same:

1. Season the chicken breast with salt and pepper; dust with flour, carefully shaking off the excess. Place the chicken pieces side by side in a pan, not too close together, with some hot melted butter. Sear and brown quickly on both sides; do not raise the heat suddenly.

2. Dip the pieces of chicken breast in melted butter, season with salt and pepper on both sides. Place in a thickly buttered pan; squeeze a few drops of lemon juice on top. Cover, place in a 425°F (220°C, gas mark 7) oven for 5–8 minutes, depending on the thickness.

3. Dip the pieces of chicken breast in melted butter, season, roll in fresh breadcrumbs, sprinkle with a few drops of melted butter or melted chicken fat, and grill at a high temperature.

Chicken breasts must be cooked only minutes before serving. This dish cannot wait. Furthermore, these pieces should never be boiled.

This way of serving chicken is not so expensive as one might imagine. The carcass is used to make or to enrich consommés or soups; the giblets and the back can be made into a stew or sautéed; the legs can be grilled, poached or diced for various uses such as cutlets, turnovers, croquettes (page 21), etc.

POACHED CHICKEN WITH TRUFFLES
Poularde de Bresse truffée mère Brazier
For 4 people

1·6–2-kg (3½–4½-lb) roasting chicken
8 large truffles, sliced
½ lemon
Salt and pepper
1 medium onion stuck with cloves
4 leeks, white part only
225 g (8 oz) new carrots
150 g (6 oz) white turnips
1 celery stalk

Prepare the chicken as usual – pluck, singe and draw it. Slide the truffle slices under the skin (4 around the breast and 2 under the skin of the thighs). Then rub the chicken on all sides with the lemon; truss it.

Put 2 l (4 pts) of water in a large pot. Add salt and pepper. Add the onion, the leeks, the carrots, the turnips and the celery.

Bring to the boil. Plunge in the chicken, lower the heat and simmer.

The chicken must be poached slowly. Allow 30–40 minutes for a 1·6-kg (3½-lb) chicken.

The chicken is served with the bouillon and the vegetables – carrots, turnips, leeks – and a rice pilaf (page 514). Serve coarse salt separately.

1·4-kg (3-lb) roasting chicken, drawn, and cut into 8 pieces
175 g (6 oz) butter
Salt and pepper
4 shallots, chopped
¼ l (½ pt) good wine vinegar

CHICKEN SAUTÉED WITH VINEGAR
Volaille de Bresse sautée au vinaigre
For 4 servings

Heat 100 g (4 oz) of butter in a pan big enough to hold the pieces of chicken. Season the pieces with salt and pepper; brown lightly. The butter should remain light in colour.

Cover, and continue cooking in a 425°F (220°C, gas mark 7) oven for about 20 minutes.

When cooked, place the pieces of chicken on a platter, cover and keep warm.

Sauté the chopped shallots without letting them brown in the butter in the pan. Deglaze with the wine vinegar. Boil to reduce by half and beat 50 g (2 oz) of butter into the sauce. Pour the sauce over the pieces of chicken, carefully coating them with the sauce.

1·8-kg (4-lb) roasting
  chicken
8 large slices of truffle
125 g (5 oz) veal fillet
6 tablespoons double
  cream
Salt and pepper
50 g (2 oz) each
  cooked diced
  carrots, turnips,
  celeriac
50 g (2 oz) cooked
  green peas
50 g (2 oz) cooked
  sliced French beans
White part of 1
  cooked leek
1 pork bladder soaked
  in salted water
1 tablespoon Madeira
10 l (20 pts) white
  chicken bouillon

Optional:
50 g (2 oz) each diced
  truffles and *foie
  gras*
Chicken liver, diced

BONED, STUFFED CHICKEN
Poularde de Bresse truffée en vessie Joannes Nandron

For 4 people

Carefully draw the chicken and bone the body, leaving the wings and the legs. Slide the slices of truffle under the skin on the breast and the thighs.

To make the forcemeat chop the veal finely in a blender. Season with salt and pepper. Place the meat in a bowl; set the bowl in a larger bowl of ice and add, beating with a wooden spoon, the cream. Mix in the cooked vegetables. Correct the seasoning.

Stuff the cavity with the vegetable and veal mixture. Insert the leek in the centre.

Close up the chicken, sewing the openings and trussing to return it to its original shape.

Turn the pork bladder inside out, and place the stuffed chicken inside, adding a pinch of salt and pepper and the Madeira. Close the bladder very tightly, tying it twice with string.

To cook, plunge the chicken in the bladder into a large saucepan of hot white bouillon, prepared with the giblets and the carcass of the boned chicken.

The chicken is poached without boiling at a slow simmer for $1\frac{1}{2}$ hours.

Serve the chicken on a platter, and remove it from the bladder in front of the guests.

Carve by first cutting away the wings and the legs. Give each guest a piece of chicken and some of the stuffing.

The chicken can be accompanied by suprême sauce (page 110) and a rice pilaf (page 514).

100 g (4 oz) green
asparagus tips
75 g (3 oz) butter
1 breast of a large
chicken
Flour
2 tablespoons double
cream
Salt and pepper
Dash nutmeg

CHICKEN BREASTS WITH ASPARAGUS

Suprême de volaille Françoise

For 1 person

In salted boiling water, cook the asparagus with the tips tied in small bunches and the tender part of the stems cut into pieces 1 cm ($\frac{1}{2}$ inch) long. Drain immediately and cook gently in butter. Season with a pinch of salt. Just before serving, remove the cut asparagus to a hot plate and coat with butter.

Untie the bunches of asparagus tips and baste them with $\frac{1}{2}$ tablespoon of melted butter.

Ten minutes before serving, season the chicken breasts with salt and freshly ground pepper, dust lightly with flour and place flat in a pan, just big enough to hold the pieces, in which 25 g (1 oz) of butter is bubbling. Baste the breast with melted butter, cover tightly and cook in a 450°F (230°C, gas mark 8) oven. Cooking time will be 5 minutes, or more, depending upon the weight of the chicken breast.

Pile the pieces of asparagus around the edge of a hot round platter, topping them with the bunches of asparagus tips. Arrange the chicken in the centre. Coat the chicken with the juices from the pan, deglazed with the cream.

The deglazing is done in the following way. After the chicken breast has been removed to a platter, pour the cream into the pan. Bring to the boil quickly; season with a pinch of salt, a turn of the pepper mill and a dash of grated nutmeg. After boiling for a few seconds, the cream liquified by the heat reduces slightly and thickens. At this point, remove from the heat and finish the sauce, without letting it boil, by adding 25 g (1 oz) of butter. Correct the seasoning and pour the sauce over the chicken.

CHICKEN BREASTS WITH TRUFFLES

Suprêmes de volaille Antonin Carême

For 4 servings, prepare potatoes Anna (see page 503) in a pan the diameter of a dessert plate, mixing in raw truffles cut in large julienne – about 1 medium truffle per serving. The potatoes should be no deeper than 2·5 cm (1 inch).

Make 5 incisions on the surface of each of 4 chicken breasts and insert pieces of raw truffle. Season with salt and pepper and cook the breasts following the preceding recipe.

To serve, unmould the potatoes Anna on to a hot round platter; place the chicken breasts on top. Deglaze the chicken juices with ¼ glass of port and 4 tablespoons of double cream. Boil to reduce by half. Finish the sauce away from the heat with 1 tablespoon of butter. Baste the chicken breasts with 3 or 4 tablespoons of butter, cooked until it is light brown. Serve the rich sauce separately in a sauceboat.

SAUTÉS AND FRICASSEES OF CHICKEN

Côtelettes de volaille, volailles sautés ou fricassées, poulets sautés

1 large frying chicken, cut up
50 g (2 oz) unsalted butter or 25 g (1 oz) unsalted butter and 2 tablespoons oil
Salt and pepper
Deglazing liquid: wine, spirits, cooking juice from mushrooms, chicken or veal stock, etc.

The best chicken to use is a *poulet à la reine* – a plump, tender medium-sized chicken. The bird is cut up in the usual way, into 7 or 8 joints.

The cooking method is the same, regardless of the sauce or the garnish.

Choose a pan just big enough to hold the pieces of chicken in one layer comfortably.

Heat 50 g (2 oz) of butter or 25 g (1 oz) of butter and 2 tablespoons of oil.

Place the pieces of chicken in the very hot butter, season with salt and pepper and brown lightly on both sides. The butter must keep its light-brown colour; the browning must be done carefully.

Cover and continue cooking in a 425°F (220°C, gas mark 7)

oven. Remove the wings and the white meat after 8–10 minutes. Cook the legs, which are thicker and firmer, 5–8 minutes more.

When cooked, place the pieces of chicken on a plate, cover and keep warm.

Then deglaze the pan. During the cooking, the juices from the meat will stick to the bottom of the pan, where they form particles of light chicken glaze. They must be dissolved so that they can be used to make the sauce, which has a distinctive flavour.

First drain off most of the fat used for browning the chicken. Add whatever liquid is specified in the recipe to the pan – wine, spirits, cooking juice from mushrooms, chicken stock or veal stock, etc.

Boil to reduce, following the recipe, and add the sauce or stock.

Simmer the pieces of the chicken in this liquid for 3–4 minutes, without letting them boil.

Arrange the pieces of chicken on a very hot long or round platter. Pour the sauce, correctly seasoned, over the chicken to coat it completely.

Note: If the chicken is going to be poached, the method is the same but the browning is omitted. Instead sear the meat in hot butter and cook it, covered, in a 325°F (170°C, gas mark 3) oven. The deglazing for the sauce is done the same way but usually with cream or with velouté (page 109), Allemande (page 109), or béchamel sauce (page 110).

1 large frying
chicken, cut up
1 tablespoon oil or
15 g (½ oz) unsalted
butter
175 g (6 oz)
mushrooms,
cleaned, washed
and thinly sliced
1 level tablespoon
flour
Salt and pepper
½ glass dry white
wine
3 dl (½ pt) veal stock
or bouillon and 2
tablespoons tomato
purée
25 g (1 oz) unsalted
butter
Chopped parsley

SAUTÉED CHICKEN WITH MUSHROOMS
Poulet sauté aux champignons

Follow the instructions for sautéed chicken (above). When the chicken has been cooked and removed from the pan the pan is ready to be deglazed.

Add oil or butter, heat and add the mushrooms. Sauté the mushrooms quickly on a high flame, and as soon as the juices have evaporated completely, sprinkle with the flour; season with salt and pepper, mix and brown lightly. Moisten with white wine; boil to reduce by half, and add the stock or bouillon and 2 tablespoons of tomato purée. Stir carefully into the flour.

Bring to the boil and boil for 5 minutes. Add the legs and thighs and simmer for 5 more minutes. Remove from the heat, and add the breast and the wings; coat the chicken with the sauce and the mushrooms; remove to a platter.

Finish the sauce by boiling to reduce it, if it is too thin; correct the seasoning, and add 25 g (1 oz) of butter; stir well, and do not boil.

Sprinkle with chopped fresh parsley.

Note: If you have any Espagnole sauce (page 108) or demi-glace sauce (page 108), use one of them as the moistening liquid and do not add flour.

SAUTÉED CHICKEN WITH SHALLOTS, TOMATO AND HERBS
Poulet sauté chasseur

Proceed as for sautéed chicken with mushrooms making these changes:

1. Before sprinkling with the flour, add 1 teaspoon of finely chopped shallots.
2. Before moistening with the white wine, add 1 tablespoon of cognac; ignite for two seconds, then snuff out the flame with the cover of the pan.

3. With the moistening liquid, add a large ripe tomato, peeled, seeded and coarsely chopped.
4. With the butter, add ½ teaspoon each of chopped tarragon and chervil.

Note: The flour can be omitted if you have some well-skimmed Espagnole or demi-glace sauce. These sauces replace the liquid used with the flour as a thickening ingredient, and produce a better result.

CHICKEN WITH CRAYFISH
Volaille de Bresse aux écrevisses
For 4 people

1·4-kg (3-lb) chicken
24 crayfish *à la bordelaise* (page 202)
50 g (2 oz) unsalted butter
50 g (2 oz) chopped shallots
50 g (2 oz) carrots, core removed, chopped finely
2 tablespoons cognac
½ glass dry white wine
100 g (4 oz) tomatoes coarsely chopped
1 garlic clove, crushed
Chopped parsley and tarragon

After singeing the chicken, draw and cut in 8 pieces.

Meanwhile, prepare the crayfish *à la bordelaise*, removing the shells of 20 of the crayfish tails and reserving the sauce.

In a heavy pan, heat 40 g (1½ oz) of butter. When the butter is hot, add the pieces of chicken, seasoned with salt and pepper. Brown the pieces of chicken lightly, turning them to brown evenly on all sides.

Add the finely chopped shallots and carrots. Cover the pan and place in the oven or on top of the stove on a low flame for about 15 minutes to half cook the chicken.

Boil the juice to reduce slightly, then degrease if necessary. Deglaze with the cognac and the white wine. Reduce again and add the chopped tomato and the garlic. Finish cooking the chicken, covered.

When the chicken pieces are cooked, remove to a plate. Again, boil the juices to reduce slightly, and add the bordelaise sauce from the crayfish. Boil for a few minutes; thicken with 15 g (½ oz) of butter or 2 tablespoons of cream.

To finish put the pieces of chicken back in the sauce, adding the 20 crayfish tails.

To blend the different flavours, let the dish simmer for a few minutes and correct the seasoning, if necessary.

To serve, place the pieces of chicken and crayfish on a shallow serving platter, coat them with the sauce and sprinkle the chopped parsley and tarragon over them.

Garnish with 4 beautiful crayfish in their shells.

SAUTÉED CHICKEN WITH WOODLAND MUSHROOMS
Poulet sauté aux morilles ou aux cèpes

1 large frying
  chicken, cut up
1 tablespoon oil
225 g (8 oz) morels or
  ceps
1 teaspoon finely
  chopped shallots
Salt and freshly
  ground pepper
½ glass white wine
6 tablespoons veal
  stock
25 g (1 oz) unsalted
  butter
Pinch chopped
  parsley

Follow the recipe for sautéed chicken with mushrooms up to the deglazing of the sauce.

After removing the chicken from the pan, add 1 tablespoon of oil and the morels or ceps, cleaned very carefully (the undersides of the caps generally contain a great deal of sand). Sauté over a high flame for 3 minutes; sprinkle with shallots, and season with salt and freshly ground pepper.

Place the pieces of chicken, except the breast and the wings, on the morels; cover, and cook in a 425°F (220°C, gas mark 7) oven for 5 minutes.

Remove from the oven, and moisten with wine. Boil to reduce almost completely; add veal stock, boil 2 minutes. Add the breast and the wings, but do not let boil. Finish away from the heat by adding butter while stirring. Correct the seasoning, and pile on a platter. Sprinkle chopped parsley over it.

CHICKEN MARENGO
Poulet sauté à la Marengo
For 6–8 people

1 large frying
  chicken, cut up
Crushed garlic clove
½ glass dry white
  wine
3 dl (½ pt) tomato
  sauce (page 111)
1½ dl (¼ pt) veal stock
Unsalted butter
Seasoning
1 dozen mushroom
  caps
6–8 small fried eggs
6–8 crayfish
6–8 croûtons, fried in
  butter
6–8 thick slices truffle
Juice of ¼ lemon
Pinch chopped parsley

Follow the directions for sautéed chicken with mushrooms for the first steps. Cook a crushed garlic clove in the butter for 1 second before deglazing the pan.

Deglaze the pan with wine; boil to reduce by two-thirds; moisten with tomato sauce and veal stock. Season with the cooked garlic.

Bring the sauce to the boil, first with the thighs and the legs. Follow the steps given in the recipe for sautéed chicken; and finish away from the heat by adding butter. Correct the seasonings.

The presentation is done the classic way for Chicken Marengo. Garnish the platter with mushroom caps, sautéed with the chicken and set aside, then coated with the sauce at the last moment; small fried eggs; crayfish (the claws turned back and stuck in the tails) cooked in a court-bouillon or sautéed in butter; heart-shaped croûtons fried in butter; and thick slices of truffle, cooked in the sauce for 2 minutes before finishing.

Squeeze lemon juice over the dish, and sprinkle with parsley.

Note: It is easier, especially given the variety of garnishes used here, to correct the seasoning of the sauce after placing the chicken on the platter. This makes it possible to simmer the mushrooms and the slices of truffle in the sauce for a few minutes and add the butter away from the heat afterward.

SAUTÉED CHICKEN WITH TARRAGON
Poulet sauté à l'estragon

1 large frying chicken, cut up
½ glass dry white wine
4 tablespoons veal stock
Chopped chervil and tarragon

Sauté the chicken according to the basic instructions (given above). Place the bird on a platter; deglaze the pan with the dry white wine. Boil to reduce by half; add the veal stock. Bring to the boil for 3 minutes, and away from the heat correct the seasoning and add some chopped chervil and tarragon to the nearly boiling juice.

Baste the chicken with this juice, which should be thick.

Serve with a bowl of small potatoes *à la parisienne*, lightly browned in butter (page 502).

SAUTÉED CHICKEN WITH ONIONS
Poulet sauté lyonnaise

1 large frying chicken, cut up
½ glass dry white wine
4 tablespoons veal stock
Chopped parsley

Cook the chicken in butter as for the sautéed chicken with mushrooms. Cook the onions in salted water.

After the breast and the wings have been removed, add the onions to the rest of the chicken which needs longer cooking.

Simmer for 5 minutes.

Place the chicken on the platter, surround it with the onions, which will have absorbed the fatty juice of the chicken and be lightly browned.

Deglaze the pan with the dry white wine. Boil to reduce by

two-thirds, and moisten with veal stock. Correct the seasoning. Bring to the boil and immediately pour the sauce over the chicken.

Sprinkle the onions with chopped parsley.

SAUTÉED CHICKEN WITH TRUFFLES
Poulet sauté aux truffes

1 large frying chicken, cut up
125 g (5 oz) raw truffles, quartered
1 glass champagne
2 tablespoons Madeira
50 g (2 oz) unsalted butter

Sauté the chicken in butter.

After removing the breast and wings add the truffles to the rest of the chicken.

Place the chicken on a platter, leaving the truffles in the pan. Deglaze with the champagne. Boil to reduce by two-thirds. Away from the heat finish the sauce with Madeira and butter. Mix the truffles into the sauce and pour over the chicken.

SAUTÉED CHICKEN WITH SPRING VEGETABLES
Poulet sauté printanier

Prepare and sauté the chicken following the classic method described above.

Deglaze the pan with 4 tablespoons of veal stock.

Place the chicken on a platter and surround it with spring vegetables: carrots, turnips cut into olive shapes, onions cooked in butter and glazed, peas and French beans steamed and coated with butter.

Pour the reduced juices over the chicken.

⫻══⫻══⫻══⫻══⫻══⫻══⫻══⫻══⫻══⫻══⫻

SAUTÉED CHICKEN WITH TOMATOES AND GARLIC
Poulet sauté à la portugaise

1 large frying
   chicken, cut up
1 onion, finely
   chopped
2 garlic cloves,
   crushed
½ glass dry white
   wine
3 large ripe
   tomatoes, peeled,
   seeded, coarsely
   chopped
Salt and pepper
Pinch chopped
   parsley
50 g (2 oz) unsalted
   butter

Sauté the chicken using half oil and half butter.

When the wings and the breast are cooked, remove the pieces of chicken from the pan. To the cooking butter add the onion; soften it slowly, then brown lightly. Add the garlic; heat for a second, then moisten with white wine. Reduce almost completely. Add the tomatoes. Be careful not to leave any seeds in the tomato pulp and season with salt and pepper; add the chicken carcass and the legs and cook, covered, in a 425°F (220°C, gas mark 7) oven for 7–8 minutes.

Remove the pieces of chicken.

If the sauce at the bottom of the pan is not sufficiently reduced, raise the heat for a few seconds. Correct the seasonings.

Season with a pinch of freshly ground pepper and chopped parsley, added to the sauce away from the heat. Coat the pieces of chicken with the sauce and place on a platter. Finish the tomato sauce with the butter and do not let it boil again.

Cover the chicken with the sauce, and sprinkle with chopped parsley.

⫻══⫻══⫻══⫻══⫻══⫻══⫻══⫻══⫻══⫻══⫻

ROASTING CHICKEN COOKED IN SALT
Poulet de Bresse au sel

For 4 people

1·4-kg (3-lb) roasting
   chicken
4 kg (8½ lb) sea salt

Prepare the chicken for roasting and remove the feet. Pepper it lightly.

Line the bottom and the sides of a braising pan with aluminium foil. Spread a generous layer of sea salt on the bottom. Place the chicken, breast down, in the centre of the pan. Cover the chicken completely with salt, and fold over the foil on top to enclose the chicken.

Place the braising pan in a 450°F (230°C, gas mark 8) oven for 1¼ hours.

To serve, place the chicken in the foil on a platter. Remove the foil.

Break the block of salt in front of your guests. If the cooking instructions have been observed, the chicken should be golden brown.

Seasoned by the iodine in the sea salt, the chicken has an incomparable flavour, and its meat is succulent.

CHICKEN ROASTED ON A SPIT
Volaille de Bresse à la broche
For 4 people

Choose a roasting chicken weighing about 1·6 kg (3½ lb). Carefully draw and truss. Season inside and outside with salt and freshly ground pepper.

Put the chicken on a spit, and brush with 50 g (2 oz) of melted butter. Place over a hot wood fire with glowing red embers. At regular intervals baste the chicken with the juice that collects in the drip pan.

For a chicken of this size, allow about 45 minutes cooking time.

To appreciate the incomparable flavour of a spit-roasted chicken it should be eaten as soon as it is finished.

Serve the concentrated juice from the drip pan in a sauceboat.

Note: You can slide truffle slices under the skin of the chicken before trussing it.

1·4-kg (3-lb) chicken
2 hearts lettuce, quartered
100 g (4 oz) fresh green peas, shelled
100 g (4 oz) young French beans
50 g (2 oz) spring turnips, cut into sticks
100 g (4 oz) young carrots, cut into sticks
4 small white onions
100 g (4 oz) unsalted butter
Salt, pepper
Pinch sugar
Flaky pastry (page 531)

CHICKEN COOKED IN A TUREEN
Poulet de Bresse en soupière

For 4 people

Prepare the chicken (draw, singe, trim and truss); place it in a large, ovenproof soup tureen.

Surround the chicken with the vegetables. Add the butter and season with salt and pepper and a pinch of sugar.

Cover the tureen tightly with a thin layer of flaky pastry.

Place the tureen in a preheated 400°F (200°C, gas mark 6) oven. 5 or 10 minutes later, cover the pastry with aluminium foil, so that it will not brown too much during cooking.

Cooking time is $1\frac{3}{4}$ hours in the heated oven, plus $\frac{1}{4}$ hour with the heat turned off.

To serve, place the tureen in front of the guests. Remove the pastry cover with the point of a knife, releasing a most appetizing smell.

Carve the chicken in the usual way. Serve a portion to each guest, with some of the delicious vegetables and a piece of the pastry cover.

100 g (4 oz) unsalted butter
1·4-kg (3-lb) spring chicken
Salt and pepper
25 g (1 oz) flour
$\frac{1}{2}$ l (1 pt) white bouillon
Bouquet garni
12 small onions
12 medium mushrooms, washed and quartered
Juice of $\frac{1}{2}$ lemon
2 egg yolks
Dash grated nutmeg
6 tablespoons double cream
Croûtons

FRICASSEE OF CHICKEN WITH ONIONS AND MUSHROOMS
Fricassée de poulet vallée d'Auge

In a pan just big enough to hold the chicken, heat 25 g (1 oz) of butter. Add the chicken, cut into pieces, and the wing tips, neck and gizzard.

Season with salt and freshly ground pepper.

Cook over medium heat to sear the meat. Do not brown. Stir often with a wooden spoon.

Sprinkle with flour, mix and cook for a few minutes without letting the flour brown. Moisten by adding the bouillon and stirring it into the flour until the liquid reaches boiling point. Add the bouquet garni. Cover, and simmer slowly for 35 minutes.

If you have no bouillon, replace it with water flavoured with 1 medium-sized carrot cut into quarters and 1 onion stuck with a clove. Add salt as needed.

While the chicken is simmering, cook the small onions, barely covered with water, with 15 g ($\frac{1}{2}$ oz) of butter and a few grains of salt. Cook the mushrooms for 4 minutes in 1 tablespoon of boiling water, a small knob of butter, the lemon juice and a pinch of salt. Remove the mushrooms to a bowl.

Prepare the thickening ingredients. Place the yolks in a bowl; add 2 tablespoons of the cooking juice from the mushrooms, 15 g ($\frac{1}{2}$ oz) of butter in bits, and a dash of grated nutmeg. Beat the cream into the egg yolks.

When the chicken is cooked, remove the pieces from the sauce and place them in another pan; sprinkle the onions and mushrooms, both drained, on top.

Slowly pour 1 ladleful of the sauce into the mixture of egg yolks and cream, stirring with a whisk. Then add the egg yolks and cream to the sauce. Heat for a minute and remove from the heat just as the sauce reaches the boiling point; it should not boil.

Away from the heat finish the sauce by stirring in the remaining butter. Correct the seasoning.

Strain the sauce through a fine sieve on to the chicken. Turn the chicken over in the sauce to coat it well, and place it on a hot round platter.

Around the chicken and vegetables arrange the bread croûtons, cut into heart shapes and fried in butter.

Note: This recipe can be used for a tender boiling fowl. The cooking time will be longer, according to its age and size. The garnish can be supplemented with about 15 tiny carrots cooked following the recipe for glazed vegetables (page 429), coated with the chicken sauce and served separately or mixed with the mushrooms and onions.

1·8-kg (4-lb) chicken
Salt and pepper
100 g (4 oz) lean
 bacon
50 g (2 oz) butter
12 small onions
100 g (4 oz)
 mushrooms,
 washed
1 tablespoon flour
2 garlic cloves,
 crushed
1 bottle red
 Burgundy
Small bouquet garni
$\frac{1}{2}$ l (1 pt) lightly salted
 bouillon or water
The chicken blood
 kept liquid with a
 little vinegar, or 3
 tablespoons pork
 blood
3 tablespoons cognac

CHICKEN IN RED WINE WITH ONIONS AND MUSHROOMS
Coq au vin à la bourguignonne

Cut the chicken as for sautéed chicken. Put the pieces, including the giblets but not the liver, on a plate, and season with salt and freshly ground pepper.

Cut the bacon into lardoons and place them in a pan. Cover with cold water and blanch for 5 minutes; drain and wipe dry.

In a fireproof earthenware casserole heat the butter and brown the lardoons slowly along with the small onions. When they are both golden, drain and set aside on a plate.

In the same butter and over high heat, cook the washed mushrooms, cut into quarters if they are too large. Brown the mushrooms slightly and add them to the onions and pork fat.

In the same butter sauté the pieces of chicken; then sprinkle the chicken with flour, mix well and let brown, uncovered, in the oven.

After 5 minutes, remove from the oven, add the garlic, stir for 1 minute and pour over the wine. Heat to boiling point, stirring continuously. Add the bouquet garni, the onions, the lardoons and the mushrooms. Add bouillon or water to cover. Cover the pan, and cook 45 minutes in a 350°F (180°C, gas mark 4) oven.

Remove from the oven and strain the liquid from the chicken through a fine sieve.

If the sauce is too thin, boil to reduce rapidly to the proper consistency before straining. Clean the casserole.

After the liquid has been strained, return the chicken and the liquid to the casserole. Bring to the boil, correct the seasoning and thicken as directed below.

Cut the chicken liver into large cubes, season with a dash of salt and pepper, sear rapidly in 1 tablespoon of butter; place in a sieve and rub through with a pestle. Combine the liver purée with the chicken or pork blood and dilute with the cognac.

Remove the casserole with the chicken from the heat to stop the boiling. Pour a little very hot sauce into the bowl with the blood, stirring well with a whisk. Then add all the liver and blood mixture to the chicken pan, shaking it round to mix the sauce and the purée so that the sauce thickens without boiling; the heat of the saucepan will cook the blood and the liver.

Correct the seasoning again, and pour the chicken and sauce

into a shallow dish or serve in the cooking pot. The pot is better, for this delicious dish should be served piping hot.

The thickened sauce should be very smooth.

This dish can be served with bread croûtons, cut into heart shapes and fried, placed on top.

COCK COOKED IN FLEURIE
Coq au Fleurie

1·8-kg (4-lb) chicken or cockerel (see recipe)
1 bottle Fleurie
1 carrot
1 onion, sliced
Bouquet garni with extra thyme
2 garlic cloves, unpeeled
10 peppercorns, crushed
1 tablespoon lard
Cognac
1–2 tablespoons flour
20 small onions, lightly glazed
100 g (4 oz) pork fat, cut into lardoons, blanched and slightly browned
500 g (1 lb) small mushrooms, sautéed in butter
Croûtons browned in butter

Ideally you should use a grain-fed cockerel for this recipe and if you are in the country you should collect the cock's blood as it is killed. Before the blood coagulates, add $\frac{1}{2}$ glass of wine and 1 tablespoon of vinegar. Failing this you can use some pig's blood. If you have neither the dish can be made without.

Prepare the chicken in the usual way, cutting the bird into several pieces (legs and wings in four). Marinate the pieces of chicken in a bowl with the Fleurie. To flavour the marinade add a carrot, an onion, a bouquet garni, with some extra thyme, garlic and peppercorns. For the marinade to be effective, the bowl must be kept in a cool place for a minimum of 24 hours.

In a pan heat 1 tablespoon of lard. Season the pieces of cock with salt; sauté quickly in the hot fat. When the pieces are browned on all sides, moisten with a little cognac, ignite, then cover to put out the flame.

Sprinkle the chicken with flour. After mixing well, place in a 425°F (220°C, gas mark 7) oven for a few minutes. Add the carrot and onion, sautéed in butter, and the bouquet garni.

Moisten with the wine used for the marinade, bring to the boil, and stir well. Simmer, covered, on a very low flame.

Depending upon the age of the cock, cooking time will be 45 minutes to 1 hour.

When the cock is cooked, remove the pieces to another saucepan. Add to them the glazed onions, lardoons and mushrooms.

The sauce in the first pan is thickened with the cock's blood or pig's like a civet of hare (page 391). After correcting the seasoning, strain the sauce on to the cock.

Serve the cock with triangular croûtons browned in butter.

1 large frying
  chicken
50 g (2 oz) unsalted
  butter
50 g (2 oz) salt pork
  or bacon, cut into
  lardoons and boiled
  10 minutes
10 very small onions,
  blanched
20 potatoes, cut the
  size and shape of
  olives, blanched
Chopped parsley

CHICKEN IN A CASSEROLE WITH POTATOES
Poulet en cocotte à la bonne femme

Use a casserole big enough to hold the chicken, with its garnish round it, resting on the bottom of the pan to cook in the juice. Do not use a large quantity of vegetables.

Heat the butter in the casserole; add the chicken, seasoned, and cook it, covered, turning and basting often.

When the chicken is half cooked, surround it with the lardoons, onions and potatoes. Continue cooking in a 425°F (220°C, gas mark 7) oven to brown the vegetables lightly. Season, taking into account that salt pork has been used. Sprinkle with chopped parsley just before serving.

ROAST CHICKEN
Volailles rôties

Roasting in the oven and on a spit are two different ways of cooking, discussed previously in the general section on roasting.

The method is the same for all types of chicken but the cooking time varies depending on size and weight.

In the oven. Place the chicken, seasoned inside and out with a pinch of salt, on a roasting pan with a rack; baste it with melted butter. The chicken should be kept on its side as much as possible and basted often with the cooking butter, but not with the cooking juices which will remain at the bottom of the pan.

If the cooking has been done carefully and slowly, the juice and the butter that have collected in the pan should be enough gravy for the chicken. If not, add 1 or 2 tablespoons of hot water before finishing the cooking.

On a spit. The intensity of heat must be adjusted to the size of the chicken. Baste with the fat that collects in the drip pan.

The juices provide a gravy for the chicken.

Roast chickens are usually served with a bunch of watercress, and the cooking juice, not degreased, is served separately.

DEVILLED CHICKEN
Poulet de grain grillé à la diable

Prepare the chicken and truss it by slipping the feet and the drumsticks into incisions made in the skin on either side. Cut the connective tissue at the leg joints to make it lie flat when the heat touches it.

Split the chicken from neck to tail down the back, open it out and flatten it slightly; season with a pinch of salt. Place on a roasting pan, baste with melted butter and roast in a 350°F (180°C, gas mark 4) oven for 10 minutes.

Then brush with mustard slightly diluted with water; sprinkle with breadcrumbs, baste with melted butter and finish cooking under the grill.

Serve with watercress, matchstick, Pont-Neuf or other potatoes, and with a sauceboat of sauce diable (page 116).

DEVILLED CHICKEN WITH BACON, TOMATOES AND MUSHROOMS
Poulet de grain grillée à l'américaine

Follow the recipe for devilled chicken (above). Place the chicken on a large long platter; on top place 6 slices of grilled smoked bacon, 6 small tomatoes and 6 mushroom caps, both grilled. Serve with a sauceboat of sauce diable (page 116).

COLD CHICKEN
Les volailles froides

A roasted or poached chicken that is going to be served cold should not be kept in a refrigerator or at a temperature below about 50°F (10°C).

If cooked chicken is overchilled it becomes tough, tasteless and unappetizing.

I advise leaving the chicken to cool on a plate in a room other than the kitchen, if possible.

Serve the cold chicken like other cold meats, with some of the suggested garnishes and sauces.

CHICKEN MAYONNAISE
Mayonnaise de volaille

Shred one or more hearts of lettuce, depending on the number of guests; salt this julienne and sprinkle with a few drops of vinegar. Mix and pile into a glass or china bowl.

Over it place pieces of chicken, skin removed, and cut into thin slices. Spread with a generous coating of mayonnaise (page 128). Decorate with designs made with beetroot, tomatoes, capers, gherkins, pitted olives, quarters of hard-boiled eggs, anchovy fillets, marinated herrings. In the centre place an opened heart of lettuce.

When ready to serve, mix well to coat all the ingredients with the mayonnaise.

CHICKEN MOUSSE
Mousse de volaille

Follow the recipe for ham mousse (page 302). Use a light-coloured aspic, the colour of champagne.

POACHED CHICKEN IN ASPIC
Poularde pochée à la gelée

Place a large roaster in a deep saucepan just big enough to hold it. Cover the chicken with a white veal stock, rich in natural gelatine, well seasoned and clarified (see page 104).

Bring to the boil, remove the scum, cover and poach at a simmer.

Place a bouquet of fresh tarragon in a bowl deep enough to

hold the chicken completely immersed in the cooking stock as it cools. Then place the chicken in the bowl, and pour the boiling cooking liquid over the top.

When the chicken has cooled, carve it carefully. Arrange the pieces of chicken in a glass bowl, and strain the chicken stock, now lightly flavoured with tarragon, through cheesecloth over them.

If the poaching has been done correctly, the chicken stock should be clear and well flavoured but not stiff enough to un-mould the chicken. This is the right consistency exactly.

Keep refrigerated until ready to serve.

TURKEY WITH TRUFFLES
Dinde de Crémieu truffée

Here, for winter, is my paternal grandfather's recipe, as it has always been made in my family.

'Take a turkey of 1·8–2·7 kg (4–6 lb). Stuff it with 500 g (1 lb) of sausage meat and the same amount of sliced truffles. Slide some truffles slices under the skin before trussing the bird. Wrap your turkey in wax paper and enclose it in a potato sack. Dig a hole in your garden not too deep, and bury the turkey. The damp cold of the earth will allow the aroma of the truffles to come out fully. Two days later, prepare a court-bouillon with carrots, celery, onions, leeks, cloves, salt, pepper, a veal shin and an ox tail cut into pieces. Poach your turkey for 1½ hours. Serve with vegetables and a rice pilaf.'

༜═སྭཱ═སྭཱ═སྭཱ═སྭཱ═སྭཱ═སྭཱ═སྭཱ═སྭཱ═སྭཱ═སྭཱ═༜

TURKEY STUFFED WITH CHESTNUTS
Dinde farcie aux marrons

Small turkey, 2–2·5
  kg (4–5 lb) drawn
  weight
Salt and pepper
Thyme
Bay leaf
300 g (10 oz) lean
  pork
300 g (10 oz) fresh
  pork back fat
300 g (10 oz) pork
  flair fat or lard
½ tablespoon spiced
  salt (page xxiv)
2 shallots, peeled and
  chopped
1 tablespoon cognac
  or fine champagne
  brandy
750 g (1½ lb) chestnuts
1 celery stalk
Bouillon
2 large pieces fresh
  pork fat

Preparation. Remove the wing tips from the turkey. Singe the bird and pull out the pinfeathers. Draw the bird by first cutting through the skin of the neck down the back; loosen the skin and without disturbing it cut the neck off at the base. Work through this hole to clean the turkey. Detach and remove the wishbone, which blocks your finger from reaching inside the bird completely. Slide your finger inside to break all the membranes holding the organs – lungs, gizzard, heart and liver.

Remove the organs one by one, being careful not to break the gall bladder attached to the liver. Remove the intestines, if they were not removed when the bird was killed, as they generally are.

Remove the tendons of the drumsticks. The bird is now ready for stuffing.

Trim the giblets: remove the pocket of bile and the stringy membranes from the liver; cut the liver in 6 pieces, season with salt and pepper and a dash of thyme and bay leaf crushed to a powder; assemble the pieces on a plate. Cut the two meaty pieces from the gizzard and remove the gristle. Place with the heart and the lungs beside the liver. Add the neck.

Stuffing. Cut the lean pork into cubes; chop it very fine with the pork back fat (rind removed). Season this mixture with the spiced salt. Add the heart, the lungs and the two pieces of the gizzard all finely chopped.

Cut the flair fat into small pieces, removing any membranes or fibres. Mash with a pestle, and put this paste into a pan, heat it very slowly to soften the mass and then rub immediately through a very fine sieve.

In another pan melt 2 tablespoons of this strained pork fat. When it is smoking, add the pieces of liver; sear quickly and drain on a plate while still rare. As soon as the liver is cold, chop fine and place in a bowl.

In the same pan place 1 tablespoon of the strained pork fat and heat it; as soon as the fat is hot, brown the chopped shallots and add the finely chopped pork mixed with the turkey giblets. Stir continuously with a wooden spatula over a high flame for a few minutes – as long as necessary to half cook the stuffing.

Just before removing from the heat, add 1 tablespoon of cognac or brandy, ignite and cover immediately.

Set aside to cool.

When this stuffing is warm, pour into the bowl with the liver. Add the remaining strained pork fat and mix well with a spatula to blend the mixture. The best result can be obtained by using a pestle and mortar.

Place the mixture in a bowl and refrigerate.

Before using, test the seasoning by poaching $\frac{1}{2}$ tablespoon of stuffing in salted water. Correct, if necessary.

Chestnuts. Slash the skins of the chestnuts and plunge them for a few minutes into boiling oil or bake them in the oven. Remove the skins while the chestnuts are still hot; both layers will come off easily.

Place the peeled chestnuts in a deep saucepan with a celery stalk; add bouillon to cover. Cook, letting the bouillon boil slowly; stop the cooking when the chestnuts are still firm and whole.

Drain the chestnuts when they are warm; add them to the stuffing, and mix well, taking care not to break the chestnuts.

Stuffing and braising the turkey. First season the cavity with salt and pepper through the hole made in the neck; then insert the stuffing and the chestnuts. Fold over the neck skin. Truss the turkey with two strings: the first one passing through the wing tips and holding the neck skin in place; the second one crossing the turkey at the level of the thigh and drumstick joints (which are folded towards the wings) then crossed over the legs at the joints of the feet. Then bard the bird with the 2 pieces of pork fat.

Place the prepared turkey in a braising pan, laying it on its side; brush it with some pork fat specially set aside for the purpose, add the neck, sprinkle with a pinch of salt and cook slowly in a 325°F (170°C, gas mark 3) oven, covered.

Turn the bird often. Towards the end of the cooking remove the cover and then the pork fat so that the turkey takes on a beautiful golden colour.

Calculate the weight of the turkey plus the stuffing, and cook 20 minutes per pound.

Remove the trussing strings and serve with the cooking juice, slightly degreased.

Note: The ingredients for the stuffing are completely or nearly cooked before being put into the turkey. This means you cook the turkey without adding any time (or very little) to the total cooking time because of the stuffing. You can braise the turkey like an unstuffed bird, and stop the cooking at just the right moment to obtain perfectly tender meat.

If the turkey were stuffed with raw ingredients, the cooking time would have to be increased and the turkey would become dry – turkey flesh becomes very crumbly when it is overcooked and in any case the chestnuts would still be completely raw.

100 g (4 oz) belly of pork or bacon
50 g (2 oz) butter
12 small white onions
3 pigeons
500 g (1 lb) green peas, shelled
Small bouquet garni
Sugar

PIGEONS WITH GREEN PEAS
Pigeonneaux aux petits pois

[*Editor's note:* The French *pigeonneau* is smaller and more tender than the English woodpigeon. It is important to keep this in mind when following these recipes.]

General rules. Draw the pigeon, but never remove the liver which does not have a gall bladder. Truss the birds by folding the legs and sliding the ends of the drumsticks through incisions made in the sides of the breast. Tie with a string, crossing the pigeon first at the wings and then around the legs.

Method. Remove the rind from the pork fat, cut into small dice, place in cold water and boil 5 minutes to blanch. Drain, wipe dry, and brown in a pan with 15 g ($\frac{1}{2}$ oz) of butter.

Drain the fat cubes with a skimmer and set aside on a plate.

In the same butter brown the onions until golden. Drain the onions with a skimmer and add to the pork fat.

Replace the onions with the pigeons and brown them on all sides, covered, for 12 minutes or longer according to age and size. Remove and keep warm between two plates.

Return the onions to the same pan, add the pork fat and the fresh green peas, the bouquet garni and a pinch of sugar. Add 2 tablespoons of water and cook, covered, on a high flame.

As soon as the peas are nearly cooked, which will take 15–20 minutes if they are fresh, add the pigeons and heat them. Do not let the birds boil.

Place the pigeons on a shallow round platter; remove the bouquet garni, and away from the heat add the remaining butter to the peas; mix well, taste and pour the garnish over the pigeons. Serve immediately.

Note: The juice from the cooking should be reduced to a syrupy glaze, but there should be enough of it to coat the peas after the extra butter is added.

---

1 medium carrot
   (core removed),
   diced finely
1 medium onion,
   diced finely
2 shallots, diced finely
100 g (4 oz) unsalted
   butter
Salt
Pepper
Pinch grated nutmeg
125 g (5 oz)
   mushrooms
1 glass good red wine
3 young pigeons
1 tablespoon cognac
Croûtons

SALMIS OF PIGEON
Pigeonnaux en salmis

Stew the carrot, the onion and the shallots in a pan with 25 g (1 oz) of butter; season with salt, pepper and nutmeg. When the vegetables are cooked, add the mushroom stems, cleaned, washed and chopped fine. Moisten with the red wine, and cook slowly until the wine is reduced by half.

Roast the pigeons in 25 g (1 oz) of butter in a 450°F (230°C, gas mark 8) oven for 12–15 minutes or longer, depending upon their weight and age. They should be rare. Remove to a plate; in the same pan sauté the mushroom caps, whole if they are small, in quarters if they are medium or large, for 2 minutes. Season with a pinch of salt.

Cut the pigeons into 5 pieces: the 2 legs, the 2 wings and the breast. Remove the skin, and replace the pieces of pigeon in the pan in which the mushroom caps have just been browned.

Remove the livers from the carcasses and put on a plate; with a fork mash them with 50 g (2 oz) of butter.

Chop the carcasses into large pieces, with the necks and the gizzards; place them in a duck press to extract all the blood and collect it in a bowl.

To complete the dish, mix the blood with the chopped vegetables cooked in wine; heat nearly to the boiling point. Stir with a whisk, but do not let boil.

Baste the pieces of pigeon with the cognac, ignite and smother the flames right away.

Strain the vegetable, wine and blood mixture through a fine sieve, rubbing the vegetables through, over the pigeon.

Heat together, stirring, without letting the sauce boil. The thickening will occur through the coagulation of the blood as it is heated.

Away from the heat add the livers mixed with the butter. Spice with freshly ground pepper.

Place the pigeons on a very hot platter and surround with bread croûtons cut into heart shapes and fried in butter.

4 pigeons
Salt and pepper
100 g (4 oz) unsalted butter
2 tablespoons fine champagne brandy
1 cup white chicken stock (page 104)
50 g (2 oz) purée of *foie gras*
50 g (2 oz) fresh *foie gras* finely diced
19 g (¾ oz) truffles, cut into julienne
4 bread croûtons (see page 91)

ROAST PIGEON WITH FOIE GRAS AND TRUFFLES
Pigeon en bécasse à l'assiette
For 4 people

After cleaning the pigeons season them; roast in 100 g (4 oz) of butter in a covered pan in a 425°F (220°C, gas mark 7) oven for 12–15 minutes, or longer depending on size and age.

When the pigeons are cooked, remove them and keep warm.

Deglaze the pan with the brandy. Moisten with the white stock. Boil for a few minutes without reducing very much. Thicken the sauce by beating in the purée of *foie gras*, the diced *foie gras* and the truffles.

On each plate place a large croûton browned in butter. On top place a pigeon cut in half.

Pour over the sauce and serve immediately.

DUCKS AND DUCKLINGS
Canards et canetons

In France the two main breeds of domestic duck are the Nantes duck (*nantais*), the smaller of the two, weighing up to 1·8 kg (4 lb), and the Rouen duck (*rouennais*) which may weigh 2·2–2·7 kg (5–6 lb). A true *caneton* or duckling is under 6 months old and usually weighs about 1·8–2·2 kg (4–5 lb) drawn weight.

There are also many varieties of wild duck which are decorative as well as delicious, but these are dealt with in the game chapter.

ROUEN DUCK
Canard rouennais

The Rouen duck is the largest of French ducks. In France it is killed in a unique way. The breeder smothers the bird, which allows the blood to remain spread throughout the meat; this gives the duck its brown colour and special taste. However, this method has the drawback of hastening the spoilage of the meat during warm weather. It is, therefore, important to be sure that the duck is very fresh, if it is going to appear on a summer menu. One can become quite ill from eating duck meat that has gone bad.

There are two ways to cook a *rouennais* duck. The classic recipe produces a superb but simple salmis, the best that one can imagine. However I really prefer another recipe which is a speciality of Normandy. I have called it 'Rouen duck from the Hôtel de la Couronne' in honour of the famous restaurant run by the brothers Dorin.

PRESSSED ROUEN DUCK
Le canard rouennaise de l'Hôtel de la Couronne

1 duck, 1·5 kg (3 lb) drawn weight
Salt and pepper
Duck's liver and 3 additional livers, cut into large dice, seasoned
50 g (2 oz) fresh pork fat
2 shallots, finely chopped
1 tablespoon calvados or cognac
50 g (2 oz) fresh breadcrumbs soaked in milk and squeezed
Spiced salt (page xxiv)
2 tablespoons cognac

Rouennaise sauce:
½ teaspoon finely chopped shallots
Dash powdered bay leaf and thyme
1 glass good red wine
6 tablespoons demi-glace sauce (page 108)
50 g (2 oz) unsalted butter

Draw the duck through the neck and set aside the liver. Season the inside with salt and pepper.

Besides the duck liver, prepare 3 additional livers (chicken livers can be used). Cut into large dice, season and mix well. Set aside on a plate.

Grate the pork fat. Melt 1 tablespoon of the fat in a pan and stew the shallots in it. When the shallots are cooked, add the 3 additional livers; reserve the duck's liver for later. Sear the livers on a high flame, keeping them rare. Moisten with calvados or cognac; ignite, and smother the flame at once.

Pour the contents of the pan into a sieve and rub the livers through it into a bowl. Mix the purée with the remaining grated pork fat and the breadcrumbs soaked in milk and squeezed.

Correct the seasoning.

Season with the spiced salt, and put the stuffing in the duck. Fold the bird's legs and truss.

Roast the duck in 450°F (230°C, gas mark 8) oven or on a spit over a hot fire for 18–28 minutes. The duck should be rare.

Carve immediately, first removing the legs, which will be very rare. Place them under the grill, cut sides towards the grill, to finish the cooking, and continue to carve. Remove the wings and then slice the breast. Place the slices on a hot round platter in the shape of a fan.

Open the carcass, remove the stuffing and pile it at the base of the fan, crossing the legs when done at the edge of the stuffing. Cover the platter with another plate or a glass bell to keep warm.

Quickly chop the carcass and place it in a duck press to extract the juices; add 2 tablespoons of cognac to the juice collected in a bowl. Coat the breast slices with the following sauce.

Rouennaise sauce

Cook the shallots in a little butter. Add the bay leaf and thyme. Moisten with good red wine and cook, reducing by two-thirds. Mix this reduced sauce with demi-glace sauce, and boil for 5 minutes. Rub the reserved duck liver through a sieve and add it to the sauce away from the heat. Add the bloody juices gathered from the duck press. Heat slowly, without letting the sauce boil.

Strain through a very fine sieve and complete the sauce by adding the butter.

Correct the seasoning and coat the duck slices and the stuffing generously with the sauce.

DUCK BREASTS
Steaks de canard
For 2 people

2 duck breasts
Salt and pepper
125 g (5 oz) butter
1 tablespoon chopped shallots
1 tablespoon old armagnac brandy
1 glass red Burgundy

Trim the two duck breasts. Season with salt and pepper.

In a pan, sear the duck breasts in 25 g (1 oz) of butter; brown them on both sides without cooking too much, because duck must remain pink, almost bloody.

When the breasts are cooked, place them on a serving platter and slice.

In the pan stew the shallots; deglaze the juices with the armagnac and Burgundy.

Boil to reduce the sauce by half, and thicken with the remaining butter.

Correct the seasoning.

To serve, coat the duck steaks with the delicious sauce and garnish with small glazed onions and turnips, mushrooms sautéed in butter and fresh leaf spinach.

Duck livers
Salt and pepper
Port
Cognac
Duck stock
Cornflour
Gelatine
Duck slices

Cooking liquid:
½ veal stock, ½ red
   Bordeaux

JELLIED DUCK BREASTS WITH DUCK LIVER
Canard Claude Jolly, création Michel Guérard

Foie gras *with pepper.*   Remove the membranes from the duck livers.

Marinate the livers for 2 days with salt, pepper, port and cognac.

Tie them in a dish cloth and cook in a duck stock with some port wine for about 10 minutes, depending on their size, and let cool.

Reduce the stock in which the duck livers have cooked; thicken it slightly (for 2 l (2 quarts) of reduced stock, use 1 tablespoon of cornflour and 8 leaves of gelatine). Chill.

Let the gelatine stiffen until you can coat the livers with a first layer of jelly. Sprinkle coarsely ground pepper over the first layer. Finish the glaze with more jelly.

Duck slices.   Cook ducks (killed so their blood remains in the meat) in a broth of ½ veal stock, ½ red Bordeaux for about 30 minutes. Remove the slices of breast and cool.

Glaze the slices with the same jellied stock used for the livers.

Serve slices of duck with a slice of duck liver coated with jelly for each helping.

[*Editor's note:* This recipe was cooked for the President of the French Republic, Valéry Giscard d'Estaing, on 25 February 1975.

SALMIS OF ROUEN DUCKLING
Caneton rouennais en salmis

Roast the duckling in a 450°F (230°C, gas mark 8) oven for 16–18 minutes maximum.

After taking the bird from the oven, let it stand for 5 minutes.

Thickly butter a long fireproof dish. Then sprinkle with 1 teaspoon of chopped shallots, a dash of nutmeg and a couple of turns of the pepper mill.

Heat the platter to brown the shallots very lightly.

Carve the duck. First the legs, place them under the grill, the cut side to the flame; then carve the wings and slice the breast. Place the duck slices flat on the heated dish.

Chop the carcass, crush it in a duck press and collect the juice in a bowl; pour 3 or 4 tablespoons of good red wine over the carcass during the pressing. To the blood and wine add the raw duck liver, which has been puréed by rubbing it through a very fine sieve.

Sprinkle the slices of duck with some pieces of butter, baste them with a liquor glass of cognac, ignite and smother the flames immediately. Coat the duck with the bloody juice from the press mixed with the puréed liver. Heat in the dish, shaking to mix and, without letting the sauce boil, place for a second in a 450°F (230°C, gas mark 8) oven. Serve, adding the legs to the dish.

Note: The sauce thickens because of the coagulation of the blood in the juice and in the puréed liver. The difficult part of this dish is to heat the juice very slowly, without allowing it to boil, until it has the consistency of a thick smooth sauce.

NANTES DUCKLING
Caneton nantais

The preparation of a duckling is always the same, regardless of the recipe or the garnish. Unless it is boned and stuffed, in which case it is generally poached, it should be roasted or braised. Avoid any method that would cause the bird to boil in liquid as this would dry the tender part – the breast.

DUCKLING WITH TURNIPS
Caneton aux navets

1 duckling

50 g (2 oz) unsalted butter

15 small onions, peeled and boiled for 5 minutes

1 tablespoon chicken fat

500 g (1 lb) turnips, cut and trimmed to look like small eggs

1 teaspoon sugar

1 level tablespoon flour

$\frac{1}{2}$ glass dry white wine

Veal stock, lightly salted bouillon, or water

Salt and pepper

1 garlic clove, finely chopped

Tiny bouquet garni (parsley, sprig thyme and $\frac{1}{4}$ bay leaf)

Chopped parsley

To prepare a duckling, singe and draw, and season it inside with salt and pepper, trussing it around the legs and barding it.

Brown the duckling slowly on all sides in a pan with 25 g (1 oz) of butter. When it is golden brown, cover and continue cooking for 25 minutes.

It is important to stop the cooking when the juice, drained from inside the duck on to a plate, is a clear pink colour.

For the duck to be tender and juicy, the meat should be somewhat undercooked. Slightly pink beads should form on the meat as the duck is carved.

If the breast slices are a dark colour, the meat will be hard and dry.

Careful cooking to just the right point is essential for the success of this delicious but tricky dish.

While the duck is cooking, prepare the garnish.

In a pan heat 25 g (1 oz) of butter and brown the onions. Drain them and set aside on a plate.

Add 1 tablespoon of chicken fat to the butter, and sauté the turnips. Season with a pinch of salt. When the turnips are lightly browned, sprinkle with the sugar, which will darken the turnips to a deep gold when it caramelizes. (If the turnips are old, boil them well before browning them.)

Sprinkle the turnips with the flour. Brown for 2 minutes, then moisten with white wine; boil to reduce by two-thirds. Then cover the turnips with veal stock, lightly salted bouillon or water. Season with salt and pepper; add the onions, garlic and the bouquet garni. Simmer until completely cooked.

When the duck is cooked, place it on a hot shallow platter. Remove the bouquet garni, and put the turnips and onions into the pan used to braise the duck.

The garnish should have cooked down into a rich, light mixture that, combined with the dripping from the duck, will make enough sauce to serve with the duck and the turnips.

Shake everything together to deglaze the bottom of the duck pan, correct the seasoning and place the vegetables on either side of the duck; pour the remaining sauce over the duck.

Sprinkle chopped parsley on the turnips.

DUCKLING WITH OLIVES
Caneton aux olives

Prepare and braise the duckling as in the recipe above. When it is cooked, put it on a platter. Pit and boil 100 g (4 oz) of green olives for 2 minutes to remove the brine taste; drain and wipe dry. Simmer in the braising juice (there will be enough if the recipe has been followed carefully; if it has reduced too much, add 1 or 2 tablespoons of veal stock, bouillon or water). Away from the heat stir 25 g (1 oz) of unsalted butter into the braising juice and the olives. Pour over the duck.

---

1 braised duckling
500 g (1 lb) fresh
  green peas *à la
  française* (page 488)
100 g (4 oz) fresh
  pork belly (rind
  removed), diced
  finely, blanched
  and browned
25 g (1 oz) unsalted
  butter
Seasoning

DUCKLING WITH GREEN PEAS
Canetons aux petits pois

Braise the duckling following the recipe for duckling with turnips (above). Place the duckling on a platter. Into the braising juice put the green peas and pork fat.

Simmer the peas in the braising juice for 5 minutes. Away from the heat stir in the butter, correct the seasoning and pour the peas and juices over the duck.

Note: Peas prepared by this method should not be too liquid; they should be lightly thickened and have a syrupy coating made smooth by the addition of butter.

---

1 duckling
Salt and pepper
75 g (3 oz) unsalted
  butter
3 oranges
2 cubes sugar
2 teaspoons vinegar
Juice of $\frac{1}{4}$ lemon
1–2 tablespoons veal
  stock
Pinch tapioca

BRAISED DUCKLING WITH ORANGE
Caneton poêlé à l'orange dit 'à la bigarade'

Season the cavity of a duckling with salt and pepper. Add a knob of butter; braise the duck very slowly in butter, following the recipe above. Cook the bird slightly rare, so it will be just pink after it has stood for 10–15 minutes.

While the duckling is cooking, remove the rind of an orange very thinly, leaving the bitter white part of the skin. Cut the rind into fine julienne and boil 5 minutes; drain and wipe dry. Set aside on a plate. Peel 2 oranges, detach the sections and remove the pips; place the sections in scallops around the edge of the platter on which the duck will be placed.

Rub the rind of one orange with the cubes of sugar. Then cook the sugar in a small saucepan until it is a light caramel colour; add 2 teaspoons of vinegar; reduce almost completely, to a thick syrup.

Squeeze the orange into a bowl and combine with the lemon juice. Strain it through cheesecloth.

When the duckling is cooked, place it in the centre of the orange sections. To the braising juice add 1 or 2 tablespoons of veal stock; strain the juices into the caramelized sugar through cheesecloth placed over the saucepan. Add a pinch of tapioca and boil for a few minutes to cook the tapioca completely; this will give the sauce its slightly syrupy consistency. Then away from the heat add the orange rind and the orange and lemon juices; thicken with the remaining butter. Correct the seasoning and coat the duck with sauce. In a sauceboat, serve the remaining sauce.

Note: Do not reduce the braising juice too much; if necessary, correct by adding veal stock.

GUINEA FOWL
Pintades et pintadeaux

January and February are the best months for guinea fowl.

The young guinea fowl (*pintadeau*), roasted, braised or casseroled, should have pink flesh when done. Its meat, once cooked, cannot wait. Cook just in time to serve.

The older bird (*pintade*) should be braised with cabbage. It would be dry if roasted; braised, it is delicious (see the recipe for partridge *en chartreuse*, page 411).

GOOSE
Oie

Goose is generally cooked in the same way as a turkey or a duck. The preceding recipes can be used.

If the goose is no longer young, make a stew. Cooked with turnips, chestnuts, onions, horseradish, rice, potatoes, kohlrabi or swede, it makes a delicious dish.

GOSLING WITH APPLE STUFFING
Oison farci à la fermière

1 gosling, 1·5 kg (3 lb) drawn weight
2 slices white bread, crusts removed
Milk
2 shallots, finely chopped
1 medium-sized onion, finely chopped
25 g (1 oz) unsalted butter
Gosling's liver
2 chicken livers
Salt and pepper
1 tablespoon cognac
50 g (2 oz) fresh pork fat, grated
½ teaspoon chopped parsley
2 sage leaves, chopped
1 egg
Dash grated nutmeg
3–4 tart green apples, peeled, quartered, seeded and chopped
2 tablespoons veal stock or water

Draw the gosling through the neck, following the instructions for a small turkey (page 364) and make the following stuffing.

Soak 2 slices of white bread, crusts removed, in milk.

Meanwhile slowly cook the shallots and an onion in butter in a pan. When cooked but not browned, add the gosling's liver and the chicken livers. Heat quickly for 3 seconds to sear; season with salt and pepper. Moisten with cognac, ignite and smother immediately with the lid.

Pour the contents of the pan into a strainer and rub the livers, shallots and onions through on to a plate; set the purée aside.

Squeeze the bread which has been soaking, and add it to the liver purée.

Place the purée in a bowl; add the pork fat, parsley, sage, egg, nutmeg, salt and pepper. Mix well with a wooden spatula.

Sauté the apples in the remaining butter until they are half cooked. Add to the purée in the bowl.

When the mixture is smooth and the seasoning right, season the gosling inside and stuff it. Truss and bard the bird. Place in a roasting pan.

Season the gosling with salt, and baste generously with melted butter. Cook in a 350°F (180°C, gas mark 4) oven for 50 minutes, basting frequently with the cooking butter.

To serve, add 2 tablespoons of veal stock, preferably, or water to the cooking butter. Boil for 2 minutes to deglaze the pan, and serve the juices without degreasing.

1 plump goose, less
than 1 year old
60 chestnuts
$\frac{1}{4}$ l ($\frac{1}{2}$ pt) consommé
2 celery stalks
50 g (2 oz) butter
200 g (7 oz) fresh
pork flair fat
225 g (8 oz) lean pork
Salt and pepper
12 chipolatas or other
small sausages
6 small pigs' trotters,
truffled
200 g (7 oz) small firm
white mushrooms
2 medium onions,
peeled and chopped
2 shallots, peeled and
finely chopped
1 tablespoon cognac
1 egg, beaten
1 tablespoon spiced
salt (page xxiv)
$\frac{1}{2}$ teaspoon fresh
chopped parsley
Pork fat for barding

CHRISTMAS EVE GOOSE
L'oie du réveillon

Preparation.   Singe the goose, clean, draw through the neck and reserve the liver after removing the gall bladder. Collect the excess fat, including the fat that surrounds the intestines.

Chestnuts.   Bake the chestnuts in the oven or plunge them in very hot oil; peel.

Divide the chestnuts in two. Take those that are less good and cook them, covered, in a court-bouillon made with consommé and 1 celery stalk. Place the best chestnuts in a pan big enough to hold them all comfortably.

Sprinkle these chestnuts with the white part of a celery stalk, finely chopped, and moisten with consommé just to cover. On top sprinkle 50 g (2 oz) of butter, cut into small pieces.

When the first batch of chestnuts are cooked but still firm, drain them. Uncover the second batch a few minutes before they are fully cooked, and boil to reduce the consommé until the liquid mixed with the butter and the natural sugar released by the chestnuts becomes a thick syrup. This step must be done carefully so that the chestnuts do not crumble.

Start cooking the best chestnuts 35 minutes before serving; those in the first batch should be cooked when the recipe is begun, for they will be used for stuffing the goose.

Stuffing.   Cut the pork fat into small pieces and remove all the membranes. Pound it in a mortar and place it on a plate in a warm place to soften. Then rub through a fine sieve. Set aside.

Chop the lean pork finely and set aside.

Cut the goose liver into large dice. Set aside.

In a pan melt 2 tablespoons of goose fat. When the fat is smoking, quickly sear the goose liver. Season with salt and pepper. Keep the liver rare; drain. Place on a plate.

In the same fat, on a high flame brown the following, one at a time and place on the plate:

1. The sausages, which have first been cooked for 2 seconds in nearly boiling water to firm the skin;
2. The truffled pigs' feet;
3. The mushrooms, cleaned, quickly washed and seasoned with a pinch of salt;
4. The chopped onions and shallots; cook slowly.

Add 3 tablespoons of goose fat to the pan; and, when it is hot, add the lean pork to the shallots and onions, and stir for 5 minutes with a spatula over a high flame. Pour in the cognac, ignite and smother immediately with the lid. Remove from the heat.

Pound the goose liver in a mortar; when it becomes a paste, first add the pork fat and mix well, then the lean pork with the shallots and onions. Finish with 2 tablespoons of raw goose fat, the beaten egg, the spiced salt and the chopped parsley. Correct the seasoning of the stuffing by poaching a teaspoon of it and tasting.

Place the stuffing in a bowl and carefully mix into it the mushrooms and the less perfect chestnuts. Stuff the goose, alternating layers of stuffing with layers of sausage and the truffled pigs' feet. Truss and bard the bird.

Braising. In a braising pan, brown the goose very slowly in melted butter or goose fat. Cover the pan and braise, basting often, for $1\frac{1}{4}$ hours. Then remove the bard and the truss and return to the oven for the final 10–15 minutes of cooking. Because the goose is cooked slowly, there should be plenty of juice. If it is too reduced, add a couple of tablespoons of water.

Presentation. Place the goose on a long platter and surround it with the best chestnuts.

Pour a little of the cooking juice over the goose and serve the remaining juice, degreased, in a sauceboat.

---

1 fat goose
Large handful spiced salt made with:
1 kg (2 lb) sea salt, finely crushed
1 teaspoon saltpetre
500 g (1 lb) sugar
4 cloves
1 bay leaf
Sprig thyme crushed to powder
Melted fat (1 part goose fat and 1 part pork fat, clarified and strained)

PRESERVED AND POTTED GOOSE
Confit d'oie et rillettes d'oie

Confit d'oie is easy to prepare and an excellent food that can be stored a long time. It is part of French regional cooking, a speciality of Languedoc, Gascony and the Béarn.

Bleed a fat goose, pluck, singe, then completely cool it. Slit the goose down the back, from neck to tail. Draw it carefully to avoid damaging the liver, which can be used in cooking other dishes. Remove the fat that surrounds the gizzard and the intestines.

Cut the goose into four pieces: the two breast pieces with the wings attached and the two legs. Leave the carcass bones attached to each quarter.

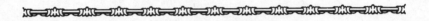

GAME

Every September in France the opening of the hunting season brings an abundance of game providing the ingredients for a variety of rich and splendid dishes.

In English the meat of *cerf* (red deer), *daim* (fallow deer) and *chevreuil* (roebuck) is known generally as venison, and recipes for the three are interchangeable, though *chevreuil* is thought to have the most delicate meat. The prime cuts are, in order of quality, the haunch, saddle and chops. The shoulder can be boned, rolled and roasted, but is more often cooked in a civet or stew with the neck.

Hare (*lièvre*) is at its best at 7–8 months old, weighing about 3 kg (6½ lb). Hares weighing 4 kg (9 lb) or even more have tough, stringy meat and are best used in pâtés and terrines.

Ordinary rabbit is not comparable to hare, but young wild rabbit (*lapereau de garenne*), which has ear cartilage which tears easily, is delicious sautéed. Older animals are more suitable for terrines.

Game birds are also best eaten young. A young pheasant (*faisan*) has a flexible beak and underdeveloped spurs, or none at all. The smaller hazel grouse (*gélinotte*) is a delicate bird. Partridge (*perdrix grise* or grey partridge is the principal species in France) is delicious when less than a year old, and is at its most succulent in October at the start of the season. In the young bird the feet are grey, the ends of the large wing feathers are pointed, and the lower beak is flexible and bends if you hold the bird up by it, between thumb and forefinger. A plump young quail (*caille*) is a great delicacy. Woodcock (*bécasse*) is one of the finest game birds. It is not drawn but the gizzard is removed. *Bécassine* (snipe) and *bécasseau* (wheat ear or white tail) belong to the same family. Woodcock makes a particularly fine salmis.

In France a number of small song birds appear on menus – larks, thrushes, ortolans – but these are unobtainable in England and many of the species are in fact protected.

The duck family has 42 varieties, so there is a wide choice of water fowl. Recommended varieties for culinary purposes are the ordinary wild duck or mallard (*canard sauvage*), the ancestor of all domestic species; *pilet* (pintail); *souchet* (shoveller duck or spoonbill), a delicate bird slightly smaller than the previous two; *garrot* (arctic duck) from Normandy, Picardy and Les Landes.

Other game birds include teal (*sarcelle*, which looks like a duck but is not one) which feeds on watercress, wild chervil and grain and has extremely delicate meat; snipe (*bécassine*) which in autumn is as plump as a quail and a gourmet's dream; and the smaller *bécasseau* (white tail or wheat ear). Two further highly regarded French delicacies are the golden or grey plover (*pluvier*) which appears beside French rivers with the autumn rains; and finally the lapwing or *vanneau*, the subject of a French saying: '*N'a pas mangé un bon morceau qui n'a mangé ni bécasse ni vanneau*' ('He who has not eaten woodcock or lapwing has missed a choice morsel').

ROAST LEG OR HAUNCH OF VENISON WITH CHESTNUT PURÉE

Gigot, cuissot ou gigue de chevreuil rôti à la purée de marrons

2 kg (4 lb) leg or haunch of venison
125 g (5 oz) fresh pork fat
Poivrade sauce (page 118)
Chestnut purée (page 479)

Marinade:
Pinch crushed sea salt
3 shallots, thinly sliced
1 large onion, thinly sliced
1 carrot, thinly sliced
Sprigs parsley
Sprig thyme
½ bay leaf
Pinch crushed peppercorns
3 dl (½ pt) white wine
4 tablespoons vinegar
4 tablespoons olive oil

Skin the leg, leaving on the foot with its skin. Protect the foot by wrapping it in wax paper before putting the meat into the oven.

Bone the butt end, remove all the tendons from the leg, and lard the meat with the pork fat in narrow rows pointing towards the foot.

Marinate the meat for 24 hours or more as follows.

Place the leg flat in a deep plate. Sprinkle on top the sea salt, shallots, onion, a carrot, parsley, thyme, bay leaf, pepper, white wine, vinegar and olive oil. Turn the leg from time to time. As the meat is very tender, avoid making the marinade too acid.

When the time comes to cook the leg drain and dry it carefully. Place on the rack of a roasting pan and baste with melted butter. Place in a 450°F (230°C, gas mark 8) oven to sear rapidly. To prevent the pan juices from burning, place between the oven shelf and the roasting pan a metal triangle 3·5 cm (1–1½ inches) thick or something similar. Baste often with the fatty part of the pan juices.

Cooking time will be about 40 minutes, or 9–10 minutes per pound, in an oven; on a spit allow 11–12 minutes per pound.

The leg should be rare; let stand for 10 minutes to obtain a nice pink colour.

Serve the leg on a long platter with a sauceboat of poivrade sauce (page 118) to which the pan juices have been added and a bowl of chestnut purée (page 479). Carve as you would a leg of lamb.

SADDLE OF VENISON WITH KIDNEY BEANS
Selle de chevereuil Saint-Hubert

Proceed as for the leg: remove all the tendons from the fillets and lard them in three rows, pointing the lardoons towards the spine; place in a marinade. Roast following the recipe above, but replace the butter with olive oil.

Serve with a sauceboat of poivrade sauce to which are added a few raisins and sliced almonds, cut lengthwise and toasted. Accompany with a bowl of boiled red kidney beans.

VENISON CHOPS WITH LENTILS
Côtelettes de chevreuil aux lentilles

Cut the ribs into chops at least 3·5 cm (1½ inches) thick. Trim, flatten slightly and sprinkle with salt and freshly ground pepper.

In a pan heat 3 tablespoons of oil, and when it is smoking, arrange the chops in one layer. Cook as quickly as possible, turning just once and keeping the meat pink inside.

Place the chops on a large platter in a circle, alternating with heart-shaped croûtons fried in butter, the same size as the chops.

Pour poivrade sauce (page 118) over the chops and with them serve a purée of lentils.

Note: After cooking the chops, drain the oil and with 1 tablespoon of sauce deglaze the pan juices sticking to the bottom; then add this liquid to the sauce.

VENISON CHOPS WITH CREAM
Côtelettes de chevreuil à la crème

6 venison chops
  sauteéd in butter
Pinch paprika
Croûtons
¼ glass Madeira
3 dl (½ pt) double
  cream
25 g (1 oz) unsalted
  butter
1 teaspoon lemon
  juice
Chestnut purée (page
  479)

Prepare the chops as above, adding a pinch of paprika to the salt and pepper.

Sauté the chops quickly over high heat in butter.

Place on a platter with croûtons, as for the chops with lentils.

Pour the Madeira into the cooking juices. Reduce to 2 tablespoons; add the cream. Boil for a few minutes; after thinning, the cream will reduce and thicken.

Away from the heat add the butter to the sauce, stirring with a wooden spoon. Finish the sauce with lemon juice. Correct the seasoning, strain through a fine sieve and serve with chestnut purée.

VENISON CHOPS WITH CELERIAC PURÉE
Côtelettes de chevreuil à la purée de céleri-rave

6 venison chops
Marinade
Oil and butter
Croûtons fried in
  butter
3 dl (½ pt) veal stock
Pinch tapioca
25 g (1 oz) unsalted
  butter
Seasoning
Celeriac purée (page
  444)

Cut the venison ribs into chops after marinating for 12 hours as indicated for the leg of venison, above.

Sauté quickly in half oil, half butter, smoking hot.

Keep the meat pink. Put on a round platter, placing between the chops heart-shaped croûtons, fried in butter.

Drain the oil from the pan; then pour in 4 tablespoons of the marinade. Boil to reduce by half. Add the veal stock and a pinch of tapioca; cook for 10 minutes, reducing again by half. Away from the heat add the butter, correct the seasoning, and strain through a fine sieve over the chops.

Serve with celeriac purée.

Note: The tapioca can be replaced by ½ teaspoon of cornflour diluted with a little cold bouillon, or by 1 tablespoon of butter mixed with ½ teaspoon of flour.

SMALL VENISON STEAKS WITH POTATO CROQUETTES
Noisettes de chevreuil à la Berny

Take 2 fillets from a saddle of roebuck, remove any gristle and place the fillets in a marinade for 12 hours, as for the leg of venison, above.

Then drain the fillets, dry carefully and cut into slices about 4·5–5 cm (1¾–2 inches) thick.

Sauté in smoking oil and place each slice on a croûton, fried in butter, about 2 cm (¾ inch) thick and the same size as the meat.

In the centre of the platter, place a mound of croquettes *à la Berny*, recipe below.

Serve with a sauceboat of poivrade sauce to which are added a handful of skinned almonds, sliced very thin and toasted, or a sauceboat of redcurrant jelly.

Potato Croquettes à la Berny

To 1 kg (2 lb) of duchess potatoes (page 497), add 100 g (4 oz) of chopped truffles and 50 g (2 oz) of almonds – skinned, chopped and toasted.

Divide the mixture into balls the size of an egg, about 50 g (2 oz) each, roll in beaten egg, then in fresh breadcrumbs.

Eight minutes before serving, while the chops are cooking, plunge the potato balls into very hot oil.

When golden brown and crisp, drain on paper towels, and sprinkle lightly with a pinch of salt.

Note: All these cuts of venison can also be served with a purée of Jerusalem artichokes or with apple sauce, unsweetened or lightly sweetened.

VENISON STEW
Civet de chevreuil, cerf ou daim

Cut the meat into 50 g (2 oz) pieces, using the shoulder, neck and upper part of the ribs. Place in a marinade for 24 hours; drain and wipe dry, then cook like a civet of hare (page 391).

WILD BOAR OR YOUNG WILD BOAR
Sanglier ou marcassin

Wild boar can be cooked according to the various recipes for venison, increasing the marinade time if the animal is not really young.

HARE
Lièvre

Hare can be cooked still warm, as soon as it is shot. If it gets cold, it should be hung for 2 or 3 days in its skin. Hanging it does not mean leaving it until it is rotten. Rigorously avoid meat that has been hung until unpleasantly high.

Whenever you can, choose a young hare, about 1 year old, with glossy fur, small paws and barely developed claws.

HARE ON A SPIT
Lièvre à la broche

After the hare has been barded whole, it can be cooked on a spit. Put a young hare on a spit without marinating it. Sprinkle with salt and pepper. Spice the inside with sprigs of thyme. Brush the hare generously with Dijon mustard. Roast in front of a good wood fire for 35 minutes. During the cooking put 1 tablespoon of chopped shallots in the drip pan; before the shallots brown, deglaze with a few drops of wine vinegar; add 3 dl ($\frac{1}{2}$ pt) cream. Boil to reduce.

Serve the hare with the sauce separately and a bowl of rice pilaf (page 514).

HARE STEW
Civet de lievre

1 young hare, less than 1 year old
Salt and pepper
Pinch of thyme and crushed bay leaf
2 large onions
2 tablespoons olive oil
1 tablespoon Armagnac
50 g (2 oz) butter
100 g (4 oz) fresh pork fat
24 small onions
100 g (4 oz) very firm white mushrooms
2 medium-sized carrots
2 tablespoons flour
2 garlic cloves, crushed
1 l (2 pts) good red Burgundy wine
Bouquet garni
½ glass cognac
4 tablespoons double cream
12 heart-shaped croûtons fried in butter
Chopped parsley

Skin the hare, draw and carefully collect the blood accumulated around the lungs and the throat in a bowl.

Set aside the liver, with the gall bladder removed.

Cut the hare into pieces, place them on a plate and season with salt and freshly ground pepper, a pinch of thyme and crushed bay leaf; add 1 onion, sliced, the olive oil and the Armagnac.

Mix well, and marinate for 3 hours; turn the hare from time to time.

Heat the butter in a heavy-bottomed pan big enough to hold the stew. Cut the pork fat into large lardoons, soak them in 2 cups of cold water, then boil for 5 minutes, drain and wipe dry. When the butter is hot, put the lardoons into the pan.

When they are half browned, add the small onions and cook until they are golden; then add the mushrooms, well cleaned and washed rapidly. Season with a pinch of salt; sauté quickly; drain, using a skimmer, and place on a plate.

In the same butter and melted fat, adding more butter if necessary, cook 1 onion and the carrots, quartered, until golden; then sprinkle with the flour. Mix well, and stir continuously with a wooden spoon over a low flame until the flour takes on a dark gold colour.

At this point, add the pieces of hare, drained and wiped dry. Sear them in this roux, stirring constantly with the wooden spoon. When the meat is seared, sprinkle the crushed garlic on top, mix well and cover with the red wine. Bring to the boil, stirring, so that the sauce thickens without lumps and is perfectly smooth. Correct the seasoning with salt; add the bouquet garni, cover and place in a 275–300°F (140–150°C, gas mark 1–2) oven for 45 minutes.

Place the pan on the kitchen table on a trivet. Next to it place another pan. Then, with a slotted spoon, remove the pieces of hare, and with a fork, slide them into the other pan.

Once all the meat has been transferred, place the lardoons, the small onions and the mushrooms on top of the hare; pour the sauce on to the meat through a very fine sieve, rubbing the garnish – onions, carrots, bouquet garni – through.

Bring the second pan to the boil, correct the seasoning once more and cover. Simmer in a 325°F (170°C, gas mark 3) oven for 45 minutes.

Rub the liver through a fine sieve on to a plate; mix with the blood; add the cognac and cream which will dilute the sauce perfectly.

Then proceed to the thickening. When the stew is cooked, remove from the oven and place on the lowest possible heat. While beating with a whisk, slowly pour a ladleful of the stew into the sauce. Heat the mixture slowly, as it will become lumpy if it is cooked too quickly. Strain all the sauce through a very fine sieve and pour it into the stew with one hand, shaking the pan with the other hand so that the whole stew is evenly coated. Rub through everything that remains in the sieve; nothing should be left. During this time the stew should not boil.

When the sauce is smooth, place the pan on a very low flame, shaking it until the first signs of boiling. Remove from the heat.

Pour the stew into a shallow dish, place the croûtons around the edge and sprinkle a pinch of chopped fresh parsley in the centre.

The sauce should be perfectly thickened, smooth and dark in colour.

YOUNG HARE WITH ONIONS, MUSHROOMS AND CREAM
Levraut Chabert

1 young hare (3–5 months old) about 1·5 kg (3 lb)

Salt and pepper

Pinch of finely crushed bay and thyme

100 g (4 oz) fresh pork fat

225 g (8 oz) onions

225 g (8 oz) mushrooms

½ glass dry white wine

4 dl (¾ pt) veal stock

Roux made with 1½ tablespoons butter and 1 tablespoon flour

1 garlic clove, crushed

Sprigs parsley

2 dl (8 fl oz) double cream

10 heart-shaped croûtons fried in butter

This dish will take 1½ hours to cook. Skin and draw the hare. Carefully collect the blood that is concentrated around the lungs; then remove the liver, getting rid of the gall bladder. Cut the young hare into pieces and season with salt, freshly ground pepper and a pinch of crushed bay and thyme. Mix well and place on a plate.

Remove the skin from the pork fat and chop the fat very fine. Melt in a pan, then add the pieces of hare and brown on a high flame.

Add the onions, cut into fine julienne, mix and lower the flame; cover, and steam for 15 minutes. The onions should not brown but be well softened.

Meanwhile, prepare the mushrooms. Clean, wash carefully and quickly; cut off the stems and place them on one plate and the caps on another.

When the onions are cooked, pour the white wine on the hare and boil to reduce almost completely over a high flame.

Moisten with the veal stock, and add the roux (cooked for 15 minutes and cooled) in small amounts; add the mushroom stems, the garlic and the parsley. The stock should just cover the hare; if there is not enough, add a few tablespoons of water.

Stir until the sauce boils, to dissolve the roux and blend it completely. Simmer on a low flame, covered, for 25 minutes.

When this is done, drain the pieces of hare with a slotted spoon and, with the help of a fork, place them in a clean pan.

Scatter the mushroom caps on top of the hare. Strain the sauce through a fine sieve and rub through the onions, so that they are puréed. Pour the sauce over the mushrooms.

Bring to the boil, correct the seasoning and simmer slowly, covered, for 20 minutes more.

When the young hare and the mushrooms are cooked, thicken the sauce. Purée the liver through a sieve and mix it in a bowl with the blood and cream. Dilute the mixture with a ladleful of the hot sauce, poured slowly to heat the mixture a little at a time. Remove the hare from the heat, and shaking the pan round to mix, slowly pour the blood mixture into the sauce.

When the sauce is well mixed, heat slowly again almost to boiling point, stirring constantly.

Remove from the heat, taste and serve.

Pour the stew into a shallow dish and place the fried croûtons around it.

HARE WITH RABBIT, MUSHROOMS AND TRUFFLE STUFFING
Lièvre farci à la Diane

1 young hare, about 2–2·7 kg (5–6 lb)
100 g (4 oz) larding fat
1 slice of pork fat

Stuffing:
Back and legs of 2 rabbits
¾ tablespoon salt
Pinch freshly ground pepper
Pinch herb and spice mixture (page xxiv)
Pinch powdered thyme, bay and marjoram
125 g (5 oz) fresh pork fat, grated
125 g (5 oz) young white mushrooms
Large raw truffle
50 g (2 oz) white bread, crust removed, soaked in a little bouillon or veal stock
1 tablespoon cognac

Sauce:
25 g (1 oz) unsalted butter
½ dl (¼ pt) dry white wine
Sprig thyme
2 large shallots, chopped fine and boiled for a few minutes
6 tablespoons double cream
Redcurrant jelly

Skin the hare, leaving the ears. Draw the innards through an opening, as small as possible, made in the skin of the belly. Collect the blood and the liver, removing the gall bladder. Plunge the ears into boiling water and remove the hair by rubbing firmly with a cloth.

Remove the tendons from the thighs and the hare fillets, exposing them.

Cut the larding fat into small lardoons as thick as a pencil and about 3·5 cm (1½ inches) long; place the hare on a cloth to avoid holding it directly with your fingers, and lard the legs and the fillets.

Stuffing

When the two rabbits have been skinned and drawn, collect the blood and the livers, removing the gall bladders. Put the rabbits' blood with the hare's blood, and set aside the livers.

Cut off the rabbits' hindquarters at the top of the ribs; remove the tendons, and bone. Cut into pieces and season with salt, pepper, spices, thyme, marjoram and bay leaf. Mix well and chop the meat coarsely along with the livers from the rabbits.

Place in a bowl.

Pound the pork fat in a mortar or grate it and add to the chopped meat

Clean the mushrooms and wash rapidly; coarsely chop the mushrooms and the truffle. Squeeze the soaked white bread and add with the cognac to the other ingredients with the chopped meat.

Mix well with a wooden spatula, and test the seasoning by poaching a small piece of the stuffing in salted boiling water. Correct if necessary.

Hare

Place the hare on its back and insert the stuffing in the cavity, evenly distributed. Sew the opening in the belly with thick thread, and place the slices of pork fat over the sewing. Hold it in place with a string. The barding fat prevents the belly from tearing while cooking and keeps the stuffing in place.

Turn the hare on its belly, and place the paws against the body as if the hare were crouched. Tie the paws in place with a string. Straighten the head in line with the shoulders. Hold it in place with a string tied around the shoulders. Protect the ears by wrapping them with well-buttered paper and tie them together.

Use a roasting pan with a rack, big enough to hold the hare comfortably. Arrange the hare, coat with melted butter, sprinkle with a pinch of salt and place in a 425°F (220°C, gas mark 7) oven to sear. Then lower the heat slightly to 400°F (200°C, gas mark 6).

Meanwhile heat the white wine with the butter and, with a sprig of thyme dipped in it, baste the hare every 7 minutes. Cook it in this way for 1 hour.

Sauce

Strain the blood and rub the liver through a fine sieve placed over a soup plate. When the hare is roasted, pour the cooking juices of the hare and the basting juice in the roasting pan through a sieve into a pan. Degrease this juice, boil to reduce by half and add the blanched shallots and the cream.

As soon as the mixture starts to boil, pour a few tablespoons of the sauce into the blood, stirring with a whisk. Then do the opposite: pour the blood and liver mixture into the sauce, away from the heat, stirring continuously with the whisk. Heat again slowly while beating with the whisk; as soon as the sauce starts to boil, remove from the heat. The sauce should not boil.

Correct the seasoning of this thick, rich sauce, which should be spiced with freshly ground pepper.

Presentation. Place the hare on a long platter on its back, remove the bard and the thread, turn it on its stomach, remove the paper from its ears.

Serve the sauce in a sauceboat, together with a dish of red-currant jelly separately.

1 hare, 2·2–2·7 kg (5–6 lb)

3–4 tablespoons goose fat

100 g (4 oz) fresh pork fat

100 g (4 oz) pork fat, sliced

1 carrot

4 medium-sized onions

4 cloves

30 garlic cloves

60 shallots

Bouquet garni

Salt and pepper

$\frac{1}{4}$ dl ($\frac{1}{2}$ pt) good red wine vinegar

2 bottles Chambertin, at least 5 years old

Utensils:

Oblong copper braising pan, well tinned, 8 inches deep, 20 inches long and 14 inches wide, with a well-fitting lid

Small bowl to hold the hare's blood, big enough to whip the blood before incorporating it in the sauce

Chopper

Large shallow platter

Strainer

Small wooden pestle

HARE BRAISED IN CHAMBERTIN
Lièvre à la royal du sénateur Couteaux

Theoretically the ideal animal for this magnificent dish is a male hare with russet-brown coat, of a good French breed – light, graceful and strong, preferably from mountain or moorland. It should weigh 2·2–2·7 kg (5–6 lb) – no longer a leveret but not yet fully grown – and should be killed neatly so that it does not lose a drop of blood.

Skin and draw the hare. Set aside the heart and the lungs. Collect the blood carefully (if you like you can add the traditional 2 or 3 small liqueur glasses of fine old Charentes cognac).

First step (preparation time: 1.30PM–5.00PM)

1.30PM. Coat the bottom and the sides of the braising pan with the goose fat and cover the bottom with a layer of sliced pork fat.

Cut off the forequarters of the hare at the shoulders, removing the neck and the head; only the saddle and the paws are left. Then place the animal lying on its back on the pork fat. Cover with a second layer of pork fat. All the sliced pork fat has then been used.

Cut the carrots into quarters, stick 1 clove into each. Add to the pan along with 20 garlic cloves, 40 shallots and the bouquet garni.

Pour over the hare the wine vinegar and a bottle and a half of the Chambertin.

Season with salt and pepper.

2.00PM. Cover the braising pan and place on the flame.

Regulate the heat so that the hare cooks for 3 hours on a low flame.

Second step (to be done during the initial cooking of the hare)

First chop the following four ingredients, separately, very fine: the fresh pork fat; the hare's liver and lungs; 10 garlic cloves; 20 shallots. The garlic and the shallots must be chopped extremely fine – this is vital for the success of this dish.

When the pork fat, the liver, the lungs, the garlic and the shallots have been chopped separately, put everything into one bowl and mix well until the forcemeat is perfectly blended.

Set this forcemeat aside.

Third step (5.00PM–7.45PM)

5.00PM.   Remove the braising pan from the heat. Remove the hare carefully; set it on a platter. Then remove all the remaining pork fat, carrots, onions, garlic and shallots that cling to the hare; put all these condiments back into the braising pan.

Now place the strainer over a large shallow platter and pour the contents of the braising pan into the strainer. Rub everything in the strainer with the wooden pestle so that all the juices can be extracted to make a purée or *coulis*.

Mix the *coulis* and the forcemeat. Heat the remaining half bottle of wine. Pour this hot wine into the mixture of *coulis* and forcemeat and mix well.

5.30PM.   Put the forcemeat and *coulis* mixture, the hare and all the bones from the legs or any other bones that came away during the cooking back into the braising pan. Place the braising pan on the stove over a low flame; continue cooking a second time for $1\frac{1}{2}$ hours.

7.00PM.   Because of the large quantity of fresh pork fat used, it is difficult to check the thickness of the sauce, so give it a preliminary skimming. The dish will not be finished until the sauce is thickened almost to the consistency of mashed potatoes. However it must not become too thick, or there will not be enough sauce to moisten the meat of the hare (which is very dry).

The hare, degreased, can continue to cook slowly until the time when the blood is added to the sauce.

Fourth step (15 *minutes before serving*)

7.45PM.   The thickening of the sauce is nearly completed The fourth and last step – adding the hare's blood – will finish it quickly.

By adding the blood now, not only will the sauce be thickened but it will also take on a nice brown colour; the darker the colour, the more appetizing the dish.

The blood should not be added more than 15 minutes before serving, after a second skimming of the fat. When this skimming is done immediately whip the hare's blood with a fork, so that if any part of the blood has curdled, it will become liquid again, (The optional cognac helps to prevent curdling.)

Pour the blood mixture into the sauce, being careful to shake the braising pan up and down and left to right, in a to-and-fro movement so that the blood runs all round the braising pan.

Taste the sauce; then add salt and pepper, if necessary. A little later (about a quarter of an hour maximum) prepare to serve.

Final preparation (8.00PM)

Remove the hare from the braising pan. Its shape will naturally have altered somewhat. Place all the meat in the middle of the serving platter – the bare bones are now discarded. Finally arrange the garnish round the meat and pour your marvellous sauce, so carefully made, all over it.

Needless to say this meltingly tender hare can be served with a spoon – the use of a knife would be sacrilege.

---

1 saddle of hare
100 g (4 oz) fresh
  pork fat
1 bottle Burgundy
2 carrots, sliced
1 medium-sized
  onion, chopped
Thyme, bay
Peppercorns, crushed
Salt
100 g (4 oz) unsalted
  butter
¼ glass cognac

Sauce:
5 tablespoons oil
500 g (1 lb) hare
  trimmings and bones
225 g (8 oz) *mirepoix*
  (very finely
  chopped vegetables)
5 tablespoons vinegar
Marinade from saddle
  of hare
Salt
½ tablespoon
  peppercorns, crushed
Small bouquet garni
50 g (2 oz) *beurre
  manié*
Small glass of hare
  blood

SADDLE OF HARE WITH POIVRADE SAUCE
Râble de lièvre sauce poivrade

For 2 people

The saddle is the part of the hare between the top ribs and the beginning of the thighs.

Choose a nice saddle of hare. After trimming it and removing the tendons, lard it with small strips of pork fat. Place in a bowl for 4 hours in a marinade made with the Burgundy, the carrots, the chopped onion, the thyme, bay and crushed peppercorns.

After marinating, drain the saddle and salt it. Roast in butter in an earthenware pan at 425°F (220°C, gas mark 7); 10–15 minutes should be enough to cook it. The hare meat, when roasted, should remain pink – but allow slightly longer if necessary.

Remove the hare, place on a serving platter and set in a warm place covered with a piece of aluminium foil to keep warm.

Deglaze the roasting pan with the cognac. Boil to reduce by half and add the wine used for the marinade.

Carve the saddle into thin slices. To serve reshape the saddle, replacing the slices on the backbone.

Serve with poivrade sauce (recipe below) in a sauceboat. This dish can be accompanied by chestnut purée (page 479), *soubise* (page 483), celeriac purée (page 444) or fresh noodles in butter.

Poivrade sauce

Put the oil in a saucepan, and in it brown the hare trimmings, cut into small pieces, and the bones. Add the *mirepoix* and stew for a few minutes.

Deglaze with the vinegar and boil to reduce until nearly evaporated. Moisten with the juice from the marinade. Season with salt and the crushed pepper.

After adding the bouquet garni, cook on a low flame Strain the sauce; thicken it with the *beurre manié*; thicken further with the blood.

After correcting the seasoning, to finish the sauce, strain again through a very fine sieve; before using, heat in a *bain-marie*.

---

1 saddle of hare
Small fresh pork
  lardoons
Salt and pepper
Olive oil
½ glass white wine
½ tablespoon vinegar
100 g (4 oz) unsalted
  butter
2 dl (¼ pt) double
  cream
Juice of ¼ lemon

SADDLE OF HARE WITH CREAM
Râble de lièvre à la crème

With the sharp blade of a knife remove the membranes that cover the fillets. Lard across the fillets with two rows of small fresh pork lardoons. Break the spine with a blow of your knife, in the middle of the saddle, to avoid contraction.

Season with salt and pepper and place in a shallow dish; baste with olive oil, white wine and vinegar. Marinate the saddle for 12 hours, turning it often.

Drain the saddle and wipe dry; roast in 75 g (3 oz) of butter in 450°F (230°C, gas mark 8) oven for 15 minutes (or slightly longer at a lower temperature if you are not sure how tender the hare will be). Keep very rare, so that the meat will remain pink after standing over a very low heat for 10 minutes.

Drain off the cooking butter that is left in the roasting pan, replace with cream. Bring to the boil and cook until reduced by half, then away from the heat add the lemon juice and remaining butter cut into small pieces; stir until the sauce thickens. Correct the seasoning, and strain the sauce through a very fine sieve.

Place the saddle (which has been kept warm) on a long heated platter and baste it with the sauce.

Serve with a bowl of chestnut purée (page 479) or celeriac purée (page 444).

Note: It is important not to allow the juices of the hare which collect in the roasting pan to caramelize while roasting. This would make the deglazed sauce bitter and unusable and the dish would lose most of its flavour.

ROAST SADDLE AND LEGS OF HARE
Train de lièvre rôti

The saddle and legs of a hare in one piece are called the *train de lièvre*.

Carefully remove the membrane from the fillets and the legs and lard with several rows of small fresh pork fat lardoons. If it is a young animal, do not place in a marinade.

Season with salt and pepper on all sides and place on the rack of a roasting pan; baste with melted butter, and roast in a 450°F (230°C, gas mark 8) oven for 20 minutes, or longer if necessary. Baste often with the melted cooking butter, and watch that the juices from the hare do not harden at the bottom of the roasting pan; they will caramelize slightly but should not go beyond a pale-brown colour.

After letting the hare stand for 5 minutes, while the roasting pan is being deglazed with $\frac{1}{2}$ cup of boiling veal stock to dissolve the juices, place the hare on a long platter and baste it with a little of its juice.

Serve the remaining juice in a sauceboat with cooked chestnuts glazed in butter, mushrooms in cream, celeriac purée (page 444) or a purée of apples unsweetened or lightly sweetened.

Note: The forequarters of the hare can be stewed.

1 1·5-kg (3-lb)
   domestic rabbit
150 g (6 oz) pork
   belly or bacon
15 small onions
150 g (6 oz)
   mushrooms
25 g (1 oz) butter
Salt and pepper
Bay and thyme
   leaves, crushed
2 scant tablespoons
   flour
2 garlic cloves,
   crushed
4 dl (¾ pt) dry white
   wine
Bouquet garni
Chopped parsley

RABBIT STEW WITH MUSHROOMS AND ONIONS
Lapin de garenne en gibelotte

Cut the pork fat into large lardoons; place them in ½ l (1 pt) of cold water and boil for 5 minutes. Drain and wipe dry. Peel and scald the onions with boiling water. Drain.

Trim the mushrooms; wash them carefully without letting them stand in the water.

In a pan big enough to hold the stew, heat the butter and half brown the pork fat; add the onions, stir often. When the onions are golden brown, add the mushrooms and sauté over a high flame for 5 minutes.

Drain with a slotted spoon and set aside on a plate.

In the same butter, adding more if necessary, brown the rabbit, cut into pieces (except the liver), and season with salt and pepper, crushed bay and thyme leaves.

Sprinkle with the flour, mix well and brown slightly. Sprinkle the crushed garlic on the rabbit, mix, add the white wine and cover with veal stock, or with bouillon or water.

Add the bouquet garni, then bring to the boil, stirring continuously; cover, and cook slowly in a 325°F (170°C, gas mark 3) oven for about 30 minutes.

Add the pork fat, onions and mushrooms; correct the seasoning and continue cooking for 25 minutes. Five minutes before the cooking is over, add the liver, after removing the gall bladder.

If the sauce seems too thin, because of the gentle cooking, remove the rabbit to a shallow platter and take out the bouquet garni. Place the sauce over a high flame for a few minutes to boil it down to the necessary consistency.

Pour the sauce over the rabbit and sprinkle with freshly chopped parsley.

2 tablespoons lard or
  pork fat
1 rabbit, cut into
  pieces
Salt and pepper
Thyme
Pinch crushed bay
  leaf
100 g (4 oz) unsalted
  butter
4 shallots, finely
  chopped
225 g (8 oz) medium
  sized mushrooms,
  cleaned and thinly
  sliced
1 glass dry white
  wine
1½ dl (¼ pt) lightly
  salted veal stock
2 tablespoons tomato
  paste
Pinch chopped
  chervil
Pinch chopped
  tarragon
Chopped parsley
Croûtons

SAUTÉED RABBIT WITH MUSHROOMS
Lapereau de garenne sauté chasseur

In a pan heat 2 tablespoons of lard or pork fat; when the fat is smoking brown the pieces of rabbit; set the liver aside.

Season with salt and pepper, thyme and bay leaf. When the pieces of rabbit are well browned, drain the fat and replace it with 50 g (2 oz) of butter; cover, and stew, in a 325°F (170°C, gas mark 3) oven if possible, for 45 minutes. Stir often.

Meanwhile, in a pan brown 4 finely chopped shallots in 50 g (2 oz) of butter; add the mushrooms.

Sauté the mushrooms on a fairly high flame, and moisten with white wine; boil to reduce almost completely, and add the lightly salted veal stock and tomato paste. Boil to reduce by one-third, correct the seasoning.

After the young rabbit has been cooked, add the broth and the mushrooms; simmer for 5 minutes. Sprinkle with chervil and tarragon; mix carefully, and pour into a shallow dish.

Sprinkle some chopped parsley on top.

Surround the dish with diamond-shaped croûtons, fried in butter.

FAISAN

Pheasant

Generally pheasant is prepared in the same way as casseroled chicken or partridge, duckling *en salmis* or any galantine of poultry.

ROAST PHEASANT
Faisan rôti

1 young pheasant
Salt and pepper
Pork fat
Melted unsalted
  butter
1 rectangular croûton
  fried in butter or
  cooking fat
1 pheasant and 1
  chicken liver
Herb and spice
  mixture (page xxiv)
1 tablespoon cognac
Watercress
1 lemon
2 tablespoons veal
  stock, bouillon or
  water

Choose a young pheasant. Pluck the bird, singe, draw and season it inside with a pinch of salt and pepper; truss and bard to protect the breast, which is extremely delicate.

Place the bird on its side on a rack in a roasting pan, baste with melted butter and season with salt and pepper. Place in a 425°F (220°C, gas mark 7) oven for 25–30 minutes, depending upon the weight.

During roasting, turn carefully so the breast is not exposed to sudden heat; baste often with the cooking butter. Five minutes before the pheasant is cooked, remove the trussing and the pork fat; reserve the fat keeping it warm, and let the breast brown. Baste often during this last brief step.

The pheasant should be pink when cooked; let stand for a few minutes before serving.

Presentation.   Cut a rectangular croûton, 25 cm (10 inches) long, 13 cm (5 inches) wide and 2 cm ($\frac{3}{4}$ inch) thick from a loaf of white bread.

Fry it in butter or the cooking fat from the pheasant roasting pan. This second method will give the croûton a less pleasant colour but a better taste.

Spread the following mixture on the croûton.

Cut the pheasant liver and 1 chicken liver in 2 or 3 pieces each, and season them with salt and pepper and a dash of herbs and spices. Dice an equal quantity of fresh pork fat and melt it in a small pan. Then add the livers, sear and half cook on a high flame. Remove from the heat; into the pan pour 1 tablespoon of good cognac to dissolve all the liver juices; pour everything into a sieve placed on top of a bowl.

Rub everything through the sieve with a small wooden pestle and collect the purée in a bowl. Work it until smooth with a wooden spatula and spread the paste on the croûton; put the croûton on a hot ovenproof platter in a 450°F (230°C, gas mark 8) oven to brown the surface lightly.

Place the pheasant on the croûton, with a bouquet of watercress placed tastefully at either end of the platter. Return the reserved barding fat, which has been kept warm, to the bird; and place 2 half lemons on each side.

Deglaze the roasting pan with 2 tablespoons of veal stock,

bouillon or water. If you use water, correct the seasoning. Serve the cooking juice in a sauceboat.

Carve the pheasant at the table after removing the barding fat. First detach the 2 legs, then the 2 wings cut with part of the breast; then cut the breast from the carcass. Place each of the 5 pieces on one-fifth of the croûton. Serve.

If the pheasant has been cooked correctly, the flesh will be pale pink with pink drops of juice coming out of the meat as the pheasant is carved. If the pheasant is overdone, the meat will be a dull grey, grainy to the teeth. It will have lost its tenderness and succulence.

One generally serves a dish of potato chips or matchstick potatoes (page 493) with this delicious dish.

BRAISED PHEASANT
Faisan en casserole

Prepare a young pheasant as if to roast it, but truss it, inserting the ends of the drumsticks into incisions in the skin, one on either side of the breast.

Place the pheasant in a pan big enough to hold it comfortably and brown, covered, in 50 g (2 oz) of unsalted butter for 25–30 minutes. Remove the barding and the trussing strings a few seconds before the end of cooking.

After cooking the pheasant until pink, pour 1 tablespoon of cognac into the pan, cover and serve immediately in the pan on a plate covered with a folded napkin.

BRAISED PHEASANT WITH ONIONS AND MUSHROOMS
Faisan à la cocotte

Prepare as for the braised pheasant (recipe above) but place it in an ovenproof earthenware pot in a 325°F (170°C, gas mark 3) oven. After about 25 minutes add 1 dozen small onions browned in butter and 100 g (4 oz) of mushrooms, well cleaned, quartered and sautéed in butter. Cook for another 10–15 minutes.

**1 young pheasant,
    barded**
**25 g (1 oz) unsalted
    butter**
**1 medium-sized
    onion, quartered**
**100 g (4 oz) firm
    white mushrooms**
**1½ dl (¼ pt) double
    cream**
Salt and pepper

PHEASANT WITH CREAM
Faisan à la crème

Pot roast the young pheasant 25–30 minutes in butter with an onion.

Meanwhile carefully clean the firm white mushrooms without letting them stand in water and cut into medium slices; sauté in butter over a high flame and moisten with the cream. Season with salt and pepper; bring to a rolling boil and pour over the pheasant when it is two-thirds cooked. At this point, remove the barding and the trussing strips.

Let the pheasant stand in the oven for 3 minutes, placed on its back to keep the breast out of the boiling cream. Then place it on a flat round platter.

Boil to reduce the cream slightly until it has the consistency of a sauce, then pour over the pheasant.

All around the edges arrange small triangular croûtons fried in butter.

Partridge, young guinea fowl and quail also can be prepared in this way.

PHEASANT WITH BRAISED
CABBAGE AND VEGETABLES
Faisan en chartreuse

Proceed as for *chartreuse* of young partridge (page 411), but in the cabbage braise an old pheasant; the only role of this pheasant is to give its flavour to the cabbage.

The pheasant that is actually served in the *chartreuse* must be a young and tender bird, roasted or braised separately.

SALMI OF PHEASANT
Salmis de faisan

There are two methods, both recommended.

First method:

1 young pheasant

3 shallots, finely
  chopped

1½ dl (¼ pt) espagnole
  sauce (page 108) or
  demi-glace sauce
  (page 108)

1 dozen small
  mushrooms

20 slices truffles

2 tablespoons cognac
  or champagne
  brandy

25 g (1 oz) unsalted
  butter

Croûtons fried in
  butter

First method

Prepare a young pheasant as if to roast it; set aside the liver.

Roast the bird in a 450°F (230°C, gas mark 8) oven for 20–25 minutes; while still rare, carve 6 pieces; the 2 legs, the 2 wings without the tips and the breast cut into 2 pieces lengthwise.

Put the pieces in a buttered pan, cover and keep warm.

While the pheasant is roasting, cook the shallots slowly, without letting them brown, in butter in a small pan. Add the espagnole sauce, reduced and well degreased, or demi-glace sauce.

Simmer for 15 minutes.

After the pheasant is carved, pound the remaining carcass in a mortar, along with the wing tips and any other trimmings; add this purée to the espagnole sauce.

In the cooking butter in the roasting pan, quickly sauté 1 dozen small mushrooms – firm, very clean and seasoned with salt and pepper. Sear the pheasant's liver, remove it, then add about 20 slices of truffles, cut rather thick; when the truffles are warm, deglaze the pan with good cognac or fine champagne brandy. Finally, pour everything over the pieces of pheasant.

Rub the liver, which should be rare, through a fine sieve and away from the heat add to the espagnole sauce, which should then be reduced by half. Mix well with a whisk, heat slowly while stirring and, as soon as the sauce starts to boil, pour into a very fine sieve placed over the pieces of pheasant. Rub everything through until the sieve is dry. Add a knob of butter cut into small pieces, shaking gently and heating the sauce without letting it boil until the butter is blended. Correct the seasoning and pour into a hot dish.

Decorate the dish with diamond-shaped croûtons, fried in butter.

At the same time place very hot plates on the table.

Second method:

1 young pheasant

50 g (2 oz) unsalted
   butter

1 carrot (core
   removed)

1 medium-sized
   onion, finely diced

2 shallots, finely diced

Pinch salt, powdered
   thyme, bay leaf

1 heaped tablespoon
   flour

1½ dl (¼ pt) veal stock
   or bouillon

1 glass dry white
   wine

1 tablespoon cognac

Second method

Cook the carrot, onion and shallots gently in 25 g (1 oz) of butter until soft; season with a pinch of salt and powdered thyme and bay leaf.

Roast a young pheasant as indicated for the first method, above.

Carve the bird, keeping the pieces warm in a covered pan; pound the carcass in a mortar, rub the liver through a fine sieve or chop it fine to purée it.

Sprinkle the *mirepoix* (carrot–onion–shallot mixture) with flour. Mix and cook this roux for 15 minutes until the flour is light brown; moisten with veal stock or bouillon. Mix well to avoid lumps, and simmer for 15 minutes.

Pour dry white wine in the roasting pan used, boil to reduce by two-thirds, and add the sauce above. Add the puréed carcass, bring to the boil for a few seconds; then away from the heat finish by adding the liver purée. Heat slowly, stirring, until the sauce reaches boiling point; remove from the heat, correct the seasoning, and pass the sauce through a very fine sieve on to the pieces of pheasant, rubbing it through.

Finish the dish with 1 tablespoon of good cognac and 25 g (1 oz) of butter Add the truffles and the mushrooms as for the first method and present the dish in the same way.

---

1 young pheasant

1 tablespoon olive oil

1 small onion, finely
   chopped

2 shallots, finely
   chopped

100 g (4 oz)
   mushrooms

300 g (10 oz) fresh
   pork fat

225 g (8 oz) truffles

½ tablespoon spiced
   salt (page xxiv)

3 tablespoons Madeira

3 tablespoons cognac

12 chestnuts

Slice fresh pork fat

PHEASANT STUFFED WITH CHESTNUTS AND TRUFFLES
Faisan farci aux marrons et aux truffes

Pluck the pheasant, draw it through the neck, removing the wishbone. Set aside the liver and the heart; season the pheasant with salt and pepper on the inside.

Heat the oil in a pan, add the finely chopped onion and shallots and brown slowly, stirring often. Add the mushrooms – cleaned, washed quickly and chopped very fine, then dried over high heat while stirring with a wooden spoon. Season with a pinch of salt.

Remove the rind and the membrane from the pork fat; cut it into small pieces and pound it in a mortar; put this paste in a bowl. Put it in a warm place to soften the fat, then rub through a strainer into a bowl.

Add the mushrooms, onion and shallots; the cleaned truffles, washed carefully and cut into quarters; the spiced salt; the Madeira; the cognac; and the liver chopped into a purée. Work vigorously with a wooden spatula to mix well.

Peel and cook the chestnuts in a little bouillon. Put the stuffing into the pheasant, adding some chestnuts here and there.

Truss the pheasant and bard with the slice of pork fat; pot roast it lying on its side, allowing 20 minutes per pound.

Be sure to protect the breast; finish cooking, and serve, with the degreased pan juices served separately.

Note: This recipe can be made without truffles.

PHEASANT STUFFED WITH FOIE GRAS
Faisan farci au foie gras dit à la Souvarov

Stuff a pheasant with fresh *foie gras* and truffles that have been cut into large cubes, seasoned, and marinated in cognac then seared in butter. Truss the pheasant, heat it in 25–50 g (1–2 oz) of unsalted butter to sear it, and cook in a 325°F (170°C, gas mark 3) oven in a covered pan, sealed with a band of dough (made of a mixture of flour and water) around the lid. This will take about 40 minutes.

Partridge can be cooked in the same way.

PARTRIDGE
Perdreaux

All the recipes for pheasant can be used for partridge and vice versa.

ROAST PARTRIDGE
Perdreau rôti

Prepare a young partridge as you would a pheasant. Put a vine leaf on the breast before covering it with the pork fat.

Cook in butter in a 425°F (220°C, gas mark 7) oven 18–20 minutes.

As for pheasant, the flesh should still be pink when the cooking is completed.

Garnish like the pheasant with croûtons, and serve with the cooking juices thinned slightly with a tablespoon of strong veal bouillon.

PARTRIDGE WITH CABBAGE (1)
Perdrix au chou

1 cabbage
100 g (4 oz) belly of pork or bacon, in the piece
Sea salt and pepper
2 partridges
1 medium-sized carrot
1 onion stuck with a clove
Bouquet garni
150 g (6 oz) garlic sausage
3 tablespoons chicken fat or lard
1 l (2 pts) bouillon
6 long chipolatas

This dish will take 2½ hours to cook.

Remove any wilted leaves and the very green leaves of the cabbage; cut out the core and separate the leaves; wash carefully.

Blanch the cabbage by dropping the leaves in a large saucepan of boiling water, then add the piece of pork or bacon. Boil for 15 minutes and drain; remove the pork or bacon, rinse the cabbage, drain again and squeeze to remove water.

Spread the leaves on a large platter, and season with crushed sea salt and freshly ground pepper.

Meanwhile roast the partridges in a 325°F (170°C, gas mark 3) oven with a little fat to start them browning for about 8 minutes.

Prepare a deep casserole, large enough to hold the cabbage, the partridges and the garnish. In the bottom of the pan, place in this order: the rind from the pork, one-third of the cabbage, the partridges, the carrot and the onion, the bouquet garni, the second third of the cabbage, the pork fat, the garlic sausage, the remaining cabbage, the chicken fat and finally enough bouillon to cover the cabbage on top. Bring to the boil.

With 3 tablespoons of bouillon deglaze the roasting juices from the partridges and pour over the cabbage. Cover with a round of wax paper cut to the diameter of the pan and greased, and then the lid. Bring to the boil on top of the stove; then cook in a 325°F (170°C, gas mark 3) oven very slowly for 1½ hours to braise it.

Remove the sausage after 30 minutes and the pork fat after 45 minutes. Grill the chipolatas.

To serve, remove the partridges to a plate; take out the cabbage with a skimmer, draining completely. Pile the leaves on a round platter and place the partridges on top. Between them, place the chipolatas and the cooked pork or bacon cut into fairly thin rectangles. Around the edge arrange thick slices of garlic sausage alternating with slices of carrot.

PARTRIDGE WITH CABBAGE (2)
Perdreau au chou

1 old partridge
1 good-sized cabbage
Salt and pepper
Lard
1 carrot
1 onion stuck with a clove
1 small bouquet garni
100 g (4 oz) unsalted belly of pork or bacon
Bouillon or water
1 young partridge

To prepare this very popular dish, an old partridge must be sacrificed to flavour the cabbage; a fine young roast partridge is served in its place.

Take a good-sized cabbage, cut it into quarters, remove the core and the thick ribs and separate the leaves. After washing the leaves well, blanch for a few minutes in boiling water and rinse; then drain. Spread the leaves on the chopping block, season with salt and pepper and chop coarsely with a knife.

Meanwhile, brown an old partridge in some lard in a stew pot. Cover the browned bird with the cabbage; flavour the dish with a carrot, an onion stuck with a clove, a small bouquet garni and the pork or bacon. Pour in bouillon or water to reach half-way up. Cover the pot and simmer for about 1½ hours.

Meanwhile, roast the young partridge in a pan or on a spit.

To serve, pile the cabbage in a mound, place the young partridge in the centre, and over the partridge and the cabbage pour the delicious juice from the roasted young partridge. Discard the old bird.

Note: To improve the dish and make it more substantial, you can add a small garlic sausage and some potatoes, cooked at the last moment with the cabbage.

CHARTREUSE OF PARTRIDGE
Perdreaux en chartreuse

Ingredients as in previous recipe, plus:

100 g (4 oz) carrots (core removed)

100 g (4 oz) turnips

100 g (4 oz) French beans

100 g (4 oz) peas

75 g (3 oz) unsalted butter

Few slices garlic sausage

1 recipe veal forcemeat (page 273)

100 g (4 oz) belly of pork or bacon

1½ dl (¼ pt) veal stock

Braise 2 or 3 partridges with cabbage, following the recipe above

Cut the carrots, turnips and beans into small sticks as thick as a pencil and 3·5 cm (1½ inches) long; cook the carrots and turnips separately in a little clear stock. Cook the peas and beans rapidly in salted water to keep them green.

Choose a straight-sided mould big enough to hold the partridge and the cabbage and butter it thickly with 25 g (1 oz) of butter.

Garnish the bottom of the mould with a ring of carrot and turnip sticks alternately. Place a pea between the sticks round the edge, and a slice of sausage, the same thickness as the vegetable sticks, in the centre. Decorate the sides of the mould, starting from the bottom, with zig-zag rows of carrot and turnip sticks alternately.

Coat the vegetable sticks, being careful not to displace them, with a thin layer of forcemeat, then cover the forcemeat with very well-drained cabbage.

Fill the mould with several layers of partridge, quartered, the pork or bacon, cut into rectangles, and the remaining well-drained cabbage.

Finish the top of the mould with a thick layer of veal forcemeat.

Place the mould in a saucepan and fill the saucepan two thirds up the mould with boiling water. Poach slowly for 40 minutes.

Then let the *chartreuse* stand for 5 minutes; unmould on to a hot round platter.

Garnish the top with slices of sausage arranged in a circle, inside the circle formed by the sticks of carrots and turnips. In the centre, pile the French beans dressed with a knob of butter.

Around the mould, pour a few tablespoons of the veal stock, reduced and thickened away from the heat with 50 g (2 oz) of butter.

PARTRIDGE WITH APPLES AND CREAM
Perdreaux à la mode d'Isigny

4 large eating apples
100 g (4 oz) butter
2 young partridges, trussed and barded
6 tablespoons double cream

Peel and core the apples and cut them into thick slices; sauté quickly in 50 g (2 oz) of butter without cooking completely; season with a pinch of salt.

Meanwhile, brown the two partridges in 50 g (2 oz) of butter in an ovenproof earthenware casserole. Place the partridges on a plate.

In the casserole spread a layer of the apples and place the partridges on top on their backs, removing the bards and untrussing them; surround the birds with the remaining apples, and pour the cream over them. Place in a 325°F (170°C, gas mark 3) oven uncovered for 18 minutes. Serve in the casserole, placed on a plate covered with a folded napkin.

SAUTÉED PARTRIDGE WITH TRUFFLES
Perdreaux sauté aux truffes

1 large partridge, cut in 6 pieces
Salt and pepper
75 g (3 oz) unsalted butter
12 truffle slices
2 tablespoons Madeira
2 tablespoons veal stock

Cut a large partridge into 6 pieces; the 2 legs, the 2 wings, the breast and the back. Season with salt and pepper.

Heat 50 g (2 oz) of butter in a pan. When the butter is hot, place the 6 pieces of partridge flat in the pan, turn them after 7–8 minutes, cook them for another 7–8 minutes, then place them on a round platter, cover and keep warm.

In the same butter heat 1 dozen truffle slices, thickly cut, for 2 minutes; sprinkle with a pinch of salt and add 2 tablespoons of Madeira and 2 tablespoons of veal stock. Bring to the boil and away from the heat add the remaining butter.

Baste the partridge with this juice, spreading the truffle slices on top.

STUFFED PARTRIDGE WITH CEPS
Perdreaux farcis à la limousine

2 young partridges
Slices fresh pork fat
Vine leaves

Stuffing:
25 g (1 oz) unsalted
   butter
1 small onion, finely
   chopped
2 shallots, finely
   chopped
Stems of fresh ceps
   (taken from the
   garnish)
2 partridge livers
2 chicken livers
50 g (2 oz) cooked
   ham
50 g (2 oz) white
   bread, crust
   removed, soaked in
   milk or bouillon
   and squeezed
1 small egg, beaten
½ teaspoon chopped
   parsley
Pinch salt and pepper
Herb and spice
   mixture (page xxiv)

Garnish:
125 g (5 oz) belly of
   pork or bacon
25 g (1 oz) butter
225 g (8 oz) fresh ceps
2 tablespoons olive oil
2 tablespoons veal
   stock
Chopped parsley

Stuffing

In butter in a small pan brown the onion and the shallots; add the stems of the ceps, chopped fine and seasoned with a pinch of salt; stir over a high flame for 3 minutes. Let cool.

Combine the partridge livers and the chicken livers, seared in butter and kept rare, the ham and stems of the ceps – all finely chopped. Add the bread, the egg the chopped parsley, salt, pepper and seasoning.

Mix well in a bowl. Season the two partridges with salt inside, and stuff them.

Truss the birds; season and bard them, putting a vine leaf under each bard of pork fat.

Garnish

Remove the rind from the pork and cut the pork or bacon into small lardoons; place in 1 l (2 pts) of cold water, boil for 5 minutes, drain and wipe dry.

Brown the lardoons in butter in an ovenproof earthenware casserole big enough to hold the 2 partridges. Remove them with a skimmer and place on a plate. Put the two partridges in the casserole and brown them on all sides.

Meanwhile slice the caps of the ceps, season with salt and pepper, brown in a frying pan with very hot oil and drain; mix with the lardoons and surround the partridge. Cover the casserole, and bake in a 425°F (220°C, gas mark 7) oven for 25 minutes.

Just before the cooking is finished, pour 2 tablespoons of veal stock into the casserole; sprinkle a pinch of chopped parsley on top. Replace the lid; boil for 1 minute on top of the stove, and serve in the casserole, on a plate covered with a folded napkin.

2 good-sized
  partridges
Salt, freshly ground
  pepper, herb and
  spice mixture (page
  xxiv)
Cognac
1 kg (2 lb) forcemeat
  (see recipe for
  chicken terrine
  Paul Mercier, page
  35)
1 large truffle
2 pieces raw *foie gras*
Pork fat
1 carrot, sliced
1 onion, sliced
¼ glass port
Jellied stock

BONED AND STUFFED COLD PARTRIDGE
Perdreaux froids Café de Paris

Bone 2 good-sized partridges (do not remove the bones from the legs) following the method given for chicken terrine Paul Mercier (page 35).

Spread the partridges on the table, season with salt, freshly ground pepper and seasonings. Sprinkle with a little cognac. Make 1 kg (2 lb) of forcemeat, following the recipe for the chicken terrine. Spread a layer of forcemeat inside each bird, as for the chicken terrine. Place lengthwise in the centre a large truffle, cut in half, and on either side 2 pieces of raw *foie gras*, as big as half an egg, marinated in cognac and seasonings. Cover with a not-too-thick layer of stuffing and shape the partridges again into their natural shape; wrap them in pork fat, and secure the fat with a string.

Spread the bones of the carcass, chopped, in a pan big enough to hold the 2 partridges, add the carrot and onion, and place the partridges on top. Put on the lid, bring to the boil, then lower the flame and simmer for 30 minutes.

Place the partridges and the liquid in a bowl, letting the birds cool in their cooking juice.

When they are cool, drain and place on a serving platter. Clarify the jelly and chill (see page 136); when it is half set, coat the partridges with a shiny coat of jelly and cover the bottom of the platter with 2 cm (1 inch) of jelly.

WOOD GROUSE, HAZEL GROUSE OR GROUSE
Coq de bruyère et gelinotte ou grouse

These delicious birds are usually roasted or braised, except for the legs of the wood grouse. If braising you can deglaze the pan with a few tablespoons of sour cream mixed with the juice of quarter of a lemon.

ROAST QUAIL
Cailles rôties

Pluck the quail, draw them and season the insides with salt; truss and bard the birds, and place in a flat pan; baste with melted butter and roast in a 450°F (230°C, gas mark 8) oven for 12 minutes.

Remove the trusses and serve the quail immediately on croûtons fried in butter.

In a sauceboat, serve the butter and the cooking juices to which has been added 1 tablespoon of veal stock or hot water to deglaze the juices sticking to the bottom of the pan.

If the butter–juice mixture were poured directly on the quail, it would be immediately absorbed by the croûtons, which would lose their crispness.

QUAIL WITH GRAPES
Cailles aux raisins

6 quails
50 g (2 oz) unsalted butter, melted
Salt and pepper
48 ripe green grapes
Veal stock

Prepare 6 quail as for roasting; place in an ovenproof earthenware casserole with the hot butter.

Season with salt and pepper, and brown the birds quickly on all sides; finish cooking in a 450°F (230°C, gas mark 8) oven. These two steps should take 12 minutes.

Meanwhile remove the skins and, with a barding needle, the pips, from the ripe green grapes; allow 8 grapes per quail.

When the quail are cooked, add the grapes to the casserole. Add a little veal stock to deglaze the pan, cover, bring to the boil, and serve immediately in the casserole, on a plate with a folded napkin.

QUAIL RISOTTO
Risotto de cailles

Allow for each quail:
Unsalted butter
25 g (1 oz) rice
1 teaspoon
mushrooms
1 teaspoon truffles
1 teaspoon lean ham
1 tablespoon chopped,
cooked tomatoes
3 tablespoons veal
stock

Roast the quail in a casserole with butter for 12 minutes. When the quail are done, keep warm between two plates. Prepare a risotto allowing 25 g (1 oz) of rice per quail. The risotto is flavoured with the mushrooms, truffles and ham, cut into julienne and cooked as described below.

In the cooking butter quickly heat first the mushrooms, then the truffles, then the ham. Pour all this mixture into the risotto; mix carefully.

To the same pan add the cooked tomatoes and 3 tablespoons of veal stock; bring to the boil for 2 minutes. Pack the rice in a mould. Unmould on a hot round plate and place the quail around it, legs in the air. Place the chopped tomatoes in the centre; baste the quail with the juice.

COLD QUAIL WITH TRUFFLES AND FOIE GRAS
Cailles froides George Sand

6 good-sized quail
2 pieces truffles
2 pieces raw *foie gras*
Salt, pepper, herb and
spice mixture (page
xxiv)
3 tablespoons cognac
Melted unsalted
butter
Julienne (1 part
carrots, 1 part
truffles, 1 part raw
mushrooms)
White jellied stock
(page 136)

Draw 6 good-sized quail and truss them by making incisions in the sides of the birds and pushing the foot joints into them, folding the drumsticks back on the thighs.

Season the inside of each quail with a pinch of salt, and then place inside 2 pieces of truffles and 2 pieces of raw *foie gras* that has been marinated with a dash of salt, pepper, seasoning and cognac.

Choose an ovenproof dish just big enough to hold the 6 quail. Place the birds in the dish close to each other. Season, baste lightly with melted butter; sear quickly in a 450°F (230°C, gas mark 8) oven for 5 minutes.

Drain the fat. Pour 3 tablespoons of cognac over the quail, ignite and smother immediately with the lid. Cover the quail with a julienne of one-third cored carrots, one-third truffles and one-third raw mushrooms, cooked gently in butter. Cover with a good jellied white stock, bring to the boil and poach slowly for 12 minutes.

Place the quail in a serving bowl; degrease the liquid and pour it over the quail along with the vegetables.

Put in a cool place and serve when the jelly is set.

Note: Since this dish is served in the bowl, the jelly should not set as firmly as if the dish were to be unmoulded.

ROAST WOODCOCK
Bécasse rôtie

1 woodcock
Pinch salt
Slice fresh pork fat
Melted unsalted
  butter
Croûton, fried in
  butter
1 tablespoon *foie gras*
Fresh pepper
15 g ($\frac{1}{2}$ oz) unsalted
  butter or *foie gras*
1 tablespoon
  champagne brandy

Pluck the bird just before cooking it. Do not draw it, but remove the gizzard. Singe lightly, remove the eyes, tie the feet together and stick the beak into the body above the legs.

Season with a pinch of salt.

Wrap the bird in a slice of fresh pork fat.

Roast the woodcock on a spit over a hot fire or in a 450°F (230°C, gas mark 8) oven, basting with melted butter.

Cooking time is 18–20 minutes, depending on the weight.

Cook the bird slightly rare.

Place the woodcock on a croûton – 6 cm (4 inches) long, 3 cm ($2\frac{1}{2}$ inches) wide and 1 cm ($\frac{1}{2}$ inch) thick – cut from white bread and fried in the cooking butter, if the woodcock is roasted in the oven. Spread 1 tablespoon of *foie gras*, if available, on the croûton.

Carve the woodcock in front of the guests; put the intestines on a hot plate, grind a little fresh pepper on top, add a knob of butter or *foie gras* for each woodcock; mash everything with a fork, adding 1 tablespoonful of fine champagne brandy.

Spread this purée on the surface of the croûton, which is then divided among the guests. Serve the cooking juice to which you have added 1 tablespoon of veal stock or hot water separately.

3 woodcocks
1 pigeon
3 large truffles
1 fresh goose liver
Salt and pepper
1 tablespoon Madeira
1 piece stale white
  bread
Hot cream
100 g (4 oz) unsalted
  butter
4 egg yolks
Fresh pork fat
French bread slices,
  1 per guest
3 lemons, quartered

ROAST STUFFED WOODCOCK
Bécasses farcies rôties

This recipe is taken from the *Livre de cuisine des familles*.

'The recipe is for six people.

'You need three raw woodcocks and one pigeon. Bone one of the woodcocks and remove the best part of the meat; cut the meat into large dice. Clean and peel three large truffles, slice them into thick slices and then cut again into squares.

'Take a fresh goose liver, cut it into cubes the same size as the woodcock meat. Place the woodcock meat and the liver in a bowl, salt and pepper, add a tablespoon of good Madeira wine, to moisten the mixture.

'Bone the pigeon, remove all the meat, and, after chopping it slightly, place in a mortar. Pound well. Moisten a piece of stale white bread the size of a fist, crust removed, with water; squeeze out the water and moisten the bread with a ladleful of hot cream. Add the bread to the mortar along with the butter and pound well to mix everything. Finally add to this stuffing four very fresh egg yolks. Add salt and pepper.

'Remove from the bowl the pieces of meat and truffles, which are now impregnated with the Madeira. Chop as finely as possible; then take the stuffing from the mortar and place it on the chopping board. Add the meat and truffles to the stuffing, mixing with your fingers and kneading together. It is with this preparation that you will stuff the two woodcocks which you have not touched yet.

'The moment has come to take care of the birds.

'After plucking, singe the birds lightly and draw them completely; throw away the crops, the gizzards and the intestines. Keep only the livers of these two woodcocks, and set them aside with the liver of the third woodcock. Then fill the insides of the two woodcocks with the stuffing that has been prepared; stuff them well, sew all the openings carefully. When this is done, truss and bard each woodcock, crossing their feet and bringing the head towards the legs. Pass the beak through the jointing of the drumsticks; the bird, this way, seems to be pierced by its long beak. Wrap each woodcock with a thin layer of fresh pork fat. Then put a metal skewer through it, being careful that each woodcock is pierced at an angle; then place the skewers on a spit.

'Roast over a good fire, which means a clear, bright fire, well tended in the grate. For this roast, the woodcocks should not be rare but, on the contrary, well done; they must cook 25–30 minutes.

'Meanwhile, cut as many slices of French bread as you have guests; first grill them. Place them in the drip pan on a metal rack; they then get the juice dripping from the game, but remain crisp. Twelve minutes before the woodcocks are roasted, remove the slices of bread, spread them with what remains of the stuffing, mixed with the livers of the three woodcocks well chopped. Your croûtons with this spread are more hygienic than when spread with the intestines of the game. As soon as the croûtons are spread with the stuffing, again place them in the drip pan; the last ten minutes of cooking are sufficient to cook the garnish.

'Now that the woodcocks are roasted, remove them from the spit, remove their bards and the strings that trussed the birds. Serve the birds on a hot platter, surrounding them with the croûtons, and accompanied by three lemons, quartered, and a sauceboat with the juice from the drip pan to which you add 1 tablespoon of good Madeira.

'Do not forget that the plates should be well-heated.'

Note: The next day you can make a delicious game soup with the carcasses of the two roasted woodcocks (what is left from the carving), the raw carcass and some of the raw meat left from the third woodcock, which was used for the stuffing. You simply cook these leftovers in 1½ l (3 pts) of bouillon from a *pot-au-feu* for 1 hour; after cooking, strain through a fine sieve.

SALMIS OF WOODCOCK
Salmis de bécasses à l'ancienne Christian Bourillot
For 4 people

2 good-sized woodcocks

Unsalted butter

Mirepoix of finely diced carrot, onion and celery

Cognac

1½ glasses white or red wine

2 dl (¼ pt) demi-glace sauce (page 108)

Cooking juice from mushrooms

25 g (1 oz) unsalted butter

Small mushrooms

Slices of truffles

Croûtons, fried in butter

Foie gras

After having removed the gizzards, truss and season 2 good-sized woodcocks. Roast over a high flame in an oven or on a spit. Cook the meat rare. Carefully separate the breasts, wings and legs and place the meat in a bowl or a shallow covered dish and keep warm. Set aside the intestines.

Meanwhile, chop the carcass and the skin; brown in butter with a *mirepoix*. As soon as the ingredients are browned, moisten with cognac, ignite and pour over the white or red wine. Boil to reduce by half. Add the demi-glace sauce and boil for a few minutes.

Pass the sauce through a fine strainer, rubbing through all the ingredients to get the best of the carcass and the flavourings. The resulting mixture should be more like a *coulis* than a sauce. Thin with reduced mushroom juice, correct the seasoning and add a knob of butter to the sauce. When the sauce is done, strain it, very hot, on to the pieces of woodcock to which have been added the 2 heads and a garnish made with small mushrooms and slices of truffles cooked in butter.

To serve, add a final touch to this delicious dish with croûtons fried in butter and spread with a stuffing made with the intestines and a little *foie gras*.

Note: The recipe for salmis of woodcock *à l'ancienne* can serve as a basic principle for a salmis of many other birds – pheasants, partridges, wood pigeon, wild duck and other water fowl.

WILD DUCK
Canard sauvage

All types of wild duck are treated in the same way.

ROAST WILD DUCK
Canard sauvage rôti

Truss the duck after seasoning the inside; do not bard it. Baste the
duck with melted butter and place in a 450°F (230°C, gas mark 8)
oven for 15–20 minutes, depending on its weight. Cook it rare.

Place the duck on a platter with a bouquet of watercress and
half a lemon. Serve with it the cooking juice mixed with butter
and 2–3 tablespoons of veal stock or hot water added to deglaze
the roasting pan.

ROAST WILD DUCK WITH
APPLE SAUCE
Canard sauvage rôti à l'anglaise

Roast the wild duck, then serve it with a bowl of unsweetened
or lightly sweetened apple sauce.

SALMIS OF WILD DUCK
Salmis de canard sauvage

Proceed as for the salmis of pheasant (page 406). Cooking time
will be 18–20 minutes. It must be rare.

WILD DUCK WITH ORANGE
Canard sauvage à la bigarade

Follow the recipe for braised duckling with orange (page 374).
Cook it pink.

VEGETABLES, PASTA
AND RICE

Vegetables play a very important part in cooking. There are so many varieties, such a wide range of flavours and so many ways of preparing them that they enhance and complete the most elaborate menus.

The basic ways of cooking vegetables are in water, steamed, à l'étuvée, deep fried and grilled.

Cooking vegetables in water

Some vegetables, notably spinach and French beans, are put into large quantities of boiling water to cook them thoroughly while maintaining their green colour.

The saucepan should be uncovered and placed over a high flame with enough water to cover the vegetables completely when they are plunged in, using $\frac{1}{2}$ tablespoon of salt to each litre (2 pts) of water. The water should be boiling and should never stop boiling during cooking. It is preferable to use the vegetables as soon as they have been cooked and drained, if they are going to be served plain, à l'anglaise or with butter.

After cooking the vegetables may be plunged into cold water to refresh them. In this case they must not stay in the water, or they will lose all their flavour. They must be thoroughly drained.

Some vegetables require special treatment, especially artichoke hearts, celery, etc. Once these vegetables have been peeled or trimmed, they blacken on contact with the air; to avoid this they have to be kept in fresh water, acidulated by the addition of lemon juice They are cooked in a liquid called a *blanc*.

Blanc à legumes

1 l (2 pts) water
1 teaspoon salt
25 g (1 oz) flour
Juice of 1 lemon
Fat or oil

The quantity of liquid is determined by the quantity of vegetables to be cooked; for 1 l (2 pts) of water use 1 teaspoon of salt, 25 g (1 oz) of flour, diluted with cold water, the juice of 1 lemon and any kind of fat or oil. The acidity of the lemon kills the tannin and the other ingredients coat the vegetables so that they do not come in contact with the air while cooking. The vegetables should be cooked in a boiling *blanc*. If the vegetables are not to be used immediately, they should be left to cool in their cooking liquid.

Cuisson à l'étuvée

Also called *à l'étouffée*, this very delicate method requires close attention and continuous surveillance. Vegetables cooked *à l'étuvée* must be young – new or spring vegetables. Among those used most often are: carrots, turnips, green peas, French beans and sorrel. One can include potatoes, although the cooking method is slightly different.

To cook vegetables *à l'étuvée*, place them in a heavy-bottomed saucepan; salt and butter them lightly. Stir the vegetables over a low flame, making them 'sweat'. The purpose of this cooking method is to make the vegetables give up some of their water, which is needed to cook them, and, at the same time, to bring out their aroma and flavour. The saucepan should be covered tightly, so that when the steam condenses on the lid, it falls back on to the vegetables. The flame should be moderate. If it is too low, the vegetables will disintegrate. If it is too high, because of the vegetables' sugar content, they may caramelize and stick to the bottom of the saucepan. When cooking is completed, the water from the vegetables should have evaporated without their becoming dry. To sum up, to obtain perfectly cooked vegetables, the cooking must be done slowly, with as little evaporation as possible, so that the liquid needed to produce the steam does not dry up.

STEAMING

Steaming is similar to cooking *à l'étuvée*. The vegetables are enclosed in a steam bath until they are completely cooked. For this you need a large saucepan or steamer made so that the vegetables are separated from the boiling water by a perforated rack. The water should be salted. It is important that no steam be lost, and so the saucepan should be tightly closed. For the vegetables to cook properly the water must boil continuously; if not, the steam will not reach the needed pressure and temperature needed to cook the vegetables.

In France this method is used mainly for potatoes. It can be used for other vegetables and for other foods such as meats, fish and shellfish. Pressure cookers are really tightly closed steamers in which the steam can reach very high pressures.

Steamed vegetables are eaten plain, with butter.

GRILLING

Grilling is one of the first methods ever used by men to cook their food. Although it is very useful for meat and fish, it is less so for vegetables. However, for some vegetables, grilling gives good results and a pleasant flavour.

Tomatoes, mushrooms and most vegetables with a high water content can be grilled very successfully. They should be first seasoned and coated with some fat, preferably olive oil. Place the vegetables on a very hot grill, turn them often and baste them with oil while they are cooking. The heat must be high so that the exterior of the vegetable caramelizes lightly. The inside pulp is cooked as its water content evaporates.

Grilled vegetables are served most often as a garnish for meat and poultry. The best heat for this method of cooking is produced by charcoal.

FRYING

Vegetables are fried by immersing them in vegetable or animal fat heated to a specific temperature. This method of cooking requires a certain degree of skill.

The vegetables that are to be fried must be rich in starch, like potatoes. Otherwise you must coat them with flour or a frying batter. Courgettes, aubergines, etc., are cooked in this way.

What happens during cooking? The vegetables, plunged into the hot oil, are sealed by the high heat. The starch in them forms a thin waterproof skin, enclosing the vegetable's water inside the pulp. The water then boils under this heat and cooks the pulp.

A correctly fried vegetable must be firm, crisp and a beautiful light-brown colour outside, and cooked and soft inside. To obtain these results the frying oil must be just the right temperature. If the heat were too high, the sugar content would caramelize too much and give a bitter taste and too dark a colour to the vegetables. The cooking time cannot be specified; it depends on the size of the vegetables. One must not fry too large an amount at one time, as the temperature of the frying oil would drop. If this happens the fat will penetrate the vegetable pulp and the pulp will disintegrate instead of permitting the protective skin to form. As soon as they are fried, the vegetables should be drained and dried on a piece of cloth or paper towel, salted and served immediately; otherwise, they get soft.

FRYING BATTER FOR VEGETABLES

**250 g (8 oz) sifted
flour**

**50 g (2 oz) melted
unsalted butter**

2 whole eggs

Salt

Optional:

**4 egg whites, beaten
stiff**

Beer

In a bowl mix the sifted flour with the melted butter and 2 whole eggs; add salt. Then dilute with enough water to obtain a semi-liquid batter, which must be prepared 1 hour before it is to be used.

Vegetables that have been boiled beforehand – such as salsify, cauliflower, etc. – can be fried. For this type of vegetable you must prepare a thicker frying batter and, just before using it, add 4 egg whites beaten stiff. One can also make the batter lighter by replacing the water with beer.

BRAISING

This method is derived from cooking *à l'étuvée*. The vegetables that are going to be braised must first be blanched to reduce their volume and neutralize their bitterness To do this, plunge the vegetables, cleaned and trimmed, into a large pan of boiling water. A few minutes of quick boiling is enough. After they have been half cooked, rinse quickly in cold water and drain the vegetables.

The main vegetables that can be braised are cabbage, celery hearts, lettuce, etc. The braising is done in a heavy-bottomed ovenproof casserole on top of a rich *mirepoix* of finely diced carrot, onion and celery. The vegetables are moistened to a quarter of their height with a fatty bouillon, salted and peppered. The cooking is done in the oven, at a simmer that produces the steam necessary to the cooking. The braising pan should be covered, and to prevent the surface of the vegetables from drying out, they should be covered with a piece of buttered paper with a hole in the centre big enough for the steam to escape and condense on the sides of the braising pan. The cooking time depends on the vegetables being cooked.

For cabbage the braising pan should be lined with slices of fresh pork fat (or bacon). In some cases one adds such ingredients as salted pork or game (pheasant, partridge, etc.).

Celery and lettuce are drained after braising and placed in a shallow casserole; add some thickened veal stock to the juices in the braising pan. Boil to reduce, correct the seasoning, then strain the sauce on to the vegetables so that they absorb the sauce and are glazed with a shiny coat.

Vegetables can also be stuffed before being braised.

Vegetables à la grecque

1 l (2 pts) water
6 tablespoons virgin olive oil
½ tablespoon salt
Juice of 3 lemons
Fennel
Celery
Coriander seeds
Pepper
Thyme
Bay leaf

This way of preparing vegetables is not, as the name might suggest, a Greek speciality. The method was studied and perfected by French cooks on the basis of Greek originals.

Vegetables cooked *à la grecque* are served most often cold as hors-d'oeuvre. Artichokes, leeks, small onions and mushrooms, are the best suited to the method.

Depending on the quantity of vegetables being cooked, the following ingredients are used: water, olive oil, salt and lemon juice. Season with fennel, celery, coriander seeds, pepper, thyme and bay leaf, using these spices in proportion to their aromatic strength. In certain cases, part of the water is replaced by dry white wine.

The vegetables are then cooked in this preparation, and after being cooked, kept in that liquid, which will have reduced in part.

GLAZING

Some vegetables, carrots, turnips, small onions, etc., are glazed to preserve and accentuate their flavour and to give them a shine without losing their natural colour and firmness. After being trimmed or rounded the vegetables are placed in a shallow heavy-bottomed saucepan, with butter, salt, a pinch of sugar and water reaching halfway up. The cooking is done by boiling to evaporate the liquid almost completely, reducing it to a syrup. Glazing is done by rolling the vegetables in the syrupy liquid to give them a shiny coating.

Glazed vegetables are used as a garnish for meats and poultry. They are also used to make bouquets of vegetables.

The term 'glaze' is also used for braised vegetables (see above), though in this case the word has a slightly different sense.

DRIED VEGETABLES

Dried vegetables are mainly pulses, such as beans, lentils and peas, picked when ripe. Dried vegetables must not be too old – preferably less than a year. As they have lost much of their own moisture they must be soaked for a few hours before cooking. However, if they are soaked for too long they will germinate and ferment which makes them difficult to digest. Before soaking the beans must be sorted and washed to remove any dirt, grit or bad beans.

Unlike fresh vegetables, dried vegetables are started in plenty of cold water, so that they will cook properly and continue to swell. To be sure of perfect cooking, the liquid must be brought to the boil slowly. Skim the top, spice with an onion stuck with a clove, carrots, garlic and a bouquet garni. Add salt after half an hour, and keep the saucepan covered. The cooking must be slow and regular; under no circumstances should the liquid stop bubbling. If the liquid evaporates, add boiling water – not cold water, which would harden the starch.

ARTICHOKES STUFFED WITH MUSHROOMS
Artichauts à la Barigoule

6 medium artichokes
1 carrot, sliced
1 onion, sliced
3 pieces fresh pork rind
Sprig thyme
½ bay leaf
½ glass dry white wine
White veal stock, lightly salted, or bouillon
3 tablespoons reduced demi-glace sauce (page 108) or 25 g (1 oz) unsalted butter

Stuffing:
50 g (2 oz) fresh pork fat, grated or cut in tiny dice
2 shallots, finely chopped
225 g (8 oz) white mushrooms
Salt and pepper
50 g (2 oz) sausage meat
1 teaspoon chopped fresh parsley
50 g (2 oz) unsalted butter

Choose 6 medium artichokes of the same size. Cut the stems off close to the leaves and trim the leaves by about 3 cm (1½ inches).

Blanch the artichokes for 15 minutes in boiling water and drain them. When cool enough to handle, remove the centre leaves, then all of the choke.

Season lightly, then fill the inside with a large tablespoon of the stuffing.

Stuffing

Grate the fresh pork fat or cut into tiny dice; slowly heat in a pan with the shallots.

Meanwhile, quickly chop the mushrooms, cleaned and washed without letting them stand in the water. Add the mushrooms to the pan with the pork fat and the shallots; dry everything on a high flame for 3 minutes, stirring continuously with a wooden spoon; season with salt and pepper.

At this point, add the fine sausage meat if liked. Remove from the heat and finish by adding 1 teaspoon of chopped fresh parsley and 50 g (2 oz) of butter. Mix well until the butter is completely incorporated. Correct the seasoning. Stuff the artichokes and cover each with a piece of fresh pork fat; tie with string.

At the bottom of a thickly buttered deep saucepan just big enough to hold the 6 artichokes, place a carrot and an onion, both sliced, 3 pieces of fresh pork rind, thyme and bay leaf. Place the artichokes on top, cover and stew for 10 minutes, simmering; moisten with dry white wine and boil to reduce almost completely. Add veal stock, lightly salted, or bouillon, to reach halfway up the artichokes. Bring to the boil, cover, and cook in a 325°F (170°C, gas mark 3) oven for 45 minutes.

Remove the lid and let the pork fat brown.

Remove the artichokes, take off the strings and place the artichokes on a hot round platter.

Strain the braising juice into a pan, degrease it and boil to reduce it to ½ cup; correct the seasoning and add 3 tablespoons reduced demi-glace sauce; or away from the heat add 25 g (1 oz) of butter.

Pour this sauce over the serving platter with the artichokes or simply serve in a sauceboat.

ARTICHOKES WITH VARIOUS SAUCES
Artichauts avec sauces diverses

Cook artichokes whole. First cut the stems off close to the leaves; with scissors, remove the pointed ends of the bottom row of leaves and trim the artichokes by one-third. Wash them, tie them to keep the leaves together while they are cooking, and plunge them into a saucepan of boiling water, let stand off the heat for 10 minutes, then drain.

Place the artichokes again in boiling salted water and cook, letting the water boil rapidly.

The artichokes are cooked when they feel soft to light pressure on the bottom or when a leaf can be detached easily.

To serve artichokes hot drain them well, standing them upside down on their leaves, and place them on a folded napkin. Serve a sauceboat of melted butter, or hollandaise (page 126), mousseline (page 127), cream (page 121) or velouté sauce (page 109).

To serve artichokes cold drain them, standing them upside down on their leaves, and let them cool. Place them on a folded napkin after removing the centre leaves, and then the chokes. Replace the bouquet of leaves that were removed, with the leaves upside down, the pointed ends inside the centre of the artichoke. Place a pinch of chopped parsley or chervil on top in this hollow.

Serve with a cold sauce: vinaigrette (page 129), light mayonnaise (page 128), with or without mustard, tartare sauce (page 131), etc.

ARTICHOKE HEARTS WITH MUSHROOM PURÉE
Fonds d'artichauts à la bressanne

12 medium-sized artichokes
1 tablespoon flour
2 tablespoons vinegar or half a lemon
1 l (2 pts) water
1½ teaspoons salt
75 g (3 oz) unsalted butter
Salt and fresh pepper
6 tablespoons double cream
½ l (1 pt) light mushroom purée (page 447)

Remove all the leaves from the freshly gathered artichokes; completely remove the chokes and trim the outsides; rub with a quarter of a lemon to keep white, and place the artichoke hearts in cold water.

Meanwhile, prepare a *blanc* made with the flour, vinegar or half lemon, water and salt. Moisten the flour with cold water and bring the liquid to the boil, stirring often.

Add the artichoke hearts and cook, simmering, for 30–40 minutes. When they are cooked, drain and wipe dry; stew in butter in a pan for 15 minutes. Season with a dash of salt and fresh pepper. Raise the heat to brown the hearts lightly on both sides, turning them carefully with a spatula.

Moisten the artichokes with 6 tablespoons of cream, boil to reduce slowly by half and add the mushroom purée.

Remove from the heat as soon as the purée is boiling, and add remaining butter, stirring well. Serve in a bowl.

ARTICHOKES A LA GRECQUE
Artichauts à la grecque

12 small artichokes
¾ l (1¼ pts) water
3 sprigs parsley
1 celery stalk
Sprig thyme
½ bay leaf
Pinch coriander
Pinch fennel
5 crushed peppercorns
Juice of 2 lemons
6 tablespoons oil
1½ teaspoons salt

Choose a dozen freshly gathered small artichokes. Quarter them, trim the leaves and throw into acidulated cold water. Drain.

Blanch the artichokes for 8 minutes by plunging them into boiling water, then drain.

Meanwhile, prepare the cooking liquid with the water, parsley, celery, thyme, bay leaf, coriander, fennel and peppercorns, the juice of 2 lemons, 6 tablespoons of oil and 1¼ teaspoons of salt.

Bring this to the boil and boil quickly for 10 minutes. Then add the artichokes; cook on a high flame for 15–20 minutes, then pour into a bowl and let cool.

Place the artichokes in a dish with a little of the cooking liquid and serve very cold.

STUFFED ARTICHOKE HEARTS
Fonds d'artichauts farcis

Trim the artichoke hearts and cook in a white court-bouillon following the directions in the recipe for artichoke hearts *à la bressanne* above. Drain, season with salt and pepper and stew in butter 15 minutes in a pan. Place in a gratin dish, and garnish with a rather thick mushroom purée (page 447); sprinkle with fresh breadcrumbs, baste with the cooking butter and brown in a 425°F (220°C, gas mark 7) oven.

Serve with a sauceboat of Madeira sauce (page 113).

ARTICHOKE HEARTS WITH CHEESE SAUCE
Fonds d'artichauts Mornay

Proceed as for the stuffed artichoke hearts above. After the artichokes are cooked and stewed, put them side by side in a gratin dish, first placing a light layer of Mornay sauce (page 120) at the bottom.

Spoon 1 tablespoon of Mornay sauce on each, then sprinkle with some grated Parmesan and Gruyère cheese, half of each, mixed with a pinch of fresh breadcrumbs.

Baste each heart with a few drops of melted butter, and brown in a 425°F (220°C, gas mark 7) oven.

ARTICHOKE HEARTS WITH ASPARAGUS TIPS
Fonds d'artichauts princesse

Prepare in the same way as the artichoke hearts with Mornay sauce above. However, when the hearts are placed in the gratin dish, garnish them with green asparagus tips, cooked in salted boiling water, drained and stewed 5 minutes in butter and coated with a few tablespoons of Mornay sauce. Finish the dish as for the artichoke hearts with Mornay sauce.

ARTICHOKE FRITTERS
Beignets d'artichauts

Prepare artichoke hearts as directed above, and cook them in a white court-bouillon, or, even better, steam them; drain and wipe dry. Then cut into 4 or 6 pieces each, depending on their size.

Place the artichoke pieces in a bowl and pour over a few drops of lemon juice and a little oil. Season with salt and pepper and add a pinch of chopped parsley and chervil; mix well, and marinate for 20 minutes.

Drain the artichoke pieces and plunge them one at a time into a frying batter (see page 428); then into very hot deep oil. When the fritters rise to the top and are golden brown and crisp, drain them on a paper towel, sprinkle with salt and pile them on a round platter covered with a folded napkin.

On top place a pinch of fried parsley.

ASPARAGUS
Asperges

Preparing asparagus is very simple. Peel the stems, being careful not to touch the tips; delicately remove the tiny leaves that surround the tips It is not enough to scrape the stalk because that does not remove the tough skin.

As the stalks are peeled and the tough part of the stem removed, place the stalks in a bowl of cold water, without leaving them in it too long. Drain them and tie in bunches of about 6–10, depending on their thickness; cook by placing the bunches in boiling water, with $1\frac{1}{4}$ teaspoonfuls of salt per litre (2 pts).

The cooking time is 18–20 minutes. [*Editor's note:* Directions are for thick white French asparagus; slender green asparagus will take less time to cook.]

The asparagus should not be overcooked; the stalks should still have some bite to them.

If the asparagus is to be served hot, cook it just before serving time. Remove each bunch with a slotted spoon and then dip it in a second pan of boiling water, correctly salted. Washing the asparagus this way will remove the strong taste of the asparagus water and make the stalks more tender and delicious. Drain the

stalks on a paper towel and place on a long platter, if possible
with a special rack for draining. Place each row of asparagus
1·5 cm ($\frac{3}{4}$ inch) behind the preceding one to display the tips well.

If the asparagus is to be served cold, follow the same method
but let the stalks cool on a paper towel.

Hot asparagus is served with a hot sauce: hollandaise page
126), mousseline (page 127) or velouté sauce (page 109) or melted
butter. Cold asparagus is served with a vinaigrette (page 129) or
light mayonnaise (page 128), etc.

ASPARAGUS WITH CHEESE SAUCE
Asperges au gratin

After cooking the asparagus as directed above, cut off the tender
part 5–8 cm (2–3 inches) from the tips. Gently cook the tips for
10 minutes in butter. Season with a dash of salt and freshly
ground pepper.

Place the asparagus in a gratin dish and follow the method given
for artichoke hearts with Mornay sauce (page 433).

Asperges à la polonaise

Just before serving the asparagus cooked by the directions above,
place it, very hot and well drained, on a long platter, arranging
one row behind the other. Sprinkle the tips with 1 hard-boiled
egg yolk (for 15–20 asparagus stalks), rubbed through a sieve, and
a large pinch of chopped parsley, slightly damp.

Over the asparagus tips pour some butter cooked until light
brown, in which some fine white breadcrumbs have been fried
till brown and crisp. Serve immediately while the butter is still
bubbling.

GREEN ASPARAGUS TIPS
Points d'asperges vertes

Green asparagus tips from stalks no thicker than a pencil are generally used as a garnish. Break off the tender part, which is no more than 8 cm (3 inches) long, by bending the asparagus between your fingers; 225 g ($\frac{1}{2}$ lb) of green asparagus gives about 100 g (4 oz) of tips.

Tie the tips in small bunches with string; cut the tender part of the stems in pieces 1 cm ($\frac{1}{2}$ inch) long. Place the asparagus in a large quantity of boiling salted water, cook on a high flame, drain well and prepare according to the recipe chosen.

AUBERGINES
Aubergines

The best aubergine for cooking is the large purple one, which is used in many different ways, either as a separate vegetable or as a garnish.

It is important to rid the aubergines of their excess water by steeping them in salt for half an hour, when they are to be cooked in butter in a covered saucepan, *au gratin* or sautéed. To remove the water, peel the aubergine then slice or quarter it, or cut into large sticks or pieces the shape of an olive, depending upon the recipe. Place the pieces in a bowl, sprinkle with sea salt, mix and let steep. Drain well, wipe dry and cook.

In addition to the ways given here, aubergine can be sliced thickly, peeled and sautéed to serve with poached or soft-boiled eggs, tournedos, noisettes, grenadins, etc.

3 large aubergines
Salt and pepper
Oil for deep frying
50 g (2 oz) butter
1 medium-sized
   onion
2 shallots
1 tablespoon olive oil
100 g (4 oz) white
   mushrooms
1 garlic clove,
   crushed
2 tablespoons tomato
   purée (page 507)
2 tablespoons
   espagnole sauce
   (page 108) or veal
   stock
3 tablespoons fresh
   breadcrumbs
Chopped parsley

STUFFED AUBERGINE BROWNED IN THE OVEN
Aubergines au gratin
For 6 people

Cut the aubergines in half lengthwise. Score the pulp lightly with the point of a knife and make an incision in each half 3 mm ($\frac{1}{8}$ inch) inside the skin around the edge. Let them steep with salt for 30 minutes.

Drain the aubergine, wipe dry and plunge into very hot deep oil, cooking just until the pulp can be removed easily with a spoon – about 5–8 minutes.

Drain on a paper towel and remove the pulp with a spoon, being careful not to damage the skins. Spread the skins, side by side, the black side down, on a well-buttered gratin dish; meanwhile, chop the pulp fine and put it in a bowl.

Chop the onion and the shallots, stew them slowly with 1 tablespoon of butter and 1 tablespoon of olive oil. When they are cooked, raise the heat and brown them. Add the mushrooms, washed and chopped. Season with salt and pepper, and cook quickly on a high flame, stirring continuously with a wooden spoon.

When the water from the mushrooms has evaporated, add the garlic, the tomato purée, the espagnole sauce or the veal stock, and the pulp from the aubergine. Simmer 5 minutes, stiffening the mixture (it should be like mashed potatoes) by adding some fresh breadcrumbs.

Remove from the heat, season and fill the aubergine skins with this mixture piled up.

Sprinkle the tops with fresh breadcrumbs, moisten with the remaining butter, melted (or oil), and brown in a 425°F (220°C, gas mark 7) oven. After removing from the oven, pour around the aubergines a border of espagnole sauce or veal stock reduced and buttered. Sprinkle each aubergine with a pinch of chopped parsley.

3 firm aubergines
Salt
75 g (3 oz) unsalted
   butter
3 dl (½ pt) double
   cream
Chopped chervil

AUBERGINE WITH CREAM
Aubergines à la crème

Peel 3 firm aubergines. Slice 6 mm (¼ inch) thick; steep in salt for 30 minutes; drain and wipe dry.

Stew the slices in 50 g (2 oz) or more of butter in a covered saucepan until completely cooked.

Just before serving, add the cream. Boil on a high flame to reduce quickly by half, stirring the aubergine but being careful not to crush the slices. When the sauce is sufficiently reduced, correct the seasoning and, stirring, add away from the heat 25 g (1 oz) of butter.

Place in a bowl and sprinkle with chopped chervil.

FRIED AUBERGINE OR AUBERGINE FRITTERS
Aubergines frites au beignets d'aubergines

Peel the aubergines, slice them 6 mm (¼ inch) thick. Season with salt and freshly ground pepper, sprinkle with 2 tablespoons of flour and mix well.

Shake off the excess flour and plunge the slices into very hot oil.

When they are golden brown and crisp, drain and place on a round platter covered with a napkin. To be really delicious, the aubergine must be crisp, so keep your guests waiting for their vegetable.

Aubergine slices can also be fried as fritters, dipped in frying batter (page 428).

3 tablespoons olive
  oil
½ onion, cut into
  julienne
1 medium aubergine,
  cut into 1·5-cm (¾-
  inch) cubes
Salt and pepper
1 teaspoon flour
½ garlic clove,
  crushed
1 tomato, peeled,
  seeded, juice
  squeezed out and
  coarsely chopped
Chopped parsley

AUBERGINE WITH GARLIC AND TOMATO
Aubergines à la provençale
For 1 serving

Heat the oil in a pan and slowly brown the onion, until golden. Add the aubergine, season with salt and pepper and sprinkle with the flour.

Stir often to keep the pieces from sticking and to brown everything lightly.

Add the garlic, crushed with a knife blade (never chop garlic); heat for a second, shaking the pan, then add the tomato.

Correct the seasoning with salt and pepper and continue to cook slowly. The juice from the tomato changes the cooking process from frying to stewing. The aubergine and other ingredients get soft until the moisture has completely evaporated. This step will take about half an hour; then the aubergine, tomato, and oil, well mixed, will look almost like jam.

To serve, correct the seasoning, pour the mixture into a hot bowl, and sprinkle chopped parsley on top.

CARDOONS
Cardons

Cardoons look like giant artichoke plants; when they reach full growth, the leaves are tied up and the plant is covered to blanch it.

The Tours variety is the best.

Only the tender centre stalks are used for the table. A 2·7-kg (6-lb) plant will yield about 1 kg (2 lb) of edible parts.

Whatever the recipe, the cardoon stalks need special preparation.

First remove the tough and wilted branches. Then, one by one, cut off the tender branches until you reach the heart. Cut the stalks into pieces 8 cm (3 inches) long, starting from the base, discarding the leafy top part, which is tough and stringy, and keeping only the thick parts, which are tender.

Peel the pieces of stalk, removing all the stringy parts, and rub them with quarter of a lemon to keep them from darkening. Place the pieces in a bowl of cold water with vinegar or lemon juice.

Prepare a white court-bouillon with 1 l (2 pts) of water, 1 tablespoon of flour diluted with 2 tablespoons of vinegar or the juice of half a lemon, and 1½ teaspoons of salt.

Stir until the liquid comes to the boil; add the pieces of cardoon, drained at the last moment.

To protect the pieces of stalk from contact with the air, which would darken them, add to the court-bouillon 100 g (4 oz) of raw veal fat, diced very fine, for each litre (2 pts) of water.

Boil slowly, covered, for 2 hours. When the cardoons are cooked, they should give when pressed. Pour the cooked cardoons into a glazed bowl and keep them until finished for serving.

1 white cardoon
3 tablespoons flour
1 lemon
Salt and pepper
50 g (2 oz) butter
1 l (2 pts) well-flavoured beef bouillon
225 g (8 oz) beef marrow
50 g (2 oz) Gruyère cheese, grated

CARDOONS WITH BEEF MARROW
Cardons à la moelle
For 6 people

Cut the tender parts of a cardoon into small sticks 3 cm (1¼ inches) long; trim them and cook in a court-bouillon made with 3¼ l (6 pts) of water to which are added 1 tablespoon of flour diluted in water, the juice of 1 lemon and 1 tablespoon of salt.

Meanwhile, in a saucepan heat 25 g (1 oz) of butter. Add the remaining flour and make a roux. Into the roux pour the beef bouillon. After mixing with a whisk, simmer for 20 minutes. Correct the seasoning.

When the cardoons are cooked, drain them, mix into the sauce and place in a buttered gratin dish.

Poach the beef marrow. Slice it. Place the marrow on the cardoons. Sprinkle the grated Gruyère on top and brown in the oven.

Serve immediately in the gratin dish.

CARROTS

Carottes

Cooked as a vegetable, a garnish or a seasoning, carrots play an important role in cooking. They are available all the year round, from the early forced varieties to the summer crop and the late varieties which will keep through the winter.

Small, bright orange, new carrots are the best to prepare as a vegetable or garnish. They need only be peeled very thinly because the nutritive elements, the sugar and the vitamins are concentrated towards the outside part, which is also the tenderest.

Young carrots should never be blanched, that is, plunged into boiling water. After peeling, cut them, depending on how large they are, into halves or quarters; round the edges to give each piece the shape of a large olive. Wash in cold water.

Cook the carrot pieces in a saucepan with just enough cold water to cover them; for each 1 l (1 pt) add a pinch of salt, 1 teaspoon of sugar and 50 g (2 oz) of butter.

Cook, covered, on a moderately high flame, until all the liquid has evaporated. The mixture of the butter, the juices from the vegetables and the reduced liquid produces a thick syrupy sauce. Sauté the carrots in this mixture until they are covered with a shiny coating.

Cooked this way, the carrots are ready to be served on their own or with a main dish.

When you have to use old carrots, use the dark-orange part. The cores are woody and strong in flavour; after being blanched they can be used in moderation to flavour stock.

Cut the carrots into large pieces, shaped like olives, and cook them in salted water before using in any recipe, this is the only way to remove the strong flavour of old carrots. The carrots can be grated or cut into thin strips and coated with cream and lemon mayonnaise (page 132) or any sauce with a mayonnaise base.

CARROTS GLAZED IN BUTTER
Carottes glacées au beurre

The word 'glaze' conjures up the shiny film which coats the carrots like a varnish when they are cooked.

Prepare by the instructions above. Away from the heat add some butter, which will mix with the syrupy juice in which the carrots were sautéed.

This vegetable should be cooked just before serving; waiting spoils the fresh sweet taste of the carrots, which then take on an unpleasant reheated flavour.

CARROTS WITH CREAM
Carottes à la crème

Prepare carrots glazed in butter (as directed above); when the sauce is reduced, moisten again, covering the carrots with double cream. Boil to reduce by half, correct the seasoning, shake everything to distribute the sauce and place in a vegetable dish.

CARROTS VICHY
Carottes Vichy

Follow the cooking method for carrots glazed in butter (above). Instead of shaping the carrots like olives, they should be thinly sliced; and add a pinch of bicarbonate of soda to the cooking water.

Place the carrots in a vegetable dish and sprinkle with fresh chopped parsley.

CARROT PURÉE
Purée de carottes

Slice the carrots very thin, add well-washed rice to equal one-fourth of their weight.

Cook together over a high heat, as for carrots glazed with butter (above). However, increase the quantity of water. Rub the cooked carrots and rice through a fine sieve, put the purée into a pan and dry it on a high flame.

Away from the heat add 100 g (4 oz) of butter for each 500 g (1 lb) of purée, and bring to the proper consistency by adding milk, cream or boiling bouillon.

Correct the seasoning, place in a vegetable dish and decorate with diamond- or heart-shaped croûtons, fried in butter.

CELERY AND CELERIAC
Pieds de céleri et céleri-rave

These are two different varieties of the same vegetable. In the celery we eat the stalks; in celeriac, the root.

Both are eaten raw or cooked. However, they are not prepared in the same ways.

In the chapter on hors-d'oeuvre there are recipes for celery and celeriac salad. The recipes given here are to be served as a separate course or as a garnish.

Trim the celery stalks or heads by removing the green leaves and by slicing off part of the base. Leave enough of the base to hold the trimmed stalks, about 20 cm (8 inches) long, around the heart.

Wash carefully, running cold water between the ribs to remove the dirt and the tiny insects that are sometimes there.

Remove the strings from the outside of the ribs, rinse the vegetables, plunge them into a pot of boiling salted water and boil for 10 minutes.

Drain and let cool; season the insides with a pinch of salt, and tie the branches with a string.

To braise, place a few slices of carrot and onion and some pork rind in a buttered fireproof casserole. Place the celery heads on top, side by side; cover them and simmer for 15 minutes. Cover with a good white veal stock not degreased, to which is added 100 g (4 oz) of chopped belly of pork or bacon per 1 l (2 pts) of stock.

Bring slowly to the boil and simmer, covered, in a 350°F (180°C, gas mark 4) oven for 2 hours.

If the celery is not to be used immediately, remove to a glazed bowl and pour over the strained juice.

Celeriac should first be washed, then peeled, cut into quarters, trimmed or thickly sliced. Rinse in cold water and blanch in salted boiling water for 5 minutes.

Drain and let cool on a paper towel. Stew in butter in a covered pan. Season with salt and pepper. After the celeriac is cooked, prepare as described above for celery stalks.

CELERY WITH VEAL GRAVY
Céleri au jus

Drain braised celery (recipe above). Cut the heads in half lengthwise. Place in a pan and cover with a good veal stock, lightly salted, adding the braising juices, one part braising juice to two parts veal stock.

Cover and simmer for 15–20 minutes.

Place the celery in a vegetable dish; if the juice has not reduced sufficiently, raise the heat, and boil for a few minutes to reduce it to the quantity needed. Away from the heat thicken with 50 g (2 oz) of butter for ½ cup of juice. Pour on the celery.

CELERIAC PURÉE
Purée de céleri-rave

This purée is made by mixing together one part celeriac purée to one part puréed potato.

Prepare like mashed potatoes; that is, dry on a high flame to evaporate the moisture. Work the purée with a spatula, away from the heat, adding 50 g (2 oz) of butter for 500 g (1 lb) of purée, and bring it back to the proper consistency with hot milk and double cream. Spice with a dash of grated nutmeg. Do not let the purée boil. Serve in a vegetable dish.

⫸━⫷━⫸━⫷━⫸━⫷━⫸━⫷━⫸━⫷━⫸━⫷━⫸━⫷━⫸━⫷━⫸━⫷

CULTIVATED MUSHROOMS
Les champignons

First method:
500 g (1 lb)
  mushrooms
6 tablespoons water
50 g (2 oz) unsalted
  butter
Juice of ½ lemon
Pinch salt

Second method:
500 g (1 lb)
  mushrooms
½ lemon
Melted unsalted
  butter
Pinch salt
2 tablespoons Madeira
2 tablespoons veal
  stock or white
  chicken bouillon

First method

Choose mushrooms that are white and firm, with their gills not visible; cut off the sandy part of the stems. Place the mushrooms in a bowl and pour some cold water over; wash them carefully and quickly in two changes of water; drain and wipe dry immediately.

Trim the mushrooms; cut the stem off, and peel the cap thinly.

Meanwhile, prepare a court-bouillon with the water, butter, the juice of half a lemon and a pinch of salt. Bring to the boil and add the mushrooms.

Boil the mushrooms in this prepared liquid for 5 minutes on a high flame, and remove them to a glazed bowl. Cover with a piece of buttered paper to prevent the tops from darkening.

Second method

As the mushrooms are peeled, rub each one with half a lemon and place them in a pan with melted butter; add the salt, Madeira and veal stock or white chicken bouillon. Cover and stew for 8 minutes. Remove to a bowl and follow the directions for the first method.

⫸━⫷━⫸━⫷━⫸━⫷━⫸━⫷━⫸━⫷━⫸━⫷━⫸━⫷━⫸━⫷━⫸━⫷

MUSHROOMS WITH CREAM
Champignons à la crème

500 g (1 lb) white
  mushrooms
175 g (6 oz) unsalted
  butter
Pinch salt and freshly
  ground pepper
1½ dl (¼ pt) double
  cream
Juice of ¼ lemon

Choose white mushrooms, preferably small, firm and very white. Remove the sandy parts; wash the mushrooms carefully, then drain and wipe dry. If the mushrooms are large or medium, quarter them.

In a pan large enough to spread out the mushrooms, heat 100 g (4 oz) of butter. When the butter is hot, raise the heat and add the mushrooms; season with a pinch of salt and a few turns of the pepper mill. Sauté on a high flame to evaporate the mushroom liquid quickly and to start to brown the mushrooms lightly.

Add the cream and the juice of a quarter of a lemon; boil to reduce by half and away from the heat thicken with 50 g (2 oz) of butter.

Place in a warm vegetable dish.

For this recipe you need young mushrooms, well formed and very white; if not, the dish, which should be a beautiful ivory colour, may turn grey.

For 1 kg (2 lb) of mushrooms add 3 dl ($\frac{1}{2}$ pt) of cream and simmer on the stove. After it reduces slightly, correct the seasoning, add a little cream to restore the whiteness to the sauce and to thicken it.

For a large dinner in order to prevent the cream from curdling, some béchamel sauce (page 110) can be added.

MUSHROOMS WITH PARSLEY AND GARLIC
Champignons à la provençale

Use the method for *cèpes à la bordelaise* (page 450); replace the shallots with chopped parsley and plenty of garlic.

GRILLED MUSHROOMS
Champignons grillés

Choose firm, white mushroom caps. After washing and drying them, season and coat with oil or melted butter.

Place them under a hot grill: turn them once and brush with melted butter or oil. Serve the mushroom caps on a plate with *maître d'hôtel* butter (page 226) in their hollow.

They are usually used as garnish for grilled chicken *à l'américaine*, mixed grill, etc.

MUSHROOM PURÉE
Purée de champignons

Carefully wash firm, white mushrooms; rub them through a metal sieve or chop them very fine with a knife. Immediately place the mushroom pulp in a pan over a high flame and stir with a wooden spoon until the water has evaporated completely.

Finish the purée by adding some béchamel sauce (page 110) made with extra cream. Add salt, pepper and a dash of nutmeg.

CHOPPED MUSHROOMS SAUTÉED IN BUTTER
Duxelles sèche de champignons

500 g (1 lb) mushrooms
Unsalted butter and oil
50 g (2 oz) finely chopped shallots and onions
Salt and pepper
Pinch chopped parsley

Finely chop the mushrooms; squeeze in a cloth to remove all the juice. Sauté the finely chopped shallots and onions in butter and oil. Add the chopped mushrooms, salt and pepper. Cook on a very high flame, stirring with a wooden spoon until the water has evaporated completely. Finish by adding a good pinch of chopped parsley.

The dry *duxelles* should be stored in a bowl covered with buttered paper; it can be used as needed, especially in stuffings.

The *duxelles* used to stuff some vegetables, tomatoes, artichokes, mushroom caps, etc., is prepared in the same way as dry *duxelles*, but towards the end of cooking add a dash of garlic, a little reduced demi-glace sauce (page 108) with tomato and fresh breadcrumbs, rubbed through a fine sieve.

SAUTÉED MUSHROOMS WITH BUTTER OR CHEESE SAUCE
Champignons sautés au beurre ou à la Mornay

Slice the mushrooms – if they are large, into 3–5 slices. Season with salt and pepper, and sauté in a pan in butter on a very high flame.

Place the chopped mushrooms in a vegetable dish and sprinkle with chopped parsley.

You can also thicken them with Mornay sauce (p. 120). Then pour the mushrooms into an ovenproof dish, sprinkle with grated Gruyère cheese and brown.

STUFFED MUSHROOMS
Champignons farcis Jean-Paul Lacombe

Large mushrooms
Salt and pepper
Melted unsalted
   butter or olive oil

Duxelles:
1 medium-sized
   onion
1 shallot
100 g (4 oz) unsalted
   butter
6 tablespoons
   espagnole sauce
   (page 108) or veal
   stock
1 tablespoon tomato
   purée
Grated garlic
1 teaspoon chopped
   parsley
Few drops of lemon
   juice
1 heaped teaspoon
   fresh breadcrumbs

Choose large mushrooms all the same size.

Clean them, wash, drain and wipe dry. Remove the stems to make a hole in each cap.

Place the mushrooms in a well-buttered ovenproof dish, season with salt and pepper and baste with some melted butter, or olive oil, if you prefer.

Start the cooking by placing the mushrooms in a 450°F (230°C, gas mark 8) oven for 5 minutes.

Remove the mushroom caps and fill each with a mound of stuffing made from the stems, chopped and cooked as a *duxelles* (see below). Sprinkle with fresh breadcrumbs. Baste with melted butter or oil, and brown in a 425°F (220°C, gas mark 7) oven.

Duxelles

For 225 g (8 oz) of mushroom stems, finely chop 1 medium-sized onion and 1 shallot and cook them in 50 g (2 oz) of butter without letting them brown. When the onion and shallot are soft, add the finely chopped mushroom stems, heat on a high flame for 3 minutes to evaporate the water and moisten with espagnole sauce or a good veal stock and 1 tablespoon of tomato purée or the pulp of a fresh tomato. Season with salt and pepper, and flavour with a little grated garlic, chopped parsley and a few drops of lemon juice.

Cook to reduce to the proper consistency for stuffing or thicken with 1 heaped teaspoon of fresh breadcrumbs. Correct the seasoning and finish away from the heat by adding 50 g (2 oz) of butter.

[*Editor's note*: The French eat several varieties of excellent woodland mushrooms which are not sold in the British Isles, though they grow here quite commonly. The main kinds are ceps, morels, girolles and *mousserons* (St George's mushrooms).]

BOLETI OR CEPS
Bolets ou cèpes

The boletus is part of the group of polypores. These beautiful mushrooms, some weighing as much as 1·8 kg (4 lb) are called ceps or boleti in cooking. They are mainly found in autumn. As they grow old, they lose a great part of their culinary appeal; sometimes they have parasites or become spongy, and they can be toxic. Whatever the variety, ceps have a tendency to fall apart in cooking and to become slimy. Here are some basic principles to counteract these drawbacks and some frequently used methods for cooking them.

SAUTÉED CEPS WITH PARSLEY AND SHALLOTS
Cèpes sautés à la boredelaise (méthode Escoffier)

225 g (8 oz) ceps
Salt and pepper
Oil
Unsalted butter
2 tablespoons ceps stems, chopped
1 teaspoon chopped shallots
Lemon juice
Chopped parsley

The ceps should be barely opened or not at all. Do not wash but wipe them; however, those that are completely opened must be washed and wiped dry.

Slice the ceps, season with salt and pepper, sauté in very hot oil until they are lightly browned. Drain, replace the oil with butter and add, for 225 g (8 oz) ceps, 2 tablespoons of ceps stems that have been chopped and set aside, and chopped shallots. Sauté the mixture for a few minutes and put into a bowl; add a little lemon juice and some chopped parsley.

500 g (1 lb) ceps
Unsalted butter or oil
1 teaspoon lemon
juice
3 tablespoons olive
oil
Salt and pepper
3 shallots, chopped
2 tablespoons fresh
breadcrumbs
1 teaspoon chopped
parsley
Lemon juice

SAUTÉED CEPS WITH PARSLEY, SHALLOTS AND BREADCRUMBS
Cèpes à la bordelaise (méthode parisienne)

Sort 500 g (1 lb) of firm ceps. Clean, wash and stew in butter or oil with lemon juice. Drain the ceps and wipe dry if they are large; slice them, reserving the stems.

In a pan big enough to hold the ceps heat 3 tablespoons of olive oil. Throw the ceps into the very hot oil to sear them; season with salt and freshly ground pepper; sauté over a high flame to brown lightly.

Just before serving, add the chopped stems and shallots, fresh breadcrumbs, chopped parsley and a little lemon juice.

SAUTÉED CEPS WITH PARSLEY AND GARLIC
Cèpes sautés à la provençale

Prepare the same way as for *cèpes à la bordelaise*, but replace the shallots with 1 teaspoon of chopped garlic.

GRILLED CEPS
Cèpes grillés

Choose medium-sized ceps caps. Peel and flute the rounded sides; salt and pepper.

Brush the caps with oil or melted butter; cook on a very hot grill. Serve with *maître d'hôtel* butter (page 226) inside the caps. They can also be stuffed with the chopped stems, stewed in butter and flavoured with chopped parsley and garlic.

MORELS
Les Morilles

Gourmets consider morels the best mushrooms.

Some suggest not washing them; this is a mistake, however, because morels have very fine sand in their cells that must be removed. To do this, after removing the sandy part of the stems, place the morels in a large quantity of cold water and then rinse each morel under the cold tap. This is a time-consuming business but it is the only effective way of eliminating the sand.

To cook the morels cut them into several pieces if they are too large. After cleaning stew them in a saucepan with salt and pepper, the juice of a lemon and 100 g (4 oz) of butter for 500 g (1 lb) of morels.

Cook over a high flame, covered, for 10 minutes.

The juices the mushrooms release is usually sufficient for them to cook in.

MORELS WITH CREAM
Morilles à la crème

After stewing the morels, following the recipe above, add, for 500 g (1 lb) of morels, 6 tablespoons of reduced cream; let simmer for a few minutes.

Just before serving, add some fresh cream to thicken and whiten the sauce; correct the seasoning.

Note: Morels are used frequently to garnish veal or chicken fricasee, and to fill pies, flaky pastry, *vol-au-vent*, etc.

GIROLLES OR CHANTERELLES
Girolles appelées aussi chanterelles

These excellent mushrooms have a fine, light aroma and do not require any special cooking preparation. After removing the sandy part of the stems, simply wash them well and stew in butter or sauté in oil or butter.

Chanterelles can be cooked *à la bordelaise* or *à la provençale*. They are also used as a garnish for meat, poultry or game.

Note: If the chanterelles are too large, it is better to cut them lengthwise; before sautéeing them they can be blanched for 1 minute in salted boiling water.

ST GEORGE'S MUSHROOMS
Mousserons — roses des prés

These mushrooms are cooked in the same way as white mushrooms, but they are at their best sautéed in butter or in an omelette.

TRUFFLES
Les truffes

In addition to their value as a flavouring, truffles are used as a garnish and for decoration.

For the skilful work of decoration pieces of tinned truffle are generally used.

These truffles are usually large, firm and very black; they are cut into very thin slices. Placed flat on the table, the truffle slices are cut with a very sharp knife or cutter into different shapes – crescent, diamond, star, flower, etc. Then the cutouts are placed on a plate with some melted aspic. The ingredients are now ready and the decorating consists of placing each truffle shape on the prepared dish with a larding needle. When the decoration is finished, glaze the dish with a coat of delicious jelly.

For cooking, it is better to use fresh, raw truffles.

Raw truffles must be cleaned carefully; soak them in warm water to remove the sand that partly coats them. Then brush each truffle under running water and with a kitchen knife remove the sand that still remains. Rinse the truffles again and thoroughly dry them. Depending on their use, dice them, cut them into small sticks, slice them or shape them like olives. The trimmings and the peels, which have a strong flavour, are chopped and used to prepare a Périgeux sauce (page 116) or for stuffing and mousses. Whatever their use, the chopped stems and peels are always stewed in butter, especially if they are raw, before being incorporated in a dish.

Finally, fresh truffles can also be cut into julienne, sticks or slices and used in mixed salads.

Poultry and game birds with truffles

This procedure is used for capons, large roasting chickens, ducks, turkeys, pheasants, partridges, etc.

First clean and peel the truffles; set aside a few slices and quarter the remaining truffles, trimming the corners.

Then place these quarters in a bowl and marinate them with a little cognac and Madeira. Season with salt, pepper and seasonings in judicious proportions.

Place the reserved slices under the skin of the bird, being careful not to tear it. Remove all the membranes from some fresh pork fat and rub it through a fine sieve. Mix with the quartered truffles. Place this stuffing inside the bird, which must be kept cool but not too cold.

The bird must be stuffed with truffles at least 24 hours before cooking. During this time poultry or game birds will absorb the truffle flavour and this flavour will develop even more during cooking.

The excess fat, melted after cooking, can be used for other purposes.

Foie gras and truffles

Truffles for studding fresh *foie gras* must be fresh, peeled and quartered, seared in cognac on the stove and cooled in a covered bowl. Truffles cooked in this way can also be used to make pâtés, terrines or galantines.

OMELETTE WITH FRESH TRUFFLES
Omelette aux truffes fraîches

Use 100 g (4 oz) of truffles for an omelette made with 6 eggs.

Slice the truffles thin. Salt and pepper them and cook them lightly in butter.

Beat the eggs lightly. Season and add three-quarters of the sliced truffles. Make the omelette as usual, so that it is well-shaped and slightly runny in the middle, without browning it too much.

Place the omelette on a long platter, put the remaining truffle slices in a row on top, and serve.

Variation.   Instead of mixing the truffles with the eggs, you can stuff the omelette with a truffle stuffing thickened with a reduced demi-glace sauce (page 108).

SCRAMBLED EGGS WITH TRUFFLES
Oeufs brouillés aux truffes

Butter small cylindrical moulds and place a nice truffle slice at the bottom of each one.

Prepare the scrambled eggs so that they remain very soft; add the truffles, diced and cooked in butter.

To 6 scrambled eggs, add 4 raw eggs; mix and season them.

Fill the moulds and poach in a *bain-marie* in the oven. Unmould on little round pieces of bread fried in butter.

Serve with a very light demi-glace sauce (page 108), with essence of truffles.

Note: This way of serving scrambled eggs is called *oeufs moulés Verdi*.

TRUFFLES COOKED IN EMBERS
Truffes sous la cendre (méthode Escoffier)

Choose beautiful fresh truffles; clean them well, but do not peel.
Salt the truffles lightly and baste with a little fine champagne
brandy. Wrap each truffle first with a thin slice of fresh pork
fat, then with a double piece of buttered wax paper; dampen the
outside piece of paper with water. Bury the wrapped truffles
under a layer of burning embers, keeping the top embers glowing.

Allow $\frac{3}{4}$ hour cooking for average truffles.

After removing the paper, place the truffles on a napkin and
serve with fresh butter.

500 g (1 lb) truffles
1 glass champagne
1 heaped tablespoon
**   *mirepoix***
**   *bordelaise***
6 tablespoons veal
**   stock**

TRUFFLES WITH CHAMPAGNE
Truffes au champagne

Season well-cleaned truffles and cook, covered, with 1 glass of
champagne and 1 heaped tablespoon of *mirepoix bordelaise* (finely
chopped carrot, onion and celery) stewed in butter.

Place the truffles in a silver bowl. Boil the cooking liquid to
reduce almost completely; add the veal stock.

Boil for 5 minutes; correct the seasoning, and strain this sauce
through a cheesecloth over the truffles.

Serve very hot without boiling.

Note: The champagne can be replaced with sherry, port or
Madeira.

500 g (1 lb) fresh
**   truffles**
Salt and pepper
50 g (2 oz) unsalted
**   butter**
Cognac or port
3 dl ($\frac{1}{2}$ pt) cream

TRUFFLES WITH CREAM
Truffes à la crème

Cut 500 g (1 lb) of fresh truffles into thick slices. Season with salt
and pepper, stew slowly with butter and a little cognac or port.

Moisten with cream and simmer on a low flame without
letting the cream separate.

Serve as soon as the sauce is thickened and the seasoning is
correct.

TRUFFLE PASTRY TURNOVERS
Rissoles de truffes à la Valromey

Sandwich together two large thick slices of truffles with a slice of *foie gras* between. Season lightly and baste with a little fine champagne brandy.

Place each pair between two layers of flaky pastry (page 531), cut with a cutter into rounds slightly larger than the truffles. Press the pastry edges to make them stick together.

Plunge the turnovers into deep hot oil to brown.

Drain and place the turnovers on a napkin, garnish with fried parsley and serve immediately with Périgueux sauce (page 116).

TRUFFLES WITH FOIE GRAS
Truffes en surprises Roger Roucou

Rub some cooked *foie gras* through a very fine sieve. Put the purée into a silver or stainless-steel bowl and place the bowl on top of shaved ice. With a wooden spoon mix in chopped truffles, cooked in Madeira.

Make small balls of *foie gras* in various sizes. Roll them in finely chopped and dried truffles.

After shaping the balls to look as much like real truffles as possible, place them on a rack in a cool place.

Glaze with a coat of very well-flavoured aspic (see page 136).

These *truffes en surprises* are served on a napkin, in a basket or in a glass bowl.

**500 g (1 lb) chicory
Salt
50 g (2 oz) unsalted
butter
Juice of ¼ lemon
3 tablespoons water**

CHICORY
Endives

Chicory (also called Witloof or Belgian endive) in its second growth, after being blanched by covering with sand, is very white and delicate.

Trim 500 g (1 lb) of chicory and wash quickly under running water – it becomes bitter if permitted to stand in water. Place in a buttered saucepan, sprinkle with salt and butter, cut into pieces; baste with the juice of a quarter of a lemon. Add 3 tablespoons of water, cover with buttered paper.

Put the lid on, then bring to the boil; continue cooking for 45 minutes at moderate heat, in the oven, if possible.

CHICORY WITH CREAM
Endives à la crème

Stew the chicory as described above, then place them in a pan, cover them with boiling double cream, and simmer until the cream has reduced by two-thirds.

Drain the endives and place them in a warm vegetable bowl; correct the seasoning of the cream. Away from the heat add 75 g (3 oz) of butter for each 1½ dl (¼ pt) sauce, and pour over the chicory.

CHICORY WITH CHEESE SAUCE
Endives Mornay

Cook the chicory as for chicory with cream (above) and place them in a gratin dish. Boil the cream to reduce almost completely, then add enough Mornay sauce (page 120) to cover the chicory.

Coat the chicory with this sauce; sprinkle on top some grated Gruyère and Parmesan cheese, half of each, mixed with a pinch of fresh breadcrumbs. Baste with melted butter and brown in a 375°F (190°C, gas mark 5) oven.

BRAISED CHICORY
Endives à la meunière

Stew the chicory as described above and drain well. Heat some butter in a pan. When the butter turns a light brown, add the chicory in one layer without squeezing them. Cook slowly, turning them one by one to brown on all sides.

Place the chicory on a long platter and baste them with the cooking butter.

CABBAGE
Choux

White cabbage, green cabbage, red cabbage, cauliflower, broccoli, Brussels sprouts and kohlrabi provide great variety, and different types of each vegetable are available throughout the year.

SAUERKRAUT WITH PORK AND SAUSAGE
Choucroute à la ménagère

1 kg (2 lb) sauerkraut
Salt and freshly ground pepper
Thin slices fresh pork fat and fresh pork rind
1 large onion stuck with a clove
1 large carrot, quartered
1 teaspoon juniper berries
100 g (4 oz) piece of smoked bacon
100 g (4 oz) salt belly of pork
Piece of salt beef brisket (optional)
Uncooked garlic sausage
Bouquet garni
Ham knuckle (optional)
100 g (4 oz) lard or goose fat
White bouillon or water
Frankfurters

Sauerkraut is made with white cabbage with a very hard white heart.

The cabbage is cut into shreds, then placed in a small barrel in layers, sprinkling each layer with coarse salt mixed with juniper berries; the proportions are $\frac{1}{4}$ cup of salt to 10 lb (4·5 kg) of cabbage.

Press the cabbage down with a piece of wood and place a stone on top; the salted vegetable juices will cover the cabbage by the next day.

Kept in a cool place, the sauerkraut will undergo fermentation which gradually becomes less. After three weeks the sauerkraut is ready to be used.

Cooking the sauerkraut. Wash the sauerkraut under running water. If it is old, soak it for 2 hours.

Drain the sauerkraut and squeeze it by handfuls. Spread on a dish towel in a thin layer. Season with salt and freshly ground pepper. Adjust the amount of salt depending on the ingredients that are going to be used with it and the liquid for moistening. Line a braising pan or an ovenproof terrine with thin slices of fresh pork fat and fresh pork rind. On top first spread a layer of about half the sauerkraut. Place on the sauerkraut the onion stuck with a clove, carrot, juniper berries, bacon and salt pork, garlic sausage (prick it a few times with the point of a knife) and a bouquet garni.

A piece of salt brisket and a ham knuckle can also be added.

Cover with the remaining sauerkraut, and on top spread the lard or goose fat, and finally, slices of fresh pork fat.

Cover with white bouillon or water.

Bring to the boil, cover and simmer in a 325°F (170°C, gas mark 3) oven for 4 hours.

After 1 hour, remove the meat and the sausage and continue cooking.

When the sauerkraut is cooked, it should be white and slightly sharp in taste, due to the fermentation. Place the sauerkraut on a platter, draining it very well; discard the onion, the carrot and the bouquet garni. Cut the bacon, the pork and the garlic sausage into thin slices and place on top; then add frankfurters poached for 5 minutes.

Serve with a bowl of very creamy mashed potatoes or boiled potatoes.

GREEN CABBAGE
Chou vert

The green 'full heart' cabbage starts its annual cycle in the spring with early varieties.

New cabbage is nearly always cooked *à l'anglaise*, which means cooked in salted water, after having been quartered and cored.

The cabbage is well drained, with the water pressed out with a slotted spoon, and served with butter, crushed coarse salt and freshly ground pepper, and a separate dish of boiled potatoes.

In spring new cabbage is added to the *pot-au-feu*. It is blanched 5 minutes, drained, held together with a thread, and cooked with the *pot-au-feu*, at the same time as the other vegetables.

Recipes for green cabbage can also be used to cook white cabbage.

BRAISED GREEN CABBAGE
Chou vert braisé

1 cabbage
Strips fresh pork fat
  and pork rind
Salt and freshly
  ground pepper
Dash nutmeg
1 onion stuck with a
  clove
1 large carrot
Bouquet garni with 2
  garlic cloves
Fatty white bouillon
3 tablespoons lard,
  goose fat or fat
  from a roast
A piece of smoked
  bacon, salt belly of
  pork or salt brisket
  of beef (optional)

For braising, use cabbage with a full white heart, which arrives later in the season.

Remove the yellow or very dark green leaves, quarter the cabbage, remove the core and the thick portions of the stems; wash the leaves carefully and plunge into a saucepan of salted boiling water. Boil for 10 minutes and drain.

Cover the bottom and the sides of a deep casserole, big enough to hold the cabbage, with strips of fresh pork fat and pork rind. In the pan place the cabbage leaves, which have been sprinkled with salt and freshly ground pepper and a dash of nutmeg; in the middle bury an onion stuck with a clove, a large carrot cut into quarters, and a bouquet garni with 2 garlic cloves.

Cover just to the top with a fatty white bouillon, add 3 tablespoons of lard, goose fat or fat from a roast. Cover with strips of fresh pork fat and bring to the boil.

Simmer, covered, in a 325°F (170°C, gas mark 3) oven for 2 hours.

You can add a piece of bacon, salted pork belly or brisket. The amount of salt should be adjusted to these other ingredients.

STUFFED GREEN CABBAGE
Chou vert farci

1 firm green cabbage
Thin slices pork fat
Stuffing (half fresh
  pork fat and lean
  pork, or any other
  leftover meats, and
  mushrooms, etc.)
Pork rind
1 medium carrot
1 onion stuck with a
  clove
Bouquet garni
Fatty white bouillon,
  lightly salted

Choose a firm green cabbage. Remove the yellow leaves or those that are too green or faded; remove the core, wash the head and blanch it, whole, in boiling water for at least 15 minutes.

Drain the cabbage head and place it on a damp towel covered with thin slices of pork fat.

Spread and carefully open each leaf until you reach the heart, and place in the centre a ball of stuffing made with equal parts of fresh pork fat and lean pork, or any other leftover meats, mushrooms, etc.

Reshape the cabbage, adding some stuffing between the leaves; season with salt and pepper while closing the cabbage.

Wrap it with strips of pork fat and tie it securely.

In the bottom of a deep casserole just big enough to hold the cabbage, place a layer of pork rind, a medium-sized carrot, sliced, an onion stuck with a clove and a bouquet garni. Add the cabbage and cover with fatty white bouillon, lightly salted.

Bring to the boil, then cover and simmer in a 325°F (170°C, gas mark 3) oven for 2 hours.

To serve set the cabbage on a plate, remove the string and the pork fat and baste with 1 teaspoon of the cooking juice, greatly reduced.

Serve the remaining reduced juice in a sauceboat with a bowl of boiled potatoes.

1·5-kg (3-lb) firm, white cabbage
500 g (1 lb) chestnuts
6 large onions
225 g (8 oz) butter
½ tablespoon salt
¼ teaspoon freshly ground pepper
3 dl (½ pt) milk, brought to the boil
Broth

CABBAGE STUFFED WITH CHESTNUTS
Chou farci aux marrons
For 8 people

This is a Carême dish, robust and delicious, requiring long, slow cooking for at least 5 hours. It is a good lunch dish.

To remove the outside skin of the chestnuts, first soak them in a saucepan of cold water, then cover and bring to the boil, and simmer for 12 minutes.

Remove from the heat. Drain a few chestnuts with a slotted spoon and remove their skins; continue to do the same with the remaining chestnuts. Set aside on a plate.

Peel the onions and slice them thinly. Place them in a deep saucepan with 50 g (2 oz) of butter; heat slowly, then cover and simmer for 15 minutes without letting the onions brown. Then add the chestnuts and 100 g (4 oz) of butter. Continue cooking, covered, very slowly. Stir often with a spatula, being careful not to break the chestnuts.

Simmer for ½ hour with the same care. The chestnuts will finally take on the colour and look of preserved chestnuts.

Sprinkle with half the salt and pepper, then remove everything – onions, chestnuts and butter – to the plate used for the chestnuts.

Cut out the core from the cabbage and remove any leaves that are too green or withered.

Plunge the cabbage into a big saucepan of boiling water and boil slowly for half an hour.

Drain well, pressing to remove all the water.

Place the cabbage on a dish towel and open the leaves, one

by one, until you reach the heart. Replace the heart with 1 heaped tablespoon of the above stuffing. Reshape the cabbage, placing 1 tablespoon of stuffing inside of each layer of leaves.

Tie up the cabbage with string like a parcel, and tie the ends on top of the cabbage, leaving them long enough that you can use them to lift the cabbage out of the saucepan.

Spread the remaining butter in the saucepan. Put in the cabbage, stalk end down; sprinkle with the remaining salt and pepper. Cover with the lid, then simmer. As it starts to simmer, the butter melts and water runs out of the cabbage to produce steam, which in turn condenses on the lid and falls in drops on to the cabbage and the pan. Continue simmering for 5 hours, preferably in a 300°F (150°C, gas mark 2) oven.

From time to time baste the cabbage with its own juice. Do not let the cabbage stick to the saucepan.

After 2½ hours of cooking, add the boiling milk, reserving 4 tablespoons; 15 minutes before serving add the remaining milk.

To serve, remove the cabbage, lifting it out of the saucepan with the string and a slotted spoon. Place on a serving platter and remove the string.

Dilute the brown juice sticking to the bottom of the saucepan with a little broth. Correct the seasoning, and pour the juices over the cabbage.

Serve as it is.

CAULIFLOWER
Choux-fleurs

Choose a very white cauliflower with very tight florets.

Generally, one eats only the cauliflower itself, but the pale green leaves that surround the florets and the white ribs can be prepared in the same way as green cabbage. The inside stalk, cut into pieces, and the stems can be prepared *à la grecque* for cold hors-d'oeuvre.

To prepare a cauliflower remove the leaves and cut the cauliflower into small bouquets with 2-cm (¾-inch) stems. Peel the stems and place the bouquets in lightly vinegared cold water.

In a saucepan, bring to the boil enough water to cover the cauliflower completely. Add the florets and boil for 10 minutes. Drain and place them in a second saucepan of salted boiling water. Boil slowly until completely cooked.

Total cooking time is about 25 minutes. Cauliflower cooked in this way never has a strong taste.

Drain the florets and place them in a bowl, reshaping the cauliflower, or place them on a plate covered with a folded napkin.

Serve with a sauceboat of hollandaise (page 126), mousseline (page 127), white (page 109), or cream sauce (page 121), or melted butter.

CAULIFLOWER CHEESE
Chou-fleur au gratin

500 g (1 lb) cauliflower
Salt and pepper
50 g (2 oz) unsalted butter
Mornay sauce (page 120)
1 tablespoon grated Gruyère or Parmesan cheese
1 teaspoon fresh breadcrumbs
Melted unsalted butter

Cook the cauliflower as directed above; spread the florets on a cloth, season with salt and pepper. In a pan heat 50 g (2 oz) of butter for each pound of cauliflower and stew the florets in the butter for 15 minutes.

Turn them once with a fork, carefully. When the water has completely evaporated and the florets have absorbed the butter, place them in a prepared gratin dish, on a layer of Mornay sauce. Place the florets in a circle, the stems facing the centre. Cover this first layer with sauce and continue making layers of cauliflower and sauce until all the cauliflower is used.

Cover completely with Mornay sauce; on top, sprinkle 1 tablespoon of grated Gruyère or Parmesan cheese mixed with 1 teaspoon of fresh breadcrumbs.

Baste with some melted butter and brown in a 425°F (220°C, gas mark 7) oven.

CAULIFLOWER WITH HARD-BOILED EGG AND BREADCRUMBS
Chou-fleur à la polonaise

1 cauliflower
225 g (8 oz) unsalted butter
Salt and freshly ground pepper
Yolk of a hard-boiled egg
1 heaped tablespoon chopped parsley
2 tablespoons fresh breadcrumbs

Cook a cauliflower as directed above, drain and lightly brown in a frying pan. To do this correctly, heat 100 g (4 oz) of butter in a pan large enough so that the florets can be placed flat in it.

When the butter sizzles and starts to turn light brown, add the florets, one at a time. Season with salt and freshly ground pepper, and sauté them over a high flame. Turn each floret with a fork, so that they brown on all sides. When they are golden brown, remove them to a bowl and sprinkle on top the yolk of a hard-boiled egg rubbed through a sieve and mixed with chopped parsley.

Add 100 g (4 oz) of butter to the pan; when the butter sizzles, add fresh breadcrumbs; as soon as the crumbs begin to brown, pour them over the cauliflower.

Serve as it is.

CAULIFLOWER PURÉE
Purée de chou-fleur

Prepare a cauliflower following the recipe for cauliflower *au gratin*. When the florets are stewed and all the water has evaporated, rub through a fine sieve. Put the purée into a saucepan, and add an equal weight of mashed potatoes. Mix well with a spatula and add cream or boiling milk to bring to the proper consistency.

Finish the purée away from the heat with 50 g (2 oz) of butter. Correct the seasoning. Do not let the purée boil.

BOILED CAULIFLOWER
Chou-fleur à l'anglaise

The cauliflower must be absolutely fresh and ripe – white, hard and tight. Remove the stem without detaching the tender leaves round the florets.

Blanch the cauliflower by plunging it into boiling water and boiling for 10 minutes. Drain and cook the cauliflower whole, in salted water, $1\frac{1}{4}$ teaspoons per litre (2 pts) of water. Cook slowly until tender.

Serve on a folded napkin with a dish of butter and half a lemon or a sauceboat of thick cream flavoured with lemon juice.

BRUSSELS SPROUTS
Choux de Bruxelles

The recipes for cauliflower can also be used for Brussels sprouts. But the best way to cook the sprouts is to sauté them in a frying pan, browning them well.

The leaves of each sprout should be very tight; remove yellow or withered leaves and cut off the stem. Wash the trimmed sprouts and put them in a saucepan of boiling water. Boil for 10 minutes, drain, and cook them again in salted boiling water.

Cook slowly, uncovered, to keep the sprouts green and to hold their shape. If the sprouts boil too quickly, the leaves will fall apart.

Drain hot in a colander; sprinkle with salt, which will help to get rid of the moisture, and place in a frying pan with sizzling butter (125 g (5 oz) of butter for 500 g (1 lb) of Brussels sprouts).

Brussels sprouts soak up a lot of fat. They are delicious sautééd in goose fat, chicken fat or dripping from a lamb or pork roast. Season with freshly ground pepper and a dash of nutmeg.

When the sprouts are well browned, place them in a very hot bowl. Sprinkle a pinch of chopped parsley on top and serve. Place a hot plate in front of each guest.

Prepared this way, Brussels sprouts are quite delicious.

1 medium-sized red
cabbage
225 g (8 oz) smoked
bacon
20 chestnuts
1 onion, stuck with a
clove
Bouquet garni
Pinch salt
Dash freshly ground
pepper
6 tablespoons
bouillon or veal
stock, lightly salted
3 tablespoons wine
vinegar
3 heaped tablespoons
goose fat or roast
pork fat

RED CABBAGE WITH BACON AND CHESTNUTS
Chou rouge à la mode alsacienne Paul Haeberlin

For 8 people

Trim off the withered leaves of the cabbage and cut off the stem at the base. Cut the head into quarters, wash and drain. Remove the cores and shred the leaves.

Bring a large saucepan of water to the boil, plunge in the shredded cabbage and blanch for 6 minutes. Drain in a colander so that all the water can easily run off.

Remove the rind and trim the outside of the bacon, which should be strongly smoked. Cut into rectangles, 10 by 8 cm (4 by 3 inches) and 1 cm ($\frac{1}{2}$ inch) thick.

Slash the outer skins of the chestnuts, and place them on a pie dish in a 350°F (180°C, gas mark 4) oven for 5–6 minutes, just long enough to loosen both the outer skin and the thinner inner skin. Remove them from the oven, 3 or 4 at a time, and peel immediately. Set aside on a plate.

Choose a deep casserole, holding about 2 l (4 pts). Divide the cabbage into three parts, the bacon and the chestnuts into two.

In the pot first spread a layer of cabbage, then a layer of bacon, then finally a layer of chestnuts. Repeat this step, adding the onion and the bouquet garni. Cover with the last part of the cabbage.

Sprinkle with salt and pepper and moisten with the bouillon or veal stock; add the vinegar, and end with the goose or pork fat.

Cover and bring to the boil. As soon as it starts to boil, place a round piece of buttered paper the size of the casserole on the cabbage. Cover again tightly and simmer in a 325°F (170°C, gas mark 3) oven for $2\frac{1}{2}$ hours.

If the braising has been done properly, there should be very little juice in the cabbage, about 4 tablespoons.

Remove the onion and the bouquet garni, and pour the vegetable into a bowl, placing the bacon on top. If there is too much juice, boil it to reduce as necessary and pour over the cabbage.

1 firm medium-sized
    red cabbage
Salt and pepper
2 teaspoons wine
    vinegar
Unsalted butter
3 cooking apples
1 teaspoon sugar

RED CABBAGE WITH APPLES
Chou rouge à la flamande

This dish is easy to cook and delicious.

Remove the stem and the withered leaves from a firm medium-sized red cabbage. Cut the cabbage into quarters, wash, remove the core and large ribs and shred the leaves coarsely.

Season the cabbage with salt and pepper and sprinkle with 2 teaspoons of wine vinegar; mix well.

Heavily butter an ovenproof earthenware pan, add the cabbage, then tightly cover and cook in a 300°F (150°C, gas mark 2) oven for $2\frac{1}{2}$ hours. After 2 hours add the apples, peeled, cored, quartered and sprinkled with 1 teaspoon of sugar. Spread the apples on the cabbage. Continue to steam for another half hour; then serve in a vegetable dish.

PICKLED RED CABBAGE
Chou rouge mariné

Trim the cabbage, quarter, wash and remove the core and the large ribs; shred thinly.

In a large preserving pan bring $4\frac{1}{2}$ l (8 pts) of water to the boil; plunge the cabbage in and blanch for 5 minutes. Drain well and let cool; salt lightly and place in an earthenware pot or a glass jar containing peppercorns, 1 sprig of thyme, $\frac{1}{2}$ bay leaf and 3 garlic cloves; fill the container with cold boiled vinegar.

Let marinate for 8 days before using the cabbage.

To serve, drain the quantity of cabbage needed and place in a dish or bowl; dress with a little olive oil.

CUCUMBERS WITH CREAM
Concombres à la crème

Thinly peel 2 cucumbers and cut them into 2·5 cm (1 inch) cubes; blanch in boiling water for 5 minutes, drain and stew in butter in a pan until all the water has evaporated.

Season with salt and pepper.

Cover the cucumbers with boiling double cream, and cook until the cream is reduced to half and the sauce has thickened.

Remove from the heat, and stir in 50 g (2 oz) of butter for each $\frac{1}{2}$ cup of cream. Correct the seasoning.

Remove to a bowl.

SPINACH
Épinards

Cooked spinach is a delicious dish – so long as the vegetable is extremely fresh and young, and it is carefully prepared just before serving.

Before the spinach leaves are cooked, remove the stems; wash the leaves in several changes of water, and remove any yellow or withered leaves.

The green colour of the spinach is a sign of a healthy plant, an indication of its nutritive values and fresh taste.

The spinach should keep its green colour until it is eaten. Two steps must be taken to ensure this easy but important result:

1. Cook the spinach quickly.
2. Do not let the spinach stand between the time it is cooked and the time it is served.

In a large enamel (not aluminium) saucepan bring to the boil enough water to cover the spinach completely so that the water will stop boiling for only a very short time when the spinach is added.

Use $1\frac{1}{4}$ teaspoons of salt for each litre (2 pts) of water, and cook over high heat. When the water boils, add the washed spinach and shake well to distribute.

Note when the water starts to boil again, pushing down the spinach with a spatula; after 8 minutes of boiling, remove a leaf and see if it is cooked by squeezing it between your fingers. If the spinach is young, it should be cooked; if not, continue boiling for a few minutes and check again.

Pour the spinach into a colander; fill the saucepan with cold water, and drop the drained spinach into it. Repeat this step twice to cool the spinach quickly.

After the spinach is rinsed and drained, squeeze the leaves by handfuls or in a dish cloth to remove all the water; then rub through a fine sieve or chop fine.

If the spinach is not to be used immediately spread it out on a china or an enamel plate. Place in a cool spot.

When spinach is not chopped, it is best if possible to blanch the leaves at the last minute, drain them, but not rinse them. Simply squeeze the leaves in a dish cloth held at each end and twisted.

When this has been done, place the leaves in a pan with sizzling butter, (50 g (2 oz) of butter for every 500 g (1 lb) of spinach), and dry them rapidly for a few seconds on a high flame. Season following the chosen recipe.

Note: For 500 g (1 lb) of cooked spinach, you need roughly 2 kg (4 lb) of uncooked spinach.

SPINACH WITH BUTTER
Épinards au beurre

Follow the recipe above to prepare the spinach. When it has been dried, add, away from the heat, 100 g (4 oz) of butter for every 500 g (1 lb) of cooked spinach. Season with a pinch of salt, a pinch of freshly ground pepper, a dash of grated nutmeg, and a dash of sugar if the spinach is rather bitter. Be careful not to sweeten the spinach.

SPINACH WITH CREAM
Épinards à la crème

Follow the recipe for spinach with butter, replacing the butter with 6 tablespoons of cream and 25 g (1 oz) of butter. Season in the same way.

FRENCH BEANS
Haricots

French beans must be cooked as soon as they are gathered. Picked green, they should be eaten green, without adding chemicals, to retain their nutritive values and delicious taste.

First choose beans as much the same size as possible, and string them by breaking off the two ends of the bean and pulling the strings off.

Wash the beans and drain, shaking them well. Plunge them into a saucepan of boiling salted water, $1\frac{1}{4}$ teaspoons of salt for every 1 l (2 pts) of water. Do not cover, and keep boiling on a high flame.

The best saucepan for cooking French beans is a large preserving pan or saucepan, preferably made of untinned copper.

After 15 minutes of boiling, pick out a bean and bite it. If it is slightly crunchy, remove the beans from the heat and drain.

Sprinkle the beans with a pinch of salt and shake them in the colander; the water will drain more quickly. Place the beans in a very hot pan, prepare them following your recipe, and serve.

French beans *à l'anglaise* are simply served with butter separately.

The beans should be naturally green and delicious.

When they cannot be cooked at the last minute for some reason, the beans should be rinsed in cold water as soon as they are cooked; then drained and spread on a cloth-covered rack.

If the beans are to be served hot, they are then stewed in a little butter and seasoned.

FRENCH BEANS WITH MAÎTRE D'HÔTEL BUTTER
Haricots verts au beurre maître d'hôtel

Follow the directions above for cooking the beans and sauté in 100 g (4 oz) of butter, cut into pieces, to every 500 g (1 lb) of beans.

The beans should be completely coated with the melted butter.

Put into a bowl and sprinkle a pinch of fresh chopped parsley on top.

Serve on very hot plates.

FRENCH BEANS WITH CREAM
Haricots verts à la crème

Proceed as for string beans with *maître d'hôtel* butter (above) but
instead of coating the beans with butter, cover them just to the top
with double cream. Bring to the boil and cook until the cream
is reduced by half; then away from the heat shake to coat the
beans with the cream.

Correct the seasoning.

Note: The cream can be replaced with a béchamel (page 110)
or a velouté sauce (page 109). Add half as much sauce and coat
the string beans without reducing the sauce.

FRENCH BEANS WITH
EGG YOLK AND CREAM
Haricots verts à la normande

Follow the recipe for beans with cream; when the reduction is
complete, just before serving, take off the heat and add an egg
yolk (1 egg yolk for every 500 g (1 lb) of beans) diluted with 1
tablespoon of cream. The concentrated heat of the beans and
the boiling cream is enough to thicken the egg yolk and partly
cook it.

PURÉE OF FRENCH BEANS
Purée de haricots verts

After cooking the beans as described above, stew them in 50 g
(2 oz) of butter for every 500 g (1 lb) of beans. Rub the beans
through a fine sieve and mix with an equal quantity of purée of
fresh green flageolet beans. Butter away from the heat with 100 g
(4oz) of butter or add some cream to bring the purée back to the
proper consistency.

MIXED BEANS WITH BUTTER
Haricots panachés au beurre

Mix together equal amounts of French beans and green flageolets, each cooked separately. Coat with butter following the recipe above.

FRESH WHITE BEANS
Haricots blancs frais

First method:
Fresh white beans
1 teaspoon salt for
each litre (2 pts) of
water
1 medium-sized
onion stuck with a
clove
2 garlic cloves
½ carrot
Small bouquet garni

Second method:
Unsalted butter
1 onion
1 carrot
1 l (2 pts) water
2 garlic cloves
Bouquet garni
150 g (6 oz)
unsmoked bacon
Fresh white beans

When the beans are ripe but still fresh, gather the pods, spread them in a cool place and shell them just before they are to be cooked.

First method

Cook the fresh white beans by plunging them into a saucepan of boiling water to which is added 1 teaspoon of salt for each quart of water, an onion stuck with a clove, garlic, carrot and a small bouquet garni.

Skim the top, cover and boil slowly.

Second method

The court-bouillon should be cooked in advance. In the saucepan in which the beans will be cooked, brown the onion and carrot in butter, add 1 l (2 pts) of water, garlic, a bouquet garni and bacon.

Bring to the boil, skim the top and cook slowly for 20 minutes; add the fresh white beans. Continue cooking at a simmer and finish following the various recipes.

DRIED WHITE BEANS
Haricots blancs secs

Dry white beans always should be from the latest harvest; then they need only 2 hours' soaking in cold water.

Before starting, pick over the beans to remove tiny stones, etc., and wash them in several different waters.

Dry white beans are cooked exactly like fresh white beans (above).

However, I advise proceeding in two steps:

1. Cover the beans with cold water, heat slowly to boiling point, let boil for 10 minutes and then drain.
2. Place the beans again in cold water, adding 1 teaspoon of salt per 1 l (2 pts) of water; bring to the boil and simmer, covered.

When the beans are cooked, prepare them according to one of the following recipes.

DRIED WHITE BEANS WITH BUTTER
Haricots blancs au beurre

For 500 g (1 lb) of beans add 75–100 g (3–4 oz) of butter just before serving.

Drain the beans not quite completely and place them in a pan with 3 or 4 tablespoons of the cooking bouillon. Add the butter, cut into pieces, and sauté slowly. The butter and the bouillon will mix together, forming a light creamy emulsion that will coat the beans. Grind some pepper on top and mix; correct the seasoning and pour into a bowl.

Sprinkle a pinch of fresh chopped parsley on top.

Cooked this way, the beans will not be dry; in addition to the butter, the bouillon will add flavour.

FLAGEOLETS WITH BUTTER
Haricots flageolets au beurre

Use the same method as for the dried white beans, above.

DRIED WHITE BEANS WITH ONION AND TOMATO
Haricots blancs à la brétonne

500 g (1 lb) cooked beans
1 onion
100 g (4 oz) unsalted butter
½ glass dry white wine
3 large tomatoes
Pinch salt
Grated garlic clove
Freshly ground pepper

For 500 g (1 lb) of cooked beans, chop an onion fine and brown it slowly in 50 g (2 oz) of butter that has been heated in a saucepan. Stir often with a wooden spoon; when the onion is cooked but not brown, moisten with dry white wine and boil to reduce to 2 tablespoons. Add the tomatoes, peeled, quartered and seeded. Do not remove all the juice. Season with a pinch of salt, garlic and a few turns of the pepper mill. Cook for 15 minutes.

If you do not have fresh tomatoes, use ½ cup of tomato purée.

Add the drained beans to the onion–tomato mixture and away from the heat mix in 50 g (2 oz) of butter, following the directions for beans with butter.

WHITE BEANS WITH HAM AND SAUSAGE
Haricots blancs ménagère

Cook the beans following the second method for fresh white beans (page 472) adding besides the bacon a ham knuckle, unsalted.

Meanwhile, prepare the sauce as for the white beans *à la brétonne* (above). Along with the chopped onion cook 1 sausage per guest, if possible the small flat sausages known as *crépinettes*.

Remove the sausages before adding the white wine, and set aside.

When the beans are added to the sauce, keep the sauce slightly more liquid by adding about ½ cup of the bean cooking liquid;

add the fresh bacon and the fresh ham, cut into large dice, with the skin well cooked and very tender.

Pour the beans into a deep earthenware gratin dish; bury the sausages in them and sprinkle with fresh breadcrumbs.

Baste with 1 tablespoon of melted butter, or goose or chicken fat, or the fat from a pork roast; put into a 325°F (170°C, gas mark 3) oven and cook for 20 minutes uncovered so that a nice brown crust forms.

Place on a serving platter on a folded napkin.

MANGE-TOUT PEAS SAUTÉED IN BUTTER
Haricots mange-tout sautés au beurre

This variety of peas or beans are eaten with their pods; they are sometimes green and sometimes yellow. They are gathered when half mature, and the pods, still tender, contain young beans, not fully grown.

Cook the same way as French beans, drain. In a pan heat 100 g (4 oz) of butter for every 500 g (1 lb) of beans; add the beans and sauté on a high heat to brown them lightly.

Season with salt and freshly ground pepper and chopped parsley.

BRAISED LETTUCE
Laitues braisées

6 small firm lettuces
1 medium carrot
1 onion
Pork rind
Very small bouquet garni
Pinch salt
Well-seasoned, fatty veal stock, lightly salted
Croûtons, fried in butter
50 g (2 oz) unsalted butter

Choose 6 small firm lettuces. Remove the yellow or withered leaves and trim the stem to a cone shape. Wash the heads without breaking the leaves and plunge them for 10 minutes into a large saucepan of boiling water so that the lettuces will be completely covered.

Drain the heads and rinse them; drain them again, then squeeze to remove all the water.

Meanwhile, in the bottom of a well-buttered fireproof casserole big enough to hold the lettuces, place 1 medium carrot and 1 onion, both sliced, some pork rind and a very small bouquet garni. On top place the lettuces with the leaves gathered together and tied with string. Sprinkle with a pinch of salt, cover and simmer for 15 minutes to extract the water, which will evaporate and, after condensing on the lid, will caramelize slightly in the bottom of the pan.

Cover the lettuces just to the top with veal stock, well seasoned and fatty, but lightly salted; bring to the boil, top with a buttered piece of paper and cover with the lid; place in a 325°F (170°C, gas mark 3) oven to simmer for 50 minutes.

To serve remove the lettuces one by one; cut each in half lengthwise; fold the halves and place them in a circle on a heated round platter, placing between each pair of lettuces a heart-shaped croûton fried in butter.

Remove the vegetables, pork rind and bouquet garni from the saucepan, reduce the juices to 6 tablespoons; add 50 g (2 oz) of unsalted butter in pieces while the reduced cooking juices are still boiling; beat over a high flame. When the sauce is well mixed and thickened, pour it over the lettuce.

Note: You can leave the flavourings in the sauce and cut the pork rind into thin strips.

STUFFED BRAISED LETTUCE
Laitues farcies et braisées

Prepare the lettuce as above. When the heads are boiled and the water has been squeezed out, cut each head in half lengthwise without removing the stem; open the halves and flatten them slightly; stuff each half with a meat stuffing – beef, pork, chicken, etc., mixed with chopped mushrooms – or any other stuffing.

Fold each lettuce half over the stuffing, tie with a string and braise the bundles as directed for the braised lettuce, above.

To serve remove the strings and place the lettuce halves whole on a round platter in a circle. Baste them with the braising juice, reduced and buttered away from the heat.

LENTILS
Lentilles

Lentils are generally sold dry and must be picked over, washed and soaked, then cooked like dry beans.

Lentils are used exactly like beans, in soups, as garnishes or as vegetables, cooked with meat (pork, bacon) or just with other vegetables (carrot, onion) for flavour.

SWEETCORN
Le maïs

Sweetcorn, which rarely appears on French menus, is a grain with nutritive values and flavour worth exploring.

The corn should be gathered when the kernels are still milky and therefore very tender.

Cut off the stems and remove the green leaves, leaving the white leaves around the ears, which are then placed in boiling water with milk added ($\frac{1}{2}$ l (1 pt) of milk to 5 l (10 pts) of water). Do not salt the water.

Cover, and let boil gently for 10 minutes.

Drain the ears; fold back the leaves, and place the corn on a plate covered with a folded napkin.

Serve with a sauceboat of melted butter or with double cream and a lemon.

The guests then scrape the cob on to their hot plates and baste the kernels with the melted butter or with the cream and a few drops of lemon juice.

The corn is then mixed and coated like English green peas.

SWEETCORN WITH BUTTER OR CREAM
Maïs au beurre, à la crème

Poach the corn as described above; shell the ears into a pan, and coat the kernels with butter or double cream.

Add a few drops of lemon juice.

SWEETCORN PANCAKES
Crêpes au maïs dites à la Marignan

Scrape the corn into an unsweetened crêpe batter (see crêpes ménagères, page 606), add butter or cream, depending on how rich you want to make the crêpes. Make the mixture the right consistency for crêpes, using about equal weights of crêpe batter and corn kernels.

Cook the crêpes, thicker than usual, in butter in a pan following the classic method.

CHESTNUTS
Marrons

The two ways to peel chestnuts are well known: make a shallow slash in the outer shell and place the chestnuts on a pastry sheet with 3 or 4 tablespoons of water; bake in a 425°F (220°C, gas mark 7) oven for 8 minutes: or after making the incision, plunge the chestnuts into boiling oil for 8 minutes. Remove the shells and the inner skins.

CHESTNUTS COOKED IN BUTTER
Marrons à l'étuvée

500 g (1 lb)
  chestnuts
White bouillon
1 celery stalk
1 lump sugar
50 g (2 oz) unsalted
  butter

Place the chestnuts, peeled as described above, in a heavy saucepan, cover with white bouillon, add a celery stalk, a lump of sugar and 50 g (2 oz) of butter.

Cook, covered, for 30 minutes. At this point the bouillon should be reduced to a syrupy liquid. Turn the chestnuts over slowly in the syrup to make them very shiny. They are then glazed. Serve.

CHESTNUT PURÉE
Purée de marrons

Cook the peeled chestnuts as above; drain, then pour them into a sieve placed above a plate and rub them through with a pestle. Put the purée into a saucepan, add a piece of butter and mix the purée with a wooden spoon. Bring to the proper consistency with milk or boiling cream.

Correct the seasoning and serve in a bowl.

CHESTNUT SOUFFLÉ
Soufflé aux marrons

500 g (1 lb)
  chestnuts
6 eggs, separated
100 g (4 oz) unsalted
  butter
Pinch salt
Dash grated nutmeg
Pinch freshly ground
  pepper
Milk or cream, if
  necessary

Purée the chestnuts following the recipe above. Mix the very hot chestnut purée with 6 egg yolks, and add the butter. Spice with a pinch of salt, a dash of grated nutmeg and grind a pinch of pepper on top. The purée should have the consistency of thick cream; add some milk or cream, if necessary. Twenty minutes before serving, beat 6 egg whites very stiff and fold into the purée with a spatula, lifting the purée carefully to avoid breaking down the whites.

Fill a buttered 1-l (2-pt) soufflé dish two-thirds full, and bake in a 375°F (190°C, gas mark 5) oven for 20 minutes.

Serve immediately. The soufflé will fall very quickly; any wait would be harmful.

Note: This recipe can be used for a dessert soufflé. In that case, omit the pepper, reduce the quantity of salt, leave the nutmeg and add 100 g (4 oz) of sugar.

TURNIPS
Navets

Spring turnips and larger turnips the rest of the year are used mainly as a garnish or to flavour other ingredients. New turnips are very digestible. Whichever way turnips are prepared, they must be cooked with plenty of fat – butter, pork, chicken or even lamb fat, with which they blend very well.

Unlike carrots which have a thin skin, turnips have a thick, fibrous skin, which must be peeled completely.

The young leaves, prepared *à l'anglaise*, are a good vegetable. Turnips can also be prepared following any carrot recipe.

GLAZED TURNIPS
Navets dits glacés

First method

Peel new turnips and cut them into pieces the size of large corks. Trim the angles to shape them like olives. Place the turnips in a pan with 50 g (4 oz) of butter, 1 teaspoon of sugar and a pinch of salt for every 500 g (1 lb) of turnips, peeled and trimmed. Cover with water and simmer until all the water has evaporated.

Add 25 g (1 oz) of butter and away from the heat turn over the turnips until they are coated and shiny.

Cooking time will be 20 minutes.

This last step should be done just before serving without letting the turnips wait.

Second method

Peel the turnips, cut and trim them and sauté in 50 g (2 oz) of butter in a frying pan rather slowly; fry them so that they do not boil but brown and take on a nice golden colour. Season with a pinch of salt and halfway through the cooking sprinkle with 1 tablespoon of sugar.

The sugar will melt, caramelize and cover the turnips with a clear coating.

Finish cooking by simmering with the juices from the main dish, and serve the turnips as garnish.

TURNIP PURÉE

Purée de navets

Cook the turnips as described above and rub through a very fine sieve; add potato purée (page 496) to equal one-third the turnips' weight.

A purée of turnips alone would be very thin unless egg yolks and cream are added and then the purée heated until it thickens. Do not let the purée boil and finish by adding unsalted butter.

ONIONS

Oignons

When onions are to be mixed with raw ingredients do not mince or chop them too fine, as this bruises them and squeezes out the juice. Instead cut them into very small dice or slice and cut into julienne as thinly as possible.

Here is a good way to cut an onion.

Cut it in half. Place the flat side of one half on the table and cut off the root end. Cut the half onion into very thin slices vertically, without cutting completely through the stem. Then slice it through horizontally and finally slice through downwards again. With some experience an onion can be cut into neat, white, regular dice in less than a minute. Use immediately.

GLAZED ONIONS
Oignons glacés
For white sauces or garnishes

Choose small onions – as small as marbles – equal in size. You will need 4 or 5 per person. Peel without spoiling their shape; to make this work easier, blanch the onions for a minute in boiling water or sprinkle them with vinegar.

Place the onions in a pan large enough to hold them evenly in one layer. Cover them with water or, if possible, white bouillon. If you are using water, add a pinch of salt and, in both cases, 100 g (4 oz) of butter per litre (2 pts) of liquid.

Bring to the boil, cover and cook slowly; the stock should be reduced when the onions are cooked. Finish the dish with 25 g (1 oz) of butter cut into pieces; roll the onions in the syrupy juice and coat them with the butter. The onions will be shiny and glazed.

For brown sauces or garnishes

After peeling the onions as described above, brown them slowly in butter. Season with a pinch of salt and sugar.

The browning and the cooking should be done at the same time. Halfway through the cooking, half cover the onions with white bouillon or water, and proceed to reduce as described above for white sauces or garnishes.

STUFFED ONIONS
Oignons farcis

Use rather large, sweet Spanish onions equal in size.

Peel the onions without spoiling their shape and make a deep incision around each stem.

Plunge the onions into boiling salted water, $1\frac{1}{4}$ teaspoons of salt per litre (2 pts) of water. Boil for 5 minutes, drain.

Guided by the incision, scoop out the onion heart, leaving a hole in the centre. Place the onion shells in a heavily buttered pan.

Sprinkle with a pinch of salt.

Quickly chop the onion hearts that have been removed and stew slowly in butter for 15 minutes. Stir often; do not let brown.

Add to the chopped onions, chopped or minced beef, poultry, game, shellfish or fish; flavour with mushrooms, tomatoes, truffles, etc.

Bring the stuffing to the desired consistency by adding brown or white stock or a brown or white sauce, depending on the meat or fish used. Leftovers lend themselves to this use very well.

Stuff each onion, giving it a dome shape with a spoon or a pastry bag. Sprinkle with fresh breadcrumbs. Baste generously with melted butter and bake slowly in a 350°F (180°C, gas mark 4) oven, uncovered, to brown. Baste often with the cooking butter.

Pour 2 or 3 tablespoons of well-flavoured pale veal gravy into a hot platter, and place the onions on top. Finish the dish by pouring the cooking butter over the onions.

ONION PURÉE
Purée d'oignons ou purée Soubise

500 g (1 lb) onions
100 g (4 oz) melted unsalted butter
Pinch salt
Pinch white pepper
Pinch sugar
Dash grated nutmeg
½ l (1 pt) béchamel sauce, reduced (page 110)
50 g (2 oz) unsalted butter
3 or 4 tablespoons double cream

Slice the onions, blanch them by boiling for 5 minutes in heavily salted water, drain and place in a saucepan with the melted butter, salt, white pepper, sugar and grated nutmeg. Stew slowly without letting them brown until soft.

Mix in béchamel sauce reduced till quite thick. Simmer for 10 minutes, then rub through a very fine sieve. Collect the purée in a saucepan; bring to the boil, boil for a few seconds, and away from the heat add the butter and cream, until the purée reaches the desired consistency. Correct the seasoning.

Note: The consistency of the purée depends upon the use that will be made of it; it can be used as a purée or as a more liquid *coulis*.

SORREL
Oseille

500 g (1 lb) cooked sorrel
25 g (1 oz) unsalted butter
1 tablespoon flour
Pinch sugar
Freshly ground pepper
1½ dl (¼ pt) bouillon or white veal stock
2 eggs or 4 egg yolks
4 tablespoons heated double cream
Unsalted butter
Fatty veal stock

Use young sorrel, which is sweeter. Remove the withered or yellow leaves and the stems. Wash very carefully in several changes of water, drain and place on the stove in a saucepan with a little water.

As soon as the sorrel wilts and some juices run out, drain in a sieve lined with a cloth.

Meanwhile, for 500 g (1 lb) of cooked sorrel, prepare a light-coloured roux with 25 g (1 oz) of butter and 1 tablespoon of flour. Cook the roux for 15 minutes, stirring often. Add the sorrel, a pinch of sugar, a few turns of the pepper mill and the bouillon or white veal stock.

Mix well with a wooden spatula, letting the sorrel boil; cover, and continue cooking in a 325°F (170°C, gas mark 3) oven for 2 hours.

Rub the sorrel through a sieve and place in a saucepan to boil; thicken with whole eggs or egg yolks – 2 eggs or 4 egg yolks for each pound of sorrel – then dilute with 4 tablespoons of heated cream. Strain the eggs through a very fine sieve to remove all the strings which would coagulate into white lumps. Mix the egg and cream mixture into the sorrel away from the heat, place back on the stove and heat, stirring without stopping, until the purée starts to boil.

Do not let it boil; remove it immediately. Add some butter – sorrel absorbs a great deal of butter – and correct the seasoning before serving by adding some rich golden veal gravy.

SORREL CHIFFONADE
Chiffonade d'oseille

Gather cleaned and washed sorrel in a bunch and cut the leaves into fine julienne.

Cook the sorrel until soft in butter in a pan with a pinch of salt and sugar.

Set the sorrel aside in a glazed bowl to use later for soup, eggs, sauce, etc.

This chiffonade can be kept for quite a long time by pouring a layer of well-cooked lard about 6 mm (¼ inch) thick on the surface.

LEEKS
Poireaux

In France leeks are used in cooking more as a seasoning than as a vegetable, though they are excellent prepared in various ways and reputedly good for the health. It is a vegetable that can be found all year round, and it is generally not too expensive compared to other vegetables.

LEEKS A LA GRECQUE
Poireaux à la grecque

Use the white parts of the leeks blanched for 5 minutes in boiling water; then drain and prepare as for artichokes *à la grecque* (page 432).

LEEKS COOKED IN BUTTER
Poireaux à l'étuvée

12 medium-sized leeks, white part only
Pinch salt and pepper
50 g (2 oz) unsalted butter
½ teaspoon lemon juice

In boiling water blanch 12 medium-sized leeks, white part only, for 5 minutes. Drain completely, sprinkle with a pinch of salt and pepper and place the leeks side by side in a well-buttered oven-proof dish. Baste with 50 g (2 oz) of butter and ½ teaspoon of lemon juice.

Place buttered paper on top, cover, and stew for 40 minutes in a 300°F (150°C, gas mark 2) oven, basting often with the cooking butter.

LEEKS VINAIGRETTE
Poireaux à la vinaigrette

Tie the white part of the leeks into bundles and blanch them for 5 minutes in boiling water; drain, and place in a large saucepan of boiling salted water. Cook slowly, drain again completely, and serve with a sauceboat of vinaigrette sauce (page 129) with mustard.

LEEKS BROWNED IN THE OVEN
Poireaux à l'italienne

Cook the white part of leeks as described above; after they are cooked, place them in a gratin dish and sprinkle generously with grated Gruyère cheese mixed with a large pinch of fresh bread-crumbs. Baste with the cooking butter and brown in a 425°F (220°C, gas mark 7) oven.

PEAS
Petits pois

Being very delicate, peas demand special care. For example they should be eaten immediately after they have been picked, to be at their most delicious. If this is not possible keep the peas in their pods, spread out in a cool place. They should be used within 12 hours. If this is not possible, the peas should be shelled. Then the best way to preserve the peas without heating them – which would spoil the finished dish – is to place them in a bowl with 100 g ($\frac{1}{4}$ lb) of butter for each litre (2 pts) of shelled peas, then mix thoroughly. Make a well, pushing the peas against the sides of the bowl, where they will stick because of the butter coating them. Keep in a cool place until ready to use.

This technique keeps the peas fresh without any extra expense, for the butter will be used later for cooking the peas.

A last bit of very important advice; freshly gathered peas are pale green and will cook in 15–20 minutes at the most. They should be cooked just before serving time. The longer the time lapse between the gathering of the peas and the cooking or the steps taken to keep them fresh, the longer the cooking will take.

BOILED PEAS
Petits pois à l'anglaise

3 l (6 pts) water
3 teaspoons salt
500 g (1 lb) shelled peas, freshly gathered
Pinch salt
Unsalted butter
1 tablespoon chopped fresh fennel
1 tablespoon chopped fresh mint
1 tablespoon chopped fresh savory

Bring 3 l (6 pts) of salted water (1 teaspoon of salt per litre (2 pts) of water) to a boil in a large enamel saucepan.

Keep the water boiling, and add the peas. Fifteen minutes later, check to see if they are done. When they are tender, drain in a large sieve or strainer; sprinkle with a pinch of salt, shake to help the water drain off and place the peas in a very hot vegetable bowl.

Serve with butter separately.

Place a very hot plate in front of each guest, letting each dress the peas for himself or herself.

Note: With the peas serve three small dishes: one with 1 tablespoon of chopped fresh fennel, another with 1 tablespoon of chopped fresh mint, and the third with 1 tablespoon of chopped fresh savory.

PEAS WITH MINT
Petits pois à la menthe

Cook the peas *à l'anglaise*, as described above; add some fresh mint leaves to the cooking water.

Drain the peas and pour into a saucepan. For each 500 g (1 lb) of shelled peas cut 50 g (2 oz) of butter into pieces and scatter over the peas; on top sprinkle a pinch of fennel or mint leaves blanched for 1 minute and chopped; away from the heat shake to coat the peas.

Add 2 or 3 teaspoons of the boiling cooking water to make the sauce lighter.

Place in a vegetable bowl.

700 g (1½ lb) shelled
  peas
12 small spring
  onions
1 lettuce heart
Bouquet garni
  (parsley root, sprig
  savory, sprig
  thyme, ½ bay leaf)
¼ teaspoon salt
25 g (1 oz) sugar
125 g (5 oz) unsalted
  butter
2 tablespoons water

PEAS WITH LETTUCE AND ONIONS (CLASSIC RECIPE)

Petits pois à la française

For 6 people

Shell enough freshly gathered peas to yield about 700 g (1½ lb) of shelled peas.

Peel 12 small spring onions.

Separate the leaves of a lettuce heart; wash the leaves and cut into julienne.

Tie a parsley root, a sprig of savory and thyme, and ½ bay leaf to make the bouquet garni.

Place everything in a bowl with salt, sugar and 100 g (4 oz) of butter.

Mix well, press down in the bowl, cover with a damp cloth and leave in a cool place for about 2 hours, to macerate.

When ready to cook, choose a deep saucepan, but not too large. Pour in 2 tablespoons of water, then the pea and lettuce mixture. Cover with a soup plate filled with cold water to produce condensation of the steam. Cook over medium heat; shake the peas from time to time. The condensation of the water should be enough to cook the peas.

After 20–25 minutes, check the peas to see if they are done, season, remove the bouquet garni, and away from the heat stir in 25 g (1 oz) of butter.

Note: If the peas have just been gathered, and the cooking has been properly done, the reduced water from the vegetables – the peas and the garnish – thickened by the butter should provide enough syrupy, lightly foamy sauce to coat the peas without being too thick or too liquid. The peas and the sauce, placed in a bowl, will hold their shape like a very light mousse. This subtle and delicate dish is a delight to eat.

PEAS WITH GLAZED CARROTS
Petits pois à la bourgeoise

Prepare 700 g (1½ lb) of green peas, following the recipe for peas
à la française; and prepare 12 small new carrots, following the
recipe for carrots glazed in butter (page 442), in the same saucepan
that will be used for the peas.

When the carrots are nearly done, add the prepared peas with
their garnish and continue cooking, raising the heat towards the
end to reduce the juice further.

Away from the heat mix in 3 tablespoons of double cream.

PEAS WITH BACON
Petits pois à la paysanne

Follow the recipe above, adding, for 700 g (1½ lb) of peas, 100 g
(4 oz) of bacon, cut into small lardoons, blanched in boiling water
for 5 minutes, and browned in butter in the saucepan in which the
peas will be cooked. Omit the carrots and the cream, and let the
peas simmer with the bacon; away from the heat mix in some
butter.

FRESH PEA PURÉE
Purée de pois frais

Preferably, use large sweet peas; cook them *à l'anglaise* or *à la
française* (see recipes above).

Drain the peas, and if they have been prepared the French way,
reserve the cooking liquid; rub the peas through a fine sieve and
put the purée into a saucepan. For 700 g (1½ lb) of peas add
125 g (5 oz) of butter, and bring to the consistency of a purée by
adding some of the cooking liquid.

If the peas are cooked the English way, add some double
cream.

SWEET PEPPERS
Piments doux

Sweet peppers do not occupy an important place in French cooking. There are three different varieties: red, yellow and green. The best peppers come from Spain.

STUFFED SWEET PEPPERS
Piments farcis

Use sweet peppers of an even size, the length of a medium-sized carrot. Grill the peppers slightly so that they can be peeled; remove the stem and the seeds; blanch the peppers in boiling water for 2 minutes.

Fill the peppers with a stuffing made with leftovers: lamb, veal, chicken, alone or mixed with rice, using two-thirds meat and one-third creole rice or rice pilaf (page 514). Mix with a couple of tablespoons of veal stock or pork stock, not degreased, and thick tomato purée. Season with grated garlic and chopped onion, cooked in butter with freshly ground pepper.

Generously oil a fireproof dish, sprinkle the bottom with chopped onions and place the peppers side by side. Cover halfway up with a light tomato *coulis* made with tomato pulp and juice. Bring to the boil, cover and bake in a 325°F (170° C, gas mark 3) oven for 35 minutes.

Place the peppers on a round platter. Boil the cooking juice to reduce and add butter away from the heat; correct the seasoning. Pour over the peppers.

Note: The reduction of the tomato pulp and juice tends to produce a kind of syrup. This sweet juice goes well with the taste of the sweet peppers.

SWEET PEPPERS WITH RISOTTO
Piments doux à la piémontaise

Prepare equal amounts of sweet peppers, ripe tomatoes and risotto *à la piémontaise* (page 514). Peel, seed and stew the peppers and tomatoes in butter or olive oil for 15 minutes.

In a gratin dish place alternating layers of the three ingredients, finishing with a layer of tomatoes or sweet peppers. Sprinkle with some grated Gruyère cheese, baste with melted butter and simmer in a 350°F (180°C, gas mark 4) oven for 20 minutes until the top browns.

SWEET PEPPER PURÉE
Purée de piments doux
Garnish for chicken

Peel and seed large red peppers and stew in butter.

Cook rice equal to one-third the weight of the peppers in a white bouillon, as for a risotto, but the rice should be softer at the end.

Pound everything in a mortar and rub through a very fine sieve.

Place the purée in a saucepan; heat it well, stirring with a wooden spatula, bringing it to the proper consistency by adding cream, milk or white veal stock. Bring to the boil, remove from the heat immediately and add as much butter as possible.

Note: The rice can be replaced by the same amounts of thick béchamel sauce (page 110).

POTATOES
Pommes de terre

In France there are many varieties of potatoes, with very different characteristics. The best are those with yellow flesh: the long Holland potatoes, the *quarantaine*, the Belle de Fontenay, the Belle de Juillet and the Esterlingen. The long, red, sausage-shaped potato with yellow flesh is excellent for purée and soups.

For potatoes to remain in good condition, they must be carefully cared for and stored properly. They should be kept in an airy, light, cool or cold place, protected from frost, and checked often to prevent any signs of germination.

Cooking methods for potatoes

The various ways of preparing potatoes are:

Frying
Boiling or steaming
Baking in the oven
Browning or stewing in fat

These four ways of cooking are the basis of innumerable recipes.

The classic French fried potato is made by the following recipe.

FRENCH FRIED POTATOES
Pommes frites dites Pont-Neuf

Peel, wash and dry the potatoes; cut them lengthwise into slices 1 cm ($\frac{1}{2}$ inch) thick; cut each slice into chips 1 cm ($\frac{1}{2}$ inch) wide.

Never cut the potato sticks thicker, otherwise each chip will contain a quantity of starch in the pulp that is not easily digestible and is unpleasant to the palate.

Place the potatoes in a frying basket and plunge them into very hot oil or well-clarified beef or veal fat.

The temperature of the fat should be close to 350°F (180°C). This seals the potatoes just enough so that they do not absorb the fat. When cold potatoes are put in, the temperature of the oil drops to 320°F (160°C). Watch the frying so that the potatoes, which are starting to brown, cook more slowly; the temperature of the fat will drop gradually to 300°F (150°C), where it should be maintained to prevent boiling.

After 5 minutes of cooking, check if the potatoes are done by pressing one fried potato stick between your fingers. If the pulp is soft, drain the potatoes in the frying basket. Reheat the oil to smoking point; the temperature should rise again to 350°F (180°C).

At the first contact with the very hot oil, each piece of potato was seared and surrounded by a thin coating which enclosed some of the water and prevented it evaporating during frying.

The potatoes, cooled or warm, are plunged a second time into the oil, heated to 330°F (175°C). The coating previously formed stiffens, turns golden and becomes crisp, while the potato stick puffs up with the expansion of the moisture inside.

The potatoes are now a beautiful golden colour. Drain them in the frying basket, sprinkle with a pinch of salt, shake and turn upside down on a platter covered with a folded napkin. Serve immediately, while appetizing and above all deliciously crisp.

MATCHSTICK POTATOES
Pommes frites allumettes

Cut the potatoes half the size of the French fried potatoes, and follow the same recipe. Pile up the matchstick potatoes and serve, golden and very crisp.

STRAW POTATOES
Pommes paille

Cut the potatoes into julienne. Wash in cold water and soak for 10 minutes to remove the starch, which might make them stick together; drain and wipe dry. Then fry following the recipe for French fried potatoes (above).

During the first frying, when they are seared, stir the potatoes gently with a slotted metal spoon, so that they do not stick to one another. Pile up the potatoes and serve, golden and crisp.

POTATO CRISPS
Pommes chips

Cut the potatoes into very thin slices; soak the slices in cold water for 10 minutes. Rub them with your hands in the water to separate them and to remove the starch, thus keeping them from sticking to one another while cooking. Drain the slices and dry carefully.

Plunge the potato slices into very hot oil and cook quickly without lowering the temperature. Stir with a slotted metal spoon; then, when the slices are golden brown and very dry, drain them, sprinkle with salt and serve. They most often accompany roasted game.

Potatoes cooked this way can also be served cold, salted as an appetizer with aperitifs, along with salted toasted almonds, olives, etc.

PUFFED FRIED POTATOES
Pommes de terre soufflés

Peel good quality potatoes with firm yellow flesh.

Dry the potatoes and cut lengthwise into even slices 3 mm ($\frac{1}{8}$ inch) thick.

Wash the slices in cold water, drain and wipe dry.

In order to fry these potatoes, it is important to have two pans of hot oil, one for the first frying and the second for puffing the potatoes.

Heat the first oil to 360°F (180°C); plunge in the frying basket with a moderate amount of potato slices. Continue cooking the potatoes without raising the temperature too much. Tip the basket and loosen the potatoes with a skimmer to stop the slices sticking together.

In 6 or 7 minutes the slices will be golden and soft and will rise to the top.

With a slotted spoon remove the potatoes in small batches, drain them and plunge them immediately into the second pan of fat heated to a temperature of 375°F (190°C) and smoking.

The phenomenon explained for French fried potatoes also takes place here; because of the shape and the thickness of the slices, each slice puffs up, becoming egg shaped.

The potato slices take on a golden colour and dry very quickly; drain them immediately on a paper napkin, sprinkle with salt, and place on a platter lined with a folded napkin or beside the grilled meat they are to accompany.

Note: Puffed potatoes can be prepared in advance: after the second cooking, drain the slices, place them on a platter and cover them with a cloth. The potatoes will sink, but this will not spoil them, as they will puff up again when they are plunged into the fat a third time, just before serving.

BOILED OR STEAMED POTATOES
Pommes de terre cuites par ébullition ou à la vapeur

Potatoes boiled in water or some other liquid are the basis of many potato recipes.

In certain cases boiling is replaced by steaming, particularly when the potatoes are to be eaten plain, *à l'anglaise*.

STEAMED POTATOES
Pommes de terres à l'anglaise

Choose potatoes equal in size, as large as a small egg, of a firm, waxy variety.

Peel them and place them in a steamer; fill the bottom with water. Cover tightly, bring the water to the boil and simmer for 20 minutes.

If you do not have a steamer, use a soup plate, placed over a saucepan to hold the potatoes above the water.

Steamed potatoes are served with fish cooked in a court-bouillon or poached, or with certain other dishes. The potatoes can also be wrapped in foil and cooked in hot coals or baked in the oven.

BOILED POTATOES WITH THEIR SKINS
Pommes en robe de champs

Potatoes can also be cooked, unpeeled, in simmering salted water. When they are nearly cooked, pour off the water and dry the potatoes for 10 minutes on top of a warm stove.

POTATO PURÉE OR MASHED POTATOES
Purée de pommes de terre

Peel, wash and quarter the potatoes. Place in a saucepan, cover with cold salted water, bring to the boil and boil until the potatoes are cooked.

From time to time prick a potato with the point of a knife to see if it is done; stop the cooking as soon as the blade penetrates the potato or when the pulp yields to the pressure of your finger. The potatoes should not be overcooked, to prevent them from getting soggy.

Drain the potatoes well, put back into the saucepan and let stand on top of a warm stove for 8–10 minutes to dry.

Place the very hot potatoes in a very fine sieve and push them through with a pestle. To purée the potatoes, push from the top to the bottom. Never sieve the pulp by pressing on the pestle with a horizontal or circular movement. These will twist the pulp, make it rubbery and change its taste.

Put the purée back into the saucepan, and set it on a very low flame to keep it hot; add 100 g (4 oz) of butter for every 500 g (1 lb) of purée, beating vigorously with a wooden spatula to make the purée lighter and whiter. Dilute the purée to the desired consistency by adding boiling milk in small quantities. Working with the spatula makes the purée creamier and lighter. Do not boil after this step.

Spice the purée with a dash of grated nutmeg and correct the seasoning.

You may keep the purée warm in a double-boiler; however, whenever possible serve the purée as soon as it is ready to enjoy it at its best, which waiting would spoil.

DUCHESS POTATOES
Pommes de terre duchesse

500 g (1 lb) potatoes
4½ tablespoons
  unsalted butter
Pinch salt
Pinch freshly ground
  white pepper
Dash grated nutmeg
1 whole egg
2 egg yolks, beaten
Unsalted butter

The mixture known as duchess potatoes is used to prepare various garnishes – croquettes, potatoes dauphine, duchess potatoes, etc.

Cook 500 g (1 lb) of potatoes as directed for a purée (above); push through a very fine sieve, put into a pan and stir with a wooden spatula over a high flame to evaporate all the moisture.

When the purée is quite dry, like a thick paste, add away from the heat 50 g (2 oz) of butter, a pinch of salt, a pinch of freshly ground white pepper and a dash of grated nutmeg. Correct the seasoning and, stirring vigorously, add 1 whole egg and 2 beaten egg yolks.

Butter an enamel or a china dish, fill with the purée and dab the top with a piece of butter on a fork, to prevent a skin forming.

The mixture is now ready to be used in different recipes, such as duchess potatoes. For this cut the purée into pieces of about 50 g (2 oz) each. Shape them into small balls or into squares, circles or rectangles about 1 cm (½ inch) thick, or into quenelles, etc. Place on buttered pastry sheets, then brush with beaten egg, and place in a 400°F (200°C, gas mark 6) oven to brown.

POTATO CROQUETTES
Croquettes de pommes de terre

Duchess potatoes
1 egg
Pinch salt
1 tablespoon olive oil
Fresh breadcrumbs

Prepare a mixture of duchess potatoes (above). Divide into pieces, and on a table dusted with flour roll each piece into the shape of a small sausage; cut each into lengths the size of a long cork.

Dip the croquettes into 1 egg beaten with a pinch of salt and 1 tablespoon of olive oil, and roll them immediately in fresh breadcrumbs. Plunge the croquettes into very hot oil; as soon as they are golden and crisp, drain on a paper towel and sprinkle with a dash of salt.

Place the croquettes in a heap on a plate covered with a folded napkin.

500 g (1 lb) medium
  yellow potatoes, all
  the same size
½ l (1 pt) milk
Salt, pepper and
  nutmeg
1 egg
100 g (4 oz) grated
  Gruyère cheese
1 garlic clove
50 g (2 oz) unsalted
  butter

POTATO GRATIN WITH GRUYÈRE CHEESE
Gratin dauphinois
For 6 people

Boil the milk and let it cool.

Peel and dry the potatoes. Slice them thin; sprinkle with salt, grind some pepper on top, add a dash of grated nutmeg and mix well. Place the potatoes in a bowl.

Beat the egg well, strain it through a fine sieve and beat in the cooled milk, mixing both well.

Spread two-thirds of the Gruyere cheese on the potatoes and mix. Pour the milk–egg mixture over them. The quantity of milk used should just cover the potatoes. Mix well with a spatula; correct the seasoning.

Rub the garlic inside a deep ovenproof gratin dish, and butter it well; pour the potatoes and milk into the dish. The potatoes should not be deeper than 6 cm (2½ inches). Fill the dish to about 1 cm (½ inch) from the top. Carefully wipe the edges. On top, sprinkle the remaining grated Gruyère cheese and the butter cut into small pieces.

Bake in a 325°F (170°C, gas mark 3) oven for 45–50 minutes. The mixture, which can be made richer by adding thick cream, will become thick and succulent, and form a magnificent golden crust.

1·2 kg (2½ lb) yellow
  potatoes
Salt and freshly
  ground white pepper
1 garlic clove
50 g (2 oz) unsalted
  butter, plus extra
  butter
2 eggs
2 dl (¼ pt) milk
2–3 tablespoons
  double cream
Grated nutmeg

POTATO GRATIN WITH CREAM
Gratin de pommes de terre Fernand Point
For 4–6 people

Peel, wash and dry the potatoes. Slice them thin. Place the slices on a cloth. Toss them in salt and pepper.

Take a large gratin dish, rub the inside with the garlic clove and butter the dish generously.

Spread the potatoes in thin, even layers. Meanwhile, in a bowl combine the eggs, the milk, the cream and the grated nutmeg. Salt lightly and mix with a whisk.

Cover the potatoes with this mixture. Sprinkle 50 g (2 oz) of butter, cut into small pieces, on top. Bake in a 350°F (170°C, gas mark 3) oven for 45 minutes.

When the gratin is cooked and golden brown, let it stand in a warm place.

Serve very hot.

POTATOES WITH CREAM
Pommes de terre à la crème

Cook the potatoes in water; they should remain firm. Peel them while still hot and cut into thick slices; place in a pan.

Sprinkle the potatoes with salt, a pinch of white pepper, a dash of grated nutmeg, and cover with boiling milk or cream, or a mixture of both.

Slowly boil until the milk or cream is completely reduced; just before serving, add away from the heat a few tablespoons of double cream. Stir to mix, and serve in a bowl.

BAKED POTATOES
Pommes de terres rôties au four

Choose large, long potatoes, all the same size, of a starchy variety. Wash and dry them and bake in a 425°F (220°C, gas mark 7) oven for 40–60 minutes.

Place the potatoes on a plate covered with a folded napkin, putting them between the napkin folds. Serve with butter.

POTATOES ROASTED IN CHARCOAL
Pommes de terre rôties dans la cendre

Prepare large potatoes as for baked potatoes (above) and bury them in a very hot charcoal; some of the coals should still be glowing.

Serve in the same way as baked potatoes.

Other dishes are based on this way of cooking potatoes, for example:

POTATO PURÉE WITH WHIPPED CREAM
Pommes de terre mousseline

500 g (1 lb) potato purée
100 g (4 oz) unsalted butter
2 egg yolks
Dash grated nutmeg
Pinch salt
6 tablespoons whipped cream
Precooked pie crust (optional)

First bake or cook the potatoes in charcoal. Then open and remove the pulp.

Push the very hot pulp through a fine sieve. Put the potato purée into a saucepan and over a very low flame stir with a whisk, adding the butter, 2 egg yolks, a dash of grated nutmeg and a pinch of salt. Do not let the purée boil; it should be hot enough to absorb the egg yolks.

When the purée is smooth and white, add the whipped cream to give it a proper creamy consistency.

The purée is served either as it is, in a bowl, or spread in a buttered gratin dish and baked in a 425°F (220°C, gas mark 7) oven or baked in a precooked pie crust browned in a 425°F (220°C, gas mark 7) oven.

POTATO PANCAKE
Pommes de terre Macaire

500 g (1 lb) potato purée
100 g (4 oz) unsalted butter
Dash grated nutmeg
Pinch salt and pepper

Remove the very hot pulp of baked potatoes. Put it into a bowl, add the butter, a dash of grated nutmeg, pepper and salt. Mix well with a fork.

Heat a knob of butter in a frying pan. When the butter is light brown, spread the potato purée in a round about 4 cm (1½ inches) thick. Cook slowly, tilting the pan as you would in making a crêpe. When the pancake is golden brown, turn the pan upside down over a plate; add a knob of butter to the empty pan and slide the pancake back in to brown the other side. Serve very hot.

SAUTÉED RAW POTATOES
Pommes sautées à cru

Cut the potatoes into thin even slices, wash under cold water, drain, dry and sprinkle with a pinch of salt.

Place the slices in a frying pan with very hot butter and cook, stirring often. The slices should be all golden brown, with crisp brown edges and soft centres.

Place the potato slices in a bowl and sprinkle with a *persillade* (parsley chopped with garlic).

SAUTÉED POTATOES WITH SHALLOTS AND BEEF MARROW
Pommes sautées à la bordelaise

Sauté 500 g (1 lb) of boiled or raw potatoes. Season them after they are browned and a few minutes before serving. Add $\frac{1}{2}$ teaspoon of finely chopped shallots and 1 tablespoon of beef marrow, diced and poached. Finish the dish with a *persillade*. Serve as for sautéed raw potatoes (above).

SAUTÉED POTATOES WITH ONIONS
Pommes sautées à la lyonnaise

As for potatoes *à la bordelaise*, but instead of the beef marrow and shallots add some onion cut into fine julienne and cooked till golden in butter, varying the quantity to taste.

SAUTÉED POTATOES WITH GARLIC
Pommes sautées à la provençale

As for potatoes *à la bordelaise*, adding a little grated garlic instead of the beef marrow and shallots.

POTATOES IN BUTTER
Pommes de terres au beurre dites 'château' ou pommes de terres rissolées

New potatoes or old potatoes are cooked the same way; only the cooking time is different.

Choose small potatoes; if the only potatoes available are large, cut them into the shape of a large walnut. The pieces should be the same size. Peel, wash, drain and dry the potatoes, and place them in a pan with sizzling butter. Sprinkle with salt and cook slowly, covered; stir the potatoes from time to time and brown them gradually. When the potatoes are cooked, they should be a uniform golden colour, soft and soaked in butter.

The softness of the potatoes results from covering the saucepan tightly in the beginning and during most of the cooking. They should be golden brown when done.

The potatoes can be cooked and browned equally well on top of the stove or in the oven (at 350°F, 180°C, gas mark 4). It is easier to check the progress of the browning when the potatoes are cooked on top of the stove.

POTATO BALLS
Pommes noisettes ou à la parisienne

Choose large potatoes; peel, wash and drain them. Cut them into round balls the size of a large hazelnut with a vegetable scoop or round spoon, turning it to make the balls. Place them in cold water, and continue until all the potatoes have been cut.

Use the remaining pulp in soups.

Potatoes *à la parisienne* are prepared the same way, but a smaller cutter is used.

The potatoes are cooked as for château potatoes (above).

Sprinkle with chopped parsley just before serving.

POTATO FONDANTS
Pommes de terre fondantes

These potatoes are prepared like château potatoes. However, they are twice as large, and they are cooked, covered, very, very slowly on top of the stove. The potatoes should be placed in one layer in the pan and turned one at a time as they brown. When they are cooked, the potatoes should be soaked with butter and very soft.

Note: This second series of potato dishes cannot be left waiting after being cooked, if you want to eat them at their best. I do not advise blanching (placing the potatoes in cold water and boiling for 5 minutes) before sautéeing potatoes. It is certainly faster, and it saves some butter, but naturally it cannot produce the same results.

POTATOES ANNA
Pommes de terre Anna

Choose long, medium-sized potatoes. Peel, wash and dry; cut into very thin even slices.

Place the potato slices in cold water; drain, dry in a cloth and season with salt and pepper.

If you do not have a special straight-sided, flat-bottomed mould, use a heavy straight-sided sauté pan, and butter the inside with clarified butter. The water or whey in unclarified butter would make the potatoes stick to the pan.

Choose slices of the same diameters and, starting from the edge, cover the bottom of the pan completely, placing the slices in circles, each slice overlapping the preceding one, and each circle overlapping the preceding one. Press a circle of potato slices overlapping one another against the sides of the pan. Inside these potatoes place a layer of potato slices 2 cm ($\frac{3}{4}$ inch) thick.

Baste this first layer of potatoes with a few tablespoons of clarified butter. Start another layer; there is no need to align these slices as carefully as at first. Baste again with butter and continue until you have 5 or 6 layers.

If necessary, add another layer of slices to fill the mould. Finish by basting with butter.

Cover the mould tightly, heat it for a moment on top of the stove, then bake in a 400°F (200°C, gas mark 6) oven for 35–40 minutes.

With the point of a knife or trussing needle, probe the potatoes to see if they are cooked. To serve unmould on to a lid placed on a plate to drain and collect the excess butter. Slide the golden-coloured potato cake on to a platter.

Serve immediately.

POTATOES WITH TRUFFLES AND *FOIE GRAS*
Pommes de terre à la sarladaise

Make layers of potatoes Anna alternating with layers of sliced raw truffles. In the layers sprinkle a few pieces of *foie gras*, diced or sliced. If the liver is raw, sear the pieces quickly in a pan on a high flame. The dish can be improved if the cooking butter is mixed by half with the fat from the *foie gras*.

POTATOES IN BUTTER WITH ONIONS
Pommes de terre à la boulangère

To 500 g (1 lb) of whole new potatoes or potatoes cut to be sautéed, add 100 g (4 oz) of very small peeled onions.

Cook together very slowly, following the recipe for château potatoes above.

This recipe can be prepared with thin potato slices and small onions or large onions cut into large strips. Spread a thin layer in a thickly buttered earthenware roasting pan, season with salt and pepper, and add a small bouquet garni. Place a piece of meat on this bed of vegetables and roast in the oven.

POTATO FRITTERS
Pommes de terre Lorette

Mix well together equal amounts of unsweetened choux pastry (page 551), not too buttery, and of potatoes dauphine (above).

Take a heaped tablespoonful of this mixture for each fritter, and with a knife blade dipped in hot water push the mixture into a saucepan full of very hot oil.

When the fritters rise to the surface and are golden brown, drain them on a paper towel, sprinkle with salt and pile on a platter covered with a folded napkin.

SALSIFY OR OYSTER PLANT, AND BLACK SALSIFY
Salsifis ou scorsonères

These are similar roots, one white, the other black on the outside, from two different plants but both cooked the same way.

Before cooking in a white court-bouillon, peel the roots very thinly; they can also be scraped, but this is not so satisfactory.

To prevent the roots from turning black, place them in cold water with lemon juice or vinegar as soon as they are peeled. Cut into pieces about 7 cm (3 inches) long.

Meanwhile, prepare a white court-bouillon with 1 tablespoon of flour, diluted with 1 l (2 pts) of cold water, 2 tablespoons of vinegar and $1\frac{1}{2}$ teaspoons of salt.

Bring to the boil, stirring often to distribute the flour well. Then add the salsify.

Cover and boil slowly. Cooking time is at least 2 hours.

Check whether the salsify is cooked by pressing a piece between your fingers; it will crush easily if it is done.

Cooked salsify can be refrigerated and kept for several days in the cooking liquid. Once the roots are cooled, place a piece of oiled or buttered paper over the liquid.

SALSIFY SAUTÉED IN BUTTER
Salsifis sautés au beurre

Drain the salsify cooked as directed above, dry and place in very hot butter in a frying pan. Season with a pinch of salt and freshly ground pepper; sauté and brown as you would for sautéed potatoes. Serve with a *persillade* (chopped parsley and garlic).

SALSIFY WITH ONIONS
Salsifis sautés à la lyonnaise

Sauté 500 g (1 lb) of salsify in butter, as directed above, then add 1 tablespoon of onion cut into thin strips and cooked in butter until soft and golden.

SALSIFY FRITTERS
Fritots ou beignets de salsifis

500 g (1 lb) salsify
Pinch salt
Pinch freshly ground pepper
1 teaspoon chopped parsley
Olive oil
½ teaspoon lemon juice
Light batter (page 601)
Bouquet fried parsley

After cooking the salsify in a white court-bouillon by the directions above, drain and dry; put 500 g (1 lb) of salsify to marinate 30 minutes in a plate with a seasoning made with a large pinch of salt, a pinch of freshly ground pepper, chopped parsley, olive oil and lemon juice. Mix well as for a salad.

A few minutes before serving, dip the salsify pieces in a light batter and drop them one at a time into very hot oil.

As soon as the fritters are golden brown and crisp, drain on a paper towel, sprinkle with a pinch of salt and arrange in clusters on a round platter covered with a folded napkin.

On top of the salsify place a bouquet of fried parsley which has been dipped for 1 second into very hot oil and drained.

SALSIFY IN VEAL STOCK
Salsifis au jus de veau

After cooking the salsify by the directions above, drain the pieces, then dry them and place in a pan, in no more than two layers. Baste with some good, well-flavoured veal stock, lightly salted and fatty, and stew for 15 minutes.

Place the salsify in a bowl and baste with the juice reduced until there is just enough to serve with the salsify.

SALSIFY WITH CREAM
Salsifis à la crème

Cook the salsify by the directions above, drain and dry. Put the pieces into a pan in one layer, not too thick. Cover with cream and simmer slowly. Serve when the cream is reduced by half. Correct the seasoning, grind some pepper on top and away from the heat stir in some butter.

TOMATO FONDUE
Fondue de tomates

Tomato *fondue* is generally used for various garnishes or as a flavouring. Depending on its final use, the *fondue* is made *au naturel, à la portugaise, à la niçoise* or *à la provençale*.

The method of cooking is identical for all of these, but the seasonings are different.

Au naturel

Cut off the stalks of the tomatoes. Dip them for 1 second in boiling water; peel. Cut each tomato in half and remove the seeds, leaving as much of the juice as possible; cut into large dice.

Season with salt and pepper and a pinch of sugar.

In a pan heat 2 tablespoons of oil or 1 tablespoon of oil and

25 g (1 oz) of butter; add the diced tomatoes and simmer until the juice is completely evaporated.

Away from the heat finish by adding 50 g (2 oz) of butter, cut into pieces, and stir well.

A la portugaise

Follow the directions above, but at the start of the cooking, cook 2 large onions, sliced thinly, in the oil without letting them brown. Finish with a *persillade* (chopped parsley and garlic).

A la niçoise

Cook as for tomatoes *à la portugaise*, and finish with 1 teaspoon composed of equal amounts of chopped parsley, chervil and tarragon, and 1 teaspoon of chopped capers. Away from the heat mix in 25 g (1 oz) of anchovy butter.

A la provençale

Finish the recipe for tomatoes *au naturel* above with a *persillade*, adding an extra grated garlic clove.

STUFFED TOMATOES
Tomates farcies

Choose medium-sized tomatoes, ripe but firm.

Cut off the tops and stems, and remove the juice and the seeds without destroying the shape of the tomatoes.

Oil or butter a gratin dish. Place the tomatoes with the open side on top; sprinkle on each a pinch of salt, a little ground pepper and a few drops of oil or a pat of butter.

Bake in a 425°F (220°C, gas mark 7) oven for 5 minutes.

Collect the juice rendered by the tomatoes and mix it with the prepared stuffing (see below); stuff the tomatoes in a dome shape, sprinkle with fresh breadcrumbs, baste with a few drops of oil or melted butter and bake again in a 425°F (220°C, gas mark 7) oven to finish cooking and to brown.

The tomatoes can be served as they are or with 1 tablespoon of veal stock, demi-glace sauce (page 108) or a light tomato sauce poured into the gratin dish.

The tomatoes are usually stuffed with forcemeat made with leftovers or sausage meat cooked with chopped mushrooms, rice pilaf, sweet peppers, onions, shallots, garlic, etc. They can also be stuffed with *duxelles* (chopped mushrooms, page 447), risotto with chicken livers, diced kidneys, etc.

GRILLED TOMATOES
Tomates grillées

Prepare the tomatoes as you would stuffed tomatoes (above); baste with a few drops oil or melted butter, season with salt and pepper.

Grill the tomatoes under a low flame. Turn them when they are half cooked.

Note: One can also grill whole tomatoes, after cutting off the stems and tops.

SAUTÉED TOMATOES
Tomates sautées

Remove the stems and cut the tomatoes in half horizontally, squeeze out the juice and the seeds, and place the tomato halves side by side in a pan in which a few tablespoons of oil mixed with butter are sizzling. Season with salt and pepper. Cook on a high flame to reduce the remaining juice rapidly and to brown the tomatoes lightly; turn them halfway through the cooking.

To finish sprinkle with a *persillade* (chopped garlic and parsley) mixed with an extra grated garlic clove (*à la provençale*). Or sprinkle with an onion, finely chopped or cut into thin julienne and cooked in butter, and chopped parsley (*à la lyonnaise*).

Or simply sprinkle with chopped parsley (*aux fines herbes*).

½ l (1 pt) tomato
fondue
Salt and pepper
Pinch sugar
6 tablespoons reduced
béchamel sauce
(page 110)
4 egg yolks, beaten
6 egg whites, beaten
very stiff
Unsalted butter

TOMATO SOUFFLÉ
Soufflé de tomates

Prepare tomato *fondue* (see recipe above), seasoned with salt and pepper and a pinch of sugar, very reduced and strained through a very fine sieve. To the very hot tomatoes, add the reduced béchamel sauce, and thicken without boiling with 4 beaten egg yolks. Mix well, correct the seasoning and add carefully, to keep them from falling, 6 egg whites beaten very stiff.

Butter a soufflé dish, fill to 2 cm ($\frac{3}{4}$ inch) from the top with this mixture, smooth the surface and cook in a 400°F (200°C, gas mark 6) oven for 15 minutes.

Note: This preparation must be made and cooked at the last moment, then served as soon as it comes from the oven. If not, the soufflé will fall rapidly and lose its character.

This mixture can also be used to stuff tomatoes or artichoke hearts, first cooked and stewed in butter (page 433). Bake them in a 425°F (220°C, gas mark 7) oven for 15 minutes.

Pasta

500 g (1 lb) sifted
flour
1½ teaspoons finely
crushed salt
6 eggs

FRESH NOODLES
Nouilles fraîches

Place the sifted flour on a table or marble slab; make a well in the centre and place in it 1½ teaspoons of finely crushed salt and 6 eggs.

Gradually mix the eggs into the flour until you have a very firm dough. To blend the two ingredients well, knead the dough by pressing pieces of dough down firmly on the table and away from you with the palm of your hand.

When the dough is very smooth, shape it into a ball; wrap it in a cloth to prevent it from forming a skin, and let stand for an hour or two, depending upon the quality of the flour, until the dough is no longer elastic.

Then divide the dough into pieces the size of a lemon, and roll them into rectangular sheets 2 mm ($\frac{1}{10}$ inch) thick.

Fold these sheets in half and place over a stretched string for about an hour to dry them.

Dust the sheets of dough with flour, roll them up and slice them into strips 2 mm ($\frac{1}{10}$ inch) wide.

Spread the strips in thin layers on baking sheets to help them dry; do this whenever the fresh noodles are not to be used immediately.

Cooking.   For 500 g (1 lb) of fresh noodles, bring 2 l (4 pts) of water to the boil with 1 tablespoon of salt. Add the noodles and when it starts to boil again, remove from the heat, cover and poach without boiling for 12–15 minutes.

Drain the noodles well to prepare for the next step. Never rinse them. This advice applies to both dry and fresh noodles, of any shape.

MACARONI WITH BUTTER AND CHEESE
Macaroni à l'italienne

Cook 225 g (8 oz) of macaroni, drain well and place the steaming macaroni back in the hot saucepan in which it was cooked, adding 25 g (1 oz) of butter and 75 g (3 oz) of grated Gruyère cheese, salt and pepper. Mix well with a wooden spoon. Serve in a bowl.

MACARONI CHEESE
Macaroni au gratin

Prepare 225 g (8 oz) of macaroni with butter and cheese as above, adding at the last moment, 6 tablespoons of boiling cream.

In a buttered gratin dish, spread the macaroni and sprinkle with grated Gruyère cheese mixed with a pinch of fresh white breadcrumbs. Baste with 1 teaspoon of melted butter.

Brown in a 425°F (220°C, gas mark 7) oven.

MACARONI WITH TOMATO
Macaroni à la napolitaine

To 225 g (8 oz) of macaroni with butter and cheese add 3 table-spoons of tomato *fondue au naturel* (page 507).

---

225 g (8 oz) macaroni
1 tablespoon truffles
2 tablespoons lean cooked ham
2 tablespoons mushrooms
Unsalted butter
1 tablespoon Madeira
6 tablespoons demi-glace sauce (page 108)

MACARONI WITH HAM AND TRUFFLES
Macaroni à la milanaise

Prepare macaroni with butter and cheese as above. To garnish 225 g (8 oz) of macaroni, use 1 tablespoon of truffles, 2 table-spoons of lean cooked ham and 2 tablespoons of mushrooms, all cut into julienne. First cook the mushrooms quickly in very hot butter; then add the truffles, then the ham, then 1 tablespoon of Madeira. Reduce by half and finish with the demi-glace sauce well-flavoured with tomato. Mix with cooked macaroni.

Serve in a bowl.

Note: The above macaroni recipes can also be used for noodles, lasagne and spaghetti.

Noodle dough (page 510)

Ravioli stuffing:
225 g (8 oz) leftover boiled or braised beef
225 (8 oz) cooked spinach
1 lamb's brain
1 medium-sized onion
2 eggs, lightly beaten
Salt, fresh pepper, dash nutmeg

RAVIOLI NICE STYLE
Ravioli à la niçoise

Roll a rectangular sheet of noodle dough (see above) about 3 mm ($\frac{1}{8}$ inch) thick. On top, in rows 5 cm (2 inches) apart, place small pieces of stuffing about the size of an olive. Follow the recipe below or use any ingredients to hand – cooked beef, chicken, etc., or a vegetable stuffing (for instance spinach purée).

Moisten the gaps between the stuffings with a feather or a brush dipped into water.

Cover with a second sheet of dough, the same size and thickness.

Stick the two layers of dough together by pressing with your fingers or a ruler on the dampened portions. Then cut with a pastry cutter or a knife into 5-cm (2-inch) squares.

Plunge the ravioli into salted boiling water and simmer 6 minutes.

Drain the ravioli in a colander and place on a cloth.

In a gratin dish, spread a few tablespoons of veal juice or any other stock. Place the ravioli flat in the dish, baste them with the same stock and sprinkle with grated Gruyère cheese mixed with a large pinch of fresh breadcrumbs, which helps the cheese to stick to the ravioli. Baste with a few drops of melted butter and brown in a 425°F (220°C, gas mark 7) oven. Serve as it is.

Ravioli stuffing

Cut the beef into tiny dice. Mix with the cooked spinach, rubbed through a fine sieve, 1 lamb's brain, poached, then mashed with a fork, 1 medium-sized onion, finely chopped and cooked in butter without letting it brown. Mix all the ingredients together in the pan used to cook the onion, and add 2 eggs lightly beaten. Heat slowly, stirring the mixture until completely mixed, without letting it boil. Season with salt, fresh pepper and a dash of nutmeg.

Rice

Industry has considerably changed rice, which in its polished form seems to be considered a first-class product.

This is a grave mistake for although it gives the rice a more attractive appearance, this process takes away its vitamins, which means its main nutritive values. I therefore advise buying unpolished rice.

Before cooking rice, wash it in cold water and drain well.

In French cookery there are three main methods for cooking rice: risotto; *à l'indienne* or *à la créole*; and rice pilaf (or pilau).

1 large onion
50 g (2 oz) unsalted butter
225 g (8 oz) rice
White bouillon or veal stock
2 tablespoons grated Parmesan or Gruyère cheese

RISOTTO WITH ONION, BUTTER AND CHEESE
Risotto à la piémontaise

Cut a large onion into thin strips and brown lightly and very slowly in 25 g (1 oz) of butter in a pan. When the onion is cooked, add the rice, washed and drained.

Stir the rice with the onion on the lowest possible flame. When the grains of rice have soaked up the butter, cover the rice with twice its volume of white bouillon or veal stock.

Bring to the boil, tightly cover and cook either in a 325°F (170°C, gas mark 3) oven or on the stove over low heat for 25 minutes.

When the rice is cooked, separate the grains with a fork, adding 25 g (1 oz) of butter and 2 tablespoons of grated Parmesan or Gruyère cheese.

RICE PILAF
Riz pilaf

Soak the rice for 2 hours in cold water before cooking, after-having carefully washed it; then drain.

Cook as for the risotto, but increase the quantity of butter to cook the onion and saturate the rice (75 g (3 oz) of butter for 225 g (8 oz) of rice).

Cover the rice with twice its volume of white bouillon or veal stock, and cook as for the risotto above.

STEAMED RICE
Riz à l'indienne ou créole

Wash the rice, then pour into a saucepan of boiling salted water. Boil for 10 minutes. Drain in a sieve; wash several times in cold water and drain again.

Pour the rice into a heavy fireproof dish or saucepan, cover tightly and place in a 275°F (140°C, gas mark 1) oven for 25 minutes, or in a steamer, until completely cooked. The grains of rice should remain whole and not stick to one another.

Rice prepared this way can be seasoned in various ways and served with numerous dishes – curry, shellfish *à l'américaine*, etc.

---

1 recipe for risotto *à la piemontaise*
4 tablespoons tomato purée or pulp of 3 fresh tomatoes
1 onion
1 tablespoon lean cooked ham
1 large truffle
3 large mushroom caps

RISOTTO WITH TOMATO, HAM AND TRUFFLE
Risotto à la milanaise

Follow the recipe for risotto (above). For 225 g (8 oz) of rice, add 4 tablespoons of tomato purée (page 507) or the pulp of 3 fresh tomatoes, cooked with an onion and added to the rice after the rice has absorbed the butter.

When the rice is cooked, add 1 tablespoon of lean cooked ham, cut into julienne.

Generally, this garnish is completed with 1 large truffle and 3 large mushroom caps, all cut into julienne and added to the rice before the tomato.

RICE WITH BUTTER
Riz au beurre

Cook 225 g (8 oz) of rice as for the rice pilaf (above) but without the onion. Pour over the rice twice its volume of water. Add salt.

When the rice is cooked, separate the grains carefully, adding 100–125 g (4–5 oz) of butter; the quantity of butter used is determined by one's purse.

RICE WITH PEAS AND BEANS
Riz à la Valenciennes

Cook 225 g (8 oz) of rice pilaf. When the rice has soaked up the butter, add 1 heaped tablespoon each of small fresh green peas and French beans cut into 2-cm (1-inch) pieces, and 1 lettuce heart shredded. Cook for a few minutes before adding the bouillon.

Finish cooking as for rice pilaf. Mix well while buttering, and serve.

RICE WITH SAUSAGE, PEPPERS AND PEAS
Riz à la grecque

225 g (8 oz) rice pilaf
(recipe above)
100 g (4 oz) butter
1 medium onion,
sliced
100 g (4 oz)
chipolatas
100 g (4 oz) shredded
lettuce leaves
100 g (4 oz) sweet red
peppers, diced
100 g (4 oz) small
fresh peas

In a heavy saucepan, melt the butter and brown the onion; then sear the sausage cut into small pieces. Add the rice, washed and drained, and heat until the rice absorbs the butter. Stir carefully to avoid breaking the sausage, and finish by adding the lettuce, the sweet pepper and the peas.

Pour white chicken bouillon or veal or any other stock to come up slightly above the rice. Bring to the boil and cover. Cook slowly on a low flame.

As the rice puffs up and absorbs the liquid, add small quantities of boiling bouillon. Stir in very carefully. Repeat this step several times.

The rice will be cooked when it has absorbed three times its volume in liquid. Cooking time will be 20 minutes.

Although the rice is perfectly cooked, it will not be crushed or stick together, and it will be very creamy. Correct the seasoning.

Note: This method of cooking rice is one of the best and can be used to make risotto.

SAFFRON RICE
Riz à l'orientale

Cook this like a risotto *à la milanaise,* but without the ham and flavoured with saffron.

Gnocchi

Gnocchi are made with semolina, *paté à choux* or potatoes. They make a delicious and inexpensive light entrée.

½ l (1 pt) boiling milk
125 g (5 oz) semolina
Salt, pepper, dash
nutmeg
50 g (2 oz) unsalted
butter
2 egg yolks diluted
with 1 tablespoon
cold milk
Grated Gruyère or
Parmesan cheese

SEMOLINA GNOCCHI
Gnocchi à la romaine

First make a porridge: pour the semolina into the boiling milk, stirring continuously with a wooden spoon.

Season with salt and pepper and a dash of nutmeg; cook very slowly for 20 minutes.

Away from the heat, when the semolina has stopped boiling but is still hot, add 25 g (1 oz) of butter and mix in 2 egg yolks diluted with 1 tablespoon of cold milk.

Correct the seasoning.

Spread this mixture in a layer about 1 cm (½ inch) thick on a pastry sheet dampened with water. When the semolina is cold, cut it into rounds 5-cm (2-inches) in diameter, or into small squares, diamonds or rectangles of 3·5–5 cm (1½–2 inches) on each side.

Thickly butter a gratin dish, sprinkle it with grated Gruyère or Parmesan cheese. Arrange a layer of gnocchi, sprinkle generously with the grated cheese, baste with melted butter and brown in a 300°F (150°C, gas mark 2) oven.

Serve very hot from the dish.

¼ l (½ pt) milk
50 g (2 oz) butter
Pinch salt, plus extra
salt
Dash grated nutmeg
125 g (5 oz) flour,
sifted
3 eggs
100 g (4 oz) grated
Gruyère cheese

GNOCCHI MADE WITH CHOUX PASTE
Gnocchi à l'ancienne

In a saucepan, combine the milk, the butter, the salt and the nutmeg. Bring to the boil; as soon as the butter is melted, add the flour, stirring with a wooden spoon. Cook the mixture on a low flame, stirring often, for 5 minutes. Then, away from the heat, beat in the 3 eggs, one by one, to obtain a very smooth dough. Stir in the cheese.

In a large saucepan bring salted water to the boil, using 1 teaspoon of salt for each litre (2 pts) of water.

Meanwhile, place the dough in a pastry bag with a plain, medium-sized nozzle, and squeeze it with your left hand over the pot of boiling water; using your right hand, with a knife dipped often into hot water, cut the dough as it comes out of the tube into pieces about 5 cm (2 inches) long. Or form pieces of the dough the size of a small walnut with a teaspoon, dipped each time into boiling water, and let the dough slide into the poaching water.

Bring the water back to the boil for about 1 minute, then simmer for 15 minutes.

The gnocchi will rise to the surface when they are cooked. To be sure they are done, drain one and check its elasticity by pressing between your fingers. Drain cooked gnocchi on a cloth. Prepare like the gnocchi *à la romaine* or *parisienne*.

GNOCCHI WITH CHEESE SAUCE
Gnocchi à la parisienne

In a gratin dish, spread a few tablespoons of a light Mornay sauce (page 120). Place on top the gnocchi made with choux paste and cover with the same sauce. Sprinkle with grated Gruyère cheese mixed with fresh white breadcrumbs, 1 part crumbs to 5 parts cheese.

Baste with a few drops of melted butter and brown in a 375°F (190°C, gas mark 5) oven.

The gnocchi will puff up to three times their initial volume.
Serve very hot.

POTATO GNOCCHI
Gnocchi Belle-de-Fontenay

500 g (1 lb) pulp from firm, yellow potatoes
75 g (3 oz) butter
Salt, pepper, grated nutmeg
1 egg yolk
1 whole egg
125 g (5 oz) sifted flour
25 g (1 oz) grated Gruyère cheese, plus extra cheese

Wash the potatoes, bake in the oven, remove the pulp while still very hot and then push the pulp through a fine sieve. Put the purée into a bowl and stir it vigorously with a wooden spoon, adding 25 g (1 oz) of butter, salt, pepper and dash of nutmeg.

Correct the seasoning when the purée is smooth and white.

Add the egg yolk and then, in small quantities, the whole egg, lightly beaten.

Finish by adding the flour, then 25 g (1 oz) of Gruyère cheese.
The dough should be perfectly smooth.

Let the dough cool; divide into small balls of about 25 g (1 oz). Place the balls on a table dusted with flour and roll them into rounds. Flatten them with a fork, pressing the fork twice in different directions to form a square pattern.

Plunge the gnocchi into a large saucepan of boiling salted water (1 teaspoon of salt per 1 l (2 pts) of water). The gnocchi should move easily in the water.

When the water starts to boil again, lower the flame to maintain a slight simmer; cover, and poach this way for 15 minutes. The poaching is done if when you press the dough with your fingers, it seems elastic. Drain the gnocchi on a cloth.

Thickly butter a round deep gratin dish; sprinkle generously with grated Gruyère cheese and arrange one layer of gnocchi. Sprinkle again with grated cheese, and make another layer of gnocchi. Cover the second layer with cheese.

Meanwhile, in a pan cook 50 g (2 oz) of butter until light brown and pour over the last layer of cheese; place in a 425°F (220°C, gas mark 7) oven for 7–8 minutes to brown, and serve immediately.

Note: The butter can be replaced by a light Mornay sauce (page 120), as for gnocchi *à la parisienne*.

DESSERTS

We must distinguish between raised dough or pastry made with yeast, and pastry made by various methods with flour and liquid or fat ingredients but no yeast.

Dough for brioches, babas, savarins, kugelhupf, etc., belong to the first group. The second group includes flaky (puff) pastry, pastry for *galettes*, short pastry, sweet flan pastry, etc.

All these doughs can be made successfully in a domestic kitchen, but the baking can be tricky. You must have an oven with heat that is uniform and regular and the bottom of the oven must be able to reach a very high temperature. It is better to take measures to keep the pastry from burning than to have to compensate for inadequate heat. A brioche cooks and flaky pastry rises because of the heat from below.

Remember that the oven temperature must be related to the size and nature of the pastry being baked. For example, the oven should be much hotter to cook a series of small brioches or small puff pastries than for a large brioche or a Pithiviers almond cake. Small pastries need a hot oven to seal them. Large ones should be baked in a moderately hot oven. These general guidelines, although important, cannot replace experience. You can acquire experience very quickly if you are aware of the problems and doubly careful.

Raised doughs

BRIOCHE DOUGH
La pâte à brioche

This triple alliance of butter, eggs and flour, combined by long-established techniques, then allowed to rise properly, will produce the most delicious cake so long as the ingredients that make up this superb mixture are of superior quality and impeccably fresh.

Brioche dough can contain more or less butter. Here I will give an average recipe which produces excellent results, without adding to the difficulties.

For about 1·1 kg (2½ lb) dough:

500 g (1 lb) plain flour

5–12 g (¼–½ oz) dried yeast (depending on the temperature)

Warm milk or water

2 teaspoons salt

6–7 whole eggs (depending on size)

10 g (½ oz) sugar

500 g (1 lb) unsalted butter

25 g (1 oz) extra sugar (optional, may be mixed with flour to produce a beautiful golden crust)

1 egg, beaten (for glazing)

Method. 1. Sift one-third of the flour and place in a mound on a table or a pastry slab. Make a well in the centre, and add the yeast. The quantity of yeast will depend upon the temperature. On hot summer days, 5 g (¼ oz) may be enough for each 500 g (1 lb) of flour, while 12 g (½ oz) will be needed if the day is cold. This difference has important consequences; the yeast produces the leavening of the dough upon which its lightness and its flavour depend. Excessive fermentation gives the dough a bitter, disagreeable taste, destroying its butter-smooth quality. Too little leavening produces a heavy, indigestible dough, and baking is difficult because the dough does not rise properly.

Sprinkle the yeast in the middle of the flour. Dissolve the yeast by pouring in 2 tablespoons of warm water or milk; then little by little mix in the flour, adding more warm water or milk very gradually until you obtain a dough that is soft but thick enough to be rolled into a ball. Place the ball of dough in a bowl and make a slash across the top. Cover the dough with a cloth, and set in a warm place to rise.

The dough will be ready when it has doubled in volume.

2. While this dough is rising (which will take 20–30 minutes) sift the remaining two-thirds of the flour on to the table in a mound. Make a well and in the centre place the salt dissolved in 2 tablespoons of water. Break 3 eggs, one by one, into a bowl to check their freshness, in case any are bad. Add the eggs to the salt in the centre of the flour. Meanwhile, cream the butter by hand to make it very malleable and smooth, and set aside on the table. Also prepare the sugar in a bowl, adding 2 tablespoons of milk or water to dissolve it. Then start to mix and knead the flour with the salt and 3 eggs.

The dough, stiff in the beginning, will absorb one by one the 4 other eggs (also checked for freshness) and then the dissolved sugar. These ingredients should be added slowly, testing the consistency of the dough by pinching it between your thumb and forefinger; work the dough with your fingers until it becomes elastic, which means very light but with enough body so that it no longer sticks to the fingers or to the table.

When the dough reaches that point, add the softened butter. This second step will be done less vigorously, and as soon as the butter is mixed into the dough, add the risen dough from the bowl, which should by then have doubled its original volume.

Mix the dough again gently, cutting through it with the side of your fingers, held rigid; place one-half of the dough on top of the other. Cut through the stacked dough again and restack until the dough is completely mixed. Place the dough in a bowl, sprinkle with flour and cover with a cloth. Set in a warm place.

3. The second period of rising now begins. It will take 5–6 hours.

After this time, place the dough on the table dusted with flour; flatten it with your hands to eliminate the air; fold several times, roll again in a ball, then place back in the bowl.

This step increases the volume of the dough and precedes the third period of rising which also lasts 5–6 hours, making a total of 10–12 hours.

It is only then that the brioche dough is ready to be used, cut into pieces and placed in moulds.

At this point the dough can be kept for a whole day before it is cooked, provided that you stop it rising by refrigerating the dough, without freezing it however.

Since this dough is to be used in a domestic kitchen, we advise baking it immediately.

4. Correctly risen brioche dough should be light and moderately elastic. Now divide it into sections and shape it by rolling each small piece of dough on the table with the palm of your hand (both lightly dusted with flour). Curve your fingers gently around the dough without pressing it and roll it round and round between your palm and the table. The dough should not stick to your hand or to the table.

If the dough is going to be used for one large brioche, it is rolled the same way, using both hands.

Roll the dough quickly so that the heat of your hands does not make it sticky.

Quickly place the ball of dough in a brioche mould (wider at the top and fluted). It is customary to top each brioche with a 'head'. This is made of a quarter of the dough used to make a brioche, rolled in a ball and then shaped like a pear; stick the pear-shaped piece (round end up) in the centre of the brioche, punching it halfway in with your forefinger.

Cover the small brioches or the one large brioche with a cloth-to prevent the dough from forming a skin and set in a warm place so that the dough rises once more.

5. When the dough in the mould or moulds has increased its volume by one-third, brush with beaten egg, being careful not to flatten the 'heads' and make a crosswise slash, using scissors dipped in water, on each top to help the dough to rise. Place the large brioche in a 350°F (180°C, gas mark 4) oven; use a 425°F (220°C, gas mark 7) oven for small ones.

The cooking time for a brioche made with 500 g (1 lb) of dough is 20–25 minutes.

To decide when the brioches are done, stick a thin trussing needle or the sharp point of a knife under one of the heads; when you remove the blade or the needle, there should be absolutely nothing sticking to it if the brioche is done.

Do not unmould the brioche immediately, because it loses its shape rapidly. Unmould after the brioche has cooled.

SPONGE BRIOCHE
Brioche mousseline

Use 500 g (1 lb) of brioche dough ready to be placed in moulds (recipe above).

Roll the dough into a thick round; on top spread 100 g (4 oz) of unsalted butter that has been softened and well creamed; fold the dough over the butter several times until the butter is completely mixed in.

Roll the dough into a ball and place in a tall, narrow, cylindrical mould, buttered and lined with a piece of white paper reaching 3 cm (1¼ inches) above the edge. This overlap will be cut with scissors into triangular points.

Allow the brioche to rise in the mould, as described in the recipe for brioche above, then brush it with melted butter, slash across the top with scissors and place in a 375°F (190°C, gas mark 5) oven for 25–30 minutes.

Unmould, but leave the paper on until ready to serve to keep this delicious cake soft.

CROWN-SHAPED BRIOCHE
Couronne de brioche

This brioche is not put in a mould. Make a ball with 500 g (1 lb) of ordinary brioche dough (recipe above). Flatten the ball and make a hole in the centre with your fingers. Pick up the dough through the hole and turn it like a skein of yarn; the hole will increase in diameter until it is about 9 cm (3½ inches) across. Place the ring of dough on a pastry sheet lightly dampened with water; correct the ring shape, cover with a cloth and let stand for its final rising.

When the dough has increased by one-third its volume, brush with a beaten egg; cut a series of notches around the top with scissors dipped in water, and bake in a 425°F (220°C, gas mark 7) oven for 25 minutes.

ORDINARY BRIOCHE DOUGH
Pâte à brioche commune

**500 g (1 lb) plain
flour
175–225 g (6–8 oz)
unsalted butter
(depending on how
much dough you
need)
4 eggs beaten with
milk
5–12 g (¼–½ oz) dried
yeast (depending
on the temperature)
2 teaspoons salt
2 teaspoons sugar**

Follow the general recipe for brioche dough above. This dough is usually used for hot pies, such as *coulibiac* (Russian fish pie, see page 180) or pastries filled with *foie gras* or other rich stuffings.

500 g (1 lb) plain flour

12–20 g ($\frac{1}{2}$–$\frac{3}{4}$ oz) dried yeast

6 tablespoons warm milk or water

2 teaspoons salt

7–8 eggs

1$\frac{1}{2}$ tablespoons sugar

350 g (12 oz) unsalted butter, softened

1 tablespoon chopped candied lemon peel

BABA OR SAVARIN DOUGH
Pâte à baba et à savarin

This dough is based on the recipe for ordinary brioche dough, but it is fluffier and lighter.

Sift half the flour into a large bowl. Make a well in the centre and place in it 12–20 g ($\frac{1}{2}$–$\frac{3}{4}$ oz) of yeast, depending upon the season. Dissolve the yeast in the warm milk or water, then slowly mix in the flour until the dough is slightly soft, adding more milk or water if needed.

Scrape the sides of the bowl with a spatula and incorporate the scrapings into the dough. Sift the remaining flour on top of the dough and sprinkle with 2 teaspoons of salt; set in a warm place to rise. When the flour that covers the leavened dough has raised and cracks appear, add 3 eggs and mix well into the flour and the dough, kneading it quickly. The dough should become elastic and detach itself from the palms of your hands. One by one add 4 or 5 more eggs, according to size. As the dough softens, knead it lightly with the tips of your fingers.

Finish the dough by adding 1$\frac{1}{2}$ tablespoons of sugar, which will give it a beautiful colour when it is baked; and add the softened unsalted butter. Scrape the sides of the bowl again with a spatula and incorporate the scrapings. Cover with a cloth and set in a warm place; let the dough rise for at least 10 hours. During that time, beat down the dough after the first 5 hours, that is, press it down to remove the air so that the dough can continue to rise. (If you do not have a pastry spatula, use a slice of a large potato instead!)

Five hours later, beat down the dough again, and add 1 tablespoon of chopped candied lemon peel.

Baba and savarin moulds are both moulds with rounded bases.

Butter the mould with clarified butter. If you are making a savarin, sprinkle almond slices in the bottom of the mould. Fill the moulds two-thirds of the way up, tap them on a folded cloth so that the dough settles and let the dough rise again.

When the moulds are nearly filled, bake in a 325°F (170°C, gas mark 3) oven for about 30 minutes.

As soon as the babas or savarins are done, unmould on a pastry rack, then soak them with syrup.

Note: The above amounts will fill at least 3 medium-sized moulds, 18–23 cm (7–9 inches) in diameter.

BABA DOUGH
Pâte à baba

Some cooks differentiate between baba dough and savarin dough
on the basis of the quantity of butter. For the baba use less butter:
225 g (8 oz) instead of 350 g (12 oz) for each 500 g (1 lb) of flour;
replace the chopped lemon peel with sultanas and currants, 50 g
(2 oz) of each.

Take any stems off the currants and sultanas, shake in a cloth
with a pinch of flour, then shake in a coarse sieve and add to the
dough just before placing it in the moulds.

The preparation, kneading, moulding and baking are same for
the two doughs. Follow the recipe above.

SAVARIN WITH RUM OR BABA WITH KIRSCH
Savarin au rhum ou baba au kirsch

Prepare a sugar syrup (see page 628) by boiling 680 g (1 lb 8 oz)
of sugar with 1 l (2 pts) of water for a few minutes in a saucepan
with a diameter larger than the savarin's. Remove from the heat
and lower the temperature to 175°F (80°C). Add a flavouring
such as rum, kirsch or another liqueur, and plunge the baba or
the savarin into the syrup.

Remove the cake carefully, place it on a rack over the top of
a bowl and baste with a few tablespoons of the syrup to moisten
the cake all the way to the centre. Finish basting with 1 tablespoon
of kirsch, rum or whatever flavour you have chosen.

Note: Small savarins or babas are baked in small moulds
shaped like crowns or bowls, following the instructions above.

125 g (5 oz) sultanas
Old rum
225 g (8 oz) sifted
 plain flour
10 g ($\frac{1}{2}$ oz) dried
 yeast
4 eggs
125 g (5 oz) unsalted
 butter
$\frac{1}{2}$ tablespoon salt
1$\frac{1}{2}$ tablespoons sugar

Syrup:
1 l (2 pts) water
1 glass old rum
500 g (1 lb) sugar

SAVARINS WITH RUM AND SULTANAS
Savarins au rhum Maurice Bernachon
For 8 people

The night before, macerate the sultanas in old rum.

In a bowl place the flour, the yeast dissolved in a little warm water and 4 eggs. Knead the dough and cover with the butter without mixing it in; let it rise for 2 hours. Then mix in the butter and $\frac{1}{2}$ tablespoon of salt, 1$\frac{1}{2}$ tablespoons of sugar and the sultanas. Fill a savarin mould. Let rise for 1 hour, and cook about 30 minutes in a 375°F (190°C, gas mark 5) oven; unmould.

Syrup

Combine 1 l (2 pts) of water and 1 glass of old rum; boil with 500 g (1 lb) of sugar. Soak the savarin in the syrup, then drain on a rack; decorate with fruits, and serve apricot sauce (optional); the savarin syrup can also be made with good quality maraschino.

KUGELHUPF DOUGH
Pâte à kouglof

Towards the middle of the seventeenth century this Alsatian pastry seems to have introduced to France the use, in pastry and then in bread-making, of dry brewer's yeast, which had been in use for a long time in Poland and Austria.

Kugelhupf dough resembles brioche and baba dough in its composition and its consistency. It has more sugar than baba dough, and it is softer than brioche dough, not so soft as the savarin dough.

The rising, moulding and baking are the same. The kugelhupf mould is special; it is very deep, with fluted sides and a hollow tube in the centre. Butter the mould and sprinkle the bottom with chopped almonds. You can also include 50 g (2 oz) of currants. Unmould as soon as the cake is cooked. Serve like a brioche.

Flaky pastry doughs

FLAKY OR PUFF PASTRY
Le feuilletage

Pastry cooks have known how to make flaky pastry since the thirteenth century, but it was during the eighteenth and nineteenth centuries that this pastry was brought to a high level of perfection.

The recipe is simple but the technique is tricky for the inexperienced cook.

Since flaky pastry plays an important role in the making of desserts, we are going to try to describe the method of making it as clearly as possible.

For about 1·3 kg (2¾ lb) dough:
500 g (1 lb) plain sifted flour
2 teaspoons salt
2–3 dl (¼–½ pt) cold water
500 g (1 lb) unsalted butter

Method.   1. Sift the flour and place in a mound on a pastry board or preferably on a piece of marble. Make a well in the centre and put the salt and half the water in it.

Dissolve the salt by stirring the water with your fingers, then gradually mix in the flour, adding part or all the remaining water to give the dough a medium consistency.

The quantity of water used depends upon the quality of the flour used and how hard the butter is. In winter the butter should be placed in a warm place; in summer, in a cool place. Then, in both cases, it should be kneaded in a cloth. This kneading is to soften the butter and make it smooth so that it can be mixed with the paste of flour and water.

The flour–water mixture should be combined without working the dough too much. Simply gather the dough into a ball; avoid giving it too much elasticity.

It is not possible to roll hard dough and soft butter, or vice versa, together. This would make the butter stick to the rolling pin, the pastry would be impossible to 'turn' correctly and the dough would separate from the butter while baking, producing leathery rather than flaky pastry.

2. Gather the dough, neither too soft nor too hard, in a lump, wrap in a cloth and set in a cool place for 20 minutes. This rest will enable the dough to lose any elasticity it may have acquired, and will make it more or less inert.

Dust the table or marble with flour and place the dough on it. Spread the dough with the palm of your hand, shaping it in an even circle about 3 cm (1¼ inch) thick.

Place the kneaded butter in the centre and spread it smoothly over the dough in a square about 4 cm (1½ inches) inside the edges. Now, one by one, pick up the four flaps of dough not covered by butter and fold them over the butter, covering it completely. The dough is now a square shape.

3. The purpose of 'turning' is to mix the butter and the dough by combining them in superimposed layers. This is why the consistency of the dough and that of the butter must be similar, since they are going to be mixed together.

Cooling the square of dough too much would also be a mistake because the butter would harden and become lumpy and it would be impossible to mix the two ingredients.

We are now assuming that the two ingredients are well matched; the dough is then ready to be 'turned' twice.

Dust the marble, or the table, and the dough with flour, and roll the dough with a rolling pin into a symmetrical rectangle about 61 cm (24 inches) long and 1 cm (½ inch) thick; always roll away from yourself.

Take the lower short edge of the rectangle and fold one-third of it towards the top edge. Press the folded edge lightly with the rolling pin; fold over it the other third of the dough. Seal the three-layered dough with the rolling pin.

This first 'turn' is followed by a second one. But before you roll, give the dough a quarter of a turn, so that the folded edges are to your right and left. Roll the dough away from you again, making it the same size (61 cm (24 inches) long) and repeating the folding and rolling of the second turn. Then put the folded dough in a cool place and cover with a cloth to prevent the top from drying out.

After letting the dough stand for 20 minutes, give the third and fourth turns, being careful, at each turn, always to roll the dough with the folded edges to your right and left, never facing you.

After letting the dough stand for another 20 minutes, or more if the flour is of good quality, give the fifth and sixth turns. The flaky dough is then ready to be used. Shape and bake in a 375°F (190°C, gas mark 5) oven without waiting.

The dough will rise and will be very light if the various steps have been followed correctly. It will have 729 layers, which explains why the dough rises so high.

The bottom of the oven must be well heated.

SEMI-FLAKY PASTRY
Demi-feuilletage

Semi-flaky pastry is the leftover trimmings of the dough. Gather the pieces into a ball, then give it two turns.

Pastry for galettes is also given this name.

GALETTE PASTRY
Pâte pour galettes

Pastry for galettes is a less-rich flaky pastry. It is prepared exactly the same way as the flaky pastry (above), but the quantity of butter is different: 225 g (8 oz) instead of 500g (1 lb) for 500 g (1 lb) of flour, and the number of turns is four instead of six.

PITHIVIERS ALMOND CAKE
Gâteau aux amandes dit 'Pithiviers'
For 8 servings

Take 500 g (1 lb) of flaky pastry with all its turns completed (recipe above).

Roll out a sheet 9 mm (⅜ inch) thick; place a plate upside down on it, or use the bottom of a 20-cm (8-inch) flan tin and with the point of a knife cut a circle. Remove the trimmings, gather them and give them two turns; make a second circle with this dough, the same size as the first one but half as thick.

Place the second circle on a pastry sheet slightly dampened with water; press the dough down with your fingers and prick with a fork three or four times. Moisten the edges with a pastry brush dipped in water. On top, 4 cm (1½ inches) inside the edge, spread a layer of almond cream (recipe below) about 2·5 cm (1 inch) thick. Place the first pastry circle on top. Press the edges with your thumbs to stick them together. Crimp the edges, brush the top with beaten egg and cut a rose design with the point of a knife.

Bake in a 375°F (190°C, gas mark 5) oven until golden brown.

A few minutes before removing the cake from the oven, sprinkle confectioners' sugar on the top; this will give it a nice dark-gold colour.

One variation on this delicious Pithiviers cake consists of sprinkling the top, after the cake is baked, with a light layer of icing sugar two minutes before removing from the oven. In that case the glazing with the beaten egg is omitted. While cooking, the sugar melts, caramelizes slightly, and gives a very nice taste to this pastry.

Serve warm.

Almond cream

500 g (1 lb) almonds
500 g (1 lb) sugar
12 eggs
500 g (1 lb) butter
1 teaspoon vanilla
    sugar
1 tablespoon rum

Boil the almonds for 2 minutes, drain and remove the skins by pressing each almond between your thumb and forefinger. This is called blanching; the almond is squeezed out by the pressure of your fingers, leaving the skin behind.

Place the almonds in a mortar and pound and crush them into a paste with cube sugar in preference to caster sugar; then add the eggs, one by one, then the slightly softened butter. Make the paste very light by working the pestle in the mortar. From time to time scrape the sides of the mortar with a pastry scraper. When the almond paste is white and creamy, place it in a bowl and add the vanilla sugar and the rum.

The paste will be extremely fine and ready to use.

Note: If you do not have a mortar, grate the almonds or crush them in some other way. Combine the nuts with caster sugar in a bowl and continue working the paste with a wooden spatula following the method above. This method is not so good as the one above.

SMALL PITHIVIERS ALMOND CAKES
Petits Pithiviers

These small cakes are made by the same recipe as the large one (above) but formed into small, individual cakes. Cut the rectangular flaky dough, rolled very thin, into circles with a fluted cutter 8–10 cm (3–4 inches) in diameter. Use the trimmings, gathered and turned, to make the bottom crusts, which are placed on a slightly dampened pastry sheet, then filled with $\frac{1}{2}$ tablespoon of almond cream each. Dampen the edges and cover with the first series of small circles. Stick the layers of dough together with a smaller pastry cutter; brush the tops with beaten egg, and make a design with the point of a knife in each one. Bake in a 375°F (190°C, gas mark 5) oven for 10–15 minutes. Two minutes before removing from the oven, sprinkle with icing sugar.

ALMOND SQUARES
Jalousies aux amandes

Roll a piece of flaky dough into a rectangle 18 cm (7 inches) wide, 28–38 cm (11–15 inches) long, and 6 mm ($\frac{1}{4}$ inch) thick.

Roll a second piece of flaky dough the same dimensions, but thinner and made with the dough trimmings.

Place the second sheet of dough on a slightly dampened pastry sheet and prick it with a fork to prevent bubbles from forming. Moisten the edges with water and spread a layer of almond cream (above) 2 cm ($\frac{3}{4}$ inch) thick and 8 cm (3 inches) wide, along its length. On top of the cream place the first sheet of pastry; stick the edges together by pressing with your fingers and trim the edges in a straight line with a knife. Crimp the two sides with the point of a knife; brush the top with beaten egg or sprinkle with caster sugar. With the point of a knife score the dough in 6–8-cm ($2\frac{1}{2}$–3-inch) squares; make a crisscross pattern on each square; bake in a 375°F (190°C, gas mark 5) oven for 12–15 minutes.

If the dough has been brushed with egg, glaze the cake before you remove it from the oven by sprinkling it with icing sugar.

When the cake is cold, cut it along the scored squares to serve it.

TWELFTH-NIGHT CAKES
Gâteau des rois

Use semi-flaky or galette pastry rolled out in a rectangle, allowing about 75 g (3 oz) per serving. Fold the corners towards the centre to form a ball; flatten the ball, then roll with a rolling pin to make dough 2 cm (¾ inch) thick and absolutely round, which can be done by turning the dough slightly each time you roll it.

Crimp the edges of the dough by pressing with the point of a knife; place the dough on a slightly dampened pastry sheet, brush with a beaten egg, make a crisscross design on top with the point of a knife, prick two or three times, and bake in a 375°F (190°C, gas mark 5) oven.

Hide a bean in the dough before putting it on the pastry sheet.

[*Editor's note:* The French bake a dried bean in the cake; the person finding the bean in the cake becomes the king or queen and chooses a consort; the guests drink to their health.]

Pie dough and short pastry

This dough is used to make pieces, timbales (filled pastries) and various other pastries such as gâteau Saint-Honoré.

FINE PASTRY DOUGH
Pâte à foncer fine

500 g (1 lb) plain flour
1½ teaspoons salt
1 teaspoon sugar
300 g (10 oz) unsalted butter
1 egg
2–3 tablespoons milk

Note: The amount of liquid – egg, water or milk – depends upon the quality of the flour rather than a rigorous mathematical rule. While making the dough, you will be aware of how much liquid to add (often only a few drops sprinkled in with the fingers) to obtain the right consistency; the dough should always be slightly firm.

ORDINARY PASTRY DOUGH
Pâte à foncer ordinaire

The ingredients are the same as above, except for the butter: use 250 g (9 oz) instead of 275 g (10 oz); omit the egg and replace it with ½ cup of water.

SWEET FLAN PASTRY (1)
Pâte surfine ou sablée

500 g (1 lb) plain flour
1½ teaspoons salt
1 tablespoon sugar
375 g (13 oz) unsalted butter
2 eggs
2–3 tablespoons milk

Do not make the dough too firm.

This is a delicious dough for small fruit tarts, such as strawberry tarts.

SWEET FLAN PASTRY (2)
Pâte royale ou sablée

500 g (1 lb) plain flour
1½ teaspoons salt
1 tablespoon sugar
500 g (1 lb) unsalted butter
4 egg yolks
6 tablespoons milk or, better, double cream

This dough is delicate to make. Do not work or knead it. Mix slowly and gather into a ball. Do not make too firm.

Method. These four doughs are usually made the same way, except where otherwise indicated.

Sift the flour and make a mound on a table or piece of marble; in a well in the centre place the salt, the sugar and the butter (previously kneaded in a cloth dusted with flour), the egg yolks or the egg and the milk, cream or water.

Dissolve the salt and slowly mix in the butter and the liquids, pushing the flour with your fingers from the outside of the well to the centre; if necessary, sprinkle in a small quantity of water with your fingers; the dough should not be too firm. To finish the dough, work it twice, except in making *pâte royale* which should not be worked at all.

Working these doughs does not involve ordinary kneading. Instead it is a method that permits all the ingredients to mix perfectly without making the dough elastic, which must be avoided because it would contract during cooking.

Here is the description of this method, called *fraisage*:

After all the ingredients have been roughly mixed for 2 or 3 minutes during the first step, the *fraisage* begins. With the heel of your hand, press down small pieces of dough on the pastry table or marble, pushing away from you; when all the dough has been pressed, gather the pieces into a ball, and start over again. This double working mixes the butter and the flour together very well.

Fraisage is not advisable for dough that is rich in butter, because it would break down the combination of eggs and butter which is the main ingredient of the mixture. Furthermore, because of the quantity of butter used, it is easy to mix the ingredients without having to work the dough.

Sweet pastry

SWEET SHORTCRUST PASTRY
Pâte sucrée

500 g (1 lb) plain sifted flour
Pinch salt
225 g (8 oz) caster sugar
125–200 g (5–7 oz) unsalted butter, depending on the fineness of the dough
3 eggs
1 tablespoon orange blossom water

Mix the dough as you would for pie dough (above). Flavour with 1 tablespoon of orange blossom water or any other flavour.

DOUGH FOR SWEET BISCUITS
Pâte à petits gâteaux sucrés pour le thé
For 100 biscuits

500 g (1 lb) plain sifted flour
Pinch salt
300 g (10 oz) sugar
300 g (10 oz) unsalted butter
1 whole egg
4 egg yolks
3 tablespoons double cream

Prepare the dough as you would for *pâte sucrée* (above). Make a ball, wrap the dough in a cloth, and let it stand in a cool place for 1 hour.

500 g (1 lb) plain sifted flour
1 teaspoon salt
1 teaspoon sugar
300 g (10 oz) unsalted butter, melted with 2 dl (6 fl oz) hot double cream or milk

DOUGH FOR SALTED BISCUITS
Pâte à petits gâteaux salés pour le thé
For 100 biscuits

Prepare the dough following the recipe for flaky pastry. Let the dough stand for 1 hour before using it.

Preparing and baking pastry cases

VOL-AU-VENT SHELL
Croûte à vol-au-vent
For 6–8 people

Roll out half a recipe of flaky pastry after six turns; roll it 2·5 cm (1 inch) thick.

Place a plate upside down (or the bottom of a 20-cm (8-inch) flan tin) on the thick layer of dough and with the point of a knife cut a circle around the edge of the plate, cutting through all the thicknesses of dough. Remove the trimmings and then the plate, turn the dough over and place it on a slightly dampened pastry sheet. Press the dough lightly to make it stick to the pan. With the blunt side of a knife, make a series of indentions all around the edge of the dough, 4 cm ($1\frac{1}{2}$ inches) apart. This step is called 'crimping'.

Place an upside-down dessert plate (or any other 13-cm (5-inch) round) on this disc of flaky pastry; cut a circle around the edge of the plate with the point of a knife, making an incision $1\frac{1}{2}$ mm ($\frac{1}{16}$ inch) deep. This inside disc will become the lid.

Brush the surface of the pastry with a beaten egg using a pastry brush or a goose feather. Be careful not to put too much egg along the incision, or to brush the edges of the dough, or to leave drips of egg with the pastry brush, which would prevent the dough from rising uniformly. With the point of a knife make a crisscross design on the disc that will serve as the lid. Bake in a 375°F (190°C, gas mark 5) oven for 20 minutes.

It is important to have an oven with heat that is regular, and preferably with a bottom made of cast iron. This determines, in great part, the success of flaky dough, which rises because of heat coming from below.

When the vol-au-vent is lightly browned, remove from the oven; with the point of a knife, cut around the cover, remove the top layers and scoop out from the shell most of the soft inside dough.

The vol-au-vent is ready to be served; keep it warm and fill it at the last minute.

COVERED PIE OR TART
Tourte

The *tourte* – which can be used for either a main dish or a dessert – dates from the early days of French cookery.

Served as an entrée, the *tourte* is prepared and baked with its filling or baked unfilled, like a vol-au-vent, and filled later.

If the shell is cooked unfilled, take one recipe of flaky pastry dough, after it has been given six turns following the usual method, and roll it into a long band 2 cm ($\frac{3}{4}$ inch) thick and as long as the circumference of the pie tin you are using. With a knife cut the dough to make a band 3 cm ($1\frac{1}{4}$ inches) wide and as long as the dough. Reserve this band.

Gather the trimmings, give them two turns and make a ball with the dough; then roll the dough 6 mm ($\frac{1}{4}$ inch) thick; cut a circle of dough to fit the pie tin. Dampen the tin with water, and place the circle of dough in the bottom. Prick the dough generously with a fork.

If the pie is to be cooked with its filling, divide the filling into small balls and cover the central part of the dough. Cover the top with another layer of dough 6 mm ($\frac{1}{4}$ inch) thick, made with the trimmings of the flaky dough. Dampen the edges of the bottom layer of dough and press down the top layer with your thumb all around the edges to stick them together.

If the shell is to be baked empty, cover the bottom with a wad of paper domed in the centre, and put the second circle of dough over it.

In both cases, moisten the edges of this last circle of dough lightly with a pastry brush or with a cloth and on top place the strip of flaky pastry prepared earlier. Stick the ends of the dough together, cutting them on the bias where they meet, and crimp the edge roughly with the point of a knife.

Brush with beaten egg on the surface of the strip of dough and the cover only. Make a crisscross design with the point of a knife on the cover.

Bake in the oven like the vol-au-vent (above).

When the pie shell is cooked empty, cut around the lid while it is still hot, lift it up and remove the wad of paper.

Fill the shell the same way you would a vol-au-vent.

If it is a dessert pie, the preparation is identical. The filling will be made of pastry cream (page 569), frangipane cream (page 568) or almond cream (page 534), cooked or uncooked fruit or fruit jam.

Sweet pies can be made without a cover. One must then be careful that there is no contact between the strip of dough and the filling, as the filling would prevent it rising.

Bake for 35–45 minutes, depending upon the thickness and the filling, in a 375°F (190°C, gas mark 5) oven. Five minutes before removing from the oven, sprinkle the pie generously with icing sugar and raise the heat to 475°F (240°C, gas mark 9) to turn the melting sugar a light-brown colour.

After the pie is baked, a light coat of fruit purée or jam can be spread over the fruit.

SMALL PUFF PASTRIES
Bouchées

Bouchées are small individual vol-au-vents.

Roll ½ recipe flaky pastry with a rolling pin, making it just over 6 mm (¼ inch) thick; then, with a scalloped pastry cutter 8 cm (3 inches) in diameter, cut 20 circles of about 25 g (1 oz) each.

Turn these circles of dough over and place on a lightly dampened pastry sheet.

Brush the circles with beaten egg on the top only; do not brush the edges – that would prevent the dough from rising. With a plain pastry cutter 3 cm (1¼ inches) in diameter, cut the top covers by pressing very lightly into the circles. Dip the cutter into warm water before each use.

Make a crisscross design with the point of a knife on each cover.

Bake in a 425°F (220°C, gas mark 7) oven 12–15 minutes. Remove the covers as soon as you take the pastries out of the oven and press the inside dough down lightly to make room for the filling.

TIMBALE SHELL
Timbale

Divide 750 g (1½ lb) of pie dough (*pâte à foncer*) into two pieces, one weighing 500 g (1 lb), the other 250 g (8 oz).

Make each piece of dough into a ball and roll the first one out in a circle 20 cm (8 inches) in diameter. Turn the pastry circle over and dust it lightly with flour, fold it in two and bring together both ends of this half circle in the centre to produce a pointed cap. You can extend the points of the dough by rolling on one side then the other.

When it is about 6 mm (¼ inch) thick all around, open the cap and slide it point down into a buttered straight-sided charlotte mould.

Press the inside of the cap against the mould, using a small ball of dough, so that the dough sticks well to the sides and the bottom of the mould. Cut off the excess dough 1 cm (½ inch) from the edge.

Prick the bottom of the pastry with a fork, and line with fine white paper; then fill with dry beans up to the edge of the mould. On top of the dry beans, place a dome of crushed paper and cover it with a thin layer cut from the reserved dough. Stick this circle of dough to the dampened edges of the bottom layer. Then, pressing with the thumb and the forefinger, shape the edge of the top dough into a ridge. Pinch this ridge on both sides with a pastry crimper or with your fingers.

Decorate the lid, placing on top tiny pieces of pastry dough in the shape of delicate rosettes, cut with a fluted cutter; mark the petals with the back of a knife blade. Make overlapping rings of these rosettes, starting from the edge of the lid and moving in towards the centre. Make a decoration as big as a marble by pressing two or three small pieces of dough in a ball shape, gathering the edges towards the centre. Place on top of the lid and then lightly mark a cross on top.

Brush well with beaten egg and bake in a 375°F (190°C, gas mark 5) oven for 40 minutes. When the shell is baked, remove the lid carefully and set aside. Remove the dry beans from inside the timbale; carefully remove the paper; brush the inside with beaten egg, and place the shell in the oven again for 5 minutes to dry the inside and give it a golden colour.

Unmould the timbale; brush the outside with beaten egg and return to the oven for a few seconds. As soon as it is a nice golden colour, remove from the oven and set aside to be filled.

SMALL INDIVIDUAL TIMBALES
Petites timbales individuelles

Make small timbales following the technique above. Use the same pie dough, and roll the cap of dough until it is 3 mm ($\frac{1}{8}$ inch) thick. Mould in small baba moulds or any other small cylindrical moulds.

TART CASE BAKED BLIND
Croûte à tarte cuite à blanc

Butter the inside of a 25-cm (10-inch) flan ring, and place it on a baking sheet slightly dampened with water.

Make a ball of $\frac{1}{2}$ recipe pie dough, using any of the four types on pages 536–537, depending on how delicate you wish to make the dessert; roll in a circle 30 cm (12 inches) in diameter.

Fold the dough in half and place it on the ring, with the fold across the centre line of the flan ring; open the pastry circle and lower it, pressing it against the sides of the ring to make it stick. Fold the excess dough down over the edge and sides and cut the excess off by running the rolling pin over the top. This last step will form a fold of dough around the edge. Take the fold of dough with both hands between your thumbs and index fingers and press it up to form a rim 6 mm–1 cm ($\frac{1}{4}$–$\frac{1}{2}$ inch) above the edge of the tin. Then crimp the outside of this rim with a pastry crimper to make a diagonal pattern.

Prick the bottom of the dough with a fork to prevent bubbles forming during cooking. Line the inside of the pastry with fine buttered paper; fill to the top with dry beans (which can be reused endlessly for this purpose); bake in a 375°F (190°C, gas mark 5) oven for 25 minutes.

Remove from the oven; take out the dry beans, the paper and remove the ring; brush the sides of the tart shell with beaten egg and replace in the oven for 2 or 3 minutes to dry and brown the crust, which is then ready to be filled with raw or cooked fruit.

SMALL TART CASES BAKED BLIND

Croûtes pour tartelettes cuites à blanc

Small tarts can be made with any of the pie doughs (pages 536–537) or trimmings from flaky pastry (page 531) or galette pastry (page 533).

Roll the chosen dough in a rectangular shape 3 mm ($\frac{1}{8}$ inch) thick; cut the dough with a fluted cutter of a diameter slightly larger than the moulds that will be used. Butter each mould and place a small circle of dough in it. Press it with a small ball of dough, lightly floured, so that each circle of dough takes the shape of the mould. Prick the bottom of each pastry and put a circle of buttered paper and dry beans or dry cherry stones inside it; bake in a 375°F (190°C, gas mark 5) oven for 10–12 minutes; finish the tarts as indicated in the recipe above.

SHELL FOR PÂTÉS COOKED IN PASTRY

Croûte pour pâtés en croûte

The moulds used for pâtés in pastry are usually deep, decorated, and round or oval; they can be the same shape as a timbale, which is the type used for *pâté de foie gras*.

The crust is generally made with ordinary pie dough. Sometimes brioche dough is used.

The method is identical to that used for making a timbale (see above). The cap of dough should be 9 mm ($\frac{3}{8}$ inch) thick. Prick the dough several times. Fill with the desired ingredients, following the directions in the recipes. Cover with a thin circle of dough; stick the two layers together and form a rim around the edge; pinch the rim as for a timbale, then on top of the pâté place a second layer made with the trimmings of flaky pastry, turned twice and about 6 mm ($\frac{1}{4}$ inch) thick.

Brush the surface with beaten egg, score it, forming rosettes or leaves with the point of a knife; make a hole in the centre (or make two holes for an oval mould) and in the hole put a cone of buttered paper, which acts as a tiny chimney to allow the steam to escape; bake in a 375°F (190°C, gas mark 5) oven, following the individual recipe as regards the cooking time.

Tarts and flans

APPLE FLAN
Flan aux pommes Jérôme
For 6 people

Butter a 25-cm (10-inch) flan ring and place on a pastry sheet.

Prepare ½ recipe pie dough (*pâte à foncer*). Gather the dough in a ball and roll it 6 mm (¼ inch) thick. To make this dough perfectly round, follow the steps described for the Twelfth-Night cake (page 536). The dough should be at least 33 cm (13 inches) in diameter.

Place the dough on the flan ring and ease it down little by little so that the dough takes the exact shape of the inside of the ring. Then press the crust against the ring using a small ball of slightly floured dough.

Fold the excess dough over the edge and cut it by running a rolling pin over it. This method will form a rim of dough. Take the rim of dough in your two hands between your thumbs and index fingers and press it up to form an even ridge. Pinch the ridge with a pastry crimper to make a twisted rope pattern.

Prick the bottom of the dough with a fork.

Meanwhile cook 1 kg (2 lb) of apples into a purée. Choose firm, well-flavoured eating apples.

First wash and peel the apples. Cook the peels, uncovered, in ½ cup of water for 15–20 minutes; drain with a slotted spoon, and remove 3 tablespoons of the juice. Reserve, and add 1 heaped tablespoon of sugar to the remaining juice. Cook this syrup 4–5 minutes; pour into a bowl. In the same saucepan, with the reserved juice, cook the apples (set aside the best one), quartered and seeded. Cover the saucepan, and cook slowly for 20–30 minutes. The apples should then be a thick purée. Add 125 g (5 oz) of sugar. Continue cooking for about 10 minutes to reduce this mixture, which will become slightly liquid when the sugar is added.

Rub through a fine sieve or mash the apples with a sauce whisk. Cool.

When ready to fill the pie, stir 1 tablespoon of kirsch into the apple purée. Then fill the pie crust two-thirds of the way up, smooth the purée, and cover with slices of the reserved apple.

To do this, peel the apple set aside, cut into quarters, seed each quarter and cut into thin slices. These thin crescent-shaped slices of fruit will be arranged, overlapping slightly, in circles starting against the flan ring, with each succeeding circle going in the opposite direction and partly overlapping the preceding one; continue until you reach the centre. Sprinkle the top with 1 tablespoon of sugar.

Bake in a 375°F (190°C, gas mark 5) oven for 30–35 minutes.

Take the tart out of the oven, remove the flan ring, brush the crust with beaten egg all around the vertical edge; place in the oven again for 3 minutes; then cover the top of the apples with the reserved 3 tablespoons of juice cooked to a jelly.

Note: This recipe can be used to make small individual tarts in the same way.

FRUIT FLANS
Flans aux fruits, mirabelles, abricotes, quetsches, reines-claudes

Use small golden plums (mirabelles), apricots, purple plums or greengages.

Make a pie dough in a flan ring as for the apple tart (above).

Sprinkle the bottom of the crust with 1 teaspoon of sugar and make circles with halves of one of the above fruits.

First stone the mirabelles or cut the apricots, greengages or plums in two and remove their stones.

Arrange the fruit halves in circles, cut sides up, each overlapping the preceding one slightly and reversing the direction of the fruit for each new circle.

Cook in a 375°F (190°C, gas mark 5) oven, preheated to sear the bottom crust so that the fruit juices do not soak into the dough.

After removing the flan from the oven, take off the ring, and sprinkle the surface of the fruit with icing sugar.

Cover the fruit with apricot jam, slightly melted, which will cool into jelly.

CHERRY TART
Tarte aux cerises

Follow the same method as for the preceding tart. Stone sweet cherries and fill the bottom of the tart, placing them close together.

After the tart is baked, sprinkle with icing sugar or coat with redcurrant jelly.

STRAWBERRY TART
Tarte aux fraises

500 g (1 lb)
  strawberries,
  cleaned and hulled
½ recipe sweet dough
  (*pâté sucrée*)
6 tablespoons
  redcurrant jelly
Kirsch

Prepare the dough following the recipe for sweet pastry. Gather into a ball and roll in a circle.

Place the dough in a flan ring on a slightly dampened pastry sheet; press the dough down so that it takes the exact shape of the ring. Bake blind (unfilled) following the general directions above.

After baking, let cool; remove the ring when the crust is nearly cold.

A few minutes before serving, arrange the hulled strawberries attractively in the pie. Glaze the surface of the berries with redcurrant jelly slightly diluted with kirsch.

APPLE OR PEAR TART WITH CUSTARD FILLING
Tarte à l'alsacienne

Place a flan ring on a slightly dampened pastry sheet and line it with fine or very fine dough (*pâte fine* or *surfine*, pages 536–537). Form a rim around the edge, prick the bottom and fill halfway up with custard filling (*crème pâtissière*, page 569).

Cut apples or pears into quarters, core, then slice lengthwise and arrange the slices on top of the cream in tight circles. Sprinkle with 1 tablespoon of sugar, and bake in a 375°F (190°C, gas mark 5) oven for 20 minutes.

As soon as the tart is baked, remove the ring; brush the vertical edge with beaten egg and place in the oven again for 2–3 minutes to finish baking.

Spread 1 tablespoon of apple jelly or apricot jam, slightly reduced, over the apples or pears.

APPLE OR PEAR TART WITH ALMOND CUSTARD FILLING
Tarte normande

Follow the recipe for Alsatian tart (above); but replace the custard filling with a *crème frangipane* (page 568) adding 1 part frangipane to 5 of double cream.

After baking, finish the tart with a layer of *crème Chantilly* (page 569) about 2 cm (¾ inch) thick.

Decorate the surface of the whipped cream with a design traced with the point of a knife or press the *crème Chantilly* through a pastry bag with a large fluted tube.

CHERRY TART WITH CUSTARD FILLING
Tarte aux cerises à la crème

The method used is nearly identical to the preceding one. After lining the flan ring with dough, fill the bottom with a layer of *crème pâtissière*, made light by adding about one-fifth double cream, or *crème anglaise* (see the section on cream fillings, pages 569–570); then cover with stoned sweet cherries macerated in a little sugar and 1 tablespoon of kirsch; cover the cherries with another layer of the cream.

Bake in a 375°F (190°C, gas mark 5) oven for 25–30 minutes.

CUSTARD TART
Tarte à la crème

Place a flan ring on a slightly dampened pastry sheet and line with pie dough (*pâte à foncer fine*, page 536); do not prick; fill with a custard made as for *crème renversée* (page 574).

Bake in a 375°F (190°C, gas mark 5) oven for 25–30 minutes. The surface of the tart should be a nice golden colour. Do not let the custard boil while baking.

PEAR TART WITH CREAM
Tarte aux poires

Line a flan circle with *pâte brisée*. Peel and slice ripe pears and place them in the pie shell.

In a bowl combine $\frac{1}{2}$ l (1 pt) of double cream, 4 eggs, 125 g (5 oz) of sugar and a pinch of salt. Stir well and pour over the pears. Bake for 30 minutes in a 375°F (190°C, gas mark 5) oven.

APPLE TART WITH SWEET FLAN PASTRY
Tarte aux pommes pâté brisée

Pâté brisée:
- **500 g (1 lb) plain flour**
- **1 tablespoon salt**
- **350 g (12 oz) unsalted butter**
- **3 whole eggs**

Pâté sablée:
- **500 g (1 lb) plain flour**
- **2 teaspoons salt**
- **225 g (8 oz) sugar**
- **300 g (10 oz) unsalted butter**
- **3 whole eggs**

Place a flan ring on a pastry sheet and line with *pâté brisée* or *pâté sablée* (ingredients on left; see page 537 for method). Let stand for 2 hours. Make a compote with 2 lightly sugared apples and sieve them. Pour the compote into the tart. Peel 4 large apples, core and slice them and line the tart, then sprinkle the apples with granulated sugar and on top scatter 225 g (8 oz) of butter, diced very small.

Bake for about 30 minutes at 375°F (190°C, gas mark 5).

◈◈◈◈◈◈◈◈◈◈◈◈◈

UPSIDE-DOWN APPLE TART
Tarte Tatin

325 g (11 oz) unsalted butter
100 g (4 oz) caster sugar
1 kg (2 lb) eating apples
225 g (8 oz) flour
1 egg
Pinch salt

Take a fairly deep cake tin or baking dish 23 cm (9 inches) in diameter and butter the bottom generously, using 100 g (4 oz) of butter, then sprinkle with half the sugar.

Peel the apples, dry with a cloth, core, cut into quarters or thick slices. Arrange the apple pieces together tightly to cover the bottom of the pan. Sprinkle the remaining sugar on top. Add 25 g (1 oz) of melted butter. Place the mould on the stove over a high heat for about 20 minutes; the sugar should caramelize but remain light brown.

Meanwhile mound the flour on a pastry board. In the centre form a well and in it place the egg, the salt and the remaining butter, softened. Mix all the ingredients together. Add some water if necessary to produce a soft dough that can be rolled in a circle, as thin as possible.

Cover the pan with this dough, pushing the edges inside the mould. Bake in a 375°F (190°C, gas mark 5) oven for 30 minutes.

Invert the tart on to a serving platter. Let it cool before serving.

Chou pastry

This dough is used in ordinary cooking, as well as in *pâtisserie*. Depending upon its use, the ingredients for the dough will vary, but the preparation of the dough is the same.

◈◈◈◈◈◈◈◈◈◈◈◈◈

FINE CHOU PASTRY
Pâté à chou fine

½ l (1 pt) water
Pinch salt
225 g (8 oz) unsalted butter
225 g (8 oz) sifted flour
7–8 eggs, or use 6–7 eggs plus 6 tablespoons milk or cream
1 tablespoon orange blossom water
Scant tablespoon sugar

Pour the water into a large heavy-bottomed saucepan. Add the salt and the butter cut into small pieces. Heat to boiling point, stirring the boiling mixture with a wooden spatula; then add the flour.

Work the dough with the spatula over a high flame. The water will evaporate little by little until the dough is completely dry and leaves the sides of the pan.

Now remove the dough from the heat, and beat it without stopping, adding the eggs, one by one, then the milk or cream.

The number of eggs needed depends upon their size and on whether or not you add milk, which saves an egg and makes the dough softer.

Flavour the dough with orange water and sugar.

The dough should be vigorously beaten with a spatula until it is smooth and light. It should not have too soft a consistency and should be stiff enough to squeeze through a pastry bag while still hot. The dough will flatten slightly on the pan.

It is then ready to use.

½ l (1 pt) water
125 g (5 oz) unsalted
  butter
Pinch salt
225 g (8 oz) flour
7–8 eggs
1 scant tablespoon
  sugar

ORDINARY CHOU PASTRY
Pâté à chou ordinaire

Proceed as for the fine chou pastry (above).

If the dough is to be used for savoury purposes omit the sugar.

½ l (1 pt) water
Pinch salt
100 g (4 oz) unsalted
  butter
300 g (10 oz) sifted
  flour
7–8 eggs, depending
  upon their size
1 level tablespoon
  sugar
1 tablespoon orange
  blossom water

BATTER FOR PUFFED FRITTERS
Pâté à beignets soufflés

Follow the instructions for ordinary chou pastry (above).

Since these fritters are fried in oil, less butter is used in the dough.

DOUGH FOR CHEESE PASTRIES
Pâté à ramequin et à gougère

Make ordinary chou pastry (above), but replace the water with milk and omit the sugar. When the dough is finished, stir in 100 g (4 oz) of grated Gruyère cheese.

COFFEE OR CHOCOLATE ÉCLAIRS
Éclairs au café ou au chocolat

For 12 regular-size éclairs, prepare 1 recipe chou pastry (above). Put the dough into a pastry bag with a plain 1-cm ($\frac{1}{2}$-inch) tube.

Press the pastry bag with the hand that holds it and guide it with the other; pipe on to a pastry sheet strips of dough about 5 cm (2 inches) long, placing them 5 cm (2 inches) apart. Each éclair uses about 25 g (1 oz) of dough.

To cut the dough when each strip is the correct length, stop pressing the bag and raise the nozzle with a little twist.

Brush the dough strips with a pastry brush dipped into beaten egg and bake in a 425°F (220°C, gas mark 7) oven. Let cool.

When the éclairs are cooled, split each one along the side, open and fill the cavity with cream flavoured with coffee or chocolate.

You can also fill the éclairs with *crème frangipane*, *pâtissière*, Saint-Honoré or Chantilly (pages 568–572).

Close the éclairs, and cover the lids with warm coffee or chocolate icing (page 629).

Place them on a board.

When the icing has hardened, remove any drips and serve the éclairs on a plate.

CREAM PUFFS
Choux à la crème

Proceed as for the éclairs (above), but instead of making strips of dough make small balls the size of macaroons, spacing them 8 cm (3 inches) apart. Brush the tops with beaten egg and bake in a 400°F (200°C, gas mark 6) oven for 15–20 minutes.

When the puffs are cool, cut off the tops, turn the cut-off pieces upside down, and put them inside the puffs and fill with *crème* Saint-Honoré or Chantilly (pages 572 or 569).

GRILLED PUFFS
Choux grillés

These puff pastries are identical to cream puffs; however, after brushing the tops with egg, flatten them slightly and coat each top with a pinch of chopped almonds covered with a pinch of caster sugar. Press lightly to make the nuts stick.

Bake in a 400°F (200°C, gas mark 6) oven for 15–20 minutes and serve after the puffs cool.

Lining pastry (*pâté à foncer fine*, page 536)
$\frac{1}{4}$ l ($\frac{1}{2}$ pt) water
125 g (5 oz) flour
125 g (5 oz) unsalted butter
3 eggs
1 egg, beaten
Crème Saint-Honoré (page 572) or Chantilly (page 569)
Sugar syrup (optional)
Granulated sugar or chopped toasted almonds (optional)

Gâteau Saint-Honoré
For 6 servings

The Saint-Honoré is an example of the pastries made by the old Pâtisserie Chiboust, near the Palais-Royal on the rue Saint-Honoré which gives this exquisite cream cake its name. The cake was created by this renowned pastry cook in the days when all fashionable Paris visited the Palais-Royal.

Method. Roll a piece of lining pastry to the diameter of an ordinary plate (about 25 cm (10 inches)) and about 1·5 cm ($\frac{5}{8}$ inch) thick.

Pierce the dough several times with a fork and cut out a circle with the point of a knife, using a plate turned upside down on the dough to guide you.

Place the circle of dough on a pastry sheet slightly dampened with water.

Make fine chou pastry with the water, flour, butter and 3 eggs (see recipe on page 550 for method).

Using a pastry bag fitted with a 1-cm ($\frac{1}{2}$-inch) plain tube, pipe a ring of chou pastry all around the edge of the circle and a spiral in the centre.

On another pastry sheet, make 30 small puffs the size of small walnuts.

Brush all the chou pastry with beaten egg and bake in a 400°F (200°C, gas mark 6) oven for 15–20 minutes.

When they are golden brown, place the base and the puffs on a rack; let cool.

Meanwhile, prepare the *crème* Saint-Honoré, or just before serving, some *crème* Chantilly (page 569). Fill the circle of dough with the cream, spreading it 4 cm (1½ inches) thick right up to the edge of the chou pastry. Then with a tablespoon, drop spoonfuls of the cream side by side on top of the layer of cream, giving each one the shape of an elongated egg. Drop each spoonful of cream with an abrupt movement; this gives it a ridge on the top.

Remove the tops of the tiny cream puffs and with the pastry bag give each one a squirt of cream filling. Then place them around the top of the ring of chou pastry, like a string of large pearls.

Stick the filled puffs to the ring of chou pastry by attaching them to the cream piled on the Saint-Honoré.

As a more complicated finishing touch you can if you like dip the tops of the tiny puffs in sugar syrup cooked to crack stage (page 628), which will form a solid transparent coating. The tops of alternate puffs are then dipped into granulated sugar or in chopped toasted almonds. With the same sugar syrup, still very hot, stick the puffs to the ring of chou pastry, turning the tops up.

If this method is used, put the tiny puffs in place before filling the circle with cream.

½ l (1 pt) cold milk
225 g (8 oz) unsalted
  butter
2 teaspoons salt
25 g (1 oz) sugar
400 g (14 oz) flour
12 eggs

Cream filling:
1 vanilla bean
Pinch salt
1 l (2 pts) milk
8 egg yolks
300 g (10 oz) sugar
75 g (3 oz) flour
Sugared almonds
Caramelized orange
  slices

Croque-en-bouche

For 10 servings

The name means literally a pastry which crunches and crumbles in the mouth.

Place the milk in a saucepan; add the butter, salt and sugar. Bring to the boil, add the flour, dry the dough on the heat for about 4 minutes, and beat in the eggs, one at a time. Butter some pastry sheets, put the dough into a pastry bag, and pipe 60 small puffs on to the sheets. Bake in a 400°F (200°C, gas mark 6) oven for about 20 minutes.

Cream filling

Steep a vanilla bean with a pinch of salt in the milk; in a bowl, mix the egg yolks with half the sugar and then add the flour; stir into the milk with a whisk and cook over a low flame for a good 5 minutes; use to fill the puffs.

Heat the remaining sugar until it melts and turns caramel colour. Oil the inside of a cone-shaped or round mould. Dip the puffs into the caramel. Starting from the point, fill the whole mould with puffs, each one dipped into caramel. Let cool. Unmould. Decorate with sugared almonds and caramelized orange slices.

Cakes

❧❧❧❧❧❧❧❧❧❧❧❧❧❧❧❧

PLAIN GENOESE CAKE
Génoise ordinaire

**500 g (1 lb) caster
sugar
16 eggs
500 g (1 lb) flour
225 g (8 oz) unsalted
butter, clarified**

Note: The proportions above can be altered; if you use only 400 g (14 oz) of flour, the dough will be lighter; if the butter is reduced or omitted, then the cake will be less fine and less soft.

Flavour with vanilla sugar, liqueur, or the grated rind of lemon or orange crushed with a lump of sugar.

Method. Place the sugar in a deep copper bowl, such as the French use for beating egg whites. If you do not have such a bowl, use an ordinary mixing or salad bowl, though the shape is less convenient. Add the eggs, breaking them one by one into another bowl to check their freshness before adding them to the sugar. Mix well with a whisk and beat as you would beat eggs for an omelette. The mass will increase in volume, become lighter in colour and creamy, until the consistency is such that it coats the wires of the whisk. The cream is ready when, if you lift the whisk, the mixture falls slowly in ribbons.

This beating with the whisk will take about 30 minutes. This time can be shortened by placing the bowl over a very low flame or on hot coals. That method is quicker but more risky, and the dough will fall more easily when the flour and the butter are added.

If you adopt this second method, remove the bowl from the heat when it is lukewarm, and continue to beat until the mixture is completely cooled.

Whatever the method chosen, when the mixture forms a ribbon, remove the whisk and start using a wooden spatula or a spoon. Sift the flour into the bowl, stirring the mixture with your right hand with a spatula while from time to time you rotate the bowl in the opposite direction with your left.

After adding the flour, add the flavouring and pour in the clarified butter in a stream, mixing it in the same way as the flour.

Pour the mixture into round, square or oval moulds, plain or decorated, buttered carefully with clarified butter, dusted with flour and shaken well. Fill each mould two-thirds full, bake in a 350°F (180°C, gas mark 4) oven for 20–25 minutes, with the oven door slightly ajar.

You will know that the cake is done when it resists slightly when pressed lightly with your finger; unmould immediately on to a rack and let cool naturally without letting the steam of the cake condense.

The mixture can be baked in a 2 large rectangular pans about 4 cm (1½ inches) deep. After baking, the cake can be cut up in various ways depending upon its use.

CHOCOLATE GENOESE CAKE
Génoise au chocolat

8 eggs
225 g (8 oz) caster sugar
200 g (7 oz) well-sifted flour
50 g (2 oz) cocoa
100 g (4 oz) ground almonds
150 g (6 oz) unsalted butter, melted
ganache à truffes (see page 631)

In a bowl, beat the eggs with the sugar; then add the well-sifted flour, cocoa and ground almonds. Mix well, and add the melted butter. Pour into a mould, set in a shallow pan of hot water and bake in a 325°F (170°C, gas mark 3) oven for 25 minutes.

Cut the cake in half horizontally and fill with *ganache à truffes* (plain chocolate mixed with double cream).

PRESIDENT'S CAKE
Gâteau du Président
Maurice Bernachon's recipe

4 eggs
125 g (5 oz) sifted flour
125 g (5 oz) sugar
100 g (4 oz) unsalted butter
½ l (1 pt) cream
600 g (1 lb 4 oz) plain chocolate
Glacé cherries

Make a *génoise* (directions above) with the 4 eggs, sifted flour, sugar and butter. Beat the eggs with the sugar as directed. As soon as the mixture forms a ribbon, add the flour, then the melted butter. Cook over a low flame for 20 minutes; butter a 20-cm (8-inch) mould and dust it with flour before pouring in the mixture. Meanwhile, cook the cream with the chocolate for 10 minutes. Remove from the heat, beat with a stainless steel whisk until completely cool. Add some glacé cherries and use this chocolate cream to fill and frost the cake. Then, with a knife make curls of chocolate to cover the cake.

Madeleine

For 48 madeleines

500 g (1 lb) caster
  sugar
12 eggs
500 g (1 lb) sifted
  flour
500 g (1 lb) unsalted
  butter
1 teaspoon vanilla
  sugar

Follow the recipe for the *génoise* (above), but mix the ingredients cold. When the mixture forms a ribbon, add first the flour, then the butter, melted and clarified. Be careful not to include the whey or scum from the clarified butter which would sink to the bottom of the moulds during cooking and cause the dough to stick to them, making unmoulding quite difficult. The cakes would not be a neat shape.

Fill the madeleine moulds, pouring the mixture in with a pastry scraper or a tablespoon, placing a little in each of the special madeleine moulds, which come 6–12 in a tin; first butter the moulds, carefully, with a little clarified butter; dust with flour, and then shake the moulds.

Bake in a 350°F (170°C, gas mark 3) oven for about 25 minutes; unmould as soon as they are done.

Plum Cake

225 g (8 oz) unsalted
  butter
8 eggs
225 g (8 oz) sugar
Sultanas and currants
50 g (2 oz) each
  candied orange and
  lemon peel
$\frac{1}{2}$ glass rum
1 teaspoon vanilla
  sugar
225 g (8 oz) sifted
  flour

Fill a large mixing bowl with boiling water and let stand until the bowl is lukewarm. Empty the water, wipe the bowl and put in the butter, which has been cut into pieces and softened by kneading it in a cloth. Work the butter with a wooden spoon until it becomes smooth and white.

Add the eggs, one by one, continuing to work the mixture with a wooden spoon. The volume of the mixture increases as the eggs are added, but it is also the long beating that makes the mixture light, white and creamy. At this point add the sugar and beat the mixture until all the sugar is absorbed.

As soon as the mixture forms a ribbon when you lift it with the spatula, add the sultanas and currants, cleaned by dusting them with flour and rubbing them on a sieve that will let the stems through. Then add the candied orange and lemon peel cut into tiny dice, the rum, the vanilla sugar and the sifted flour.

Adding these ingredients should not weigh down the egg–butter mixture.

Use a rectangular cake tin, about 13 cm (5 inches) high, 10 cm (4 inches) wide at the top and 9 cm (3½ inches) wide at the base. Butter the tin with clarified butter and line with buttered white paper. Cut the paper 2 cm (¾ inch) higher than the mould and zigzag the top in triangles.

Spoon the mixture into the tins. Fill only two-thirds of the way up. Tap the tin on a folded dishcloth so that the mixture is level.

Bake in a 350°F (180°C, gas mark 4) oven for about 1 hour.

One teaspoon of baking powder can be added to the cake mixture. Under the action of this baking powder, the top of the cake cracks and rises in a point. If you omit this ingredient, it is necessary to split the top of the cake lightly lengthwise with a knife during baking. This helps the cake to rise and keep it light.

After removing the cake from the oven, unmould it but leave it wrapped in the paper, and cool on a rack.

In order to cut the cake easily into 1 cm ($\frac{1}{2}$ inch) slices, keep it a day or two before serving.

This cake, one of the finest, originated as the name suggests in England.

SAVOY SPONGE-CAKE
Biscuit de Savoie

500 g (1 lb) caster sugar
12 eggs, separated
500 g (1 lb) sifted flour
1 teaspoon vanilla sugar
Clarified butter

Place the sugar and the 12 egg yolks in a large bowl.

Mix with a spatula and beat the mixture vigorously until it has tripled in volume and is white, creamy and slides from the spatula in a thick, smooth ribbon.

At this moment add the flour, folding it into the mixture with the spatula; add the vanilla sugar and one-quarter of the egg whites beaten very stiff. Mix very well; finish by folding in the remaining beaten egg whites, but this time fold very gently to keep the mixture from becoming heavy.

Moulds for this cake are round and deep with a central funnel and generally decorated. Butter 3 moulds carefully with clarified butter and turn them upside down to let them drain. Dust the inside with a mixture of equal parts of flour or cornflour and caster or icing sugar.

Fill the tins two-thirds full and tap them on a folded cloth to make the mixture level.

Bake in a 325°F (170°C, gas mark 3) oven for 40 minutes.

The Savoy sponge-cake should be a pale golden colour.

The dusting of sugar inside the mould forms a delicate, slightly crisp coating.

After removing the cakes from the oven, let them stand for 5 minutes before unmoulding.

**500 g (1 lb) caster
sugar
16 eggs, separated
400 g (14 oz) sifted
flour
1 tablespoon vanilla
sugar**

SPONGE FINGERS
Biscuits à la cuiller

Follow the directions for Savoy sponge-cake, above.

Put the mixture into a pastry bag with a plain nozzle 2·5 cm (1 inch) in diameter. Close the bag, and follow the steps described in the recipe for éclairs (page 552).

Make strips about 13 cm (5 inches) long on a buttered pastry sheet dusted with flour or covered with wax paper. Leave a 5-cm (2-inch) space between each.

Sift some caster sugar on top of the strips, let them stand for 2 minutes, then lift the pan or the paper and shake off the excess sugar.

Using a brush dipped in water and shaken to remove the excess, sprinkle small drops of water on to the sugar left on the fingers. These drops of water, mixed with the sugar while cooking, will turn into little pearls.

Place the pastry sheet in a 300°F (150°C, gas mark 2) oven for 25 minutes. When they are done, the sponge fingers should be just browned. When they have cooled, detach them from the paper or the pastry sheet and pair them two by two, back to back. Place in an airtight tin where they will keep fresh.

**500 g (1 lb) caster
sugar
18 egg yolks
Vanilla
3 tablespoons rum
400 g (14 oz) sifted
flour
300 g (10 oz) unsalted
butter
12 egg whites, beaten
very stiff**

MIXED-UP SPONGE-CAKE
Biscuit manqué

Follow the recipe for Savoy sponge-cake above, adding to the beaten sugar and egg yolks the vanilla, the rum, the flour, the butter and the egg whites, in that order.

GENOA CAKE
Pain de Gênes

The Genoa cake is one of the best cakes of this type. It is somewhat difficult to make it perfectly, but with care and experience, you can surmount the problems even if you are not a professional cook. Two methods can be used, depending upon the equipment you have.

First method:
225 g (8 oz) unsalted butter
300 g (10 oz) caster sugar
250 g (9 oz) blanched almonds and 1 bitter almond, finely ground
8 eggs
2 teaspoons curacao
50 g (2 oz) flour

Second method:
225 g (8 oz) blanched almonds and 1 bitter almond
6 eggs
325 g (11 oz) caster sugar
50 g (2 oz) flour
125 g (5 oz) unsalted butter, melted
1 teaspoon anisette

First method

Soften the butter in a bowl by working it with a spatula. Add the sugar; mix well, beating vigorously with the spatula to lighten and whiten the mixture. Add the ground almonds and, one at a time, 4 whole eggs and 4 yolks.

The mixture will become lighter, creamier and increase in volume. At this point, carefully add the curaçao, the flour and the 4 egg whites, beaten stiff. Fold the mixture with a spatula, lifting the batter very gently.

Second method

Pound the almonds in a mortar. When they form a paste, beat in, one at a time, the 6 eggs, then the sugar; work the batter vigorously to make it creamy and light. When it is ready add the flour and the melted butter, folding them into the mixture with a spatula very carefully.

Flavour with anisette.

[*Editor's note:* Bake following the instructions for Savoy sponge-cake above.]

Petits fours

BISCUITS MADE WITH FLAKY PASTRY
Petits gâteaux feuilletés

Roll a piece of flaky dough (page 531) with a rolling pin until you have a sheet about 6 mm ($\frac{1}{4}$ inch) thick. Cut this dough into small diamonds, rectangles or squares about 6–8 cm ($2\frac{1}{2}$–3 inches) a side, or similar-sized rounds or ovals cut with a fluted cutter.

Place each biscuit upside down on a slightly dampened pastry sheet. Brush the top surface with beaten egg, decorate using the point of a knife, and bake in a 400°F (200°C, gas mark 6) oven for 12–14 minutes.

Just before the biscuits are done, remove from the oven and sprinkle icing sugar on the top; place back in the oven for 1 minute, long enough to melt the sugar, which will give a pleasant taste and a nice colour.

PALM LEAF BISCUITS
Palmiers

Use a piece of flaky pastry that has had four 'turns'. Let stand for 15 minutes, then give the fifth and sixth turns but, instead of sprinkling the table with flour, sprinkle generously with sugar.

When the dough has had six turns, fold it, then roll out the dough as if you were going to give it another turn until it is about 40 cm (16 inches) long and 9 mm ($\frac{3}{8}$ inch) thick. Fold each end of the dough towards the centre so that the ends touch; then fold one half on top of the other again, like a wallet.

The rectangle of dough should be 10 cm (4 inches) long and 4 cm ($1\frac{1}{2}$ inches) thick. With a knife cut slices 9 mm ($\frac{3}{8}$ inch) thick and put them, cut side down, on a slightly dampened pastry sheet, placing them 13–15 cm (5–6 inches) apart. Bake in a 400°F (200°C, gas mark 6) oven for about 15 minutes, watching them carefully. While baking, the biscuits will open like palm leaves, and the sugar in them will caramelize quickly.

SUGAR BISCUITS
Palets au sucre

With a fluted cutter cut some flaky pastry or trimmings from flaky pastry (page 531) into circles about 6 mm ($\frac{1}{4}$ inch) thick.

Dust the table with sugar; and with a rolling pin, roll each circle in the sugar until it becomes oval.

Turn the thin ovals over and place them on a slightly dampened pastry sheet, the sugared surface on top.

Bake in a 400°F (200°C, gas mark 6) oven for 10–12 minutes, keeping a careful eye on them, as with the *palmiers*.

PASTRY TWISTS
Sacristains

Use trimmings of flaky pastry (page 531) pressed into a ball. Roll the dough on sugar until it is 9 mm ($\frac{3}{8}$ inch) thick, giving it a rectangular shape; trim with a knife to make it 15 cm (6 inches) wide.

Brush with beaten egg, cover with chopped almonds and sprinkle generously with sugar. Stick the almonds and the sugar to the dough by pressing lightly with the flat part of a knife blade.

Turn the strip of dough over, placing it almond side down on the table sprinkled with sugar. Repeat the steps: brush with egg, cover with almonds, sprinkle with sugar and press down with a knife blade.

Then cut crosswise into small strips 3 cm ($1\frac{1}{4}$ inches) wide; take these little strips, one by one, and give each one a double twist before placing it on a slightly dampened pastry sheet.

Bake in a 400°F (200°C, gas mark 6) oven for 10–12 minutes. Check while baking, because the sugar caramelizes very quickly.

Note: The above biscuits, made from flaky pastry, can be made very small to be served as *petits fours*.

SHORTBREAD BISCUITS
Gâteaux sablés fins

350 g (12 oz) unsalted butter

2 eggs

500 g (1 lb) flour

225 g (8 oz) caster sugar

225 g (8 oz) almonds, crushed or finely ground

1 or 2 egg yolks (optional)

1 teaspoon vanilla sugar or 1 tablespoon rum

Mix together the butter and eggs with the flour combined with the sugar and crushed or finely ground almonds.

Knead the dough quickly. If the dough is too firm and breaks, add 1 or 2 egg yolks.

Flavour with 1 teaspoon of vanilla sugar or 1 tablespoon of rum.

Wrap the dough in a cloth and let stand 20 minutes.

Then roll with a rolling pin into a sheet 3 mm ($\frac{1}{8}$ inch) thick, and cut into small squares using a fluted rolling pastry cutter. Place each biscuit on a pastry sheet, prick with a fork to avoid bubbles and bake in a 400°F (200°C, gas mark 6) oven for 15–20 minutes.

These delicious crumbly biscuits should be a nice light-brown colour when done.

Keep them in an airtight tin.

CATS' TONGUES
Langues de chat
Ordinary recipe

125 g (5 oz) caster sugar

1 teaspoon vanilla sugar

1 egg

6 tablespoons single cream or milk

125 g (5 oz) flour

In a bowl, combine the sugar, the egg and the cream or milk; add the flour, sifted. Mix well.

Place the mixture in a pastry bag with a plain 1-cm ($\frac{1}{2}$-inch) nozzle and pipe small strips about 8–10 cm ($3\frac{1}{4}$–4 inches) long on a lightly buttered pastry sheet.

Keep the strips about 6 cm ($2\frac{1}{2}$ inches) apart so that the dough can spread.

Bake in a 375°F (190°C, gas mark 5) oven for 7–8 minutes. The cats' tongues should be a light golden-brown colour, edged with darker brown.

Remove the cats' tongues from the pastry sheet when they are completely cold, and keep them very dry, in a tightly closed tin, so that they will remain crisp.

125 g (5 oz) butter
75 g (3 oz) sugar
3 eggs, separated
100 g (4 oz) sifted flour
25 g (1 oz) vanilla-flavoured icing sugar

CATS' TONGUES
Langues de chat
Special recipe

Warm a small bowl with boiling water, pour out the water and dry the bowl; put in the butter, cut into pieces, and work with a wooden spatula until it is soft and smooth. Then add all the sugar, beating vigorously until the mixture is creamy; and finish by beating in the egg yolks, one by one. Add the flour, then the three egg whites, beaten stiff. Put the mixture into a pastry bag and pipe strips on to a buttered pastry sheet and bake as described in the preceding recipe.

125 g (5 oz) currants
2 tablespoons rum
125 g (5 oz) unsalted butter
125 g (5 oz) caster sugar
3 eggs
125 g (5 oz) flour

CURRANT BISCUITS
Palets aux raisins

Pick over the currants and rub them with a pinch of flour in a sieve coarse enough to let the stems through. Macerate in the rum.

In a slightly warmed bowl, soften the butter, cut into small pieces, and work it with a spatula to make it creamy. Add the sugar, and work the mixture again; add the eggs, one by one, the flour, and the currants, beating after each addition. Flavour with rum.

Fill a pastry bag with a plain tube and pipe small balls of the mixture on to a buttered pastry sheet. Place them about 5 cm (2 inches) apart so that the biscuits do not stick to one another as they spread when they are baked.

Bake in a 350°F (180°C, gas mark 4) oven and keep in a tightly closed tin, like the cats' tongues.

125 g (5 oz) pounded
   or ground almonds
1 teaspoon cornflour
150 g (6 oz) caster
   sugar
1 tablespoon vanilla
   sugar
2 egg whites and 1
   yolk
Sliced almonds

ALMOND BISCUITS
Tuiles aux amandes

In a bowl, work the pounded or ground almonds with a wooden spatula, adding the cornflour, the sugar and 1 egg white. When the mixture is smooth and creamy, add the egg yolk and, a few seconds later, the other egg white.

This mixture should be soft and spread slightly; if it is too thick, add more egg white.

Using a pastry bag with a 1-cm ($\frac{1}{2}$-inch) tube or a teaspoon, make small balls of the mixture as big as walnuts on a buttered pastry sheet. Place them about 6 cm ($2\frac{1}{2}$ inches) apart, since the dough will spread. Sprinkle a few slices of almonds on each small biscuit and bake in a 300°F (150°C, gas mark 2) oven until they begin to brown on the edges.

To make the biscuits curved, while they are still hot place each one on the side of a rolling pin. While they are warm, they are very pliant and will take the shape of the rolling pin, and keep this shape when they cool and become very crisp and crunchy.

Keep them dry in a tightly closed tin.

Pastry desserts

Most pastry desserts combine cake and cream, cake and jam or cake and icing.

Any type of cake can be used as a foundation for a dessert. The most delicate one is the madeleine mixture (page 557) baked in a cake tin.

These cakes can be filled with a variety of creams: butter cream in any of a number of flavours, or *crème frangipane*, *pâtissière*, Chantilly or *à Saint-Honoré* (see pages 568–572).

A cake can be coated with sugar, chopped pistachio nuts, chopped or sliced almonds, sugared or toasted almonds or grated chocolate. Icings are usually flavoured with coffee, chocolate, kirsch, anisette, maraschino, rum, etc.

500 g (1 lb) caster
  sugar
16 eggs
500 g (1 lb) sifted
  flour
1 tablespoon vanilla
  sugar
Moka cream (page
  570)
Sugar

COFFEE CAKE
Moka

This cake was invented in 1857 but is still a great favourite, combining the fresh flavour of best butter with the exquisite aroma of coffee. Besides the other suggested mixtures, here is an extra recipe for a light cake which is most suitable for the Moka cake and in general for any cake to be filled with butter cream.

Method.   Beat the sugar in a large bowl with the eggs. Place the bowl on charcoal or a warm corner of the stove. When the mixture forms a ribbon, add the sifted flour, mixing carefully with a spatula. Flavour with 1 tablespoon of vanilla sugar. Pour into a cake tin and bake in a 350°F (180°C, gas mark 4) oven. Unmould on a rack, and let cool completely before filling with butter cream.

When the cake is cold, with a long thin knife cut it horizontally into three parts. Spread a layer of moka cream about 1 cm ($\frac{1}{2}$ inch) thick on the bottom layer; place the second layer of cake on top, then spread with a second layer of moka cream and place the third layer of cake on top. Then coat the cake on the sides and the top with a thick layer of moka cream. This last step is done by placing the cake on a rack slightly smaller than the cake, which will allow you to smooth the cream evenly on the sides of the cake.

Finish the sides by pressing on some granulated sugar. Do this step over a sheet of paper to catch the sugar that spills.

With a small pastry bag fitted with a very fine fluted tube decorate the top of the cake with 2 tablespoons of moka cream; carefully pipe a design of rosettes, garlands and tiny roses. Refrigerate until ready to serve.

CHOCOLATE CAKE WITH PRALINE
Chocolatine pralinée

Make this like the coffee cake (above), using butter cream flavoured with cocoa or chocolate.

Cover the sides with chopped almonds coated with sugar and caramelized. Decorate the top with chocolate cream in the same way as the moka cake.

GENOESE OR SPONGE-CAKE WITH BUTTER CREAM
Gâteau mascotte

Fill several round or square layers of Genoese cake (page 555) or any other sponge-cake with moka cream (page 570) or chocolate butter cream. Follow the steps for the moka cake above, keeping the rounded surface on the top. Put slightly more filling in the centre so that the cake curves slightly on top. Cover the sides with cream as for the moka cake. Sprinkle the top and sides with praline – chopped almonds, sugared and caramelized. Finally dust with vanilla-flavoured icing sugar.

CHRISTMAS LOG
Bûche de Noël

This is a moka cake traditionally made at Christmas time.

The Genoese (page 555) or any other sponge mixture is baked in a long semi-cylindrical mould. If you do not have a special mould, bake a flat rectangle of cake, spreading it in a very flat pan lined with a piece of waxed paper or simply on a piece of paper on a pastry sheet. Once the cake is baked and cooled, remove the piece of paper and spread a layer of moka (page 570) or chocolate cream about 1 cm ($\frac{1}{2}$ inch) thick on top of the cake, then roll the cake to make a log. Whatever method you use for making the cake, the bottom of the cake should be iced with moka cream and then stuck to a base of cooked pastry (*pâte sablée, pâte à foncer fine* or *pâte sucrée,* see pages 536–538) with a layer of cream; this base should be about 3–4 cm (1¼–1½ inches) larger than the cake. Then cover the top of the cake with rows of cream from a pastry bag fitted with a fluted flat tube. These rows of cream should imitate the rough bark of a log.

With a little skill you can make the stumps of one or two cut branches from a piece of cake with rough edges that is covered with cream. Cover the joins with plain butter cream; and, here and there, place a small amount of chopped almonds, tinted green, to imitate moss. The decoration of the cake is a matter of imagination and taste – there are plenty of possibilities: meringue mushrooms, imitation leaves, etc.

CREAMS, CUSTARDS, MOULDS AND HOT PUDDINGS

Creams and custards

ALMOND CUSTARD FILLING
Crème frangipane

1 l (2 pts) milk
1 vanilla bean
225 g (8 oz) flour
225 g (8 oz) caster sugar
Pinch salt
4 eggs
6 egg yolks
100 g (4 oz) unsalted butter
4 tablespoons macaroon crumbs

In a heavy-bottomed saucepan holding about 2 l (4 pts), boil the milk with a vanilla bean.

Meanwhile, in a bowl, mix the flour with the sugar and salt; then stir in the egg yolks.

While the milk is still very hot, pour it slowly into the egg mixture, beating with a whisk, and pour the mixture back into the saucepan; heat to boiling point, stirring continuously. Remove from the heat and add the butter and macaroon crumbs.

Pour the frangipane cream into a bowl and stir it with a wooden spoon until completely cold. This last step prevents the formation of a skin on top of the cream which would eventually produce lumps. A skin can also be avoided by dabbing the surface with a piece of butter. Keep refrigerated until ready to use.

1 l (2 pts) hot milk
500 g (1 lb) caster
  sugar
125 g (5 oz) flour
Pinch salt
12 egg yolks
Vanilla

CUSTARD FILLING
Crème pâtissière

Follow the recipe for frangipane cream (above), changing the quantities of the ingredients as instructed.

When the mixture reaches boiling point, pour into a bowl and stir often with a wooden spoon until completely cold.

This cream should be flavoured with vanilla, but you also can add essence of coffee, cocoa, orange or lemon rind – steep the rind in the boiling milk, covered.

Note: When these creams are cold, scrape the sides of the bowl to incorporate whatever has stuck to the sides while stirring; after each stirring, smooth the top surface of the cream and cover with buttered white paper.

WHIPPED CREAM
Crème Chantilly

Use very thick fresh double cream and keep it on ice or in the refrigerator during hot weather.

Pour the cream into a bowl and whip, beginning slowly, with a small, flexible whisk. The cream will slowly increase in volume until doubled. When cream reaches that point, whip faster, and stop only when the cream stands in peaks and stays in the whisk when you lift it, as egg whites do when beaten stiff.

Be careful not to beat too much or butter will start to form; you need only 2 or 3 seconds too long to make whipped cream into butter.

Carefully add 125–225 g (5–8 oz) of sugar to every 1 l (2 pts) of whipped cream, depending on its use.

Note: Since this cream can be whipped so quickly, we advise whipping it just before serving.

¾ l (1½ pts) boiled
milk with a split
vanilla bean steeped
in it, covered, after
milk has boiled
225 g (8 oz) sugar
8 egg yolks

CUSTARD CREAM
Crème anglais
For 1 l (2 pts)

This cream is the base for, or is served with, many hot or cold desserts and ice-cream *parfaits*.

In a bowl mix the sugar and the egg yolks; beat this mixture with a wooden spoon until it is frothy, thick and nearly white. Then slowly add the milk.

Pour the mixture back into the saucepan, and cook on a low flame; stir continuously with the spatula, moving it all around the bottom of the pan to prevent the egg yolks from coagulating.

As the sauce heats, the egg yolks will thicken the cream. As soon as the cream starts to coat the spoon, which is when it is about to reach boiling point, remove from the heat and pour into a bowl to hasten the cooling and to stop the egg yolks scrambling into tiny particles, losing their binding and thickening properties.

Making this cream requires some experience. It is possible to make up for lack of practice by adding 1 teaspoon of cornflour to the milk for each litre (2 pts).

Note: If you want to make an even finer, smoother custard, you can increase the number of egg yolks to about 20 for 1 l (2 pts) of milk and add, after the custard has cooled, 2 dl (8 fl oz) of double cream.

COFFEE CREAM (1)
Crème moka

Among custard creams, this butter cream is the supreme mixture of sugar, egg yolks and butter. These are various good methods for making this cream, but the two following recipes are recommended because they are simpler to make in a domestic kitchen.

First method

In a saucepan, mix 225 g (8 oz) of sugar and 8 egg yolks; beat the mixture with a wooden spatula to make it white and creamy. Then slowly add ¼ l (½ pt) of good strong black coffee and heat slowly, stirring continuously as in making a custard cream. As soon as the cream approaches boiling point, thickens and coats the back of the spatula, stop the boiling at once and remove quickly from the heat, pouring it in a bowl to cool it and stop the egg yolks from cooking.

When the cream is lukewarm, add 350 g (12 oz) of fine unsalted butter, cut into small pieces, and mix with a whisk into a smooth paste; then whip vigorously with a sauce whisk.

When mixed, the cream becomes smooth, creamy and shiny. The colour is light brown, with a delicious strong coffee flavour.

Use the moka cream immediately without refrigerating, which would harden the cream and make it difficult to use.

Second method

Prepare ¼ l (½ pt) of *crème anglaise* (above). When it is still warm add, following the first method, 225 g (8 oz) of unsalted butter. Finish the cream by adding 1 teaspoon of coffee essence.

Instead of *crème anglaise* you can use ¼ l (½ pt) of *crème pâtissière* which is rather less delicate. Finish the cream as above.

Note: It is an invariable rule that equal amounts of butter and cream must be used. Not enough butter causes the two ingredients to separate, though this is easy to correct, by readjusting the proportions.

COFFEE CREAM (2)
Crème moka délice

In memory of Master Chef Urbain Dubois

8 egg yolks
1 tablespoon icing sugar
6 tablespoons syrup made with sugar and strong, fresh coffee (in the proportions 100 g (4 oz) sugar to 4 tablespoons liquid
350 g (12 oz) unsalted butter

With a whisk beat in an unlined copper bowl over charcoal, 8 egg yolks with 1 tablespoon of icing sugar; slowly add the syrup.

When the cream coats a wooden spoon like custard, remove from the heat and continue to whip until the cream is lukewarm. Then pour the cream on to the butter, first softened into a paste in a bowl.

Work the mixture vigorously with a whisk.

¼ l (½ pt) milk

25 g (1 oz) flour or
  cornflour

125 g (5 oz) sugar

6 eggs

½ teaspoon vanilla
  sugar

2 sheets gelatine (⅛ oz
  powdered gelatine)
  softened in water

SAINT-HONORÉ CREAM
Crème à Saint-Honoré

Follow the recipe for *crème pâtissière*. When the cream is cooked, add the gelatine away from the heat; then, while the cream is still hot, add the egg whites, beaten stiff.

Here are two ways to mix the cream and the egg whites.

Either slowly pour the boiling cream into the beaten egg whites, folding carefully with a spatula, lifting the mixture to prevent the whites from falling.

Or first pour the very hot cream into a bowl and then fold in the beaten egg whites, in small quantities, as above.

This second method is preferable.

Saint-Honoré cream should be used right away, before it sets and hardens.

CREAM WITH CHESTNUT PURÉE
Crème à la purée de marrons

Prepare a butter cream (see the recipes for moka cream, omitting the coffee of course) and, when it is finished, add chestnut purée equal in weight to the sugar used in the cream.

To make the purée, rub broken *marrons glacés* through a sieve, or remove the double skins from fresh chestnuts, cook and rub them through a sieve. Mix with a little sugar syrup or milk.

This purée should be creamy and rather firm.

BEATEN EGG WHITES
Blancs d'oeufs en neige

To make white of eggs frothy, smooth and white, two utensils are needed: an unlined copper bowl for beating eggs and a wooden-handled whisk with tinned-steel wires. To this day no electrical appliance has been able to replace the wrist, except a machine made for laboratories, run by a motor, with joints that can reproduce exactly the movements of the arm and wrist.

Very fresh egg whites have a tendency to turn grainy and separate at the end of the whipping. This problem can be overcome by adding a pinch of salt at the beginning of the whipping and a couple of tablespoons of caster sugar at the end.

In the beginning, beat slowly as for an omelette – with the bowl held slightly inclined and the whites at the bottom. As the albumin coagulates and increases in volume, it is important to increase the speed of the whipping and finally to change the movement of the whisk, moving it round quickly and pushing against the sides of the bowl. The egg whites are sufficiently beaten when they become firm and can be lifted by the wires of the whisk. If you notice the egg whites separating, add the sugar.

When the egg whites are firm, they should be used immediately.

To mix beaten egg whites with other ingredients, use a spatula and fold them in, lifting the mass carefully to keep the whites from falling.

CUSTARD CREAM WITH GELATINE
Crème pour bavaroises, plombières, puddings, charlottes glacés

Prepare a custard cream (*crème anglaise*, page 570), with at least 12 egg yolks for each 1 l (2 pts) of milk.

Add 12 sheets (15 g ($\frac{1}{2}$ oz) of powdered) gelatine softened in cold water to every 1 l (2 pts) of mixture. Add the gelatine after the milk is mixed into the egg yolks.

After cooking, strain through a fine sieve, pour into a bowl and stir until completely cool to prevent the formation of a skin or lumps.

BAKED CUSTARD
Crème renversée

1 l (2 pts) boiled milk

200 g (7 oz) sugar, dissolved in the milk

4 whole eggs and 8 egg yolks or 8 whole eggs

The function of the egg whites in this custard is to make the custard set as it is cooked. The role of the yolks is to make it smooth. Therefore, the higher the proportion of egg yolks and the lower the portion of egg whites, the finer the custard will be. However, four egg whites are the minimum for a custard stiff enough to unmould properly.

Crème renversée is flavoured by steeping a vanilla bean in the milk; using orange or lemon rind; melting chocolate in the milk or using cocoa; adding to the milk a chosen flavour such as coffee or tea or any other liquid, being careful to subtract an equal amount of milk from the liquid used.

Combine the sugar and the eggs in a bowl and beat the mixture with a wooden spoon for a few minutes. Pour the boiling milk into it, stirring constantly. Strain through a fine sieve, remove the froth that floats on top and pour into a mould – a cake tin with a funnel in the centre, a sponge tin or any other shallow tin or small individual moulds.

Place the mould in a shallow baking pan and fill the baking pan two-thirds up with nearly boiling water; bake in a 325°F (170°C, gas mark 3) oven for at least 1 hour.

The water should never boil, because boiling would partially separate the custard and make it watery. If the water should start to boil, stop it by adding a few tablespoons of lukewarm water.

Check the cooking by touching the surface and insert a fine needle or a thin knife blade; if it comes out clean, the custard is baked.

Let cool in the mould. Unmould just before serving.

CARAMEL CUSTARD
Crème renversée au caramel

Dissolve 2 tablespoons of sugar in 2 tablespoons of water. Cook this mixture slowly until the water has completely evaporated and the sugar starts to dissolve; remove from the heat when its colour is light brown.

Rapidly plunge the bottom of the saucepan into cold water to prevent the sugar from burning, or the taste will become bitter; or pour the caramel immediately into the mould in which the custard will be baked and spread it, tipping the mould in all directions to give it a coating of caramel about 3 mm ($\frac{1}{8}$ inch) thick.

If you wish to serve a caramel syrup with the custard, double the quantity of sugar and water, pour half the finished caramel into the mould and add $\frac{1}{2}$ cup of water to the remaining syrup in the saucepan; cook to a syrup and set aside to serve with the custard.

Meanwhile, prepare the custard as in the recipe above. Pour it in the mould coated inside with caramel and bake in a *bain-marie* in a 325°F (170°C, gas mark 3) oven for at least 1 hour. It is preferable to prepare this dessert 6 hours before serving. While it stands, the moisture will dissolve the caramel, which will soak into the custard producing a beautiful colour when the dish is unmoulded.

INDIVIDUAL CUSTARD CREAMS
Pots de crème

Of all the cooked custard creams, the most delicate to prepare are *pots de crème*. These custards are served in their own individual small moulds, not unmoulded, which allows you to omit the whites of eggs completely. The quantities are easy to adjust. Use 1 egg yolk at least per pot (if the pots hold about 6 tablespoons of liquid). The combined volume of the egg yolks and the sugar equals one-quarter of the capacity of the pots, so we can calculate the quantity of milk or, even better, single cream needed on the basis of these figures and the number of pots to be used. Measure the quantity of egg yolks, adding a scant 20 g ($\frac{3}{4}$ oz) of sugar per mould, then add three times this amount of milk or cream. Beat well and pour into the pots. After filling the pots, let them stand for a few minutes. Carefully remove the foam that rises to the tops.

Poach the covered pots of custard in a *bain-marie* in the oven very carefully, because of the extreme sensitivity of the custard. Being covered, the tops of the cream will not brown; if flavoured with vanilla, they will be golden-yellow; if with chocolate, brown and shiny.

FLOATING ISLANDS
Oeufs à la neige Gisou

8 extremely fresh
eggs, separated
225 g (8 oz) caster
sugar
½ l (1 pt) boiled milk
with a split vanilla
bean steeped in it,
covered, after
boiling

This family dessert is always popular. Its success depends on the freshness of the eggs.

In a saucepan, combine 8 egg yolks with half the sugar; beat cold with a whisk until the mixture forms a ribbon.

Add the milk. Place the saucepan on the stove and heat, stirring with a wooden spoon. As soon as the custard thickens and coats the spoon, remove from the heat. Do not let it boil. Immediately strain through a fine sieve into a bowl; stir until completely cold.

Place 8 egg whites in a large stainless steel or copper bowl. With a whisk, start to stir them and whip them slowly. Beat faster until the whites are quite firm. They will form a light froth that sticks to the wires of the whisk. At that point add the remaining sugar, a little at a time, to keep the egg whites very light.

Take a large shallow saucepan, fill it three-quarters with water. Bring the water to the boil.

Using a wooden spoon preferably, form the egg whites into large ovals the size and shape of eggs.

Place each spoonful on the surface of the simmering water, giving a little tap on the edge of the saucepan to detach the egg white from the spoon.

Poach about 6 at once. With a slotted spoon turn them over after a minute or two to poach them on all sides.

Drain the egg whites on a cloth or a fine sieve placed over a bowl. Let cool.

Place the cold custard in a large deep dish. Place the 'floating' egg whites on top, overlapping them slightly.

You can sprinkle the eggs with slivers of toasted almonds or pour a stream of caramel over them or even dust them with powdered chocolate.

This delicious dessert is eaten cold but not iced.

Note: To get more volume into the egg whites, add a pinch of salt or a drop of lemon juice.

※═⊃米⊂═⊃米⊂═⊃米⊂═⊃米⊂═⊃米⊂═⊃米⊂═⊃米⊂═⊃米⊂═⊃米⊂═⊃米⊂═⊃米⊂═⊃米⊂═⊃※

ZABAGLIONE
Les Sabayons

For 1 l (2 pts):
10 egg yolks
**400 g (14 oz) caster
sugar**
**2 glasses dry white
wine**
**Flavouring or liqueur
(see recipe)**

Sabayons are served as an accompaniment to hot or cold desserts. They are always prepared in the same way, and with the same combination of ingredients; only the flavouring element changes, depending on the dessert it is to be served with.

Method.   In a saucepan combine the egg yolks and the sugar, and beat the mixture as for *génoise* cake (page 555). When the mixture is nearly white and forms a ribbon from the wires of the whisk, add the white wine. Then, still beating, heat the mixture in a *bain-marie* until it is like a light cream and just hot enough so that the egg yolks are beginning to cook, as *crème anglaise* (page 570). This will keep the mixture light and smooth.

At this point, pour into a bowl and let cool, whipping often, or pour into a double saucepan and keep warm.

Flavour just before serving with one of the flavourings or liqueurs: vanilla, orange or lemon sugar; $\frac{1}{2}$ glass rum, kirsch, kummel, maraschino, Grand Marnier or apricot brandy.

If the flavouring is to be wine (Madeira, port, sherry, marsala, Samos, or champagne) omit the white wine and replace with the chosen wine.

Orange, tangerine or lemon sugar

An easy method that gives very good results: rub 1 or more cubes of sugar on the skin of the fruit until all the surfaces of the sugar are covered with rind from the fruit. Then scrape the sugar with a knife and rub the rind again until you have the quantity of sugar needed; stop while the fruit still has some coloured skin left as this is the part that is flavoured.

Dessert Sauces

CHOCOLATE CREAM SAUCE
Sauce crème au chocolat

225 g (8 oz) plain
   chocolate or 100 g
   (4 oz) cocoa
6 tablespoons water
2 dl (8 fl oz) double
   cream
25 g (1 oz) unsalted
   butter

Cook the chocolate or cocoa slowly for 15 minutes with the water, stirring from time to time. Just before serving, add away from the heat the cream and the butter. Whip vigorously for 2 minutes.

Note: If cocoa is used, add 100 g (4 oz) of sugar when it is dissolved.

APRICOT SAUCE
Sauce aux abricots

For 1 l (2 pts):
700 g (1½ lb) apricot
   jam
2 dl (¼ pt) water
50 g (2 oz) sugar

Combine the ingredients in a saucepan, boil slowly for 5 minutes, skim and strain through a fine sieve, pushing through the pieces of fruit. Keep warm in a double boiler.

Flavour before using with kirsch or maraschino and vanilla.

For other sauces follow the method above, substituting the corresponding jam. For strawberry sauce, flavour with kirsch; for raspberry sauce, flavour with maraschino; for redcurrant sauce, flavour with kirsch; for orange sauce, flavour with curaçao and add one-third of apricot sauce.

CREAM SAUCE WITH PRALINE
Sauce crème pralinée

To 1 l (2 pts) of *crème anglaise* or zabaglione made with champagne, add 3 tablespoons of almonds, pastachios or hazelnuts, finely chopped, sugared and caramelized.

CHERRY SAUCE
Sauce Montmorency

225 g (8 oz) fairly acid cherries
225 g (8 oz) redcurrant jelly
Juice of 100 g (4 oz) raspberries (optional)
Juice of 2 oranges
Pinch ginger
50 g (2 oz) glacé cherries
2 tablespoons kirsch

Crush the cherries to get the juice. Put the juice into a bowl with the partially melted redcurrant jelly, made from raw currants. Add the juice of the raspberries. Then add the orange juice, ginger and glacé cherries macerated in kirsch with 1 tablespoon of warm water so that they swell.

If possible use jelly made with half raspberries, half redcurrants and omit the raspberry juice.

Blancmange

Blanc-manger or blancmange, which is a very old recipe, remains among the most delicious of desserts. Simple and French in its taste, it seems to be forgotten more and more by modern cooks, which is very regrettable. I wanted it to keep its place in this book, remembering that it is the delicate ancestor of the modern French Bavarian creams, iced puddings and so on.

225 g (8 oz) sweet almonds mixed with 2 bitter almonds
4 dl (¾ pt) single cream
100 g (4 oz) sugar loose or in cubes
½ teaspoon vanilla sugar
15 g (½ oz) gelatine
6 tablespoons double cream

Method. Blanch and skin the almonds, rinse; soak 1 hour in cold water to make them very white, drain and dry. Then pound in a mortar, moistening them, in the beginning, with 2 tablespoons of water. Slowly add the single cream in small quantities as you pound. Pour this mixture into a dishcloth or linen towel and squeeze by twisting the ends in opposite directions over a bowl.

Dissolve the sugar in this cold almond milk. Add ½ teaspoon of vanilla sugar, then the gelatine softened in a little of the cold almond milk and heated to dissolve.

The almond milk, sugar and gelatine together will be just over 3½ dl (½ pt) of liquid. When the mixture is about to set add 6 tablespoons of thick, whipped cream, lightly sweetened.

Pour the almond milk into a mould, and refrigerate exactly like a Bavarian cream. It is served in the same way.

Bavarian Cream

Bavarian cream and all the other chilled desserts that derive from it take the place of a cream or fruit ice in making up a menu.

The advantage these chilled desserts have over ice-cream is that they can be made with limited kitchen equipment. They are also always very popular.

225 g (8 oz) caster
sugar

8 egg yolks

½ l (1 pt) boiled milk
with a split vanilla
bean steeped in it,
covered, after milk
has boiled

15 g (½ oz) gelatine
softened in cold
water

½ l (1 pt) double
cream

2 tablespoons icing
or caster sugar

BAVARIAN CREAM WITH CUSTARD BASE
Bavaroises à base de crème

Follow the recipe for *crème anglaise* (page 570); while hot, add the gelatine, stir until dissolved and strain through a fine sieve into a glazed bowl.

Let the cream cool, stirring often. When it is nearly cold and starts to jell, carefully add the double cream, whipped and sweetened with 2 tablespoons of icing, preferably, or caster sugar. At the same time, add the flavouring and the chosen garnish.

Moulding. Bavarian creams are nearly always made in a ring mould with a hollow centre tube with or without decoration. If you do not have such a mould, you can use any other straight-sided, sloping-sided or ring mould. Or even more simply, a glass or silver bowl. In that case do not unmould the cream; the gelatine can be reduced by half, which increases the delicate texture of the dessert.

If the Bavarian cream is to be unmoulded, oil the mould lightly with almond oil before filling it, or coat the mould with caramel, very light in colour, which is much better.

When the mould is filled with the cream mixture, tap it lightly on a folded cloth so that the contents settle into the shape of the mould; place the mould in a bowl of crushed ice or refrigerate for at least 3 hours.

To unmould dip the mould for one second into warm water, wipe it and turn it over on to a serving platter.

The Bavarian cream can be served with a plate of small, soft vanilla and chocolate macaroons.

BAVARIAN CREAM WITH LIQUEURS
Bavaroises aux liqueurs

Grand Marnier, Cointreau, Marie-Brizard, apricot liqueur, kirsch, maraschino, rum, fine champagne brandy, plum brandy, etc.; almonds, hazelnuts, walnuts, praliné, lemon, orange, coffee, chocolate, port, Marsala, Frontignan – all may be used to flavour a base of Bavarian cream.

In the springtime Bavarian creams can be prepared with flowers such as violets, rose petals, acacia flowers, orange blossoms, elder flowers or carnations; gather them fresh and choose those with the strongest scent.

The simplest method is to steep the flowers, covered, in the boiling syrup prepared for this dessert. When they have steeped, strain the syrup through a very fine sieve and continue as for the Bavarian cream with fruit (below).

BAVARIAN CREAM WITH FRUIT
Bavaroises aux fruits

Bavarian cream based on fruit purées is made with equal parts of fresh fruit purée and sugar syrup. Combine 750 g (1 lb 10 oz) of sugar and $5\frac{1}{2}$ dl (1 pt) of water to make 1 l (2 pts) of syrup, and follow the instructions on page 628. For 1 l (2 pts) of fruit and syrup, add the juice of 3 lemons or 3 oranges, 30 g (1 oz) of gelatine softened in cold water and dissolved in the hot syrup, and $\frac{1}{2}$ l (1 pt) of whipped cream.

The method is the same as for the basic Bavarian cream above. When the sugar syrup has cooled and is close to setting because of the gelatine, add the fruit purée, the lemon or orange juice, and then the cream.

The best fruits to use are: strawberries, raspberries, blackberries, pineapple, peaches, apricots, bananas, cherries and melon. All these fruits must be very ripe to obtain the maximum flavour. Here is another simple recipe.

NECTARINE BAVARIAN CREAM
Bavaroise nectarine

30 ripe nectarines or
  peaches
225 g (8 oz) sugar
  (caster, icing or
  loaf)
18 g ($\frac{3}{4}$ oz) gelatine
2 tablespoons kirsch
3 dl ($\frac{1}{2}$ pt) double
  cream, whipped
6 tablespoons light
  sugar syrup
30 strawberries,
  hulled
Redcurrant jelly

Remove the skins and the stones of the ripe, very fruity peaches or nectarines; put the fruit into a large bowl with half the sugar (preferably loaf sugar). Mix carefully, cover with a cloth and place in a cool place to macerate for 30 minutes. Stir from time to time.

Then pour the fruit into a fine sieve placed over a bowl and rub through to make a purée, to which you add the remaining sugar.

Soften the gelatine in cold water and then dissolve in $\frac{1}{4}$ cup of hot water and add, stirring, to the fruit purée. Mix without stopping until the gelatine starts to set.

At this point, add to the mixture 1 tablespoon of kirsch and the whipped cream. Mould following the directions given above, and refrigerate.

While the mould is chilling, bring the light sugar syrup to the boil; remove from the heat, pour in 1 tablespoon of kirsch and add the strawberries. Stir to coat the fruit, cover, let cool and refrigerate immediately.

To serve, unmould the Bavarian cream, following the instructions above, on to a round platter. Surround it with a circle of glazed strawberries. Coat everything with redcurrant jelly, made with raw fruit, partially melted and diluted with a few tablespoons of the syrup from the strawberries. Serve with a tray of almond *tuiles* (page 565).

CANDICE AND STÉPHANIE'S DREAM
Rêverie Candice et Stéphanie

1 Genoa cake (*pain de Gênes*) about 25–30 cm (10–12 inches) in diameter (page 560)

Maraschino

¼ l (½ pt) cream

125 g (5 oz) caster sugar

1 teaspoon cornflour

4 egg yolks

25 g (1 oz) gelatine

Cube sugar rubbed on orange skin

150 g (6 oz) wild strawberries

75 g (3 oz) raspberries

75 g (3 oz) wild blackberries

225 g (8 oz) icing sugar

1 tablespoon maraschino or kirsch

20 g (⅔ oz) gelatine

3 tablespoons hot light sugar syrup

¼ l (½ pt) double cream, whipped and sugared like *crème* Chantilly (page 569)

Crystallized violets (page 630)

Prepare and cook a Genoa cake about 25–30 cm (10–12 inches) in diameter; soak with maraschino. Refrigerate.

Make a *crème anglaise* (for method see page 570) with the cream, caster sugar, cornflour, 4 egg yolks, and 10 g (⅓ oz) softened gelatine; cook until the cream coats a spoon and then strain through a very fine sieve into a bowl. Stir in until completely cool. Flavour with a cube of sugar rubbed on an orange skin.

At this point it will begin to set. Pour the cream into a ring mould at least 6 cm (2½ inches) smaller than the diameter of the cake. Cool the cream on a bed of crushed ice, turning and tipping the mould so that the cream coats the inside completely. Refrigerate.

Pick over and hull the strawberries, raspberries and wild blackberries, freshly gathered. Collect the berries in a bowl and sprinkle with icing sugar. Moisten with 1 tablespoon of maraschino or kirsch. Mix with a silver spoon, cover with a cloth and macerate in the refrigerator for 15 minutes. Pour into a fine sieve placed over a large bowl and rub all the fruit through the sieve.

Mix this fruit purée with:

20 g (⅔ oz) of gelatine softened in cold water, then dissolved in 3 tablespoons of hot light sugar syrup, and at the moment when the gelatine is setting, add:

1 cup of whipped *crème fraîche*, sugared like *crème* Chantilly.

Pour this fruit cream into the mould coated with the custard cream and refrigerate for at least 3 hours.

To serve place the cake on a round platter large enough to accommodate the garnish; dip the mould into hot water, wipe and turn over on to the cake. At the base of the Bavarian cream place a row of crystallized violets; and around the edge of the cake place a row of blackberries rolled in sugar.

Serve with a bowl of redcurrant jelly partially melted, and a plate of shortbread biscuits (page 563).

½ l (1 pt) boiled milk
with a split vanilla
bean steeped in it,
covered, after milk
has boiled
5 egg yolks
225 g (8 oz) sugar
25 g (1 oz) gelatine
50 g (2 oz)
  crystallized fruit
100 g (4 oz) sponge
  fingers (page 559)
100 g (4 oz) raisins
Macaroons
Rind ¼ lemon

ICED PUDDING
Pudding glacé du prélat
For 6 people

While the vanilla bean is steeping in the hot milk (for 15 minutes), combine the egg yolks and the sugar in a bowl and beat the mixture with a wooden spoon until it is white and creamy; beat in the hot milk. Return to the saucepan and heat slowly, stirring, to boiling point; do not let boil. The mixture will thicken, becoming smooth, and coat the wooden spoon. Add the gelatine, softened in cold water; as soon as it has dissolved, strain the cream through a very fine sieve and set aside in a bowl.

Choose a charlotte mould or a ring mould. Oil the inside with almond oil or very pure olive oil that is absolutely tasteless.

Arrange the preserved fruit, quartered or diced, on the bottom of the mould in an attractive pattern; on top arrange the sponge fingers, each cut into 6 pieces. Then, over the whole, sprinkle the raisins dipped in lukewarm water, seeded and dried; then the macaroons, crumbled into small pieces; on top of them, a pinch of chopped lemon rind. Repeat these layers until all the ingredients are used, pouring in the hot custard in small quantities to soak the pieces of cake and the pieces of macaroon, which, as they slowly absorb the custard, will settle in the mould and not rise to the top. It is important that the custard, the cake and the fruit should be equally distributed in the mould all the way up.

Let the mould cool, then refrigerate or place it in crushed ice for 7 hours.

Unmoulding the pudding is quite easy: slide the blade of a knife all round the edges of the mould or dip the mould into a bowl of hot water. Turn the mould over on a large platter and cover the pudding completely with some of the following raspberry sauce.

Raspberry sauce

Raspberry sauce:
225 g (8 oz) very ripe
  raspberries
6 tablespoons sugar
1 teaspoon lemon juice
1 tablespoon kirsch
6 tablespoons thick
  whipped cream

Rub very ripe raspberries through a fine sieve, removing the stems. Put the juice and the pulp in a glazed bowl; avoid letting them touch metal or tin, which would darken the juice.

In a saucepan combine 6 tablespoons of sugar, 3 tablespoons of water and 1 teaspoon of lemon juice and bring to the boil; skim and continue cooking until a drop of the syrup put on a plate will harden without running, keeping its round shape.

Then pour the raspberry pulp into the syrup, mix with a silver spoon and remove from the heat immediately without boiling the raspberries, which would lose their flavour.

Pour into a glazed bowl, cool, then refrigerate.

When the sauce is quite cold, add kirsch and whipped cream.

Serve the extra raspberry sauce in a glass bowl; it should be a strong, beautiful red.

This recipe for iced pudding finishes the series of Bavarian creams. It is included here because it is closer to a cream then a real pudding.

Charlottes

APPLE CHARLOTTE
Charlotte reine du Canada

1 kg (2 lb) large sweet eating apples
3 tablespoons sugar
50 g (2 oz) butter, plus melted butter
1 vanilla bean
Zest ½ lemon
2 tablespoons dry white wine
1 loaf white bread, crust removed
4 tablespoons apricot jam, rubbed through a sieve

Peel the apples, quarter, core and place in a saucepan. Sprinkle the sugar and butter, cut into pieces, on top; bury the vanilla bean, quartered, and the lemon zest among the apples and add the white wine. Cook slowly, stirring often, on a high flame to produce a thick apple sauce; remove from the heat, mix in the strained apricot jam and cool.

Thickly butter the bottom and sides of a charlotte mould (straight-sided). Cut part of the bread into slices 6 mm (¼ inch) thick, and from these slices cut a dozen triangles of a size that will completely cover the bottom of the mould. Dip one side of each triangle into melted butter and place the triangles to form a rosette in the bottom of the mould, putting the buttered side down against the bottom of the mould.

Then cut most of the remaining bread into slices 1 cm (½ inch) thick and cut the slices into rectangles 4 cm (1½ inches) wide and at least 2 cm (¾ inch) longer than the height of the mould, unless the mould is very deep – in that case, cut them to fit.

Proceed as for the bottom of the mould; dip each rectangle of bread into melted butter and apply them, overlapping, to the sides of the mould.

Fill the mould with the apple sauce, removing the vanilla bean and the lemon zest, and cover the top with a round slice of bread about 6 mm (¼ inch) thick dipped into melted butter; place the buttered side of the bread towards the apple sauce. This round covering of bread can be made in two pieces.

Place the charlotte in a 425°F (220°C, gas mark 7) oven to brown the bread immediately to keep it from getting soggy. Cook for 40 minutes.

Let stand at least 15 minutes before unmoulding; then serve immediately.

STRAWBERRY CHARLOTTE
Charlotte de la Saint-Jean

125 g (5 oz) wild strawberries mixed with 1 tablespoon raspberries

2 tablespoons sugar

2 tablespoons kirsch

$\frac{1}{4}$ l ($\frac{1}{2}$ pt) milk

125 g (5 oz) caster sugar

4 egg yolks

$\frac{1}{2}$ vanilla bean

15 g ($\frac{1}{2}$ oz) gelatine

225 g (8 oz) sponge fingers (page 559)

$\frac{1}{4}$ l ($\frac{1}{2}$ pt) double cream, whipped

Large strawberries and raspberries all the same size, for garnish

Candied angelica

Remove the stems from the berries and place them in a bowl with the sugar and the kirsch; mix carefully, and let stand for 45 minutes.

With the milk, sugar, egg yolks and vanilla, prepare a *crème anglaise* (page 570).

As soon as the custard coats a wooden spoon, strain through a fine sieve into a glazed bowl, add the gelatine softened in cold water and stir until completely cool.

While the cream cools, trim the sponge fingers so that the sides and the ends are cut neatly; cover the bottom of a charlotte mould with a round piece of buttered paper, and on it place the sponge fingers, cut into triangles, to form a rosette. Line the sides of the mould with the sponge fingers, placed side by side, very close together. The curved side of the biscuits should be placed against the mould, so it will show when unmoulded.

When the custard is cold and starts to stiffen because of the gelatine, fold in the whipped cream, lightly sweetened, then the fruit.

Pour the custard into the mould; sprinkle the trimmings from the sponge fingers on top, and refrigerate for at least 4 hours.

To serve, unmould the charlotte at the last moment on to a round platter covered with a fine doily; remove the paper and around the base of the charlotte place strawberries and raspberries, like a ring of large rubies. In the centre of the charlotte stick three diamond-shaped leaves cut from a piece of candied angelica.

325 g (11 oz) caster
  sugar
3 eggs
100 g (4 oz) sifted
  flour
50 g (2 oz) unsalted
  butter, melted
1 teaspoon vanilla
  sugar
3 macaroons, crushed
300 g (10 oz) *marrons
  glacés* pieces
25 g (1 oz) unsalted
  butter
4 dl ($\frac{3}{4}$ pt) double
  cream, whipped
  and sugared like
  crème Chantilly
  (page 569)
Vanilla
Large *marrons glacés*

CHESTNUT CHARLOTTE
Charlotte de la Saint-Martin

Prepare a madeleine dough (for method see page 557) with 125 g (5 oz) of sugar, 3 eggs, the sifted flour, melted butter and 1 teaspoon of vanilla sugar. Add 3 crushed macaroons at the same time as the flour. Bake this cake in a square 20- or 23-cm (8- or 9-inch) mould, buttered and floured. Let stand at least 2 days.

With 150 g (6 oz) of sugar and 1 cup of water, make a syrup and boil for 2 minutes.

With pieces of *marrons glacés* and one-third of the syrup, make a purée, first softening the chestnuts, then mashing them with 25 g (1 oz) of butter.

Moulding.   Place a round piece of white paper in the bottom of a 1-litre (2-pt) charlotte mould.

Cut the cake into rectangles the height of the mould and 3 cm (1$\frac{1}{4}$ inches) wide by 6 mm ($\frac{1}{4}$ inch) thick.

Line the sides of the mould, overlapping the pieces until the mould is completely lined.

Whip the double cream; add sugar as for *crème* Chantilly, and flavour with vanilla.

When the cream is stiff and has doubled its volume, put one-third into the refrigerator.

Beat the chestnut purée with a wooden spatula and add the remaining syrup to thin it. When the purée is smooth, add the remaining two-thirds of the whipped cream. This mixture should be folded in carefully, lifting the purée.

Pour the purée into the mould, sprinkle 1 tablespoon of cake crumbs on top, and refrigerate for at least 3 hours.

To serve, place a fine doily on a round platter and unmould the dessert a few minutes before serving.

Remove the round piece of paper; and in its place pipe a decoration with the refrigerated whipped cream, using a pastry bag with a fluted tube.

At the edge of the charlotte, make a circle of large *marrons glacés*, set in small fluted paper cups.

Note: This very rich dessert sets because of the butter mixed with the chestnut purée.

**20 sponge fingers
(page 559)**

**100 g (4 oz) caster
sugar**

4 egg yolks

**2 dl ($\frac{1}{4}$ pt) milk or
half and half milk
and double cream**

1 vanilla bean

6 g ($\frac{1}{4}$ oz) gelatine

**3 dl ($\frac{1}{2}$ pt) whipped
cream**

2 tablespoons sugar

**$\frac{1}{2}$ teaspoon vanilla
sugar**

Charlotte à la russe

The outside of this dessert is the same as for the Charlotte de la Saint-Jean. Follow the recipe (above).

A 1$\frac{1}{2}$-l (3-pt) charlotte mould will require about 20 sponge fingers.

Before placing the sponge fingers, it is a good idea to line the sides and the bottom of the mould with white paper, a round piece at the bottom and a strip for the sides.

The fingers should be 1–2 cm ($\frac{1}{2}$–$\frac{3}{4}$ inch) higher than the mould. They should all be cut the same length so that the charlotte balances when unmoulded.

Fill the inside of the mould with a *crème anglaise* (page 570) made with 100 g (4 oz) of sugar, 4 egg yolks, the milk, or milk and cream, and a vanilla bean.

When the custard coats the wooden spoon, remove immediately from the heat and add the gelatine, softened in cold water; stir until dissolved.

Strain the mixture through a fine sieve into a glazed bowl as soon as the gelatine is completely mixed.

Let the custard cool on ice or refrigerate, stirring often. As soon as it starts to set, carefully add the whipped cream flavoured with 2 tablespoons of sugar and $\frac{1}{2}$ teaspoon of vanilla sugar.

Pour the mixture into the lined mould, filling it to the top. Smooth the surface with a knife blade and sprinkle with a pinch of cake crumbs; refrigerate for at least 2 hours

To serve unmould on a round platter covered with a fine doily.

Note: The above custard can be replaced by a Saint-Honoré cream (page 572).

Charlotte Chantilly

This recipe has the advantage of being prepared quickly. Line the charlotte mould the same way as for the charlotte *à la russe* (above). This part can be done in advance.

A few minutes before serving the dessert, in a glazed bowl set in a bowl of ice, whip $\frac{1}{2}$ l (1 pt) of double cream, adding 125 g (5 oz) of icing sugar and 1 teaspoon of vanilla sugar.

Fill the mould to the brim and sprinkle cake crumbs on top; unmould the dessert on a round platter lined with a doily. Serve immediately.

RASPBERRY CHARLOTTE
Charlotte Antonin Carême

Follow the recipe for the charlotte *à la russe*, and add to the custard ½ cup of raspberry purée before adding the whipped cream.

Select some large raspberries all the same size; macerate in kirsch, drain on a plate and one by one sprinkle heavily with granulated sugar, which will give the fruit a crystallized coating. Unmould the charlotte on a round silver platter and surround the base with a row of the raspberries.

Hot Puddings

PEACH AND RASPBERRY SOUFFLÉ/PUDDING
Pudding soufflé Victoire

225 g (8 oz) unsalted butter
10 egg yolks
225 g (8 oz) caster sugar
3 tablespoons peach purée
3 tablespoons raspberry purée
6 egg whites, beaten stiff
Sponge cake
Banyuls or Frontignan wine
Raspberries
Redcurrant jelly
1 tablespoon champagne brandy

In a bowl soften the butter to a paste, then add the egg yolks, one by one, beating the mixture until each is absorbed. Then add the sugar; continue working with a wooden spatula until the cream is frothy and white.

At this point add the very fine peach purée and raspberry purée; finish by adding the egg whites. For this last step fold the egg whites into the mixture, lifting with the spatula each time. The difficulty, easily eliminated with a little experience, is to get a well-blended mixture without allowing the egg whites to fall.

Thickly butter a mould with a hollow tube in the centre and fill it with the mixture in layers. In between the layers, sprinkle some pieces of sponge cake dipped into a few tablespoons of very good quality Banyuls or Frontignan dessert wine.

Place the mould in a *bain-marie* and poach in a 375°F (190°C, gas mark 5) oven for 25–30 minutes. When the pudding is done, it is slightly resistant to light pressure with the back of a spoon or any other utensil.

Unmould on a round platter and garnish the centre of the pudding with raspberries coated with partially melted redcurrant jelly flavoured with 1 tablespoon of Banyuls or Frontignan wine mixed with 1 tablespoon of fine champagne brandy.

150 g (6 oz) unsalted
butter
150 g (6 oz) sugar
1 teaspoon vanilla
sugar
150 g (6 oz) sifted
flour
$\frac{1}{2}$ l (1 pt) boiled milk
with a split vanilla
bean steeped in it
and cooled
Pinch salt
9 eggs, separated

VANILLA PUDDING WITH CHOCOLATE SAUCE
Pudding de l'Aiglon

In a heavy, slightly heated saucepan, soften the butter. With a wooden spoon, work in the sugar and vanilla sugar; then add the softened flour. Moisten this dough with the vanilla milk. Add a pinch of salt, heat slowly, stirring constantly with a wooden spatula. The mixture should be very smooth. Keep on the flame until the dough dries up and detaches itself from the pan, as for chou pastry.

Remove the saucepan from the heat, let cool; then beat in the egg yolks one by one. Then following the recipe for a soufflé omelette (page 615), add the egg whites, beaten stiff.

Pour the mixture into a well-buttered soufflé dish or a charlotte mould and poach in a *bain-marie* in a 375°F (190°C, gas mark 5) oven for 30–35 minutes.

Check whether the pudding is done by pressing the top lightly.

During the baking be careful not to subject the pudding to high heat in the beginning, or a crust will form on top that would prevent the heat from penetrating inside the pudding. Protect the top from the heat, if necessary, with a piece of buttered paper.

Unmould on a warm round platter; then coat the pudding with a hot chocolate cream (page 578) mixed with the same amount of *crème* Chantilly or with the sauce in the recipe below.

Serve the remaining chocolate sauce separately in a silver sauce-boat, and a plate of cats' tongues (page 564).

Chocolate sauce

Chocolate sauce for
desserts:
225 g (8 oz) milk
chocolate
6 tablespoons thick
whipped cream
Vanilla sugar or a
vanilla bean

Break the milk chocolate into small pieces; melt with 2–3 table-spoons of water. Make an absolutely smooth thin paste, then add 2 dl ($\frac{1}{4}$ pt) of water.

Cook slowly for 15 minutes to produce a syrup with the consistency of a custard cream; just before serving, add the whipped cream. Flavour with vanilla, either with vanilla sugar or by cooking a vanilla bean with the chocolate.

ALMOND PUDDING
Pudding Henry Clos-Jouve
For 8 people

75 g (3 oz) sweet
almonds and 1
bitter almond,
freshly skinned
¼ l (½ pt) single cream
or milk
Zest 1 lemon
75 g (3 oz) tapioca
Pinch salt
6 eggs, separated
50 g (2 oz) unsalted
butter
100 g (4 oz) caster
sugar
Caramel (page 574)
Sabayon sauce (page 577)
Praline (page 630)
Macaroons
Red sugared almonds

Make almond milk by soaking the almonds in water so they become very white. Then drain, dry and crush in a mortar, moistening from time to time with a few drops of water so that they do not become too oily. To this paste add the cream or milk. Collect the thinned paste in a cheesecloth and squeeze all the liquid into a saucepan. Heat the almond milk and steep the zest of 1 lemon in it for 5 minutes. Remove the zest, boil the milk and pour in the tapioca, stirring with a wooden spoon. Add the salt. After boiling for 3 minutes remove from the heat. The mixture should then be a thick paste; pour it into a large bowl.

Immediately add the 6 egg yolks, one by one, then the butter and the sugar, beating the mixture vigorously with a wooden spoon. The mixture should soften, becoming lighter and smooth like baba dough.

Just before cooking the dessert, beat the 6 egg whites until stiff and fold them into the dough, following the classic recipe for soufflé omelette (page 615).

Immediately pour the mixture into a charlotte mould lined with very pale caramel. The mould should be half filled.

Place the mould in a deep *bain-marie* so that the water reaches three-quarters of the way up the mould. Poach in a 325°F (170°C, gas mark 3) oven for 45 minutes. The pudding should not be subjected to very high heat; protect the top of the dessert with paper while baking.

To serve unmould on a hot round platter.

Pour all around a few tablespoons of sabayon sauce, very creamy and made with half almond milk, half champagne and 1 tablespoon of praline or crushed macaroons. Serve the remaining sabayon in a glass bowl and serve with it a plate of soft macaroons glazed with vanilla icing.

Just before serving, sprinkle a good pinch of red sugared almonds, coarsely crushed, over the pudding; on top of the bowl of sabayon sprinkle 2 additional tablespoonfuls. Just before serving the first guest, mix the sugared almonds with the pudding before the sugar has time to melt. It is delightful to crunch the pleasantly flavoured sugar while eating the pudding.

RAISIN PUDDING WITH RUM
Pudding Gaston Lenôtre
For 8 people

½ l (1 pt) milk
Zest ½ lemon
100 g (4 oz) cornflour
50 g (2 oz) caster
   sugar
Pinch salt
25 g (1 oz) unsalted
   butter
3 eggs
50 g (2 oz) raisins
50 g (2 oz) currants
1 tablespoon rum

Sauce:
1 teaspoon cornflour
6 tablespoons
   redcurrant jelly
25 g (1 oz) sugar
Rum

Boil the milk, steeping the lemon peel in it and being careful the bitter white pith is removed.

When the milk is cooled, remove the lemon peel and mix the liquid with the cornflour, sugar and salt. Add the butter, cut into pieces, and heat to boiling point, stirring constantly with a wooden spatula.

The mixture will thicken until it forms a dough similar to chou pastry. Continue cooking until the dough is dry enough to detach itself easily from the sides of the saucepan and the spoon.

Remove from the heat, and after waiting a couple of minutes for the dough to cool slightly, add the eggs, one by one, beating vigorously after each addition to make the dough very smooth and light.

Then add the raisins and currants, washed in warm water, drained carefully and dried; then the rum.

Beat the dough for another few minutes, as for baba dough, to aerate it completely. Thickly butter a charlotte mould, dust with flour and shake out the excess. Pour in the mixture, filling the mould to two-thirds of its capacity; shake the mould to settle the dough; place in a deep *bain-marie* in a 325°F (170°C, gas mark 3) oven, avoiding any sudden rise in heat. Cook for about 1 hour.

To serve unmould the pudding on a hot round platter and pass the following sauce, prepared 8–10 minutes before serving.

In a flame-proof porcelain or enamel pan, mix 1 teaspoon of cornflour in ½ cup of water; add 25 g (1 oz) of sugar and 6 table-spoons of redcurrant jelly.

Heat slowly, without boiling, to produce a mixture with the consistency of syrup; remove from the heat, add a little rum and serve in a sauceboat.

35 g (1½ oz) almonds, plus 1 bitter almond
3 dl (½ pt) boiled milk with a split vanilla bean steeped in it, covered, for 20 minutes after milk has boiled
125 g (5 oz) butter
100 g (4 oz) caster sugar
75 g (3 oz) cornflour
6 egg yolks
Sabayon sauce (page 577) or vanilla custard (recipe below)

TOASTED ALMOND PUDDING
Pudding mousseline de la vieille Catherine
For 8 people

Skin the almonds by plunging them into boiling water. Let stand in the water for 5–6 minutes, drain, spread on a cloth, and taking them one by one between your thumb and forefinger, squeeze each almond, which will be forced out of its skin. Then wash the almonds in cold water, drain and dry in a dishcloth. Sort out the larger ones and cut them into thin slices lengthwise. Spread the almond slices in a pie tin.

Chop the remaining almonds very fine and spread them also in a pie tin. Place both almond pans in a hot oven, leaving the door ajar. Watch the almonds closely: they will first dry then toast. Stir often and remove from the oven as soon as the nuts are uniformly light brown. Set aside.

Meanwhile, soften the butter, kneading it in a dishcloth. Use 25 g (1 oz) to butter the mould and place the remaining butter, exactly 100 g (4 oz) in a 3-l (6-pt) saucepan. In a warm place work the butter to a paste with a wooden spoon. Add the sugar; beat the paste again until it becomes white and creamy, add the cornflour, then dilute the paste, little by little, with the vanilla milk.

Put on the stove; heat slowly, stirring continuously. It will thicken little by little up to boiling point; remove from the fire and beat in, one by one, 6 egg yolks. Then add the toasted chopped almonds. Spoon into the mould, filling it two-thirds full. Shake the pudding to level the top.

Place the mould in a deep *bain-marie*, cover with a lid, and bake in a 425°F (220°C, gas mark 7) oven for 40 minutes. Remove the lid towards the end of the cooking time.

Remove from the oven; let stand 5 minutes in the *bain-marie*, then unmould on to a warm round platter, wiping the mould before this last step. Coat the pudding with the following custard or with a sabayon and sprinkle with sliced toasted almonds.

Custard:

3 dl (½ pt) milk
  boiled with a
  vanilla bean
75 g (3 oz) sugar
3 egg yolks
I tablespoon
  cornflour
I teaspoon kirsch or
  rum

Custard

Boil the milk flavoured with vanilla; when cool pour in slowly, stirring, a mixture of the sugar, 3 yolks and cornflour. Heat slowly, stirring constantly, and as soon as the custard starts to boil, remove from the heat immediately.

Just before using the cream, flavour with I teaspoon of kirsch or rum.

125 g (5 oz) semolina
¼ l (½ pt) milk
¼ l (½ pt) single cream
75 g (3 oz) sugar
Pinch salt
100 g (4 oz) unsalted
  butter
4 egg yolks
I tablespoon
  chopped pistachios
3 egg whites, beaten
  stiff
Macédoine of fruit
Apricot jam
  flavoured with
  maraschino

SEMOLINA PUDDING WITH PISTACHIOS AND FRUIT
Pudding Ile-de-France

Pour the semolina into a boiling liquid made with milk, cream, sugar and salt. Heat, stirring with a wooden spoon until the mixture reaches boiling point; add a knob of butter, cover with a lid, then cook in a 300°F (150°C, gas mark 2) oven about 30 minutes.

When cooked, put the semolina into a bowl, without scraping the saucepan. Thicken with 4 egg yolks, adding them one by one, and the remaining butter, cut into small pieces. Work the mixture with a spatula to make it smooth; add the chopped pistachios, and fold in 3 egg whites beaten stiff.

Butter a mould with a hollow tube in the centre, fill two-thirds full with the mixture and bake in a *bain-marie* in a 325°F (170°C, gas mark 3) oven for 20 minutes.

Unmould when ready to serve on a warm round platter, and place in the centre of the pudding a macédoine of fruit cooked in syrup and mixed with a few tablespoons of apricot jam flavoured with maraschino.

Serve with a sauceboat of sabayon sauce (page 577) made with one part apricot jam flavoured with maraschino to four parts sabayon.

225 g (8 oz) unsalted
  butter
150 g (6 oz) sugar
150 g (6 oz) sifted
  flour
½ l (1 pt) boiled milk,
  lukewarm
2 cubes sugar
1 orange or lemon
8 egg yolks
6 egg whites
Sabayon sauce (page
  577)

LEMON OR ORANGE PUDDING
Pudding au citron ou à l'orange

In a saucepan, near the stove, soften the butter, and work it
with a wooden spoon. Beat in the sugar and the flour. Dilute with
the milk. Bring the mixture to the boil, stirring, then dry the
dough as for chou pastry.

Remove from the heat and immediately add 2 cubes of sugar
that have been rubbed on the rind of a lemon or an orange, to
soak the sugar with the flavour of the fruit rind; beat in the
yolks, one by one, then fold in the whites, beaten very firm.

Pour the mixture into a charlotte mould or a ring mould,
thickly buttered, and bake in a *bain-marie* in a 325°F (170°C, gas
mark 3) oven for 30–35 minutes.

Unmould on to a warm round platter; serve with a sabayon
sauce flavoured with lemon or orange and a plate of almond
tuiles (page 565).

PUDDING WITH PORT
Pudding au porto

Follow the recipe for the pudding Ile-de-France (above). Before
folding in the stiffly beaten egg whites, add 1 tablespoon of port.
Fill a buttered ring mould one-third; sprinkle small pieces of
sponge cake soaked in port over the mixture, cover with an
equal quantity of the mixture and bake in a *bain-marie* in a 325°F
(170°C, gas mark 3) oven for 20 minutes.

Just before serving, unmould the pudding and coat with a
sabayon sauce flavoured with port and with cubes of sugar rubbed
on an orange skin; add one-quarter of its volume of *crème
Chantilly* (page 569). Serve with the pudding the remaining
sabayon sauce and a plate of currant biscuits (page 564).

Note: The port can be replaced with a French dessert wine –
Frontignan, Banyuls, Château-Yquem, etc.

FRENCH CHRISTMAS PUDDING
Pudding de Noël à la française

500 g (1 lb) *marrons glacés* pieces, crushed fine and flavoured with vanilla

100 g (4 oz) unsalted butter

Few tablespoons double cream

8 egg yolks

6 egg whites, beaten very stiff

Chocolate macaroons with apricot jam

Crush the pieces of *marrons glacés* fine and flavour with vanilla and work in the butter. Dilute this paste with a few tablespoons of cream, until it is like chou pastry.

Pour this purée into a sieve placed on top of a bowl and rub the chestnuts through with a pestle. Beat with a wooden spatula, add 8 egg yolks and fold in 6 egg whites, beaten very stiff.

Fill a well-buttered charlotte mould two-thirds, and bake in a *bain-marie* in a 325°F (170°C, gas mark 3) oven for 30 minutes.

Unmould to serve, and coat the pudding with a chocolate cream sauce (page 578).

Serve with a sauceboat of chocolate sauce and a plate of soft chocolate macaroons sandwiched together with a little thickened apricot jam.

CUSTARD PUDDING
Pudding à la crème

25 g (1 oz) each sultanas and currants, washed in lukewarm water

3 tablespoons candied fruit, diced small

½ glass kirsch, rum or Grand Marnier

Angelica and candied cherries

6 sponge fingers (page 559), cut in half lengthwise, then in half horizontally, and soaked in the same liqueur

Apricot jam

½ l (1 pt) *crème renversée* mixture (page 574)

Sabayon sauce (page 577) or *crème anglaise* (page 570)

Macerate the sultanas and currants and the candied fruit in the kirsch, rum or Grand Marnier. Carefully butter a ring mould and decorate the inside with angelica and candied cherries. Spread on top the half sponge fingers, then sprinkle on some raisins and fruit, macerated and well drained. Place teaspoons of apricot jam here and there, and continue, alternating the sponge fingers and the fruit.

Pour in the prepared *crème renversée*, a little at a time, so that the sponge fingers will soak it up and not dislodge the garnish.

When the mould is full, bake in a *bain-marie* in a 325°F (170°C, gas mark 3) oven for about 40 minutes, with the same precautions as for the *crème renversée*.

Let stand for 10 minutes before unmoulding, and serve hot with a sabayon sauce flavoured with vanilla or port or with a *crème anglaise*.

100 g (4 oz) candied
  orange peel, diced
100 g (4 oz) candied
  lemon peel, diced
25 g (1 oz) crystallized
  ginger, diced
225 g (8 oz) peeled
  and chopped apples
500 g (1 lb) mixed
  raisins, sultanas and
  currants, washed in
  lukewarm water
  and dried
½ glass rum, plus
  extra rum
250 g (9 oz) white
  bread, crusts
  removed
125 g (5 oz) sifted flour
500 g (1 lb) chopped
  beef suet
350 g (12 oz) brown
  sugar
100 g (4 oz) chopped
  blanched almonds
Juice of ¼ lemon
Juice of ¼ orange
½ teaspoon chopped
  lemon and orange
  peel
Large pinch mixed
  spices with extra
  cinnamon and
  nutmeg
2 eggs
½ glass Madeira
½ glass cognac
1½ teaspoons salt
1 glass beer
Crème anglaise (page
  570), flavoured with
  rum (optional)
Sugar

ENGLISH PLUM PUDDING
Pudding à l'anglaise

Macerate all the fruit in the rum for 2 hours.

Combine all the ingredients in a bowl and mix well.

Pack this mixture into china pudding bowls. Or grease a dish-cloth soaked in cold water, dust it with flour and wrap it around a ball of the mixture; close the dishcloth, gather the ends and tie securely, bringing the string around the ball to hold it tightly. If using bowls cover with white paper and then wrap in a cloth.

Place the bowl or ball in boiling water and simmer for 3 hours.

Take out the pudding and let drain and cool. Remove from the bowls or dishcloth, cut into 6-mm (¼-inch) slices, and place them on a very hot platter. Set in a hot oven for a few minutes. Sprinkle with sugar and pour on some heated rum; ignite the rum at the table to flame it, or serve with a hot custard cream flavoured with rum.

Serve on very hot plates.

Note: In England of course plum pudding is prepared many days in advance; it is also served whole, reheated in its bowl in simmering water for 20 minutes.

GERMAN BREAD PUDDING
Pudding à l'allemande

150 g (6 oz) rye
  bread, crusts
  removed
½ l (1 pt) Moselle or
  Rhine wine or beer
100 g (4 oz) brown
  sugar
2 eggs and 3 yolks
Large pinch
  cinnamon
100 g (4 oz) melted
  unsalted butter
3 egg whites, beaten
  stiff
Breadcrumbs
Apricot syrup (page
  578)

Soak the bread in the wine or beer with the sugar, then rub through a sieve. Collect the mixture in a bowl, and slowly add the whole eggs, the yolks, the cinnamon, the butter, and then fold in the beaten whites of eggs.

Butter a kugelhupf mould (a deep ring mould), line with fine breadcrumbs, fill with the mixture and bake in a *bain-marie* in a 325°F (170°C, gas mark 3) oven for 35 minutes.

Unmould on a hot round platter and serve with apricot syrup.

Note: I have already mentioned a French pudding, *Pudding glacé du prélat*, in the section on Bavarian creams (page 584).

Rice desserts

In desserts rice can be the main ingredient or an accompaniment. In either case it is cooked in the same way.

Use long grain rice such as Carolina or Patna rice. Wash it in several changes of cold water until it drains clear; blanch it by placing it in boiling water, then drain and wash it again in lukewarm water, and drain completely. Then cook it.

First method

4 dl (¾ pt) milk
1 vanilla bean
Zest of orange or
  lemon
Pinch salt
100 g (4 oz) rice
3 egg yolks
1 tablespoon cream or
  boiled milk
25 g (1 oz) unsalted
  butter
50 g (2 oz) sugar

Boil the milk with the vanilla bean, and the orange or lemon zest and salt; boil 10 minutes, remove the bean and zest, scatter in the rice and stir with a wooden spoon; when the milk boils again, cover. Bake in a 325°F (170°C, gas mark 3) oven for 35 minutes. Do not stir the rice. Remove from the oven and let cool slightly; then add the yolks, diluted with the cream or boiled milk, and mix in the butter cut into small pieces. Mix the yolks and butter into the rice carefully with a fork, in order not to break the grains of rice.

The sugar is sprinkled on the rice when it is removed from the oven before adding the eggs. If it is added to the milk in the beginning, it prevents the rice cooking perfectly.

Second method

Only the manner of cooking is different from the first method.
The rice is first blanched, washed and drained, as explained above.
Pour in ½ cup of boiling milk with 1 tablespoon of butter and a
pinch of salt. Stir and continue boiling slowly, covered. When all
the milk is absorbed and the rice puffs out with liquid, add a
second ½ cup of boiling milk and continue in the same way until
all the milk is used. Stir the mixture each time carefully with a
fork.

After the rice is cooked, add the sugar and thicken with the
egg yolks as explained in the first method.

This second method of cooking rice will give a creamier
dessert and is preferable to the first method. It is based on a common Italian method of making desserts in the domestic kitchen.

RICE CAKE
Gâteau de riz

Prepare dessert rice, cooked and thickened as described above;
add 50 g (2 oz) of mixed sultanas and currants, cleaned by rubbing
them in a cloth dusted with flour and then in a coarse sieve to rub
off the stems and shake away any debris.

Beat 3 egg whites very stiff, then fold in the rice. The flavouring
(orange or lemon, or kirsch, rum, etc.) is added at the same time
as the sultanas and currants.

Pour the rice in a 1-l (2-pt) mould lined with a very thin layer of
pastry (*pâte à foncer fine*, page 536), or with caramel (page 574),
or simply buttered carefully.

Bake in a 375°F (190°C, gas mark 5) oven for 45 minutes.

Protect the top of the cake from the heat either with the lid of
the mould or with buttered paper. Test to see if the cake is done
by inserting a needle, which should come out clean and very hot.

Remove from the oven and let stand for about 10 minutes
before unmoulding on a round plate.

Serve this dessert warm rather than hot, with a syrup or custard
sauce.

RICE CAKE WITH CARAMEL
Gâteau de riz au caramel

Follow the recipe above. Line the mould with caramel; flavour the rice with vanilla and lemon peel. Serve with a caramel syrup or with a custard flavoured with caramel syrup.

RICE CAKE WITH SABAYON SAUCE
Gâteau de riz au sabayon

Follow the recipe above. Line the mould with pastry (*pâte à foncer fine*, page 536); flavour the rice with kirsch. Serve with a sabayon sauce (page 577), made with kirsch, and vanilla.

RICE CAKE WITH CUSTARD SAUCE
Gâteau de riz à la crème

Follow the recipe above. Butter the mould; flavour the rice with maraschino and lemon peel or curaçao and orange peel. Make a *crème anglaise* (page 570) with maraschino and add one-quarter its volume of whipped cream. When the dessert is unmoulded coat it with this mixture and serve the remaining custard separately.

Fritters, Crepes, Omelettes and Soufflés

This group of desserts starts with a recipe for frying batter. The batter may be made at the last minute and used immediately, or it can be prepared in advance.

In the first case the batter must be lightly beaten, to prevent its becoming elastic, which would make it tough and prevent it sticking to the ingredients that will be dipped into it. In the second case beating the dough warms it and starts off the processes which make it lighter. Letting the batter stand breaks down the stiffness produced while beating it.

FRYING BATTER
Pâte à frire

For 1 l (2 pts):
225 g (8 oz) sifted
flour
Pinch salt
2 eggs, separated
2 dl (¼ pt) beer
2 dl (¼ pt) water or
milk
2 tablespoons melted
butter or olive oil

In a bowl combine the flour, the salt, and the egg yolks; dilute little by little with the beer and the water or the milk, then the butter or oil.

Let the batter stand for at least 2 hours in a warm place to start the fermentation. Just before using, add 2 egg whites beaten stiff.

The frying dough should be like a light, slightly fluffy cream.

Note: This recipe can be used for frying all kinds of foods. The fermentation can be increased by adding a pinch of yeast or a spoonful of frying batter a few days old and well fermented.

Frying batter for fruit fritters

To the above ingredients add 1 teaspoon of caster sugar and follow the same procedure.

APPLE FRITTERS
Beignets de reinettes

With the point of a knife or with a corer, carefully remove the cores and pips of large apples (1 per serving). Then peel the apples and cut them into slices 6 mm (¼ inch) thick.

Spread these slices on a large plate or on several plates; sprinkle each slice with sugar and baste generously with cognac, rum or kirsch; macerate for 20 minutes covered with an upside down plate or plates.

Eight minutes before the fritters are to be served, dip the apple slices one by one in the batter, then plunge each immediately into very hot oil.

The fritters should be seared immediately, so they will fry and not boil, to keep the batter from soaking up oil, which would give a disagreeable taste and make them indigestible.

Fried quickly, the batter will be transformed into a crunchy protective coating of a golden brown.

Drain the fritters on a paper towel, wipe them carefully; sprinkle with icing sugar and place them flat on a pastry sheet.

Slide under the grill for 1 minute to caramelize the surface lightly. Serve on a warm round platter.

PEAR FRITTERS
Beignets de poires

Use whatever pears are in season at different times of the year.

Follow the recipe for the apple fritters exactly; however, to remove the pips more easily, peel the fruit and cut into thin slices, then remove the core from each slice with a pastry cutter. Sprinkle the slices with sugar and macerate in a liqueur – maraschino, Grand Marnier, etc.

Note: The pears must be very ripe.

PINEAPPLE FRITTERS
Beignets d'ananas

Choose a large pineapple to make about a dozen fritters.

If the pineapple is fresh, peel, remove the hard core, and cut into 6-mm ($\frac{1}{4}$-inch) slices. Spread the slices on a plate, sprinkle with sugar and baste with kirsch; macerate, covered, for 20 minutes.

Then follow the recipe for apple fritters (above).

PINEAPPLE FRITTERS WITH FRANGIPANE CREAM
Beignets d'ananas marquisette

1 fresh pineapple
Rum
2 dl ($\frac{1}{4}$ pt) milk
40 g (1$\frac{1}{2}$ oz) sifted
  flour
40 g (1$\frac{1}{2}$ oz) sugar
1 egg
1 vanilla bean steeped
  in milk
25 g (1 oz) unsalted
  butter
2 egg yolks
1 tablespoon
  blanched, chopped
  pistachios
Icing sugar
Light frying batter
  (page 601)
Frying oil

Peel a fresh pineapple, cut in half lengthwise and cut each half in 6-mm ($\frac{1}{4}$-inch) slices. Remove the centre core from each slice.

Place the pineapple slices on a plate, sprinkle with sugar and baste with rum. Cover with an upside-down plate and macerate for 20 minutes.

Meanwhile, prepare 3 dl ($\frac{1}{2}$ pt) of frangipane cream: mix the milk with the sifted flour, sugar, egg, vanilla bean steeped in the milk almost at boiling point. Stir with a whisk without stopping until the custard starts to boil; remove from the heat and finish by adding the butter and 2 egg yolks. Stir the cream while it is cooling to prevent the formation of lumps; then add the pistachios.

Drain the slices of pineapple, dip them one by one into the lukewarm cream, being careful to coat each one well, and place them on a plate dusted with icing sugar.

Let the slices stand until the cream sets.

When the cream is firm, follow the recipe for frying fritters, just 8 minutes before serving.

Separate the slices of pineapple, being careful not to dislodge the cream, and dip them, one by one, in a light frying batter. Plunge them, one by one, into hot oil to sear them perfectly.

Drain the fritters and wipe dry; sprinkle with icing sugar, place under the grill to glaze them and serve arranged in a circle on a platter.

BANANA FRITTERS
Beignets de bananes

Peel the bananas; cut each in half lengthwise and place on a plate. Sprinkle with sugar, and baste with cognac or fine champagne brandy. Macerate for 20 minutes.

Then cook following the recipe for apple fritters (above), frying in very hot oil.

Glaze and serve them in the same way as the apple fritters.

½ l (I pt) water
100 g (4 oz) unsalted
  butter
½ teaspoon salt
1½ teaspoons sugar
300 g (10 oz) sifted
  flour
6–7 eggs
Rum or other
  alcohol or liqueur
Frying oil
Icing sugar

SOUFFLÉ FRITTERS
Beignets soufflés

The batter for soufflé fritters is an ordinary chou pastry made with water, butter, ½ teaspoon of salt and 1½ teaspoons of sugar.

In a saucepan combine all these ingredients; bring to the boil, and away from the heat add the sifted flour. Mix over a high flame to dry the dough, stirring vigorously with a wooden spatula.

The dough is ready when it detaches itself from the side of the saucepan in one mass.

Remove from the heat, then add, one at a time, 6–7 eggs, depending on their size, beating the dough vigorously during this last step.

The batter should be smooth and medium thick; flavour with rum or any other alcohol or liqueur.

With a tablespoon and a knife drop the batter in pieces the size of a small walnut into hot deep oil.

This step is easy to do. Fill the tablespoon with batter, then with the blade of a knife, dipped each time into hot water, push the dough out by sliding the end of the knife along the bowl of the spoon. The dough will gather into a ball the size of a walnut and will fall from the damp blade into the oil.

Increase the heat of the oil slowly as the fritters start to cook and double their volume at least; cook until golden brown and dry.

Drain on paper towels; sprinkle with icing sugar and pile on a folded napkin.

SOUFFLÉ FRITTERS WITH CHOCOLATE CREAM
Beignets soufflés à la créole

Prepare the soufflé fritters (recipe above) and stuff each one using a pastry bag with a plain 3-mm (⅛-inch) tube filled with whipped cream with finely grated chocolate; keep the cream on ice before using.

This is done just before serving so the piping hot fritters are dished up filled with ice-cold cream.

Place the fritters in a ring round a mound of the same cream, decorated with a fluted tube.

⚜──⚜

GRANDMOTHER BOCUSE'S WAFFLES
Gaufres de grand-mère Bocuse

500 g (1 lb) flour
Pinch salt
Pinch yeast
3 teaspoons sugar
1 cup milk
¾ l (1¼ pts) cream
8 egg yolks
1 tablespoon rum
300 g (10 oz) melted unsalted butter
4 egg whites, beaten stiff

In a bowl, mix the flour with the salt, the yeast and the sugar.

Moisten the mixture first with the milk, then the cream, the egg yolks and the rum. After this has been done carefully, add the melted butter and fold in the egg whites, whipped very stiff.

Heat and butter a waffle iron; pour a quantity of batter on one side, covering all the squares.

Close the waffle iron and turn it over, so that the batter sinks into the pattern on the other half.

Cooking this way produces a very crisp waffle.

The waffles can be eaten sprinkled with icing sugar or filled with *crème* Chantilly (page 569) or any good homemade jam.

Crêpes

Traditionally crêpes are eaten during Lent. But in fact this delicious dessert is eaten all the year round since there are so many different kinds, from the crêpes for family meals, which do not need a festive occasion, to the delicate lacy crêpes that are one of the best accompaniments for a frozen dessert.

Whether the batter used for the crêpes is ordinary or very fine, the method for preparing them is always the same.

Method. In a bowl combine the flour, the sugar and the salt. Add the eggs, one at a time, beating to produce a perfectly smooth, homogeneous batter. Continue by adding the milk in small quantities, beating it into the mixture.

It is important to prepare this batter at least 2 hours before using it; keep it in a warm place to produce an almost imperceptible fermentation.

Finish the batter by adding a flavouring, just before using it.

Cook them in a very hot frying pan lightly brushed with clarified butter. The crêpes should be thin, light and golden brown on both sides. Turning them over is a traditional feat which requires more dexterity than explanation.

Sprinkle the crêpes with sugar as you make them, and place them on a napkin.

Here are some variations:

SIMPLE CRÊPES
Crêpes ménagères

225 g (8 oz) sifted flour
Pinch salt
100 g (4 oz) caster sugar
4 dl ($\frac{3}{4}$ pt) boiled milk
3 eggs
Flavouring: orange blossom water, rum, kirsch

Follow the recipe above to cook and serve.

CRÊPES WITH CHESTNUT CREAM
Crêpes châtelaines à la crème de marrons

Frangipane cream

Frangipane cream:
100 g (4 oz) sugar
50 g (2 oz) flour
6 egg yolks
4 dl ($\frac{3}{4}$ pt) milk
1 vanilla bean
40 g (2 oz) unsalted butter
125 g (5 oz) *marrons glacés*, well crushed

Make a frangipane cream (for method see page 568), with the sugar, flour, yolks, milk and vanilla bean. As soon as the cream boils, remove from the heat and add the butter and the *marrons glacés* – whole or in bits – well crushed.

Crêpes batter

Crêpes batter:
225 g (8 oz) sifted flour
100 g (4 oz) sifted chestnut flour
Pinch salt
100 g (4 oz) caster sugar
7$\frac{1}{2}$ dl (1$\frac{1}{4}$ pts) boiled milk
6 eggs
Flavouring: cognac

Mix together all the ingredients. Let the batter rest for a while if possible.

Cook following the basic recipe (above). As the crêpes are made, spread each one with the frangipane cream.

Fold the crêpes in four with the cream inside and place them on a long platter, overlapping them; sprinkle with icing sugar and place them for 1 minute in a 475°F (240°C, gas mark 9) oven to melt the sugar and glaze the crêpes.

CRÊPES WITH ORANGE BLOSSOM WATER
Crêpes à l'eau de fleur d'oranges

225 g (8 oz) sifted
  flour
Pinch salt
100 g (4 oz) sugar
50 g (2 oz) melted
  unsalted butter
2 tablespoons double
  cream
6 eggs and 2 yolks
Light brown sugar
Flavouring: cognac (2
  tablespoons), few
  drops orange
  blossom water

Follow the basic directions above. Do not make the crêpes too thin, and cook them in two large well-buttered frying pans; they can be served to two people without waiting.

Before turning them, prick each one with a fork; the moisture will evaporate immediately.

When the crêpe is cooked, slide on to a hot plate sprinkled with brown sugar; sprinkle the crêpe with brown sugar and with a few drops of orange blossom water; slide a second crêpe on top of the first one, sugar it, then sprinkle with the orange blossom water and serve right away.

While the guests are enjoying these, make a new batch of crêpes.

LIGHT CRÊPES
Crêpes légères

225 g (8 oz) sifted
  flour
Pinch salt
100 g (4 oz) sugar
1½ teaspoons yeast
6 tablespoons boiled
  milk
6 eggs, separated
½ l (1 pt) whipped
  cream

Make a batter following the general directions above, using 6 egg yolks. Let the batter rise for 2 hours in a warm place; then fold in 6 egg whites, whipped stiff, and the whipped cream.

Let stand 10 minutes.

Spread 2 or 3 tablespoons of batter in to a well-buttered frying pan of the proper size, and cook following the recipe given above.

Sprinkle the crêpes with icing sugar and place in a 450°F (230°C, gas mark 8) oven for 1 minute to glaze.

CRÊPES WITH MARASCHINO
Crêpes Vatel

225 g (8 oz) sifted
  flour
Pinch salt
75 g (3 oz) caster
  sugar
3 eggs
3 egg yolks
½ l (1 pt) boiled milk
2 dl (¼ pt) double
  cream
100 g (4 oz) unsalted
  butter
Flavouring:
  maraschino

Mix and cook following the general recipe for crêpes above.

CRÊPES FLAMBÉES WITH GRAND MARNIER
Crêpes flambées au Grand Marnier

225 g (8 oz) sifted
  flour
4 eggs
2 egg yolks
Pinch salt
1 tablespoon
  granulated sugar
½ l (1 pt) milk
225 g (8 oz) unsalted
  butter, melted, plus
  extra butter
6 tablespoons Grand
  Marnier
2 tablespoons icing
  sugar

In a bowl, combine the flour, the eggs, the yolks, the salt and the granulated sugar.

Pour in the milk slowly, stirring, to get a smooth batter without any lumps; finally add the melted butter and the Grand Marnier.

Heat the crêpes pan and pour in a full tablespoon of the batter. As soon as the crêpe detaches from the pan, shake it and flip it, and cook the second side.

Slide the crêpe on to a buttered ovenproof dish; sprinkle with icing sugar, and brown the sugar under the grill.

Serve the crêpes basted generously with Grand Marnier and flame in front of the guests.

Serve 3 or 4 crêpes per guest.

Note: Since this batter is made with butter, there is no need to grease the crêpe pan for each crêpe. The thinner the crêpes, the better they are.

PANCAKES
Pannequets

225 g (8 oz) sifted flour
8 eggs, separated
½ l (1 pt) milk
6 tablespoons double cream
50 g (2 oz) sugar
Pinch salt
125 g (5 oz) unsalted butter, melted
2 crushed bitter almonds
1 teaspoon vanilla sugar

This dessert consists of a variety of crêpes filled with infinitely varied stuffings.

All the various crêpe batters can be used. Here is one that is excellent:

Mix the sifted flour in a bowl with the yolks, adding them to the flour one at a time; stir in the milk, cream, sugar, salt and butter, melted.

Flavour with 2 crushed bitter almonds and 1 teaspoon of vanilla sugar.

Let the batter stand 2 hours; just before making the pancakes, fold in the egg whites, beaten very firm.

Make the crêpes very thin in a small frying pan or crêpe pan, thickly buttered. Be careful to spread the batter thinly and evenly in the pan.

When they are cooked, keep the crêpes warm, piling one on top of the other, while finishing them.

SOUFFLÉ PANCAKES
Pannequets soufflés

The crêpes are cooked very thin. In the centre of each crêpe, place 1 tablespoon of kirsch soufflé mixture (page 616). Fold the crêpe to enclose the mixture completely, giving the pancake a rectangular or semi-circular shape, like an apple turnover.

Place the pancakes on a round ovenproof platter; sprinkle some icing sugar on top and place in a 425°F (220°C, gas mark 7) oven for 3 minutes, just to glaze the sugar and to make the soufflé rise.

Serve immediately, accompanied by a bowl of kirsch-flavoured sabayon sauce (page 577).

PANCAKES WITH CREAMED RICE
Pannequets à l'impératrice

Make the pancakes following one of the recipes for crêpes above. Fill each cooked pancake with 1 tablespoon of hot dessert rice (page 598), folded into 1 tablespoon of whipped cream flavoured with maraschino. Finish each with 1 tablespoon of diced pear poached in syrup and macerated in maraschino.

Fold the crêpes like apple turnovers and place them on a round ovenproof platter in a circle, overlapping slightly; sprinkle with icing sugar, then bake for 1 minute in a 450°F (230°C, gas mark 8) oven, just long enough to glaze them.

Decorate the centre with beautiful pear halves poached in syrup flavoured with maraschino and well drained. Stand them upright leaning against each other, allowing one for each guest.

Coat the pears with a few tablespoons of chocolate sauce to which the reduced poaching syrup has been added.

Serve the remaining chocolate sauce in a sauceboat separately.

PANCAKES WITH JAM
Pannequets aux confitures

Any kind of jam can be used to fill pancakes made from one of the recipes for crêpes above.

The jam must be quite thick, so that it does not melt into a syrup as soon as it comes in contact with heat. Coat the pancakes on one side with a layer of jam, then fold them as directed in the recipes above.

Place the folded pancakes in a circle on a plate, sprinkle with icing sugar and bake in a 450°F (230°C, gas mark 8) oven just long enough to glaze them.

You can fill the centre of the dish with a mound of fruit of the same variety as the jam, poached in syrup, whole, cut in half or diced.

If you do that, baste the fruit with a little sauce made with the fruit used, flavoured with kirsch; serve the same sauce separately.

PANCAKES WITH PINEAPPLE AND APRICOT SAUCE
Pannequets tonkinois

Make the pancakes by one of the recipes for crêpes above.

Prepare diced cooked pineapple in an apricot syrup thickened with apple jelly, reduced, and flavoured with maraschino.

Fill the pancakes, fold them and arrange in a circle on a plate; sprinkle with icing sugar and glaze in the oven. In the centre of the ring of shiny golden pancakes, place a pyramid of stewed pineapple in apricot syrup, considerably reduced to coat the fruit and flavoured at the last moment with maraschino.

Serve apricot sauce (page 578) separately.

PANCAKES WITH FRANGIPANE CREAM
Pannequets à la crème frangipane

Make the pancakes by one of the recipes for crêpes above. Fill each pancake with 1 tablespoon of frangipane cream (page 568), place the pancakes on a plate, sprinkle with icing sugar and glaze in a 425°F (220°C, gas mark 7) oven.

PANCAKES WITH CHESTNUT PURÉE
Pannequets à la crème de marrons

Prepare a chestnut purée with pieces of *marrons glacés* (page 572); make it light and smooth by adding whipped cream. Make the pancakes by one of the recipes for crêpes above. Fill them with this purée as explained.

Serve the same way. They are delicious accompanied by a bowl of sabayon sauce (page 577) flavoured with maraschino.

PANCAKES WITH FRUIT
Pannequets aux fruits

All kinds of fruit make an exquisite filling for pancakes. Make the pancakes by one of the recipes for crêpes above. Pears, apples, pineapples, bananas or peaches should be poached in syrup, diced, drained and coated with *crème pâtissière* (page 569) flavoured with a few drops of pastis. Stone cherries, poach and coat in the same way.

Strawberries and raspberries, picked small and coated in the same way, are also good choices.

The preceding recipes show the range that dessert pancakes offer. There is vast scope for anyone with imagination.

Dessert Omelettes

There are three different types of dessert omelettes; sweet omelettes, omelettes with liqueur and omelettes with jam.

6 eggs, or 4 eggs plus 3 egg yolks
Pinch salt
½ teaspoon sugar
2 tablespoons double cream or boiled milk
Icing sugar

SWEET OMELETTE
Omelette au sucre
For 2 people

Whatever the name, the basic preparation is the same: 6 eggs, or 4 eggs plus 3 egg yolks, beaten lightly with a pinch of salt, ½ teaspoon of sugar and 2 tablespoons of whipped cream, or more economically, boiled milk.

Make the omelette (following the recipe on page 60), turn it out on a hot plate, and sprinkle it with icing sugar.

Heat a metal skewer until red hot and apply to the omelette, making a dark-gold crisscross design by caramelizing the sugar.

OMELETTE WITH LIQUEUR
Omelette aux liqueurs

Make an omelette as you would a sweet omelette, above, being careful to turn it out on to a very hot plate. After sprinkling it with icing sugar, pour on any chosen liqueur or spirits, previously heated.

Serve the omelette immediately; ignite the liqueur and let it flame on the omelette until it burns itself out.

The best liqueurs or spirits to use for an omelette are: rum, kirsch, fine champagne brandy or cognac, armagnac, calvados, mirabelle, raspberry or blackberry brandy, Grand Marnier, Cointreau, anisette, Pernod, chartreuse·

OMELETTE WITH JAM
Omelette aux confitures diverses

This type of omelette differs from the two sweet omelettes above only in that a filling is added. Before rolling it, in the centre spread 3 tablespoons of the chosen jam which should be quite thick.

Finish the omelette, turn it out on a plate, sprinkle with icing sugar and decorate with a red-hot skewer (as for sweet omelette, above).

PINEAPPLE OMELETTE
Omelette tahitienne

3 slices pineapple, fresh or canned
3 tablespoons apricot jam, melted
2 tablespoons maraschino
Sweet omelette made with 6 eggs and 2 egg yolks
Icing sugar

Dice 3 slices of fresh or canned pineapple, removing the core. Place in a pan with 3 tablespoons of melted apricot jam, bring to the boil and stew slowly for 15 minutes. Away from the heat flavour with 2 tablespoons of maraschino. Prepare a sweet omelette with 6 eggs and 2 egg yolks, fill it with the diced pineapple; fold the omelette, sprinkle with icing sugar and glaze in a 425°F (220°C, gas mark 7) oven or under the grill just long enough so that the sugar melts and takes on a golden colour.

Surround the omelette with some of the apricot syrup used to stew the pineapple.

CHERRY OMELETTE
Omelette aux griottes

225 g (8 oz) bitter
   cherries
6 tablespoons water
4 tablespoons sugar
1 teaspoon kirsch
Sweet omelette made
   with 6 eggs and 2
   yolks
Icing sugar

Remove the stems from the cherries and cook one-quarter of them for 15 minutes in a syrup made with the water and sugar. Crush the remaining three-quarters of the cherries, with their stones, very fine and cook the *coulis* with equal its weight in sugar. When the *coulis* has the consistency of jam, remove it from the heat, pass through a fine sieve and then strain. Put into a bowl, flavour with 1 teaspoon of kirsch and add the stewed cherries, stones removed.

Make a sweet omelette (above) and fill with this delicious purée.

Sprinkle the omelette with icing sugar and flame with kirsch.

OMELETTE WITH ALMOND CREAM
Omelette de la belle Aurore

4 tablespoons
   frangipane cream
   (page 568)
2 tablespoons
   whipped cream
1 teaspoon liqueur
Sweet omelette made
   with 6 eggs and 2
   yolks
Icing sugar

Prepare 4 tablespoons of frangipane cream, replacing the macaroons with 1 heaped tablespoon of caramelized almonds and pistachios (half of each) crushed to a very fine paste. Flavour with 1 teaspoon of liqueur, preferably one made from fruit stones.

Lighten the mixture with 2 tablespoons of whipped cream. Fold it into the frangipane cream carefully and fill a sweet omelette (above), made with extra cream to keep it moist.

Sprinkle lightly with icing sugar, and make a design with a red-hot skewer.

BANANA OMELETTE
Omelette Côte-d'Ivoire

2 large bananas, sliced
  into 3-mm ($\frac{1}{8}$-inch)
  slices
Pinch sugar
Unsalted butter
2 tablespoons sweet
  almonds, freshly
  skinned
1 blanched bitter
  almond
1 heaped tablespoon
  sugar
2 tablespoons double
  cream
Sweet omelette

Sprinkle the bananas with a pinch of sugar. Melt a large piece of butter in a pan; when it is very hot, add the sliced bananas and cook quickly.

Meanwhile, in a mortar pound the almonds, add the sugar and the cream gradually. Strain quickly through a fine sieve, or leave as it is and use this delicious almond cream to coat the warm sliced bananas.

Make a sweet omelette and fill with the bananas.

Sprinkle the omelette with sugar and glaze in a 425°F (220°C, gas mark 7) oven, or under the grill.

Make a 2-cm ($\frac{3}{4}$-inch) slash on top of the omelette, and through this opening pour 1 tablespoon of almond cream; pour the remaining cream around the omelette.

SOUFFLÉ OMELETTE
Omelette soufflée

The method for making a soufflé omelette is always basically the same, and it can also be used for a long list of surprise omelettes.

I advise using the recipe below for vanilla soufflé omelette; you can vary it to make all the surprise omelettes.

VANILLA SOUFFLÉ OMELETTE
Omelette soufflé à la vanille
For 2–3 people

150 g (6 oz) caster
  sugar
4 egg yolks
Cube sugar rubbed on
  orange skin
1 teaspoon vanilla
  sugar
6 egg whites,
  whipped very stiff
Icing sugar

In a bowl, combine the sugar and 4 egg yolks. Beat this mixture with a wooden spatula for at least 15–20 minutes, until the mixture is thickened and creamy, and is a pale yellow in colour.

Rub all the sides of a sugar cube on the skin of an orange. When the sugar is soaked with the rind, crush it and add to the mixture with 1 teaspoon of vanilla sugar.

Then when the mixture has reached the point described above, whip 6 egg whites until very stiff and fold them in carefully in the following way. First add a quarter of the egg whites into the egg–sugar mixture; mix until smooth and light. Then fold in the remaining whites, lifting the mixture with the spatula held in your right hand while your left hand rotates the bowl in the opposite direction. You must not allow the mixture to fall; it must keep its lightness, which is its most important property.

Butter a long ovenproof platter generously, then sprinkle it with sugar. On the platter place the mixture in an oval mound and smooth it with a spatula or a knife. In the centre make a hole on the top to permit the heat to penetrate and decorate the omelette by making designs with the point of a knife or with some of the egg mixture piped through a pastry bag with a fluted nozzle.

Bake immediately in a 375°F (190°C, gas mark 5) oven; look at it after about 20 minutes. You must be careful that it does not brown too rapidly or get too dark. The cooked omelette should be a pale coffee colour.

After baking it about 20 minutes, sprinkle the omelette with icing sugar; the sugar will melt in a few seconds. Watch the dessert continuously. The sugar melts and caramelizes very quickly. A beautiful glaze will then cover the omelette. It must be served immediately; and the guests must wait for it. If the omelette has to wait it will be a great disappointment – it will fall and become heavy and very unappetizing.

When such a dessert is part of your menu, you should time the length of the dinner so that you can fix exactly the time to start the soufflé omelette, taking into account the time to prepare (15–20 minutes), to decorate (5 minutes) and to cook (25 minutes).

SOUFFLÉ OMELETTE WITH LIQUEUR
Omelette soufflée aux liqueurs

This dessert derives from the one above and is prepared in the same way, using the same ingredients, but adding to the mixture when it is creamy 2 teaspoons of rum, kirsch, maraschino, curaçao, raspberry liqueur or the like.

When the omelette is cooked and glazed pour 4 tablespoons of the liqueur used in the omelette (first heated) through the hole in the top and light it in front of your guests.

SOUFFLÉ OMELETTE WITH GRAND MARNIER
Omelette soufflée au Grand Marnier
For 2–3 people

225 g (8 oz) caster
 sugar
4 egg yolks
I cube sugar
I orange peel
I teaspoon vanilla
 sugar
I tablespoon Grand
 Marnier
6 egg whites
Butter
Icing sugar

In a bowl beat the sugar and the egg yolks with a wooden spatula for at least 15–20 minutes.

Rub all the surfaces of the sugar cube on the skin of an orange. When the sugar is soaked with the rind, crush it and add to the mixture with the vanilla sugar and the Grand Marnier. Mix well.

Next, whip the egg whites until stiff and fold in carefully in the following way. First add a quarter of the egg whites and mix quickly, making the mixture smooth and light; then fold in the remaining whites, lifting the mixture with the spatula held in your right hand while your left hand rotates the bowl in the opposite direction. The mixture must not fall; it must remain light.

Butter a long ovenproof platter and sprinkle it with sugar. Pile the omelette mixture in the centre in an oval mound and smooth with a spatula. Make an opening in the centre so that the heat can penetrate.

Bake immediately in a 375°F (190°C, gas mark 5) oven; look at it after about 20 minutes.

The cooked omelette should be a pale coffee colour. After baking it about 20 minutes, sprinkle the omelette with icing sugar; the sugar will melt and caramelize very quickly. Serve immediately.

SURPRISE OMELETTES
Omelettes surprises

The surprise effect of these omelettes comes from the contrast between cold and hot ingredients.

All follow the same pattern: a cake bottom, forming a base for an ice-cream, covered with a soufflé-omelette mixture, baked in the usual way and served hot.

100 g (4 oz) caster
  sugar
3 egg yolks
1 cube sugar rubbed
  on a lemon or
  orange skin until
  soaked with the oil,
  then crushed fine
1 teaspoon vanilla
  sugar
5 egg whites
20-cm (8-inch)
  Genoese cake (page
  555), baked in an
  oval tin or cut to
  this shape
1–2 tablespoons
  liqueur (choice
  depends on the
  flavour of the ice-
  cream)
½ l (1 pt) ice-cream

BAKED ALASKA
Omelette norvégienne
For 6–8 people

Prepare a soufflé omelette (above) with the listed ingredients.

Lightly moisten the Genoese cake, which should not be more than 4 cm (1½ inches) high, with a few tablespoons of the chosen liqueur.

Unmould the ice-cream or spoon it on to the cake and completely cover it with the thick mixture for the soufflé omelette. Smooth with a pastry spatula and decorate by piping the same mixture through a pastry bag with a large fluted tube.

It is baked very much like an ordinary soufflé omelette. Here, however, one must not brown the omelette too much. In a 425°F (220°C, gas mark 7) oven a protective crust immediately forms, which shields the ice-cream from the heat.

The baking time for baked Alaska and the other desserts that derive from it, is less than for a soufflé omelette; 6–7 minutes is enough.

For all these recipes the omelette should remain very creamy because, if it is not cooked very much inside, it will keep the ice-cream firm.

These desserts must be served as soon as they are removed from the oven. Waiting would ruin them.

You must time the length of your lunch or dinner exactly to know when to start preparing the dessert.

STRAWBERRY AND VANILLA SURPRISE OMELETTE
Omelette princesse Élisabeth

Follow the recipe for Norwegian omelette (above); replacing the Genoese cake with a Genoa cake (page 560). Moisten the cake lightly with kirsch. Place on top, in layers parallel to the cake, strawberry ice-cream and vanilla ice-cream. Into the omelette mixture, flavoured with kirsch, mix 1 tablespoon of crystallized violets (page 630).

When removing the dish from the oven, put a few crystallized violets on top of the dessert.

PEACH SURPRISE OMELETTE
Omelette surprise aux pêches

Stone and peel several small, quite ripe peaches, all the same size. Poach in maraschino syrup and refrigerate.

You will need a long platter big enough for the peaches to be placed between the ice-cream and the inside rim of the platter.

Use the same recipe as for the Norwegian omelette (above); moisten the Genoese cake (page 555) with a few tablespoons of any liqueur made from fruit stones. Fill with two ice-creams, one made with a custard for ice-cream *bombe* (page 638), flavoured with maraschino and praline (page 630), and the other a strongly flavoured, creamy peach ice-cream. Flavour the omelette mixture with maraschino.

When the omelette is baked and glazed, surround it with a row of peaches. Coat each peach with 1 tablespoon of redcurrant jelly, partially melted.

CHERRY SURPRISE OMELETTE WITH KÜMMEL
Omelette moscovite

Follow the recipe for Norwegian omelette (above). Moisten the cake base with a few tablespoons of kümmel; top the cake with the ice-cream. Cover with a soufflé-omelette mixture lightly flavoured with Pernod or anisette liqueur. Flavour very creamy vanilla ice-cream (page 636) with kümmel. Stir in some preserved cherries, macerated in kümmel.

Drain some cherries soaked in brandy and dip in fondant (page 629) flavoured with kümmel. Set aside in the refrigerator. After baking and glazing the omelette place each cherry in a fluted paper sweet case. Put a row of them around the edge of the omelette.

6–7 pears, peeled,
   stems on, cored
   from bottom
Maraschino
Norwegian omelette
   (page 618), made
   with madeleine
   mixture (page 557)
   for the base
4 heaped tablespoons
   finely crushed
   macaroons
Vanilla-flavoured ice-
   cream *bombe* (page
   638)
Pear ice-cream,
   coloured pink
Champagne sabayon
   (page 577)
Whipped cream

PEAR SOUFFLÉ OMELETTE
Omelette soufflée merveilleuse

Poach the pears in a light-pink syrup flavoured with maraschino. Set aside in the syrup and refrigerate.

Follow the recipe for a Norwegian omelette above, using for the base cake a madeleine mixture, with 4 heaped tablespoons of finely crushed macaroons added. On the cake sprinkle drops of maraschino and cover with 3 cm ($1\frac{1}{4}$ inches) of vanilla-flavoured ice-cream *bombe*; then add a second layer, 6 cm ($2\frac{1}{2}$ inches) thick, of pear ice-cream, coloured pink; cover with a third layer, identical to the first one.

Cover the cake and the ice-cream with a fine soufflé omelette flavoured with maraschino and decorated by piping the mixture with a pastry bag with a large fluted tube; bake in a 425°F (220°C, gas mark 7) oven. Meanwhile, drain the pears.

When the omelette is baked and glazed, arrange the pears around the omelette inside the edges of the platter, which should be large enough to hold the ice-cream and the garnish.

To finish the dessert coat each pear with 1 tablespoon of champagne sabayon flavoured with maraschino and mixed with one-quarter of its volume of whipped cream. It should have the consistency of a custard cream. This consistency can be adjusted by mixing in 1 or 2 tablespoons of the poaching syrup. Serve a glass bowl of very cold sabayon sauce separately.

Soufflés

There are two kinds of soufflés, one based on cream or milk thickened with egg yolks and the other based on sugar syrup cooked to the hard-crack stage, to which a fruit purée is added. In both cases the egg whites are beaten very stiff before being folded into the mixture.

25 g (1 oz) flour or
  cornflour
2 dl (¼ pt) milk
50 g (2 oz) caster
  sugar
Vanilla bean
4 egg yolks
20 g (¾ oz) butter
Flavouring
5 egg whites

CREAM SOUFFLÉ OR VANILLA SOUFFLÉ

Soufflé à la crème

For 6 people

Moisten the flour or cornflour first with a little cold milk. Boil the milk with the sugar and the vanilla bean; steep the bean for 5 minutes, remove and mix the still-warm milk with the flour. Heat gently, stirring, just to boiling point. Remove from the heat; the mixture should be very smooth. Add away from the heat the egg yolks, the butter and the flavouring. Then fold in the stiffly beaten egg whites.

The whites must be folded in very gently so that they do not fall.

While whipping the egg whites, you may often notice that just as they start to get stiff, the albumen separates and the mixture becomes grainy. As soon as you notice the problem, add 1 tablespoon of sugar and continue beating. This graininess often occurs in very fresh eggs.

Add 1 tablespoon of beaten egg whites to the prepared mixture and mix well with a wooden spatula. This first tablespoon will lighten the mixture, making it easier to fold in the remaining egg whites. Folding, as explained before in this book, consists in cutting the mixture with a spatula in a movement from bottom to top, starting from the centre and going towards the left. At the same time, the bowl is rotated in the opposite direction. The soufflé thus becomes well mixed, while the whites keep their fluffy consistency.

Moulding and cooking.   Soufflés are always served in the moulds in which they are baked – special silver moulds or ovenproof porcelain soufflé dishes, round and no deeper than 18–20 cm (7–8 inches); the diameter of the base is quite large and can stand easily in the oven.

Butter a soufflé mould and sprinkle the inside with icing or granulated sugar.

Fill the mould to three-quarters of its capacity, smooth the surface of the soufflé with a knife, make a rosette design on the surface with a knife and bake.

Place the mould for 1 minute on the floor of a 375°F (190°C, gas mark 5) oven to heat the bottom and to prepare the contents to rise; then place the mould in the centre of the oven. Watch the cooking attentively. Turn the mould a quarter turn several times; this step must be done quickly to avoid leaving the oven door open too long.

Eighteen–20 minutes later, the soufflé should have risen 9–10 cm ($3\frac{1}{2}$–4 inches) above the edges of the mould and started to take on a dark-golden colour; begin then to glaze the soufflé. Quickly sprinkle the surface with icing sugar and replace the mould in the centre of the oven; in 2 seconds the sugar will melt. Sprinkle again with sugar; do this at least 6 times.

You will get a transparent glazed coating, with a beautiful colour and drops like large golden pearls, like enamel tears on a stone statue.

Then place the soufflé dish on a platter covered with a lace doily and serve at once to the waiting guests.

Time the dinner carefully so that the delay is kept to a minimum.

Two last tips

1. The cook who watches the soufflé must not be distracted from the work; it requires complete attention.
2. Do not be tempted to serve the soufflé as soon as it has risen. To be delicious, a soufflé must also be cooked; the heat must penetrate the soufflé so that the egg whites lose the raw albumen taste one often encounters – a technical and gastronomic mistake that must be avoided.

If you study and understand these instructions it is impossible not to make a soufflé correctly and to cook it perfectly; all the following recipes are based on the instructions above.

LEMON SOUFFLÉ
Soufflé au citron

This is a soufflé mixture flavoured with lemon zest. Rub a couple of sugar cubes over the rind, then dissolve them in the milk, with 2 tablespoons of candied lemon peel, cut into tiny dice, and add to the mixture before folding in the whites.

ORANGE SOUFFLÉ
Soufflé à l'orange

Follow the directions for the lemon soufflé (above), replacing the lemon with orange.

SUGARED ALMOND SOUFFLÉ
Soufflé aux pralines

Add to the soufflé mixture 2 tablespoons of praline or nougat (pages 629–630), pounded into a powder. Add 6 caramelized almonds, coarsely chopped, to the mixture while folding in the egg whites, then sprinkle 5 or 6 caramelized almonds on top of the soufflé just before it is baked.

ORANGE SOUFFLÉ WITH SPONGE-CAKE AND GRAND MARNIER
Soufflé Martine

Garnish the orange soufflé with small sponge fingers (page 559) soaked in Grand Marnier. Place these pieces of cakes between two layers of the soufflé mixture when filling the mould.

CHOCOLATE SOUFFLÉ
Soufflé au chocolat

Follow the vanilla soufflé recipe (above). Omit the flour or cornflour and add 75 g (3 oz) of plain chocolate; break up the chocolate, melt and cook for 10 minutes with 2 tablespoons of water. Add it to the milk, cook to reduce to the consistency of a thick syrup and away from the heat thicken with egg yolks. Continue following the directions given in the general recipe.

COFFEE SOUFFLÉ
Soufflé au café

Flavour the basic recipe with 1 tablespoon of strong fresh coffee or 1 teaspoon of coffee essence.

ALMOND SOUFFLÉ
Soufflé dame Blanche

Follow the basic recipe. Replace the milk with almond milk (see the recipe for blancmange, page 579). Before folding in the egg whites add 2 tablespoons of chopped toasted almonds, slightly sugared, to the mixture.

HAZELNUT SOUFFLÉ
Soufflé aux avelines

Follow the recipe for almond soufflé (above), using the almond milk, but replacing the sugared almonds with hazelnuts.

SOUFFLÉ WITH SPONGE-CAKE AND KIRSCH
Soufflé Palmyre

Follow the basic recipe and add pieces of sponge fingers soaked in kirsch. Place in layers in the mixture when filling the mould.

SOUFFLÉ WITH FRUIT AND KÜMMEL
Soufflé Rothschild

Make the basic mixture adding 3 tablespoons of candied fruit, diced and macerated in kümmel. When the soufflé is baked, around the edge quickly place a row of wild strawberries or candied cherries.

SOUFFLÉ WITH FLOWERS
Soufflé aux fleurs

Make the basic soufflé mixture, adding 2 tablespoons of crystallized flowers (page 630), roughly chopped.

For *soufflé de Parme* add crystallized violets; for *soufflé Printanier* add crystallized acacia flowers; and for *soufflé France* add crystallized rose petals.

100 g (4 oz) sugar
1 teaspoon vanilla sugar
6 eggs, separated
3 tablespoons coarsely chopped walnuts
1 teaspoon liqueur made from fruit stones
6 tablespoons whipped cream

SOUFFLÉ WITH WHIPPED CREAM
Fin soufflé de bonne-maman
For 6 people

In a bowl combine the sugars and add the egg yolks, one at a time, beating the mixture with a wooden spatula. Mix well for about 10 minutes, so that the mixture whitens and becomes light. At this point add the walnuts, the liqueur and the whipped cream; then fold in the 5 egg whites, beaten stiff.

To fold in the whites, follow the instructions given in the basic recipe.

Fill a well-buttered soufflé mould and bake following the basic recipe.

Note: This soufflé has no flour or starch; it is thickened only by the rich whipped cream which gives the sought-after softness. This is an exquisite mixture of great delicacy and lightness.

❧❧❧❧❧❧❧❧❧❧❧❧❧❧❧

FRUIT SOUFFLÉS
Soufflés aux fruits
For 6 people

This series of soufflés are related to the preceding group only by the manner of presentation and by the sugar and the egg whites they contain.

250 g (9 oz) sugar
200 g (7 oz) fresh fruit purée
5 egg whites

Method. Prepare the fruit purée, rubbing it through a fine sieve. Set aside in a bowl.

Place the sugar in a heavy pan and sprinkle with 4 tablespoons of water. After dissolving the sugar, heat and boil; skim carefully and cook until the sugar cracks (about 280°F, 140°C).

At this point, add the fruit purée; do not let boil unless the addition of the fruit lowers the temperature of the sugar below the hard ball stage (about 250°F, 120°C).

While the mixture is still very hot, pour the fruit purée in a stream on to the very stiffly beaten egg whites, lifting them with a spatula to mix well.

The moulding and baking are the same as for a cream soufflé.

The best fruits for these soufflés are strawberries, raspberries, apricots, peaches, melons, blueberries, redcurrants and pineapple; these must be ripe and uncooked. Apples, pears and quince should all be cooked to a jam consistency then puréed.

It is important to add a few pieces of sugar rubbed on the rind of an orange or a lemon to give more flavour to the fruit used.

You should add a small quantity of liqueur to these mixtures, about 2 teaspoons of kirsch, maraschino, any liqueur made from fruit stones or rum. The liqueur is added when the fruit and the sugar are mixed into the egg whites.

SOUFFLÉS WITH LIQUEUR AND WINE
Soufflés aux liqueurs et vins

Rum, curaçao, Grand Marnier, apricot brandy, Cointreau, anisette, kümmel, chartreuse, kirsch, crème d'abricots, crème de cacao, Marsala, port, Frontignan, Madeira – all can be used to flavour a cream or milk-based soufflé. The liqueur is added to the cornflour or flour and eggs.

Use the basic recipe, taking into account the quantity of liqueur or wine added. The consistency of the basic mixture will depend upon the quantity of liqueur added.

Note: To finish this series of desserts let us add that, in the basic recipe, you can substitute half *crème pâtissière* (page 569) or frangipane (page 568). You can use flour and make a quick white roux with the given amount of butter. The proportions of sugar and eggs are unchanged.

I prefer to use cornflour or, even better, the recipe for soufflé with whipped cream (above).

SOUFFLÉ ORANGES
Oranges soufflées
For 4 people

4 large oranges
sugar
75 g (3 oz) caster
sugar
4 eggs, separated

Cut off a third of each orange and scoop out the pulp with a spoon. Reserve the removed tops. Rub the pulp through a fine strainer. In a pan boil the pulp to reduce it; add 1 tablespoon of finely chopped blanched orange rind, made with the reserved tops.

Add the sugar, and cook for a few minutes. Cool away from the heat and thicken with the egg yolks. Beat the egg whites very stiff, and fold a little at a time into the mixture.

Fill the emptied orange shells with this mixture. Bake in a 375°F (190°C, gas mark 5) oven like any other soufflé, for 15–18 minutes.

Serve on a platter immediately.

SUGAR, MERINGUES AND ICES

Cooking sugar

The instructions that follow are designed to explain the principles of cooking and storing sugar syrups and jams.

They also make it easier to do small sweet-making jobs with the limited means of the domestic kitchen.

Sugar syrup

In a saucepan, combine the quantity of sugar, granulated or in cubes, and water specified in the recipe, using, for example, 500 g (1 lb) of sugar and 6 tablespoons of water.

Put it on the fire, heat slowly, stirring now and then until the sugar is dissolved and almost at boiling point.

As the syrup heats, impurities will rise to the surface; skim carefully. Then add 1 teaspoon of glucose to keep the sugar from becoming grainy during the cooking.

Boiling makes the water in the syrup evaporate and thickens it; it is soon covered with tiny bubbles very close to one another. The temperature will be about 180°F (82°C).

Thereafter the pan must be watched attentively, for the syrup changes very rapidly, and easily caramelizes or burns. From this point on it is essential to use a sugar thermometer and be vigilant. The syrup should be boiled for at least 3 minutes at 200–210°F (93–99°C).

Consult the individual recipes for the proportions for specific syrups.

FRESH RASPBERRY SYRUP
Sirop de framboises au naturel

Rub 1 kg (2 lb) of beautiful, ripe raspberries through a fine sieve. Add an equal weight of sugar to the raspberry pulp, and stir until dissolved. Raspberry syrup is used mainly to top dishes of ice-cream with fruit.

FONDANT ICING
Fondant ou glacé

In a heavy stainless steel pan melt 500 g (1 lb) of sugar with a few tablespoons of water. Place on the stove and cook to the soft ball stage (234–240°F, 111–116°C). Skim carefully while cooking. Pour on to a piece of marble, into a frame made with 4 metal bars; the marble and the bars (sold at confectioners' suppliers) should be oiled. When the sugar is lukewarm, remove the bars and work the mixture with a spatula, folding the edges towards the centre. During this step the sugar will become white and harden, and then be transformed into a smooth paste, pliable and creamy.

Place in a bowl and cover with a fresh cloth for later use.

The flavour is added when the fondant is used. Heat the fondant gently to soften it and make it slightly liquid, without its losing its shine. Half a teaspoonful of glucose can be added at this stage.

ICING
Glace

At a low temperature mix icing sugar with a flavoured syrup and a little glucose until it reaches the consistency of a thick cream.

ALMOND BRITTLE
Nougat aux amandes

Place 225 g (8 oz) of sugar in a heavy stainless steel saucepan, heat slowly, stirring constantly with a spatula.

Sugar melts, dry, at a temperature of 320°F (160°C). It then has a light-golden colour. As soon as the sugar reaches the syrup stage, pour in 225 g (8 oz) of almonds, skinned, chopped and dried, which have been kept warm. Away from the heat mix the two ingredients and pour on to a lightly oiled tin. Keep the mixture warm. Mould it on a piece of marble into thin sheets, which are then put into flat oiled tins to harden.

Unmould when hard.

CARAMELIZED CHOPPED ALMONDS
Praline

Combine equal amounts of sugar, chopped skinned almonds and chopped skinned hazelnuts. Follow the recipe for almond brittle (above); after the brittle has cooled, crush in a mortar or in some other way.

Keep in a jar covered with oiled paper.

CRYSTALLIZED FLOWERS
Fleurs pralinées

Violets, acacias and petals of roses and lilies are most commonly used for crystallized decorations.

Measure sugar and an equal amount of flowers (stems removed). Place the sugar in a heavy stainless steel saucepan, pour in a little water and cook as directed to 230°F (110°C).

At this point plunge the flowers into the syrup. Bring to the boil, and with a slotted spoon drain the flowers on to a plate. Continue cooking the syrup to the soft ball stage (234–240°F, 111°–116°C), remove from the heat and stir the sugar with a spatula. It will slowly become white and grainy. Return the flowers and mix until the flowers are coated with the sugar. Spread on a baking sheet and dry out in a very low oven or warming oven for 10 hours. Then sift carefully, gathering only the flowers coated with sugar.

The sugar can be dyed the same colour as the flowers used.

CANDIED CHESTNUTS
Marrons confits

Peel large chestnuts without breaking them. Cook slowly in a white court-bouillon (water mixed with a small quantity of flour). Drain and place in a glass or glazed earthenware jar with a vanilla bean, and cover with boiling sugar syrup made according to the instructions on page 628, using 725 g (1 lb 10 oz) of sugar to 1 l (1¾ pts) of water. After 48 hours drain off the syrup. Put it in a saucepan and add an extra 100 g (4 oz) of sugar to it, dissolve and bring to the boil. Then pour over the chestnuts. Repeat this operation twice more at 48-hour intervals. Finally, on the ninth day, glaze the chestnuts. Drain off the syrup, add another 100 g (4 oz) of sugar to it, bring to the boil and stir with a spatula until the syrup becomes whitish. Then dip the chestnuts in this syrup.

TRUFFLES
Truffes

1 l (2 pts) double cream
1·5 kg (3 lb) plain chocolate, melted
225 g (8 oz) good quality unsalted butter
Cocoa

Boil the cream, then add it to the chocolate, melted in a double boiler. Let it stand in the refrigerator overnight. The next morning, with the mixture still in a double boiler, heat slightly, adding the butter. Put the mixture into a pastry bag, form into pieces and roll them in cocoa.

Meringues

Meringues can be made in four ways:

Ordinary meringue
Italian meringue
Cooked meringue
Swiss meringue

The first meringue is a cold mixture of 8 egg whites beaten very stiff with 500 g (1 lb) of sugar poured on the whites in a stream while they are being whipped. The proportion of whites varies from 6–12 for this quantity of sugar, depending upon how the meringue will be used. The quantity of 8 whites is an average. This mixture is frequently used in *pâtisserie*.

The second meringue is a mixture of 500 g (1 lb) of sugar in syrup cooked to the soft-ball stage (234–240°F, 111–116°C) and poured into 6–8 egg whites whipped very stiff. It is used for desserts.

The third meringue is made with egg whites whipped with icing sugar, this time over low heat, until the consistency of a very thick cream is reached. It is used for *petits fours* and other fancy biscuits.

The fourth meringue is made by beating with a spatula 500 g (1 lb) of icing sugar, 2 egg whites and a few drops of acetic acid (or ½ teaspoon of lemon juice). When the mixture is thick, firm and creamy, add the remaining egg whites, whipped very stiff. This is used for decorations and glazing, sometimes sprinkled with *praliné*.

ORDINARY MERINGUES
Meringues ordinaires

Make the mixture by the first method above and flavour with vanilla. Pour into a pastry bag with a 1-cm (½-inch) plain tube; on a buttered and floured pastry sheet pipe meringue shells into oval puffs about the size and shape of an egg. Bake in a 225°F (110°C, gas mark ¼) oven for at least 1 hour to dry the meringues and give them an ivory colour.

Before baking, proceed as for sponge fingers, by sprinkling the meringue shells with sugar mixture containing 1 part granulated sugar and 4 parts icing sugar. Shake off the excess sugar and keep it for later use; then sprinkle the meringues with drops of water which will form pearls. When you take the shells from the oven, press down the inside of each one lightly, using an egg.

Once cooled, the meringue shells will remain crisp for a very long time if kept in an airtight tin.

FILLED MERINGUES
Meringues garnies

Meringue shells (recipe above) are generally used in pairs, joined with *crème* Chantilly (page 569), garnished with more cream, ice-cream or fruit. There should be a 2·5 cm (1-inch) space between the two shells which is filled with cream. Saint-Honoré cream (page 572) can also be used.

This is a very delicate dessert and can be used in many different ways. A whole range of delicious ideas can be thought up, like the following suggestions.

STRAWBERRY MERINGUES
Bouchées exquises

Join pairs of meringue shells (recipe above) with *crème* Chantilly
(page 569) coloured pink with a few tablespoons of strawberry
purée and a dash of maraschino. Lay each pair of filled shells
on its side and coat with a very light, white fondant icing (page
629) flavoured with kirsch that is transparent enough to let the
pink tint of the cream show. Place the meringues on a cake stand
covered with a doily.

MERINGUES WITH RUM
ICE-CREAM
Zéphirs antillais

These are meringues filled with vanilla ice-cream flavoured with
rum. Pile to look like rocks.

Accompany with a light chocolate sabayon (page 577), served
very cold in a glass bowl, and a plate of cats' tongues (page 563).

MARASCHINO FLOATING
ISLANDS
Mousselines au marasquin

Prepare ordinary meringue (above), flavoured with vanilla.
Boil milk with sugar and vanilla in a shallow saucepan. Add the
meringue, moulded with a tablespoon, and poach the egg shapes
in the simmering milk.

A few minutes later turn the meringues over so that they cook
on both sides. When the meringue eggs are firm to the touch,
drain on a cloth, then place in a large bowl. With the cooking
milk, make a *crème anglaise* (page 570), thickened with 10 egg
yolks for 1 l (2 pts) of milk.

When the custard is cool, flavour with maraschino and pour
over the eggs. Serve very cold with a plate of small shortbread
biscuits (page 563) or a sponge brioche (page 526).

Ice-creams and ices

This section includes cream ices, fruit ices, *bombes*, mousses and parfaits, and sorbets.

There are 4 main steps in making an ice.

1. Prepare the mixture;
2. Pack the *sorbetière* (the special freezer apparatus for making ices);
3. Freeze the mixture, stirring it all the while;
4. Mould and freeze again.

1. Instructions for preparing the mixture are given in the recipes which follow.

2. The *sorbetière* is placed on its pivot in a special bucket. It is surrounded with crushed ice, mixed in layers with coarse salt and saltpetre: 1·5 kg (3 lb) of salt and 150 g (6 oz) of saltpetre to 10 kg (20 lb) of ice. Pound down the ice to pack it tightly and lower its level to about two-thirds the height of the container. Cover the salted ice with a cloth.

3. According to type, ices are either first frozen in a *sorbetière*, then moulded and frozen again, or put directly into moulds and frozen.

In the first case the mixture, prepared and cooled, is poured into the *sorbetière* after it has been placed in position. Open the *sorbetière* and fill with mixture to halfway up. Close tightly – whether the apparatus is turned by hand or mechanically, it must be closed hermetically to prevent any salt getting into the mixture accidentally. Now set the apparatus going.

The old-fashioned method was simple and can still be used if you do not have more sophisticated modern equipment. The *sorbetière* itself has hardly changed since the days of Procopio, the Sicilian who reputedly introduced ice-cream to France in 1660. It consists of a deep tinned cylinder with a curved base; it has a lid which closes hermetically to which a strong handle was attached. This handle has disappeared in modern freezers which are worked mechanically.

In the early days the cook would half fill the container, close it and pack salted ice all round. Then he would grip the handle on the lid and turn it round and round energetically, throwing the mixture against the sides of the *sorbetière* where it would freeze. At regular intervals he would take off the lid and scrape the sides, mixing the frozen mixture back into the rest until all the mixture had set.

I have described this method, which did not produce such good results as modern mechanical equipment, to show that it is possible to make ices without highly developed machinery.

Modern *sorbetières* have beaters inside which whisk the mixture efficiently beneath the lid. The mixture is thrown against the sides of the container and freezes in thin layers which are immediately scraped off by the revolving spatulas and thrown back into the mass of the mixture. With the constant beating the mixture gradually becomes light, smooth and creamy.

4. The frozen mixture can then be served immediately in small bowls or piled in a mound on a folded napkin, using a tablespoon dipped in warm water.

However, generally ice-cream is shaped in simple moulds or special decorated ones. The ice-cream is spooned into the mould, which should be tapped on the table to fill any spaces. When the mould is filled to the brim, cover with a piece of white paper with a diameter slightly larger than that of the mould; butter the edges of the lid, place it on the mould and place the mould in a container filled with crushed ice, mixed with salt and saltpetre as for freezing the ice-cream. Leave the moulds in the bucket of ice for at least 1 hour before serving.

If the ice-cream is moulded without being frozen beforehand, place on ice, as above, and leave for at least $2\frac{1}{2}$ hours.

Serving.   At the last moment remove the moulds from the salted ice, wash each one and dip it for a second in warm water. Wipe, remove the lid and turn the mould over on a folded napkin placed on a serving platter.

Serve with a plate of biscuits or small cakes.

Note: The use of ice to make ice-cream will soon belong to the past; it has been replaced by dry ice, which is now readily available. The advantage of dry ice over ordinary ice with salt and saltpetre is that it eliminates these three ingredients and their dampness. Dry ice goes from the solid state to a gas very slowly.

But dry ice itself has been quickly overtaken by the increasing use of electric freezers with very low temperatures. An ice-cream, unmoulded after a certain time in such a freezer, will be so hard that it cannot be eaten until it has been out of the freezer a few hours. This process represents scientific progress and convenience, but it adds nothing to – even detracts from – the high quality of ice-cream made with methods that some may consider quite old-fashioned.

[*Editor's note:* As the average English kitchen does not have a special ice-cream freezer, you can experiment with making ices in the freezer compartment of your refrigerator, setting it to the lowest possible temperature. The important thing is to stir the ice frequently, mixing the frozen sides into the middle, to replace the action of the mechanical ice-cream freezer described above. The texture may not be as perfect as by authentic methods, but the results can be delicious.]

$\frac{3}{4}$ **l ($1\frac{1}{4}$ pts) milk**
1 vanilla bean
300 g (10 oz) sugar
8 egg yolks

ICE-CREAM
Glaces à la crème
For 8–10 people

Boil the milk with the vanilla bean; steep for 5 minutes.

Meanwhile, in a bowl combine the sugar and the egg yolks; beat with a wooden spatula until the mixture is light and forms a ribbon when poured from the spatula.

Slowly beat the milk into the mixture. After they are blended, pour back into the saucepan, heat slowly without boiling, and as soon as the mixture thickens like a light custard (coating the spatula), remove from the heat and pour it into a bowl through a fine sieve. Stir to accelerate the cooling process.

Cooking this custard is rather tricky and requires either experience or a great deal of attention. The smoothness comes from the egg yolks and if they are cooked too quickly they will become grainy and lose their thickening and enriching properties. The number of egg yolks can be increased up to 16 yolks for 1 l (2 pts) of milk and the sugar increased proportionately to 400 g (14 oz) to obtain a finer, richer custard.

The milk can be replaced in part or totally by single cream.

COFFEE ICE-CREAM
Glace au café

Use the same proportions as for ice-cream (above). To flavour steep 50 g (2 oz) of freshly ground coffee in the boiling milk. Cover the saucepan. Strain through a fine sieve.

CHOCOLATE ICE-CREAM
Glace au chocolat

Replace the coffee with a chocolate syrup made by melting 225 g
(8 oz) of plain chocolate with ½ cup of water. Decrease the
quantity of sugar by about 100 g (4 oz). Boil slowly for 10 minutes.
You may use unsweetened cocoa, allowing 150 g (6 oz). In this
case do not reduce the amount of sugar.

ICE-CREAM WITH SUGARED ALMONDS
Glace pralinée

To every 1 l (2 pts) of ice-cream add 100 g (4 oz) of praline: caramelized almonds or hazelnuts pounded in a mortar and then
rubbed through a sieve (page 630).

**1 kg (2 lb) ripe
redcurrants
½ l (1 pt) sugar syrup,
made with 400 g
(14 oz) sugar and
2½ dl (½ pt) water
(see page 628)**

REDCURRANT ICE
Glace à la groseille

Squeeze the redcurrants in a dish towel to extract the juice.
There should be about 6 dl (1 pt) of juice. Mix the syrup and the
currant juice.
Freeze, following instructions above, mould and harden.

**500 g (1 lb)
strawberries or
wild strawberries
½ l (1 pt) sugar syrup
made with 400 g
(14 oz) sugar and
2½ dl (½ pt) water
(see page 628)
Juice of 1 lemon
and 1 orange**

STRAWBERRY ICE
Glace aux fraisis

Mash the washed and hulled strawberries into a purée and rub
through a fine sieve.
Mix the fruit purée and the syrup in equal quantities (½ l (1 pt) of
each), add the lemon and orange juice, and freeze, following the
method for redcurrant ice, above.

½ l (1 pt) water
500 g (1 lb) sugar
Juice and rind of 4
    oranges or
    equivalent amount
    of tangerine juice
Juice and rind of 1
    lemon

ORANGE OR TANGERINE ICE
Glace à l'orange ou à la mandarine

Boil the sugar and water, steeping the rind of the oranges and the lemon; strain, and let cool. Then add the orange or tangerine juice and the lemon juice. Freeze, mould and harden, following instructions above.

First method:
1 l (2 pts) milk
1 vanilla bean
Rind of 3 lemons
400 g (14 oz) sugar
10 egg yolks

Second method:
½ l (1 pt) water
500 g (1 lb) sugar
4 lemons

LEMON ICE
Glace au citron

First method

Make like the ice-cream (*glace à la crème*) above, and freeze in the usual way.

Second method

Follow the recipe for orange ice (above), and replace the orange juice with the juice of 4 lemons.

1 l (2 pts) sugar syrup
    made with 700 g
    (1 lb 9 oz) sugar and
    6 dl (1 pt) water
    (see page 628)
32 egg yolks
1½ l (3 pts) double
    cream

ICE-CREAM BOMBE MIXTURE
Appareils à bombe glacée

Combine the syrup and the egg yolks in a large stainless steel bowl.

Place over a very low flame and whip it as for a Genoese cake (page 555) until the egg yolks are partially cooked as for a *crème anglaise* (page 570). The mixture will expand and form a ribbon. At this point remove the bowl from the heat and continue to whip until completely cold.

Add the chosen flavour, then the whipped cream, folded in carefully. Put into moulds.

This mixture is not frozen in an ice-cream freezer first but is moulded directly.

Generally the inside of a *bombe* mould is first lined with a thin layer of ice-cream of a different flavour from the *bombe* – vanilla ice-cream, for example – which acts as a support for the very delicate *bombe* mixture.

Close the mould following the directions above (page 635) and pack in ice and salt. Leave it in the container filled with ice for at least 2 hours; just before serving unmould on to a folded napkin, and serve with a plate of *petits fours*.

MOUSSE MIXTURE
Pâte à mousse

There are two kinds of mousse, one made with syrup and one with cream.

The syrup mousses are easy to make. Generally, one can use the following proportions: for 1 l (2 pts) of sugar syrup, combine 700 g (1 lb 9 oz) of sugar with 6½ dl (1¼ pts) of water, and follow the directions on page 628.

Syrup-based mousse

Combine 1 l (2 pts) of syrup made in the proportions above with 1 l (2 pts) of strained fruit purée and 2 l (4 pts) of stiffly whipped cream.

This quantity will fill 4 moulds of 1 l (2 pts) each and serve 35 people. The quantities can easily be adapted to make more or less as needed.

Put into not-too-deep moulds and pack in ice and salt to freeze for 2½–3 hours, following the method described above (page 635). The moulds can also be placed in the freezing compartment of a refrigerator for 4 hours.

Cream-based mousse

500 g (1 lb) caster sugar
16 egg yolks
½ l (1 pt) milk
½ l (1 pt) double cream
20 g (1 oz) gelatine
½ l (1 pt) strained fruit purée

Using the sugar, 16 egg yolks and milk, prepare a *crème anglaise* (for method see page 570). When the custard is cold, add the double cream, the gelatine dissolved in warm water and the strained fruit purée.

Place the bowl containing this custard on crushed ice and whip the mixture vigorously to make it frothy and very light.

Mould and close tightly, pack in ice and salt to chill as directed for the syrup-based mousse, or place in the refrigerator for 4 hours; the mousse should be set but not frozen.

❉══❉══❉══❉══❉══❉══❉══❉══❉══❉══❉══❉══❉

COLD CHERRY SOUFFLÉ
Soufflé glacé aux cerises

Prepare 1 l (2 pts) of the mousse mixture (above) with cherries cooked in syrup flavoured with maraschino.

With a string tie a strip of paper around a soufflé dish so that the dish can be filled 4 cm (1½ inches) above the brim.

Fill the mould to 1 cm (½ inch) from the top of the paper with the mixture, smooth the surface and cover completely with whole stoned cherries, their stems removed, poached and cooled in a maraschino-flavoured syrup.

Refrigerate for 3 hours.

Just before serving, remove the strip of paper and coat the cherries lightly with a *coulis* of fresh raspberries (see the recipe for fresh raspberry syrup, page 628). Serve with a ring-shaped brioche (page 527), cut in 1-cm (½-inch) slices; sprinkle each slice with vanilla-flavoured icing sugar and place under a hot grill for a few seconds – just long enough to colour the sugar.

❉══❉══❉══❉══❉══❉══❉══❉══❉══❉══❉══❉══❉

NEAPOLITAN ICE-CREAM
Appareils à biscuits glacés

**500 g (1 lb) sugar
12 egg yolks
½ recipe Italian meringue (page 631) made with 4 egg whites, beaten very stiff, and 125 g (5 oz) sugar
1 l (2 pts) whipped cream**

Prepare and whip the eggs and sugar with a whisk as for a Genoese cake (see page 555), beaten hot and partially cooked like a *crème anglaise* in a double boiler. When the mixture rises and forms a ribbon, remove from the hot water and continue whipping until completely cold.

Finish by adding ½ recipe Italian meringue and the whipped cream.

The Italian meringue is made with 4 egg whites, beaten very stiff, into which, while beating, you pour a stream of sugar cooked to a syrup at the soft-ball stage (234–240°F, 111–116°C).

The moulding is done in special square or rectangular moulds with two deep lids. These moulds make it possible to use three layers of ice with different flavours and colours, since the lids are filled as well as the mould itself.

Pack in a container of ice and salt to set, following the general directions, or place in a refrigerator like the mousses.

1 l (2 pts) syrup
32 egg yolks
1 l (2 pts) whipped
   cream
Coffee essence

Parfaits

A parfait was originally a fine coffee ice-cream.

The mixture is made like a *crème anglaise* (see page 570) in which the milk is replaced with 600 g (1 lb 5 oz) of sugar and $7\frac{1}{2}$ dl ($1\frac{1}{4}$ pts) of water (see page 628).

When the custard, heated slowly, coats the spatula, strain it through a very fine sieve into a bowl, and whip it until completely cold. Then place the bowl on crushed ice and continue to whip for at least 15 minutes. Finish by adding the whipped cream.

Flavour with coffee essence.

Mould in a *bombe* mould and pack in ice and salt as directed in the general instructions.

Nowadays different flavours are added to this mixture. I simply suggest adding 3 tablespoons of crushed, sieved praline per 1 l (2 pts) of parfait mixture.

Note: The preceding recipes could be followed by an impressive list of the many possible combinations. I have tried to give the basic essentials for making delicious ices which will never be a disappointment, so long as the procedures are carefully followed. This should not be a problem, for although making ices demands care and attention, it does not present any particular difficulties.

Of all the possible flavourings, I would like to suggest the following in particular to my readers.

Coffee, chocolate, vanilla and tea;
Almonds, hazelnuts, pistachios, walnuts and praline;
Oranges, tangerines and lemons;
Redcurrants, raspberries, strawberries, cherries and apricots (for all red fruits add a few tablespoons of orange juice or lemon juice to give tartness to the flavour);
Bananas, pineapples and melons;
Crystallized violets and rose petals;
Maraschino, Benedictine, Grand Marnier, Pernod or any other aniseed liqueur, Cointreau, Marie Brizard apricot, chartreuse, etc.;
Rum, kirsch, raspberry liqueur, etc.

As regards presentation, there are other possibilities besides moulds. For example, pineapple ice can be put into the shell of the fruit just before serving and decorated with pineapple leaves. An orange tangerine or lemon ice can fill the carefully emptied fruit shells, the tops of the fruit used as lids, and perhaps a few leaves.

Give your imagination free rein, as long as the rules of good taste and harmonizing flavours are not forgotten.

The names of some ice-creams indicate that they are made with more than one flavour, but the ingredients are not always evident from the name. For example:

AIDA: Line the mould with raspberry ice filled inside with vanilla ice-cream; after unmoulding, decorate with a pastry bag with a fluted tube filled with *crème* Chantilly.

AIGLON: Line the mould with pineapple ice; fill the inside with tangerine ice.

AMBASSADEUR: Line the mould with strawberry ice; fill the inside with *crème* Chantilly sprinkled with strawberries macerated in a little kirsch.

ARCHIDUC: Line the mould with apricot ice; fill the inside with vanilla ice-cream with fresh walnuts, peeled and pounded.

CENDRILLON: Line the mould with cherry ice; fill the inside with a vanilla mousse sprinkled with fresh or candied fruits macerated in maraschino.

MIREILLE: Line the mould with apricot ice; fill the inside with maraschino ice.

NELUSKO: Line the mould with vanilla ice-cream; fill the inside with chocolate ice-cream.

VICTOIRE: Line the mould with redcurrant ice; fill the inside with a raspberry mousse, sprinkled with strawberries macerated in raspberry liqueur.

This list could contain a hundred or more combinations involving different moulds and decorations.

Sorbets

Sorbets are classified into four categories, very like light water ices: *granités, marquises, punches* and *spooms*.

In fact they are derivatives of liqueur ices, made entirely with syrup. Make a syrup with 450 g (1 lb) of sugar to 7·3 dl (26 fl oz) of water. Add the liqueur, about ½ glass of liqueur per 1 l (2 pts) of syrup.

If wine is used – champagne, port, Madeira, Samos, sauternes such as Chateau-Yquem – make a syrup with 550 g (1 lb 4 oz) of sugar and 6·7 dl (24 fl oz) of water. Mix $\frac{1}{2}$ l (1 pt) wine with an equal amount of syrup, plus the juice of 2 lemons and 1 orange.

Fruit juice can be used – redcurrant, raspberry, strawberry, pineapple, melon and cherry are suitable; use half juice and half syrup. The strength of the syrup depends how sweet the fruit is. Use somewhere between 450 g (1 lb) of sugar to 7·3 dl (26 fl oz) of water and 550 g (1 lb 4 oz) of sugar to 6·7 dl (24 fl oz) of water.

When the mixture is ready, freeze it not too long before serving and do not freeze it too hard; its consistency should be nearly that of a drink. Sorbets are served in small fruit dishes or glasses.

For 12 people, you will need 1 l (2 pts) of sorbet.

Granités

Granités are made only with acid fruit juices: oranges, lemons, redcurrants or cherries mixed with a syrup made in the proportions mentioned above.

Because this mixture is very light, freezing produces a grainy texture that gives the ice its name.

Marquises

This sorbet is usually made only with pineapple juice, kirsch or puréed strawberries, using a sugar syrup made with 550 g (1 lb 4 oz) of sugar to 6·7 dl (24 fl oz) of water.

The mixture is frozen rather stiffer than an ordinary sorbet. Then add $\frac{1}{2}$ l (1 pt) of whipped cream for 1 l (2 pts) of sorbet.

Punches

Make a syrup of 550 g (1 lb 4 oz) of sugar to 6·7 dl (24 fl oz) of water. Steep the zest of 1 lemon and 1 orange in the syrup. Prepare a mixture of $\frac{1}{2}$ l (1 pt) of syrup, $\frac{1}{2}$ l (1 pt) of champagne brut and the juice of 2 oranges and 2 lemons. Freeze in the usual way.

After freezing, add 3 egg whites, beaten stiff with 100 g (4 oz) of sugar (Italian meringue, page 631), and finish by pouring in $\frac{1}{2}$ glass of rum. Serve in glasses or fruit dishes like a sorbet.

Spooms

Of all the four sorbets, *spooms* are the thickest. They are prepared with a sugar syrup made with 500 g (1 lb 2 oz) of sugar to
7 dl (25 fl oz) of water. They nearly always are made with champagne, muscatel or sauternes, and are exceedingly light and frothy.
To reach that point, the mixture is frozen and then combined
with an equal amount of Italian meringue (page 631) folded in
carefully. This is also served in fruit dishes.

12 large oranges
**3 dl (½ pt) light sugar
 syrup**

Sorbet:
**1 l (2 pts) juice from
 the oranges and 2
 lemons**
225 g (8 oz) sugar

SORBET IN ORANGES
L'orange a l'orange
For 6 people

With a knife, peel the zest of 6 of the oranges; cut the zest into fine
julienne and cook for a few minutes in the syrup.

Trim the remaining pith from the 6 oranges that have been
peeled. Cut the pulp into thin slices. Place the orange slices in a
deep dish and sprinkle them with 1 generous tablespoon of the
sauce.

Meanwhile, scoop out each of the remaining 6 oranges to leave
them hollow and keep the shells cold; reserve the pulp and juice
of the oranges to make the sorbet. Finally fill each orange shell
with some of the sorbet, the slices of oranges and the zest, drained
and cooled.

The sorbet is made from the orange juice, lemon juice and sugar,
frozen in the usual way.

Fruit Desserts

12 large ripe apricots
150 g (6 oz) sugar
3 dl (½ pt) water
1 vanilla bean
**1 tablespoon kirsch or
 liqueur made from
 fruit stones**

STEWED APRICOTS
Compoté d'abricots

Make a light syrup with the sugar, water and a vanilla bean.
Plunge large, ripe apricots for a moment into boiling water, and
peel at once. Cut in two, stone them and break 4 of the stones.
Cut the kernels in two and add to the syrup, along with the
apricots.

Bring the apricots slowly to the boil and poach, simmering, for 8 minutes. Cook gently, so that the apricots do not become soft or lose their shape.

Keep in the syrup in a glazed bowl until time to use.

Flavour the syrup when it is lukewarm with 1 tablespoon of kirsch or liqueur.

BAKED APRICOTS WITH MARASCHINO
Abricots compotés au marasquin

Spread 2 tablespoons of double cream on an ovenproof porcelain plate. Side by side on the cream, arrange apricot halves peeled as for stewed apricots, above.

Sprinkle with icing sugar and bake in a 350°F (180°C, gas mark 4) oven.

After making, baste with 1 tablespoon of maraschino and serve warm in the baking dish.

APRICOTS WITH RICE
Abricots Condé

First stew 10 apricots by the recipe above and prepare 125 g (5 oz) of dessert rice (see page 599). As soon as the rice is cooked (tender and fluffy), add beaten egg whites and flavour with kirsch. Pour into a ring mould – a savarin mould with a curved bottom. Poach as for the *gâteau de riz*, then unmould on a round platter. Drain the apricot halves, which have been kept warm in the syrup, and place 16 of them on the rice, overlapping them around the curved top of the ring. Decorate the apricots with designs in angelica and candied fruits, glacé cherries, candied peel, etc.

Baste everything with a sauce made by boiling the syrup to reduce it to a scant cup. Rub the 4 remaining apricot halves through a fine sieve and mix with the syrup. Flavour the sauce with 4 teaspoons of kirsch.

Note: Out of season, use canned apricots in syrup and thicken the syrup with apricot jam.

FLAN WITH ALMOND CREAM
Abricots Bordaloue

Poach 12 apricots as for stewed apricots (above). Flavour with 4 inside kernels.

Prepare $\frac{1}{2}$ l (1 pt) frangipane cream (page 568). Pour the cream into a fine flan crust made with *pâte sablée* (page 537) and baked unfilled.

Carefully drain the apricot halves and arrange them on the cream. Sprinkle generously with crushed dry macaroons; dust lightly with icing sugar and bake in a 425°F (220°C, gas mark 7) oven for a few minutes to caramelize the sugar and to form a fragrant crust.

Serve with a bowl of apricot sauce flavoured with kirsch, adding the poaching syrup, reduced.

DEEP-FRIED APRICOTS
Abricots Colbert

50 g (2 oz) semolina
2 dl ($\frac{1}{4}$ pt) boiling milk, sweetened, flavoured with vanilla
Pinch salt
2 egg yolks
25 g (1 oz) unsalted butter
12 apricots
1 egg
Fresh breadcrumbs
Frying oil
Icing sugar
Apricot sauce (page 648) flavoured with kirsch or maraschino

Sprinkle the semolina into the boiling milk, sweetened and flavoured with vanilla and a pinch of salt.

Poach, covered, in a 375°F (190°C, gas mark 5) oven for 30 minutes. After removing from the oven, separate the grains with a fork and thicken with the egg yolks and $\frac{1}{2}$ oz of butter.

Poach the apricots, whole, following the recipe for stewed apricots (above), keeping them rather firm. Drain and half open each one to remove the pit and replace it with an equal quantity of the cooked semolina.

Close the apricots and dip them, one at a time, into 1 egg beaten with 15 g ($\frac{1}{2}$ oz) of melted butter, then roll each one in fresh breadcrumbs.

Plunge the coated apricots in a deep fryer with very hot oil, 8 minutes before serving.

Drain on a cloth, sprinkle lightly with icing sugar and pile on a napkin.

Serve with a bowl of apricot sauce flavoured with kirsch or maraschino.

APRICOTS WITH MERINGUE
Abricots meringués Clairette

20-cm (8-inch) Genoa cake (page 560)
Fruit-stone liqueur
50 g (2 oz) dessert rice (page 599)
Vanilla
12 large apricots, stewed whole (page 644)
Crushed macaroons
Unsalted butter
2 egg whites
125 g (5 oz) sugar
Pinch vanilla sugar
Meringue (page 632)
Redcurrant or apricot jelly

Prepare:

A Genoa cake and soak it with liqueur.

Dessert rice flavoured with liqueur and vanilla.

Stewed apricots. Remove the stones, replace them with small balls made with 1 part crushed macaroons and 1 part butter flavoured with a few drops of liqueur.

Egg whites (reserved from the yolks used in the rice), whipped stiff with the sugar and a pinch of vanilla sugar.

Place the Genoa cake on a large platter. Spread the rice on top in an even layer; arrange the apricots, carefully closed, on top and cover everything with a meringue (ordinary meringue, page 632), following the method for a Norwegian omelette (see page 618).

Smooth the meringue with a spatula, and decorate with rosettes, roses, etc., made with a pastry bag with a fluted tube.

Bake in a 375°F (190°C, gas mark 5) oven, sprinkle with sugar and remove from the oven when the meringue is a light-brown colour.

In the centres of the rosettes or roses, place a little redcurrant or apricot jelly.

This dessert is excellent served cold. In that case, make sure that the meringue is completely cooked or use a meringue made with sugar syrup.

APRICOTS FLAMED WITH GRAND MARNIER
Abricots flambés au Grand Marnier

12 whole apricots
1 tablespoon chopped almonds
2 inside kernels from apricot stones
Vanilla sugar
Pinch cornflour
1 tablespoon Grand Marnier per serving

Poach whole apricots (see recipe for stewed apricots, above) and place on an ovenproof porcelain platter.

Remove the stones from the apricots and keep the fruit warm in the syrup, which should be as thick as possible.

Sprinkle the tops of the apricots with chopped almonds with which you have included 2 kernels, then sprinkle with vanilla sugar and brown the tops lightly in a 425°F (220°C, gas mark 7) oven.

In the bottom of the plate pour a few tablespoons of the poaching syrup thickened slightly with a pinch of cornflour.

Heat to boiling before serving. Then, at the table, pour 1 tablespoon of Grand Marnier per serving on the apricots and ignite.

APRICOT SAUCE
Sauce abricot

6 ripe apricots
2 dl (¼ pt) sugar syrup
Liqueur
Knob of unsalted butter (optional)

Rub 6 ripe apricots through a fine sieve. Mix the pulp with the sugar syrup; place the mixture in a heavy saucepan and cook like jam. Flavour with the chosen liqueur when the sauce is warm or cold.

If used warm, add away from the heat a large piece of butter.

APRICOT JELLY WITH ALMOND SAUCE
Abricots Robert l'Ardeuil

2 dl (¼ pt) water
125 g (5 oz) sugar
20 g (¾ oz) gelatine
10 ripe apricots
Juice of 1 orange
Juice of ½ lemon
10 apricots
175 g (6 oz) sugar
2 dl (¼ pt) water
50 g (2 oz) sweet almonds with 1 bitter almond
6 tablespoons single cream or milk

Prepare an unclarified jelly by heating 2 dl (¼ pt) of water with 125 g (5 oz) of sugar and the gelatine soaked in cold water.

Stone 20 apricots and reserve the stones. Make a purée with the apricots, rubbing them through a fine sieve; put into a bowl.

Break the apricot stones, remove the kernels, skin them after blanching them 1 minute in boiling water and slice thin.

Combine the fruit purée, the apricot kernels and the jellied syrup before it is set. Add the juice of 1 orange and of ½ a lemon.

Oil a bowl or a domed mould and fill with the mixture just before it starts to set.

Refrigerate for 3 hours before serving.

While the purée is refrigerated, slowly poach 10 apricots, stoned carefully to keep the fruit intact, in a syrup made with 50 g (6 oz) of sugar and 2 dl (¼ pt) of water.

Poach in barely simmering syrup until the fruit is barely tender.

Drain on to a plate and refrigerate.

Boil the syrup to reduce by half.

Skin the sweet almonds with 1 bitter almond and soak in cold water. Pound them in a mortar.

Moisten the almonds slowly, while they are being pounded, with cream or milk.

Place the paste in a dishcloth or linen towel and squeeze out the milk. Mix the almond milk, away from the heat, into the syrup; strain through cheesecloth into a bowl. Refrigerate.

To serve unmould the apricot mould by dipping it for a second into hot water, shake and turn over on to a large plate. Surround the base with the poached apricots and baste with the almond syrup. Serve a bowl of the remaining syrup separately. Everything should be very cold.

PINEAPPLE
Ananas

Because of its rare digestive properties, and delicious flavour which are impaired by cooking, pineapple should always be eaten fresh and uncooked. It can be prepared in marvellous ways.

PINEAPPLE WITH RICE
Ananas Condé

Peel a pineapple; cut in half lengthwise and remove the very hard core; or leave the fruit whole and remove the centre core.

Cut into 1-cm ($\frac{1}{2}$-inch) slices, sprinkle with caster sugar and place on a plate to macerate with a few tablespoons of kirsch.

Prepare some dessert rice (page 599). Mould it in a round mould, poach and unmould on a round platter; while the rice is very hot, arrange the slices of pineapple, well drained, on top in a rosette.

Coat the rice with apricot sauce (page 648) flavoured with kirsch and the juices from the pineapple.

PINEAPPLE WITH MERINGUE
Ananas meringué

Follow the recipe for apricots with meringue Clairette (above), except that the pineapple is peeled, sliced, then cut into large dice, macerated as for moulded rice with pineapple (above) and spread in one layer on the rice. Cover with the meringue, decorate and bake.

1 very ripe pineapple
50 g (2 oz) sugar
1 tablespoon apricot
  liqueur or
  Cointreau
50 g (2 oz) semolina
4 egg yolks
4 egg whites
Pinch vanilla sugar
2 large eating apples,
  peeled, seeded
  quartered
15 g (½ oz) unsalted
  butter
1 teaspoon water
Vanilla
Crème Chantilly (page
  569)
Apricot sauce (page
  648), flavoured with
  apricot liqueur or
  Cointreau
Candied cherries

PINEAPPLE WITH APPLE MERINGUES
Ananas et zéphirs normands

Peel a very ripe pineapple and cut in half slices after removing the core. Dice 3 slices in 1-cm (½-inch) cubes, sprinkle with sugar and pour over 1 tablespoon of apricot liqueur or Cointreau. Macerate the remaining slices with sugar and liqueur in another bowl.

Prepare the semolina as for apricots Colbert (above) but thicken with 4 egg yolks and add 2 egg whites whipped very stiff.

Flavour, after adding the yolks but before adding the whites, by adding the macerated diced pineapple. Add the vanilla sugar.

Pour into a round buttered mould. Poach in a *bain-marie* in the oven.

Whip the 2 other egg whites with sugar into a meringue (page 631) and, with a pastry bag or a tablespoon, form small meringue shells as large as pullets' eggs on a pastry sheet and bake.

Cook the apples in a pan with 15 g (½ oz) of butter, 1 tablespoon of sugar, and 1 teaspoon of water. Stew slowly until all the pulp is soft. Mash with a fork, add vanilla and mix with half its volume of *crème* Chantilly.

Make an apricot sauce flavoured with liqueur, as above.

Presentation. Carefully put the meringue shells together in pairs with a filling of the apple and cream mixture.

Unmould the semolina on to a large round platter. On the very top place the half slices of pineapple, overlapping.

In the spaces between the pineapple slices and around the edges of the plate, pour the apricot sauce to show up its golden colour.

Then, around the pineapple slices and round the edge of the plate, place a row of the pairs of meringues.

Between the meringues place a candied cherry. On top group three meringues and one cherry.

Coat the pineapple very lightly with the apricot sauce, and serve the remaining sauce separately. Add the liqueur and juice from the pineapple to the reserved sauce.

PINEAPPLE WITH LIQUEUR
Ananas aux liqueurs

Prepare pineapple slices and macerate as in the preceding recipe.

Place the pineapple slices on a hot platter sprinkled with icing sugar, then sprinkle more on the slices. Pour on the chosen liqueur, heated beforehand.

Ignite the liqueur and present to the guests while still burning. Baste the slices until the flames are extinguished naturally.

PINEAPPLE PAUL AND RAYMONDE
Ananas Paul et Raymonde

1 large well-flavoured
  pineapple
Thick sugar syrup
Kirsch
$\frac{1}{2}$ l (1 pt) Bavarian
  cream (page 580)
4 tablespoons
  strawberries
1 tablespoon sugar
1 slice Genoese cake
  (page 555), 3 cm
  (1$\frac{1}{2}$ inches) thick
Whole strawberries
Juice of $\frac{1}{2}$ blood
  orange

Choose a large well-flavoured pineapple of a beautifully golden colour. Cut off the top, leaving about 1 cm ($\frac{1}{2}$ inch) attached to the leaves.

Scoop out the fruit from the shell, cutting it all around 1 cm ($\frac{1}{2}$ inch) from the skin with a long thin blade, turning it so that the pineapple is removed in one piece.

Cut the pulp into two equal parts lengthwise and remove the hard core. Then cut half the pineapple pulp into 1 cm ($\frac{1}{2}$-inch) slices, and the other half into 1-cm ($\frac{1}{2}$-inch) dice.

Poach the two batches of cut fruit separately in a thick sugar syrup. Pour into two bowls, flavour with kirsch, and refrigerate.

Prepare the Bavarian cream, flavour with kirsch and add the poaching syrup from the pineapple. Just as the cream is about to set, add the diced pineapple and 4 tablespoons of strawberries macerated in kirsch with 1 tablespoon of sugar.

Before the mixture sets, pout it into the pineapple shell. Pack in crushed ice or refrigerate for 3 hours.

Presentation. On a large platter place a thick slice of Genoese cake with a circle cut out in the centre to hold the pineapple standing up.

On top of the pineapple and around the edges of the cake place circles of macerated strawberries; and on the very top place the pineapple top with its leaves.

At the base of the cake arrange a garland of half slices of pineapple. Fill the centre of each half slice with a strawberry.

Squeeze the juice of $\frac{1}{2}$ a blood orange into the poaching syrup. and add 2 tablespoons of kirsch; pour over the pineapple slices. The excess syrup will be absorbed by the cake. After serving the Bavarian cream, cut the cake into small wedges and serve.

BANANAS
Bananes

Bananas, peeled and poached in syrup, can be prepared *à la Bourdaloue* (page 646), with dessert rice (page 599) or with meringue (page 631).

You can also make excellent banana cream soufflés: slice the bananas in half and cook slowly in butter; sprinkle with sugar, and purée before adding the basic soufflé mixture (page 621).

Instead of baking and serving the banana soufflé in a soufflé dish, you can make a delicious fantasy, soufflé bananas with praline. When you peel the fruit, be careful not to spoil the peels of half the bananas; place the skins in their natural shape in a circle on an ovenproof dish. Add 1 tablespoon of praline (page 630) or crushed macaroons to the banana soufflé mixture. Using a pastry bag with a large tube, fill the banana skins with the mixture. Sprinkle the praline on top of each banana, then dust with icing sugar. Bake in a 425°F (220°C, gas mark 7) oven for 5 minutes and serve.

FLAMING CHERRIES
Cerises flambées

Remove the stones and the stems from large cherries and poach them in a syrup flavoured with liqueur. Follow the method for apricots flamed with Grand Marnier (page 647).

STRAWBERRIES WITH LEMON ICE
Fraises mignonnes glacées

1 kg (2 lb) strawberries
50 g (2 oz) sugar
4 teaspoons vanilla sugar
½ glass curaçao
½ glass champagne
1 l (2 pts) lemon ice
100 g (4 oz) crystallized violets (page 630)
4 dl (¾ pt) single cream
20 crystallized orange flowers (page 630)
½ tablespoon candied orange rind

Place the strawberries in a bowl, sprinkle with sugar and 1 teaspoon of vanilla sugar; baste with curaçao and champagne. Refrigerate for 30 minutes, stirring the fruit from time to time so that the berries are completely soaked in the liqueur syrup.

Prepare the lemon ice (page 638) not frozen too hard but still fairly soft.

Coarsely crush the crystallized violets. Sweeten the cream with 3 teaspoons vanilla sugar and keep refrigerated.

Prepare 20 crystallized orange flowers and ½ tablespoon of candied orange rind cut into tiny dice.

Just before serving, spread the lemon ice in a glass fruit bowl or a silver dish, then, in one layer on top, the strawberries, drained and basted with the syrup strained through cheesecloth. Coat everything with the sweetened cream and on top sprinkle the crushed violets mixed with the diced candied orange peel.

Decorate here and there with the 20 crystallized orange flowers.

These last preparations should be done very quickly.

1 medium-sized
  pineapple, very
  ripe and well-
  flavoured
Sugar syrup flavoured
  with kirsch
2 golden yellow
  bananas
500 g (1 lb)
  strawberries
3 tablespoons sugar
1 orange

STRAWBERRIES WITH PINEAPPLE AND BANANA
Fraises aux fruits d'or

Peel the pineapple, cut it in half lengthwise and remove the centre core; cut the thickest part of the pineapple into 12 half slices and dice the remaining pineapple in 1-cm ($\frac{1}{2}$-inch) cubes.

Place the half slices in a deep dish and baste them with a few tablespoons of sugar syrup flavoured with kirsch; refrigerate.

Peel the bananas, dice them like the pineapple and add them to the pineapple.

Wash the strawberries quickly in cold water, remove the stems and add the berries to the pineapple and bananas. Sprinkle the fruit with 3 tablespoons of sugar and baste with the juice of 1 orange and 1 tablespoon of kirsch. Refrigerate to macerate; mix the fruit carefully from time to time.

In a fruit bowl place the half slices of pineapple in a circle round the edge; then in a mound in the centre, the pineapple, strawberries, and bananas. Baste everything with the macerating juice strained through cheesecloth.

CHESTNUT MONT-BLANC
Mont-Blanc aux marrons

Push pieces of *marrons glacés* through a fine sieve over a plain ring mould. The chestnuts will fall into the mould in the shape of vermicelli. Finish filling the mould by spooning up the chestnuts that fall around it.

Turn the moulded chestnuts out on a serving platter and with a spoon fill the centre of the ring with a mound of *crème* Chantilly (page 569) flavoured with chartreuse.

ICED MELON
Melon royal

Use 2 ripe melons with good flavour.

Rub the pulp of one of the melons, seeds removed, through a fine sieve and with it prepare a light sorbet (*granité*, page 643) flavoured with curaçao.

Cut the top off the other melon to make a hole big enough to remove the seeds; then scoop out the pulp with a silver tablespoon – each piece of pulp removed should be as big as a small egg.

The skin of the melon should remain intact. To keep it firm, refrigerate.

Place the pieces of melon in a bowl, sprinkle with icing sugar and baste with 1 part curaçao and 2 parts fine champagne brandy. Let macerate 1 hour.

To serve place the melon shell on a base of crushed ice and fill with layers of melon sherbet and macerated melon. Cover with the top part of the melon.

MELON WITH PORT
Melon de la bonne auberge

Choose small melons, of the Charentais variety, which have an especially good flavour and are rarely a disappointment if well chosen.

Allow 1½ melons per guest; 9 melons for 6 servings, for example.

Scoop out 6 melons following the method in the preceding recipe, keeping the skins intact; peel the other 3 and reserve their pulp along with the rest.

Refrigerate the shells and put the pieces of pulp to macerate in a bowl with some vintage port and, for each melon, 1 tablespoon of fine champagne brandy. Cover the bowl tightly and refrigerate. Leave 30 minutes.

To serve fill the empty melon shells with the macerated pulp, dividing the port among the 6 melons.

Place the melon shells on a bed of crushed ice, cover the top of each melon with the piece cut off, and serve.

This is a superb combination; the pieces of melon tinged with juice the colour of rosewood.

PEACHES
Pêches

You should always remove the skin of peaches to get a clean, velvety fruit; dip them for a second or two, depending how ripe they are, into boiling water.

Poach peaches in sugar syrup, either whole or cut in half.

Prepare peaches following any of the apricot recipes.

PEACHES WITH SEMOLINA AND CRÈME PÂTISSIÈRE
Pêches archiduc

125 g (5 oz) semolina
½ l (1 pt) boiling milk
Vanilla
Pinch salt
175 g (7 oz) sugar
½ l (1 pt) *crème pâtissière* (page 569)
Crème Chantilly (page 569)
2 tablespoons kümmel
2 dl (¼ pt) water
1 vanilla bean
6 large peaches
3 egg yolks
Italian meringue (optional, page 631)
6 tablespoons single cream
12 teaspoons strawberry or raspberry purée

Cook the semolina, sprinkling it into the boiling milk flavoured with vanilla, seasoned with a pinch of salt, then sweetened with 75 g (3 oz) of sugar.

Cover, and bake in a 325°F (170°C, gas mark 3) oven, without stirring, for 30 minutes.

While the semolina is cooking, prepare the *crème pâtissière*, adding one-quarter of its volume of *crème* Chantilly, flavoured with 1 tablespoon kümmel.

In a syrup made with 100 g (4 oz) of sugar, 2 dl (¼ pt) of water and a vanilla bean, poach 6 large peaches, peeled, cut in half and stoned. Set aside in a bowl in the refrigerator.

When the semolina is cooked, while it is still very hot, separate it with a fork, adding 3 egg yolks. Cool in a bowl. Separate the grains from time to time, so that the mixture does not become too compact. When very cold, add another tablespoon of kümmel and one-quarter of the semolina's volume of *crème* Chantilly or Italian meringue made with 3 egg whites, whipped stiff, and cooked sugar (page 631).

Presentation. Lightly oil a plain ring mould with sweet almond oil; fill with the semolina and let stand for 15 minutes in the refrigerator. Unmould on to a round platter after dipping the mould for a second in hot water and wiping it.

In the centre pour half the *crème pâtissière*. On top arrange peach halves in a circle. Thin the remaining *crème* with single cream, and pour some of this mixture over the semolina. Serve the remaining portion in a bowl with the dessert.

Complete the dish by coating each peach half with a teaspoon of strawberry or raspberry purée lightly sweetened and flavoured with kümmel.

Sprinkle a pinch of crushed macaroons round the edge of the plate.

PEACHES WITH APPLE AND PEACH PURÉE
Pêches du bocage

12 large peaches
Sugar syrup made with 375 g (13 oz) sugar and 2·7 dl (10 fl oz) water
1 tablespoon calvados
6 large apples, peeled, cored, sliced
2 tablespoons sugar
25 g (1 oz) unsalted butter
Piece lemon zest
Peach purée
Strawberries
Wild blackberries

Dip the peaches in boiling water for a few seconds, and remove the skins and then the stones by cutting down from the stem end being careful not to hurt the fruit.

Poach the peaches, keeping them slightly firm, in sugar syrup. Do not let them boil. Remove from the heat, drain and place in a bowl. Baste them with 1 tablespoon of calvados; then add the poaching syrup and refrigerate.

Meanwhile, prepare some apple sauce with well-flavoured eating apples, stewed with the sugar, butter and a piece of lemon zest.

Keep this purée quite thick and rub it through a fine sieve; place in a bowl and refrigerate.

When the apple purée is very cold, add equal its volume of good quality uncooked peach purée, made by peeling and stoning peaches and pushing them through a sieve.

Pile the purée in the centre of a fruit bowl; around its base place the 12 poached peaches, drained.

Coat the peaches with a *coulis* of uncooked red fruit, half strawberries and half wild blackberries, sugared with a couple of tablespoons of poaching syrup, reduced and iced. Serve the remaining *coulis* in a bowl.

Serve a plate of crisp, thin pancakes, with this dessert.

CHILLED PEACHES WITH SYRUP
Pêches glacées au sirop

Choose good quality peaches all the same size; remove the skins without blanching if the peaches are quite ripe. One at a time plunge them into sugar syrup made in the proportions 875 g (1 lb 15 oz) of sugar to 4·7 dl (17 fl oz) of water.

Poach the peaches slowly, keeping them firm, then place them in a glass bowl with the syrup, which should barely cover them.

When the peaches are cold, baste them with 1 tablespoon of kirsch, maraschino or other liqueur, and refrigerate for 1 hour. Serve in the same bowl.

PEACH MELBA
Pêches Melba

This dessert was created by Chef Auguste Escoffier in honour of the famous singer Dame Nellie Melba on a visit to London

Poach large peaches; when they are cold, let them stand in the syrup in the refrigerator.

Fill a glass bowl with vanilla parfait (page 641). On top arrange the fruit, well drained and with the stones carefully removed. Coat the peaches with raspberry purée lightly sweetened and flavoured with kirsch.

PEACHES WITH PISTACHIO ICE-CREAM
Pêches sultane

Proceed as for Melba peaches, replacing the vanilla parfait with pistachio ice-cream and coating the fruit with the reduced poaching syrup. This should be very cold and flavoured with essence of roses.

GODDESS PEACHES
Pêches déesses

Peel and poach large peaches as for Melba peaches. Let them cool in the syrup, and when cold, flavour with liqueur.

Meanwhile, prepare a light frangipane cream (page 568), using $\frac{1}{2}$ l (1 pt) for 12 peaches; make it rather thick and flavour with macaroons.

In a fruit bowl large enough to hold them easily, place the peaches in a circle, stem side down. In the centre pile the frangipane cream in a mound, coat the peaches with shiny partially melted redcurrant jelly prepared with uncooked fruit, and sprinkle a few petals of sugared roses over the cream.

Serve with a glass bowl of redcurrant jelly prepared with raw fruit.

PEACHES WITH STRAWBERRIES
Les pêches de mon moulin

12 peaches
Sugar syrup made with 450 g (15 oz) sugar and 2·5 dl (9 fl oz) water
Cherry brandy
500 g (1 lb) strawberries
3 tablespoons sugar
1 tablespoon kirsch
Vanilla-flavoured whipped cream

Peel the peaches after plunging them in boiling water and poach in syrup. Place in a bowl with the syrup and refrigerate; flavour with cherry brandy and let macerate.

Macerate the strawberries with 3 tablespoons of sugar and 1 tablespoon of kirsch.

Drain the peaches; remove the stones carefully and replace each one with a macerated strawberry of the same size; arrange the stuffed peaches in a circle in a fruit bowl.

Coat the remaining strawberries with vanilla-flavoured whipped cream and place in a mound in the centre of the peaches.

Baste the peaches with a teaspoon of the poaching syrup with cherry brandy.

PEACHES WITH ORANGE ICE AND BLACKCURRANT SYRUP
Pêches Astoria

Prepare 12 large peaches as for Melba peaches (page 658). When they are chilled, drain and remove the stone from each fruit without spoiling the shape of the peach and replace with an equal volume of praline (page 630) crushed in butter, 1 part butter to 1 part almonds.

Fill a glass fruit bowl with orange ice (page 638) made only with orange juice (no lemon); place the very cold poached peaches on the ice and coat the fruit with fresh blackcurrant juice, sweetened to a syrup with icing sugar and lightly flavoured with kirsch.

Sprinkle the dessert with crystallized rose petals.

Note: The blackcurrant juice is made by squeezing the ripe fruit in a cloth and mixing the cold juice with icing sugar, 750 g (1 lb 10 oz) of sugar to every 1 kg (2 lb) of fruit. Crush a piece of clove and add it to the fruit before sqeezing it in the cloth.

Serve very cold with a plate of small *palmier* biscuits (page 561).

PEARS
Poires

Soft, ripe pears should be peeled and poached in a flavoured syrup. Use the same recipes as for apricots, apples and peaches.

FLAMING PEAR FLAN
Flan de poires flambées

I flan crust of *pâté à foncer fine* (page 536), 30–35 cm (12–14 inches) in diameter
Cinnamon
I tablespoon walnuts
6 ripe pears
2 glasses red wine
225 g (8 oz) sugar
Piece stick cinnamon
½ lemon rind
12 sugared hazelnuts
½ glass old marc or calvados
15 g (½ oz) unsalted butter

Prepare:

One flan crust baked unfilled.

Apple sauce made following the recipe for *pommes exquises* (page 668); flavour with cinnamon and mix with I tablespoon of walnuts, coarsely chopped, lightly sugared and toasted.

Six pears poached in a syrup made with red wine, sugar, cinnamon and lemon rind.

With all the ingredients warm, pour the apple sauce into the crust; cut each pear in half and scoop out the core with a spoon, filling the hole with a hazelnut. Arrange the pear halves on top of the apple sauce, stem ends towards the centre. Over the fruit pour the marc or calvados (first heated); ignite and serve to the guests immediately. Serve the poaching syrup reduced to ½ a cup and lightly buttered separately.

Crème renversée au caramel:

½ l (1 pt) milk
1 vanilla bean, steeped in the milk
100 g (4 oz) sugar
4 egg yolks
2 whole eggs
3 tablespoons caramel syrup

Pears:

6 medium-sized ripe pears
12 small pears, all the same size
350 g (12 oz) sugar
3 dl (½ pt) water
Vanilla bean
1 glass red wine
Pinch cinnamon
3 dl (½ pt) double cream
1 teaspoon vanilla sugar
5 red sugared almonds, crushed
Redcurrant jelly, partially melted

PEARS WITH CRÈME CARAMEL
Poires Félicia

Prepare the *crème renversée* (follow the instructions on page 574); pour it into a ring mould lined with sugar cooked to a dark caramel colour and bake in a *bain-marie* in a 325°F (170°C, gas mark 3) oven for at least 1 hour. After it is cooked, let the custard cool in the mould.

Peel the pears; remove the cores from the bottom and prepare a poaching syrup by simmering 225 g (8 oz) of sugar, water and a vanilla bean.

Divide the syrup in half; to one part add the red wine, a pinch of cinnamon and 100 g (4 oz) of sugar.

Poach the 6 pears, cut into quarters, in the plain syrup; cook the 12 small pears in the syrup with the wine.

After poaching, pour the pears with their syrups into two fruit bowls; cool and refrigerate or place over crushed ice.

Presentation. Before unmoulding and assembling the dish, drain the small pears on a rack.

Unmould the *crème renversée* on to a round platter with a diameter 10 cm (4 inches) larger than that of the mould.

In the centre place the quartered pears, well drained, in a pyramid; whip the cream and sweeten it with 1 tablespoon of sugar and 1 teaspoon of vanilla sugar and completely cover the pear pyramid. Sprinkle coarsely crushed sugared almonds on top.

Just before serving dip the small pears in partially melted redcurrant jelly to coat and place them in a circle around the *crème renversée*.

Serve with a tray of small shortbread biscuits (page 563).

Genoa cake (page 560) flavoured with maraschino, baked in a 20-cm (8-inch) round tin

6 large ripe pears

½ l (1 pt) sugar syrup made with 450 g (15 oz) sugar and 2·5 dl (9 fl oz) water

Maraschino

50 g (2 oz) praline (page 630)

50 g (2 oz) unsalted butter

Kirsch

Jelly made with fresh redcurrants and raspberries

3 dl (½ pt) *crème* Chantilly (page 569) flavoured with vanilla

Crystallized rose petals

ALMOND PEARS WITH GENOA CAKE
Poires Rose-Marie

Bake the Genoa cake following the recipe on page 560.

Peel the pears, cut them in two, remove the cores and poach in the syrup. Place in a bowl; when cooled, flavour with maraschino. Refrigerate.

Mash the praline with the butter; set aside on a plate.

Unmould the Genoa cake on to a round platter or shallow fruit bowl; soak the cake with kirsch, then cover it with a thick ayer of redcurrant jelly. Return to the refrigerator for 10 minutes so that the jelly sets.

Arrange the pear halves, drained, in a rosette on top, and fill the cavities in the pear halves with nut-sized balls of praline and butter.

Using a pastry bag with a fluted tube filled with *crème* Chantilly, pipe a braid between the pears. Colour some of the *crème* Chantilly pale pink by adding partially melted redcurrant jelly, and with the pastry bag pipe a beautiful rose in the centre of the dessert.

Sprinkle the edge of the plate with crystallized rose petals.

Serve with a plate of cats' tongues (page 563).

CRÊPES WITH PEAR PURÉE
Marmelade de poires
For 6 people

Crêpe batter:
500 g (1 lb) sifted
  flour
6 egg yolks
¾ l (1¼ pts) milk,
  boiled and cooled
Pinch salt
1 tablespoon sugar
1 teaspoon vanilla
  sugar
100 g (4 oz) unsalted
  butter, softened

Pear purée:
Sugar syrup made
  with 450 g (15 oz)
  sugar, 1·7 dl (6 fl
  oz) water, 0·8 dl (3
  fl oz) Anjou white
  wine
3 large ripe pears,
  peeled
2 tablespoons double
  cream
Cointreau
Champagne brandy

Crêpes

Mix the flour with 6 egg yolks and the milk, boiled and cooled; add a pinch of salt, 1 tablespoon of sugar and 1 teaspoon of vanilla sugar. When the dough is smooth and fluid, add the softened butter.

The mixture should not be too light; depending on the type of flour reduce, if necessary, the quantity of milk. Let the batter stand at least 3 hours in a warm place, covered with a cloth. Fermentation will start while the dough stands, and the flour will lose the body that it may have acquired during the mixing.

Make the crêpes (following the cooking method on page 605). Spread each one with a layer of very cold pear purée (recipe below); fold in four. Place the crêpes in a circle on a large, very hot platter and baste them with Cointreau mixed with an equal quantity of fine champagne brandy, heated without boiling, and ignite, in front of the guests.

Pear purée

To make the purée prepare the sugar syrup. In it poach the ripe pears. Place the pears in a bowl and let them cool in the syrup. As soon as the fruit is cold, rub the pears through a fine sieve and put the purée in a bowl. Thicken with 2 tablespoons of thick cream and a little of the poaching syrup, reduced. Store in the refrigerator.

6 large pears
1 bottle Beaujolais
  wine
150 g (6 oz) sugar
1½ teaspoons
  powdered
  cinnamon
1 clove
2 slices orange
2 slices lemon
5 black peppercorns
  (indispensable)

PEARS WITH BEAUJOLAIS WINE
Poires à la beaujolaise

Peel the pears, leaving the stems on, and cook them in a Beaujolais syrup made with the remaining ingredients.

They will take about 15 minutes to cook.

Serve this dessert cold.

APPLES
Pommes

Apples can be prepared by any of the recipes for apricots, though some recipes are designed especially for apples.

BAKED APPLES
Pommes bonne femme

Wipe several large apples; cut out the cores with a knife or an apple corer, making a cylindrical hole in each centre about 2 cm (¾ inch) in diameter from the stem to the bottom of the apple, and removing all the seeds. With the point of a knife make an incision about 1½ mm ($\frac{1}{16}$ inch) deep at the midpoint of each apple, going all around it. Place the fruit in an ovenproof baking dish; in the bottom of the dish pour a few tablespoons of water or white wine; fill the hole in each apple with sugar and place a piece of butter on top. Bake in a 400°F (200°C, gas mark 6) oven for 30–60 minutes.

While the apples are baking, prepare a 9-mm (⅜-inch) thick croûton for each apple. Fry slices of bread in butter (or make small cakes with Genoese, Genoa or madeleine dough, (pages 555–560) and place them on a serving platter; set a cooked apple on each one.

Pour the cooking juice around the croûtons; sprinkle the holes with icing sugar or pour on some half-melted redcurrant jelly, flavoured with kirsch.

APPLE FLUFF WITH WALNUTS
Mousseline de reinettes aux noix

11 medium-sized apples

50 g (2 oz) unsalted butter

150 g (6 oz) sugar

1 teaspoon vanilla sugar

Piece lemon rind, chopped very fine

2 dl ($\frac{1}{4}$ pt) water

1 vanilla bean

2 dl ($\frac{1}{4}$ pt) double cream, whipped

3 whole eggs, lightly beaten

3 egg yolks

2 tablespoons walnuts, coarsely chopped

Liqueur made from fruit stones

Peel, core and slice 8 apples; stew them with 25 g (1 oz) of butter, 3 tablespoons of sugar, 1 teaspoon of vanilla sugar and a piece of lemon rind, chopped very fine.

Cut the remaining apples into 8 pieces each, and poach them in a syrup made with the water, the rest of the sugar and 1 vanilla bean. This poaching should be done very slowly, and at the end the fruit should be barely tender.

Remove 15 pieces of apple at this point and let the remaining 9 pieces cook until they are soft; then drain. Reserve the syrup.

With a fork mash up the apples in the first sauce as soon as they are cooked and boil to reduce the sauce over a high flame, stirring with a spatula until all the water has evaporated and you are left with a real fruit paste.

At this point remove from the heat.

While the apple paste is still hot, stir in 6 tablespoons of cream, whipped, 3 eggs, lightly beaten, 3 egg yolks, 2 tablespoons of walnuts, coarsely chopped, and, to finish, the 15 lightly poached apple pieces.

Butter a charlotte mould and pour the apple mixture in it; tap it slightly to remove the bubbles and bake in a *bain-marie* in a 325°F (170°C, gas mark 3) oven for 40 minutes.

Check to see if the baking is done by pressing lightly with your finger. The mixture should have the consistency of a baked custard.

To serve let the mould stand for about 10 minutes after taking from the oven; then unmould on to a warm round platter.

Make a sauce by boiling down the syrup in which the 9 apple slices were cooked until it is reduced to $\frac{1}{2}$ a cup; rub the syrup and the 9 slices through a fine sieve and cook to make a purée, then add away from the heat 25 g (1 oz) of butter and the remaining whipped cream. Flavour with liqueur. Coat the dessert with the sauce.

Serve with a plate of cats' tongues (page 563) or any other small, crisp biscuits.

✕═══✕

BAKED APPLES WITH ALMOND CREAM AND RUM
Pommes au four Martiniquaise

Choose large equal-sized apples of good quality that will not lose their shape when cooked.

Peel the apples and core from the stem to the eye with a corer 2 cm ($\frac{3}{4}$ inch) in diameter; bake as for baked apples above.

When the apples are baked, place each one on a Genoa cake (page 560) moulded in small tart moulds and lightly soaked with rum; fill the empty hole with chopped pineapple macerated in rum and mixed with 1 or 2 tablespoons of frangipane cream (page 568).

Coat the apples generously with frangipane cream lightened and flavoured with rum; sprinkle with crushed macaroons. Scatter a few pieces of butter on top and brown quickly in a 425°F (220°C, gas mark 7) oven.

✕═══✕

APPLES WITH CHESTNUT PURÉE
Pommes à la limousine

6 large apples, peeled and cored
$\frac{1}{2}$ l (1 pt) water
525 g (1 lb 2 oz) sugar
2 vanilla beans
500 g (1 lb) chestnuts
Pinch salt
1 vanilla bean
6 dl (1$\frac{1}{2}$ pts) milk
Few tablespoons double cream
Handful of almonds
3 egg yolks
1 heaped tablespoon flour
2 cups hot boiled milk
25 g (1 oz) unsalted butter

Poach the apples in a light syrup made with 225 g (8 oz) of sugar and a vanilla bean.

Watch the poaching, which must be done very slowly so that the apples keep their shape perfectly.

While the apples are poaching, prepare the chestnuts. Make a slash in each one, and put them in a pot of cold water; bring to the boil and boil for 5 minutes. You will be able to remove both the outer and inner skins easily while they are still hot.

Put the peeled chestnuts into a deep saucepan, add a pinch of salt and a vanilla bean, cover with about 3 dl ($\frac{1}{2}$ pt) of milk, and cook for 40 minutes.

When the chestnuts are cooked, rub them through a sieve and put the pulp into a pan with 125 g (5 oz) of sugar; bring to the boil and thin to the consistency of a light purée with a few tablespoons of cream.

Blanch a handful of almonds by boiling them for 1 minute

and slipping the skins off; slice the nuts and sprinkle them on a flan tin, mixed with a pinch of sugar, and brown them lightly in the oven.

In a bowl mix 125 g (5 oz) of sugar with 3 egg yolks. Beat this mixture with a wooden spoon for 15 minutes; it should become white and creamy. Add 1 heaped tablespoon of flour, then slowly dilute with $\frac{1}{2}$ l (1 pt) of hot boiled milk; add a vanilla bean. Put into the saucepan used to boil the milk and bring to the boil, beating without stopping.

As soon as the cream starts to boil, remove from the heat and add 25 g (1 oz) of butter.

To serve, spread the chestnut purée on a serving platter; place the 6 apples in a circle on top; coat with the prepared cream and sprinkle with the browned almonds.

125 g (5 oz) Carolina or Patna rice
Kirsch
Light caramel sugar (page 574)
125 g (5 oz) unsalted butter
8–9 apples
4 tablespoons sugar
225 g (8 oz) redcurrant jam
6 caramelized almonds (see page 629)

APPLES WITH RICE AND REDCURRANT JELLY
Pommes exquises

Cook the rice as for a rice cake (page 599), flavouring it with kirsch. Pack into a ring mould, after coating the mould with a light caramel sugar.

Melt 50 g (2 oz) of butter in a pan and add 4–5 apples, peeled, cored and sliced; sprinkle with 2 tablespoons of sugar. Cook the apples until they are soft and mash them into a fine purée. Away from the heat add 50 g (2 oz) of butter.

Peel 4 nice apples, core and cut into slices about 1 cm ($\frac{1}{2}$ inch) thick; put them into a bowl, sprinkle with sugar, pour on 1 table-spoon of kirsch and macerate for at least 15 minutes.

Partially melt the redcurrant jam made with uncooked fruit (or jam made with the last apples and the first strawberries in spring). Strain the jam and put this ruby-coloured *coulis* in a bowl with 2 tablespoons of sugar and 1 tablespoon of kirsch. If you are using redcurrant jelly flavour it with kirsch, too.

Unmould the ring of rice on a warm round platter. Drain the apple slices well and sprinkle them lightly with flour; brown on both sides in a pan where 25 g (1 oz) of butter is sizzling. These slices should be barely tender and gold coloured. Place the sautéed apple slices on top of the rice ring, overlapping them. In the centre pile the apple sauce.

Coat the apple slices with either the redcurrant jelly or the *coulis* of strawberries.

Decorate the top with 6 roughly crushed caramelized almonds (see page 630).

APPLES BAKED IN ANJOU WINE
Pommes belle angevine

6 large baking apples
50 g (2 oz) unsalted butter
Anjou wine
6 teaspoons sugar mixed with 1 teaspoon vanilla sugar
6 small savarins (page 528)
Sugar syrup made with 4 dl ($\frac{3}{4}$ pt) water and 150 g (6 oz) sugar
Cointreau
6 fresh walnuts
1 tablespoon sugar

Choose 6 large baking apples, well shaped and sweet smelling. Wipe the apples with care; make an incision about $1\frac{1}{2}$ mm ($\frac{1}{16}$ inch) deep with the point of a knife all around each apple at the midpoint and core them with an apple corer or a knife. Place the apples on an ovenproof porcelain plate, buttered and moistened with $\frac{1}{2}$ glass of Anjou wine with a fine bouquet, such as wine from the vineyards of Layon.

Inside each apple pour 1 teaspoon of vanilla-sugar mixture. On top of each apple place a piece of butter; then bake in the oven following the method described for baked apples above.

Baste the apples often, adding tablespoons of wine as it evaporates and reduces. When the apples are cooked, they should retain their shape and have a nice golden colour topped by a circle of dark brown from the caramelizing of the vanilla sugar and the fruit sugar in the wine. The wine will be almost all absorbed by the apples; what remains will make a thick, rich syrup.

Let the dish cool, then set in the refrigerator or in a very cool place.

Prepare 6 small savarins baked in small ring moulds used for individual cakes.

Soak the cakes in the sugar syrup flavoured with Cointreau. Drain on a pastry rack and keep in a cool place.

Coarsely chop 6 fresh walnuts; if they are fresh, remove the thin skin that protects them, which is very bitter in the first weeks after the harvest. Spread the nuts on a flan tin, sprinkle with 1 tablespoon of sugar and place them in a 425°F (220°C, gas mark 7) oven for a few minutes to glaze them to a light-brown colour. Let cool.

Presentation.   In a circle on a large platter – a beautiful silver one if possible – arrange the 6 small savarins; soak each one again with 1 teaspoon of Cointreau.

Place a baked apple on each of the savarins and sprinkle the chopped sugared walnuts on top.

In the centre of the ring of apples spoon a mound of *crème* Chantilly flavoured with the juice from the apples which is carefully spooned up by just warming the cooking dish over low heat for a moment or two.

The *crème* Chantilly can be replaced with frangipane cream (page 568) or a Saint-Honoré cream (page 572), though these will not be so good.

PRUNES IN BURGUNDY
Pruneaux au vin de Bourgogne

1 kg (2 lb) dried prunes
1½ l (3 pts) red Burgundy
225 g (8 oz) sugar
1 orange, sliced
1 lemon, sliced
20 g (1 oz) cinnamon stick

Soak the prunes in cold water for a couple of hours. Drain and place them in a saucepan. Moisten with the red wine. Add the sugar, the cinnamon stick and the slices of orange and lemon.

Bring to the boil; remove the saucepan from the heat at once and let cool.

Serve the prunes in a bowl with their syrup and the slices of orange and lemon.

FRUIT SALADS
Fruits rafraîchis ou macédoines de fruits

Various kinds of ripe raw fruit can be cleaned, peeled, stoned and cut into small dice, or sliced or left whole, washed if necessary in water with lemon juice added. Macerate this fruit salad for at least 3 hours with sugar and kirsch, maraschino or any other liqueur or wine, such as champagne, in a cool place.

Mix from time to time so that the ingredients of the fruit salad are well blended. Place in a bowl 15 minutes before serving and set on crushed ice.

125 g (5 oz) Carolina
or Patna rice
$\frac{1}{2}$ l (1 pt) boiling milk
1 vanilla bean
Pinch salt
75 g (3 oz) unsalted
butter
75 g (3 oz) sugar
3 tablespoons apricot
jam
100 g (4 oz) glacé
fruit
4 tablespoons kirsch,
maraschino or
Grand Marnier
$\frac{1}{2}$ l (1 pt) *crème
anglaise* (see page
570)
6 g ($\frac{1}{4}$ oz) gelatine
3 dl ($\frac{1}{2}$ pt) whipped
cream
Fruit sauce

RICE WITH GLACÉ FRUITS AND CUSTARD CREAM
Riz à l'impératrice

Pick over the rice and wash in several changes of water until the water comes out clear; then boil for 5 minutes. Drain and rinse again; then sprinkle the rice into the boiling milk with a vanilla bean and a pinch of salt. Add a good knob of butter, cover and bake in a 275°F (140°C, gas mark 1) oven for 35 minutes without stirring.

Remove from the oven and sprinkle with 50 g (2 oz) of caster sugar; mix carefully with a fork, adding 3 tablespoons of apricot jam and the glacé fruit, diced and macerated in 4 tablespoons of kirsch, maraschino or Grand Marnier.

While the rice is still hot, add the hot *crème anglaise* and stir in the gelatine softened in cold water; stir until it is dissolved. Refrigerate the mixture, but before it sets, add the whipped cream sweetened with 25 g (1 oz) of sugar.

Using almond oil, lightly coat a mould with sides decorated or not, or a tube baking pan, and fill it with the rice mixture.

Bury the mould in crushed ice or refrigerate to set the rice without hardening it.

Unmould on a round platter and decorate the edges with candied fruit. Serve with a fruit sauce made with cherries, apricots, redcurrants, etc., flavoured with kirsch.

RICE WITH FRUIT
Fruits divers à l'impératrice

The rice mixture above can be served alone, but it is usually served with a fruit poached in syrup – for example, peaches, pears, apples, apricots or bananas *à l'impératrice*.

Peel, seed and cut the fruit (except the apricots) in half. Poach in a syrup made in the proportions 875 g (1 lb 15 oz) of sugar to 4·7 dl (17 fl oz) of water. Cool in the poaching syrup flavoured with liqueur.

Mould the rice mixture in a ring mould with straight sides. Unmould and garnish with the halved fruit either round the edges or in the centre.

Then coat everything with a fruit sauce (page 648) or with sabayon sauce (page 577).

In this way you can make a variety of delicious desserts with fruit that is either fresh or preserved in syrup.

DIPLOMAT PUDDING WITH FRUIT
Diplomate aux fruits

Virtually any fruit is suitable for this dish.

Prepare a bottom layer with madeleine mixture (see page 557).

Make a Bavarian cream with fruit (page 580), and mould in a ring mould 8–10 cm (3–4 inches) smaller in diameter than the cake base.

Poach fruit in a syrup with the chosen flavour.

All the ingredients must be very cold.

Spread the cake with apricot jam somewhat reduced and flavoured with liqueur. Place the cake on a serving platter and unmould the Bavarian cream on top of it.

Place the poached fruit, drained, all around the base of the Bavarian cream. Cover everything with a fruit sauce (page 648), a creamy sabayon sauce (page 577) made with champagne, or a *crème anglaise* (page 570) made with port.

GENERAL INDEX

INDEX OF FRENCH
RECIPE TITLES